THE HANDY

DINOSAUR ANSWER BOOK

ALSO FROM VISIBLE INK PRESS

ABOUT THE AUTHORS

Thomas E. Svarney is a scientist, naturalist, and artist. With Patricia Barnes-Svarney, he is the author of numerous science books, including *Skies of Fury* and *The Handy Ocean Answer Book*. He has also contributed to several books, including *The New York Public Library Desk Reference*.

Patricia Barnes-Svarney has been a nonfiction science and science fiction writer for more than 15 years. She has a master's degree in geography/geomorphology and has worked professionally as a geomorphologist and oceanographer. She has written or coauthored more than 20 books, including *The New York Public Library Science Desk Reference,* and has written more than 300 articles for science magazines and journals.

*To Dave Bilcik, for his friendship and humor—
and for years of jawless fishes. . . .*

THE HANDY DINOSAUR ANSWER BOOK™

Thomas E. Svarney • Patricia Barnes-Svarney

VISIBLE
INK
PRESS

DETROIT • SAN FRANCISCO • LONDON • BOSTON • WOODBRIDGE, CT

THE HANDY DINOSAUR
ANSWER BOOK™

Most Visible Ink Press books are available at special quantity discounts when purchased in bulk by corporations, organizations, or groups. Customized printings, special imprints, messages, and excerpts can be produced to meet your needs. For more information, contact Special Markets Manager, Visible Ink Press, 27500 Drake Rd., Farmington Hills, MI 48331-3535. Or call 1-800-776-6265.

Art Director: Michelle DiMercurio
Typesetting: The Graphix Group
ISBN 1-57859-072-8

Contents

IN THE BEGINNING . . . 1

The Birth of the Solar System . . . Early Earth . . . The Beginnings of Life

FORMING FOSSILS . . . 35

Geologic Time . . . First Fossils . . . More Recent Fossils . . . Dinosaur Fossils

EVOLUTION OF THE DINOSAURS . . . 65

Classifying Animals . . . Evolving Ideas about Evolution . . . Dinosaur Ancestors . . . Dinosaurs Appear . . . Dinosaurs in the Mesozoic

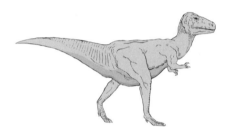
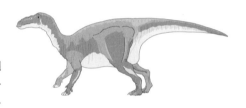

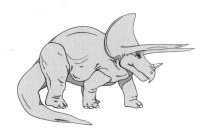

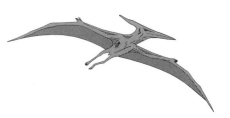

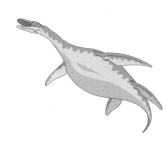

Introduction

In today's world, we are surrounded on land by animals no larger than the African bush elephant and, in the seas, no greater (that scientists know of) than the blue whale. Our backyard wildlife consists of small squirrels, songbirds, and the occasional opossum or deer. In fact, when we see a hawk, condor, or owl, we are mesmerized by its size—a flying creature larger than the usual cardinal or blue jay that visits the birdfeeder.

That is what fascinates the general public when it comes to dinosaurs: It's almost impossible to believe that something larger than a house once stomped on the grounds of our school or workplace—or in our own backyards. Admittedly, the land has changed over 65 million years—but just to think that a *Tyrannosaurus rex* may have looked for dinner on a distant hill, or a *Parasaurolophus* may have waded in a stream that once flowed nearby, is almost beyond our ken.

Everyone loves to hear and read about dinosaurs for other reasons as well—and their interest has been provoked by discoveries made in the past decade. We know now that dinosaurs had diverse behaviors. Some were strictly herbivores, while others were omnivores or carnivores. None were found in the oceans or in the sky, but rather made their home over most of the known landmasses. Their defenses varied, as did their body shape and height. Some of them may have been warmblooded. Many wandered in herds and had social groups. And one of the most perplexing questions in science has to do with dinosaurs: How and why did such a wide range of reptiles die out at such a seemingly rapid rate?

Still other questions intrigue: From what animals did the dinosaurs evolve? Who found the first dinosaur remains? What other plants and animals lived at the same time as the dinosaurs? How many dinosaurs lived on the planet? How do scientists classify these creatures? What were the continents like during the time of the dinosaurs? Did dinosaurs have muscles? What is the largest dinosaur claw ever found? What is the largest dinosaur bone ever found? How accurate was the movie *Jurassic Park?*

The Handy Dinosaur Answer Book attempts to answer these questions, taking you through the highlights of three main periods of geologic history: the Triassic, Jurassic, and Cretaceous—the age of the dinosaurs. As with all sciences, it is good to remember that the field of dinosaur study is in a constant state of flux. One reason is that scientists—amateur and professional—are continually discovering new dinosaur bones. They are digging deeper into the layers of rock, using new instruments and tools to analyze the bones—and discovering new connections between dinosaurs and other species. We've made every effort to ensure the accuracy and reliability of this book's contents; but even as we wrote the text, new discoveries were being made. It seemed as if every week we were adding to the text—covering the latest, greatest findings, along with the accompanying shifts in dinosaur theory.

Because of these recent discoveries, the study of dinosaurs prompts some great debates. Are birds really dinosaurs? Were any of the dinosaurs warmblooded? What was the cause of the dinosaurs' demise? All these questions and more are constantly being examined and discussed—and will continue to be for decades to come.

The Handy Dinosaur Answer Book is meant to take you deep into the world of dinosaurs—a great ride through what we currently know (and are debating) about these creatures and their surroundings. It will pique your interest and expand your knowledge of the field. It may even convince you to study dinosaurs, or to go out to seek fossils in your own backyard—not only of dinosaurs, but also of other ancient life.

And who knows? You may be the one to find the next major dinosaur discovery!

Acknowledgments

This book would not have been possible if not for the hard work and dedication of the editors at Visible Ink Press. Many thanks go out to Christa Brelin and Michelle Banks for their efforts in overseeing this project and crossing many bridges that arose; Julia Furtaw for her guidance and insight on this project; and Michelle DiMercurio for her page and cover designs.

Additional thanks must be extended to Gina Misiroglu for careful copyediting; Rebecca Nelson-Ferguson for advice and for the creation of a detailed resource section; Justin Karr, Sarah Chesney, Pam Reed, and Mike Logusz for photo identification, permissions, cropping, and scanning; Dean Dauphinais, Diane Maniaci, Brad Morgan, Matt Nowinski, Carol Schwartz, and Christine Tomassini for proofreading and coding; and Marco Di Vita of the Graphix Group for expert typesetting.

Cover photo of *Apatosaurus* model courtesy of Corbis.

Cover photo of *Triceratops* courtesy of Francois Gohier/Photo Researchers Inc.

Cover photo of fossil trilobite courtesy of JLM Visuals.

Back cover photo of dinosaur tracks courtesy of Tom Bean/Corbis.

Back cover photo of *Triceratops* courtesy of University of Michigan Exhibit, Museum of Natural History.

Timeline of Major Dinosaurs of the Mesozoic Era

GEOLOGIC TIME

		Geologic Time Scale	
Era	**Period**	**Millions of Years Ago**	**Life Form(s) at That Time**
Cenozoic	Quaternary	2	Modern life, including man, evolves; man takes the place of dinosaurs and becomes the dominant creature of the land.
	Tertiary	65	Flowers begin to flourish and mammals diversify into myriad shapes and sizes.
Mesozoic	Cretaceous	144	As many dinosaurs become extinct, flowering plant life appears.
	Jurassic	136	Huge dinosaurs (divided into herbivores and carnivores) roam the land, toothed birds appear along with the first primitive marine life and reptiles.
	Triassic	245	Dinosaurs evolve from thecodont ("socket-tooth") reptiles; dicynodonts ("two dog tooth") or primitive mammals such as *Kannemeyeria,* and early placental mammals such as *Zalambdalestes,* appear.
Paleozoic	Permian	250	Seed plants (gymnosperms) begin to grow; insects, snails, and other invertebrates face mass extinction.

Era	Period	Millions of Years Ago	Life Form(s) at That Time
	Carboniferous	290	Forests flourish with fern trees; huge insects, amphibians, and evolving reptiles take advantage of the growing foliage.
	Devonian	350	Cartilaginous fishes (sharks and eels) are abundant; first amphibians, invertebrates, and land plants appear.
	Silurian	400	Invertebrates dominate the land and wide coral reefs cover the planet; agnathans (fish without jaws) and armored fish flourish.
	Ordovician	510	First vertebrates (agnathans) appear, along with marine invertebrates of all shapes and sizes.
	Cambrian	550	Only marine invertebrates exist, along with few land creatures.
Pre-Cambrian		600 mil.–4.6 bil.	Origin of the solar system and Earth, only one-celled, soft-bodied marine organisms exist.

MAJOR DINOSAURS OF THE TRIASSIC PERIOD (250 TO 205 MILLION YEARS AGO)

Major Triassic Period Dinosaurs

Name	Meaning	Age (millions of years ago)	Locality	Length (feet/meters)
Anchisaurus	Near Lizard	200 to 190	USA	Up to 6.5/2
Coelophysis	Hollow Form	225 to 220	USA	Up to 10/3
Eoraptor	Dawn Hunter	225	Argentina	Up to 3/1
Herrerasaurus	Herrera Lizard	230 to 225	Argentina	Up to 10/3
Plateosaurus	Flat Lizard	about 210	France, Germany, Switzerland	Up to 23/7

MAJOR DINOSAURS
OF THE JURASSIC PERIOD
(205 TO 144 MILLION YEARS AGO)

Major Jurassic Period Dinosaurs

Name	Meaning	Age (millions of years ago)	Locality	Length (feet/meters)
Apatosaurus	Deceptive Lizard	154 to 145	USA	up to 70/21
Allosaurus	Other Lizard	150 to 135	USA	up to 50/15
Archaeopteryx*	Ancient Wing	147	Germany	up to 1.5/.5
Barosaurus	Heavy Lizard	155 to 145	USA	up to 80/24
Brachiosaurus	Arm Lizard	155 to 140	USA, Tanzania	up to 75/23
Camarasaurus	Chambered Lizard	155 to 145	USA	up to 65/20
Camptosaurus	Bent Lizard	155 to 145	USA	up to 16/5
Coelurus	Hollow Tail	155 to 145	USA	up to 8/2.4
Compsognathus	Pretty Jaw	147	Germany	about 2/.7
Dacentrurus	Pointed Tail	157 to 152	France, England, Portugal	about 20/6
Diplodocus	Double Beam	155 to 145	USA	up to 90/27
Dryosaurus	Oak Lizard	155 to 140	USA, Tanzania	up to 13/4
Kentrosaurus	Spiky Lizard	140	Tanzania	up to 10/3
Mamenchisaurus	Mamenchi Lizard	155 to 145	China	up to 72/22
Massospondylus	Massive Vertebra	208 to 204	England, South Africa	up to 13/4
Megalosaurus	Big Lizard	170 to 155	Tanzania	up to 30/9
Ornitholestes	Bird Robber	155 to 145	USA	up to 6.5/2
Pelorosaurus	Monstrous Lizard	150	England	unknown
Scelidosaurus	Limb Lizard	203 to 194	England	up to 13/4
Stegosaurus	Roof Lizard	155 to 145	USA	up to 30/9
Tuojiangosaurus	Tuojiang Lizard	157 to 154	China	up to 21/6.4

*Dinosaur origin/nature has been debated since the first fossil was found in 1861.

xvii

Major Jurassic Period Sauropods

Sauropod	Dinosaur	Comments
Diplodocidae	*Diplodocus*	This dinosaur gives this group its name; it was 89 feet (27 meters) in length, with an estimated weight of 11 to 12 tons.
	Apatosaurus	Commonly known as *Brontosaurus,* it was shorter and stockier than the *Diplodocus.*
	Barosaurus	Similar to *Diplodocus,* but its cervical vertebrae were 33 percent longer.
	Seismosaurus	One candidate for the longest known dinosaur; it is estimated to have been between 128 and 170 feet (39 and 52 meters) long; its weight was probably more than 100 tons.
	Supersaurus	Another candidate for the longest dinosaur; it is estimated to have been about 130 feet (40 meters) long.
Brachiosauridae	*Brachiosaurus*	This dinosaur gives its name to the group; the late Jurassic dinosaur was approximately 75 feet (23 meters) long; it was 39 feet (12 meters) high, about the height of a four-story building, with an estimated weight of 55 tons
	Ultrasaurus	This may be a very large *Brachiosaurus;* only a few bones have been discovered; the estimates from the bones give a length greater than 98 feet (30 meters), and a weight of 140 tons.
Camarasauridae	*Camarasaurus*	A relatively small sauropod; it was approximately 59 feet (18 meters) long; its forelimbs were not as proportionally long as the brachiosaurids.

Major Jurassic Period Theropods

Theropod	Dinosaur	Comments
Ceratosauria	*Syntarsus*	Small and slender, similar in form to *Coelophysis.*
	Dilophosaurus	Up to 20 feet (6 meters) long and fairly slender; the skull had a double crest of thin, parallel plates on its nose and forehead; it was fancifully portrayed in the motion picture *Jurassic Park* with a frill, spitting poison, and much smaller than in actuality.
	Ceratosaurus	A large, heavy carnivorous dinosaur up to 23 feet (7 meters) long; it had short bladelike

Theropod	Dinosaur	Comments
		crests over the eyes, and a short triangular nose horn; it was the largest known ceratosaur, and appeared in the late Jurassic period; some scientists believe the dinosaur was an oddball: it appeared long after the other ceratosaurs, and may not even belong to this group; in fact, some people put it with the carnosaurs.
Carnosauria	*Allosaurus*	A large predator, with fairly long and well-muscled forelimbs and huge claws; it had large legs with heavy, clawed feet, and large, narrow jaws.
	Megalosaurus	The first dinosaur to be described; it was thought to be up to 30 feet (9 meters) long, but recently studies of the fragmentary remains indicate that they may actually be parts of different carnosaurs.
Coelurosauria	*Compsognathus*	A small coelurosaur that evolved during the late Jurassic; one example is the *Compsognathus longipes,* found in the limestone quarry of Solnhofen, Germany, where the first known bird, *Archaeopteryx lithographica,* was also discovered.
	Gallimimus	An ornithomimosaur that evolved during the late Jurassic; the Gallimimus bullatus was featured in the motion picture *Jurassic Park,* and were thought to have been some of the fastest dinosaur runners, judging from their long hindlimbs.

Major Jurassic Period Ornithischians

Ornithischian	Ornithischian Sub-group	Dinosaur	Comments
Thyreophora	Stegosauria	*Huayangosaurus*	These animals had small plates in skin, with spikelike armor and equal length front and rear legs; they were approximately 13 feet (4 meters) long, with a short snout; they are considered the most primitive of the stegosaurs.
		Stegosaurus	A late Jurassic dinosaur weighing approximately one to two tons; it had an array of bony plates along

Ornithischian	Ornithischian Sub-group	Dinosaur	Comments
			the length of the back, with tail spikes; the hindlegs were long, with short, massive forelegs; the head was small and elongated, and the brain size was extremely small for an animal of this size.
		Kentrosaurus	This dinosaur had spines on tail, hip, shoulder, and back; its bony plates, similar to those on *Stegosaurus,* were also present on the neck and anterior part of the back.
	Ankylosauria	*Sarcolestes*	This nodosaurid dinosaur ("flesh robber") developed in the middle Jurassic period, and was thought to be the first ankylosaur; it had a large piece of armor plating on its outer surface.
		Dracopelta	The Dracopelta ("armored dragon") was a small late Jurassic period nodosaurid from Portugal.
Cerapoda	Ornithopoda	*Camptosaurus*	A medium-sized, bipedal herbivore; it weighed up to 1,000 pounds, reaching lengths up to 23 feet (7 meters); it is thought to be the ancestor to many of the highly successful plant-eating dinosaurs in the Cretaceous period.
		Heterodontosaurus	This dinosaur was only about 3 feet (1 meter) in length; it had caninelike teeth and relatively long arms, with large hands; its teeth were designed for cutting.

MAJOR DINOSAURS OF THE CRETACEOUS PERIOD (144 TO 65 MILLION YEARS AGO)

Major Cretaceous Period Dinosaurs

Name	Meaning	Age (millions of years ago)	Locality	Length (feet/meters)
Albertosaurus	Alberta Lizard	76 to 74	Canada	Up to 30/9
Avimimus	Bird Mimic	about 75	Mongolia	Up to 5/1.5
Baryonyx	Heavy Claw	about 124	England	34/10
Centrosaurus	Horned Lizard	76 to 74	Canada	Up to 16/5
Chasmosaurus	Cleft Lizard	76 to 74	Canada	Up to 16/5
Corythosaurus	Helmet Lizard	76 to 74	Canada, USA	Up to 33/10
Craspedodon	Edge Tooth	86 to 83	Belgium	Unknown
Deinocheirus	Terrible Lizard	70 to 65	Mongolia	Unknown, arms about 10/3
Deinonychus	Terrible Claw	110	USA	Up to 11/3
Dromaeosaurus	Running Lizard	76 to 74	Canada	Up to 6/1.8
Dryptosaurus	Wounding Lizard	74 to 65	USA	About 16/5
Edmontonia	Of Edmonton	76 to 74	Canada	About 13/4
Edmontosaurus	Edmonton Lizard	76 to 65	Canada	Up to 43/13
Euoplocephalus	Well-armored Head	About 71	Canada	Up to 20/6
Gallimimus	Chicken Mimic	74 to 70	Mongolia	Up to 18/5.5
Gilmoreosaurus	Gilmore's Lizard	80 to 70	China	About 20/6
Hadrosaurus	Big Lizard	83 to 74	USA	Up to 26/8
Hylaeosaurus	Woodland Lizard	150 to 135	England	Up to 13/4
Hypsilophodon	High Ridge Tooth	about 125	England	Up to 7.5/2
Iguanodon	Iguana Tooth	130 to 115	USA, England, Belgium, Spain, Germany	Up to 33/10
Kritosaurus	Noble Lizard	80 to 75	USA	Up to 26/8
Lambeosaurus	Lambe's Lizard	76 to 74	Canada	Up to 30/9
Maiasaura	Good Mother Lizard	80 to 75	USA	Up to 30/9
Ornithopsis	Birdlike Structure	about 125	England	Unknown, perhaps 65/20
Orodromeus	Mountain Runner	about 74	USA	Up to 6.5/2
Ouranosaurus	Brave Monitor Lizard	about 115	Niger	Up to 23/7
Oviraptor	Egg Thief	85 to 75	Mongolia	Up to 6/2

Name	Meaning	Age (millions of years ago)	Locality	Length (feet/meters)
Pachycephalosaurus	Thick-headed Lizard	about 67	USA	Up to 26/8
Pachyrhinosaurus	Thick-nosed Lizard	76 to 74	Canada, USA	Up to 20/6
Parasaurolophus	Like *Saurolophus*	76 to 74	Canada, USA	Up to 33/10
Parksosaurus	Park's Lizard	76 to 74	Canada	Up to 10/3
Protoceratops	First Horned Face	85 to 80	Mongolia	Up to 6/2
Psittacosaurus	Parrot Lizard	124 to 97	China, Mongolia, Russia	Up to 6/2
Rhabdodon	Rod Tooth	83 to 70	Austria, France, Spain, Romania	Up to 10/3
Saurolophus	Ridged Lizard	74 to 70	Canada, Mongolia	Up to 40/12
Saurornithoides	Birdlike Lizard	80 to 74	Canada, Mongolia	Up to 6.5/2
Scartopus	Nimble Foot	About 95	Australia	Unknown
Segnosaurus	Slow Lizard	97 to 88	Mongolia	Up to 13/4
Struthiosaurus	Ostrich Lizard	83 to 75	Austria, Romania	Up to 6.5/2
Styracosaurus	Spiked Lizard	85 to 80	Canada, USA	Up to 18/5.5
Tenontosaurus	Sinew Lizard	110	USA	Up to 21/6.4
Triceratops	Three-horned Face	67 to 65	USA	Up to 30/9
Troodon	Wounding Tooth	75 to 70	Canada, USA	Up to 8/2.4
Tyrannosaurus	Tyrant Lizard	67 to 65	USA	Up to 40/12
Velociraptor	Quick Plunderer	84 to 80	China, Mongolia	Up to 6/12

Major Cretaceous Period Sauropods

Sauropod	Dinosaur Species	Comments
Titanosaurids	*Saltasaurus*	A relatively small—about 39 feet (12 meters) long—sauropod with bony plates covering its back in a kind of chain-mail body armor.
	Alamosaurus	This dinosaur was up to 69 feet (21 meters) long, with relatively long forelimbs; some paleontologists question whether this dinosaur was truly a titanosaur; it is thought to be the only North American Cretaceous period sauropod.
	Argentinosaurus	A good candidate for the most massive of all dinosaurs; it was thought to be as large as the largest diplodocids of the late Jurassic period.

Major Cretaceous Period Theropods: Ceratosauria order

Species	Comments
Carnotaurus	This bizarre dinosaur grew up to 30 feet (9 meters) long; it had a short head with a horn, and stumpy arms.

Major Cretaceous Period Theropods: Carnosauria order

Species	Comments
Spinosaurus	This dinosaur grew to 40 feet (12 meters) long, and was similar in appearance to *Allosaurus;* it had 6-foot- (2-meter-) long spines on its back that are thought to have supported a sail; this structure may have played a part in the dinosaur's thermo-regulation; most of the remains have been found in North Africa.

Major Cretaceous Period Theropods: Coelurosauria order

Family	Genus	Species	Comments
Ornithomimids		*Gallimimus*	This dinosaur ("chicken mimic") probably ate insects and small animals; it lived in Mongolia about 70 million years ago and is the largest and most completely known of the ornithomimosaurs; this dinosaur was featured in the movie *Jurassic Park*.
		Deinocheirus	Only a pair of 10-foot- (3-meter-) long forelegs and hands have been found of this dinosaur, which may have been one of the largest of the ornithomimosaurs; the forelegs are on display at the American Museum of Natural History in New York.
Maniraptora	Dromaeosaurs	*Deinonychus*	This dinosaur measured up to 10 feet (3 meters) long and weighed approximately 180 pounds, about the size of a mountain lion; these dromaeosaurs had large sickle-shaped claws on the feet; some

Family	Genus	Species	Comments
			fossil evidence indicates a pack-hunting behavior; fossils have been found in North America.
		Velociraptor	This dinosaur name means "quick plunderer" or "swift seizer"; it was a dromaeosaur about the size of a large dog, almost 6 feet (1.8 meters) long, with a weight of approximately 100 pounds; it had a sickle-shaped slashing claw on each foot; fossils are found in Mongolia and it was prominent in the movie *Jurassic Park*—but in reality, the dinosaur was much smaller.
		Utahraptor	This dinosaur was up to 21 feet (6.5 meters) long, with a large, sickle-shaped claw on its foot; it is the largest known dromaeosaur found in North America.
	Troodontids	*Saurornithoides*	This troodontid from Mongolia, meaning "birdlike reptile," was a carnivorous dinosaur about 6.5 feet (2 meters) long; its skull had a long, rather birdlike narrow muzzle; the teeth were small, with many teeth in the upper jaw; the teeth's back edges were serrated; it had a large brain and large saucerlike eyes, probably for hunting small animals at dusk.
		Troodon	This troodontid, found in North America, had large eyes and possible binocular vision; it was similar to its cousin, the *Saurornithodes*.
	Therizinosaurs (or Segnosaurs)	*Therizinosaurus*	This therizinosaur, possibly herbivorous, had a relatively short tail, and huge forelimbs with enormous sickle-shaped

Family	Genus	Species	Comments
			claws; they are thought to be closely related to birds.
		Alxasaurus	A therizinosaur from Mongolia; it had longer finger bones than the *Therizinosaurus;* it is thought to be the most primitive known member of the therizinosaurs.
		Erlikosaurus	This therizinosaur is from Mongolia; one fossil of this animal is currently the only therizinosaur skull known; it is long, with elongated external nasal openings and a toothless beak.
		Segnosaurus	The *Segnosaurus* is a therizinosaur from Mongolia; they had massive arm bones and grew up to 13 feet (4 meters) long.
	Oviraptorosaurs	*Oviraptor*	The "egg snatcher or thief" had a bizarre head crest; it was originally thought to prey on others' eggs, but more recent findings show them brooding eggs in nests, although it is still debated as to weather or not they ate eggs; most scientists believe the animals' jaws were not useful for eating eggs, but for crushing food.
		Caenagnathus	This oviraptorosaur, "recent jawless," grew up to 6 feet (2 meters) in length; like all oviraptorosaurs, it had a toothless jaw that was well muscled and perfect for crushing.
Tyrannosaurids		*Albertosaurus*	The "lizard from Alberta" is found in Canada; it grew to up to 30 feet (9 meters) long.
		Nanotyrannus	The "dwarf tyrant" is a small version of at tyrannosaur from

Family	Genus	Species	Comments
			Montana; there is debate as to whether the discovered bone were from an adult or juvenile.
		Daspletosaurus	The "frightful lizard" is from Canada, and was slightly smaller than the *Tyrannosaurus rex*.
		Tarbosaurus	Very similar—almost a mirror image cousin—to the *Tyrannosaurus rex;* the "terror lizard" is from Mongolia.
		Tyrannosaurus	One of the largest and most famous of the land-dwelling carnivores; it reached up to 46 feet (14 meters) long and 18.5 feet (5.6 meters) tall; fossils suggest the females were larger than the males.

Major Cretaceous Period Ornithischians: Thyreophora order

Species	Comments
Ankylosaurus	These dinosaurs grew up to 33 feet (10 meters) long; they had a wide head, with triangular horns and bony plates covering their bodies; for defense, they used their stiffened club-shaped tail; many fossils are found in North America.

Major Cretaceoud Period Ornithischians: Ceropoda order

Family	Genus	Species	Comments
Ornithopods	Iguanodontids	*Tenontosaurus*	This animal's fossils are found mostly in North America; it was a transitional form to the more advanced iguanodontians; it was up to 13 feet (4 meters) long with a very long, stiffened tail.
		Iguanodon	Iguanodon fossils are found in Europe and North America; it was also the first dinosaur fossil ever found; it grew up to about 33 feet (10 meters) long and probably chiefly moved on all fours; it had a

Family	Genus	Species	Comments
			conical thumb spike on the first digit of its hand.
	Hadrosaurs	*Edmontosaurus*	These are the true "duck-bills" with broadened, flat snouts; fossils are found in North America.
		Shantungosaurus	This largest known hadrosaur is found in China; it measured approximately 50 feet (15 meters) long—as big as many sauropods.
		Hadrosaurus	This is a flat-headed dinosaur; the fossils are found in North America and was the first skeleton ever to be mounted.
		Saurolophus	Solid, narrow, backward-pointing crest above the eyes; most fossils are from North America.
		Gryposaurus	The prominent, "Roman-nosed" snout was produced by the animal's arched nasal bones; many fossils are from North America.
		Maiasaura	This dinosaur means "good mother reptile or lizard"; it is known from nesting sites, fossil eggs, and hatchlings; one main site was found in North America.
		Corythosaurus	This North American dinosaur has a flat-sided, rounded crest on its head.
		Parasaurolophus	This dinosaur's head crest is the shape of an elongated tube that extends backward behind the skull; many fossils are from North America.
	Hypsilophodontids	*Orodromeus*	This North American dinosaur was found in Montana; it was up to 6 feet (2 meters) in length.
		Hypsilophodon	The "high-ridged tooth" dinosaur may have been one of the fastest running ornithischian dinosaurs; at one time, scientists thought it lived in trees, but there is little indication of this; it had a horny beak to cut vegetation and its teeth could easily grind plants.

Family	Genus	Species	Comments
	Heterodontosaurs	*Heterodontosaurus*	This dinosaur, the "different-toothed lizard," averaged about 3 feet (1 meter) in length; some scientists believe it may have burrowed in the ground in the summer.

Major Cretaceous Period Ornithischians: Marginocephalia order

Family	Species	Comments
Pachycephalosaurs	*Pachycephalosaurus*	This dinosaur's thickened skull was ornamented with bony knobs, and is thought to have been used in head butting; most fossils come from North America.
	Stegoceras	This dinosaur was about 6 feet (2 meters) long; the females and males had different thicknesses in skulls.
Ceratopsia	*Psittacosaurus*	This dinosaur's fossils are found in Mongolia; the "parrot lizard" was a primitive ceratopsian; it was bipedal, with a very rudimentary frill, and is therefore often considered to be frill-less; it was only recently discovered to be a ceratopsian.
	Protoceratops	This Mongolian dinosaur was quadrupedal, with a prominent, but short, frill, and is therefore often considered to be frill-less.
	Leptoceratops	A small-bodied ceratopsian from the late Cretaceous period in Montana, U.S. and Alberta, Canada; it had no horns or large neck frill.
	Styracosaurus	This animal had a frill bordered by long spikes; most fossils are found in North America.
	Triceratops	The *Triceratops* is another well-known dinosaur from North America; it had a nose horn, and paired horns over the eyes; it was up to 26 feet (8 meters) long, with a short, solid frill, and was one of the last species of dinosaurs to roam the earth.

Family	Species	Comments
	Torosaurus	This North American dinosaur had a longer frill than *Triceratops;* its 6-foot (2-meter) skull is one of the longest of any known land animal.

IN THE BEGINNING

THE BIRTH OF THE SOLAR SYSTEM

What is the **solar system**?

Our solar system consists of stars, planets, satellites, comets, asteroids, meteoroids, and interplanetary dust and gas. It is presumed that there are other solar systems besides our own. Our solar system includes the following:

The Sun—The Sun is at the center of our solar system, and is an average star when compared with other stars in the universe. It is classed as a typical G2-class star, represents about 99.86 percent of the mass of the solar system, and is about 864,000 miles (1,390,180 kilometers) in diameter, or about 109 Earth diameters across. It is thought that the Sun arrived at its present brightness about 800 million years ago, and will probably burn for another 7 billion years.

Nine known planets—From the Sun outward, the planets are Mercury, Venus, Earth, Mars (which are known as the inner, or terrestrial, planets); Jupiter, Saturn, Uranus, Neptune (the outer, or gaseous, planets, which are also known as gas giants), and Pluto (which is more similar in characteristics to the terrestrial planets).

Moons—More than 64 moons (satellites) circle the various planets. In addition, a moon has also been found around the small minor planet (asteroid) Ida, and some scientists believe such tiny moons around asteroids may be common. Saturn has the most known moons (more than 22); Earth and Pluto have one each; and Mercury and Venus have none.

Comets—Numerous short- and long-term comets swing through our solar system. Short-term comets pass by the Sun in an elliptical orbit, taking up to

200 years to complete an orbit. For example, Halley's comet is a short-term comet, swinging by Earth once every 76 years. Long-term comets take thousands of years to complete an orbit. Many long-term comets probably just pass once through our solar system, then disappear altogether.

Asteroids—More than 6,500 asteroids have been found and catalogued, most in a rocky belt between the orbits of Mars and Jupiter; others are found in stray orbits around the solar system. Scientists believe there are more than 10,000 asteroids in our solar system, ranging in size from more than 100 feet (30.5 meters) to 600 miles (1,000 kilometers) across. They are thought to be very old, and the best representatives of objects that existed in the early solar system.

Dust and gas—Traces of interplanetary (and probably interstellar) dust and gases are found in our solar system. Most of these microsized particles are from the collision between other space bodies, such as meteor and early asteroid collisions; the release of dust and gases from comets; and interstellar particles encountered as the solar system moves through space. Such rare particles, however, are often more difficult to detect and distinguish from other interplanetary dust and debris.

Why is the **Sun** crucial for **life on Earth**?

Over time, a complex balance has been achieved between the amount of radiation absorbed by the planet's surface and atmosphere, and the amount of heat returned to space. Thus, the Sun's radiant energy supplies fuel to Earth's atmospheric heat engine. This radiation also maintains Earth's life-sustaining thermostat, and over time has allowed life to adapt to the planet in its own way. For example, the warm rays of the Sun help maintain water in a liquid state, perfect for most animals and plants to use; and the Sun provides light for photosynthesis in most plants.

What are some of the **physical characteristics** of the **planets**?

The nine planets of the solar system all have unique characteristics depending on a multitude of reasons—known and unknown. For instance, Mercury has no atmosphere mainly because of its closeness to the Sun; Saturn has the most extensive ring system, although Jupiter, Uranus, and Neptune also have rings, though much smaller, but no one truly knows why.

What were the **early ideas** on the formation of the **solar system**?

There were several early theories on the formation of the solar system. In 1796, Marquis Pierre Simon de Laplace (1749–1827), a French mathematician, astronomer, and

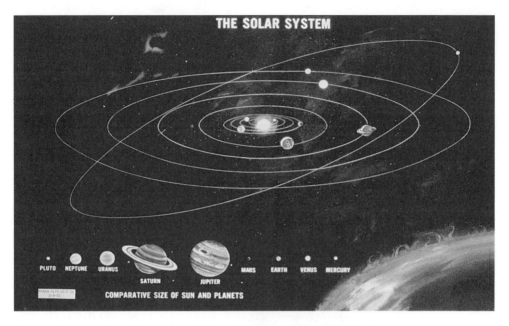

Diagram of the solar system. (Photo courtesy of National Aeronautics and Space Administration.)

physicist (and who is also called the "French Newton"), proposed the nebular hypothesis. He believed that the solar system developed from a rapidly rotating disk of hot gas, with the outer part of the disk experiencing a centrifugal force that caused a ring of material to form and eventually condense into the planets. Independently, German philosopher Immanuel Kant (1724–1804) also proposed that the solar system started as a dust cloud. He even extended the idea, suggesting that systems similar to our own formed in the same way elsewhere in the universe.

In the eighteenth century, French naturalist Comte de Georges Louis Leclerc Buffon (1707–88) suggested that the solar system formed from a more or less tangential collision between the Sun and another star. The strike knocked enough material off the Sun to form the planets. Still another theory that involves another star was developed around the turn of the eighteenth century. The tidal, or Chamberlin-Moulton, theory was proposed by American astronomer Forest Ray Moulton (1872–1952) and American geologist Thomas Chrowder Chamberlin (1843–1928). In 1905, they suggested that a star passed by, pulling off a ribbon of material from the forming Sun, the debris of which eventually formed the planets.

What is the **inflationary theory**?

The inflationary theory is a recent addition to the big bang theory. It attempts to answer such questions as why matter is so evenly distributed throughout the universe.

3

What is the big bang theory of the universe?

The big bang theory consists of the following: 15 to 20 billion years ago, a big bang, or explosion, occurred, creating the universe. The universe began as an infinitely dense, hot fireball, a scrambling of space and time. Within the first second after the bang, gravity came into being. The universe expanded rapidly and became flooded with subatomic particles that slammed into one another, forming protons and neutrons. Three minutes later, when the temperature was a mere 500 billion degrees Fahrenheit (280 billion degrees Celsius), protons and neutrons formed the nuclei of hydrogen, helium, and lithium (the simplest elements).

It took another 500,000 years for atoms to form and 300 million more years for stars and galaxies to begin to appear. Countless stars, condensed from swirling nebulae (masses of gas and dust), evolved and died before our own sun and its planets came into being in a galaxy named the Milky Way. And it was only 4.5 billion years ago that our solar system was formed from a cloud of dust and gas.

The theory was developed in 1980 by American astronomer Alan Guth (b. 1947) and says, in short, that at its earliest stages, the universe expanded at a rate much faster than it is expanding today.

What is the **steady-state theory** of the universe?

The steady-state theory claims that the universe has always been essentially the same as it is today, and that it will continue that way forever. The theory stems from the cosmological principle, which states that the universe is the same everywhere. It proposes, in other words, that the same objects and gases fill the universe from end to end and that the view from one galaxy is not much different than the view from any other galaxy. The originator of the steady-state theory applied this concept of sameness to time as well as space to come up with the steady-state theory, claiming that the universe should look the same, not only in all places, but at all times—past, present, and future. The steady-state theory was offered in response to the other major theory of how the universe began, the big bang theory.

What is the **plasma theory** of the origin of the universe?

Originated by Swedish astrophysicist Hannes Olof Gösta Alfvén (1908–95), the plasma theory argues that 99 percent of the matter in the universe is composed of plasma. Alfvén's theory states that electrical currents in plasma interact with each other to produce swirling strands, which initiate a chain reaction. The strands cause matter to clump together, which produces greater swirling, followed by more matter, and so on. According to the theory, stars, planets, and other celestial objects were formed by this process.

Why is the theory of **solar system formation** put forth by **Laplace** and **Kant** so intriguing?

There are two major pieces of evidence that favor Laplace's and Kant's solar system formation theory. First, if the solar system did originate from a spinning disk of hot gas or dust, the planets that formed should follow this original turning motion. And all the planets in our solar system do indeed rotate around the Sun in the same direction.

Second, because a spinning disk would flatten as time went on, all planetary orbits should lie more or less along the same plane. And, with the exception of Pluto, all planets in our solar system lie more or less in the same plane. Pluto may have once been a giant asteroid, captured by the Sun's or outer planets' gravitational field—and thus is not in the same plane as the original planets. In fact, there is currently a movement afoot to "demote" Pluto to a minor planet, similar to an asteroid. But until scientists truly determine the definition of a planet, Pluto remains our ninth planet.

What is the **most widely accepted modern theory** of how the **solar system formed**?

Today, the most widely accepted theory of solar system formation is a variation of Laplace's and Kant's nebular hypothesis—that the system formed from a solar nebula. But there are also two variations of this theory, as the processes that occurred after the formation of the solar nebula are not well understood. (What is known is that nuclei, or cores of material, formed and eventually grew—a process called accretion—into the planets we know today.)

One idea is called the planetesimal theory. In 1944, German physicist Baron Carl Friedrich von Weizsäcker (b. 1912) made the nebular hypothesis more acceptable by suggesting that small bodies called planetesimals were attracted to each other to form the planets. In this scenario, the solar nebula started with grains of dust from which larger aggregations of material developed as the cloud cooled. The material condensed into small, rocky bodies; then more collisions formed large bodies. Some collections of the bodies smashed into one another, forming even larger planetesimals. Eventually, some of the collisions produced planetary-sized bodies, with Earth and other planets formed by this accretion.

The other major variation is the protoplanet hypothesis, which also states that the system started as an immense cloud of dust and gas. But in this case, it was a hot, heterogeneous accretion, with the collapsing dust and debris forming large and massive

5

Stellar view of Mars, a planet scientists have been studying for signs of past or present life forms. (Photo courtesy of National Aeronautics and Space Administration.)

protoplanets due to gravitational instabilities in the nebula. The planetesimal theory seems to best support the formation of the inner planets, their gaseous atmospheres probably blown away or greatly reduced when the Sun went through a time of intense early activity. The huge gaseous planets of the outer solar system seem to be best supported by the protoplanet hypothesis. These planets kept much of their original gases; in addition, the Sun's early activities did not affect the outer planets as much, allowing the gas giants to maintain their thick atmospheres.

What is the **age** of the **solar system**?

The nebula that formed the solar system is believed to have developed about 5 billion years ago. The planets and satellites we see today are thought to have formed about 4.6 billion years ago. To compare, the universe is thought to be about 15 to 20 billion years old. These dates are highly debated, as recent satellite data continue to puzzle astronomers—some interpretations suggesting that the universe may be as young as 8 to 12 billion years old.

Are there **other solar systems** in the universe?

Astronomers have long suggested that there are extrasolar planets (planets existing outside our solar system) in other solar systems, but the majority of claims have been

Is there life on planets in other solar systems?

Because of the great distances, it has been impossible for scientists to determine whether or not planets in other solar systems contain life. If we were able to gather certain data about the extrasolar planets, we may be able to tell if there is life on a planet other than our own. In particular, the presence of carbon dioxide could tell us that the planets have an atmosphere; a significant amount of water vapor (which is unique to Earth's atmosphere in our solar system) would tell us that a planet has an ocean; and finally, ozone, the layer of gas that protects life on Earth from the ultraviolet radiation from the Sun, may tell us if a planet has life. In many ways, it would be exciting to know that Earth was not unique in the universe. It would also be interesting to find out if there is any life out there similar to humans—or to dinosaurs.

refuted. It took new techniques and advances in technology before the existence of extrasolar planets was verified. In 1991, Polish astronomer Alexander Wolszczan and American astronomer Dan Frail found the first evidence of extrasolar planets orbiting pulsar PSR B1257+12, discovered by picking out the minute variations in the pulses sent from the spinning, dying neutron star. The planets had masses of 2.8 and 3.4 times that of Earth; in 1993, Wolszczan found evidence of another planet around the same pulsar. By 1995, Swiss astronomers Michael Mayor and Didier Queloz found a planetary companion around star 51 Pegasi b. Currently, close to a dozen such planets have been discovered.

These planets are extremely distant from Earth. To reach the nearest stellar system at Alpha Centauri 4.4 light years away (26 trillion miles, or a billion trips around Earth) traveling at the same speed as the *Voyager 1* spacecraft, it would take 40,000 years. For a planetary system similar to one found recently, the trip would be much longer, as the planet is about 35 light years away.

What is **Mercury**?

Mercury is a small, bleak planet, and the closest object to the Sun. Mercury is the second smallest planet in the solar system; only Pluto is smaller. Mercury's diameter is a little over one-third Earth's, yet it has just 5.5 percent of Earth's mass. On average, Mercury is 36 million miles (58 million kilometers) from the Sun. One effect of the Sun's intense gravitational field is to tilt Mercury's orbit and to stretch it into a long ellipse (oval). Mercury is named for the Roman messenger god with winged sandals. The planet was given its name because it orbits the Sun so quickly, in just 88 days. In contrast to its short year, Mercury has an extremely long day. It takes the planet the equivalent of 59 Earth days to complete one rotation.

Surface view of Mercury. (Photo courtesy of National Aeronautics and Space Administration.)

How **visible is Mercury** from Earth?

Because of the Sun's intense glare, it is difficult to observe Mercury from Earth. Mercury is visible only periodically, just above the horizon, for about one hour before sunrise and one hour after sunset. For these reasons, many people have never seen Mercury.

What forms **Mercury's core**?

The space probe *Mariner 10* gathered information about Mercury's core, which is nearly solid metal and is composed primarily of iron and nickel. This core, the densest of any in the solar system, accounts for about four-fifths of Mercury's diameter. It may also be responsible for creating the magnetic field that protects Mercury from the Sun's harsh particle wind.

What is **Venus**?

Venus is the second planet out from the Sun and the closest planet to Earth. Beginning in 1961, the United States and former Soviet Union have deployed a long string of space probes that have examined the Venusian atmosphere and peered beneath its dense cloud cover. The probes have revealed that Venus is an extremely hot, dry planet, with no signs of life. Its atmosphere is made primarily of carbon dioxide with some nitrogen and trace amounts of water vapor, acids, and heavy metals. Its clouds are laced with sulfur dioxide.

What is the **cause** of the **tremendous heat on Venus**?

Venus provides a perfect example of the greenhouse effect. Heat from the Sun penetrates the planet's atmosphere and reaches the surface. Atmospheric carbon dioxide prevents the heat from escaping back into space. The result is that Venus's surface temperature is a fierce 900 degrees Fahrenheit (482 degrees Celsius), even hotter than that of Mercury, its neighbor closer to the Sun.

What are the **surface features** of **Venus** like?

U.S. and Soviet space probes studying Venus uncovered a rocky surface covered with volcanoes (some still active), volcanic features (such as lava plains), channels (which look like dry riverbeds), mountains, and medium and large craters. No small craters exist, apparently because small meteorites cannot penetrate the planet's atmosphere. Another set of features found on the surface are arachnoids. These features are circular formations ranging anywhere from 30 to 137 miles (48 to 220 kilometers) in diameter, filled with concentric circles which extend spokes outward.

What is **Mars**?

Mars, the fourth planet out from the Sun in Earth's solar system, is about half the size of Earth and has a rotation period just slightly longer than one Earth day. Since it takes Mars 687 Earth days to orbit the Sun, its seasons are about twice as long as ours. Mars has two polar caps. The northern one is larger and colder than the southern. Two small moons, Phobos and Deimos, orbit the planet.

What are the so-called **canals** seen on Mars?

Mars is marked by what appear to be dry riverbeds and flash-flood channels. These features could mean that ice below the surface melts and is brought above ground by occasional volcanic activity. The water may temporarily flood the landscape before boiling away in the low atmospheric pressure. Another theory is that these eroded areas could be left over from a warmer, wetter period in Martian history.

What are **conditions like on Mars**?

Spacecraft sent to Mars revealed a barren, desolate, crater-covered world prone to frequent, violent dust storms. They found little oxygen, no liquid water, and ultraviolet radiation at levels that would kill any known life form. The high temperature on Mars was measured at -20 degrees Fahrenheit (-29 degrees Celsius) in the afternoon, and the low was -120 degrees Fahrenheit (-84 degrees Celsius) at night.

EARLY EARTH

Why is **Earth** considered a **unique planet** in our solar system?

Earth is unique in many ways. The most important reason is that our planet is at "the right place at the right time." Earth's orbit is just far enough away from the Sun to be in a belt called the "life" or "hospitable" zone. Its atmosphere is the only one with mostly nitrogen and oxygen gases. It has a thin crust consisting of moving plates, and has the most liquid water of any planet. And most importantly, as far as we know, Earth is the only planet in our solar system that contains life.

How do scientists think **Earth formed**?

Although there is continuing debate on the exact process by which Earth formed, many scientists think there were four basic steps involved. First, particles in the nebular cloud around the forming Sun smashed into each other, forming large chunks of rock called planetesimals. These planetesimals collided with each other, forming even larger masses, and continued to attract material from the nebular disk. In the second step, as more and more mass was added to the forming planets, the gravitational force grew. In the case of Earth, this compacted the material into a denser and smaller body—our planet reaching this point approximately 4.6 billion years ago.

The third step came when the interior of Earth began to heat up, caused by the compression from gravity and radioactive decay. As the amount of heat increased, the interior began to melt. In this hot mixture of melted material, iron was the heaviest element. Melting iron droplets slowly began to sink toward the center of Earth, condensing and forming the core of the planet. The fourth step came when the slow movement of molten iron sped up to catastrophic proportions, in a process called the "iron catastrophe." This final step set up the overall structure of the planet—eventually producing the three major layers of the core, mantle, and crust.

Did the discoverer of Halley's comet try to determine the **age of Earth**?

English astronomer Edmond Halley (1656–1742) theorized that one could estimate the age of Earth by calculating the amount of salt the rivers had dumped into the seas over the years. Based on Halley's presumption, Irish geologist John Joly (1857–1933) calculated that Earth and its oceans formed 80 to 90 million years ago. Astronomers currently believe Earth was formed with the rest of the solar system about 4.6 billion years ago.

What does **Earth's atmosphere** consist of?

Earth's atmosphere is made of 78 percent nitrogen, 21 percent oxygen, and 1 percent argon, with minute quantities of water vapor, carbon dioxide, and other gases.

A view of Earth from space. (Photo courtesy of U.S. National Aeronautics and Space Administration.)

How old is Earth?

Earth is currently believed to be about 4.6 billion years old, but scientists arrived at that number after centuries of debate. In 1779, French naturalist Comte de Georges Louis Leclerc Buffon (1707–88) caused a stir when he announced 75,000 years had gone by since Creation: it was the first time anyone had suggested that the planet was older than the biblical reference of 6,000 years. By 1830, Scottish geologist Charles Lyell (1797–1875) proposed that Earth must be several hundred million years old based on erosional rates; in 1844, British physicist William Thomson (1824–1907), later first baron of Largs (Lord) Kelvin, determined that Earth was 100 million years old, based on his studies of the planet's temperature. In 1907, American chemist and physicist Bertram Boltwood (1870–1927) used a radioactive dating technique to determine that a specific mineral was 4.1 billion years old (although later on, with a better knowledge of radioactivity, the mineral was found to be only 265 million years old). Using different adaptations of Boltwood's methods, scientists now estimate that Earth is about 4.6 billion years old.

How old is the **oldest rock and mineral** so far found on **Earth**?

The oldest rock is a 3.96 billion-year-old granite, found in the tundra of northwestern Canada near the Great Slave Lake. The oldest mineral is 4.3 billion years old, found in 1983 in Australia. The mineral was zircon in the from of crystals, which had eroded from the original rock.

How **far away and how big is Earth's moon**?

On average, Earth's moon is 238,900 miles (384,390 kilometers) from Earth. It measures about 2,160 miles (3,475 kilometers) across, a little over one-quarter of Earth's diameter. Earth and its moon are the closest in size of any known planet and satellite, with the possible exception of Pluto and its moon, Charon.

How strong is **gravity on the Moon**?

Gravity on the lunar surface is about one-sixth that of Earth.

What is the **Moon made of**?

The Moon is covered with rocks, boulders, craters, and a layer of charcoal-colored soil from 5 to 20 feet (1.5 to 6 meters) deep. The soil consists of rock fragments, pulverized rock, and tiny pieces of glass. Two types of rocks are found on the Moon: basalt, which

Granite patterns in the Wallowa Mountains of Oregon. Granite is among the oldest of Earth's rocks. (Photo courtesy of Gary Braasch/Corbis.)

is hardened lava; and breccia, which is soil and rock fragments that have melded together. Elements found in moon rocks include aluminum, calcium, iron, magnesium, titanium, potassium, and phosphorus. In contrast with Earth, which has a core rich in iron and other metals, the Moon appears to contain very little metal.

How old is the **oldest rock** so far found on the **Moon**?

The oldest rock carried back from the Apollo Moon missions is called the "Genesis rock," and is 4 billion years old. Scientists know there are probably older rocks on the lunar surface, as Earth's satellite no doubt formed at the same time as our planet.

How old are **rocks** on **Mars**?

Based on data collected from spacecraft sent to Mars, such as the Viking and Pathfinder craft, the rocks on Mars differ in age, depending on location. In fact, the planet is almost divided into two hemispheres, one younger than the other. In addition, most of the younger rocks are found around volcanic areas. But no matter where they are found, all of the rocks are thought to be several billions of years old.

How do scientists determine the **ages of rocks** from **distant planets**?

Because scientist have never collected rocks from such faraway places as Mars, Venus, or Mercury, they can only estimate the age of these planets' surfaces. They do this by

Earth's moon is about 2,160 miles across, a little over one-quarter of Earth's diameter. (Photo courtesy of National Aeronautics and Space Administration.)

determining the distribution and number of known impacts on one of these planets, comparing the numbers to the known impact crater distribution and surface ages on Earth and the Moon. From there, scientists extrapolate the planet's surface dates.

How does **Martian geology** differ from Earth's geology?

Mars is smaller, about half the size of Earth, with a radius of 2,108 miles (3,393 kilometers) compared to 3,963 miles (6,378 kilometers) for Earth. As a result, the Martian interior cooled more quickly than Earth's—thus, it has less volcanic activity than Earth. The red planet also has no plate tectonics. Its crust is rigid, unlike the constantly moving crust of the Earth. Therefore, Mars does not have extensive mountain chains, ocean troughs, or lines of volcanoes, such as those found on Earth.

What are the **layers** of Earth?

As Earth cooled, it settled into several layers like a giant onion, with each layer having its own particular characteristics. In general, from the inside out, the layers include the inner and outer core, the mantle, and the crust.

There is little direct evidence of what lies beneath our feet. The deepest mines extend to just over 2 miles (3.3 kilometers), and the deepest boreholes are only about 9 miles (15 kilometers) below the surface—mere scratches on a planet that has an average radius of nearly 4,000 miles (6,400 kilometers). Most of what we know about Earth's interior is based on the study of seismic waves generated by earthquakes, as the waves pass through—or don't pass through—certain layers of the interior.

What are the **masses** of Earth's **core, mantle,** and **crust**?

The crust accounts for 0.4 percent of Earth's mass. The mantle represents 67.1 percent of the planet's mass, and the core, about 32.5 percent.

How did scientists determine that Earth has an **inner and outer core**?

Researchers used generated earthquake waves to determine that there was an inner and outer core to our planet. The inner core was first identified in 1936, and by 1946 scientists had indirect proof that it was solid by observing how seismic waves change abruptly when passing through the region. Scientists knew that P-waves, or compressional waves, travel through materials by shaking molecules in a parallel direction to the waves; they cannot pass through solids. S-waves, on the other hand, move molecules side to side; they can pass through solids, but not liquids. Simply put, by watching the P- and S-waves from a multitude of earthquakes, scientists discovered that our planet's inner core was solid and the outer core was a liquid.

Which elements are contained in **Earth's crust**?

The most abundant elements in Earth's crust are listed in the following table below. In addition, nickel, copper, lead, zinc, tin, and silver account for less than 0.02 percent, with all other elements comprising 0.48 percent.

Element	Percentage
Oxygen	47.0
Silicon	28.0
Aluminum	8.0
Iron	4.5
Calcium	3.5
Magnesium	2.5
Sodium	2.5
Potassium	2.5
Titanium	0.4
Hydrogen	0.2
Carbon	0.2
Phosphorous	0.1
Sulfur	0.1

When did Earth's **crust** become **solid**?

Earth's crust solidified at the same time as the rest of the inner planets—and even the Moon—about 4.6 billion years ago. The early crust was not as stable as today, as the heat from the planet's formation continually created cracks, spectacular volcanic activity, and huge mountain chains. Today, the crust has cooled more and settled down considerably, although it is still extremely active with volcanoes, earthquakes, and continental movements. The crust is not the same thickness everywhere, either: it is typically only about 4 miles (6 kilometers) thick under the oceans, and about 20 miles (32 kilometers) under the continents.

How many **kinds of volcanoes** are there?

Volcanoes are usually cone-shaped hills or mountains built around a vent connecting to reservoirs of molten rock, or magma, below the surface of Earth. At times the molten rock is forced upward by gas pressure until it breaks through weak spots in Earth's crust. The magma erupts forth as lava flows or shoots into the air as clouds of lava fragments, ash, and dust. The accumulation of debris from eruptions causes the volcano to grow in size. There are four kinds of volcanoes:

Cinder cones are built of lava fragments. They have slopes of 30 to 40 degrees and seldom exceed 1,640 feet (500 meters) in height. Sunset Crater in Arizona and Paricutin in Mexico are examples of cinder cones.

Composite cones are made of alternating layers of lava and ash. They are characterized by slopes of up to 30 degrees at the summit, tapering off to five degrees at the base. Mount Fuji in Japan and Mount St. Helens in Washington are composite cone volcanoes.

Shield volcanoes are built primarily of lava flows. Their slopes are seldom more than 10 degrees at the summit and two degrees at the base. The Hawaiian Islands are clusters of shield volcanoes. Mauna Loa is the world's largest active volcano, rising 13,653 feet (4,161 meters) above sea level.

What is the **Late Heavy Bombardment,** also called the **Great Bombardment**?

While Earth's crust was in its infancy, the solar system was still in the process of formation. The area was cluttered with chunks of debris orbiting the Sun. From about 4.0 to 3.8 billion years ago, large rocks and debris were attracted to, and thus constantly bombarded, the largest planets and satellites—including Earth and the Moon. This Great Bombardment is most evident on our own Moon, seen as the hundreds of large and small craters on the lunar surface. Because the Moon has no atmosphere, these large craters and basins are essentially "fossils," showing the massive bombardment phase that took place. Today, there are fewer space objects striking Earth and the

Moon. But every year, Earth attracts more than a million tons of new material from outer space. Luckily, the majority of the debris and dust is small enough to burn up in our atmosphere.

What caused early Earth's **water** and **atmosphere** to form?

No one really knows how the oceans filled with water. One theory is that volcanoes released enough water vapor to condense and fill the oceans. Another theory states that comets bombarded our planet just after the formation of the solar system, bringing enough water to eventually fill the oceans.

The origin of Earth's atmosphere is also debated, but not as intensely. In this case, it is more likely that some of the atmosphere originated from the gases that were part of the solar nebula; other gases were produced from volcanic activity. Earth probably would have had a thicker atmosphere, too, but the young active Sun's heat boiled away the lighter materials—elements that are still found today around the "gas giant" planets (Jupiter, Saturn, Uranus, and Neptune).

What **gases** began to **accumulate** after Earth's crust finally solidified?

As Earth's crust solidified, gases began pouring out of fissures and volcanoes, accumulating in the forming atmosphere. These same gases still emanate from modern volcanoes, and include carbon dioxide (CO_2), water vapor (H_2O), carbon monoxide (CO), nitrogen (N_2), and hydrogen chloride (HCl).

As these gases interacted in the atmosphere, they combined to form hydrogen cyanide (HCN), methane (CH_4), ammonia (NH_4), and many other compounds. Needless to say, this atmosphere would be lethal to most present-day life-forms. Over the next 2 to 3 billion years, the atmosphere continued to change, until it reached close to its present-day composition.

What does the atmosphere of **Venus** have in common with **Earth's early atmosphere**?

Scientists believe that Earth's early atmosphere—before plants developed photosynthesis and started producing oxygen—was somewhat similar to the atmosphere of Venus. The early atmosphere had a great deal of carbon dioxide, mostly in the form of gases spewed out by volcanic activity. Venus continued to build up carbon dioxide, the gas produced by the intense solar heat, scorching carbonate rocks. This created a condition now called the greenhouse effect—the global temperatures rise when certain gases, including carbon dioxide, trap the Sun's energy and keep it within the global atmosphere. But things changed for Earth: the carbon dioxide in the atmosphere gradually dwindled over millions of years. Life on Earth eventually produced oxygen, using carbon dioxide for photosynthesis; and even more carbon dioxide was absorbed by carbonate rocks.

How do the **atmospheres of Venus, Earth, and Mars** compare today?

The atmospheres of these three inner planets (Mercury is the other inner planet but has no true atmosphere) vary considerably. Overall, Venus's and Earth's atmospheres are the thickest; Venus's atmospheric composition (carbon dioxide) and closeness to the Sun cause it to have one of the hottest surface temperatures in the solar system.

How did **oxygen** form on **early Earth**?

The early atmosphere was composed mainly of water vapor, carbon dioxide and monoxide, nitrogen, hydrogen, and other gases released by volcanoes. By about 4.3 billion years ago, the atmosphere contained no oxygen and about 54 percent carbon dioxide. Just over 2 billion years ago, plants in the oceans began to produce oxygen by photosynthesis, which involved taking in carbon dioxide. By 2 billion years ago, there was 1 percent oxygen in the atmosphere and only 4 percent carbon dioxide—reduced from the intake by plants and taken up by carbonate rocks. By about 600 million years ago, atmospheric oxygen continued to increase as volcanoes and climate changes buried a great deal of plant material—plants that would have absorbed oxygen from the atmosphere if they had decomposed in the open. Today, our planet's atmosphere levels measure 21 percent oxygen, 78 percent nitrogen, and only 0.036 percent carbon dioxide.

How is **energy produced in the Sun**?

Energy in the form of heat and light is produced by a reaction called nuclear fusion in the Sun's core. The pressure at the core (312,000 miles, or 500,000 kilometers, below the Sun's surface) is great enough to squeeze gas molecules into a material 10 times as dense as gold. And the temperature is 27 million degrees Fahrenheit (15 million degrees Celsius). In that intensely hot, pressurized environment, four hydrogen nuclei combine into one helium nucleus, releasing a tremendous amount of energy in the process.

Which **planets experience** the **greenhouse effect**?

A prime example of the greenhouse effect can be found on Venus. There solar radiation penetrates the atmosphere, reaches the surface, and is reflected back into the atmosphere. The re-radiated heat is trapped by carbon dioxide, the primary constituent of Venus's atmosphere. The result is that Venus has a scorching surface temperature of 900 degrees Fahrenheit (480 degrees Celsius). The greenhouse effect can also be found on Earth and in the upper atmospheres of the giant planets: Jupiter, Saturn, Uranus, and Neptune.

> ## What is the greenhouse effect?
>
> The greenhouse effect, as its name implies, describes a warming phenomenon. In a greenhouse, closed glass windows cause heat to become trapped inside. The greenhouse effect functions in a similar manner on the scale of an entire planet. It occurs when a planet's atmosphere allows heat from the Sun to enter but refuses to let it leave.

How does the **greenhouse effect work on Earth**?

On Earth, solar radiation passes through the atmosphere and strikes the surface. As it is reflected back up, some solar radiation is trapped by atmospheric gases (such as carbon dioxide, methane, chlorofluorocarbons, and water vapor), resulting in the gradual increase of Earth's temperature. The rest of the radiation escapes back into space.

What **causes Earth's greenhouse effect**?

Human activity is largely responsible for the buildup of greenhouse gases in Earth's atmosphere, and hence Earth's gradual warming. For instance, the burning of fossil fuels (such as coal, oil, and natural gas) and forest fires add carbon dioxide to the atmosphere. Methane buildup comes from the use of pesticides and fertilizers in agriculture. Large amounts of water vapor are emitted as an industrial by-product. And chlorofluorocarbons (CFCs) are produced by some aerosol spray cans and coolants in refrigerators and air conditioners.

How **serious** is the **greenhouse gas buildup** in Earth's atmosphere?

Between the start of this century and 1970, the atmospheric carbon dioxide level rose 7 percent and that rate is on the rise. The resulting temperature increase has caused more water to evaporate from the oceans (as well as some ice to melt in the Arctic), which, in turn, increases the clouds in the atmosphere. While the greater cloud cover blocks some solar heat from entering our atmosphere, it also worsens the greenhouse effect by trapping more of the heat that does make it down to the surface. With a slow but steady increase in the world's temperature, Earth could, far in the future, become scorching like Venus.

What is **ozone** and how does it benefit **Earth**?

Ozone, or three molecules of oxygen (O_3, as compared with the O_2 we breathe), usually refers to a blanket of gas found between 9 and 25 miles (15 and 40 kilometers) up in

19

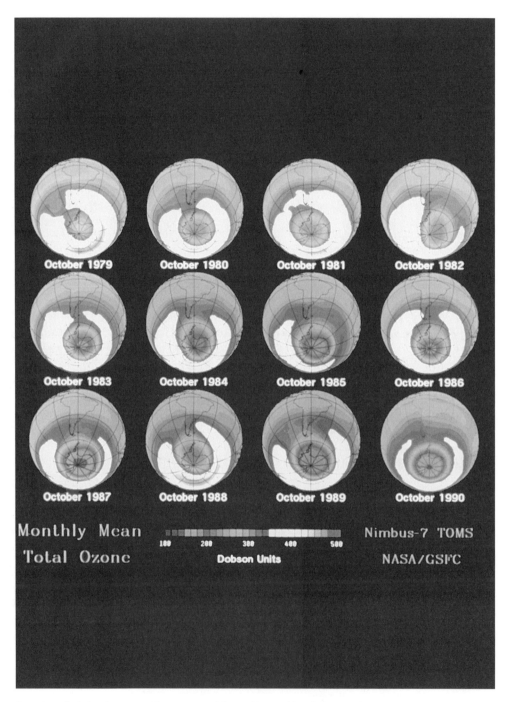

Ozone layer depletion since 1979. (Chart courtesy of National Aeronautics and Space Administration.)

Earth's atmosphere (in the layer called the stratosphere). The so-called "ozone layer" is produced by the interaction of the Sun's radiation with certain air molecules. The blue-tinged ozone gas is also found in the lower atmosphere. While beneficial in the stratosphere, ozone forms what is called photochemical smog at ground level. This smog is a secondary pollutant produced by the photochemical reactions of certain air pollutants, usually from industrial activities and cars.

The stratosphere's ozone layer is important to all life on the planet because it protects organisms from the Sun's damaging ultraviolet radiation. Scientists believe that about 2 billion years ago, oxygen was being produced by shallow-water marine plants undergoing photosynthesis. This sudden, geologically speaking, outpouring of oxygen helped build up the ozone layer. As the oxygen levels increased, ocean animals also arose. Once the protective ozone layer was in place in the atmosphere, it allowed the marine plants and animals to safely spread onto land.

Why are people **concerned** about the **ozone layer today**?

The stratosphere's ozone layer blankets the entire planet. During certain times of the year, the ozone layer over the Southern Hemisphere's Antarctic continent diminishes, creating an "ozone hole." Over the years, scientists have been measuring the ozone hole using Earth-orbiting satellites, and have noticed an increase in the size of the hole. There is also concern that an ozone hole detected recently over the Arctic in the Northern Hemisphere is also increasing. The reason for concern about the ozone holes is understandable: the loss of ozone means some sensitive organisms—and those vital to Earth's food chain—may be killed by exposure to intense ultraviolet radiation from the Sun.

No one knows the actual reason for the increase in the ozone holes, but many scientists have pointed to chlorofluorocarbons, organic compounds containing chlorine and fluorine (CFCs) as the culprit. Although the United States banned the use of fluorocarbon aerosols in 1978, and other measures have been taken to reduce the use of CFCs around the world, scientists have not yet noticed a dramatic shrinkage of the ozone hole. Some researchers believe that it will take time for Earth's ozone to "adjust" to the lower levels of CFCs—but no one knows how long. Other scientists believe that CFCs are not the culprit, and that the ozone hole expansion may be a natural change.

THE BEGINNINGS OF LIFE

When did **life first** begin on **Earth**?

No one knows the precise time that life began on Earth. One reason is that early life consisted of single-cell organisms. Because the soft parts of an organism are the first

Meteorite ALH84001, which is 4.5 billion years old, may contain evidence of former life on Mars. (Photo courtesy of National Aeronautics and Space Administration.)

to decay and disappear after death, it is almost impossible to find the remains of such organisms. In addition, because the organisms were so small, they are difficult to detect in ancient rocks. Some modern viruses are only about 18 nanometers (18 billionths of a meter) across, and modern bacteria typically measure 1,000 nanometers across—much larger than the early organisms. Despite such obstacles, scientists estimate that the first life began about 4 billion years ago. These organisms did not survive on oxygen, but on carbon dioxide.

What did the **earliest life on Earth** look like?

Because scientists have found so little fossil evidence, it is difficult to know all the true shapes of the earliest life. Scientists believe that early life was composed of primitive single-cells and started in the oceans. The reason is simple: life needed a filter to protect it from the incoming ultraviolet energy from the Sun—and the ocean waters gave life that protection.

Is there **life** on any of the **planets or satellites** in our solar system?

So far, scientists have found no verifiable evidence of life on any planet in the solar system except Earth. Recent images taken by spacecraft of various moons around the planets have caused scientists to speculate about other life in the solar system. For example,

> ## Why did life develop on Earth and not on the other planets?
>
> Scientists recognize something called the "life zone," a region around a star in which life can develop if the conditions, especially temperatures, are right. Earth had the right temperature to allow water to circulate in all three states—solid, liquid, and water vapor—conditions that eventually helped to produce life as we know it.

Europa, one of the largest moons around Jupiter, may have a huge ocean underneath its thick cover of surface ice. Some scientists believe that such an ocean may harbor some type of life. The largest moon around Saturn, called Titan, has the thickest atmosphere of any satellite in the solar system—and includes hydrocarbons necessary for life to form. All this is pure speculation until scientists can gather better data.

The closest scientists have come to finding life within the solar system is based on a meteorite that allegedly came from Mars. In 1996, meteorite ALH84001, found in Antarctica years before, reportedly showed fossil evidence of minuscule bacteria, bio-generated materials, and organic compounds suggestive of life. Whether or not the rock contains the traces of life is highly debated. Some scientists say that the carbonates found were deposited at temperatures far above the boiling point of water, and would thus destroy the life; others say that the tiny worm shapes and ovid features are artifacts of the techniques used to analyze the rock. The jury is still out on this finding—at least until more Martian rocks can be examined. But if true, it would be one of most significant scientific discoveries of all time.

Who found **ALH84001,** the celebrated "life on Mars" meteorite?

In 1984 Roberta Score, a member of the Antarctic Search for Meteorites (ANSMET) team, found the famed meteorite that may contain indication of ancient life on Mars. More than 60 research groups are now studying pieces of ALH84001.

What **conditions on early Earth** could have **led to life**?

Two major theories explain how life could have grown on early Earth. The first theory states that life grew from a primordial "soup," a thick stew of biomolecules and water. Chemical reactions were then triggered—either by the Sun's ultraviolet rays, lightning, or even the shock waves from a violent meteor strike. These reactions produced various carbon compounds—including amino acids, which make up the proteins found in all living organisms. This theory was first postulated after a famous experiment performed at the University of Chicago in 1954, by then-graduate student Stanley Miller (b. 1930), and his advisor, chemist Harold Urey (1893–1981). They showed

23

that the amino acids could be formed from chemicals thought to exist in Earth's early atmosphere, when these were combined with water and zapped by lightning.

The second theory of life conditions centers around a more recent discovery: hydrothermal vents, which are cracks caused by volcanic magma seeping through the deep ocean floor. There were probably many more hydrothermal vents on early Earth, as the crust was newer, and thus thinner, than today's cooled, thicker crust. The organisms around these vents did not need to rely on photosynthesis for energy. Today's volcanic vent organisms live off the bacteria around the vents, which in turn extract energy from the hot, hydrogen sulfide-rich water found around the sunless cracks in the ocean floor. Early organisms could have survived in much the same way.

In actuality, the conditions described by both theories could have existed simultaneously to produce the planet's early life.

When were the **hydrothermal vents** called **black smokers** discovered?

Special types of hydrothermal vents called black smokers were discovered in 1977 in the ocean off the Galapagos Islands. They were found by scientists investigating the ocean floor in the deep-diving submersible *Alvin*, a "mini-sub" built by the Woods Hole Oceanographic Institution in Woods Hole, Massachusetts.

How do these **black smokers** form?

Black smokers form as a consequence of volcanic activity on the ocean floor. These areas of activity can be thought of as gigantic heat engines, forcing seawater through the crust, where it is heated to temperatures as high as 752 degrees Fahrenheit (400 degrees Celsius). This super-heated water dissolves and transports many elements, including sulfur, zinc, copper, and gold; the mineral-laden water is then forced out of the crust in a plume at a hydrothermal vent. Reaction of the hot water with the surrounding cold ocean water causes precipitation of sulfide and sulfate minerals, and gives the flowing plume a black color. These minerals are deposited around the plumes, sulfide chimneys build up, through which black water continually flows out—hence the name black smokers. Some chimneys recovered from the ocean floor measured 5 feet (1.5 meters) tall, and ranged in weight from 1,200 pounds to more than 4,000 pounds.

Where are **black smokers** usually found?

Black smokers tend to occur on volcanically active midocean ridges, though not every ridge has them. To date, only a relatively few sites with black smokers have been found because only a small portion of the world's approximately 31,070 miles (50,000 kilometers) of ridges have been fully explored. The great depths, darkness, and enormous pressures make it difficult to explore these areas.

Is there **life** growing around modern **hydrothermal vents**?

Yes, a variety of life grows around hydrothermal vents. For example, different types of microbes live in the interiors of the black smoker chimneys, some of which are "heat-loving," or thermophilic. Currently, these microbes are some of the most primitive forms of life known on Earth. The organisms use hydrogen sulfide from the hot water plume as their primary energy source. There are also other animals surrounding the vents, such as white crabs that resemble those found elsewhere on the ocean floor—but they move around without the use of their small eyes. Huge white clams grow around the vents; and huge red and white tubeworms called *Riftia* (named after being discovered around deep sea rifts) cluster around the open vents. This unique ecosystem is the only one on Earth in which the immediate source of energy is not the Sun's rays.

Did **life** arrive **from space**?

There is another theory (known as panspermia) of how the precursors of life were brought to Earth: by the early bombarding of comets and asteroids that contained complex organic materials. In the late 1960s, radio astronomers discovered organic molecules in dark nebulae. Since that time, other sources have been discovered, including organic molecules in such space bodies as asteroids, comets, and meteorites. In 1969, analysis of a meteorite showed at least 74 amino acids within the chunk of rock. Scientists began to speculate that the organic molecules could have traveled to Earth via meteorites, cometary dust—or, during the early years of Earth, by way of comets and asteroids. Although many scientists argue that the heat from the impact of a giant asteroid or comet would fry the organics, many other scientists disagree. They propose that only the outer layers of a large body would have been affected; or that the fine, unheated dust of comets could have brought the necessary amino acids to early Earth. If this theory is true, as many scientists say, we are apparently all—from dinosaurs to humans—made of "starstuff." Also, if there is more scientific evidence to support such a theory it would simplify the search for the origin of life on Earth.

Who originated the idea called **panspermia**?

Panspermia is the idea that microorganisms, spores, or bacteria attached to tiny particles of matter have traveled through space, eventually landing on a suitable planet and initiating the rise of life there. The word panspermia means "all-seeding." The British scientist Lord Kelvin (1825–1907) suggested in the nineteenth century that life may have arrived here from outer space, perhaps carried by meteorites. In 1903, the Swedish chemist Svante Arrhenius (1859–1927) put forward the more complex

The chemical composition of pyrite (pictured here) may have sparked cells into self-replicating. (Photo courtesy of Field Mark Publications.)

panspermia idea that life on Earth was "seeded" by means of extraterrestrial spores, bacteria, and microorganisms coming here on tiny bits of cosmic matter.

How did **life** begin to **replicate itself** on Earth?

Early Earth no doubt had organic compounds, most likely held in a watery soup many have termed the "primordial soup." But in order for early life to form and self-replicate, there had to be some mechanism to encourage the early biomolecules to "stick" together. There are plenty of theories; the following lists the rock surfaces and/or conditions that could have allowed small organic molecules to assemble into self-replicating biomolecules:

Pyrite—Pyrite, or iron sulfate, may have been a catalyst, the surface of the rock allowing the molecules to adhere and begin an energy-producing reaction—perhaps something similar to an early form of photosynthesis.

Zeolites—Zeolites, a silica-rich mineral, is hydrophilic (waterloving), tending to absorb water from its surroundings. Among the zeolites is a recently discovered type called mutinaite, a naturally occurring organophilic zeolite that prefers to absorb organic materials out of water. It is possible that mutinaite, which has aluminum in place of silica, loses aluminum at its surface as it weathers. If such zeolites were at the right place at the right time, the remaining aluminum within the rock would have provided centers for organic molecules—especially amino acids—to assemble and thus eventually produce life.

Clay—Surfaces of clay, a sedimentary rock, may have been perfect places to produce self-replicating biomolecules. One reason is that clay can store energy, change it, and then release it in the form of chemical energy. This release of energy may have been harnessed by the early biomolecules, advancing the growth of life.

Bubbles—One of the more interesting ways of growing biomolecules is through bubbles—similar to those that appear at the foamy edge of the water on a beach. The bubbles could have "gathered" the biomolecules, encouraging the growth of life.

Spontaneous reaction—One of the most simple theories (but harder to explain) is that organic molecules eventually and spontaneously produced self-replicating biomolecules.

When did the **basic form** of life **develop** on Earth?

It is thought that about 3.5 billion years ago, a basic form of life was present on Earth. This life took the form of tiny cells, which were surrounded by membranes to isolate and protect their interiors from the surrounding environment. The cells had a basic genetic system similar to those in modern cells; this allowed the cells to self-replicate. Scientists classify these earliest life forms as prokaryotes, comprised of such organisms as bacteria and cyanobacteria.

When did **larger cells** develop?

Larger cells classified as eukaryotes began to develop approximately 1.9 to 1.5 billion years ago, according to the known fossil record. Before this time, rock layers contained only tiny prokaryotes, such as bacteria and blue-green algae.

What was the **nature** of these **larger cells**?

The eukaryotes were symbiotic (coactive) colonies of the smaller prokaryotes; they also had a nucleus. Many of these smaller cells "within" the larger cells eventually evolved into organelles, independently replicating themselves with their own DNA (deoxyribonucleic acid) sequences. For example, the mitochondria organelle processed oxygen, and the chloroplast organelles carried out the process of photosynthesis. The larger cells developed into protozoa, certain algae, and eventually all multicellular life.

When did the first **multicellular forms** of life develop?

Based on the known fossil record, the first primitive forms of multicellular life apparently developed around 650 million years ago. One of the first such organisms is thought to have been a primitive form of sponge. The first fossil records of burrows are also found around the same time.

What was the **nature** of these first multicellular **organisms**?

These first multicellular organisms are called Ediacara assemblages. They all seemed to have large surface areas, perhaps in response to their need to absorb oxygen, as there were very small concentrations of this gas present in the atmosphere at that time. They appear to have lived in shallow environments.

Could life have **survived impacts** and the resulting **extreme climate changes**?

Scientists believe life could have survived extreme changes. In particular, the areas around deep ocean black smokers could have been "safe havens" for primitive forms of life during extreme impact events of comets or asteroids. These impacts would have caused the extinction of other, more advanced organisms that lived in shallow waters or relied on the Sun's light—light that was blocked by the debris thrown into the atmosphere by the impact. The smaller organisms in the deeper water around the smokers would have survived as their food was provided by the volcanic vents. Then, as conditions slowly returned to equilibrium, life could have again spread outward from the smokers.

What are the **oldest known fossils** found in rock on Earth?

The oldest known fossils in rock have been found in Australia. One set of fossils found in western Australia are dated between 3.45 and 3.55 billion years old. They show evidence of layered mounds of limestone sediment called stromatolites, formed by primitive microorganisms similar to blue-green algae called cyanobacteria. Scientists know that stromatolites exist today: the fossils look amazingly like the stromatolites from the shallow waters off the coast of modern Australia.

There are other contenders for the oldest known fossils: tiny simple cells have also been found in ancient cherts (rocks) from Australia and similar ones from Africa. These cells are preserved by the silica from the chert, and appear to show a cell wall of some kind.

What is the **oldest known land life** found in rock on Earth?

In 1994, the earliest known land life was allegedly found in Arizona—fossil tubular microorganisms dating from 1.2 billion years ago. With better detection techniques, more such ancient fossils will be found—confirming this find, and determining what type of life existed so long ago.

What are **flora** and **fauna**?

Flora and fauna are scientific terms for plants and animals, respectively.

When did the **first plants** appear in the **oceans**?

The first fossil evidence of plants—and the earliest recorded evidence for life on Earth—was found in Australian rock dated between 3.45 and 3.55 billion years old. But scientists believe that life actually started long before that, about 4 billion years ago. There are two reasons that scientists have not found fossils that are old enough to substantiate this belief. First, it is difficult to find rock that has not been changed by heat, pressure, or erosion over the past 4 billion years. Second, because the single-cells are so small, they are difficult to find; and because they were made of soft parts only, they probably decayed after death—leaving no evidence of their existence.

What were the **first primitive plants** to appear on **land**?

The first primitive plants appeared on land about 470 million years ago, according to recent findings. But these plants did not look like the lush greenery we see around us today. Rather, they were rootless patches of thin, leaflike plants called liverworts, so named because some species resemble green livers; they used a specialized filament, called a rhizoid, to absorb water and adhere to rocks.

After the Cambrian Explosion of life, about 544 million years ago, the oceans teemed with multicellular plants and animals. But the land remained empty of life, except for an occasional microbe—probably in shallow pools. Animals in the oceans had no incentive to colonize the land, because there was nothing for them to eat. So it was up to the plants, specifically the liverwort, to make the great leap from the oceans and become the first multicellular organisms to live on dry land.

We still have liverworts in the world today, such as the common and braided liverworts in the United States. They, too, lead mosslike lives, and are often shaped like a flat, green liver. But so far, scientists do not know how the familial relationship among the more than 8,000 species present on Earth fits in with the lineage of the ancient liverworts.

29

Jellyfish were among the first soft-bodied creatures to appear in the oceans. (Photo courtesy of Jeffrey L. Rotman/Corbis.)

When did the **first true plants** appear on **land**?

Fossils reveal that the first true plants to colonize land appeared about 420 million years ago, and included flowerless mosses, horsetails, and ferns. They reproduced by throwing out spores, or minute organisms that carried the genetic blueprint for the plant. The ferns eventually bore seeds, but it took until about 345 million years ago. Vascular plants—those with roots, stems, and leaves—evolved about 408 million years ago.

How do scientists know that **liverworts** were probably the **first plants** to colonize the land?

Because of recent research into plant genetics, scientists know that liverworts were the first plants to colonize dry land. For a long time, scientists believed that plants made the transition to land just once, as opposed to the apparent repeated transitions of animals. Their conclusion, then, was that the first land plant was the ancestor of all living plants.

The problem was to determine which plant was truly the first. The two contenders for this title were the most simple, primitive plants known—the mosses and liverworts, both of which are related to the ocean's green algae. Unfortunately, the fossil record is incomplete—with no good indications of which plant was the original colonist.

Recently researchers turned to genetic research, focusing on extraneous pieces of genes known as introns, which are found in more than 300 modern plants. Over the course of evolution, introns have "pushed" their way into the genes of plants; they get "cut out" of the gene before it makes a protein. Scientists narrowed their research to three ancient introns, none of which are present in green algae. They found that trees, flowers, and other common modern plants have at least two of the three ancient introns present, as does moss. The liverworts, on the other hand, lacked all three ancient introns, making them the closest relatives to the water-loving green algae. And because of this relationship—and knowing that green algae was one of the oldest types of organisms—many scientists now believe liverworts were the first plants to colonize the land.

What is a **spore**?

Spore plants reproduce asexually or sexually with spores, microparticles that grow into new plants. They are loosely divided into the vascular plants such as ferns, which survive in semiwet habitats, and semiterrestrial mosses and others plants with hairlike rootlets that absorb water and nutrients.

What is a **seed**?

A seed is a container in which a plant embryo develops. It has a hard or sturdy outer shell, and contains food for the embryo, such as sugars, starches, and proteins.

What was the **advantage** of a plant evolving **seeds to reproduce**?

The advantage of seeds was—and continues to be—for easier reproduction of land plants. In particular, unlike early plants, seed plants no longer needed large bodies of water for reproduction. This allowed the plants to spread across diverse areas of the dry land. Because of their relatively hard coatings, seeds could be dispersed by winds and water. Fauna also ingested seeds, with the covering protecting the plant embryo until they were dispersed elsewhere in the animals droppings.

When did the **first soft-bodied animals** appear in the oceans?

Fossils reveal that the first soft-bodied animals appeared about 600 million years ago in the oceans, and included a form of jellyfish and segmented worms.

What were the **first land animals**?

Fossils reveal that the first animals to conquer the land may have been the arthropods, such as scorpions and spiders. Many of these creatures have been found in Silurian period rock layers, usually in association with fossils of the oldest known vascular land plants.

Insects and spiders appeared on land before dinosaurs dominated the Earth. (Photo courtesy of Field Mark Publications.)

Why did animals **first move** onto the **dry land**?

No one truly knows why the first animals moved from the oceans to dry land—but there are plenty of theories. One is that animals wanted to expand their territory, similar to the way many modern animals behave. Another possibility was for a better food source: as more animals evolved, there would be a higher demand for food. By adapting to land life—and the "new" food sources on land—these organisms would have a better chance of survival.

How long did it take for **dinosaurs** to evolve from the **first land animals**?

The first land animals evolved around 440 million years ago and the dinosaurs evolved around 250 million years ago. Thus, it took about 190 million years for dinosaurs to appear after the first land animals. These numbers are based on the currently known fossil record, and could change if new fossils are found.

What **percent** of the **geologic time scale** did **dinosaurs** live?

Scientists estimate that dinosaurs existed on Earth for about 150 million years. Thus, dinosaurs only lived 3.1 percent of the time that has passed since the formation of

Earth.

When did the first primitive dinosaurs appear?

The first primitive dinosaurs appeared about 230 million years ago. They were much smaller and less fierce than the *Tyrannosaurus rex* we often think of when someone mentions the word dinosaur.

When did the **first humans appear**?

The first appearance of anatomically modern humans known as *Homo sapiens* occurred approximately 130,000 to 100,000 years ago—meaning we have been around in our current form for an extremely short period, geologically speaking. Our sub-species of humans, *Homo sapiens sapiens*, have only been around for less than 100,000 years. But our humanoid ancestors have been around for 4 to 6 million years—a blink of time when one considers that Earth is about 4.6 billion years old.

How can you visualize the **amount of time humans** have been on **Earth**?

Humans have been on Earth for an incredibly short period of time, compared to the age of the planet. One way to understand relative time was suggested by author John McPhee in his book *Basin and Range:* Stand with your arms held straight out to each side. The extent of Earth's history—represented by the geological time scale—is the entire distance from the tip of your fingers on the left hand to the tip of your fingers on the right. If someone were to run a nail file across the fingernail of your right middle finger—and that chunk of nail represented time—it would erase the amount of time humans have been on the planet.

FORMING FOSSILS

GEOLOGIC TIME

What is **geologic time**?

Geologic time is the immense span of time that has elapsed since planet Earth first formed—almost 4.5 billion years ago—to the recent times.

What **principles** led to a way of **keeping track** of geologic time?

Danish scholar Nicolaus Steno (Nils Stensen, 1638–86) devised principles that would eventually allowed scientists to keep track of geologic time. He wrote the first real geological treatise in the seventeenth century, postulating four principles of stratigraphy (the study of rock layers). One of the most important was the principle of superposition, also known as Steno's law. In it, he stated that rock layers were laid down in chronological order, with the oldest being the deepest, and the youngest being nearer the surface. Steno's principles laid the groundwork, as it were, for the geologic time scale.

What is the **geologic time scale**?

The geologic time scale is a way of putting our planet's vast history into an orderly fashion, giving a better perspective of events. At the turn of the nineteenth century, William Smith (1769–1839), an English canal engineer, observed that certain types of rocks, along with certain groups of fossils, always occurred in a predictable order in relation to each other. In 1815, he published a map of England and Wales geology, establishing a practical system of stratigraphy, or the study of geological history layer by layer. Simply put, Smith proposed that the lowest rocks in a cliff or quarry are the oldest, while the highest are the youngest. By observing fossils and rock type in the various layers, it was possible to correlate the rocks at one location with those at other locations. Smith's work, combined with the first discoveries of dinosaur fossils in the early 1800s, led to a framework (the geologic time scale, with its various, arbitrary divisions of time including eras, periods, and epochs that scientists still use today in order to divide planet Earth's long history). Established between 1820 and 1870, the time divisions are a relative means of dating; that is, rocks and fossils are dated relative to each other as to which are older and younger. It was not until radiometric dating was invented in the 1920s that absolute dates were applied to rocks and fossils—and thus, also the geologic time scale.

What does the **geologic time scale** look like?

The geologic time scale divisions have changed significantly over time, mainly because of new fossil discoveries and better dating techniques—and it will no doubt continue to change. The following is a general listing of the geologic time table, based on current interpretations of rocks and fossils, indicating how many millions of years ago each era ended.

Geologic Time Scale

Era	Period	Millions of Years Ago	Life Form(s) at That Time
Cenozoic	Quaternary	2	Modern life, including man, evolves; man takes the place of dinosaurs and becomes the dominant creature of the land.
	Tertiary	65	Flowers begin to flourish and mammals diversify into myriad shapes and sizes.
Mesozoic	Cretaceous	144	As many dinosaurs become extinct, flowering plant life appears.
	Jurassic	136	Huge dinosaurs (divided into herbivores and carnivores) roam the land, toothed birds appear along with the first primitive marine life and reptiles.
	Triassic	245	Dinosaurs evolve from thecodont ("socket-tooth") reptiles; dicynodonts ("two dog tooth") or primitive mammals such as *Kannemeyeria,* and early placental mammals such as *Zalambdalestes,* appear.
Paleozoic (Time of Early Life)	Permian	250	Seed plants (gymnosperms) begin to grow; insects, snails, and other invertebrates face mass extinction.
	Carboniferous	290	Forests flourish with fern trees; huge insects, amphibians, and evolving reptiles take advantage of the growing foliage.

Era	Period	Millions of Years Ago	Life Form(s) at That Time
	Devonian	350	Cartilaginous fishes (sharks and eels) are abundant; first amphibians, invertebrates, and land plants appear.
	Silurian	400	Invertebrates dominate the land and wide coral reefs cover the planet; agnathans (fish without jaws) and armored fish flourish.
	Ordovician	510	First vertebrates (agnathans) appear, along with marine invertebrates of all shapes and sizes.
	Cambrian	550	Only marine invertebrates exist, along with a few land creatures.
Pre-Cambrian		600 mill. –4.6 bill.	Origin of the solar system and Earth, only one-celled, soft-bodied marine organisms exist.

How are the divisions on the **geologic time scale named**?

Most of the major divisions on the geologic time scale are based on Latin names, or areas in which the rocks were first found. For example, the Carboniferous period gets its name from the Latin words for "carbon bearing," in reference to the coal-rich rocks found in England, and after which the period is named. The Jurassic period is named after the Jura Mountains along the border of France and Switzerland, where rocks from the period were found. The names of the stages or ages most often depend on city and regions where the rocks were found; this is why division names frequently vary on geologic time scale charts from different countries.

What are the **major time units** used in the geologic time scale?

There are six major time units on the geologic time scale. The units are—in order of descending size—eons, eras, periods, epochs, ages, and subages. The eon represents the longest geologic unit on the scale; an era is a division of time smaller than the eon, and is normally subdivided into two or more periods. An epoch is a subdivision of a period; an age is a subdivision of an epoch; and a subage (although it is not used as often) is the subdivision of an age.

What is **relative time** in relationship to geologic time?

Relative time is a way to establish the relative age of rocks and fossils. It is based on the location of a rock layer in comparison to the location of other rock layers; that is,

The geologic time scale is not an arbitrary listing of our planet's natural history, nor are the divisions fanciful either. Each boundary between divisions represents a change or an event that delineates it from the other divisions. In most cases, a boundary is drawn to represent a time when a major catastrophe or evolutionary change in animals or plants (including the evolution of specific species) occurred.

it is only relative, not absolute, time. In many cases, rock layers are laid down in order, the older below the younger layers. For example, a fossil found in a higher rock layer is usually younger than a fossil found in a rock layer below it. During the nineteenth century, scientists used this method to date rock layers relative to each other—and to establish and construct the first geologic time scale.

What is **absolute time** in relationship to geologic time?

Absolute geologic time is the (approximate) true age of the rock; that is, the absolute time that the rock layer formed. Most often, radiometric techniques, which measure the amount of radioactive decay in rocks, are used to determine absolute time.

When were radiometric dating techniques **discovered**?

The basic principles and techniques of radiometric dating were not discovered until the turn of the twentieth century. In 1896, French physicist Antoine Henri Becquerel (1852–1908) accidentally discovered radioactivity when a photographic plate left next to some uranium-containing mineral salts blackened, proving that uranium gave off its own energy. In 1902, British physicist Lord Ernest Rutherford (1871–1937) collaborated with British chemist Frederic Soddy (1877–1966) to discover that the atoms of radioactive elements are unstable, giving off particles and decaying to more stable forms. These findings led United States chemist Bertram Borden Boltwood (1870–1927) to argue that by knowing the decay rate of uranium and thorium into lead, the dating of rock would be possible. In 1905, Boltwood and John William Strutt (1842–1919) dated various rocks, obtaining ages of 400 to 2,000 million years for various rock sample—showing such dating could be done.

What are the **basic principles** of **radiometric dating**?

The basic principles of radiometric dating, which makes the measurement of absolute geologic time possible, were first worked out by Ernest Rutherford (1871–1937) in 1902. They are:

1. There is some amount of a radioactive element present in a crystal of a mineral when it forms.

2. As the original ("parent") radioactive element decays, the resulting ("daughter") element remains in the crystal.

3. No "extra" amount of the "daughter" element can be present.

4. The decay rates of the radioactive element must be known.

5. The ratio of the amount of the "daughter" element to the "parent" element present can be used to calculate when the crystal formed.

The gorgon, formally called *gorgonopsid,* was a mammal-like reptile that lived before the age of dinosaurs. The first saber-toothed animals, gorgons were the largest predators of the late Paleozoic era, and ranged in size from that of house cats to as much as 800 pounds. (Drawing courtesy of University of Washington/ Associated Press.)

Who first developed an **absolute geologic time scale** using radiometric dating?

In 1911, British geologist Arthur Holmes (1890–1965) began to formulate a geologic time scale based on absolute time, using the uranium-lead dating method to determine the age of rocks. In 1913, he published *The Age of the Earth,* in which he outlined how radioactive decay methods, in conjunction with geological data, could be used to construct an absolute geologic time scale.

What was the first estimate of **Earth's age** using radiometric techniques?

The first estimate of the age of Earth's crust, based on radiometric techniques, was approximately 3.6 billion years old. This was determined in 1927 by British geologist Arthur Holmes (1890–1965).

What is the **Pre-Cambrian era**?

The Pre-Cambrian era represents the time of Earth's beginning to just before the big explosion of life in the oceans—from about 4.6 billion to about 600 million years ago. During this time, the planet was cooling, developing its oceans, and building the continental crust; in addition, scientists believe that during the early part of the Pre-Cambrian life began. The following lists the three Pre-Cambrian periods, the approximate dates, and major evolutionary events during these times:

Archaeon—4.6 to 2.5 billion years ago, a time in which blue-green algae and bacteria (some photosynthetic; some anaerobic) evolved.

Proterozoic—2.5 billion to 610 million years ago, a time in which protoctista, fungi, and photosynthetic plants evolved.

Vendian—610 to 600 million years ago, a time in which multicelled eukaryot (cells with a definitive nucleus) evolved. These organisms were the beginning of animal life.

What possibly happened during the **late Pre-Cambrian era**?

Chemical and isotopic analysis of rocks found in Africa show that our planet may have gone through at least four ice ages between 750 and 570 million years ago. These were very deep ice ages, essentially turning Earth into a "snowball planet." From the evidence to date, some scientists think the oceans were covered with ice almost 300 feet (91 meters) deep, and the land was completely dry and barren—with no life.

What could account for the **Pre-Cambrian ice ages**?

Some scientists believe the Pre-Cambrian ice ages may have been caused by Earth's tilt toward the Sun: the planet may have been tilted at a much larger angle—upwards of 55 degrees—than today's angle of 23.5 degrees. This large degree of tilt meant that the polar areas received most of the Sun's warmth, keeping them ice free. But the areas around the equator would have been colder, allowing glaciers to form.

This recreation of the Cambrian period shows the vast marine life that existed. (Photo courtesy of University of Michigan Exhibit, Museum of Natural History.)

How could **Earth's tilt** have moved to its current position?

The buildup and melting of the glaciers around the equator during the Pre-Cambrian era may have created enough force to move the planet's axis to its modern position. Some scientists have equated this process to repeatedly pushing on a swing at just the right moment in its movement, adding energy to make it go higher. The influence of the alternating advance and retreat of the glaciers could have caused the axis to straighten to its present angle.

Why did the Pre-Cambrian **ice ages end**?

Some scientists believe the "heroes" that thawed the snowball planet and paved the way for an explosion of life were none other than volcanoes. As these surface blisters erupted toward the end of the Pre-Cambrian era, they sent massive amounts of carbon dioxide into the atmosphere, an increase of approximately 350 times its present concentration. This increase trapped re-radiating solar energy, warming the planet as it created a super greenhouse effect. The temperatures rose enough to melt the ice-covered oceans and end the ice age.

Could Earth become a **snowball planet** again?

Although the planet has gone through numerous ice ages over its history—with perhaps more in store for the future—the chance of another severe Pre-Cambrian-type ice age is unlikely. There are two major reasons for this: the Sun is approximately 7 percent hotter now, and there is a warming blanket of gas covering Earth. This blanket is kept in equilibrium by higher life-forms, as carbon within organisms is naturally and continuously cycled back into the atmosphere over their lifetimes—keeping Earth's natural thermostat in working order.

What was the **Cambrian Explosion**?

Just after the end of the Pre-Cambrian era, about 600 million years ago (during the Cambrian period), a great burst of evolutionary activity began in the world's oceans. For some reason, new animals appeared at breakneck speed, geologically speaking, filling the oceans with life. No one really knows why the animals started to appear, and scientists have suggested theories ranging from a change in climate to the idea that a natural threshold had been reached. For example, some scientists believe temperature or oxygen levels reached a point that allowed the proliferation of organisms.

Recently researchers have begun looking at the genes common to modern animals to try to determine a possible cause for the proliferation of life. One study found that an ancient common ancestor—a wormlike animal from which most of the world's animals subsequently evolved—had special genetic machinery that was so successful that it survives to this day. These genes, used to grow appendages (arms, legs, claws, fins, and antennae), were operational at least 600 million years ago. With appendages, animals swam faster, grabbed tighter, and fought with greater efficiency, and thus, could eventually dominate the planet.

What was the **rate of growth** during the **Cambrian Explosion**?

Based on the fossil record of the Cambrian period, scientists estimate that the number of orders of animals doubled roughly every 12 million years. At this time, too, most of the modern phyla (broad categories) of animals began to appear in the fossil record.

What are some possible **geological causes** for the **Cambrian Explosion**?

Scientists have suggested various explanations. One theory includes the gradual breakup of a supercontinent into the continents as we know them today, which may have led to just the right distribution of oceans and continental masses. This breakup would have allowed currents to stir the ocean waters, distributing oxygen and other nutrients around the world. Another suggestion is that there was a change in sea water chemistry, as water ran around and through volcanically active midocean ridges. In addition, rock sediment and fragments eroded from mountains and were dumped in the oceans, also changing the chemistry of the sea water.

Are there any recent attempts to explain why the **Cambrian Explosion** occurred?

A recent study places the blame, or credit, for this evolutionary explosion on our planet itself—and although not everyone agrees, it is an interesting theory.

Some scientists theorize that more than 500 million years ago shifting masses within Earth essentially unbalanced the planet, or "tipped" it, causing the entire surface to reorient itself in an effort to become balanced again. In a process called true polar wander, the ancestral North America moved from near the South Pole up to the region of the equator; the large continent of Gondwanaland (made up of present-day South America, Antarctica, Australia, India, and Africa) traveled all the way across the Southern Hemisphere. This movement all happened at more than twice the rate of continental drift found in the present-day shifting of the planet's crust.

Evidence for this new theory comes from our planet itself. During the formation of rocks, the minerals inside naturally align themselves with the existing magnetic field of the planet. By studying the orientation of grains in the minerals, scientists can determine the position of ancient continents relative to the magnetic north pole, which almost always lies close to Earth's axis of rotation. When the positions of the continents were plotted using this data, scientists found that there was a major movement of the continents within a relatively short period of time around the Cambrian era. The data showed that ancestral North America moved to the equator between 540 and 515 million years ago, while Gondwanaland shifted between 535 and 500 million years ago.

How could **"tipping"** of the planet have led to the **Cambrian Explosion**?

If Earth did "tip" during the Cambrian period, with the accompanying rapid movement of the continents, there would have been dramatic changes in the worldwide climate and oceans. Many ecological systems could have been disrupted; but at the same time, many new ecological niches would have been created. This would have opened up many new opportunities for life, leading to rapid evolution and expansion of new species—which is just what occurred during this time frame.

Some scientists feel that the rapid diversification of life had already begun 10 million years before this "tipping" event, and was caused by different factors. However, this continental movement could have reinforced and even strengthened an explosion of life that might already have been under way.

Could there be other explanations for the **Cambrian Explosion**?

Yes, there may have been biological factors—or factors dealing with organisms—that helped spur the Cambrian Explosion. Many scientists believe that the complex webs of living organisms would have been extremely vulnerable to changes in the environment such as the rapid movement of the continents—and thus, such changes would have decreased, not increased, the number of animals.

Instead, many scientists point to the decline in the growth of stromatolites (algal mats) at the end of the Pre-Cambrian era as an indication that there was competition between animals. And when animals compete for territory, they often increase in diversity and numbers. Plus, early animals were developing skeletons at this time. If the skeletons evolved as a form of armor against predators, and competition was intense, a great diversity of animals with hard parts would emerge in a relatively short time—in a kind of biological "arms race."

What are the **Paleozoic, Mesozoic,** and **Cenozoic eras**?

The divisions between the eras on the geologic time scale represent major changes on the planet. The division between the Pre-Cambrian and Paleozoic, about 600 million years ago, represents an increase of life. The division between the Paleozoic and Mesozoic represents a major decrease in plant and animals species (called an extinction) about 250 million years ago. It is also called the "Permian Extinction" or the "Great Dying," in which up to 90 percent of all species died out. The division between the Mesozoic and Cenozoic, about 65 million years ago, also represents a major extinction of plant and animal species—including the dinosaurs. This extinction was not as extensive as that of the Great Dying; only about 50 percent of all species died out at this time.

What are the **divisions** of the **Mesozoic era**?

The Mesozoic era, often referred to as the "age of reptiles" or the "age of dinosaurs" (even though dinosaurs did not evolve until well into the Mesozoic), lasted from approximately 250 to 65 million years ago. It is divided into three periods: the Triassic, Jurassic, and Cretaceous.

What are the **more recent time divisions** on the **geologic time scale**?

The Cenozoic era is divided into the Tertiary and Quaternary (or Anthropogene) periods. The Quaternary is further divided into the Pleistocene epoch, a period of advances and retreats of huge ice sheets; and the Holocene epoch, or recent times, which began about 10,000 years ago.

Fossil of the prehistoric fish *Lepidotes maximus,* from the Mesozoic era. (Photo courtesy of Jonathan Blair/Corbis.)

FIRST FOSSILS

What is **paleontology**?

Paleontology is the study of ancient life, which usually entails studying the remains of plants and animals in the form of fossils. Since paleontology includes the study of past plants and animals, the field has been divided into two subdisciplines: paleozoology, or the study of ancient animal life; and paleobotany, the study of plant life of the geologic past.

What is **micropaleontology**?

Micropaleontology is the study of very tiny fossils—those so small as to require a microscope for examination.

What is a **fossil**?

The remains of plants and animals that have been preserved in the earth's crust, close to their original shape, are called fossils. This word comes from the Latin *fossilis,* meaning "something dug up." The different types of fossils depend on the remains and conditions present at the time the organism died. Fossils may be formed from the hard parts of an organism, such as teeth, shells, bones, or wood; they may also be

45

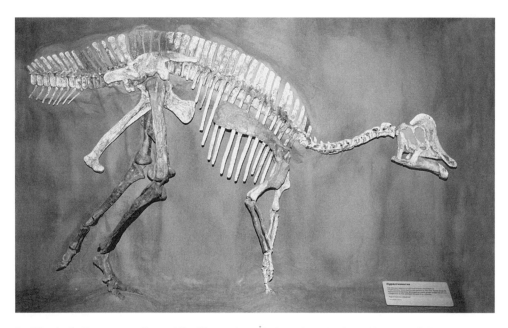

Fossil bones of a *Hypacrosaurus*. The word "fossil" comes from a Latin word meaning "something dug up." (Photo courtesy of Tom Bean/Corbis.)

unchanged from their original features, the entire organism replaced by minerals such as calcite or pyrite. Animals and plants have also been preserved in other materials besides stone, including ice, tar, peat, and the resin of ancient trees. Fossils of single-celled organisms have been recovered from rocks as old as 3.5 billion years. Animal fossils first appear in rocks dating back about 1 billion years. The occurrence of fossils in unusual places, such as dinosaur fossils in Antarctica and fish fossils on the Siberian steppes, is due to the shifting of the plates that make up the earth's crust and environmental changes (such as ice ages) over time. The best explanation for dinosaurs in Antarctica is not that they evolved there, but that Antarctica was once part of a much larger landmass with which it shared many life-forms.

How does a **fossil form**?

There are a number of ways a fossil forms, based on the type of remains and the environment. In general, the process for most fossils is much the same: the hard parts of animals, such as bones, teeth, and shells, as well as the seeds or woody parts of plants, are covered by sediment, such as sand or mud. Over millions of years, more and more layers of sediment accumulate, burying these remains deep within the earth. The sediment eventually turns to stone, and often the remains are chemically altered by mineralization, becoming a form of stone themselves (these are the type of fossils often viewed as the recreated dinosaur skeletons seen in many museums). The same process

Fossil of a prehistoric reptile. Most fossils are found in sedimentary rock. (Photo courtesy of Kevin Schafer/Corbis.)

also produces petrified wood, coprolites (petrified excrement), molds, casts, imprints, and trace fossils.

Most fossils are found in sedimentary rocks, those rocks produced by the accumulation of sediment such as sand or mud. Wind and other weathering conditions wash away sediment on land, depositing it in bodies of water. For this reason, fossils of sea creatures are more common than those of land creatures. Land animals and plants that have been preserved are found mostly in sediments in clam lakes, rivers, and estuaries.

A fossil may also consist of unaltered original material. Bones and teeth are not uncommonly preserved this way. However, far more often the pores of bones and teeth are filled in with minerals, in a process called permineralization (what many have called petrifying). Circulating ground water carries silica or calcium carbonate that fill the pores.

How is **petrified wood** formed?

Petrified wood is formed when water containing dissolved minerals such as calcium carbonate ($CaCO_3$) and silicate infiltrates wood or other structures. The process takes thousands of years. The foreign material either replaces or encloses the organic matter and often retains all the structural details of the original plant material. Botanists find these types of fossils to be very important since they allow for the study of the internal structure of extinct plants. After a time, wood seems to have turned to stone because the original form and structure of the wood have been retained.

What are **carbon films**?

Under the temperatures and pressures of burial, the flesh of many soft-bodied animals will completely decay, leaving behind only a carbon film. However, this film will sometimes preserve the outlines of the animal's body. Much of the fauna of the Burgess Shale in British Columbia has been preserved this way. And a well-known specimen of an ichthyosaur (an extinct marine reptile of the Mesozoic) was preserved with a carbon film outlining the body shape. From this, paleontologists learned that the ichthyosaur had a fleshy dorsal fin that did not possess skeletal elements. Also, the group of organisms known as graptolites appear as carbon films in fine black shales. These animals lived in colonies in small tubular chambers strung along a threadlike axis. They were very tiny and decayed quickly, but the chambers were slightly more durable; upon burial these became flattened into distinctive films that look a little like a band saw blade. It is not uncommon for the leaves of some plants to be preserved as carbon layers. The outline of a leaf and a hint of the pattern of veins may be all that can be recognized, but this is often sufficient to identify the plant from which the leaf came.

How **likely** is it that an **organism becomes a fossil**?

Not all organisms survive to become fossils, and the chance of a living organism becoming a fossil is generally very low. Many organisms completely decay or are chewed apart by other animals. Because of this, some scientists estimate that although billions of flora and fauna have lived on this planet, very few survived into fossil form. Thus, the fossils we do find on the earth represent only a small fraction of the animals and plants that have ever lived on our planet.

An organism has the best chance to become a fossil if it is quickly covered by moist sediment after death, protecting the decaying organism from predators, scavengers, and bacteria. The soft parts of the organism (such as skin, membranes, tissues, and organs) quickly decay, leaving behind teeth and bones. The majority of found fossils are from almost 500 million years ago, when organisms first began to develop skeletons and other hard parts.

The following are the steps in the fossilization process, using a dinosaur as an example. This outline also shows how difficult it is for a dinosaur to become a fossil:

Scavenging and decay—When a dinosaur died, it didn't take long for scavengers to remove the soft, fleshy parts of its body. Those parts that were not eaten decayed at a fast or slow rate, depending on the prevailing climate. In any case, within a short time, only a skeleton would remain. But even the remaining hard body parts were not impervious to change. They were often weathered by wind, water, sunlight, and chemicals in the environment, rounding the bones or reducing them to small pieces.

Location—If the dinosaur's skeleton was in an area in which rapid burial did not take place, then the chances of fossilization were slim. The bones would break and scatter, often moved by the action of changing river courses or flash floods. But occasionally, this transport increased the chance of fossilization, moving the bones to a better area for preservation, such as a sandbank in a river.

Burial—The most crucial step in the fossilization process is burial. The sooner the burial of the dinosaur bones, the better the chance a good fossil was created. If the bones were covered by mud or sand, whether before or after transport, then the amount of further damage would have been lessened; in addition, oxygen is lessened, thus reducing additional decay of the dinosaur bones. Some damage might still have occurred, however, primarily from the pressure created by the increasing amount of sediment on top of the bones, or even from acidic chemicals that can dissolve into the sediment.

Fossilization—The fourth step is the actual process of fossilization itself. Here, the sediments surrounding the fossil slowly turned to stone by the action of pressure from the overlying sediment layers and loss of water. Eventually the grains became cemented together into the hard structure we call rock. The dinosaur bones fossilized, as the spaces in the bone structures filled with minerals, such as calcite (calcium carbonate) or other iron-containing minerals; or the actual mineral component of the bone itself, apatite (calcium phosphate), may have recrystallized.

Exposure—Lastly, deeply buried dinosaur bones must be exposed on the surface where they can be discovered. This process involves the uplift of the bone-containing sedimentary rock to the surface, where erosion by wind and water expose the fossilized skeleton. If the bones are not found in time, the action of the wind and water can destroy the precious record of the ancient species.

How do scientists determine the **age** of **fossils**?

A number of methods are used today to date fossils. Most of the methods are indirect—meaning that the age of the soil or rock in which the fossils are found are dated, not the fossils themselves. The most common way to ascertain the age of a fossil to determine where it is found in rock layers. In many cases, the age of the rock can be determined by other fossils within that rock. If this is not possible, certain analytical techniques are often used to determine the date of the rock layer.

One of the basic ways to determine the age of rock is through the use of radioactivity. For example, radioactivity within the earth continuously bombards the atoms in minerals, exciting electrons that become trapped in the crystals' structures. Using this knowledge, scientists employ certain radiometric techniques, including electron spin resonance and thermoluminescence, to determine the age of the minerals. By determining the number of excited electrons present in the minerals—and comparing that number with known data that represents the actual rate of increase of similar excited electrons—the time it took for the amount of excited electrons to accumulate can be calculated. In turn, this data can be used to determine the age of the rock—and the fossils within the rock.

There are other methods for determining fossil age. For example, uranium-series dating measures the amount of thorium-230 present in limestone deposits. Limestone deposits form with uranium present, and almost no thorium. Because scientists know the decay rate of uranium into thorium-230, the age of the limestone rocks and the fossils found in them can be calculated from the amount of thorium-230 evident within a particular limestone rock.

Why are there **gaps** in the **fossil records**?

Gaps in the fossil records—eras or evolutionary stages that are "missing" from the known collection of fossils—are most often the result of erosion. This geologic process wears away layers of rock and embedded fossils, usually by the action of wind, water, and ice. Gaps in fossil records can also be caused by mountain uplift, which destroys fossils, and volcanic activity, which can bury fossil evidence with hot magma rock that physically changes the rock, and thus fossils.

Besides fossilization, how else have **human remains** been preserved?

Human remains are not only found in hard rock layers. More recent—that is, thousands of years old—human remains have been preserved naturally in peat, ice, and desert sand. Humans remains have been found almost intact in peat, partially decayed

Anthropologist Donald Johanson with his famous fossil find, Lucy. (Photo courtesy of Morton Beebe-S.F./Corbis.)

vegetation that forms a thick spongy mat. If a human accidentally died in this boglike environment, he or she would be buried with the peat. The peat would "smother" the body and decrease its decay by oxygen. Human remains from these regions are often very well preserved.

Other human remains can be preserved in the cold of icy regions, with the body being deep frozen. Such "icemen" have been found in many mountainous regions. For example, in 1991 a 40-year-old man was found frozen in the Austrian Alps—a man who was about 5,300 years old. Deserts also desiccate human remains, literally sucking the water out of the body. For example, the mummified remains of a 4,000-year-old human have been found in one of the driest places on the earth, the valley of the Atacama Desert in South America.

Is there another way of **preserving human remains**?

Yes, one of the better known ways of preserving human remains is not natural, but is done by humans to humans—mummification. The first embalmed mummies, mostly bodies of Egyptian notables, date from about 2,000 B.C. The practice survived until 642 A.D., when Egypt was conquered by the Muslim Arabs. Amazingly, the entire process of mummification, at its most sophisticated, took about 70 days to complete.

A paleontologist exposes dinosaur tracks—one type of "trace fossil"—in a Mojave formation at a dinosaur trackway site in the Painted Desert in Arizona. (Photo courtesy of Tom Bean/Corbis.)

Where did the term **mummy** originate?

The term mummy is not from the Egyptians, but is derived via Arabic from the Persian word *mummia,* meaning "bitumen" or "tar." Mummies were named this because ancient people who came across the aged and blackened corpses thought they were a source of tar.

What are **molds** and **casts**?

Molds and casts are types of fossils. After burial, a plant or animal often decays, leaving only an impression of its hard parts (and less often, soft parts) as a hollow mold in the rock. If the mold is filled with sediment, it can often harden, forming a corresponding cast.

What are **trace fossils**?

Not all fossils are hardened bones and teeth, or molds and casts. There are also fossils that are merely evidence that creatures once crawled, walked, hopped, burrowed, or ran across the land. Trace fossils are just that: the traces a creature left behind, usually in soft sediment like sand or mud. For example, small animals bored branching tunnels in the mud of a lake bed in search of food; and dinosaurs hunted for meals along a riverbank, leaving their footprints in the soft sand. Similar to the fossil formation of hard parts, the footprints and tunnels were filled in by sediment, then buried by layers of more sediment over millions of years, eventually solidifying. Today we see the results of this long-ago activity as trace fossils. Many originators of trace fossils are unidentifiable—in other words, there are no hard fossils of the creatures left in the area, just their tracks. Some of the most famous trace fossils are those of dinosaurs tracks (for example, in Culpepper, Virginia, and near Golden, Colorado) and of human-like footprints (such as those found in East Africa)—all found in hardened sediment.

What can some **trace fossils** of **dinosaur tracks** tell us?

The numerous fossilized dinosaur footprints, called a trackway, that are located north of Flagstaff, Arizona, on the Navajo Reservation indicate much about the dinosaurs' speed. This site was first discovered by Barnum Brown of the American Museum of Natural History in the 1930s, but had been lost until recently. It includes an example of a running dinosaur that left tracks with an 8-foot (2.4-meter) space between the right and left prints; from these prints, scientists calculated that the dinosaur ran at a speed of 14.5 miles (23.3 kilometers) per hour—one of the faster dinosaurs known. The speed record, however, is presently held by a Jurassic carnivore that left a 16-foot (5-meter) gap between the right and left tracks, in a Glen Rose, Texas, trackway. The calculated speed of this dinosaur was about 26.5 miles (42.8 kilometers) per hour, faster than the speediest human.

What is the difference between **tracks and trails**?

Tracks are generally the traces of distinct footprints, whereas trails may have been produced by an animal dragging its feet or some other appendage as it moved. Tracks, therefore, are more distinctive, and different animals can be distinguished by their own peculiar footprints. Trails can seldom be associated with a particular animal.

MORE RECENT FOSSILS

What and when were the **ice ages**?

In 1795, Scottish naturalist James Hutton (1726–97) was the first to publish the idea that, in the past, Alpine glaciers had been much more extensive than they are today. He based his observations on strangely shaped glacial boulders called erratics near Geneva. (Ironically, although he recognized the evidence of glaciation in Switzerland, he never realized the abundant evidence in his Scottish homeland.) It took several more decades before J. Esmark, in 1824, proposed that glaciation on a continental scale occurred in the past. By 1840, prominent Swiss biologist Louis Agassiz (1807–73) became the leading champion of continental glaciation, proposing that ice once covered nearly all of northern Europe, including Britain. Later, he also found evidence of this phenomenon in New England.

Today, scientists describe an ice age as any part of geologic time when huge glacial ice sheets covered more of the earth's surface than during modern times. The most recent ice age—often referred to as the "Ice Age" or the "Great Ice Age"—began about 2 million years ago (at the beginning of the Quaternary period) and ended about 10,000 years ago.

It is thought that the plains of North America cooled in the latter half of the Cenozoic era (and the beginning of the Quaternary era, Pleistocene epoch), about 2 million years ago. Ice sheets soon spread south from Canada's Hudson Bay area, and eastward from the Rocky Mountains. Toward the end of the Pleistocene epoch, the ice sheets advanced and retreated numerous times—each event lasting from about 10,000 to 100,000 years. The last retreat occurred about 10,000 years ago. In the United States, the last ice age advance and retreat is called the Wisconsinan stage; in Europe, it is called the Würmian stage. Erosional and depositional glacial features from this latter stage are still evident in many of the regions once covered by the huge ice sheets.

At their maximum extent, the Pleistocene ice sheets reached into the upper part of the northern United States, Greenland, northern Europe and Asia (although Siberia was little glaciated because it was too dry), Antarctica, southern South America, and high spots throughout Asia including the Himalayas. Altogether, geologist believe that up to 10 percent of this planet was once buried in ice (though not simultaneously) during the various ice age periods, the ice often miles thick.

How **many ice ages** occurred over geologic time?

Geologic records show that there have been relatively few times that ice ages have occurred—perhaps only less than 1 percent of the time in the last 600 million years. The first known large-scale ice age occurred about 2.3 billion years ago, during the Pre-Cambrian era.

A great deal of what scientists know about the ice ages they have learned from the study of mountain glaciers. For example, when a glacier moves downward out of its mountain source, it carves out a distinctive shape on the surrounding land. The "footprints" left by continental glaciers formed during the ice ages are comparable to those formed by mountain glaciers.

The transport of materials from one part of the earth's surface to another part is also evidence of continental glaciation. Rocks and fossils normally found only in one region of the earth may be picked up and moved by ice sheets and deposited elsewhere.

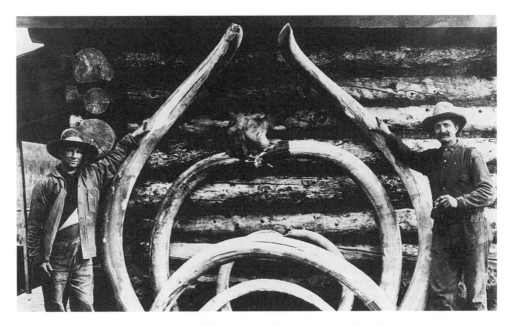

These mammoth tusks were found underground. Mammoths probably migrated from Asia to North America during the Great Ice Age. (Photo courtesy of National Archives/Corbis.)

The "tracks" left by the moving glacier provide evidence of the ice sheet's movement. In many cases, the moving ice may actually have left scratches on the rock over which it moved, providing further evidence of changes that took place during an ice age.

What **changes** did the **Great Ice Age** cause?

There is no doubt that the Great Ice Age caused major changes in the earth's overall climate over the past millions of years. Global mean (average) temperatures fluctuated radically up and down. For example, during the most recent ice age, the temperatures were about 10 degrees Fahrenheit cooler than today; and during the interglacial times, when the ice sheets retreated, the temperatures averaged 5 degrees Fahrenheit warmer than today.

The Great Ice Age was also responsible for the migration and movement of animals over the past 2 million years. Because sea levels fell as the ice sheets advanced, narrow land bridges were often exposed and used by many living things to search for new territory and better food supplies. For example, a narrow land bridge (at the Bering Strait) between Asia and North America is believed to have allowed North American native animals, such as camels, horses, and cheetahs, to migrate to Asia during the Ice Age; while mammoths, mastodons, bison, and muskox crossed from Asia to North America. In fact, this land bridge was probably also used by our own species—*Homo sapiens*.

Did the **Great Ice Age** really **end**?

Some scientists believe that the Great Ice Age never truly ended, and that we are merely in the middle of a warming trend during this ice age; others believe that we are living during an interglacial period, and thus, the temperatures will continue to rise. But since no one knows how an ice age actually begins or ends, it is difficult to tell if we are in the advance or retreat of an ice age cycle.

How fast did the **earth warm** at the **end** of the Ice Age?

Recent studies suggest that our planet's climate warmed by 20 degrees Fahrenheit or more—and all within a normal human's lifetime. This extremely rapid change occurred approximately 12,500 years ago, ending the most recent ice age.

Scientists have examined new ice cores taken from Antarctica and Greenland. Those from the southernmost continent of Antarctica showed a temperature increase of approximately 20 degrees Fahrenheit occurred in a very short time. The cores from Greenland show an even greater increase—almost 59 degrees Fahrenheit. Both ice cores showed that these rapid increases happened at the same time, and occurred within a period of 50 years. Because the northern and southern regions of the planet warmed at approximately the same time, scientists believe the temperature increase was a global phenomena, not a localized one.

What caused the **rapid warming** that ended the Ice Age?

Antarctic ice cores show a temperature rise about 12,500 years ago, along with a sudden rise in methane at this time. Methane is one of the major greenhouse gases—and an increase of this gas in the atmosphere could have trapped more heat, leading to a general warming across the planet. Scientists have yet to determine the cause of the sudden rise in methane levels.

Why is the end of the **Ice Age rapid warming** so **disturbing** to scientists?

The evidence of rapid climate change at the end of the Ice Age is disturbing to scientists for two reasons: the cause of the change itself and the short interval in which it occurred. Recent ice cores have linked rapid temperature increases to sudden rises in methane, a greenhouse gas. As our planet's human population increases, the burning of fossil fuels and other processes are increasing the amount of greenhouse gases in the atmosphere. Such a rapid increase in these gases, geologically speaking, could trigger a global climate change—similar to past increases.

If the planet warms very rapidly—within the average lifetime of humans—all organisms on the planet would find it extremely difficult to adjust to such major changes. For humans especially, there would be no time to modify agriculture, trans-

What are the La Brea Tar Pits?

The La Brea Tar Pits of Los Angeles, as the name implies, are huge pits filled with thick, gooey tar. The importance of the pits is the animals they trapped—animals of the Ice Age, including mammoths, mastodons, giant ground sloths, dire wolves, and saber-toothed cats. The animals were trapped as they entered the area and accidentally walked into the tar pits. As they struggled to get free, other predatory animals would often attack, and they, too, would become ensnared in the tar. Soon, the tar would encase the animals, preserving them by cutting off oxygen that would otherwise decay the bones, and protecting their bodies from being chewed by other animals. The fossils in La Brea are well preserved—so much so that DNA (deoxyribonucleic acid) from the bones of a 14,000-year-old saber-toothed cat found at the pit have been analyzed. The data showed that this cat was closely related to modern cats, such as lions and tigers.

portation, and the use of energy. In addition, this could lead to huge shifts in population in attempts to adapt to the new resulting climates.

What is the **difference** between a **mammoth** and a **mastodon**?

Contrary to what most people think, mammoths and mastodons were two different animals. The mastodon seems to have appeared first. It appeared in the Oligocene epoch (about 25 to 38 million years ago) and survived until less than 1 million years ago. The mastodon lived in Africa, Asia, Europe, and North and South America, and grew to a maximum of 10 feet (3 meters) tall. Mastodons were covered with dense, woolly hair, and had tusks straight forward and nearly parallel to each other.

The mammoth may have been a side branch of the mastodon, and lived in North America, Europe, and Asia. Mammoths evolved less than 2 million years ago, and died out about 10,000 years ago, at the end of the Ice Age. They grew to about 9 to 15 feet (2.7 to 4.5 meters) tall, and had long tusks that curled upward and out. They also had dense woolly hair, with an additional coarse layer of outer hair that protected them from the cold.

No one really knows why the mastodons and mammoths died out. Scientists theorize that the mastodon died out because of climate changes, and the resulting changes in the environment. Mammoths may also have died out because of climate changes, as ice sheets retreated about 10,000 years ago. In addition, early humans may have hastened the extinction process by hunting the mammoths.

Mammoths, like this one, evolved after mastodons. (Photo courtesy of Jonathan Blair/Corbis.)

Are there any **"living fossils"** on the earth?

There are some modern animal and plant species that are almost identical to those living millions of years ago. Many of these "living fossils" were discovered as actual fossils before they were found as modern living organisms. Plants such as the horsetail existed during the Devonian period almost 380 million years ago; one species of modern ginko survives from the Triassic period about 220 million years ago; and the magnolia, one of the earliest true flowering plants, existed during the Cretaceous period, about 125 million years ago. Living fossils of animals include the tuatara, the only living survivor from a reptile group that was abundant during the Triassic period; didelphids, which are marsupials, including the modern opossum, that lived at the end of the Cretaceous period; and the modern brachiopod *Lingula,* which is scarcely distinguishable from its ancestor that lived during the Devonian period. Ancient insects include cockroaches and dragonflies, which evolved during the early Carboniferous period about 350 million years ago.

One explanation for the longevity of a certain species may be its ability to adapt and live in stable ecological niches. For example, the *Lingula* live in the intertidal zone, a specialized niche along coastal areas. Even if the sea levels changed, these brachiopods could adapt by changing location with the water levels.

One of the most famous of all "living fossils" is the coelacanth, a fish that has a three-lobed tail and fins with armlike bases. The first such fish was found as a fossil in Devonian period rock; it was thought to have become extinct about 60 million years

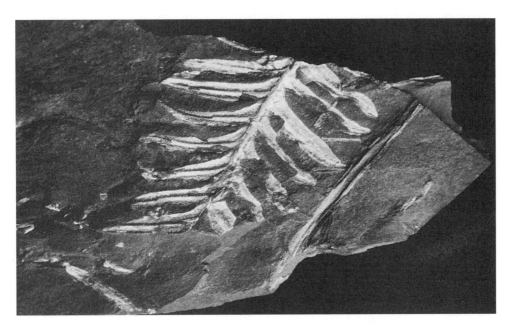

This fossil of a white fern leaf is 320 million years old. (Photo courtesy of Field Mark Publications.)

ago, at the beginning of the Cenozoic era. But in 1938, fisherman Captain Hendrik Goosen caught a living coelacanth in the Indian Ocean off the coast of South Africa. The ichthyologist who identified the fish, Professor J. L. B. Smith of South Africa, offered a reward of £100 (about $50 in current American currency) to anyone who found a second one. It took until 1952 for someone to catch another modern specimen. Since that time, many have been photographed alive in water 200 to 1,310 feet (60 to 400 meters) deep off the coast of the Cormoro Islands near Madagascar.

Will **animals** and **plants** that die **today** become fossils?

In many cases, yes, if the conditions are right. Many organisms will quickly decay, as sunlight, water, or air interacts with them, especially if the organisms do not have resistant hard parts. If the organisms do have hard parts, those that are quickly buried have the best chance of becoming fossils, as sediment stops much of the decay. Most of the future fossils will be from oceans, lakes, and rivers—areas in which quick burial, and thus fossilization, is more likely to occur.

What is the **oldest known living organism** on the earth today?

In northern Michigan, a huge *Armillaria bulbosa* fungus spawned from a single spore 1,500 or more years ago; it covers about 30 acres and weighs about 100 tons. The fungus is actually known as the button or honey mushroom, and feeds on decaying matter, such as dead wood.

This grove of aspen trees in Utah grows from one root system, making it the largest known living organism. (Photo courtesy of Galen Rowell/Corbis.)

What is the **largest known living organism** on the earth today?

Contrary to popular belief, blue whales and giant sequoia trees are not the largest known organisms in the world. The acknowledgment goes to a grove of aspen trees in the Wasatch Mountains, south of Salt Lake City, Utah. The 106-acre aspen system contains about 50,000 aspen stems and is estimated to weigh about 6,000 tons. The grove may look like separate trees, but in reality, they are different parts of the same plant, all growing from one root system. Scientists have determined that the aspen grove is one unit—the leaves all have identical sizes and shapes, and turn the same colors at the same time each fall.

DINOSAUR FOSSILS

What is a **dinosaur**?

Dinosaur is a term used to describe certain types of animals that lived during the Mesozoic era in geologic history. It is difficult to generalize about dinosaurs, but two things are definitely agreed upon: they were, in general, the largest creatures to ever

Who invented the term dinosaur?

The term dinosaur was invented by the well-known British anatomist Sir Richard Owen (1804–92). He coined the term in 1842 to describe the 175-million-year-old fossil remains of two groups of giant reptiles that corresponded to no known living creatures. In 1854, Owen prepared one of the first dinosaur exhibitions for display at Crystal Palace, the famous museum in London, England.

walk on the earth, even though there were many small dinosaur species; in addition, these animals were some of the most successful organisms that ever lived.

What does the term **dinosaur mean**?

Dinosaur comes from the term *dinosauria,* which is a combination of the Greek words *deinos* and *sauros. Deinos* means "terrible" and *sauros* means "lizard" or "reptile." Thus, dinosaur means "terrible lizard."

How do paleontologists **identify species of dinosaurs** from other fossils?

One of the best ways to identify dinosaur fossil bones is by size, as many of the bones are huge. For example, the upper leg bone, or femur, of an adult *Apatosaurus* often measures over 6 feet (1.8 meters) long.

But size is not everything, as many dinosaurs were the same size as a chicken or cat. The way scientists detect the differences between dinosaurs and other animals species is by the construction and orientation of their bones—including heads, tails, and hipbones. In addition, dinosaur fossils are often found in association with other dinosaurs at a site. Many times these fossils represent dinosaurs—from meat-eaters to plant-eaters—that gathered together along the shore of a lake or ocean. The dinosaurs were all in search of food along the banks of the water, a place that would attract many animals and plants.

Of course, not all dinosaur fossils are found in the conventional way. In 1998, an amateur fossil collector saw the movie *Jurassic Park* and recognized that a fossil he had—which he had thought was a bird—was actually a dinosaur. The specimen, only 9.5 inches (24 centimeters) long, is a young dinosaur that had just hatched before it died. In this case, the dinosaur remains probably washed into oxygen-starved waters where it was quickly buried. This may be one of the most important dinosaur fossils ever found, as many of its soft body parts were preserved, including the intestines, muscle fibers, and maybe even the liver.

When was the first **dinosaur bone** collected and described?

The fossilized bones of dinosaurs have probably been found throughout human history, but no records or descriptions were kept until fairly recently. References to fossilized sharks' teeth and shells are recorded from the European Medieval period, but because Medieval Europeans believed that no animal or plant made by God could become extinct, they explained the findings in other ways. For example, many of the fossils were interpreted as the remains of modern species as opposed to ancient, extinct species; others were thought of as merely pebbles that resembled the remains of animals and plant species.

The first recorded description of a dinosaur bone was made in 1676 by Robert Plot (1640–96), a professor of chemistry at the University of Oxford, England, in his book *The Natural History of Oxfordshire.* Although he correctly determined that it was a broken piece of a giant bone, Plot did not know the bone came from a dinosaur. Instead, he felt it belonged to a giant man or woman, citing mythical, historical, and biblical sources. In 1763, the same bone fragment was named *Scrotum humanum* by Richard Brookes (1721–63) to describe its appearance, but the name never gained wide or serious acceptance. Based on Plot's illustration, modern scientists believe the bone fragment is actually the lower end of a thighbone from a *Megalosaurus,* a meat-eating dinosaur from the middle Jurassic period that roamed the area now known as Oxfordshire, England.

In 1787, Caspar Wistar (1761–1818) and Timothy Matlack (1736–1829) discovered a large fossil bone in the state of New Jersey. Although they reported their finding, it was ignored and unverified—but may have been the first dinosaur bone ever collected in North America.

What connection does the first evidence of **dinosaur fossils in Italy** have to **literature**?

Prior to the discovery of dinosaur tracks in the Alps near Trento, Italy, in the early 1990s, there was virtually no evidence of dinosaurs in Italy. The dinosaur tracks were found around the area of an eighth-century landslide, a geological feature that served as the model for the stairway to the pits of hell in Dante's *Inferno.*

Why didn't the **Chinese** study **dinosaur fossils** sooner?

The Chinese have been collecting dinosaur fossils for over 2,000 years, but they never identified the pieces as being from ancient creatures. The Chinese thought the fossils were the remains of dragons—a prominent symbol in Chinese culture. Even today, ground up "dragon's" teeth are thought to have medicinal healing properties.

With much scientific evidence to dismiss the Chinese association of huge bones with the existence of dragons, concerted efforts have been made to investigate the lands of China, where many great archeological and paleontological finds have been made.

> ## What did the American Indians think dinosaur fossils were?
>
> Several American Indian tribes found large old bones, but did not identify them as dinosaur fossils. Because of their great size, the dinosaur bones were called the grandfathers of the buffalo, one of the largest animals the Indians knew.

In the early 1900s, the bones of a stegosaur and of a hadrosaur were found in desert regions of China. In a southwest region of Beijing, the famed Peking Man (the fossilized skeleton found in a Pleistocene cave) was discovered in 1926.

Throughout the latter half of the twentieth century, joint ventures by Chinese and Canadian anthropologists and paleontologists and other field workers have excavated over 60 tons of important fossils that have helped professionals around the world better study the life-forms and conditions of life millions of years ago.

What was the possible connection between the **mythical griffin** and **dinosaurs**?

The griffin, a mythical creature, often depicted by the Greeks and Romans until about 3 A.D., was more than likely based on skeletons of the dinosaur *Protoceratops*. This dinosaur existed during the Cretaceous period about 65 to 141 million years ago; its skeletons are found in profusion in Mongolia's Gobi Desert, south of the Altai Mountains. If nomads crossing the desert were to see the skeletons of the large creatures embedded in the rock—especially fossils of its sharp beak, elongated shoulder blade, and neck shield—they might have interpreted the fossils as the remains of the mythical creature, spreading the stories as they traveled and traded with Western cultures.

What did the early **English** think **dinosaur fossils** were?

Before discovering the bones' true nature in the nineteenth century, some English, including chemist Robert Plot (1640–96), believed that dinosaur fossils were actually the remains of elephants that had been brought to England by the Romans. Later, some believed the bones to be those of a giant human. Another early English theory, and one closer to the truth, suggested that the bones came from giant lizards.

What did the early **Australians** think dinosaur fossils were?

Early Australians called dinosaur bones they found the Kadimakara, and thought they had fallen from the great Sky Land.

A Brazilian scientist studies one of the oldest dinosaur fossils ever found. The 220-million-year-old bones of three prosauropods were discovered in southern Brazil. (Photo courtesy of Ricardo Chaves/Associated Press.)

What are some of the **oldest dinosaur fossils** found to date?

There are several dinosaur fossils that scientists claim to be the oldest ever found—and most of them have been discovered in South America. The oldest dinosaur skull was found in Argentina—a *Herrerasaurus*, a meat-eating dinosaur that lived some 230 million years old. The *Eoraptor*, a 228-million-year-old dinosaur, was also found in Argentina, and is currently thought of as the most primitive dinosaur known. More recently, paleontologists also discovered the fossilized bones of three prosauropods, plant-eating dinosaurs that lived approximately 220 million years ago, in Santa Maria, an area of southern Brazil.

EVOLUTION OF THE DINOSAURS

CLASSIFYING ANIMALS

Why was **Aristotle** important to **early animal studies**?

Greek philosopher Aristotle of Stagira (384–322 B.C.) considered by many to be one of the greatest philosophers of all times, applied the principles of logic to his physical and biological investigations and came up with a classification system for animals. He did not, however, formulate a real classification system for plants.

What was Aristotle's **classification system**?

Aristotle classified animals in a *scala naturae* ("chain of being"). This "chain," which also included plants and nonliving matter, consisted of, from the top down: God, man, mammals, oviparous with perfect eggs (such as birds), oviparous with nonperfect eggs (such as fish), insects, plants, and nonliving matter. He labeled each link in the chain a "species."

To develop his own system, Aristotle made taxonomic studies of more than 500 animals—and even dissected about 50 animals to determine their details. His animal classification system differed from the previous Greek attempts, which made use of categories such as feet or footless and winged or wingless; Aristotle's system was closer to our modern scheme. His observations of animals were published in his book, *Historia animalium* (History of Animals).

How long were **Aristotle's views** of animals regarded as true?

When it came to the study of animals (zoology), it took until the nineteenth century for much of Aristotle's work to be questioned or changed. British naturalist Charles

Darwin (1809–82) was mostly responsible, with his theories on the evolution of species.

What other **early attempts** were made to **classify organisms**?

Aristotle's *History of Animals* (and his *Parts of Animals* and *Generation of Animals*) was translated into Latin around 1220 by Scottish scientist Michael Scot (c. 1175–1234). This was the impetus for the classification of European animals by German scientist Albertus Magnus (c. 1200–80) around 1250. His work also classified plants and vegetables into several basic types.

There were many more early attempts at classification of organisms in the sixteenth and seventeenth centuries:

In 1539, Hieronymus Bock (Jerome Boch, 1498–1554) attempted a natural classification of plants, arranging them by relation or resemblance.

In 1551, Swiss naturalist Konrad (also known as Conrad) von Gesner (1516–65) described each known animal species in the form of a classification system, and wrote the first volume of *Historiae aimalium* (The History of Animals), helping to found the field of modern descriptive zoology.

In 1554, Italian naturalist Ulisse Aldrovandi (1522–1604) proposed a systematic study of plant classification in his publication *Herbarium*.

In 1623, Swiss biologist Gaspard Bauhin (1560–1624) introduced, in his book *Pinax theatri botanici,* the two name system of classifying plants, with one name for genus and one for species, now called binomial classification.

In 1660, Italian histologist Marcello Malpighi (1628–94) tried to classify all living organisms on one scale, based on the relative size of the organism's respiratory system and his perceived "level" of the organisms. In Malpighi's classification scheme, plants were at the bottom of the scale and humans were at the top.

Who first developed a **modern classification system** for all living organisms?

The first person to develop a modern classification system for the entire natural world was Swedish naturalist Carolus Linnaeus (Carl von Linné, 1707–78). For this herculean effort, he became known as "God's Registrar."

When did **Carolus Linnaeus** introduce his classification system?

Linnaeus first introduced his classification system—the first to keep track of all the known organisms on the earth—in 1735, in his book *Systema naturae*.

What **books** by Carolus Linnaeus described **plant classification**?

In 1737, Linnaeus published *Genera plantorum* (Genera of Plants), in which he explained his method of systematic botany, and classified 18,000 species of plants. And with the publication of *Species plantarum* (Species of Plants) in 1753, he introduced binary nomenclature to botany.

But his most influential work was published in 1751: *Philosophia botanica,* in which he claimed that a natural classification system could be derived from God's original creation of all species. He relied on the sexual parts of plants for his classification, and used a binomial nomenclature (two names) to name specific plants—in this case, genus and species.

What **method** did Carolus Linnaeus use to classify organisms?

Linnaeus developed a taxonomic hierarchy to classify all the known—and to be discovered—plants and animals of the world. Taxonomy (also called systematics) is a way of describing, naming, and classifying organisms. In Linnaeus' system, species were the fundamental units. Although Linnaeus believed species were fixed, he also realized they could be categorized together in larger groupings (or taxa) using similarity of structure. These groupings grew larger, with more general traits, the higher up the hierarchy they occurred.

How are **humans classified** according to the Linnaen system?

According to the Linnaen system, humans can be classified as follows (only the main groupings are shown):
Kingdom: Animalia
      Phylum: Chordata
         Class: Mammalia
            Order: Primates
               Family: Hominidae
                  Genus: *Homo*
                     Species: *sapiens*

What **groupings** did Carolus Linnaeus use to classify animals?

The most important groupings, from large and general, to smaller and more specific, are: kingdom, phylum, class, order, family, genera (genus), and species (both upper and lowercase first letters are used, depending on the context). There can also be other groupings, such as subclass and infraclass, between these main groupings.

Linnaeus defined a species as a group of organisms capable of freely interbreeding. He called this a "unity of type," and recognized the basic unit of natural classification was not the individual, but the species. In most cases, the individual members of a species tend to have the same morphology; that is, they look more similar to each other than to members of other species. And although it appears that species tend to be identified by their morphology, the real test is the ability for interbreeding.

Since this is an inclusive hierarchy, each large grouping contains several smaller groupings. Kingdoms consist of and contain classes, which in turn consist of and contain orders; orders consist of and contain families, which in turn have many genera, which consist of and contain many species. With this system, Linnaeus could classify each species and place it within the larger hierarchy of living organisms.

How does the Linnaeus classifications of **plants differ from** that of **animals**?

Plants are also classified as kingdom (Plantae), class, order, family, genus, and species. But there are two major differences: instead of phylum, plants use the term division; after species, plants include varieties.

How did Linnaeus **name the various species**?

Linnaeus gave each species a unique, scientifically descriptive name consisting of two parts, also known as a binary notation or nomenclature. The name is written in Latin or Greek, and consists of the genus name followed by the specific species name; this name is always either italicized or underlined. The other levels of the hierarchy, such as class, family, or order, are only capitalized as proper names, such as Class Mammalia.

For example, the greater horseshoe-nosed bat's scientific name is *Rhinolophus ferrumequinum,* from *rhinos* (Greek for "nose"), *lophos* (Greek for "crest"), *ferrum* (Latin for "iron"), and *equinum* (Latin for "horse"). In this name, the genus is *Rhinolophus* and the specific species name is *ferrumequinum.* This is a good description of this animal because the bat's fleshy nose protrusion is in the shape of a horseshoe.

The genus name can be used alone, but the specific species name cannot. For example, humans can refer to themselves as *Homo sapiens,* or by abbreviating the genus name, as *H. sapiens,* but never as just *sapiens.*

How many species of animals and plants exist?

Currently, it is estimated that between 5 and 30 million species of flora and fauna exist on the planet. Some types of organisms, such as mammals and birds, consist of a few hundreds of thousands of species; insects include the most species, but their true numbers are unknown. Scientists estimate more than 90 percent of all the species that ever lived on the earth are now thought to be extinct.

Did Linnaeus believe that species changed over time?

Not at first. In fact, when Linnaeus developed his classification system, he catalogued species as permanent entities created by God. But the occasional hybrids he observed seemed to suggest species might not be fixed. Later in his life, he suggested that species changed in form through time and that species were "children of time"—in other words, species could evolve.

How are dinosaurs classified according to the Linnean system?

In general, in the Linnean system, the hierarchy to dinosaurs is as follows: Animalia (kingdom), Chordata (phylum), Reptilia (class), and Dinosauria (infraclass).

EVOLVING IDEAS ABOUT EVOLUTION

What is evolution?

The term evolution actually represents two basic ideas: First, it is the theory that living organisms change over time, adapting to environmental conditions to which they are exposed over that time. Second, it is the theory that life on the earth developed gradually, geologically speaking, from one or several simple organisms to more complex organisms, also called organic evolution.

Where did the word evolution come from?

The word evolution comes form the Latin word meaning "unrolled." It referred to the Roman books, which were written on parchment and rolled on wooden rods. As they were unrolled, or evolved, they were read.

How did the theory of evolution develop?

The theory of evolution is a relatively recent concept, its true origins extending back less than 200 years. The theory was an outgrowth of the explosion in naturalist studies, especially in the nineteenth century. The discovery of diverse plants and animals around the world brought about new questions—one of which was how all these different species emerged. The discovery and recognition of fossils and the suggestion that plants and animals went extinct served to fuel scientific debates on origins and history of life. Evolution was a theory that seemed to solve some of these origin dilemmas—but it was also an idea in direct conflict with the prevailing creationist theories of the time.

What were some **early theories** of evolution?

There were numerous evolution ideas—but they were not called "evolution theories." As more scientific evidence was literally uncovered, the theories on evolution went through an evolution of their own. Here are a few early evolution ideas:

In 1748, French naturalist Benoît de Maillet proposed that evolution was the result of the retreating sea. He believed that the universe was filled with "seeds" that fell into the oceans. When the oceans gradually retreated, the seeds would grow and evolve into land animals.

In 1809, French philosopher Jean Baptiste de Lamarck (1744–1829)—now considered to be one of the first true evolutionists—proposed that the environment caused species to evolve. He suggested "the existence in organisms of a built-in drive toward perfection; the capacity of organisms to become adapted to 'circumstances' ['environment' in modern terminology]; the frequent occurrence of spontaneous generation; and the inheritance of acquired characters, or traits."

During the time period 1800 to 1812, French naturalist and anatomist Baron Georges Léopold Chrétien Frédéric Dagobert Cuvier (1769–1832) studied fossil bones of animals from the New World and other locations. Based on his comparisons of the fossils with modern species, he deduced that some plants and animals had indeed gone extinct over the history of the planet—an idea again in direct conflict with the prevailing creationist theories. Cuvier proposed many "revolutions or catastrophes" in the world's long history, causing numerous species of flora and fauna to go extinct. He was one of the first proponents of catastrophism, which is one of today's leading camps in evolution theory.

Who was **Charles Darwin**?

English naturalist Charles Darwin (1809–82) developed the theory of evolution, publishing his famous thesis in 1859, called *On the origin of species by means of natural selection of the preservation of favoured races in the struggle for life* (often shortened to *On the Origin of Species* or *Origin of Species*). At the age of 23, Darwin participated as an unpaid naturalist onboard the HMS *Beagle* during an around-the-world voyage from 1831 to 1835. During the trip, he studied the plants and animals found in remote parts of the planet. He specifically recorded flora and fauna from isolated areas, such as the Galapagos Islands. From the accumulated data, he developed his theory of evolution—the concept that animals and plant types have their origin in other preexisting types, and that the distinguishable differences are due to modifications in successive generations.

What was **the book that shook the world**?

"The book that shook the world" was Charles Darwin's thesis *On the origin of species by means of natural selection of the preservation of favoured races in the struggle for life.* It was published on November 24, 1859, and the first edition sold out that same day. This book changed forever the field of biology, and the ideas that scientists and everyday people had about the natural world. It was extremely controversial, refuting the creationist beliefs of Victorian England by introducing the theories of evolution and natural selection. *On the Origin of Species* proposed that all life evolved from a common ancestor—including humankind, which shared a common ancestor with the great apes. No longer were humans thought of as the pinnacle of creation—and no longer was the world thought of as unchanging, created by God for human enjoyment. Even today, Charles Darwin's explanation of natural evolution generates controversy among scientists and the general public.

What **two species** led to Darwin's theory of evolution?

Two species studied by Darwin—and which are still studied today—are found in the remote, isolated Galapagos Islands: finches (called "Darwin's Finches") and giant land tortoises. He studied the two species during the voyage of the HMS *Beagle*.

What is **natural selection**?

Charles Darwin felt that the process of natural selection was the engine behind evolution, leading to continual and gradual changes in organisms and creating new species. He felt certain organisms—through random genetic mutations during the reproductive process—had traits allowing them to better survive and reproduce in the surrounding environment than others of their own species. Organisms with unfit adaptations will die off; those with traits favorable to the environment will survive. In essence, nature "selects" the enduring traits. The actual process of natural selection occurs over long time spans.

What is **gradualism**?

Gradualism, also known as gradual evolution, is actually the theory of evolution first put forward by Charles Darwin. It states that the changes in organisms brought about by genetic mutation and natural selection are small, and gradually build up over extremely long periods of time—on the order of millions of years.

How did **"survival of the fittest"** fit into Darwin's ideas of natural selection?

Darwin observed the continual struggle of organisms to survive in his studies of nature. He also read Thomas Malthus's *An Essay on the Principle of Population*, which showed that human populations always breed much faster than the increase in available food. When this situation occurred, certain processes happened to maintain the "correct level" of the population. Darwin also believed this occurred with animals and plants, the main process being the production of too many young to survive. In general, of those young, only the strongest—such as those with brighter feathers or stronger bones—survived.

Thus, Darwin developed the idea that only the fittest—or the best adapted—survived. Organisms with the "right" traits lived to reproduce and pass on those traits that enabled their progeny to survive. These positive traits carried through succeeding generations, "changing" and adapting the species to the environment, allowing a better survival rate.

When was theory of **evolution** first **made public**?

The theory of evolution we are so familiar with today was introduced to the public in 1858, by Charles Darwin and naturalist Alfred Russel Wallace (1823–1913). Wallace presented the paper, "On the Tendencies of Varieties to Depart Indefinitely from the Original Type" at a meeting of the Royal Society in England, along with Darwin's "abstract" on natural selection.

Who was **Alfred Russel Wallace**?

Alfred Russel Wallace (1823–1913) was a Welsh-born scientist who devised the theory of evolution independently of Charles Darwin. Wallace's early life included many family moves to rural surroundings. This exposure was probably critical in turning Wallace to a life as a naturalist. He studied the flora and fauna of Brazil and Southeast Asia in the 1840s, and as a result developed his own theory on evolution. In fact, he wrote his theory in two days, during a bout of malaria in the jungles of Borneo in Southeast Asia. It took years for Darwin to develop his evolution ideas.

Why did it **take so long** for Darwin to announce his theory of evolution?

Charles Darwin may have gathered information about evolution on the HMS *Beagle* from 1831 to 1835, but he didn't publish his ideas on evolution until 1858. There were a number of reasons for this almost 20-year gap. In particular, it took Darwin many years to complete his studies of specimens gathered on his historic voyage. And it took even more years to develop his theory of evolution.

In fact, Darwin might not have published his theory at all, if it weren't for Alfred Wallace, who had mailed his similar theory to Darwin—thus, persuading Darwin to announce his discovery. Ever generous, Darwin decided to go public jointly with Wallace in 1858, announcing the theory of evolution to the world. He did this so neither one would have priority, although Darwin had formulated his ideas many years earlier.

Some scientists speculate that the theory of evolution would not have gained such prominence so quickly if it hadn't been for Darwin. Wallace was not as well known—but Darwin had already won a great following based on his account of the HMS *Beagle*'s voyage, and for his scientific work during the expedition.

What was the public reaction to the **Darwin–Wallace** evolution theory?

Many people were not convinced that the theory was valid, especially those who believed Darwinism was atheistic (Darwin did not consider his idea or himself to be atheistic). After all, it was a big step to go against the predominate teachings of creationism that dominated the era. Evolution meant that God had not created all life in one act—and that all life, including humankind, could have evolved from a common ancestor. Many people rejected the idea that humans and great apes shared an ancestor. Eventually, most people accepted the idea of evolution, except those who believed it contradicted the biblical account of creation.

Since Darwin and Wallace announced their theory of evolution, known as gradualism, modifications have been proposed. All of the modified theories mention changes in organisms, but brought about through different processes; the timing of the changes is also different. Examples of these include the theories of punctuated equilibrium, catastrophism, and theistic evolution.

What was an **early problem** with the Darwin–Wallace theory of evolution?

The early problem with the Darwin–Wallace theory of evolution was that intermediate forms between major groups, as forecast by gradualism, were not present in the known fossil record. Darwin initially regarded this as a bit of an embarrassment. To work around the lack of fossil evidence, Darwin insisted that the fossil record was incomplete, and that there were gaps in the rock layers. Today, scientists know that such gaps do exist—most due to very rapid changes in organisms brought about by large-scale catastrophes.

What is **punctuated equilibrium**?

Punctuated equilibrium was a theory of evolution proposed in 1972 by Niles Elredge and Stephen Jay Gould. This idea attempts to explain gaps found in the fossil record, as well as incorporating the latest findings on impact craters on the planet. It proposes that once species are found, they remain unchanged for most of their history; that is, they are stagnant. But when an evolutionary change does occur, it happens quickly, and is followed by another period of stagnancy until the next burst. The rapid changes occur over hundreds of thousands of years—short periods of time when compared to the overall geologic time scale, but much longer than a human life span. In this theory, gaps in the fossil record are not indicative of incompleteness, but are merely times of sudden changes.

What is **catastrophism**?

Catastrophism is a theory of evolution emphasizing the effects of sudden, short-lived, catastrophic, worldwide events and their effects on the earth's organisms. In this theory, periodic devastations wipe out almost all of the existing species, and new organisms replace the extinct ones. Catastrophism was first proposed by French naturalist and anatomist Baron Georges Léopold Chrétien Frédéric Dagobert Cuvier (1769–1832) in the early 1800s.

Catastrophism was based on geological and fossil evidence that indicated periodic catastrophes and species extinction. But major gaps in scientific knowledge during the early 1800s led to several problems with its interpretation. Because of this—and because many geologists and naturalists of the time had religious leanings—many people flavored this theory with a religious, or creationist, point of view. But eventually, primarily because of Darwin's predominately scientific evolution theory, catastrophism fell into disfavor.

When was the theory of **catastrophism reborn**?

The theory of catastrophism was essentially reborn in 1980, based on solid, scientific results. In that year, the team of Luis (1911–88) and Walter (b. 1940) Alvarez, Frank Asaro, and Helen Michel published a study of a thin clay layer found at the Cretaceous-Tertiary (K-T) boundary in Italy. This layer had a high concentration of iridium, a noble metal that is almost completely absent from the earth's crust. The high levels of iridium, subsequently discovered at worldwide K-T boundaries, had two potential sources: from outer space by means of large impacts, or from the earth's core by means of volcanic action. With the subsequent discovery of large impact craters around the world, such as the buried Chixculub crater in Mexico, the catastrophic theory of evolution has again gained prominence, with one caveat: the relationship between impacts, volcanic activity, and extinctions is still being worked out.

What is the **modern theory** of catastrophism?

The modern theory of catastrophism states that sudden, worldwide events—such as impacts of large space objects and/or large amounts of volcanic activity—caused the mass extinction of certain existing species at specific times in the earth's history. This resulted in low species diversity and a high number of ecological gaps. These gaps were then filled by the remaining species, subsequently giving rise to further variations and adaptations within the earth's species. Thus, in modern catastrophism, evolution is the process of extinction, followed by (after a pause) the filling of empty ecological gaps by new species. In addition, in catastrophism, natural selection is seen as a stabilizing force rather than the engine of evolution.

What is **theistic evolution**?

Theistic evolution is a modern theory of evolution that is a combination of biblical and scientific attitudes. This theory has a divine force (or God) behind creation, as proposed by biblical beliefs. However, this divine force works through the process of evolution, as revealed by modern science.

In evolution, what factors lead to a **greater diversity of species**?

The factors that lead to a greater diversity of species are small populations, isolation, and extreme conditions, which results in intense selection.

How did Darwin's theory of evolution affect early interpretations of **dinosaur fossils**?

In particular, Darwin's theory of evolution filled in the missing blanks when interpreting the first dinosaur remains found in the late 1800s in England. Thanks to the theory of evolution—in which it was realized that species could evolve and split into different groups, or even disappear altogether—scientists finally accounted for the origin and disappearance of the dinosaurs. They also visualized the vast potential for variations in dinosaur species over time, including an increase or decrease in body size, a change from walking on four feet to two feet, and changes in diet or habitat.

DINOSAUR ANCESTORS

How did **life evolve** after the early single-celled organisms?

Over hundreds of millions of years after the evolution of single-celled organisms, the oceans abounded with a huge variety of life. The first soft-bodied animals, such as worms and jellyfish, evolved toward the close of the Pre-Cambrian era; the first animals with hard parts, such as shelled mollusks, evolved during the Cambrian period of the Paleozoic era.

What are the **vertebrates**?

The first vertebrates, or animals with backbones, evolved during the late Cambrian to early Ordovician periods as jawless, freshwater fish. By the Devonian period (the "age of fishes"), jawed and armored fishes dominated the oceans. But during the same time period, a line of fish with a bony skeleton developed air-breathing lungs and "limbs" strong enough to support them. These were the precursors to the amphibians, creatures that made their first move toward land probably in response to the spread of plants to land around the early Silurian period.

What are the **amphibians** and when did they first live?

Amphibians were the first air-breathing land vertebrates; the first fossil record of their existence supports that they appeared approximately 360 million years ago, during the late Devonian period. These early amphibians were direct descendants from the early fish, and represent a transition stage from complete water dwellers to land dwellers. Amphibian comes from the Greek *amphi,* meaning "both," and *bios* meaning "life,"

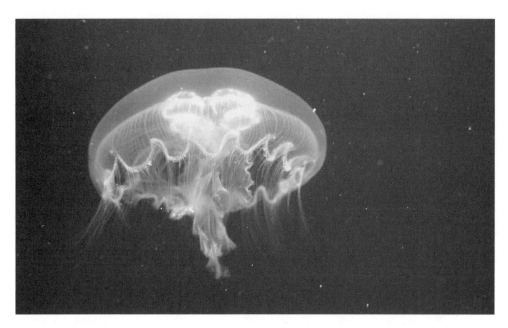

The first soft-bodied animals, such as this jellyfish, evolved toward the end of the Pre-Cambrian era. (Photo courtesy of Amos Nachoum/Corbis.)

signifying that these animals could live both in and out of the water. The Carboniferous period of the Paleozoic age, from approximately 360 to 290 million years ago, was known as the "age of amphibians." During that time, the climate was warm and humid, and there were many swamps, marshes and lakes—perfect for the water needs of the amphibians.

From what animals did the **amphibians evolve**?

The fossil records of amphibians are scarce, so the precise ancestry of amphibians may never be known. However, scientists do agree that amphibians first evolved from a group of animals known as the lobe-finned fishes during the Devonian period. In fact, these four-legged land vertebrates, called tetrapods, had fishlike heads and tails, and their limbs were no more than jointed, lobed fins. But these animals could do something that no fish could do: breathe air, with the change over from gills to lungs coming during the early larval stage of the amphibian. Amphibians were also the first vertebrates to eventually have true legs, tongues, ears, and voice boxes.

What is the **earliest known amphibian**?

Fossils of the earliest known amphibian, the *Ichthyostega,* have been uncovered in Greenland. This early amphibian lived in the swamps of the late Devonian period, in

Amphibians, such as this Asian tree frog, are able to live both on land and in water. (Photo courtesy of Field Mark Publications.)

mild, warm climates. By this time, too, insects had evolved on land, providing food for the slow-moving amphibian. The *Ichthyostega* was a 3-foot- (1-meter-) long animal with four limbs and a fin on its tail—a combination of amphibian and fish features that allowed it to climb on land and swim. This was the earliest known common ancestor of today's modern amphibians.

What were some of the **problems** as amphibians moved from **water to land**?

The early amphibian's main problem was support. In the water, a body is virtually "weightless," supported by the buoyancy of water. But on land, the amphibian's body had to be held up from the ground, and the internal organs protected from being crushed—thus, a strong ribcage was needed. The backbone, ligaments, and muscles also had to strengthen, supporting not only the weight of the body between the front and hind legs, but also the head. The limbs and limb muscles also had to change to allow walking; hind limbs turned on the strengthened pelvis, and the skeleton as a whole was made stronger.

Another problem was adapting to breathing on land. The amphibians had to modify their respiratory system (changing from gills to lungs), as lungs took over more and more of the breathing. The reproductive system, water balance, and senses also had to adapt to the new life in and out of the water. For example, the first amphibians probably spent much of their time in the water, giving birth to totally aquatic young (tadpoles) that would eventually be able to live both in and out of water. An amphibian's water balance adapted by allowing the creature to live out of water as long as it at

The salamander is one of many species of amphibians living today. (Photo courtesy of Field Mark Publications.)

least stayed damp. Their senses also had to adapt—their sight, smell, and hearing taking on more important roles as they started living more on land. For instance, amphibian eardrums developed to enable the semi-land-dwelling animals to hear sounds in the air. Their eyes had to be modified to see in air instead of water; protective eyelids developed; and tear ducts evolved, allowing their eyes to be continually moistened with tears.

Even after all these changes, amphibians still were tied to ponds, lakes, or the edges of the oceans, especially since the eggs still had to be laid and hatched in water. Evolution did not change the amphibians too much—modern amphibians are still tied to water.

Which **amphibians** are living **today**?

Names of modern amphibians are familiar to us: frogs, toads, salamanders, and newts. They represent the descendants of groups that did not become extinct at the end of the Mesozoic era (when dinosaurs died out). Of the modern amphibians, the newts and salamanders are probably the most similar to the early amphibians, although they are much smaller.

The vertebrate class Amphibia today includes about 3,500 species in three orders: frogs and toads (order Anura), salamanders and newts (order Caudata), and caecilians (order Gymnophiona). There is, however, a much larger number of extinct species of

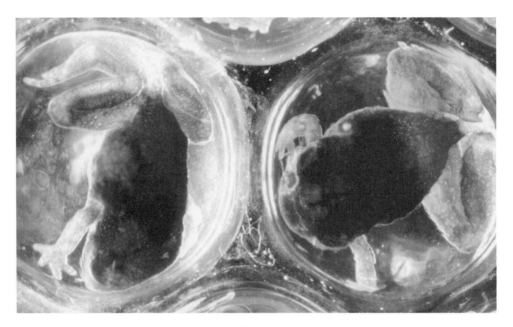

The eggs of amphibians, like these frogs, lack the hard shell of reptile eggs and must be laid in water or in damp places. (Photo courtesy of Michael and Patricia Fogden/Corbis.)

amphibians, because this ancient group of animals were the first vertebrates to begin to exploit terrestrial environments, where they fell prey to other species.

When did **reptiles** first **evolve** from amphibians?

It is thought that during the Carboniferous period, a group of amphibians gave rise to the reptiles. The first reptiles were small, lizard-sized animals, but they had many differences from their amphibian ancestors—including waterproof skins and thick-shelled eggs. This made it unnecessary for the reptiles to stay near water, to keep moist, or to lay their eggs in water. In fact, the evolution of the reptiles, geologically speaking, occurred very rapidly—and within about 40 million years, the reptiles had produced thousands of different species.

What is the **difference** between a **reptile and an amphibian**?

Reptiles are clad in scales, shields, or plates, and their toes have claws; amphibians have moist, glandular skins, and their toes lack claws. Reptile eggs have a thick, hard or parchmentlike shell that protects the developing embryo from moisture loss, even on dry land. The eggs of amphibians lack this protective outer covering and are always laid in water or in damp places. Young reptiles are miniature replicas of their parents in general appearance if not always in coloration and pattern. Juvenile amphibians

What were some of the earliest known reptiles?

Two of the earliest known reptiles, the *Hylonomus* and *Palaeothyris,* both descended from amphibians during the mid–Carboniferous period of the Paleozoic era. The best evidence of the change from amphibian to reptile were the early reptiles' high skulls, evidence of additional jaw muscles, and thicker egg shells. The *Hylonomus* lived about 310 million years ago, and the *Palaeothyris* evolved about 300 million years old. The fossils of the reptiles are found near Nova Scotia, Canada, in ancient tree stumps. Apparently the animals fell into the stumps in pursuit of insects and worms; they were trapped inside and eventually died.

pass through a larval, usually aquatic, stage before they metamorphose (change in form and structure) into the adult form.

What was one of the **most important changes** that enabled **reptiles** to become true land-dwelling animals?

The development of the amniote egg freed the reptiles completely from life in the water by allowing them to fully reproduce on land. Unlike the young of amphibians, who had to go through a larval stage in the water before metamorphosing into an adult, the amniote egg acted as a sort of "private pond" for the young reptiles.

The egg itself had a hard shell, which contained numerous small pores. These pores allowed air to enter, but the shell prevented the inside from drying up as long as the surroundings were humid. The eggs were fertilized inside the mother's body before being laid. There were three very thin bags inside the shell itself, each of which had a specific function. The first bag held the developing young and a liquid (which took the place of the pond or stream); this area was called the amnion, from which the egg gets its name. The next bag contained the yolk, the source of food for the developing embryo. The third bag was in contact with the air diffusing in through the shell. Thus, the young reptiles had food, air, protection from predators, and an aquatic environment in which to grow. The young would eventually hatch into a miniature version of its parents, able to fend for itself. Because of the egg, the reptiles no longer had to have a source of water to reproduce, and could spread out—populating the land as well as hunting for its prey well away from water.

What is a **pelycosaur**?

The pelycosaurs are a group of mostly medium to small carnivorous and insectivorous reptiles. However, included in the group are two relatively well-known gen-

The ability for reptiles to reproduce with an amniote egg allowed for these creatures to evolve into exclusively land animals. (Photo courtesy of Field Mark Publications.)

era—*Dimetrodon* and *Edaphosaurus*. These were among the largest of the pelycosaurs, reaching up to almost 10 feet (about 3 meters) in length and having great extensions of the vertebrae extending up from their spines. The most probable purpose of these "sails" would be for regulating body temperature. Both of these animals had a rather sprawling gait and were probably not very agile. *Dimetrodon* probably benefited as a carnivore by turning broadside to the morning sun, raising its body temperature and therefore becoming more active before its intended prey. *Edaphosaurus* may represent the defensive response to this threat, for it was a herbivore and might well have been the target of *Dimetrodon*'s hunger. So, it too developed a "sail" to absorb heat quickly, which would speed up the animal's response time. Of course, this is a speculative answer—the evidence is not conclusive by any means.

Why did the **reptiles dominate** during the Mesozoic?

Besides the ability to not depend on water as much as amphibians, there are probably two main reasons why reptiles became dominant in the Mesozoic. First, reptiles developed adaptations in their skeletal and bone structure, allowing them to move much quicker than amphibians. Second, during the Permian period, the climate became hotter and drier, and many water sources disappeared. The reptiles' new adaptations—from the development of scales to hold in water, to eggs that could survive without staying in water—allowed them to thrive at the expense of the amphibians.

Did some **reptiles return to the oceans**?

Yes, as the reptiles spread out over the land, some of them returned to the water. Over a period of time, they evolved and adapted to the water again. Their legs gradually evolved into fins and flippers; their eyes adapted to seeing in the water; and their bodies became streamlined for better speed in the water. In addition, they could no longer lay their eggs on land. Thus, they evolved a way of producing living young within their bodies, a process called ovoviviparous. The ichthyosaurs, or "fish lizards," were the most fishlike true reptiles.

How are **reptiles grouped**?

During the next 100 million years after the first reptiles appeared, various reptile lines continued to evolve. Today, 16 orders of reptiles are recognized, but only four have survived to present day (crocodiles, lizards and snakes, *Sphenodon,* and turtles and tortoises). The others died out over time.

The 16 orders are divided into four distinct groupings (or subclasses), called the anapsids, synapsids, diapsids, and euryapsids—all recognized by the pattern of openings in the skull. The anapsids had no openings in the skull and eventually evolved into today's turtles and tortoises. The synapsids, or "same hole," had a low skull opening, and were the ancestors of modern mammals. It was the animals of the diapsid line, or "two skull openings," that eventually gave rise to the dinosaurs. One of the more debatable lines is the euryapsids, characterized by a single opening on the side of the skull. They evolved into the placodonts ("plate tooth") ichthyosaurs and plesiosaurs—none of which were dinosaurs—and into all marine reptiles that quickly went extinct.

DINOSAURS APPEAR

How did the **reptiles** give rise to the **dinosaurs**?

It was the diapsid group of the reptiles that eventually produced the dinosaurs. The jaw muscles in these reptiles were attached to the two openings on each side of the skull, giving their jaws better leverage and strength. Sometime in the Permian period, the diapsid line branched into two groups, called the lepidosaurs and archosaurs. The lepidosaur group evolved into today's lizards and snakes, while the archosaurs gave rise to the dinosaurs.

What were **early archosaurs** like?

One of the first archosaurs—and probably typical of many archosaurs—was the big-headed *Shansisuchus,* an early Triassic period creature that lived in the area now known as China. It was about 12 feet (4 meters) long, and had long back legs and short front legs.

What were **other archosaurs** like?

Archosaurs varied in many ways. Some, like the *Gracilisuchus,* could run on their hind legs over short distances; others like the *Chasmatosaurus* were heavy carnivores that walked on all fours. The *Lagerpeton* had very peculiar hind limbs; its feet had elongated lateral digits that may have been used for perching.

What are **thecodonts**?

Thecodonts ("socket teeth") were thought to be a group within the archosaurs that eventually gave rise to the dinosaurs—and perhaps crocodiles, birds, and pterosaurs.

Do all scientists think **thecodonts** were the **direct ancestors** of the dinosaurs?

No, just like many fields of science, the study of early dinosaurs is constantly changing, and differences in opinion abound. By the mid-1980s, many scientists proposed that there was *not* a group called the thecodonts that evolved from the archosaurs. In fact, many scientists believe Thecodontia as a group does not exist. Scientists sight that some of the animals listed in this group are more closely related to the crocodiles, some to dinosaurs, and some to the entire group of archosaurs. Other scientists believe that while thecodonts may not be a true group, the term is a handy way to describe certain creatures with socketed teeth within the archosaurs.

At this time, no one really agrees on what to do with the thecodonts. Until more fossils are found to explain the early rise of dinosaurs, the thecodont question will continue to be a subject of controversy.

What was the **next stage** in the **evolution** toward true dinosaurs?

As time went on, another phase of dinosaur evolution took place: the animals' skeletal structure changed—especially the hips, which gave many of the dinosaurs the ability to run on two legs. *Euparkeria* was a small lizardlike reptile that lived on land and

> ## How were the dinosaurs unique among the reptiles?
>
> **D**inosaurs, unlike other reptiles, had their legs tucked in underneath their bodies. This gave them the ability to run and walk very efficiently, eventually leading to some species becoming totally bipedal (two-footed). They also had a keener sense of smell, sight, and hearing, unlike the amphibians and primitive reptiles.

walked on all fours, but could run on two legs when in a hurry. Further along in time was *Ornithosuchus,* or "bird crocodile," which was a two-legged predator. Its front limbs were too small to use for walking on all fours, and its thighs were nearly vertical. From this evidence, it appears that *Ornithosuchus* walked only on its hind legs.

What are some of the **earliest** known **primitive dinosaurs**?

Two of the earliest known primitive dinosaurs were both fast-running carnivores: the *Eoraptor,* or "dawn hunter," a small, 3-foot-long (1-meter-long) dinosaur; and the *Herrerasaurus,* measuring from 9 to 18 feet (3 to 6 meters) long. Both lived approximately 230 million years ago, in the area known today as Argentina. Still another earlier dinosaur was the *Staurikosaurus,* a carnivore with a fully upright gait that allowed for speed. After the evolution of these early specimens, other dinosaurs evolved quickly, becoming more and more diverse, and reaching out into all the ecological niches.

What were **early carnivorous** and **herbivorous dinosaurs** like?

The earliest carnivorous dinosaurs, or meat-eaters, came in many different shapes and sizes. It is thought that the *Dilophosaurus* was a typical carnivore: the dinosaur had strong hind legs, but short, weak forelimbs. It also had thin parallel ridges on its forehead, which could have acted as radiators to control temperature, or as decoration, possibly for territorial or mating displays. The earliest herbivorous dinosaurs, or plant-eaters, also came in many different shapes and sizes. One typical herbivore was the *Heterodontosaurus,* a small, turkey-sized dinosaur that had sharp incisors, caninelike tusks, and grinding teeth for chewing plants.

How are **dinosaurs classified**?

Dinosaurs are in the Reptilia class of animals—thus, they are called reptiles. They are from the subclass of diapsids, and in their own infraclass of Dinosauria. They are

Visitors walk among the saurischian (meaning "lizard-hipped") skeletons at the Metropolitan Museum of Art in New York. (Photo courtesy of Michael S. Yamashita/Corbis.)

divided into two main groups, based historically on their hipbone structure. Those with hips that had the two lower bones pointing in opposite directions, with the pubis bone pointing forward, were called saurischian, or lizard-hipped, dinosaurs. Those with hips that had the two lower bones lying together behind the back legs, and the pubis bone pointing backward, were called ornithischian, or bird-hipped, dinosaurs. The *Tyrannosaurus rex* is an example of a lizard-hipped dinosaur, while the *Iguanodon* is an example of a bird-hipped dinosaur.

How are **dinosaurs named**?

Dinosaur names come from a number of places, but in general, they are named after a characteristic body feature (for example, the *Hypsilophodon,* or high-crowned tooth); after the place in which the first bones were found (for example, the *Muttaburrasaurus*); or after the person(s) involved in the discovery (for example, the *Leaellynasaura*).

In many cases, the names include two Greek or Latin words, or even combinations of the words. For example, *Tyrannosaurus rex* is a combination of Greek and Latin, which translates as "king of the tyrant lizards." Overall, the two names, known as the genus and species names, are used by biologists to describe all organisms on the earth, such as humans (*Homo sapiens*), domestic dogs (*Canis familiaris*), or rattlesnakes (*Crotalus horridus*).

How many **species of dinosaurs** are currently known?

Currently, approximately 700 species of dinosaurs have been named. But there is a major caveat: only about half of these specimens are complete skeletons—and usually only complete (or nearly complete) skeletons allow scientists to confidently say the bones represent unique and separate species. All of the species are listed in the approximately 300 verified dinosaur genera—which are groups (such as the *Tyrannosaurus,* or "tyrant lizards") of species linked by common characteristics. Amazingly, many scientists speculate there may be 700 to 900 more dinosaur genera that have yet to be discovered!

How do the number of known **dinosaur species compare** to some modern species?

Even if there are truly 700 valid dinosaur species, the number is still less than one-tenth the number of currently known bird species; less than one-fifth the number of known mammal species; and less than one-third the number of known spider species.

Workers at the Natural History Museum in London, England, reassemble a plaster-cast skeleton of a *Diplodocus,* made from fossils found in the U.S.A. The *Diplodocus* is a type of saurischian. (Photo courtesy of Hulton-Deutsch Collection/Corbis.)

What kinds of dinosaurs were in the **saurischian** group?

The saurischians were a diverse group of dinosaurs that included both carnivores and herbivores. They exhibited two-legged and four-legged means of propulsion.

The carnivores included the large, two-legged *Allosaurus, Ceratosaurus, Tarbosaurus,* and the *Tyrannosaurus.* There were smaller, two-legged carnivores, such as *Ornithomimus,* and the *Dromaeosaurus,* which had specialized feet and their unique, slashing, raptorial claws.

The herbivorous saurischians that are best known are the large, four-legged sauropods, the largest dinosaurs to have walked the earth. These dinosaurs had long necks and tails, with relatively tiny heads. Included in this group are *Brachiosaurus, Camarasaurus, Diplodocus, Mamenchisaurus,* and *Seismosaurus.*

What **kinds of dinosaurs** were in the **ornithischian** group?

The ornithischians were all herbivores and had two and four-legged types. There were the four-legged armored dinosaurs such as *Ankylosaurus* and *Stegosaurus.* There were large, horned dinosaurs such as *Eucentrosaurus* and *Triceratops.* Two-legged types included *Iguanodon,* and many of the duck-billed dinosaurs (hadrosaurs), such as *Corythosaurus, Lambeosaurus,* and *Maiasaura.*

How did **dinosaurs evolve**?

The following chart offers a simplified vision of dinosaur evolution. Ideas expressed on this chart will no doubt modify over time, as more dinosaur fossils are discovered.

Evolutionary Tree of the Dinosaur

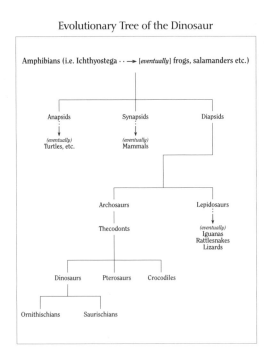

DINOSAURS IN THE MESOZOIC

What **events** led to the **dominance** of dinosaurs in the **Mesozoic** era?

Approximately 250 million years ago, at the end of the Permian period, or the beginning of the Triassic period (and thus, the end of the Paleozoic era and the beginning of the Mesozoic era), there was a mass extinction. This extinction eliminated close to 90 percent of all the species present on our planet—coming extraordinarily close to total extinction on the earth. The extinction was not selective; it eliminated organisms in the oceans and on land, including many invertebrates, armored fish, and reptiles.

The true reasons for the extinction are unknown, although there are several theories. One is that a collision of the earth with an asteroid or comet caused dust and debris to fly into the upper atmosphere, cutting off sunlight and radically changing the global climate. Another idea is that the moving continents changed the climate, sea levels, and thus, habitats, causing some species to change and adapt, while others died out. Still another theory focuses on Siberian flood basalts, in which tons of volcanic material erupted over a huge area in Asia toward the end of the Permian period, changing the climate and certain habitats.

Whatever the scenario, species that survived did so by adapting to the ecological niches that became vacant, allowing them to further evolve. After the Permian extinction and throughout the Mesozoic era, it was the reptiles in general, and the dinosaurs specifically, who diversified the most and became the dominant species on the planet.

When—and for **how long**—did dinosaurs live?

Dinosaurs were the dominant species for approximately 140 to 150 million years. They lived during the Mesozoic era, often referred to as the "age of reptiles," which lasted from approximately 250 to 65 million years ago. It includes the Triassic, Jurassic, and Cretaceous periods.

It is interesting to note that at the beginning of the Mesozoic, there were no dinosaurs; other reptiles were dominant. But, by the end of the Triassic period, the dinosaurs became dominant—and stayed that way for about 140 to 150 million years. Dinosaurs were not the only form of life that existed during this time. For example, there were smaller, lizardlike reptiles, small early mammals, insects, amphibians, invertebrates, and a wide variety of plants. In fact, these organisms helped the dinosaurs to stay dominant—as many of the dinosaurs used this abundance of life for their sustenance and growth.

When did the **age of dinosaurs end**?

The age of the dinosaurs came to an end approximately 65 million years ago. From this point onward, there are currently no known dinosaur fossils. The time of the great dinosaur (and other species) extinction is used by scientists to delineate the end of the Cretaceous period as well as the end of the Mesozoic era. After this point, the Cenozoic era (in which we still live) begins, starting with the Tertiary period.

TRIASSIC PERIOD

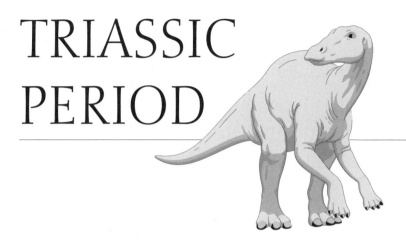

What is the **Triassic period** and how did it get its **name**?

The Triassic period follows the Permian period on the geologic time scale. During this time, dinosaurs first began to evolve from the early reptiles, the first primitive mammals appeared, and the armored amphibians and mammal-like reptiles died out. The Triassic was one of the first labeled divisions on the geologic time scale. It is named after three (or "tri-") layers of sedimentary rocks representative of the time period—from bottom to top, a sandstone, limestone, and copper-bearing shale—first found and analyzed in Germany. The Triassic is the first of three periods (the others are Jurassic and Cretaceous) making up the Mesozoic era.

When was the **Triassic period** first named?

The Triassic period was first named in 1834, by German geologist Friedrich August Von Alberti (1795–1878), to describe a three-part division of rock types in Germany. It was originally called the Trias, and is still called this by many European geologists. The three distinct rock formations are, from the bottom up, the Bunter (mostly early Triassic), the Muschelkalk (middle Triassic), and the Keuper (mostly late Triassic).

How long did the **Triassic period last**?

The geologic time scale is not exact, and depending on the country or scientist, the dates of the Triassic period can vary by about 5 to 10 million years. On the average, the Triassic period is said to have lasted from about 250 to 205 million years ago, for a total of about 45 million years in length.

What are the **divisions** of the **Triassic period**?

In general, the informal way to define parts of the Triassic period is to use the terms lower, middle, and upper Triassic. More formally, they are capitalized (Lower, Middle, and Upper) by scientists, and include subdivisions within those groupings. The following table lists a general interpretation of the Triassic epochs (although note that many researchers use slightly different notations; for example, many do not list the Rhaetian age).

Triassic Period

Epoch	Age	Millions of Years Ago (approximate)
Late	Rhaetian	210 to 205
	Norian	221 to 210
	Carnian	227 to 221
Middle	Ladinian	234 to 227
	Anisian	242 to 234
Early	Olenekian	245 to 242
	Induan	250 to 245

What did the **Triassic period signify**?

The Triassic period represented the time after the great Permian period extinctions. It also was important as a time of transition—when the old life of the Paleozoic era gave way to a more highly developed and varied form of life of the Mesozoic era. The Permian period extinctions wiped out most of the animals and plants on the planet (about 90 percent of all species), making the very early Triassic an eerie place, almost completely devoid of the abundant life that existed for perhaps hundreds or thousands of years before. Certain flora and fauna still dotted the land, and eventually, after about 10 million years or more, life began to emerge in full force again. But it still took even longer for larger animals, coral reefs, and other specialized animals to recover or evolve after the extinction at the end of the Permian period.

THE CONTINENTS DURING THE TRIASSIC PERIOD

Do the earth's **continents change positions**?

Yes, the continents continually change positions, but it takes them millions of years to shift and move great distances. The continents are actually part of the thick plates that

A *Plateosaurus* roams the land during the Triassic period. (Image courtesy of University of Michigan Exhibit, Museum of Natural History.)

make up the planet's crust, all of various sizes and shapes. These plates fit together like a jigsaw puzzle. They don't move fast—only fractions of an inch to inches per year.

What are **continental drift** and **plate tectonics**?

The reason (or reasons) for the earth's crustal movement is still somewhat of a mystery. The most accepted theory of plate movement is called continental drift, and the theory of its mechanism is called plate tectonics. These theories suggest that the continental plates move laterally across the face of the planet, driven by the lower, more fluid mantle of the earth. At certain plate boundaries, molten rock from the mantle rises at a midocean ridge (such as the Mid-Atlantic Ridge, a long chain of volcanic mountains that lie under the Atlantic Ocean) or at its equivalent on land, the rift valley (such as the one in eastern Africa), the magma solidifying and moving away to either side of the ridge. At other plate boundaries, plates are pushed under an adjacent plate, forming a subduction zone, in which the crust sinks into the mantle again. And at other boundaries, plates just slip by, which is what happens at the San Andreas Fault in California, where a part of the North American plate slides by the Pacific plate.

But not everyone agrees on these theories. One reason is because, although the idea of moving plates seems logical, the mechanisms for developing plate tectonics are not fully understood. Therefore, some scientists believe in continental drift, but not plate tectonics. Most of these scientists believe that the reason the continents shift is

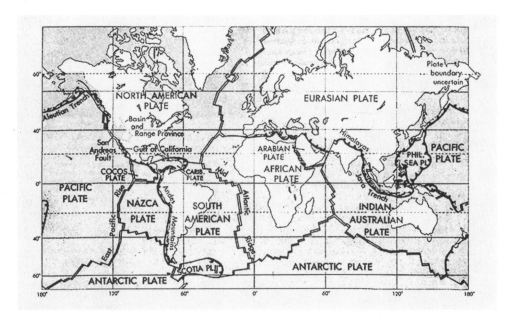

Continental drift is the most accepted theory explaining the earth's crustal movement, and plate tectonics describes its mechanism. Illustrated here are the divisions between crustal plates.

that the earth is actually expanding, causing a false illusion of movement (although no one can explain why or how the earth is expanding). Another hypothesis is called surge tectonics, in which the features of the earth's surface are explained by the sudden surge of plate movement, as opposed to a constant flow created by the steady movement of the mantle. And still others suggest that the continents have always been in the same positions.

Overall, no one really can explain the reason for the continual movement of the plates. One thing is certain: the plates do move. Since the advent of earth-orbiting observation satellites, scientists have been able to track the plates using sophisticated laser-ranging instruments that measure the minute movements.

When did scientists **determine** the jigsaw puzzle **fit of the continents**?

The actual connection between the continental fit (the idea that the continents fit together like the pieces of a jigsaw puzzle) was first proposed in 1858, by Antonio Snider. Other scientists mentioned this idea for years afterward, but it was not until 1912 that German meteorologist and geophysicist Alfred Wegener (1880–1930) expanded the theory, suggesting that the continents at one time formed a supercontinent he called Pangea (or Pangaea). Wegener's theory was not taken seriously until about the 1960s, when scientists believed they had finally worked out a mechanism (plate tectonics) for the movement of the continental plates.

How did **fossil evidence** support the theory of continental drift?

Scientists discovered the fossils of many identical-appearing species on widely separated continents. They had two theories for this. First, they theorized that separate species developed identically across the far-flung continents, a notion that was highly unlikely. The second theory was that the continents had been in contact with each other millions of years ago, and had somehow drifted apart.

For example, fossils found in South America were related to those in Australia and Antarctica. These landmasses were in contact sometime in the past, allowing species to roam freely, die, be buried, and become fossilized across these continents. The fossilized remains in the rock layers of the continents drifted with the landmasses, leading to widely separated—but nearly identical—fossils.

German meteorologist and geophysicist Alfred Wegener suggested a supercontinent he called Pangea. (Photo courtesy of UPI/Corbis-Bettman.)

Who discovered **seafloor spreading**?

Harry Hess (1906–69), an American geologist and professor of geology at Princeton University, discovered seafloor spreading. Based on material brought up from the ocean floor during an ocean drilling project, he determined that rocks on the ocean floor were younger than those on the continental landmasses. He also discovered rocks on the ocean floor varied in age: there were older rocks farther from the midocean ridges and younger rocks around midocean ridges. Hess proposed that the seafloor was spreading as magma erupted from the earth's interior along the ocean's

95

midocean ridges. The newly created seafloor slowly spreads away from the ridges, and later sinks back into the earth's interior around deep-sea trenches.

What **magnetic evidence** did scientists use to verify **seafloor spreading**?

When molten lava is expelled from midocean ridges, it cools, creating new ocean floor. And as the rock cools, specific minerals with magnetic properties line up with the prevailing magnetic field of the earth. This preserves a record of the magnetic field orientation at that particular point in time. Changes in the rocks' magnetic field records, called magnetic anomalies, happen when the earth's field reverses—or when the northern and southern magnetic poles change places—usually over hundreds of thousands of years. Scientists still do not know what causes these magnetic reversals, but it may have something to do with the giant convection currents in the earth's interior.

The theory of seafloor spreading was confirmed by measuring such magnetic anomalies in rocks on the ocean floor. Scientists discovered a symmetrical, striped pattern of magnetic anomalies on the ocean floor, spreading out on either side of the Mid-Atlantic Ridge. This ridge is a long volcanic mountain range that runs down the Atlantic Ocean seafloor between the continents of North America, Europe, Africa, and South America. The pattern and distribution of these stripes showed that the magnetic fields had reversed many times over millions of years—and only could have formed if the seafloor had been spreading apart over those millions of years.

What is the driving **force** behind the movement of the continental plates?

Not everyone agrees on why the continental plates move across the earth—but there are some theories. In general, the continental plates are made of light material that "floats" on the heavier, molten material of the earth's interior (called the mantle). As the upper part of the mantle circulates and moves, it slowly "carries" the plates around the planet.

The Nations of the World

©1994 MAGELLAN Geographix℠Santa Barbara, CA (800) 929-4MAP   Robinson Projection

A map of the world as it looks today. (Map courtesy of Magellan Geographix/Corbis.)

What are the **consequences** of continental plate movements?

As the term implies, the movement of the continental plates change the positions of the continents. Along the continental boundaries, volcanoes and mountains form, as the plates interact with each other. Some continents slowly crash into one another, forming huge mountain chains, such as the Himalayas in Asia (from the collision of the Indian and Asian plates). Other plates slide under one another, in areas called subduction zones. The Andes mountains are the result of a subduction zone between the Nazca and South American plates. Still other plates slip right by one another, such as the Pacific and North American plates. In this case, the slipping of the plates creates the San Andreas fault in California.

But there are other consequences of continental plate movement. In particular, this process also opens and closes the seas, changing ocean currents—and thus climates—around the world. In addition, volcanoes and earthquakes can also form as plates sink under each other.

What are **volcanoes**?

Volcanoes are features that form as magma (or hot, liquid rock) erupts at the surface through openings in the earth's crust. Magma can erupt as oozing lava, or explode as huge bombs, ash, dust, and gases. The result of the eruptions is usually a cone-shaped mountain; the "throat" of the volcano forms a crater (caldera) at the center of the

97

What effect did volcanoes have on the dinosaurs?

Volcanoes were often important during the time of the dinosaurs because they affected not only these reptiles but all organisms either locally or globally. If a volcano erupted, it would often spew out thousands of tons of material into the upper atmosphere. Such dust and debris could change the local climate by blocking out the sunlight. In addition, if the effects were more widespread, volcanic eruptions could modify the climate. And if the climate changed, so could vegetation—leading to changes in the landscape and the availability of food for plant-eating dinosaurs. In turn, if the plant-eating dinosaurs died off, the meat-eating dinosaurs would also lose their food sources, and the food chain would collapse.

mountain. The word volcano is derived from the island of Vulcano, located off the northern tip of Sicily, where a volcano erupted in ancient times. You've probably heard of some of the more famous volcanoes, such as the Hawaiian Islands, Cascade Mountains in the western United States (of which Mt. St. Helens is a member), Mt. Etna in Italy, and Mt. Pinatubo in the Philippines.

What is the **world's most active** volcano?

The world's most active—and largest—volcano is Hawaii's Mauna Loa. It is 13,650 feet (4,160 meters) above sea level; to compare, the tallest continental mountain, Mt. Everest, is 29,022 feet (8,846 meters) above sea level. But if you measured the volcano from its base on the ocean floor, it would be almost as tall as Mt. Everest.

What is the **Ring of Fire**?

Most volcanoes form along continental plate boundaries—and about 75 percent of the world's active volcanoes are found ringing the Pacific Ocean, called the Ring of Fire. The ring marks the boundaries between numerous continental plates around the perimeter of the Pacific Ocean. At the plates move apart, slip under, or pass by each other, liquid magma easily "slips through the cracks," forming volcanoes and earthquakes.

What is **paleoceanography**?

Paleoceanography is the study of ancient oceans. Because it includes information from the fields of geology, biology, physics, and chemistry, it is considered an interdisciplinary field. One of the goals of paleoceanography is to piece together how the oceans have changed over geologic time. Most of this data is derived from the collection of rock and sediment samples from the ocean floor.

Why is **paleoceanography important**?

Paleoceanography helps interpret not only the past ocean currents, but ancient climates. In particular, by studying ancient ocean sediments, scientists now better understand what the oceans and climates were like in the past—including the time of the dinosaurs.

What is **biogeography**?

Biogeography examines the distribution of plants and animals in terms of climate; barriers to the spread of the organisms (such as where the organisms are in relationship to barriers such as the oceans, mountains, and deserts); geographical distribution of resources and rock types; and the evolutionary history of the organisms.

Why is **biogeography** important to the study of **ancient life**?

Biogeography helps scientists discover information about the past distributions of plants and animals; understand the position and movement of the continents, oceans, and islands over time; and interpret past climates. Overall, the field is called paleobiogeography.

Paleobiogeography is also one of the reasons scientists discovered that the continental plates actually moved across the earth's surface. Initially, scientists found that the *Dryosaurus* from the late Jurassic of North America's Rocky Mountains seemed to be closely related to the *Dysalotosaurus* of the late Jurassic of southern Tanzania, Africa. The researchers speculated that the creatures must have somehow lived close to each other, even though today the continents are far apart. Now they know, based on paleobiogeography, seafloor spreading, and other evidence, that Africa was adjacent to South America and not far from North America during the late Jurassic. Thus, the two species were put into a single genus, *Dryosaurus,* based on geographical grounds.

Paleobiogeography has since been used to discover additional information about the planet's early fauna (animals) and flora (plants). For example, it showed that the position and movement of the continents had a profound effect on the distribution of the early ancestors of the dinosaurs—and eventually, on the dinosaurs themselves.

What did our **planet look like** at the start of the Triassic period?

Similar to today, most of the planet during the Triassic period was ocean, but the distribution of the landmasses was not the same. Scientists believe there was

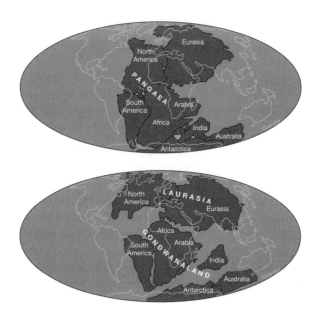

After having become one supercontinent, Pangea again broke apart during the Triassic period to form Laurasia and Gondwanaland. (Photo courtesy of AP/Wide World.)

essentially one large expanse of water called the Panthalassa Ocean. It surrounded the one very large landmass, or supercontinent, called Pangea, meaning "all earth." This giant landmass straddled the planet's equator roughly in the form of a "C"; the smaller body of water enclosed by the "C" on the east was known as the Tethys Sea (or Ocean). Only a few scattered bits of continental crust were not attached to Pangea, and lay to the east of the larger continent. They included pieces of what we now call Manchuria (northern China), eastern China, Indochina, and bits of central Asia. In addition, the sea level was low, and there was no ice at the polar regions.

What led to the original **formation of the supercontinent Pangea**?

Scientists believe the same process that would eventually break apart Pangea led to its formation—the continents seemingly moving around the planet like icebergs on an ocean. There were two large landmasses on earth during the Paleozoic era—Laurasia (made up of present-day North America and Eurasia) to the north of the equator, and Gondwanaland (or Gondwana; including South America, Africa, India, Antarctica, and Australia) to the south of the equator. These two continents slowly collided during the late Paleozoic era, forming the supercontinent of Pangea. By the beginning of the Mesozoic era, Pangea was still the only true continent on the planet.

How did **the supercontinent Pangea** change during the **Triassic period**?

In the early Triassic period, Pangea gradually began to break apart into two major continents again, the result of a seafloor-spreading rift. (This rift was similar to today's midocean ridge in the Atlantic Ocean, a volcanic seam that continues to spread, and along which the volcanic island of Iceland was born.) The Triassic rift extended westward from the Tethys Sea across what is today the Mediterranean Sea. The action of this rift separated northern Laurasia from southern Gondwanaland, which would eventually lead to the opening of the proto-Atlantic (or early Atlantic) Ocean. As northern Africa split from southern Europe, there was a gradual rise in sea level that flooded south and central Europe.

Toward the middle and late Triassic period, the spreading rift between northern Africa and Europe grew westward, and began to separate northern Africa from the eastern part of North America. The resulting rift valley was the first true stage in the formation of the proto–Atlantic Ocean.

How did this continental **configuration affect the dinosaurs**?

During the early Triassic period, the supercontinent Pangea allowed the precursors of dinosaurs to roam all over the huge landmass. As the supercontinent slowly split in two, it eventually cut off certain emerging dinosaur species from other species. The movements also caused certain ocean areas to widen, and led to the inundation of parts of the landmasses, thus changing shorelines. This also changed the types of vegetation and animal life in certain regions.

It is difficult to mention all the minute changes that occurred over such a broad expanse of time, but there are generalities. For example, as the Atlantic Ocean opened, lakes that eventually became the ocean grew larger and smaller—and even divided. These changes were often accompanied by an absence or abundance of sea life. Shorelines often grew rich in plant and animal life. We know that some dinosaurs came down to eat and drink around these changing lakes, as their tracks have been discovered in sediment that once lay along the shorelines.

Where are **Triassic period rocks** found?

Layers of Triassic period rocks are found in many countries around the world. They occur in certain localities in eastern and western North America, South America, the British Isles, western Europe, Asia, Africa, and Australia. The thickest Triassic period rock layer so far discovered lies in the Alps and it measures about 25,000 feet (7,500 meters) thick.

What is the **Newark Supergroup** and why is it **significant**?

The Newark Supergroup is a layer of Triassic period rocks located in the eastern United States; it is famous for its rocks and fossils from this period. The rock layers represent the remnants of several thousands of feet of sedimentary and volcanic rocks deposited in a chain of basins over a span of 45 million years. This layer is found in many locations, including New Jersey, Virginia, and North Carolina. The sedimentary strata (layers) contain a good cross section of fossils from the late Triassic period, including insects, fish, turtles, archosaurian reptiles (including dinosaurs, lizards, and snakes), lissamphibians (frogs, salamanders, and caecilians), and numerous plant fossils. Paleontologists hope to find additional vertebrate fossils in the Newark Supergroup layers that will shed more light on the stages that lead to the evolution of groups of many organisms—especially the dinosaurs—during the Triassic period.

How did the **Newark Supergroup form** and why does it contain so many Triassic fossils?

The movement of the continental plates was mainly responsible for a westward-spreading tear in the earth's crust between North America and northern Africa. This area of thinning and stretching became a rift valley, similar to the one found today in northeast Africa. The valley, with its shallow lakes, streams, and swamps, became one of the prime habitats for many flora and fauna of the Triassic period. As death occurred, the organisms' remains were apparently quickly buried by the large amounts of sediments eroding from the Appalachian Mountains to the west. Over millions of years, the pressures changed the sediments to rock and preserved the remains as fossils.

For what else is the **Newark Supergroup** famous?

The Newark Supergroup—indeed most of the area of the rift valley called the Atlantic Rifting Zone—is famous for reptile footprints, with tens of thousands of extremely well-preserved tracks from the Triassic and Jurassic periods. The tracks were first recognized in 1836, by U.S. paleontologist Reverend Edward Hitchcock (1793–1864), professor of natural theology and geology at Amherst College; he also described the Connecticut River Valley dinosaur footprints. These tracks are important because they show evidence of the evolution and eventual dominance of the dinosaurs.

What **other rock layers** contain large amounts of **Triassic fossils**?

Some of the other major areas with large amounts of Triassic fossils are the Keuper formation, found in Europe; the Fleming Fjord formation, found on the east coast of Greenland; and the Chinle group of western North America.

What is the Ischigualasto formation and why is it important?

The Triassic rocks of the Ischigualasto formation of Argentina are thought to be some of the richest fossil deposits, and include the earliest known, well-preserved fossils of such dinosaurs as *Herrerasaurus ischigualastensis, Eoraptor lunensis,* and *Pisanosaurus mertii.* The drab, gray rocks of this formation were deposited in a humid environment. The area where this formation is found—the Ischigualasto Valley, or the "valley of the moon"—is located to the east of a subduction zone. Consequently, it also received deposits of volcanic ash during the Triassic. Dating of this ash has enabled scientists to determine an age of approximately 228 million years for this formation, placing it in the middle to late Triassic period.

Vertebrate land fossils are abundant in the formation, including skeletons of advanced forms of synapsids, and odd, beaked reptiles called rhynchosaurs. There are also large carnivores called rauisuchians, and smaller archosaurs, but the most prevalent fossils in the formation are of dinosaurs. In fact, based on these dinosaur fossils and ones found in the Santa Maria formation of Brazil, some scientists suggest that perhaps dinosaurs arose in South America.

The Keuper formation of Germany was formed in a basin, part of the Atlantic rift system, that extended into Europe. It is famous for its rich assemblages of archosaurs—and in particular, its dinosaurs, such as the *Plateosaurus*—but the rock layers are mostly covered by vegetation or human development. The Fleming Fjord formation includes spectacular outcrops of red bedrock along the east coast of Greenland. Here, vertebrate remains similar to those found in the Keuper formation have been discovered.

Converging continental plates on the west side of North America led to very broad sags in the crust, creating a multitude of basins that filled with thin layers of sediment during the Triassic. This eventually formed the Chinle formation, which extends from Texas north to Alberta, Canada. In areas of the southwestern United States, such as New Mexico, the rock layer is rich with Triassic fossils. One of the best known dinosaur fossils discovered in this rock formation is the *Coelophysis.*

What were the **major oceans** during the **Triassic period**?

There was only one large ocean during the Triassic period, the Panthalassa Ocean. A smaller body of water was called the Tethys Sea (or Ocean), which was actually a huge bay to the east of the supercontinent Pangea. Eventually, late in the Triassic period, Pangea's separation into northern Laurasia and southern Gonwanaland led to the opening that became the early Atlantic Ocean.

What were the first true dinosaurs like?

Based on current fossil finds, the first true dinosaurs emerged in the late Triassic period, between about 230 to 225 million years ago. They were small, agile, carnivorous reptiles whose unique characteristics, such as two-legged motion, enabled them to quickly dominate the available ecological niches.

Apparently, by the time dinosaurs evolved, they had already split, even at this early stage, into two major groups: the ornithischians and the saurischians. These two main groups of dinosaurs are based historically on their hipbone structure.

What were the major **ocean currents** during the **Triassic period**?

Because there was one major continent during the Triassic period, the ocean currents were much different than they are today. There were warm currents generated around the equator, slipping up the east coast of the supercontinent Pangea in a general northward direction. Cooler currents ran by the western coast of the continent, one from the north and one from the south—with both converging at the equator. The Tethys Ocean (also called the Tethys Sea) also contained several cooler currents, all of which flowed southward past the west coasts of the larger islands and toward the equator.

What was the **climate** like during the **Triassic period**?

Because the landmass Pangea straddled the earth's equator, the temperature on land during the Triassic period was constantly warm and dry. There were no polar ice caps or large inland seas to truly change the conditions or affect the climate. Because of this, too, there was little seasonal variation in temperatures, and the climate around the equator stayed relatively stable all year long. The only differences in climate came toward the end of the Triassic period, when the land became hotter and drier. The fossil record does show one puzzling finding: the plant life between northern and southern Pangea seemed to be extremely diverse and distinct, indicating a difference in climate. But so far, scientists have no explanation for the difference in plant life.

What was the **landscape** like during the **Triassic period**?

There were many changes in the landscape during the Triassic period—far too many to outline on in this chapter. In summary, during the early Triassic period (and the late Permian period), the area we now know as Siberia released huge fields of volcanic material, called the Siberian Traps. Volcanic activity was also occurring in the areas we know today as Europe, North and South America, and northwestern Africa. This activity created the opening that became the Atlantic Ocean. Pangea also began to break up slowly into two large continents; and as the planet's crust stretched in response, huge areas collapsed (or subsided), creating many large basins that filled with water.

During the middle and late Triassic period, several mountains were being pushed up by the movement of the continental plates, including a swath of land extending from present-day Alaska to Chile—a process that is similar to the current rising of the Andes Mountains of South America—created as the Pacific Ocean crust wedged (subducted) beneath the Americas.

MAJOR TRIASSIC DINOSAURS

Were there many **dinosaurs during the Triassic period**?

Based on the current findings in fossil records, there were not many dinosaurs living during the Triassic period. Dinosaurs began to evolve from the reptiles toward the end of the Triassic period, but great numbers of the creatures did not flourish until the Jurassic period.

Why did the **dinosaurs** begin to **thrive** in the **late Triassic period**?

Scientists theorize that there were a number of reasons for the emergence of dinosaurs in the late Triassic period. One reason was that dinosaurs evolved to become biologically superior. For example, they developed an erect posture with bipedal (two-footed) motion. This development gave them a longer stride and quickness, enabling them to catch and devour semi-erect reptiles. Another adaptation might have been warm-bloodedness—although this idea is highly controversial. If it is true that the reptiles developed a form of warm-bloodedness, it would have allowed them to be more active than their cold-blooded cousins.

Still other scientists feel that these adaptations were not the reason for the dominance of dinosaurs. Instead, they believe a major extinction of the therapsids (reptilian ancestors of mammals), rhynchosaurs (lizardlike reptiles), and early archosaurs (reptiles comprising dinosaurs, pterosaurs, and crocodilians) in the middle of the Triassic period opened up ecological niches that the dinosaurs then filled.

What were some of the **early dinosaurs**?

The following partial list definitely describes some early dinosaurs of the Triassic period. It will undoubtedly change in the future as more dinosaur fossils are found and dated.

105

Selected Triassic Period Dinosaurs

Name	Common Name	Approximate Age (millions of years ago)	Locality	Length (feet/meters)
Anchisaurus	Near Lizard	200 to 190	USA	Up to 6.5/2
Coelophysis	Hollow Form	225 to 220	USA	Up to 10/3
Eoraptor	Dawn Hunter	225	Argentina	Up to 3/1
Herrerasaurus	Herrera Lizard	230 to 225	Argentina	Up to 10/3
Plateosaurus	Flat Lizard	about 210	France, Germany, Switzerland	Up to 23/7

What were some **early problems** in **classifying certain reptiles** as dinosaurs?

The earliest problems in classifying certain reptiles as dinosaurs had to do with an incomplete fossil record and the inability to date the rocks. In the mid-1800s, there were very few complete fossils of dinosaurs from the early and middle Triassic period. In addition, many fossils were incorrectly named. For example, archosaurs were named dinosaurs because of their similarities; scientists did not yet know that some archosaurs were relatives of the dinosaurs, but not dinosaurs themselves. Only after more archosaur and dinosaur fossils were found did some of these discrepancies disappear.

How has the **definition** of dinosaur **changed** over the years?

In 1842, Sir Richard Owen (1804–92) assumed dinosaurs all descended from a common ancestor (in paleontological terms, they were a monophyletic group). This meant all dinosaurs shared some common characteristics. And when finally determined, the characteristics could be used to differentiate true dinosaurs from other organisms.

In 1887, Harry Seeley (1839–1909) discovered there were two major dinosaur groups: the saurischians and the ornithischians. This led scientists to assume there was more than one common ancestor. To further complicate matters, discoveries of diverse dinosaur species pointed to many ancestors. As a result of this, dinosaurs were seen as a group of reptiles with few characteristics in common. They became a polyphyletic group, arising from many sources among the archosaurs. Interpreted this way, there was no longer one set of common characteristics dinosaurs shared.

Recently, with the use of cladistic analysis, all dinosaurs were found to have many unique characteristics in common. Once again, these reptiles are a defined as a monophyletic group descending from a common ancestor. And with the development of this modern cladistic "test," true dinosaurs can be distinguished from their closely related, but non-dinosaur, contemporaries.

What makes a reptile a dinosaur?

Using cladistic analysis, a reptile is a dinosaur if it has several specific characteristics in its fossilized skeleton, including some of the following: an elongated deltopectoral crest on the humerus; three or fewer phalanges in the fourth finger of the hand; the absence of a postfrontal bone; a crest on the tibia; three or more sacral vertebrae; a fully open hip socket; a ball-like head on the femur; and a well-developed ascending process on the astragalus, fitting on the front face of the tibia. In other words, identifying a dinosaur has a great deal to do with its skeletal anatomy. Although these characteristics are very technical, the main point is that scientists now have a clear test to determine if a fossil skeleton is truly that of a dinosaur.

Why is *Herrerasaurus ischigualastensis* thought to be one of the **earliest dinosaurs** known?

Based on the characteristics of its skeleton—a blend of archosaur and dinosaur features—scientists believe the *Herrerasaurus ischigualastensis* was an early dinosaur. Initially, scientists knew this 10- to 13-foot (3- to 4-meter) carnivorous reptile had a skull and foot similar to other archosaurs such as the *Euparkeria*. Based only on this evidence, it was impossible to determine if the *Herrerasaurus* was truly a dinosaur. But using the modern cladistic test, the *Herrerasaurus* skeleton shows all but a few of the characteristics that define dinosaurs. In particular, *Herrerasaurus* lacks bone in the center of the hip socket, a key characteristic that defines this reptile as a true dinosaur—and one of the earliest known.

Is the *Eoraptor lunensis* the most **primitive dinosaur**?

Yes, the *Eoraptor lunensis* ("dawn hunter") fossils discovered in the Ischigualasto formation in Argentina are thought to be those of the most primitive dinosaur known. This is because the *Eoraptor* fossils are a mix of primitive and specialized characteristics—a blend of features expected for the "first" dinosaur. The *Eoraptor* had a three-fingered hand, which connected them to the theropod dinosaurs. But *Eoraptor* fossils lack the specialized features that would place this reptile in any specific major group of dinosaurs.

Which **Triassic period dinosaurs** were **herbivores**?

There were numerous herbivorous dinosaurs that evolved at the end of the Triassic period. The *Thecodontosaurus*, a small herbivore, was one of the first Triassic dinosaurs ever found; it was reported in England in 1836. The *Plateosaurus* was also a plant-eating

107

dinosaur that lived during the Triassic period; the first fossils were found in Germany in 1837. They were considered the first really large dinosaurs, and had peglike teeth and huge thumb claws that were perhaps used to gather plants from taller trees.

What is the **earliest** known **herbivorous** dinosaur?

The earliest known herbivore, or plant-eating dinosaur, was the *Pisanosaurus mertii,* found in the Ischigualasto formation of Argentina. The dinosaur is dated at approximately 230 million years old. And like its relatives *Herrerasaurus ischigualastensis* and *Eoraptor lunensis,* the *Pisanosaurus* was relatively small, lightweight, and bipedal.

Which **Triassic period dinosaurs** were **carnivores**?

The first carnivores, or meat-eating dinosaurs, in the Triassic period were the *Eoraptor* and *Herrerasaurus*. Both dinosaurs were small and bipedal, with powerful hindlimbs and long tails for balance. The later *Coelophysis* was also a meat-eater. Some of the first fossils of this dinosaur were found in the southwestern United States—and were the first to show evidence of a herding behavior.

What was *Coelophysis* like?

Coelophysis ("hollow form") was a small, relatively delicate dinosaur, measuring up to 10 feet (3 meters) in length. It had an elongated neck, strong grasping hands, and a long slender skull with sharp teeth. As it walked on two legs, *Coelophysis* used its long, slender tail for balance. Its feet were narrow, with only three prominent toes, a distinctive characteristic of the theropods. The *Coelophysis* were part of a carnivorous dinosaur group that later included the *Tyrannosaurus rex* and *Velociraptor*.

What were the **smallest dinosaurs** known to have existed during the **Triassic period**?

At present, the smallest Triassic period dinosaurs known to have existed were the early, carnivorous bipeds, *Eoraptor* and *Herrerasaurus*. The *Eoraptor* was about 3 feet (1 meter) long; whereas the *Herrerasaurus* was about 9 to 18 feet (3 to 6 meters) in length.

Were there other reptiles in the **middle to late Triassic** period that may have been **early dinosaurs**?

Yes, the *Herrerasaurus* may have had some other dinosaur relatives in North and South America during the middle to late Triassic period. Some scientists believe the

Plateosaurus, the largest member of the prosauropod group, reached lengths of up to 26 feet. This dinosaur fed on ground-level plants and the leaves of tall trees, its long neck enabling it to seek food at various heights. Its fossilized remains have been found in what is now Germany. This model, one-tenth the actual size, represents the body structure common to all prosauropods.

The *Plateosaurus*, a major herbivore during the Triassic period, was the largest known herbivore during that period. (Photo courtesy of University of Michigan Exhibit, Museum of Natural History.)

Staurikosaurus pricei from southern Brazil and northwestern Argentina, and the *Chindesaurus briansmalli* from the Chinle formation in North America, were close relatives. But there are still disagreements as to where to put these dinosaurs on the overall family tree. One thing is certain: this important group gives us some idea of the time that dinosaurs first appeared—and what these early creatures looked like.

What was the **largest dinosaur** known to have existed during the **Triassic period**?

At present, the largest dinosaur known to have existed during the Triassic was the herbivorous *Plateosaurus,* with a length of up to 23 feet (7 meters).

What was the *Plateosaurus* like?

The *Plateosaurus* ("flat lizard") had a long neck, large stocky body, and a pear-shaped trunk. Its skull was deeper than that of a *Coelophysis,* though still small and narrow compared to the size of its body. The reptile's teeth were set in sockets, and were small, peglike, and leaf-shaped, with coarse serrations. The eyes were directed to the sides, rather than to the front, which reduced its depth perception but gave the *Plateosaurus* a wider field of view to detect predators.

109

The foot of the *Plateosaurus* was very similar to that of *Herrerasaurus* and the structure of the legs indicates that this dinosaur was not a fast runner. A unique feature of *Plateosaurus* was its broad, apron-shaped pubis, forming a "shelf" that may have provided support for its huge gut. The animal's tail could be bent sharply upward near its base—a good characteristic to have when rearing up against trees.

Did any **Triassic period dinosaurs** live in the **oceans**?

No. There were a variety of marine reptiles in the water, but at no time did marine dinosaurs exist. The entire classification of dinosaurs is limited to land-dwelling reptiles with specific characteristics.

OTHER LIFE IN THE TRIASSIC PERIOD

What were the **major groups of land organisms**?

The true numbers, types, names, and evolutionary events of the Triassic land animals is often highly debated—which is typical when we try to interpret our ancient past. (Fossils are subject to explanations that sometimes vary from scientists to scientist—often making it difficult to arrive at any definite statements about these animals.)

The following are the major Triassic land organisms.

Amphibians

Primitive amphibians: Only a few large, primitive amphibians, called labyrinthodonts, survived into the Mesozoic era after the Permian period extinction; they gradually declined in abundance and diversity during the Mesozoic; most of them were aquatic, the majority living in freshwater environments.

Primitive frogs, toads: First links to these modern amphibians (or lissamphibians) evolve during the early Triassic; the oldest member of the frog group was the *Triado-*

batrachus, which is the only known link between the true frogs with jumping motion and the primitive ancestors of frogs.

Reptiles (anapsids, diapsids, and euryapsids)

First turtles: Of the several Paleozoic groups of anapsids, only turtles and procolophonids survived into the Mesozoic; the oldest subgroup, proganochelydians, were moderately large, but the animal could not pull its head inside its shell.

Procolophonids: Lizardlike in their overall habits and shape, these amphibians probably ate insects and smaller animals, and some plant material; even though they looked like lizards, the true lizards did not appear until the late Jurassic.

Rhynchosaurs: These short-lived diapsid reptiles of the group Archosauromorpha were herbivorous, walked on all fours, and had huge beaks that helped them bite off vegetation; they were so widespread during the Triassic that their fossils are often used to correlate deposits on different continents.

Tanystropheids: These very short-lived diapsid reptiles of the group Archosauromorpha lived near (and sometimes in) marine waters; they had an extremely odd shape, with a tiny head on an extremely long neck, and a short, medium-sized body; the reason for such a long neck is unknown, but one theory suggests that it helped the tanystropheid stretch its neck low over the water in order to catch fish.

Archosaurs: Part of the diapsid reptile group Archosauromorpha, and the dominant tetrapods on the continents during most of the Mesozoic, the archosaurs ("ruling reptiles") were the precursors to dinosaurs; they are characterized by their better adaptation of legs, feet, and hips, giving them agility on land; others categorize the archosaurs by the openings in their skull; the earliest archosaurs were relatively large and carnivorous, and either lived on land, or led a semi-aquatic existence.

aetosaurs: heavily armored, herbivorous archosaurs.

phytosaurs: lived during the late Triassic only, and looked very much like modern crocodiles.

crocodylomorphs: a group that includes crocodiles, alligators, caimans, and gavials, known to exist from the late Triassic to the present; not all survived to the present, including the fast-running saltoposuchians.

rauischians: the creature's upright front and hindlegs were under the trunk of the body, making them the dominant land predator during the Triassic period.

ornithosuchians: relatively large (10 feet [3 meters] in length), land predators that may have walked on all fours, but ran fast only on hindlegs; the most dinosaur-like of the non-dinosaur archosaurs.

ornithodira: the middle and late Triassic group of archosaurs to which the dinosaurs belong; it also includes the pterosaurs, birds, and some early forms of creatures that appear to be closely related to dinosaurs and pterosaurs.

Aerial Reptiles (diapsids)

Gliding reptiles: The three main late Triassic gliding reptiles used either skin membranes on the wings and legs (such as the *Sharovipteryx*), scales (*Longisquama*), or fanlike wings (*Kuehneosaurus*)—all of which acted as an airfoil, allowing the reptiles to glide through the air; they probably did not flap their "wings" for powered flight.

Flying reptiles: The pterosaurs (also called pterodactyls, which actually refers to only one subgroup of pterosaurs) had front legs (or arms) that were modified into true wings by the elongation of the fourth finger, which supported a skin membrane stretching to the body; they probably flapped their wings occasionally for powered flight; they lived from the ocean shores and inland, eating fish, insects, and other small animals; they evolved during the late Triassic period.

Mammals and Their Reptilelike Relatives (synapsids)

Therapsids: These more advanced synapsids make up a varied group of mammal-like reptiles that apparently evolved from the pelycosaurs, the earliest known mammal-like reptiles that evolved in the late Carboniferous period, about 290 million years ago, and went extinct in the late Permian period; the biggest change was their ability to walk more efficiently with their limbs tucked beneath their body, whereas pelycosaurs walked with their limbs in a sprawled position; one group of therapsids gave rise to mammals, known from the late Triassic to today.

anomodonts: the most common subgroup were the dicynodonts, large, herbivorous, mammal-like reptiles; it includes the *Lystrosaurus*, a piglike animal 3 to 6 feet (1 to 2 meters) long that has been found as fossils in Australia, South Africa, India, China, and Antarctica, and hippopotamus-like *Kannemeyeria,* a 10-foot- (3-meter-) long animal with two big caninelike teeth in the upper jaw that died out during the late Triassic period.

cynodonts: carnivorous, mammal-like therapsid reptiles; they walked more upright, with limbs held more underneath their bodies; some were probably wolflike animals, and some seem to have had whiskers, pointing to the possibility that they had fur, and thus, may have been warm-blooded; they evolved during the late Permian to the middle Jurassic; at least one group of cynodonts evolved into mammals.

therocephalians: existed from the late Permian to middle Triassic period, these therapsid reptiles had their peak during the late Paleozoic era; they were small to middle sized, walked on all fours, and ate insects or small animals.

True mammals: These small mammals, about the size of a rat or mouse, with the largest about the size of a cat, were probably nocturnal; they probably ate insects or small animals, and at least one group ate plants; they evolved in the latter part of the Triassic, at the same time as the dinosaurs first appeared.

triconodonts: late Triassic to late Cretaceous mammals; among the oldest fossil mammals; three cusps of teeth in a straight row give them their name.

haramyoids: late Triassic to middle Jurassic mammals; among the oldest fossil mammals; their teeth had many cusps in at least two parallel rows.

Other Creatures

Insects: Many types of insects were profuse at this time.

Spiders: Very profuse; spiders had been around for millions of years already, appearing in fossils dating back to the Cambrian period.

Earthworms: Very profuse; earthworms had been around for millions of years already, appearing in fossils dating back to the Cambrian period.

If the dinosaurs were just evolving, which **land and marine animals dominated** the **Triassic period**?

On land, the true dominant species of the Triassic period, even after the dinosaurs started to evolve during the late Triassic, were the non-dinosaurian predators, the archosaurs; the main herbivores were the dicynodont (synapsids). In the oceans, many types of reptiles and fishes dominated.

What are the **tetrapods**?

Tetrapods ("four feet") is a term used to describe the four-legged creatures that left the water to live on land. The first tetrapods were the amphibians; dinosaurs were also tetrapods. In fact, all modern amphibians, reptiles, birds, and mammals are tetrapods.

Where did **tetrapods live on Pangea** during the late Triassic period?

The distribution of the tetrapods was not uniform during the late Triassic period—even though Pangea was a huge connected landmass. The major reason for this nonuniform distribution was the very pronounced climate zones over the very large continental landmass. The equator had a narrow, humid zone; humid temperate climates existed from around 50 degrees north and south latitudes to the poles. In between, at approximately 30 degrees north and south latitude, were wide arid zones.

The distribution of tetrapods followed these climatic variations. For example, the prosauropods, a group of dinosaurs that included the *Plateosaurus,* had a range   113

Were there any flying animals during the Triassic period?

The first true flying animals were reptiles called pterosaurs. One of the first of these flying creatures was the *Eudimorphodon*. This reptile probably skimmed the surface of the water looking for fish, using the end of its long tail as a "rudder" to steer through the air. With a sufficient wing span and structure, *Eudimorphodon* is considered to have been a heavy flyer, similar to a modern bird. Other reptiles also took to the air, but only glided. For example, the *Kuehneosaurus* used a membrane stretched over its elongated ribs as a kind of parachute. The creature would then close the membranes when resting in a tree, folding both sides like fans close to the sides of its body.

roughly corresponding to the temperate zones in both hemispheres; prosauropods shared this area with large amphibians. Phytosaurs, distant relatives of the crocodiles, were limited to the Northern Hemisphere and the coastal regions of the Southern Hemisphere. And some tetrapods, such as rauisuchians, crocodylomorphs, and aetosaurs, were distributed over all of Pangea.

What Triassic period crocodiles **galloped**?

Although it seems hard to believe—given what we know about present-day crocodiles—certain types of crocodiles ran very fast, even galloped, during the Triassic period. Modern crocodiles inspire awe as they slowly swim, or explode onto land to capture some animal. The thought of a crocodile moving like a horse staggers the imagination!

The early ancestors of crocodiles were very different in appearance from their modern descendants. They were a diverse group, with many different shapes and sizes. Some of these animals lived on land rather than in water; they were small and quick, with long, slender legs. The name of this archosaur group is crocodylomorph, and included the crocodilians and their relatives.

Recently, a 3-inch (7.6-centimeter) fossil skull of a small crocodile was found in an exposed road cut in the Connecticut River Valley. This animal resembled another early crocodile, *Erpetosuchus,* whose remains were discovered in Scotland over a century ago. It is thought the Connecticut crocodile had a fully erect stance, similar to modern mammals—and very different from the more familiar semisprawling stance of modern crocodiles.

What does this mean? Scientists believe this small, ancient crocodile could run very fast indeed—galloping with all four feet off the ground simultaneously at times.

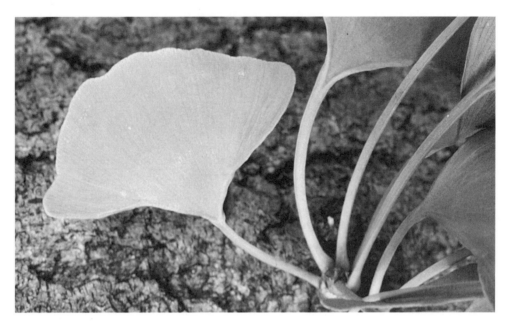

Ginkos were among several plants flourishing in the Triassic period. (Photo courtesy of Field Mark Publications.)

Modern-day Australian crocodiles, with their semisprawling stance, can move at speeds up to 15 miles (24 kilometers) per hour. This Triassic crocodile could probably run at even higher speeds.

What were the **major land plants** living during the **Triassic period**?

The Triassic land plants flourished in the hot climate. The main vegetative types were conifers, which could easily adapt to changing water conditions (dry or damp). Gymnosperms bore seeds, including conifers, cycads, and ginkos. The following table lists some of the major plants.

Major Triassic Land Plants

Cycads	Leaves are similar to palm fronds, with unbranched, usually bulbous trunks; they had specialized pollen and seed cones for reproduction; 10 genera survive today.
Horsetails	Massive plants similar to the horsetails we find in the wild today.
Conifers	Grew as trees and shrubs; the trees would reproduce with seeds found on the projecting scales of the conifer cones; the petrified wood found in the late Triassic layer of the Chinle formation, at Arizona's Petrified Forest, are conifers (they are almost identical to the modern Norfolk Island pines).

115

Major Triassic Land Plants

Ginkos	The leaves were fan-shaped, and similar to the one remaining species, the *Gingko biloba*; the sex organs were on stalks, with separate male and female trees.
Cycadeoids (bennettitales)	Leaves are similar to palm fronds, and thus, somewhat similar to cycads; a fruiting stalk contained the pollen and seeds for reproduction; they may be more closely related to flowering plants than cycads, as the fruiting stalks somewhat resembled primitive flowers; none survive today, as the cycadeoids became extinct at the end of the Cretaceous period.

What were the **major marine animals** living during the **Triassic period**?

There were many marine animals that swam the oceans of the Triassic, and many of the species still continue to this day. In general, the oceans held the animals listed in the following table, although with new fossil discoveries, this list may eventually change.

Reptiles (euryapsids)

Ichthyosaurs	Known as "fish reptiles," these were predatory sea reptiles that probably preyed mostly on shellfish, fish, and other marine reptiles; they looked similar to, and probably had some of the same habits of, modern dolphins, whales, and sharks; they lived in the oceans from the early Triassic to middle Cretaceous periods, probably outcompeted by the mosasaurs of the middle Cretaceous period.
Plesiosaurs	These medium to large, long- to short-necked reptiles had bulbous bodies; their four legs were modified into paddles; they probably ate mostly fish; they lived mostly in marine environments, but some also lived in freshwater lakes; they lived from the early Triassic to the end of the Cretaceous period and are often sighted as the model for what the Loch Ness monster is presumed to look like.
Placodonts	Large marine reptiles that had long trunks and tails, with feet that were probably webbed; their teeth were used for crushing, and they probably ate clams and other shelled invertebrates from the ocean floor.
Nothosaurs	Small to moderate-sized marine reptiles with long necks and sharp, conical teeth for spearing fish; their legs were modified flippers, rather than the paddle-shaped legs of the more advanced eurapsids; they lived from the early to late Triassic period.

Other Marine Creatures

Sea urchins	The few pencil urchins that survived the Permian period extinction are also the ancestors of all modern urchins; the Triassic period was also the time of the first burrowing urchins.

Other Marine Creatures

Corals	The first relatives to the modern corals evolved during the Triassic period.
Crabs and lobsters (crustaceans)	The first close relatives of modern crabs and lobsters evolved during the Triassic period.
Ammonoids	Ammonoids, or chamber-shelled organisms, rapidly diversified during the Triassic period.
Bony fishes	Found in salt, brackish, and fresh water, bony fishes could often move back and forth among the three; they are divided into two groups, based on their structure: the ray-finned (for example, the Triassic period's *Perleidus*) and lobe-finned (for example, the Triassic period's *Diplurus*).
Sharks	During the Triassic, the intermediate form between primitive and modern sharks evolved; the earliest sharks evolved during the Paleozoic era, middle Devonian period, about 130 million years before; one of the modern survivors of this group is the Port Jackson shark.

What was the earliest known **ichthyosaur**?

To date, the earliest known ichthyosaur ("fish lizard") was the *Utatsusaurus hataii*, found in Utatsu, Miyagi, Japan.

What were the **most vicious marine reptiles** in the **Triassic period seas**?

Probably the most notorious marine reptiles were the plesiosaurs, or "near lizards," giant reptiles that evolved during the Triassic period and became extinct at the end of the Cretaceous period. They lived in the water and ate fish to survive; but one group of plesiosaurs, the pliosaurs, became very large, feeding on other, large marine reptiles. The plesiosaurs have been described as "a snake drawn through the body of a turtle," with long necks and bulbous bodies. Most of them lived in the oceans, but there were some species that adapted to freshwater lakes.

What **discovery** was recently made about the **plesiosaur's diet**?

Recently, a partial plesiosaur skeleton was excavated out of an outcrop along a river on the island of Hokkaido, Japan. In the stomach area of the fossilized skeleton, pieces of tiny, beaklike ammonite jaws were found, measuring less than six-tenths of an inch (1.5 centimeters) long. Ammonites were spiral-shelled mollusks that are now extinct. Scientists feel that these jaws did not get there by accident, but were preserved as dietary remains within the digestive tract of the plesiosaur. The size of the jaws also suggests that the mollusks were very small.

Two ammonite fossils. Plesiosaurs probably ate these small mollusks. (Photo courtesy of Maurice Nimmo, Frank Lane Picture Agency/Corbis.)

The teeth of smaller plesiosaurs have long been regarded as being too slight to crush the hard shells of ammonites, but this latest evidence suggests that these marine predators did indeed make ammonites part of their diet. The way scientists see it, the plesiosaurs simply swallowed the small ammonites whole—a kind of plesiosaur popcorn!

What animals lived near **freshwater rivers, lakes, and ponds** during the **Triassic**?

These animals included several types of broad-headed amphibians and phytosaurs, distant relatives of the crocodiles. These animals were in search of the shellfish and fish that lived in the rivers and lakes. Other reptiles would frequent the shorelines of the lakes and ponds, including several of the early dinosaur species, and smaller reptiles.

JURASSIC PERIOD

THE JURASSIC PERIOD

What is the **Jurassic period** and how did it get its **name**?

The Jurassic period follows the Triassic period on the geologic time scale. Though the dinosaurs had their origins and approximately 25 million years of evolution in the Triassic period, it wasn't until the Jurassic period that this group really blossomed. This was the time when the giant, herbivorous sauropods like *Apatosaurus* roamed the land; when plated dinosaurs like *Stegosaurus* first appeared; and when large carnivorous species like *Allosaurus* preyed on the other dinosaurs. It was also when *Archaeopteryx*—a creature that many paleontologists consider to be the first ancestor of the birds—flew through the air.

The name Jurassic comes from the Jura mountain range, a chain of mountains that straddle the border between France and Switzerland. It was here that the first Jurassic period sedimentary rock and accompanying fossils were found. The Jurassic is the second of three periods (the first is the Triassic and the last is the Cretaceous) making up the Mesozoic era.

How long did the **Jurassic period last**?

The Jurassic period lasted from approximately 202 (or 205) to 141 million years ago, a time period of approximately 60 million years. The exact dates are debated, of course, and there are some variations of the dates in the literature, but the time frame is close.

Museum goers in Paris, France, gaze up at a model of an *Allosaurus,* a carnivore from the Jurassic period. (Photo courtesy of Jonathan Blair/Corbis.)

What are the **divisions** of the **Jurassic period**?

The Jurassic period has been divided into three main divisions, or epochs: scientists use the Early, Middle and Late; more informally, the period is labeled with lowercase letters, or the early, middle, and late Jurassic. In turn, each of these main epochs is further broken up into subdivisions. To make things more confusing, these small ages have different names (and often dates) depending on whether you are using European, North American, or Australian and New Zealand nomenclature. The following table gives the general North American divisions of the Jurassic period. These dates are not absolute, and may vary slightly from source to source.

Jurassic Period

Epoch	Age	Millions of Years Ago (approximate)
Late	Morrison	156 to 141
	Sundance	163 to 156
Middle	Twin Creek	170 to 163
	Gypsum Springs	178 to 170
Early	Navajo	195 to 178
	Kayenta	202 to 195

What Jurassic dinosaur is Utah's State Fossil?

The *Allosaurus*—a dominant predator of North America during the late Jurassic period that rivaled the *Tyrannosaurus rex* as the supreme Mesozoic meat-eater—is Utah's State Fossil. *Allosaurus* fossils have been found in Utah's Morrison formation.

What is the **Morrison formation** and where is it found?

The Morrison formation is a layer of sedimentary rocks that are world famous for the number and diversity of their Jurassic period dinosaur fossils. This formation, named for Morrison, Colorado, is found throughout a large region of western North America.

What events led to the **development** of the **Morrison formation**?

In the late Jurassic, subduction (crustal plate movement) along the west coast of North America began to uplift land inland; it eventually became the Sierra Nevada mountains. A shallow sea, called the Sundance Sea, flooded the basin created to the east of the uplifting Sierra Nevada mountains, inundating what is now Montana, the Dakotas, Wyoming, Utah, Colorado, and Nebraska. Toward the end of the Jurassic period, this interior seaway began to retreat as the continuing uplift of the Sierra Nevadas caused Nevada, Utah, and Idaho to rise. The climate in this area, along with the numerous flood plains, rivers, and lakes, supported large numbers of dinosaurs. When they died, they were quickly covered with sediment that was flowing down from the eroding Sierra Nevadas. This late Jurassic layer of dinosaur-rich sedimentary rock is the world-famous Morrison formation of western North America.

What are some **Jurassic dinosaurs** from Utah's **Morrison formation**?

There are numerous Jurassic dinosaur fossils found in Utah's Morrison formation, including *Allosaurus, Apatosaurus, Barosaurus, Brachiosaurus, Camarasaurus, Camptosaurus, Ceratosaurus, Diplodocus, Dryosaurus, Dystrophaeus, Marshosaurus, Stegosaurus, Stokesosaurus,* and *Torvosaurus.*

What is the **Tendaguru formation**?

The Tendaguru rock formation formed during the late Jurassic period, with the best outcrops found in Tanzania in East Africa. It was discovered in the early 1900s, and is considered one of the greatest dinosaur graveyards in the world. Several expeditions to

121

the area were carried out by German and British scientists early in the century—but very few in more recent years.

The Tendaguru is often compared to the Morrison formation because the overall fauna are similar in both of the dinosaur fossil–rich layers of rock. For instance, *Brachiosaurus* fossils found in both formations are strikingly similar. One reason for these similarities is that the continental landmasses remained close together during the Jurassic period, allowing the dinosaurs to remain widely distributed. But there are differences, too, including the absence of large theropod dinosaur fossils in the Tendaguru when compared to the Morrison formation.

What **event occurred** at the division between the Triassic and Jurassic periods, and why was this **important to the dinosaurs**?

There was apparently a major extinction between these two periods that led to the almost complete disappearance of many marine groups, such as some of the ammonoids (a type of mollusk with a flat, spiral shell); as well as the complete disappearance of some reptiles, including some types of archosaurs, phytosaurs, aetosaurs, and rauisuchians. Though many scientists speculate that this extinction was caused by an asteroid impact, the crater that is the leading candidate in support of this theory, Manicouagan in British Columbia, Canada, has been dated at 10 million years too early. There are thus heated debates as to the causes of this extinction event.

Some scientists feel that the end-of-the-Triassic-period extinction event opened up more ecological niches into which the dinosaurs dispersed, allowing them to flourish and become dominant. However, others feel that the dinosaurs were already on their way to dominance due to the major extinction event at the end of the Permian period. The real sequence of these events may never be known, but in any case, the dinosaurs did start to become dominant during the early Jurassic period.

There is another theory that tries to explain the extinction event between the Triassic and Jurassic periods: there were very large lava flows for approximately 600,000 years close to the division between the Triassic and Jurassic periods—among the largest such events known to have occurred on our planet. The side effects of these flows, such as the emission of carbon dioxide and sulfur aerosols, may have contributed to the mass extinctions at this time by changing the atmosphere's composition and/or climate.

Another suggestion is that an impacting asteroid or comet may have actually caused the lava flows, or worked in conjunction with the flows, to create an even harsher environment. The resulting environmental changes—from climate to vegetation—could have led to the mass extinction event between the Triassic and Jurassic periods.

THE CONTINENTS DURING THE JURASSIC PERIOD

Where were the **continents located** during the Jurassic period?

In the early Jurassic period, the continents were still clustered around the equator roughly in the shape of a "C" that bordered the Tethys Sea. However, unlike the Triassic period, in which the continents were all part of one giant landmass known as Pangea, a split formed during the Jurassic period that divided Pangea into two large landmasses. This split was caused by the action of plate tectonics.

What were **Laurasia** and **Gondwanaland**?

Laurasia and Gondwanaland (or Gondwana) were the two major continents of the Jurassic period. As the gap between North America and Africa widened, driven by the spreading rift, so did the gap between North and South America. Water filled this gap, separating Pangea into the northern continent of Laurasia, and the southern continent of Gondwanaland. Despite the separation of the huge continent, scientists have found fossil skeletons of the *Brachiosaurus* and plated *Stegosaurus* in both Africa (in Gondwanaland) and North America (in Laurasia). This indicates that although the continents were separating, there were probably land bridges that popped up from time to time, allowing the species to spread to both continents.

What is the difference between **Gondwanaland** and **Gondwana**?

There really is no difference between the terms Gondwanaland and Gondwana. They are synonymous, and the use of the terms appears to be a personal preference.

What **modern-day continents** were linked together to form **Laurasia**?

Laurasia included the present-day continents of Europe, North America, and Siberia. Also included in this large landmass was Greenland.

123

What **modern-day continents** were linked together to form **Gondwanaland**?

Gondwanaland included the present day continents of Africa, South America, India, Antarctica, and Australia.

Where were parts of the present-day **Asia located** during the Jurassic period?

Sections of Asia were essentially found in pieces during the Jurassic, as large islands in the Tethys Ocean. The islands that contained modern central Asia and southeast Asia were off the east coast of Gondwanaland, and the islands that contained today's China and Manchuria were off the east coast of Laurasia.

What were the **major oceans** and how did they **change** during the **Jurassic period**?

The major ocean continued to be the Panthalassa Ocean, which covered most of the planet. But as the gap between North Africa and North America widened, the North Atlantic Ocean began to grow.

What was the **climate** like during the **Jurassic period**?

The evidence to date seems to suggest that for the majority of time during the entire Jurassic, the climate was warm and moist over much of the landmasses, with only

Plants such as ferns flourished during the Jurassic period. (Photo courtesy of Field Mark Publications.)

small temperature differences from the equator to the poles. Similar to the Triassic period, there were no ice caps at the poles.

What caused the **climate** to **change** from hot and arid during the Triassic period to warm and moist during the Jurassic period?

The previous period, the Triassic, had been hot and arid; during the Jurassic, temperatures fell slightly and rainfall increased, allowing lush tropical vegetation to grow over large areas. The climate during the Jurassic period was probably affected by the breakup of Pangea and creation of the large seas—and no doubt the accompanying changes in sea level and ocean currents.

Did **climate conditions** lead to **new dinosaur groups** in the Jurassic period?

Yes, scientists believe the climate turned milder in the Jurassic period and lush, tropical vegetation began to grow. This gave rise to new dinosaur groups, including the long-necked sauropods (plant-eaters)—and the increase in the amount of vegetation allowed these animals to grow quite large. Their long necks might have allowed them to reach food that was out of reach for most other dinosaurs. And with abundant food supplies, these greenery-eating animals continued to grow from generation to generation.

125

What were the **most common plants** growing during the **Jurassic period**?

Because the climate had turned moist and tropical, vegetation was lush. Among the most common plants were cycads and lycopods (small treelike plants); ginkos and tree ferns covered the areas near rivers and lakes—some of which eventually became the coal seams we mine today. There were also extensive numbers of ferns and horsetails covering the ground, and forests of tall conifer trees—for example, sequoias and monkey puzzles—dominated the land.

What were the major **ocean currents** during the **Jurassic period**?

Ocean currents during the Jurassic period changed in some ways from the Triassic period, mainly because of the changes in the continents. The warm currents of the equator still swept northward along the east coast of what was once Pangea, and was now Laurasia and Gondwanaland. And along the western coastlines of both continents, colder currents flowed south along Laurasia and north along Gondwanaland, both currents heading toward the equator. Smaller currents also set up in the more open oceans, the cooler currents flowing from the north and south, toward the equator.

Were there any **major geologic events** that occurred during the **Jurassic period**?

During the early Jurassic, the east coast of what was now Laurasia and Gondwanaland was quietly accumulating sediment. As the rifting continued between North and South America, starting the Gulf of Mexico, the sea dropped layers of evaporites. Today, we see evidence of this: the evaporites eventually pushed upward as salt domes through younger sediments, forming petroleum traps—with Texas and Gulf of Mexico oil wells today taking advantage of the deposits.

During the late Jurassic, the westward drift of North America also started a period of mountain building in the areas of today's Rocky Mountains and the Sierra Nevadas. A huge basin called the Sundance Sea formed across Montana, the Dakotas, Wyoming, Utah, Colorado, and Nebraska during the West Coast mountain building. Much of northern and central Europe flooded; the resulting lagoon, protected by a bank of reefs, produced a fine-grained limestone.

MAJOR JURASSIC DINOSAURS

What are some of the major **dinosaurs** that lived during the **Jurassic period**?

There were two groups of dinosaurs during the Jurassic: the saurischians (reptile or "lizard-hipped"), divided into the sauropods (herbivores) and theropods (carnivores);

How did dinosaurs become so prolific between the Triassic and Jurassic periods?

Scientists believe that the end of the Triassic was one of the busiest times in the history of land vertebrates. There were all types of animals (except birds)—crocodiles, turtles, lizard relatives, pterosaurs, therapsids, giant amphibians, the first mammals, and dinosaurs. But during a short period of time—maybe only about 5 to 10 million years—at the beginning of the Jurassic, dinosaurs began to dominate the land, filling almost every available niche.

There are several theories that attempt to explain why. The first one is competition, as the dinosaurs out-competed the other animals for food. The second theory is opportunism, in which the dinosaurs took advantage of their specialized characteristics to take over the territories of other animals. Another suggestion is that the dinosaurs' specialized anatomy allowed them to beat out competitors, with the dinosaurs able to walk upright because of the way their hips were put together. This gave the dinosaurs an edge, allowing them to free their forearms to grasp prey—something no other animals could do.

and the ornithischians ("bird-hipped"), such as the stegosaurs, ankylosaurs, ornithopods. This latter group were all herbivores. The following table lists some of the dinosaurs that lived during the Jurassic. New fossil finds are occurring all the time and the list will subsequently grow.

Jurassic Period Dinosaurs

Name	Meaning	Approximate Age (millions of years ago)	Locality	Length (feet/meters)
Apatosaurus	Deceptive Lizard	154 to 145	USA	up to 70/21
Allosaurus	Other Lizard	150 to 135	USA	up to 50/15
*Archaeopteryx**	Ancient Wing	147	Germany	up to 1.5/.5
Barosaurus	Heavy Lizard	155 to 145	USA	up to 80/24
Brachiosaurus	Arm Lizard	155 to 140	USA, Tanzania	up to 75/23
Camarasaurus	Chambered Lizard	155 to 145	USA	up to 65/20
Camptosaurus	Bent Lizard	155 to 145	USA	up to 16/5
Coelurus	Hollow Tail	155 to 145	USA	up to 8/2.4
Compsognathus	Pretty Jaw	147	Germany	about 2/.7
Dacentrurus	Pointed Tail	157 to 152	France, England, Portugal	about 20/6

Name	Meaning	Approximate Age (millions of years ago)	Locality	Length (feet/meters)
Diplodocus	Double Beam	155 to 145	USA	up to 90/27
Dryosaurus	Oak Lizard	155 to 140	USA, Tanzania	up to 13/4
Kentrosaurus	Spiky Lizard	140	Tanzania	up to 10/3
Mamenchisaurus	Mamenchi Lizard	155 to 145	China	up to 72/22
Massospondylus	Massive Vertebra	208 to 204	England, South Africa	up to 13/4
Megalosaurus	Big Lizard	170 to 155	Tanzania	up to 30/9
Ornitholestes	Bird Robber	155 to 145	USA	up to 6.5/2
Pelorosaurus	Monstrous Lizard	150	England	unknown
Scelidosaurus	Limb Lizard	203 to 194	England	up to 13/4
Stegosaurus	Roof Lizard	155 to 145	USA	up to 30/9
Tuojiangosaurus	Tuojiang Lizard	157 to 154	China	up to 21/6.4

*Dinosaur origin/nature has been debated since the first fossil was found in 1861.

SAURISCHIAN DINOSAURS

How are the **saurischian** dinosaurs **classified**?

Paleontologists divide the saurischian dinosaurs into two general groups: the plant-eating sauropods (Sauropoda) and the carnivorous theropods (Theropoda). Both of these general groups contained numerous diverse species, which led to further subdivisions of these groups.

Like all classifications, there are differences from system to system, and there are continual debates and changes within each classification scheme. For example, in some classifications, the saurischians are divided into the theropods and the sauropodmorphs; the sauropodmorphs are further divided into the sauropods and prosauropods. But since the prosauropods died out early in the Jurassic period, other classifications concentrate mainly on the sauropods.

The general classification system used here is only one version: the sauropods in the Jurassic were subdivided into the diplodocids (Diplodocidae) and the brachiosaurids (Brachiosauridae); the camarasaurids (Camarasauridae) are either added as a subdivision of the brachiosaurs or are sometimes considered to be a separate group.

The theropods were subdivided into the ceratosaurs (Ceratosauria) and the tetanurans (Tetanurae); the tetanurans were further divided into the coelurosaurs (Coelurosauria) and carnosaurs (Carnosauria)—also known as the allosaurs

(Allosauria). Some classification systems further divide the coelurosaurs into the ornithomimosaurs (Ornithomimidae) and the maniraptorans (Maniraptora).

What were some **general characteristics** of the sauropods?

The sauropods were quadrupeds (four-footed) animals that ranged from the relatively small (approximately 23 feet [7 meters] long) to the longest land animals ever known (up to 131 feet [40 meters] long). They had very long tails and necks, five-toed hands and feet, massive limbs, very small heads, and peglike teeth. Sauropods were herbivorous, and had the lowest ratio of brain mass to estimated body mass (called the encephalization quotient) of all the dinosaurs. These animals first appeared in the early Jurassic period; by the late Jurassic period, they had reached the pinnacle of their evolution and diversity.

What characteristics determine if a dinosaur **skeleton is a sauropod**?

Paleontologists use several technical characteristics to determine if a dinosaur skeleton is that of a sauropod:

1) twelve or more neck (cervical) vertebrae;

2) four or more sacral (between the hipbones) vertebrae (most modern reptiles have two; birds have over 10; and most modern mammals have three to five);

3) massive, vertical limbs with long, solid bones;

4) ilium (part of the pelvis bone) expanded to the back;

5) extra neck vertebrae—an evolutionary feature that developed at the expense of the back (dorsal) vertebrae. In addition, their skulls were weakly attached; thus the skull is often missing from the rest of the fossil skeleton. Additional skeletal characteristics are often used to classify fossils into groups and species, including the tail chevrons and the socket structure between the vertebrae.

What were the **prosauropods**?

The prosauropods (Prosauropoda) were some of the first dinosaurs to be discovered and described in the 1830s—even before the term dinosaur was coined to describe these huge reptiles. The name prosauropod, or "precursor of the sauropods," is a misnomer, as the earliest known creatures were already too specialized to be the ancestors of the sauropods—but the name is still used today.

The prosauropods evolved during the late Triassic period some 230 million years ago, and apparently disappeared at the end of the early Jurassic period. Most prosauropods had blunt teeth, long forelimbs, and extremely large claws on the first finger of the forefoot. They were mostly herbivores, but never gained the huge size or special adaptations of the later herbivorous dinosaurs.

It is currently difficult to pin down the classification of the prosauropods. In certain classifications, saurischian dinosaurs were also divided into the suborder Sauropodomorpha, with another division Prosauropoda; another classification suggests the Sauropodomorpha were divided into the Sauropoda, Prosauropoda, and Segnosauria; still other classifications just list the prosauropods as an extinct offshoot of the saurischians.

What **prosauropod fossils** have been **discovered**?

In 1836, not long after the discovery of the first dinosaur fossils (although the term had not yet been coined), one of the earliest fossil prosauropods was found: a *Thecodontosaurus.* The next year, a *Plateosaurus* was found—today considered the best known and most extensively studied of all the prosauropods. Other prosauropod fossils have been discovered over the years, including the *Azendohsaurus, Sellosaurus, Camelotia,* and *Riojasaurus*—all from the late Triassic period. From the early Jurassic period, the most common prosauropods were the *Massospondylus, Yunannosaurus,* and *Lufengosaurus.*

What is the **most primitive sauropod** known?

The most primitive sauropod known is the *Vulcanodon,* an early Jurassic period dinosaur discovered in Zimbabwe, Africa. Unfortunately, the skull and vertebrae (except for the tail and part of the pelvic bone) have not been found. It is thought that the dinosaur walked on all fours and was about 33 feet (10 meters) long; the bones show features that were both prosauropod- and sauropod-like.

What were the **cetiosaurids**?

The cetiosaurids (Cetiosauridae) were a group of early sauropods. In fact, this group was an amalgamation of many different types of sauropods that had relatively simple vertebrae. Although some lived until the late Jurassic period, the dinosaurs in this loose group retained some primitive features. Scientists believe that the cetiosaurids led the way, evolutionarily, for the more advanced forms of sauropods, such as the diplodocids, brachiosaurs, and camarasaurs.

Some well-preserved specimens of this group have recently been found in China, complete with skulls. These sauropods were distinguished by the lack of an opening in the jaw and five pelvic vertebrae, among other features. The cetiosaurids include the middle Jurassic *Shunosaurus,* with a tail that ended in a club of bone; and the late Jurassic *Mamenchisaurus,* with an extremely long neck containing 19 elongated vertebrae. The *Mamenchisaurus* was close to diplodocid line, but still retained a number of primitive characteristics that distinguished it from them.

What were the **diplodocids**?

The diplodocids (Diplodocidae) were a group of advanced sauropods living in the late Jurassic period—and included some of the longest known dinosaurs. The diplodocids had long, whiplike tails with at least 80 vertebrae, vertebrae with tall spines, small, long, and slender skulls with elongated muzzles, peglike teeth only located in the front of the mouth, and nostrils on top of the head.

What were the **brachiosaurids**?

The brachiosaurids (Brachiosauridae) were another group of sauropods. These Jurassic period dinosaurs were much more massive than the diplodocids. Their most unique characteristic was front legs as long as—or even longer than—their rear legs. This, combined with their long necks, gave them a giraffe-like posture. In addition, the brachiosaurids had a relatively short tail comprised of about 50 small vertebrae, nostrils perched on a protrusion on top of the head, and a very long neck with 13 large vertebrae.

What were the **camarasaurids**?

Depending on the classification system, the sauropods called camarasaurids (Camarasauridae) can be listed as part of the brachiosaurids or placed in a group of their own. They were shorter and heavier than the diplodocids, with front and rear legs more similar in length. These late Jurassic period dinosaurs had 12 neck vertebrae, low, thick spines, vertebrae with extensive, deep cavities; large nostrils in front of the eyes, and large spoonlike teeth set in a short, blunt skull.

Where are **camarsaurid fossils** commonly **found**?

The camarasaurid *Camarasaurus* is the most common sauropod in the Morrison formation in the western United States. In fact, it is one of the only dinosaurs whose osteology—or the anatomy and structure of the bone—is completely known.

What were some **Jurassic period sauropods**?

The following lists the most prominent Jurassic period sauropods and some of their characteristics:

Jurassic Period Sauropods

Sauropod	Dinosaur	Comments
Diplodocidae	*Diplodocus*	This dinosaur gives this group its name; it was 89 feet (27 meters) in length, with an estimated weight of 11 to 12 tons.

Sauropod	Dinosaur	Comments
	Apatosaurus	Commonly known as *Brontosaurus,* it was shorter and stockier than the *Diplodocus.*
	Barosaurus	Similar to *Diplodocus,* but its cervical vertebrae were 33 percent longer.
	Seismosaurus	One candidate for the longest known dinosaur; it is estimated to have been between 128 and 170 feet (39 and 52 meters) long; its weight was probably more than 100 tons.
	Supersaurus	Another candidate for the longest dinosaur; it is estimated to have been about 130 feet (40 meters) long.
Brachiosauridae	*Brachiosaurus*	This dinosaur gives its name to the group; the late Jurassic dinosaur was approximately 75 feet (23 meters) long; it was 39 feet (12 meters) high, about the height of a four-story building, with an estimated weight of 55 tons
	Ultrasaurus	This may be a very large *Brachiosaurus;* only a few bones have been discovered; the estimates from the bones give a length greater than 98 feet (30 meters), and a weight of 140 tons.
Camarasauridae	*Camarasaurus*	A relatively small sauropod; it was approximately 59 feet (18 meters) long; its forelimbs were not as proportionally long as the brachiosaurids.

What were some **general characteristics** of the other saurischian group—the **theropods**?

The theropods had many general characteristics: Because they were carnivores, their teeth tended to be bladelike, with serrated ridges. Their claws, especially on the hands, were often recurved and tapered to sharp points. The outer fingers of the hand were either reduced in size or were completely lost. Most theropods were long-legged, bipedal (two-footed), slender, and quick—all characteristics that enabled the animals to more easily catch their prey. They also had three walking toes on the hindfeet.

Theropods had hollow limb bones; some went one step further and had air-filled (pneumatic) bones in certain parts of their body. For example, in some dinosaurs, pneumatic bones were found in the middle of the tail; in others, the air-filled bones were present at the back of the skull.

What characteristics determine if a **dinosaur skeleton** is that of a **theropod**?

There are many unique skeletal characteristics paleontologists use to determine if certain dinosaur bones belong to a theropod. Here are a few of the less technical characteristics:

> ## What evidence shows that large theropods were active hunters, not just scavengers?
>
> There is a good deal of evidence that larger theropods attacked other animals. For example, sauropod bones found in Colorado show the bite marks from large theropods—and sometimes the bones indicate that the prey survived the attack. At other sites, trackways show the footprints of theropods chasing or stalking smaller sauropods.

1) The bone in front of the eye (lacrimal) extends onto the top of the skull.

2) The lower jaw has an extra joint.

3) The shoulder blade (scapula) is straplike.

4) The upper arm bone (humerus) is less than half the length of the upper leg bone femur).

5) The elongated hand has lost (or has shrunken) two outer fingers.

6) The top of the bones in the palm of the hand (metacarpals) has pits where ligaments were attached.

7) The fingers have elongated bones between the second-to-last and last joints.

8) Near the head of the upper leg bone (femur) is a shelflike ridge for the attachment of muscles.

What were the **ceratosaurs**?

The ceratosaurs (Ceratosauria, or "horned reptiles") is one of the two theropod divisions. These were among the earliest theropods, arising during the Triassic period and evolving into much larger animals during the Jurassic period.

What were some **general characteristics** of the **ceratosaurs**?

Similar to all known theropods, the ceratosaurs had hollow bones—bones that were much stronger and easier to bend than solid ones. The ceratosaur dinosaurs had strongly curved S-shaped necks, similar to those exhibited by modern birds—but on a much larger scale, of course. (Scientifically, this is expressed by saying the ceratosaurs began to exhibit birdlike features, or more appropriately, birds show ceratosaurian features.)

Another ceratosaur characteristic included its upper jaw bone structure: there was a loose attachment between the two upper jawbones, known as the premaxilla (a front bone of the upper jaw) and the maxilla (main upper jaw bone, behind the premaxilla). The notch formed by this arrangement was filled by a large tooth in the lower jaw when the mouth was closed.

What were the **tetanurans**?

The tetanurans (Tetanurae) are considered to be a sister group of the ceratosaurs. They are all the theropods not classified as ceratosaurs, and are subdivided into the carnosaurs and the coelurosaurs. It was a large and diverse group, and was comprised of many species—including most of the well-known theropods.

What were some **general characteristics** of the **tetanurans**?

The unique characteristics of this group include a special row of teeth, a large pubic boot, the presence of a large opening in front of the jaw, and the rear half of the tail stiffened by interlocking rodlike projections of vertebrae. The tetanurans also had a three-fingered hand.

What were the **carnosaurs**?

The carnosaurs (Carnosauria, or "meat-eating lizards") were one of the two main groups making up the theropods called tetanurans; in some classifications this group is also known as Allosauria. They first appeared in the middle Jurassic (some say late Jurassic) period and lasted until the end of the Cretaceous period. They included the families of Megalosauridae, Sinraptoridae, and Allosauridae.

What were some **general characteristics** of the **carnosaurs**?

The dinosaurs that made up the carnosaurs were large, heavy predators. In addition to being large in size, these dinosaurs shared other unique characteristics, such as a large cavity in the lacrimal bone of the skull; this cavity, located in front of and above the orbit (eye opening in skull), may have held a gland. Other characteristics included large eye openings in a long, narrow skull, femurs (thighbones) larger than the tibia (shinbone), and neck vertebrae with a ball joint on the front and a socket on the back. Carnosaurs also had fairly good-sized forelimbs.

What were the **coelurosaurs**?

The coelurosaurs (Coelurosauria) made up the other group of tetanurans. In the past, this classification included all the small-bodied theropods, while the carnosaurs

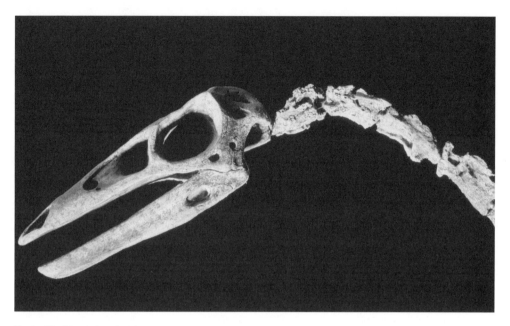

The fossilized head of an *Ornithomimus,* a type of dinosaur that resembled modern-day birds such as ostriches. (Photo courtesy of Michael S. Yamashita/Corbis.)

included all the large-bodied theropods. This is not the case today—and although several alternate classifications have been proposed, none is universally accepted.

Because this group of theropods was extremely diverse, the group's definition, the dinosaurs within the group, and the relationships between the various species are currently in continual flux. Currently, the major subgroups of coelurosaurs are the ornithomimosaurs (Ornithomimidae), maniraptorans (Maniraptora)—and a fairly recent addition to the coelurosaurs, the tyrannosaurs (Tyrannosauridae). Some of the dinosaurs in this group evolved during the late Jurassic period, but the majority reached their peak in the Cretaceous period.

What fairly **recent addition** to the **coelurosaurs** was once classified as a **carnosaur**?

The tyrannosaurs, also known as tyrannosaurids, depending on the text, include the *Allosaurus* and *Tyrannosaurus.* They used to be classified by most scientists as carnosaurs. But recent cladistic analysis shows that the tyrannosaurs are more closely related to the coelurosaurs.

What were the **general characteristics** of the **coelurosaurs**?

These carnivorous dinosaurs were more birdlike in characteristics and appearance than the large carnosaurs. In fact, birds are classified in the coelurosaur subgroup

135

known as the maniraptorans. Coelurosaurs had very long forelimbs and well-developed hinge-like ankles—although later dinosaurs in this group may have lost these features or had modified versions. Some other characteristics of the coelurosaurs included some special bone structures, such as a triangular bulge on the lower part of the pelvis and a protrusion on the ankle bone.

What were the **ornithomimosaurs**?

The ornithomimosaurs, also known as ornithomimids (Ornithomimidae, or "bird mimics"), were a subgroup of the coelurosaurs that—from general superficial appearances—resembled modern-day ratite birds such as ostriches. These dinosaurs were slender, with flexible necks, small heads, toothless beaks, long slim hindlimbs, elongated arms, and grasping hands with three powerful fingers. Ornithomimosaurs arose in the late Jurassic period and died out at the end of the Cretaceous period.

These dinosaurs were not limited to small sizes; some could reach up to 20 feet (6 meters) in length. Because of their lower leg bones and foot structure, some scientists think that these dinosaurs, like the ostrich, could run very fast. Estimates for one species, the *Struthiomimus,* range from 22 to 37 miles (35 to 60 kilometer) per hour.

What were the **maniraptorans**?

The maniraptorans (Maniraptora, or "seizing hands") were the second subgroup making up the coelurosaurs. They are defined as all dinosaurs closer to birds than the ornithomimosaurs. In fact, many paleontologists believe birds came from maniraptorans—evolving from this group during the Jurassic period.

The maniraptorans were a very diverse group—and looked (at first glance) to be totally unrelated to the coelurosaurs. However, they all shared some common characteristics that made them part of this group. The maniraptorans included the dromaeosaurids, troodontids, therizinosaurs (or segnosaurs), oviraptorosaurs—and more recently, of course, the aves (birds).

Were there any **dromaeosaurs, troodontids, therizinosaurs,** or **oviraptorosaurs** in the Jurassic period?

There is little evidence of dromaeosaur, troodontid, therizinosaur (or segnosaur), and oviraptorosaur fossils in Jurassic period rock, although dromaeosaurid and troodontid teeth have been reported in late Jurassic rock. It is currently thought that the creatures evolved in the late Jurassic, and were very prolific in the Cretaceous period. Thus, they are covered in the next chapter on the Cretaceous.

What were the **tyrannosaurs**?

The tyrannosaurs (or tyrannosaurids) are the last subgroup making up the coelurosaurs (they were once classified as carnosaurs). Although some probably evolved during the late Jurassic period, most of them dominated the Cretaceous period—and thus are covered more fully in the next chapter on the Cretaceous.

What were some **Jurassic period theropods**?

The following lists the most prominent Jurassic period theropods and some of their characteristics:

Jurassic Period Theropods

Theropod	Dinosaur	Comments
Ceratosauria	*Syntarsus*	Small and slender, similar in form to *Coelophysis*.
	Dilophosaurus	Up to 20 feet (6 meters) long and fairly slender; the skull had a double crest of thin, parallel plates on its nose and forehead; it was fancifully portrayed in the motion picture *Jurassic Park* with a frill, spitting poison, and much smaller than in actuality.
	Ceratosaurus	A large, heavy carnivorous dinosaur up to 23 feet (7 meters) long; it had short bladelike crests over the eyes, and a short triangular nose horn; it was the largest known ceratosaur, and appeared in the late Jurassic period; some scientists believe the dinosaur was an oddball: it appeared long after the other ceratosaurs, and may not even belong to this group; in fact, some people put it with the carnosaurs.
Carnosauria	*Allosaurus*	A large predator, with fairly long and well-muscled forelimbs and huge claws; it had large legs with heavy, clawed feet, and large, narrow jaws.
	Megalosaurus	The first dinosaur to be described; it was thought to be up to 30 feet (9 meters) long, but recently studies of the fragmentary remains indicate that they may actually be parts of different carnosaurs.

137

Theropod	Dinosaur	Comments
Coelurosauria	*Compsognathus*	A small coelurosaur that evolved during the late Jurassic; one example is the *Compsognathus longipes,* found in the limestone quarry of Solnhofen, Germany, where the first known bird, *Archaeopteryx lithographica,* was also discovered.
	Gallimimus	An ornithomimosaur that evolved during the late Jurassic; the Gallimimus bullatus was featured in the motion picture *Jurassic Park,* and were thought to have been some of the fastest dinosaur runners, judging from their long hindlimbs.

ORNITHISCHIAN DINOSAURS

How are the **ornithischian dinosaurs classified**?

The ornithischian dinosaurs, except for some early primitive forms, are all members of a group called the Genasauria. In one frequently used classification, the Genasauria are divided into the thyreophorans (Thyreophora) and the cerapods (Cerapoda). The thyreophorans are further divided into the stegosaurs (Stegosauria) and the ankylosaurs (Ankylosauria), although in some classifications, these two divisions are combined into one group; the cerapods are divided into the ornithopods (Ornithopoda) and the marginocephalians (Marginocephalia). The ornithischian dinosaurs developed in the middle to late Triassic period, evolving and increasing in number by the Jurassic and into the Cretaceous period.

What **general characteristics** were shared by **all ornithischian dinosaurs**?

Besides the hip structure of the animals, the other main characteristic shared by the ornithischian (Genasauria) dinosaurs was a deeply inset tooth row. This manifested itself in the skull as a deep concavity on each side—a structure some paleontologists use to support the idea of cheeks in some of these dinosaurs. (Since all ornithischian dinosaurs were herbivorous, cheeks would have been an important feature for keeping the food in the mouth during the chewing process.)

What were two of the **earliest known ornithischian** dinosaurs?

Two of the earliest known ornithischian dinosaurs were *Lesothosaurus* and *Heterodontosaurus*—both of whose remains were discovered in early Jurassic rock of the

Stormberg group in southern Africa. The *Lesothosaurus* was a small, slender biped about 3 feet (1 meter) long, with long hindlegs, delicate, short arms, and a five-fingered hand. Although this dinosaur had the characteristic ornithischian hip structure, it lacked a deeply inset tooth row, meaning its cheeks were not well developed. Therefore, some paleontologists suggest that the *Lesothosaurus* was the most primitive known ornithischian dinosaur.

The *Heterodontosaurus,* another dinosaur about 3 feet (1 meter) long, differed from *Lesothosaurus* in the skull and hands. Its skull had a deeply inset tooth row, the tooth pattern was more complicated, and it had thicker outside enamel on the upper and inside of the lower teeth. The *Heterodontosaurus* was more advanced than *Lesothosaurus,* exhibiting characteristics shared by later ornithischian dinosaurs.

What were the "fabrosaurs"?

The "fabrosaurs" are a name some scientists give to a strange, supposed ornithischian dinosaur, but no one agrees on these animals! They were small—less than 6 feet (2 meters) long—and appeared in the late Triassic period, not surviving past the early Jurassic. Some scientists have taken the fabrosaurs out of the ornithopod classification (a division of the ornithischians), as the creatures lacked some major physical characteristics of this group—including no cheeks.

Other scientists say the fabrosaurs *are* ornithopods because they were similar to most Jurassic ornithopods: small, light, and fast dinosaurs that liked to feed on the undergrowth. The most famous dinosaur thought to be a fabrosaur, the *Lesothosaurus,* was not found as a complete skeleton, and no associated skulls have yet been found—something that would help scientists discover the true classification of this small dinosaur.

What were the main **characteristics** of the **thyreophorans**?

The thyreophorans (Thyreophora, or "shield bearers") make up one of the two main Genasauria dinosaur divisions. This group was characterized by the presence of bony armor on their bodies. The thyreophorans were further subdivided based on their type of armor: the stegosaurs (Stegosauria, or "plated dinosaurs") had armor manifested as bony plates or spines on their backs; the ankylosaurs (Ankylosauria, or "crooked or bent reptiles") had armor as a covering, or small plates over their backs. In some classifications, there is no division between the stegosaurs and ankylosaurs.

What were some **early thyreophorans**?

Some early thyreophorans were the *Scutellosaurus* and *Scelidosaurus.* The *Scutellosaurus*—an early Jurassic period dinosaur whose remains were discovered in North

America—was small and bipedal (two-footed), similar to the *Lesothosaurus*. The *Scutellosaurus* also had numerous small bony skin plates, and was among the smallest of the armored dinosaurs, growing from just over 1 foot (.5 meter) to 3 feet (1 meter) in length. This creature may also have been the earliest thyreophoran.

The *Scelidosaurus* was an early Jurassic period dinosaur living in western Europe and England about 180 million years ago. It was a quadruped (four-footed) and was much heavier than *Scutellosaurus,* growing to a length of approximately 13 feet (4 meters). It had heavy, bony plates, and hooflike claws.

What were the **stegosaurs**?

The stegosaurs (Stegosauria) were one of the two groups comprising the thyreophorans (although some classifications group them with the anklyosaurs in the thyreophorans division). These quadruped, "plated" dinosaurs first appeared in the Middle Jurassic. They were medium in size, from 13 to 26 feet (4 to 9 meters) long, with a small, long skull with simple teeth, and a long toothless beak. They also had armor consisting of one or two rows of vertical bony plates or spines along their tail, back, and neck. Fossils of stegosaurs—each species with a unique arrangement of spines and plates—are found in Jurassic and Cretaceous periods rock layers around the world, but they were most abundant in the Jurassic.

What was the **famous poem** written about a stegosaur's **second brain**?

In 1912, Bert L. Taylor, a columnist for the *Chicago Tribune*, wrote the following poem about the supposed second brain of the *Stegosaurus:*

> Behold the mighty dinosaur,
> Famous in prehistoric lore,
> Not only for his power and strength

But for his intellectual length.
You will observe by these remains
The creature had two sets of brains—
One in his head (the usual place),
The other at his spinal base.
Thus he could reason *a priori*
As well as *a posteriori.*
No problem bothered him a bit
He made both head and tail of it.
So wise was he, so wise and solemn,
Each thought filled just a spinal column.
If one brain found the pressure strong
It passed a few ideas along.
If something slipped his forward mind
'Twas rescued by the one behind.
And if in error he was caught
He had a saving afterthought.
As he thought twice before he spoke
He had no judgment to revoke.
Thus he could think without congestion
Upon both sides of every question.
Oh, gaze upon this model beast,
Defunct ten million years at least.

What were the **ankylosaurs**?

The ankylosaurs (Ankylosauria) were one of the two groups that made up the thyreophorans (the stegosaur was the other). Paleontologists divide the Ankylosauria into two families—the Nodosaurids and Ankylosaurids—based on differences in skulls, shoulder blades, and armor.

The ankylosaurs were medium-sized quadruped dinosaurs. They were short-legged and squat, with long, wide bodies. Their heads ranged from the long and narrow to wide with broad muzzles. All of the ankylosaurs had bony plates of armor over their bodies, often with spines, spikes, or studs projecting outward. Some even had bony clubs on the ends of their tails. Armor consisted of plates of bone, known as scutes, embedded in the skin; some dinosaurs even had their heads covered with this armor. They were the "tanks" of the dinosaur world—able to fight off any predator.

Unfortunately, very little is known about these dinosaurs since so few complete fossils have been found. The ankylosaurs first appeared during the early to middle Jurassic period, but they became most numerous and diverse during the Cretaceous period. Most of the ankylosaurs belonged to the Nodosaurid subgroup early in the Cretaceous period (although one genus, *Sarcolestes,* is from the Jurassic); the subgroup Ankylosaurid were more prevalent in the latter Cretaceous period, and were distinguished by their broad heads, spikes in the back of their skulls, and clublike tails.

What were the **cerapods**?

The cerapods (Cerapoda, or "horn-footed") were the second group within the Genasauria. They are divided into the ornithopods (Ornithopoda) and marginocephalians (Marginocephalia).

What were the **general characteristics** of the **cerapods**?

In general, the characteristics of the cerapods included only five or fewer premaxillary teeth, with the enamel distributed differently on the sides of their teeth. This difference allows scientists to subdivide these cerapods into the margincephalians and ornithopods.

Were there any **marginocephalians** in the Jurassic period?

Currently, some paleontologists believe there were no marginocephalians during the Jurassic period. This group was apparently a latecomer in dinosaur evolution, showing up in the early Cretaceous period and dividing into the Ceratopsia and Pachychephalosauria. They are covered in the next chapter on the Cretaceous period.

What **ornithopod dinosaurs** lived in the Jurassic period?

One of the most well-known—and earliest discovered dinosaurs—was the *Iguanodon.* Ornithopods also included the hadrosaurs (the "duck-billed" dinosaurs with the famous crests), the iguanodontids, the heterodontosaurs, the hypsilophodontids, and various other dinosaurs. But many of these dinosaurs were not prolific until the Cretaceous period.

What were some **general characteristics** of the **ornithopods**?

In general, the ornithopods were bipedal, ranging in size from small, less than 3 feet (1 meter) tall and 6 feet (2 meters) long, to large, about 23 feet (7 meters) tall and 66 feet (20 meters) long. The ornithopods were plant-eaters, evolving early in the Jurassic period and continuing to the end of the Cretaceous. They lived on every continent, including Antarctica. And they were the first herbivorous dinosaurs to have multiple tooth rows, cheek pouches, and the ability to truly chew.

What were some Jurassic period **ornithischian dinosaurs**?

The following are some examples of the ornithischian dinosaurs that made up this group during the Jurassic period:

Jurassic Period Ornithischians

Ornithischian	Ornithischian Sub-group	Dinosaur	Comments
Thyreophora	Stegosauria	*Huayangosaurus*	These animals had small plates in skin, with spikelike armor and equal length front and rear legs; they were approximately 13 feet (4 meters) long, with a short snout; they are considered the most primitive of the stegosaurs.
		Stegosaurus	A late Jurassic dinosaur weighing approximately one to two tons; it had an array of bony plates along the length of the back, with tail spikes; the hindlegs were long, with short, massive forelegs; the head was small and elongated, and the brain size was extremely small for an animal of this size.
		Kentrosaurus	This dinosaur had spines on tail, hip, shoulder, and back; its bony plates, similar to those on *Stegosaurus,* were also present on the neck and anterior part of the back.
	Ankylosauria	*Sarcolestes*	This nodosaurid dinosaur ("flesh robber") developed in the middle Jurassic period, and was thought to be the first ankylosaur; it had a large piece of armor plating on its outer surface.
		Dracopelta	The Dracopelta ("armored dragon") was a small late Jurassic period nodosaurid from Portugal.
Cerapoda	Ornithopoda	*Camptosaurus*	A medium-sized, bipedal herbivore; it weighed up to 1,000 pounds, reaching lengths up to 23 feet (7 meters); it is thought to be the ancestor to many of the highly successful plant-eating dinosaurs in the Cretaceous period.
		Heterodontosaurus	This dinosaur was only about 3 feet (1 meter) in length; it had caninelike teeth and relatively long arms, with large hands; its teeth were designed for cutting.

> ## What were the smallest dinosaurs known in the Jurassic period?
>
> Currently, the smallest dinosaur on record that lived in the Jurassic was the *Echinodon*, a herbivorous ornithischian that was about the size of a modern chicken.

GENERAL JURASSIC DINOSAUR FACTS

Which major Jurassic period dinosaurs were **herbivores**?

The largest dinosaurs in the Jurassic period tended to be the plant-eaters (herbivores). The best known examples include the long-necked sauropods like *Brachiosaurus* and *Apatososaurus,* creatures that ate leaves off the tops of high trees. In addition, all of the ornithischians were herbivores, such as the plated *Stegosaurus* and the ankylosaurs. Ornithopods such as *Camptosaurus* competed with the large sauropods for vegetation.

Which major Jurassic period dinosaurs were **carnivores**?

The theropods were all carnivores, and evolved into large predators, such as the *Megalosaurus* and the well-known *Allosaurus.*

What were the **largest dinosaurs** known in the **Jurassic period**?

Some of the dinosaurs living during the Jurassic period had evolved into the largest creatures ever to live on land—the majority being plant-eaters. And it seems as if every year brings a new fossil discovery that unearths another, larger dinosaur.

There are many famous, large herbivorous sauropods that lived during the Jurassic period. One is the *Diplodocus,* one of the longest plant eaters, measuring 90 feet (27 meters) in length. At one time, scientists believed that this huge creature had to live in the water to support its great bulk, but the latest research suggests that the dinosaur was able to carry its weight on land. (This dinosaur may not end up being the longest Jurassic dinosaur, though: a possible 150-foot [46-meter] dinosaur called a *Seismosaurus* is still being dug out from a chunk of sandstone found in New Mexico.)

Another large sauropod was called the *Apatosaurus,* otherwise known as the *Brontosaurus,* which weighed up to 51 tons. But the true winner for sauropod weight may prove to be the *Brachiosaurus,* a 75-foot (23-meter) animal with unusual longer front legs and shorter back legs. Its weight is disputed, ranging from 32 to 78 tons—but either way, it was a heavyweight. Still another large plant-eating dinosaur was the *Baro-saurus*—an animal closely related to the *Diplodocus*—that had an enormously elongated neck, rivaling even the long neck of the *Brachiosaurus*. The neck of the *Brachiosaurus* reached about 43 feet (13 meters), higher than the average three-story building; to compare, a giraffe grows to about 18 feet (5.5 meters).

There may have been even larger herbivorous sauropods, but many of these are still debated, as not many fossils of these dinosaurs have been found. In North America, one such relatively rare set of dinosaur bones includes the huge sauropod *Supersaurus*. This giant dinosaur measured 80 to 100 feet (24 to 30.5 meters) long and 54 feet (16.5 meters) high; other reports say that the dinosaur was closer to 130 feet (40 meters) long, making this sauropod the longest known land animal. Another possibility was also found on the same continent—the *Ultra-saurus*, or *Ultrasauros*, which may have grown to at least 100 feet (30.5 meters) long. The actual existence of this dinosaur is highly debated—but if it is designated as a separate species (some scientists believe it may be a large *Brachiosaurus*, while others believe it is often mistaken for a *Supersaurus*), it will be classed as one of the Jurassic period's largest.

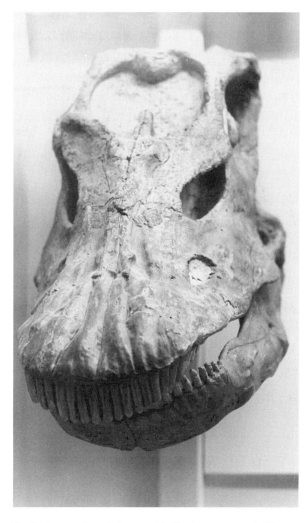

The *Apatosaurus*, formerly known as the *Brontosaurus*, was a herbivore during the Jurassic period. (Photo courtesy of University of Michigan Exhibit, Museum of Natural History.)

Larger carnivorous dinosaurs included the *Allosaurus*, measuring about 50 feet (15 meters) in length. Scientists believe the attack of the *Allosaurus* was amazing: it would open its mouth to the furthest extent, running headlong into its victim. Its 60 curved, daggerlike teeth would plunge into its prey, driven by two tons of dinosaur.

What happened to the *Brontosaurus*?

The *Apatosaurus* was formerly known as the *Brontosaurus*. Fossils from the *Apatosaurus* were officially named in 1877, while the *Brontosaurus* fossils were named in 1878. It wasn't until later that it was noticed that the fossils of the two dinosaurs were really the same. Since the *Apatosaurus* had been named first, it was adopted as the official designation for this animal.

Did the first **dinosaur fossil to be named** come from the **Jurassic period**?

Yes, the first dinosaur fossil to be named was the *Megalosaurus,* named by geologist William Buckland (1784–1856) in 1824. The fossil came from the middle Jurassic, and was found in Oxfordshire, England.

What **Jurassic period** dinosaurs were the **longest lived** of the dinosaur lines?

The herbivorous ornithopods were the longest lived of dinosaurs lines, from the early Jurassic to the late Cretaceous period. They include a series of successively larger and more massive dinosaurs that spread throughout most of the continents. One was the *Heterodontosaurus* of the early Jurassic period, a quick, 4-foot (1.3-meter) dinosaur, with strong front canine tusks and flexible hands used for digging and grasping vegetation.

OTHER LIFE IN THE JURASSIC PERIOD

What were the **major land plants** living during the **Jurassic**?

The major land plants were similar to those in the Triassic period (see the plant table on page 115 for more information), but were more profuse. Ferns and horsetails covered the ground; ginkos and tree ferns lined rivers and lakes; and cycads, conifers, and sequoias forested thousands of square miles of the drier lands. The biggest difference was the diversification and increase in abundance of the cycads (the Jurassic is often referred to as the "age of cycads") and conifers, with most of the modern families evolving, such as cypresses, redwoods, yews, and junipers. The first truly modern ferns also appeared at this time.

What were the **more profuse small marine plants** living during the **Jurassic**?

In the early Jurassic, coccolithophorids (calcareous nanoplankton) first appeared. These were very small, single-cell algae that were covered with calcium carbonate disks.

Were there any **insects** during the Jurassic period?

Because of the mild climate and lush vegetation, flying insects were very profuse during the Jurassic period. In addition, the early ancestors of the bees and flies developed (although some scientists believe that early ancestors of the flies may have evolved even earlier, during the late Triassic).

Besides dinosaurs, what **other land animals** were present during the **Jurassic period**?

Although the dinosaurs were the dominant animals, there were other animals that existed during the Jurassic period. Because of the relative stability of the climate and the lush vegetation, many land animals diversified and increased in numbers. But not all creatures survived through the Jurassic period; many became extinct, probably because competition increased.

Non-dinosaurian Land Animals of the Jurassic Period

Class	Animal	Description
Amphibians	Frogs, salamanders	First modern frogs and salamanders appeared.
Reptiles	Turtles	First modern turtles appeared in the early Jurassic period; they were able to retract their heads into their upper shell.
	Lizards	First true lizards appeared in the middle Jurassic period.
	Crocodylians	First true crocodylians appear, and were small, 3-foot- (1-meter-) long reptiles that walked on all fours; they had longer hindlegs, indicating that their ancestors were bipedal.
	Therapsids	Few families of therapsids, or mammal-like reptiles, lived into the middle Jurassic period; the anomodonts and therocephalians no longer existed, but the cynodonts did survive into the middle Jurassic.
Mammals	Small mammals	Small mammals became more profuse and diverse during the Jurassic period; they were still very small animals, about the size of a mouse or rat, with the largest the size of a cat; they were mostly nocturnal (active at night).
	Triconodonts	Late Triassic to late Cretaceous mammals; one of the oldest fossil mammals; three cusps of teeth in a straight row give them their name.

147

The *Ichthyosaurus* was a marine reptile during the Jurassic period. (Photo courtesy of University of Michigan Exhibit, Museum of Natural History.)

Class	Animal	Description
	Haramyoids	Late Triassic to middle Jurassic mammals; one of the oldest fossil mammals; their teeth had many cusps in at least two parallel rows.
	Symmetrodonts	Late Jurassic to early Cretaceous mammals; they had upper and lower cheek teeth with many cusps in a triangular pattern.
	Docodonts	Middle to late Jurassic period mammals; they had elaborate cheek teeth, with most of the cusps in a T-shape.
	Multituberculates	The multituberculates were the largest group of mammals in the Mesozoic, first appearing in the late Jurassic period.

Were there any **animals in the air** during the **Jurassic**?

Similar to the Triassic period, there were many gliding and flying animals—all of them reptiles—during the Jurassic period. They became more diverse, and some much larger than in the Triassic period. The pterosaurs, the flying reptiles, became extremely diverse and abundant, flying over all the continents. They included the *Rhamphorhynchus,* with a 6-foot (1.75-meter) wing span, and the *Pterodactylus,* with a 8-foot (2.5-meter) wing span.

The first birds also may have developed during this time, although the actual lineage is still often debated. The most famous fossils of the late Jurassic period, besides those of dinosaurs, are of the *Archaeopteryx*. Only about five fossils of this reptile have been found in late Jurassic period limestone rock in Germany, each retaining many distinctive dinosaur features, pointing to the idea that birds probably evolved from small, meat-eating dinosaurs.

What were the **major marine animals** living during the **Jurassic**?

There were many marine animals that thrived during the Jurassic period, ranging from small seabed dwellers, to large swimming predators. Most of these animals were similar to those found in the Triassic period, although many had diversified and increased in number during the Jurassic period.

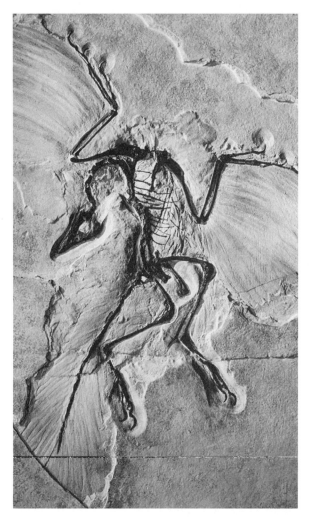

This *Archaeopteryx* fossil features wing impressions. (Photo courtesy of James L. Amos/Corbis.)

Modern shark families developed at this time; bony fishes, the teleosts, with symmetrical tails diversified (they account for the great majority of modern fishes—over 20,000 species). The first oysters evolved; modern squids and cuttlefishes appeared; and squidlike belemnites diversified. The ammonoids almost disappeared during the late Triassic extinctions; one family survived (out of eight) and quickly diversified during the Jurassic period.

The ichthyosaurs ("fish reptiles"), such as the *Ichthyosaurus* and *Stenopterygius,* flourished in the Jurassic period oceans. Plesiosaurs were also abundant, such as the *Muraenosaurus,* a late Jurassic period reptile with a 36-foot (11-meter) neck (it   **149** included 40 vertebrae); and the *Liopleurodon,* a short-necked pliosaur with a huge, elongated neck, was 39 feet (12 meters) long, with a 10-foot (3-meter) head.

What was so **special** about the evolution of the **ichthyosaurs**?

Ichthyosaurs were a group of streamlined, dolphin-shaped reptiles—but their backgrounds differed from many reptiles living around them: these creatures' ancestors went back to the sea from the land. Some scientists believe that ichthyosaurs were the first major group of reptiles to return to the sea. At first, they no doubt stayed close to the shoreline, similar to seals and walruses. But after millions of years, the creatures went into the oceans, spread, and eventually became totally fish-shaped.

The oldest ichthyosaur fossils, and the most primitive so far, are 240-million-year-old fossils found in Japan. The primitive ichthyosaur, measuring about 9 feet (2.7 meters) long, probably lived its entire life in the water. Its shape was not yet like a dolphin; and its pelvis bone was still attached to the vertebrae—similar to those of land animals and dissimilar to the later ichthyosaurs. The primitive ichthyosaurs also had fins that were similar to the limbs of land reptiles (with splayed fingers). In other words, this primitive fossil shows the first step the ichthyosaurs took from the land to the oceans.

There was one other strange characteristic of the ichthyosaurs: for unknown reasons (as evident in the fossil record), about 135 million years ago, the animals began to fade away—becoming totally extinct between 90 and 100 million years ago. This was much earlier than the demise of the dinosaurs—animals that became extinct about 65 million years ago.

CRETACEOUS PERIOD

THE CRETACEOUS PERIOD

What was the **Cretaceous period** and how did it get its **name**?

The Cretaceous period followed the Jurassic period on the geologic time scale; it was the last period in the Mesozoic era. Most of the Jurassic's large sauropods, stegosaurs, and theropods disappeared in the early part of this period, but were replaced by an incredibly large diversity of new dinosaur groups. These included the horned types, the duck-billed, the armored, and new types of theropod carnivores.

The Cretaceous period got its name from the type of rock deposited along the northern shores of the Tethys Sea at this time, in a band running from what is now Ireland and Britain to the Middle East. This rock—formed from the metamorphosed deposits of the tiny limestone skeletons of algae known as diatoms—is known as chalk. The Latin word for chalk is *creta*; hence, the name Cretaceous.

Where and when did the **term Cretaceous** first come into use?

"Cretaceous" was first used to describe a rock found in France called chalk, a white, soft limestone. In 1822, d'Omalius d'Halloy, employed by Baron de Monbret—who was in charge of statistical information in France at that time—used the name "Terrain Cretacé" to describe the strata and associated units of chalk (*craie* in French) found in that country. These same strata were also present across the English Channel, and English geologists began calling them the Cretaceous system.

Marine life during the Cretaceous period. The Cretaceous is named for the type of rock deposited along the shores of the Tethys Sea during that period. (Photo courtesy of University of Michigan Exhibit, Museum of Natural History.)

What **painter** frequently painted the **Cretaceous chalk cliffs** of France?

The strikingly beautiful Cretaceous period sea cliffs, found around Etretat on the Brittany coast, were frequently painted by the famous nineteenth-century French artist Claude Monet.

How long did the **Cretaceous period last**?

The Cretaceous period lasted from approximately 144 to 65 million years ago, or approximately 80 million years. The geologic time scale is not exact, and the dates of the Cretaceous period can vary by about 5 to 10 million years.

What are the major **divisions** of the **Cretaceous**?

Scientists divide the Cretaceous into two divisions, or epochs: the Early Cretaceous (also called the Lower Cretaceous), from approximately 144 to 89 million years ago; and the Late Cretaceous (also called the Upper Cretaceous), from approximately 89 to 65 million years ago. They are less formally referred to in this text as early Cretaceous and late Cretaceous. Each of these main epochs is broken up into smaller ages. The following chart gives the European nomenclature for each age.

		Cretaceous Period
Epoch	**Age**	**Millions of Years Ago (approximate)**
Late	Maastrichtian	74 to 65
	Campanian	83 to 74
	Santonian	87 to 83
	Coniacian	89 to 87
Early	Turonian	93 to 89
	Cenomanian	97 to 93
	Albian	112 to 97
	Aptian	125 to 112
	Barremian	132 to 125
	Hauterivian	135 to 132
	Valanginian	141 to 135
	Berriasian	144 to 141

Why did the dinosaurs **thrive and diversify** during the **Cretaceous**?

Although there is no clear answer to this question, paleontologists know that a revolution in life occurred during this time period. This took place as many types of modern flora and fauna made their first appearances. Some scientists theorize that it was the development, and eventual dominance, of a new group of plants, the angiosperms (flowering plants), in harmony with the development of new groups of insects, that provided fresh sources of food that could be exploited by the dinosaurs. These new food sources allowed the dinosaurs to continue to dominate throughout the Cretaceous period.

THE CONTINENTS
DURING THE CRETACEOUS PERIOD

What was the **earth** like during the **Cretaceous period**?

During the Cretaceous period, what we recognize as our modern-day continents were becoming much more distinct. The breakup of Pangea into Laurasia and Gondwanaland continued, and these two large continents themselves began to break apart. Sea levels rose worldwide, inundating many formerly dry areas. Similar to the Jurassic period, it was warm and humid, with no ice caps at the poles. By the end of the late

153

Cretaceous, the planet closely resembled our modern world. But today, of course, we lack the small and large dinosaurs roaming our continents—although some scientists believe that birds are truly dinosaurs and therefore these creatures never really completely died away!

How did **Laurasia** and **Gondwanaland** change during the **Cretaceous period**?

During the Cretaceous period, both Laurasia and Gondwanaland separated from each other and each fragmented into smaller landmasses. The whole motif of the Cretaceous was change—change from the ancient topography to the more familiar forms we see today.

In the early Cretaceous period, Laurasia began to break up due to the action of an extension of the Mid-Atlantic Ridge, with North America and Greenland separating from Eurasia. Rifting occurred in Gondwanaland, with South America and Africa beginning to separate. In the middle of the Cretaceous period, Gondwanaland had separated into four major landmasses: South America, Africa, the combined India and Madagascar, and the combined Antarctica and Australia.

By the late Cretaceous, North America and Greenland began to split, as did Australia and Antarctica, and India and Madagascar. The Atlantic Ocean continued to widen, and India and Australia moved northward. By the end of the Cretaceous, the continents began to assume their modern outlines and headed toward their current destinations on the planet's surface. This also led to the development and widening of the modern oceans and seas.

What was the **climate** like during the **Cretaceous period**?

Similar to the Jurassic period, the early and middle Cretaceous period climate was warm and humid over most of the continents. By the middle Cretaceous, pronounced summer and winter seasons developed, but the temperatures never dropped below freezing, even in the polar regions. And in the late Cretaceous, the mean global temperatures were as high as any time during the past 500 million years.

What was the **global sea level** like during the **Cretaceous period**?

The global sea level continued to rise through the Cretaceous period; but by the late Cretaceous, mean sea level reached as high as any time during the past 500 million years—about 600 feet (200 meters) higher than present levels. This led to extensive flooding of many land areas, including most of Europe, North Africa, the Middle East, and western Russia. The fluctuations in sea level also brought about the appearance and disappearance of many land bridges between landmasses.

What is the Wealden Basin and why is it significant?

The Wealden Basin was an area of northwest Europe that extended over southern England, northern France and Germany, Belgium, and northeast Spain. In the early Cretaceous period, this area was not yet flooded by the rising sea level. It was a low-lying area with broad streams, lakes, and scattered forests—prime habitat for the dinosaurs of the time. Because of this, some of the best early Cretaceous period dinosaur fossils have been found in the rock of this region, including the second and third dinosaurs to be named: the *Iguanodon* and *Hylaeosaurus* were both named by fossil hunter Gideon Mantell (1790–1852) in the early 1800s. (The first dinosaur fossil to be named was the *Megalosaurus* of the middle Jurassic period.)

The reason for this rise in mean sea level is highly debated. Some scientists point to the fact that there were no polar ice caps, so the water that filled the oceans was at its peak. One theory for the dramatic rise in mean sea level was the increase in the volume and height of the sea floor: the increased amount of the oceanic crust—due to the spreading midoceanic ridge—displaced the water upward, causing the rise in sea level.

What were the **major oceans** during the **Cretaceous period**?

As Laurasia and Gondwanaland continued to separate during the Cretaceous, water began to fill in the gaps. The Panthalassa Ocean continued to be the largest ocean on the planet, slowly taking its modern-day shape as the Pacific Ocean. The Tethys Sea (Ocean) continued to shrink; millions of years after the Cretaceous period ended, it would evolve into today's Mediterranean Sea. The North and South Atlantic oceans continued to widen, a process that continues today.

What were the major **ocean currents** during the **Cretaceous period**?

The Cretaceous period ocean currents differed greatly from the Triassic and Jurassic periods, as the continents of Laurasia and Gondwanaland continued to break apart. A cold current ran up South America's west coast toward the equator; another cold current rushed between the ever-spreading area between Africa and Antarctica, India, and Australia; and two more cold currents continued from the north, past Europe and Siberia, and into the Tethys Sea. Warmer currents still ran to the west along the equator; another flowed north along the east coast of North America; and still another ran south, past the east and west coasts of Africa.

Were there any **major geological events** that occurred during the **Cretaceous period**?

The westward movement of North America led to further mountain uplift along the west coast, which continued throughout this period. Rifting in Gondwanaland, with the movement of South America, led to the start of mountain building along the west coast, and eventually resulted in today's Andes Mountains. Mountain building also caused an increase in erosion, and thus there were great areas in which sediments were deposited all over the globe. There were several major volcanic eruptions that spewed out huge volumes of volcanic material. One of the most famous is called the Deccan Traps that formed at the end of the Cretaceous period; the highlands of India formed from these ancient lava flows.

MAJOR CRETACEOUS DINOSAURS

What were the **major dinosaurs** during the **Cretaceous period**?

During the Cretaceous period, many of the Jurassic period dinosaurs disappeared, replaced by new, more diverse forms. Of the saurischian sauropods, only the titanosaurids (late Jurassic or early Cretaceous period) remained as a major group—and these herbivores were mostly found on the landmasses of Gondwanaland until the end of the Cretaceous period. (These creatures present a problem to scholars, however, because no complete skeleton or skull as ever been found.) Many of the saurischian theropods became extinct during the Cretaceous period; others diversified into a wide range of animals, from large carnivores like *Tyrannosaurus,* to speedy, agile predators like *Velociraptor.*

The ornithischian dinosaurs were the most numerous and diverse of all the dinosaurs in the Cretaceous period. They included the ornithopods, such as the *Iguanodon,* and the duck-billed dinosaurs, like the *Edmontosaurus* and *Maiasaura;* the armored ankylosaurs, including the *Ankylosaurus,* with its protective plating and tail-club; the thick-headed pachycephalosaurs, thought to engage in head butting, such as the *Stegoceras;* and the ceratopsians, four-legged animals with long bony frills and horns, like the *Triceratops.*

What were some of the **dinosaurs** that lived during the **Cretaceous period**?

The number of dinosaurs that lived during the Cretaceous period was immense—and too many to list in this volume. And as more fossils are found, the number continues to grow. What follows is a partial listing of cretaceous dinosaurs.

Skull of a *Triceratops,* which is just one of the many ornithischians that flourished during the Cretaceous period. (Photo courtesy of University of Michigan Exhibit, Museum of Natural History.)

Cretaceous Period Dinosaurs

Species Name	Common Name	Age (Millions of Years Ago)	Locality	Length (feet/meters)
Albertosaurus	Alberta Lizard	76 to 74	Canada	Up to 30/9
Avimimus	Bird Mimic	about 75	Mongolia	Up to 5/1.5
Baryonyx	Heavy Claw	about 124	England	34/10
Centrosaurus	Horned Lizard	76 to 74	Canada	Up to 16/5
Chasmosaurus	Cleft Lizard	76 to 74	Canada	Up to 16/5
Corythosaurus	Helmet Lizard	76 to 74	Canada, USA	Up to 33/10
Craspedodon	Edge Tooth	86 to 83	Belgium	Unknown
Deinocheirus	Terrible Lizard	70 to 65	Mongolia	Unknown, arms about 10/3
Deinonychus	Terrible Claw	110	USA	Up to 11/3
Dromaeosaurus	Running Lizard	76 to 74	Canada	Up to 6/1.8
Dryptosaurus	Wounding Lizard	74 to 65	USA	About 16/5
Edmontonia	Of Edmonton	76 to 74	Canada	About 13/4
Edmontosaurus	Edmonton Lizard	76 to 65	Canada	Up to 43/13
Euoplocephalus	Well-armored Head	About 71	Canada	Up to 20/6
Gallimimus	Chicken Mimic	74 to 70	Mongolia	Up to 18/5.5

157

Species Name	Common Name	Age (Millions of Years Ago)	Locality	Length (feet/meters)
Gilmoreosaurus	Gilmore's Lizard	80 to 70	China	About 20/6
Hadrosaurus	Big Lizard	83 to 74	USA	Up to 26/8
Hylaeosaurus	Woodland Lizard	150 to 135	England	Up to 13/4
Hypsilophodon	High Ridge Tooth	about 125	England	Up to 7.5/2
Iguanodon	Iguana Tooth	130 to 115	USA, England, Belgium, Spain, Germany	Up to 33/10
Kritosaurus	Noble Lizard	80 to 75	USA	Up to 26/8
Lambeosaurus	Lambe's Lizard	76 to 74	Canada	Up to 30/9
Maiasaura	Good Mother Lizard	80 to 75	USA	Up to 30/9
Ornithopsis	Birdlike Structure	about 125	England	Unknown, perhaps 65/20
Orodromeus	Mountain Runner	about 74	USA	Up to 6.5/2
Ouranosaurus	Brave Monitor Lizard	about 115	Niger	Up to 23/7
Oviraptor	Egg Thief	85 to 75	Mongolia	Up to 6/2
Pachycephalosaurus	Thick-headed Lizard	about 67	USA	Up to 26/8
Pachyrhinosaurus	Thick-nosed Lizard	76 to 74	Canada, USA	Up to 20/6
Parasaurolophus	Like *Saurolophus*	76 to 74	Canada, USA	Up to 33/10
Parksosaurus	Park's Lizard	76 to 74	Canada	Up to 10/3
Protoceratops	First Horned Face	85 to 80	Mongolia	Up to 6/2
Psittacosaurus	Parrot Lizard	124 to 97	China, Mongolia, Russia	Up to 6/2
Rhabdodon	Rod Tooth	83 to 70	Austria, France, Spain, Romania	Up to 10/3
Saurolophus	Ridged Lizard	74 to 70	Canada, Mongolia	Up to 40/12
Saurornithoides	Birdlike Lizard	80 to 74	Canada, Mongolia	Up to 6.5/2
Scartopus	Nimble Foot	About 95	Australia	Unknown
Segnosaurus	Slow Lizard	97 to 88	Mongolia	Up to 13/4
Struthiosaurus	Ostrich Lizard	83 to 75	Austria, Romania	Up to 6.5/2
Styracosaurus	Spiked Lizard	85 to 80	Canada, USA	Up to 18/5.5
Tenontosaurus	Sinew Lizard	110	USA	Up to 21/6.4
Triceratops	Three-horned Face	67 to 65	USA	Up to 30/9
Troodon	Wounding Tooth	75 to 70	Canada, USA	Up to 8/2.4
Tyrannosaurus	Tyrant Lizard	67 to 65	USA	Up to 40/12
Velociraptor	Quick Plunderer	84 to 80	China, Mongolia	Up to 6/12

How did the distribution of dinosaur species change during the Cretaceous period?

The earlier Triassic and Jurassic periods were characterized by joined land-masses throughout the planet. By the time the Cretaceous began, these landmasses began to separate, isolating some species of dinosaurs, and leading to different areas having different species. For example, the amphibious titanosaur sauropods were mostly present in former Gondwanaland areas, such as South America, while the horned ceratopsians and hadrosaurs (a type of ornithopod) were found mainly in Laurasia. But many interpretations are highly debated: one of the main reasons for the present uncertainty about the overall distribution of dinosaurs is the incompleteness of the known dinosaur fossil record.

SAURISCHIAN DINOSAURS

How were **Cretaceous period saurischian** dinosaurs different?

When compared to the Jurassic period, the Cretaceous period saurischian ("lizard-hipped") dinosaurs were still divided into the large plant-eating sauropods (Sauropoda) and the carnivorous theropods (Theropoda). However, the only important family of sauropods in the Cretaceous were the titanosaurids (Titanosauridae); the other groups, such as the diplodocids and brachiosaurs, lost their dominance. And, overall, the theropods became more diverse.

What were the **titanosaurids**?

The titanosaurids were the major group (and really the only dominant group) of sauropods that lived during the Cretaceous period. They represent a great mystery for paleontologists, too: no one has yet found a complete articulated skeleton or a complete skull of a titanosaurid.

What were the **general characteristics** of the **titanosaurids**?

The titanosaurids had small, slender, pencil-like teeth, similar to the diplodocids. Because of this, until recently, paleontologists put the diplodocids and titanosaurids into the same family—even though parts of both dinosaurs' skulls were very different. In general, the titanosaurids ranged from about 23 feet (7 meters) to 82 to 98 feet (25 to 30 meters) long. All the titanosaurids' spines were unforked, and their sacrum had

159

six vertebrae. Their tail vertebrae are very distinctive, too; they also had bony body armor composed of embossed plates.

Where did most of the **titanosaurids live**?

Most of the titanosaurids lived in the southern continents of Gondwanaland—especially the southern parts of today's South America and India. Bones of these dinosaurs have also been found in many other places, including Brazil, Malawi, Spain, Madagascar, Laos, Egypt, Romania, France, and the southern United States.

Where there any **other sauropods** that survived into the Cretaceous period?

There were very few sauropod species that survived into the Cretaceous period. Most of them, except the titanosaurids in Gondwanaland, were almost extinct. But there were still a few: for example, although they were abundant in the late Jurassic period, some brachiosaurs survived into the early Cretaceous, with fossils found in Europe and Africa. There were probably more, but fossil evidence—especially whole skeletons—of Cretaceous sauropods (except for the titanosaurids) is scarce.

Sauropods

Sauropod	Dinosaur Species	Comments
Titanosaurids	*Saltasaurus*	A relatively small—about 39 feet (12 meters) long—sauropod with bony plates covering its back in a kind of chain-mail body armor.
	Alamosaurus	This dinosaur was up to 69 feet (21 meters) long, with relatively long forelimbs; some paleontologists question whether this dinosaur was truly a titanosaur; it is thought to be the only North American Cretaceous period sauropod.
	Argentinosaurus	A good candidate for the most massive of all dinosaurs; it was thought to be as large as the largest diplodocids of the late Jurassic period.

How did the **theropods change** during the Cretaceous period?

During the Cretaceous period, the theropods became much more diverse, with ceratosaurs and the tetanurans well represented. The subgroups of the tetanurans, the carnosaurs and coelurosaurs, evolved new species. For instance, the coelurosaurs, composed of the ornithomimosaurs and maniraptorans, became very diverse; although some, such as the carnosaurs, became less dominant.

What were the carnosaurs like in the Cretaceous period?

The carnosaurs seemed to grow larger in the Cretaceous period. For example, the carnosaur *Giganotosaurus* from South America and *Carcharodontosaurus* from North America were two huge theropods—probably heavier than the well-known *Tyrannosaurus rex*. In fact, some scientists believe the fossil skull of a *Carcharodontosaurus* found in Africa in 1995 indicates that the dinosaur may have been the largest meat-eater of all—although this is highly debated. Another carnosaur was the *Spinosaurus,* from the late Cretaceous period, in Niger and Egypt, Africa; they are known for the tall spines on their back.

Did any **ceratosaurs** live in the Cretaceous period?

There were some ceratosaurs (Ceratosauria, or "horned reptiles")—theropods that arose during the Triassic period and grew in number during the Jurassic period—in the Cretaceous period. One is from a group of unusual ceratosaurs, called the Abelisauridae, from South America. The up-to-30-foot- (9-meter-) long, strange-looking, horned dinosaur was called a *Carnotaurus* ("flesh bull").

What **two carnosaurs** became famous in **World War II**?

In 1944, two carnosaurs were among several dinosaurs destroyed by allied bombers at the Barvarian State Museum in Munich, Germany: a *Spinosaurus* and *Carcharodontosaurus*. Other dinosaur skeletons destroyed were types of *Aegyptosaurus* and *Bahariasaurus*.

What were the **coelurosaurs** like in the Cretaceous period?

During the Cretaceous period, there was little change in the coelurosaurs (Ceratosauria), except they continued to diversify. They were still composed of ornithomimosaurs, maniraptorans, and tyrannosaurs.

What were the **ornithomimosaurs** like in the Cretaceous period?

The ornithomimosaurs (Ornithomimidae, or "bird mimics"), were ostrich-like dinosaurs, similar to those in the Jurassic period. They had long, flexible necks and a small head; they also had long forelimbs. These dinosaurs had no upper teeth and their lower teeth were not well developed. Ornithomimosaurs probably reached lengths of up to 20 feet (6 meters).

What were the **maniraptorans** like in the Cretaceous period?

The maniraptorans (Maniraporta, or "seizing hands") greatly diversified during the Cretaceous period. They included the dromaeosaurs, troodontids, therizinosaurs, and oviraptorosaurs.

What were the **unique characteristics** of the **dromaeosaurs**?

The dromaeosaurs, also known as dromaeosaurids (Dromaeosauridae), are dinosaurs the general public associates with the term "raptor." These dinosaurs were members of the maniraptorans and, therefore, may share a common ancestor with birds; some paleontologists even speculate that birds are highly evolved dromaeosaurs.

This group ranged widely in size—from just about the size of a large dog to 30 feet (9 meters) long. These dinosaurs had large, clawed, grasping hands, a stiffened tail that may have acted as a stabilizer, muscular toothy jaws, and a large, retractable, slashing claw on the second toe of each foot. They were probably agile, predatory dinosaurs. The discovery of their remains revolutionized the way we view dinosaur metabolism and behavior.

What were the **unique characteristics** of the **troodontids**?

The troodontids (Troodontidae) are a small group within the maniraptorans, with only a few fossils remains found (there are currently only about five known species). They are only known from a few incomplete specimens found in North America and Mongolia.

These dinosaurs were about the size of a small adult human, with a long skull, unique recurved and saw-edged teeth, large, flexible hands, and long, slender legs. The troodontids were probably fast, agile hunters. And although they had an enlarged claw on their feet, it was not as large as those of the dromaeosaurs—and was probably not used in the same way.

The most unique characteristic of the troodontids was the size of their brain case—it was the largest, relative to body size, of all the dinosaurs. This may indicate that the troodontids were the most intelligent of all the dinosaurs, although this is only speculation. The skull had large eye openings (orbits), and there appears to be evidence for well-developed centers for sight and hearing. Unfortunately, the fossil record for these dinosaurs is very rare and incomplete.

What were the **unique characteristics** of the **therizinosaurs** (or segnosaurs)?

The therizinosaurs (Therizinosauridae), also known as segnosaurs (Segnosauridae), were completely unique. These dinosaurs had so many unique characteristics that they were first grouped with the sauropods. They were then made into a separate

What were the unique characteristics of the oviraptorosaurs?

The oviraptorosaurs (Oviraptoridae, or "egg snatchers") were once thought to be ornithomimosaurs, but are now considered to be maniraptorans. The oviraptorosaurs were human-sized, with distinctive skull features, grasping hands, and slender limbs.

The skull is the most unique feature of these animals, with a prominent crest containing a large nasal cavity. The function of this crest is unknown, but it may have been used for heat regulation or making sounds. The short, deep skull also had toothless jaws, but they were well-muscled for crushing food. Originally thought to have eaten eggs, the oviraptorids are now thought to have used their muscled jaws to crush mollusks—or perhaps they were omnivorous, eating small animals and some plants.

group of the saurischians, and most recently placed with the maniraptorans based on various features of their skulls, pelvis, and forelimbs.

The therizinosaurs were very large, with a heavy build; they had four toes, similar to sauropods, and were quadrupeds (four-footed). They had large leaflike teeth; the skull shows evidence of cheeks, which means they probably ate plants. They also had hollow bones of the theropods, a pubis bone that pointed backwards, a relatively short tail—and enormous, 3-foot- (1-meter-) long claws on each hand.

Because not many therizinosaur fossils have been found, little is known about their behavior. Some scientists suggest that these animals were amphibious fish-eaters; others believe these dinosaurs were herbivores, based on their teeth, possible cheeks, and snout. It is also thought that the therizinosaurs were slow-moving animals.

What were the **tyrannosaurs**?

The tyrannosaurs, also known as tyrannosaurids (Tyrannosauridae, or "tyrant lizard"), were extremely large carnivores that lived during the Cretaceous period. These "tyrant lizards" were the dominant predators of the time, growing close to 50 feet (15 meters) long. They were characterized by a long muscular tails, tiny arms, beady eyes, short, deep jaws, and long legs.

Are the **tyrannosaurs** classified as **carnosaurs or coelurosaurs**?

The tyrannosaurs, of which *Tyrannosaurus rex* is the most well-known member, have traditionally been placed in the carnosaur group. After all, this group included the large, bipedal (two-footed), carnivorous dinosaurs—and the *Tyrannosaurus rex* certainly fit all those criteria! However, modern cladistic analysis has shown that the tyrannosaurs are more closely related to the coelurosaurs than the carnosaurs—and are now placed in the former group.

What are some examples of **theropods** in the Cretaceous period?

The following tables, describing the Ceratosauria, Carnosauria, and Coelurosauria orders, are some examples of the various theropod dinosaurs of the Cretaceous period.

Ceratosauria

Species	Comments
Carnotaurus	This bizarre dinosaur grew up to 30 feet (9 meters) long; it had a short head with a horn, and stumpy arms.

Carnosauria

Species	Comments
Spinosaurus	This dinosaur grew to 40 feet (12 meters) long, and was similar in appearance to *Allosaurus;* it had 6-foot- (2-meter-) long spines on its back that are thought to have supported a sail; this structure may have played a part in the dinosaur's thermo-regulation; most of the remains have been found in North Africa.

Coelurosauria

Family	Genus	Species	Comments
Ornithomimids		*Gallimimus*	This dinosaur ("chicken mimic") probably ate insects and small animals; it lived in Mongolia about 70 million years ago and is the largest and most completely known of the ornithomimosaurs; this dinosaur was featured in the movie *Jurassic Park*.
		Deinocheirus	Only a pair of 10-foot- (3-meter-) long forelegs and hands have been found of this dinosaur, which may have been one of the largest of the ornithomimosaurs; the forelegs are on display at the American Museum of Natural History in New York.
Maniraptora	Dromaeosaurs	*Deinonychus*	This dinosaur measured up to 10 feet (3 meters) long and weighed

Coelurosauria

Family	Genus	Species	Comments
			approximately 180 pounds, about the size of a mountain lion; these dromaeosaurs had large sickle-shaped claws on the feet; some fossil evidence indicates a pack-hunting behavior; fossils have been found in North America.
		Velociraptor	This dinosaur name means "quick plunderer" or "swift seizer"; it was a dromaeosaur about the size of a large dog, almost 6 feet (1.8 meters) long, with a weight of approximately 100 pounds; it had a sickle-shaped slashing claw on each foot; fossils are found in Mongolia and it was prominent in the movie *Jurassic Park*—but in reality, the dinosaur was much smaller.
		Utahraptor	This dinosaur was up to 21 feet (6.5 meters) long, with a large, sickle-shaped claw on its foot; it is the largest known dromaeosaur found in North America.
	Troodontids	*Saurornithoides*	This troodontid from Mongolia, meaning "birdlike reptile," was a carnivorous dinosaur about 6.5 feet (2 meters) long; its skull had a long, rather birdlike narrow muzzle; the teeth were small, with many teeth in the upper jaw; the teeth's back edges were serrated; it had a large brain and large saucerlike eyes, probably for hunting small animals at dusk.
		Troodon	This troodontid, found in North America, had large eyes and possible binocular vision; it was similar to its cousin, the Saurornithodes.
	Therizinosaurs	*Therizinosaurus*	This therizinosaur, possibly herbivorous, had a relatively short tail, and huge forelimbs with

165

Family	Genus	Species	Comments
			enormous sickle-shaped claws; they are thought to be closely related to birds.
		Alxasaurus	A therizinosaur from Mongolia; it had longer finger bones than the Therizinosaurus; it is thought to be the most primitive known member of the therizinosaurs.
		Erlikosaurus	This therizinosaur is from Mongolia; one fossil of this animal is currently the only therizinosaur skull known; it is long, with elongated external nasal openings and a toothless beak.
		Segnosaurus	The *Segnosaurus* is a therizinosaur from Mongolia; they had massive arm bones and grew up to 13 feet (4 meters) long.
	Oviraptorosaurs	*Oviraptor*	The "egg snatcher or thief" had a bizarre head crest; it was originally thought to prey on others' eggs, but more recent findings show them brooding eggs in nests, although it is still debated as to weather or not they ate eggs; most scientists believe the animals' jaws were not useful for eating eggs, but for crushing food.
		Caenagnathus	This oviraptorosaur, "recent jawless," grew up to 6 feet (2 meters) in length; like all oviraptorosaurs, it had a toothless jaw that was well muscled and perfect for crushing.
Tyrannosaurids		*Albertosaurus*	The "lizard from Alberta" is found in Canada; it grew to up to 30 feet (9 meters) long.
		Nanotyrannus	The "dwarf tyrant" is a small version of at tyrannosaur from Montana; there is debate as to whether the discovered bone were from an adult or juvenile.

Coelurosauria

Family	Genus	Species	Comments
		Daspletosaurus	The "frightful lizard" is from Canada, and was slightly smaller than the *Tyrannosaurus rex*.
		Tarbosaurus	Very similar—almost a mirror image cousin—to the *Tyrannosaurus rex;* the "terror lizard" is from Mongolia.
		Tyrannosaurus	One of the largest and most famous of the land-dwelling carnivores; it reached up to 46 feet (14 meters) long and 18.5 feet (5.6 meters) tall; fossils suggest the females were larger than the males.

ORNITHISCHIAN DINOSAURS

How are the **ornithischian dinosaurs** of the Cretaceous period **classified**?

The ornithischian dinosaurs were the most numerous and diverse of the Cretaceous period dinosaurs. Similar to the ornithischian dinosaurs of the Jurassic period, these dinosaurs were all members of the group Genasauria, which is subdivided into the thyreophorans (Thyreophora) and the cerapods (Cerapoda). In the Cretaceous period, the thyreophorans are represented by the stegosaurs (Stegosauria) and the ankylosaurs (Ankylosauria), as they were in the Jurassic period.

The Cerapoda are more difficult to classify—because there is still no universally accepted classification of the ornithopods as a whole. The main reason is obvious: there are so few fossils found of some of these animals that it has been difficult to truly classify the creatures. Here are a few examples of the disagreements:

1) In some classifications, the Cerapoda are divided into the Ornithopoda (or Euornithopoda) and the Marginocephalia—both of which diversified tremendously during the Cretaceous period.

2) In another classification, the ornithischians are divided into the Ornithopoda, Thyreophora, and Marginocephalia.

167

3) In yet another classification, the Ornithopoda are divided into the Euornithopoda, which is then subdivided into the Hypsilophodontidae and Iguanodontia; and the Iguanodontia are further divided into iguanodontids and hadrosaurs.

This volume uses the first classification mentioned for the cerapods.

What **changes** occurred in the **thyreophorans** during the Cretaceous period?

There were many changes in the thyreophoran subgroups of the stegosaurs and ankylosaurs. In particular, few species of the stegosaurs survived into the Cretaceous period.

The ankylosaurs fared much better, with the best-preserved fossils coming from Mongolia and China; others are also known from North America, Europe, and Australia. In fact, these plant-eating animals were so huge and heavily armored by the end of the Cretaceous period, they probably didn't have to worry about predators!

What **changes** occurred in the **cerapods** during the Cretaceous period?

There were more major changes in the cerapods during the Cretaceous period than in the thyreophorans; these ornithopods became more diversified and the marginocephalians evolved.

What were the **changes** in the **ornithopods** during the Cretaceous period?

Overall, the Cretaceous period ornithopods still carried the characteristics that made them ornithopods—but they did increase in number and diversify. They were still medium to large plant-eaters and, in general, mostly bipedal (two-footed); they ranged from small, less than 3 feet (1 meter) tall and 6 feet (2 meters) long, to large, about 23 feet (7 meters) tall and 66 feet (20 meters) long. And they further developed their teeth, cheeks, and ability to chew over the millions of years of the Cretaceous period.

The animals also seemed to change certain physical characteristics. In particular, the ornithopods could walk, or in some cases trot, on all four feet; at higher speeds, they were probably mostly bipedal. Their feet also started to change, with some evolving into more hooflike shapes. Others developed hands that could probably grasp vegetation. And still others, as they grew in size, changed their structures to support more weight—including the number of back vertebrae connecting the pelvis to the backbone.

In the Cretaceous period, the ornithopods included such dinosaurs as the heterodontosaurids, hypsilophodonts, iguanodontians, and hadrosaurs. This list includes one of the earliest discovered dinosaurs, the *Iguanodon,* as well as the famous crested and "duck-billed" hadrosaurs—the most diverse and successful groups under the ornithopods.

What were the **heterodontosaurs** like?

The heterodontosaurs were fast-moving herbivorous dinosaurs that averaged about 3 feet (1 meter) long. They had caninelike teeth, relatively long arms, and large hands. They were also some of the most primitive ornithopods. Some scientists believe that the animals may have been the first ornithopods with teeth—long fangs used for cutting and slicing vegetation or for defense. The animals' hands also may have had some grasping abilities—and they may have used their hands to dig burrows that could have been used as shelter or as aestivation "dens" (aestivation is lying dormant during the hotter times of the year, the opposite of hibernation some animals experience in the winter). Some heterodontosaurs may have also replaced all their teeth at once—depending on the amount of wear.

What were the **hypsilophodontids** like?

The hypsilophodontids were a family of dinosaurs that arose in the Middle Jurassic—and are considered one of the first ornithopod groups to appear worldwide. They were a bit longer than the heterodontosaurs—about an average of 5 feet (almost 2 meters) long—and some scientists compare the animal's size and movements to today's gazelles. They had chisel-shaped cheek teeth overlapping each other, heavy hindlegs (most likely for stability when running), and had a light build. They may have also nested at the same roosting place each year.

No complete skeletons have ever been found, but a recent discovery of such an animal in Texas rock layers may add new information. One fossil did show something strange: a *Hypsilophodon* with a broken leg that apparently healed. This could mean the animal was able to survive a severe injury—or, as some scientists speculate, it may indicate that other *Hypsilophodons* tended the injured member until it healed.

169

What were the **iguanodons** like?

The first dinosaur ever discovered by Gideon Mantell was an *Iguanodon.* The iguanodons evolved in the early Cretaceous period, and were one of the early ornithopods. This dinosaur was larger than the heterodontosaurs and hypsilophodontids, and was fast and strong. They had long, heavy forelegs, and probably walked on all fours. They measured about 33 feet (10 meters) long, had up to 29 teeth per tooth row (on the sides of their jaws for chewing)—and a unique, conical thumb "spike" on the first digit of their hands that may have been used for defense.

What were some **general characteristics** of the **hadrosaurs**?

The hadrosaurs ("duck-billed" dinosaurs), were some of the most peculiar dinosaurs that thrived during the Cretaceous period—and the last ornithopod group ever to appear. Amazingly, these dinosaurs were similar to modern ducks: they had beaks, webbed feet, and a pelvis like a duck. Hadrosaurs also had stiff tails supported by strong, bonelike tendons, and their lost teeth were rapidly replaced. These dinosaurs probably spent most of their life close to bodies of waters, feeding on tough plants; they apparently had their young on higher ground in large nesting areas.

Most of the duck-billed dinosaurs are found in late Cretaceous rocks in Europe, Asia, and North America. They are close relatives—and some say descendants—of the earlier iguanodontid dinosaurs. The two subfamilies of the hadrosaurs were the Lambeosaurinae and the Hadrosaurinae.

How did the **Lambeosaurinae** and **Hadrosaurinae**—subfamilies of the hadrosaurs—**differ**?

Several of the hadrosaur dinosaurs are noted for the spacious and bizarre-shaped sinus regions in their skulls. In particular, the Lambeosaurinae had a crest on the skull; the Hadrosaurinae, such as the *Maiasaura* and *Edmontosaurus,* lacked any crest.

The crest on the lambeosaur's skull contained nasal passages looping through the crest and into some very large chambers before they went into the airway. There have been many suggestions as to the reason for such a crest, including its use as a snorkel (but it had no opening to the outside) or as a way to warm the air they breathed (but the climate was already warm). But the most accepted idea is that the crest acted like a resonance chamber, allowing the animals to make deep, loud calls to attract mates (either by the noise, by the odd shapes, or both), scare away predators, or keep a herd or young together.

Why are **marginocephalian** dinosaurs listed only in the **Cretaceous** period?

The marginocephalians were actually latecomers in dinosaur evolution, first appearing in early Cretaceous sediments, chiefly in North America and Central Asia. They are divided into the pachycephalosaurs (Pachycephalosauria, or "thick-headed reptiles") and the ceratopsians (Ceratopsia, or "horned dinosaurs").

What were the **marginocephalians**?

The marginocephalians were one of the three major groups of ornithischians. They were closely related to the ornithopods; some scientists believe the marginocephalians may have originated from the ornithopods, especially the heterodontosaurs. The marginocephalians, or "fringed heads," were herbivorous dinosaurs that had a slight shelf or frill at the back of their skull. The frill or shelf differed in the two main subgroups of the marginocephalians—the "bone-headed" pachycephalosaurs and the frilled ceratopsians.

What were the **pachycephalosaurs** like?

The pachycephalosaurs ("thick-headed reptiles") were bipedal dinosaurs, with short forelimbs. Some scientists believe the animals' thick skulls were used for head butting: the angle of the skull and backbone indicates that the animal's normal posture was head down with the dome of the head forward.

What were the **ceratopsians** like?

The ceratopsians ("horny faces") appeared in the early Cretaceous; by the late Cretaceous, about 100 million years ago, the animals began to diversify in North America and Asia. They were the biggest of all the dinosaur families and lasted a total of about 35 million years. There were frill-less and hornless ceratopsians, including the *Protoceratops* from Mongolia, and the unusual, bipedal *Psittacosaurus*. The huge, horned, frilled ceratopsians were found only in the late Cretaceous period of North America—and were some of the last known dinosaurs to have roamed the planet.

Some ceratopsians were bipedal, some quadruped; it is thought that the quadruped ceratopsians evolved from bipedal dinosaurs, as their front legs are shorter than their rear legs. They also evolved very strong front legs—strong enough to hold up their massive heads. And they ranged from turkey- to elephant-sized animals.

The ceratopsians probably traveled in herds. One reason for this suggestion are the huge number of bones from hundreds of individual, same-species ceratopsians discovered in the western United States—in so-called "bone beds." Such a large number of the animals in one place suggests the dinosaurs were traveling together when a

171

Why did some ceratopsians have head frills?

The ceratopsian frills may have been the animal's armor to protect itself from predators such as the *Tyrannosaurs rex,* which lived at the same time and locale as the *Triceratops.* There are other ceratopsians that had smaller frills or frills with large openings—not good for defense. Thus, some scientist suggest the frills may have been used as heat radiators, signaling devices, or for attracting mates. In fact, recent studies of the inside of the bony frill indicate that certain parts held different temperatures—supporting the idea of heat radiators.

tragedy hit, killing them all. Traveling in such large groups, the larger animals (with their threatening huge horns and frills) could circle and protect the weaker and young ceratopsians; other times, the group could stampede to escape or attack predators.

What were the **general characteristics** of the *Triceratops*?

The *Triceratops* ("three-horned face") was a ceratopsian that measured up to 30 feet (9 meters) long; it had beaked jaws and three large horns (two long and one short). They also had huge, heavy frills around their long heads, but they don't hold the record for the largest frills, just the most lasting: the *Triceratops*' bones are some of the strongest, most solid dinosaur bones known—so well built that many have survived over 65 million years. The animals had also become well adapted to feed on tough vegetation. They had beaks to slice the plants and rows of teeth to chew.

What were some **ornithischian** dinosaurs during the Cretaceous period?

The ornithischian dinosaurs were even more diverse and numerous than the saurischian dinosaurs during the Cretaceous period. The following tables, describing the Thyreophora, Ceropoda, and Marginocephalia orders, describe some examples of the types of dinosaurs present in this group.

Thyreophora

Species	Comments
Ankylosaurus	These dinosaurs grew up to 33 feet (10 meters) long; they had a wide head, with triangular horns and bony plates covering their bodies; for defense, they used their stiffened club-shaped tail; many fossils are found in North America.

A *Styracosaurus* model stands on a riverbank at Dinosaur Provincial Park in Alberta, Canada. A spiked collar and rhino–like horn helped the animal fend off his main enemy, *Albertosaurus,* during the late Cretaceous period. (Photo courtesy of Jonathan Blair/Corbis.)

Ceropoda

Family	Genus	Species	Comments
Ornithopods	Iguanodontids	*Tenontosaurus*	This animal's fossils are found mostly in North America; it was a transitional form to the more advanced iguanodontians; it was up to 13 feet (4 meters) long with a very long, stiffened tail.
		Iguanodon	Iguanodon fossils are found in Europe and North America; it was also the first dinosaur fossil ever found; it grew up to about 33 feet (10 meters) long and probably chiefly moved on all fours; it had a conical thumb spike on the first digit of its hand.
	Hadrosaurs	*Edmontosaurus*	These are the true "duck-bills" with broadened, flat snouts; fossils are found in North America.

Family	Genus	Species	Comments
		Shantungosaurus	This largest known hadrosaur is found in China; it measured approximately 50 feet (15 meters) long—as big as many sauropods.
		Hadrosaurus	This is a flat-headed dinosaur; the fossils are found in North America and was the first skeleton ever to be mounted.
		Saurolophus	Solid, narrow, backward-pointing crest above the eyes; most fossils are from North America.
		Gryposaurus	The prominent, "Roman-nosed" snout was produced by the animal's arched nasal bones; many fossils are from North America.
		Maiasaura	This dinosaur means "good mother reptile or lizard"; it is known from nesting sites, fossil eggs, and hatchlings; one main site was found in North America.
		Corythosaurus	This North American dinosaur has a flat-sided, rounded crest on its head.
		Parasaurolophus	This dinosaur's head crest is the shape of an elongated tube that extends backward behind the skull; many fossils are from North America.
	Hypsilophodontids	*Orodromeus*	This North American dinosaur was found in Montana; it was up to 6 feet (2 meters) in length.
		Hypsilophodon	The "high-ridged tooth" dinosaur may have been one of the fastest running ornithischian dinosaurs; at one time, scientists thought it lived in trees, but there is little indication of this; it had a horny beak to cut vegetation and its teeth could easily grind plants.

Paleontologist Paul Sereno walks behind a model of the five-foot-long *Carcharodontosaurus* skull his team discovered in the Moroccan Sahara. This is the most complete skull ever found from the close of the dinosaur era in Africa. (Photo courtesy of Denis Paquin/Associated Press.)

Ceropoda

Family	Genus	Species	Comments
	Heterodontosaurs	*Heterodontosaurus*	This dinosaur, the "different-toothed lizard," averaged about 3 feet (1 meter) in length; some scientists believe it may have burrowed in the ground in the summer.

Marginocephalia

Family	Species	Comments
Pachycephalosaurs	*Pachycephalosaurus*	This dinosaur's thickened skull was ornamented with bony knobs, and is thought to have been used in head butting; most fossils come from North America.
	Stegoceras	This dinosaur was about 6 feet (2 meters) long; the females and males had different thicknesses in skulls.

175

What is the oldest known hadrosaur?

The oldest known hadrosaur ("duck-billed"), and the most primitive, was the *Protohadros byrdi;* a 95.5-million-year-old fossil of this animal was recently discovered in Texas. This plant-eating dinosaur was about 15 to 20 feet (4.6 to 6 meters) long and 6 feet (1.8 meters) high at the shoulder. It could probably walk on two legs as well as four, and had a complex way of chewing.

The discovery of *Protohadros byrdi* in Texas, along with its age and primitive features, makes North America a good candidate location for the origin of duck-billed dinosaurs. Previously, paleontologists believed these types of dinosaurs originated more than 90 million years ago in eastern Asia.

Marginocephalia

Family	Species	Comments
Ceratopsia	*Psittacosaurus*	This dinosaur's fossils are found in Mongolia; the "parrot lizard" was a primitive ceratopsian; it was bipedal, with a very rudimentary frill, and is therefore often considered to be frill-less; it was only recently discovered to be a ceratopsian.
	Protoceratops	This Mongolian dinosaur was quadrupedal, with a prominent, but short, frill, and is therefore often considered to be frill-less.
	Leptoceratops	A small-bodied ceratopsian from the late Cretaceous period in Montana, U.S. and Alberta, Canada; it had no horns or large neck frill.
	Styracosaurus	This animal had a frill bordered by long spikes; most fossils are found in North America.
	Triceratops	The *Triceratops* is another well-known dinosaur from North America; it had a nose horn, and paired horns over the eyes; it was up to 26 feet (8 meters) long,

Marginocephalia

Family	Species	Comments
		with a short, solid frill, and was one of the last species of dinosaurs to roam the earth.
	Torosaurus	This North American dinosaur had a longer frill than *Triceratops;* its 6-foot (2-meter) skull is one of the longest of any known land animal.

GENERAL CRETACEOUS DINOSAUR FACTS

Which **major dinosaurs** from the **Cretaceous period** were **herbivores**?

All of the remaining sauropods, such as *Saltasaurus, Alamosaurus,* and *Argentinosaurus,* were plant-eaters. The most numerous and diverse herbivores in the Cretaceous, however, were the ornithischians (whose hips resembled those of birds), including the duck-billed ornithopods, the horned ceratopsians, the thick-headed pachycephalosaurs, and the armored ankylosaurs.

Which **major dinosaurs** from the Cretaceous period were **carnivores**?

The major carnivorous dinosaurs of the Cretaceous period were from the saurischian (lizard-hipped) groups, and were theropods. They included the large carnosaurs such as *Giganotosaurus, Carcharodonotosaurus,* and *Tyrannosaurus,* as well as the smaller, more agile dromaeosaurs, such as *Velociraptor, Deinonychus,* and *Utahraptor.*

What were the **smallest dinosaurs** known in the **Cretaceous period**?

It is difficult to determine the smallest dinosaurs known from the Cretaceous period—there were very few, as most of the "smaller" dinosaurs were about 5 to 6 feet (1.5 to 2 meters) in length, such as the *Avimimus*. In general, the smallest herbivorous and carnivorous dinosaurs could be as small as a chicken. Most of the carnivorous ones ate insects as their main supply of food; and of course, the smallest herbivores ate plants.

What were the **largest dinosaurs** known in the **Cretaceous period**?

Scientists probably have yet to uncover the largest dinosaurs of the Cretaceous period, although they will likely come from the *Sauropoda* suborder. The herbivorous

177

The last dinosaurs apparently lived in the western regions of North America. Their remains have been found through the late Cretaceous period rocks. In other regions of the world they disappeared well before the end of this period.

sauropods have small heads, long necks, and long tails. One of the largest and most relatively complete skeletons comes from the *Brachiosaurus* of Tanzania, Africa, which measured up to 75 feet (23 meters) in length. But this sauropod didn't make it through the Cretaceous—it evolved around the late Jurassic period and died out during the early Cretaceous.

More recent fossil discoveries may lead to even larger sauropods. One includes the massive herbivorous dinosaur *Argentinosaurus huinculensis,* a South American sauropod of the Titanosauridae family. But this fossil is still difficult to interpret, as it is only known from vertebrae and limb bone fossils.

The largest carnivorous dinosaur from the Cretaceous period seems to be a toss-up between the perennial favorite and two newcomers. The favorite is the theropod *Tyrannosaurus* found in North America and Asia and measuring over 40 feet (12 meters) in length. The two new challengers are the *Giganotosaurus* of South America and the *Carcharodontosaurus* of North Africa. Both of these huge, meat-eating theropods are thought to have been bigger—and even heavier—than the *Tyrannosaurus.*

What was the **largest ornithomimosaur,** the ostrich-like dinosaur, known from the **Cretaceous period**?

The largest currently known ornithomimosaur was the *Gallimimus,* a late Cretaceous dinosaur that grew up to 20 feet (6 meters) in length. The *Deinocheirus* may have been a large ornithomimosaur, but the only fossil evidence to date is a pair of 10-foot (3-meter) forelegs and hands.

What was the **top predator** among the Cretaceous dinosaurs?

It's a matter of opinion which Cretaceous dinosaur was the "top predator." The carnivorous dinosaurs were all vicious as they attacked their prey. Some, like *Tyrannosaurus,* used their size to catch their meals; while others, like pack-hunters such as the *Velociraptor,* trapped their prey as a unit. Or was it better to be fast or even agile, such as the *Utahraptor* or *Megaraptor*? Answers vary among scientists and laypeople alike.

What is the **oldest known horned** dinosaur?

The oldest known horned dinosaur is the *Zuniceratops christopheri.* The fossil remains of this animal were recently discovered by Chris Wolfe, an eight-year-old third-grader from Phoenix, Arizona! This dinosaur lived some 90 to 92 million years ago, had three horns, and might have been 10 to 12 feet (3 to 3.7 meters) long, with a weight of approximately 500 pounds. The remains were discovered in western New Mexico and include jaw parts, the brain case, teeth, a horn, and the brow.

What recently discovered dinosaur may have **eaten fish**?

Dinosaurs called spinosaurids—which lived in areas of modern Africa, Europe, and South America between 90 and 120 million years ago—may have eaten fish. Three other spinosaurids have been found, but *Suchomimus tenerensis,* a previously unknown species, is the most unique: its remains were recently discovered in the Tenere Desert of Africa—complete with features ideal for catching and eating fish.

Of course, approximately 100 million years ago, the fish were a little bigger, upwards of 6 feet (2 meters) long. To catch the fish, *Suchomimus tenerensis* had to be larger—about 36 feet (11 meters) long to be exact! The name *Suchomimus tenerensis* comes from *souchos,* the Greek word for "crocodile," and *tener,* referring to the desert where the remains were discovered.

How did *Suchomimus tenerensis* **catch and eat fish**?

Suchomimus tenerensis had a large variety of features enabling it to catch and eat fish: it had a long, pointy snout, razor teeth, and foot-long curved claws. The recently discovered remains of *Suchomimus tenerensis* were not yet fully grown, but was still 36 feet (11 meters) long, as big as a *Tyrannosaurus rex;* a fully grown adult would probably be 3 to 4 feet (1 to 1.2 meters) bigger. To get an idea of this animal's size, an averaged-sized human standing next to *Suchomimus tenerensis* would reach the dinosaur's knee level. The shape of *Suchomimus tenerensis* was also similar to a *Tyrannosaurus rex*—it had two large hindlegs, forearms, a powerful tail, and a large head.

The most distinctive feature of *Suchomimus tenerensis* was its long pointy snout, similar to that of a crocodile. This snout contained approximately 100 lightly curved and hooked teeth, similar to today's fish-eating crocodiles. The end of the snout had an extra chinlike projection, known as a rosette, containing the largest teeth. The teeth would mesh together when the jaws were closed, in order to securely hook the prey. The snout and teeth were not used for chewing, but for grabbing, securing, then swallowing fish.

The hands of *Suchomimus tenerensis* were also adapted for grabbing fish. The thumbs were approximately 16 inches (.4 meter) long, and tipped with sickle-shaped 1-foot (.3-meter) claws. The two fingers of each hand also had curved, but shorter, claws.

Which **animal** probably **competed** with *Suchomimus tenerensis* **for fish**?

The crocodile probably competed with the *Suchomimus tenerensis* for fish, since both lived at the same time. Both animals lived around the area now in central Africa because of its lushness and the presence of water—and fish that grew up to 6 feet (2 meters) long. But these ancient crocodiles were much larger than modern crocodiles. They were long-snouted and had skulls up to 6 feet (2 meters) long, making these crocodiles a formidable 50 feet (15 meters) long. You can imagine what it was like: the huge *Suchomimus tenerensis* and giant crocodiles constantly fighting over fish!

Did any **dinosaur species survive** the extinction at the **end of the Cretaceous** period?

The general consensus among scientists is that no dinosaur species survived the mass extinction at the end of the Cretaceous period. There are a few paleontologists who don't believe that the dinosaurs died off at the end of the Cretaceous period, but actually lived on, dying out gradually during the Cenozoic era. This theory will continue to be highly debated until dinosaur fossils are proven to exist past the Cretaceous period in rocks. Some scientists claim they have found such evidence, but their findings are still controversial.

In addition, if the definition of dinosaurs includes the birds, then, yes, this family of dinosaurs did survive the extinction. After the Cretaceous period, birds greatly diversified into numerous species—and as we all know, these are species that are living everywhere on the planet today.

What was the **last** dinosaur **species** to arise?

Scientists have determined there were two late-arriving species. The latest known species of dinosaurs to arise in the late Cretaceous period were the *Triceratops,* a herbivore, and *Tyrannosaurus rex,* a carnivore.

OTHER LIFE IN THE CRETACEOUS PERIOD

Were there any **insects** during the **Cretaceous period**?

In addition to some earlier forms, such as dragonflies that had survived into the Cretaceous period, many new groups of insects evolved and diversified. Their success is thought to be due to their joint evolution with the new flowering plants that arose during this time period.

Cretaceous Period Insects

Insect	Description
Dragonflies	Diversified in Carboniferous and Permian periods; many groups continued to modern times
Beetles	Continued from Jurassic
Flies	Continued from Jurassic; some believe fly ancestors may have evolved during the Triassic period
Butterflies	Fossils known only from early Cretaceous onward
Moths	Fossils known only from early Cretaceous onward
Ants	Fossils known only from early Cretaceous onward
Bees	True bees developed; fossils known only from early Cretaceous onward
Wasps	Fossils known only from early Cretaceous onward
Termites	Fossils known only from early Cretaceous onward
Hymenopterans	Sawflies evolved from the Triassic

What kind of **plants** made their **first appearance** during the **Cretaceous period**?

The kind of plants that made their first appearance during the Cretaceous period were the angiosperms, or flowering plants. These plants had flowers and a fully enclosed ovule. Their pollen was present on long stamens found around a central area that contained the ovaries. This pollen was transported to the stigma, a sticky surface above the ovule, by the action of the wind or, more importantly, by insects looking for nectar.

The plant's ability to flower and more controlled pollination allowed the angiosperms to become the dominate form of plant life by the end of the Cretaceous period. And as we can see just by looking around us, this has continued up to modern times.

What was the **earliest known flowering plant**?

The earliest known angiosperm, or flowering plant, was the *Archaefructus liaoningensis*. A fossil of this plant has been dated at 140 million years old, more than 25 million years older than the previous oldest-known angiosperm. The fossil remains of *Archaefructus liaoningensis* were found near the town of Beipiao, in China's Liaoning Province. Millions of years ago, the area was a lush, steamy forest. Many fine, well-preserved fossils have been found here—including the "feathered" dinosaurs.

However, there is still some debate about the age of the rock containing this ancient plant fossil. Some scientists believe the rock is 120 million years old—not 140 million years old. Even if this turns out to be true, *Archaefructus liaoningensis* would

Dragonflies and other insects thrived during the Cretaceous period. (Photo courtesy of Field Mark Publications.)

still be the earliest known angiosperm by at least 5 million years.

What are some characteristics of the *Archaefructus liaoningensis*?

From the fossil remains, paleontologists can only speculate on the height of *Archaefructus liaoningensis*. It was probably shrublike, perhaps several feet tall. The remains show two 3-inch- (7.6-centimeter-) long stems, with about two dozen carpels sprouting off them (carpels are pods that contain seeds). The *Archaefructus liaoningensis* carpels were leaflike structures, the fruit essentially being little more than few leaves wrapped around the seeds. Scientists think that *Archaefructus liaoningensis* was the earliest angiosperm, or flowering plant, because its fossil remains show the earliest known presence of these leafy, seed-containing carpels.

Carpels are the defining characteristic for angiosperms, whose very name means "seeds in vessels"; only flowering plants have carpels. But there were no flower petals or tasty fruits at this stage of evolution—angiosperms didn't develop showy flowers until some 70 million years ago, after bees evolved.

Based on *Archaefructus liaoningensis,* how did **angiosperms** probably **evolve**?

Some paleontologists believe angiosperms evolved from seed ferns, plants that produced their seeds on open leaves. Over time, a type of plant evolved that began to fold its leaves around the seeds, producing the first carpel and primitive fruit. The earliest

> ## What was the largest flying animal of the Cretaceous period?
>
> The largest flying animal of all was the *Quetzalcoatlus,* a late Cretaceous period pterosaur found in Texas. This giant of the sky, though not a dinosaur, was comparable in size to our modern small airplanes, with an estimated wingspan of 36 to 50 feet (11 to 15 meters).

known plant showing this characteristic is *Archaefructus liaoningensis,* with its leafy carpels. In this plant, the primitive fruits were essentially folded leaves containing the seeds—thus, it is considered to be the first angiosperm.

What were the **most common plants** growing during the **Cretaceous period**?

Some species of plants continued to evolve from previous periods, while others are known only from the Cretaceous onward. In the early Cretaceous, the cycads began their decline, leaving the conifers to dominate. Also in this time period, the angiosperms, or flowering plants, made their first appearance—considered the biggest environmental change during this time. The flowering plants diversified during the middle Cretaceous, taking over many areas that once held only the ferns and horsetails; by the end of the period, angiosperm diversity had surpassed that of the conifers. Of the 500 modern families of flowering plants, 50 appeared during the Cretaceous period, including the sycamore, magnolia, palm, holly, and trees of the willow and birch family.

The reason for the rapid spread of the flowering plants during the Cretaceous period may have been the dinosaurs themselves: as larger dinosaurs of the early Cretaceous began to trample the low-growing angiosperms, the plants grew back very rapidly—similar to today's flowering plants that respond to cutting by growing even more profuse. In addition, insects, passing dinosaurs, flying or gliding reptiles, and wind probably carried the angiosperm seeds to other areas.

What types of **small marine plants** lived during the **Cretaceous period**?

Tiny plants called diatoms (single-celled forms of algae, or plants with silica shells) came in many forms in the oceans. Their abundance led to great chalk deposits, such as the strip that runs from Great Britain to the Middle East, as the diatom "skeletons" or shells metamorphosed into a chalky limestone. Called *creta* in Latin, this chalk is the substance for which the Cretaceous period is named.

183

Model of a Pterosaur, one of the winged creatures of the Cretaceous period. (Photo courtesy of University of Michigan Exhibit, Museum of Natural History.)

Besides dinosaurs, what **other animals** were present during the **Cretaceous period**?

As in the Jurassic, many other animals surrounded the dinosaurs, competing for space and food. Most of them are familiar from the Triassic and Jurassic periods, while others diversified and evolved. But not all creatures survived; many became extinct, probably because competition increased.

Non-dinosaurian Land Animals of the Cretaceous Period

Class	Animal	Description
Amphibians	Frogs, salamanders, newts toads, caecilians	All modern amphibians; they continue to evolve and diversify.
Reptiles	Turtles	*Archelon,* a large sea turtle, grows up to 4 feet (1.2 meters) in length.
	Snakes	Earliest known snakes appear.
	Crocodiles	Many crocodiles become massive, including the *Deinosuchus,* a large terrestrial crocodile that reached 50 feet (15 meters) in length.
	Lizards	True lizards continue to evolve and diversify.

Non-dinosaurian Land Animals of the Cretaceous Period

Class	Animal	Description
Mammals	Triconodonts	Late Triassic to late Cretaceous mammals; one of the oldest fossil mammals; three cusps of teeth in a straight row give them their name.
	Symmetrodonts	Late Jurassic to early Cretaceous mammals; they had upper and lower cheek teeth with many cusps in a triangular pattern.
	Multituberculates	Late Jurassic to late Eocene mammals; they had cheek teeth with many cusps in more than one row; they probably filled a "rodent" niche that had once been filled by cynodont therasids, and was later filled by true rodents.
	Monotremes	First appearance; early Cretaceous to the present; these animals eventually lead to the true mammals (especially with hair and mammary glands); the only living form lays eggs (like a reptile duck-billed platypus).
	Early marsupials	First appearance; middle Cretaceous period to the present; these pouched animals had distinct lower and upper cheek teeth.
	Early placentals	First appearance; middle Cretaceous period to the present; the mother nourished her developing fetus through a placenta; the cheek teeth were even more elaborate; the late Cretaceous placental mammals include insectivores, or mammals that ate insects.

Were there any **flying animals** during the **Cretaceous period**?

The flying animals during the Cretaceous period were the pterosaurs, birds, and various winged insects. There were over 50 species of pterosaurs, and they were found everywhere except Antarctica. They all disappeared at the end of the Cretaceous period.

The birds, winged reptiles that began during the Jurassic period, greatly diversified during the Cretaceous period. There were also forms with reduced wings, such as the flightless, ground-dwelling *Patagopteryx* that looked like a chicken with very short wings; and the aquatic diving bird, *Baptornis,* also with tiny wings, webbed feet, and sharp teeth.

Winged insects also greatly diversified during the Cretaceous period—and quickly, probably in response to the arrival of the flowering plants.

How did the **pterosaurs** get around on the **ground**?

Similar to most birds today, the pterosaurs did not constantly fly in the sky. There were times that the animals had to land, either to rest or to feed. But how did these creatures get around on the surface?

In the past few years, paleontologists have found numerous footprints that reveal the possibilities. In the western United States, hundreds of fossilized tracks recently found are attributed to pterosaurs. The fossil impressions appear to be made by forelimbs and hindlimbs of the animals, suggesting that they walked on all fours like a bat. The trace fossils also show distinct toe and finger impressions, indicating that the pterosaurs had a four-toed triangular foot and three short, clawed fingers. A very elongated fourth finger also developed to support the wing, which the pterosaurs would fold backward over their body. Although most of the tracks in the United States showed only the three finger impressions, trace fossils of pterosaurs in France do show the impressions of a fourth finger.

But not all scientists agree: many believe these reptiles actually walked and ran on two legs (bipedal), similar to birds. Still other scientists don't believe the tracks found in the United States or France are those of pterosaurs, but suggest they were made by crocodiles (or crocodile-like reptiles). The problem is familiar: even though the impressions look like those a pterosaur would make, there are no other fossils—bones or other hard parts—around the site to confirm the identity.

What were the **major marine animals** living during the **Cretaceous period**?

As with all life in the Cretaceous, there was a mixture of the older groups and the emergence of modern, living groups. The Mesozoic "marine revolution" occurred during the Cretaceous period, and included the appearance of new, modern predators that could feed on the older, hard-shelled forms.

Many modern families of marine animals appeared during the Cretaceous period, including the modern crabs, clams, and snails; sharks also evolved into their modern families by the late Cretaceous. Larger animals included mollusks and lobsters. Amazingly, many bony fishes continued to evolve from much earlier periods than the Mesozoic era.

Marine reptiles still lived in the seas, most of them until the end of the Cretaceous. Mosasaurs, or marine lizards with paddlelike flippers that grew up to 33 feet (10 meters) in length, were around until the late Cretaceous. Plesiosaurs and ichthyosaurs still swam in most of the oceans, but died out in the late Cretaceous. And there were also a few marine crocodiles left over from the Jurassic period.

DINOSAUR BONES

GROWING BONES

Why are **fossil bones important** to our understanding of dinosaurs?

The study of fossil bones is extremely important to our understanding of dinosaurs because, in most instances, this is the only way to obtain knowledge about these animals. Other than footprints and rare fossil remains of skin, eggs, and intestines, dinosaur fossilized bones (and teeth) are the only parts that survive over long spans of time. And depending on the way the bones lie, they are important clues as to how these animals looked, ate, walked, socialized, lived—and in some cases, died.

What does the **dinosaur skeleton** tell us about the animal's **soft parts**?

There are several ways in which scientists interpret soft parts based on a dinosaur's skeleton. For example, some muscles leave attachment scars on well-preserved bones. The size of the animal's skull sometimes tells us the relative size of the brain. The holes and hollow spaces in the bones could indicate pathways for nerves. And, most importantly, the comparison of dinosaur bones to those of living animals can give us a good idea of the size, anatomy, and strength of certain dinosaurs—and sometimes the internal configuration of a dinosaur's organs.

What is the **study of bones** called?

The field of science that deals with the study of bones is called osteology.

What is the **composition** of most dinosaur bones?

Most dinosaur bones—and teeth—are made of calcium phosphate, a material that is very hard and resistant to destruction. This explains why many dinosaur bones survive in rock layers. Those bones that didn't survive were usually destroyed by certain geologic processes. For example, many were crushed by moving rock (from earthquakes or volcanic eruptions), or dissolved by naturally occurring acidic water moving through cracks in the rock.

Dinosaur bone fossil at Dinosaur Quarry in Colorado's Dinosaur National Monument. The study of bones is called osteology. (Photo courtesy of Tom Bean/Corbis.)

What is **histology**?

Histology is the study of tissue structure. To study the bone tissues of dinosaurs, scientists cut out thin slices of bone and examine them using an optical microscope. Using a more complex instrument capable of viewing the bone tissue at very high magnifications, scientists search for very small features of the bone tissue structure.

What were **dinosaur bones made of**?

Contrary to popular belief, there is not just one type of dinosaur bone; these complex structures formed the skeletons of complex animals. There are volumes of dinosaur bone tissue studies—most based on the various stages of growth and development—and they cannot be completely explained in this text.

Overall, there were three main types of dinosaur bone tissue: the primary bone, Haversian (or secondary) bone, and growth ring bone tissue. These varied between the different bones in a dinosaur, and sometimes even within individual bones. And they certainly differed from dinosaur to dinosaur.

When did **primary bones** develop during a dinosaur's life?

Scientists believe primary bones, also called fibro-lamellar bones, were formed during the rapid growth phase of a dinosaur's life—in particular, when the dinosaur was young. These bones were very similar in structure to bones with blood vessels found in birds and mammals; the dinosaur's primary bones also contained blood vessels, which helped them to grow fast. These tissues are especially noticeable in fossilized dinosaur leg bones.

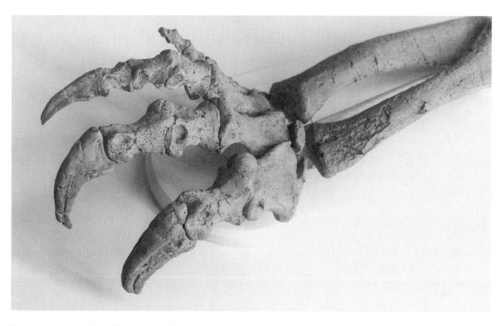

The bone structure of an *Allosaurus* hand. The bones of a dinosaur and a modern reptile are very similar. (Photo courtesy of University of Michigan Exhibit, Museum of Natural History.)

When did **Haversian (or secondary) bone tissue** develop during a dinosaur's life?

In some dinosaurs, the primary bone tissue was later replaced by Haversian bone tissue in a process called remodeling. These tissues had many blood vessels with dense, bony rings around them. This type of bone, similar to those of large modern mammals, had more strength and was more resistant to stress.

When did **growth ring bone tissue** develop during a dinosaur's life?

The growth ring bone tissue, found in some dinosaur bones and modern, cold-blooded reptiles, looks similar to growth rings found in trees. Tree rings grow each year, responding to changing seasonal conditions—and by counting the rings, it is sometimes possible to tell the approximate age of a tree.

The presence of similar structures in certain dinosaur bones suggests the animals' growth rates slowed later in life; one interpretation is that the animals became more reptilelike. One major problem is interpreting a dinosaur's growth ring bones: unlike a growth ring on a tree, no one knows the amount of time represented by each growth ring in a dinosaur bone.

189

How does bone composition compare between dinosaurs and modern reptiles?

The bones of a dinosaur and a modern reptile are very similar—with few minor additions or subtractions to bone composition over the millions of years of evolution. Scientists determine this by analyzing specially prepared bone tissues. The tissues are embedded in a synthetic polymer, sectioned and ground to the right thickness, then thinly carbon-coated for analysis in a scanning electron microscope (SEM).

In one instance, the bones of a modern alligator and a *Tyrannosaurus rex* were compared using an SEM with an energy dispersive X-ray (EDX) analyzer. The results showed that both bones had calcium and phosphorous as their major elements—with both elements present in the same ratios in ancient and modern bones. Some trace elements, such as magnesium, aluminum, silicon, and sodium, were also present.

What do these **three types of bone tissue** indicate about **dinosaurs**?

The presence of these three bone tissue structures (primary, secondary, and growth ring) suggests dinosaurs had a unique physiology—probably somewhere in between cold-blooded reptiles, and warm-blooded birds or mammals. Perhaps this unique physiology made dinosaurs extremely adaptable, and enabled them to dominate the land for about 150 million years.

Where are **extremely large dinosaur bones** being found and why?

Some of most consistently large dinosaur bone discoveries are being made in South America—especially in northwest Patagonia, in Argentina; this includes such examples as the *Giganotosaurus, Argentinosaurus,* and *Megaraptor.* And although scientists believe they know why these animals evolved differently from their northern counterparts, they truly don't know why the animals became so large.

One theory to explain the large South American animals involves locality. At the beginning of the Mesozoic era, all the land on the planet was merged into the continent of Pangea. During the Jurassic period, the supercontinent broke into the continent of Laurasia (which would eventually become North America, Europe, and Asia) and Gondwanaland (eventually Africa, Antarctica, Australia, India, and South America). And not long afterward, South America and Africa began to split apart.

Most scientists theorize these splits were the pivotal points in these large dinosaurs' evolution. For a short time, the dinosaurs crossed a land bridge from North to South America; geologic activity eventually destroyed the bridge, cutting off access and allowing creatures like the migrated *Megaraptor* to evolve separately in the south. The North American animals, such as the *Tyrannosaurus rex,* developed specialized skull, forelimbs, and pelvis; the South American dinosaurs, such as the *Giganotosaurus,* maintained most of the general features of their ancestors—and became much larger.

Other scientists believe that southern *Megaraptors* and their northern counterparts originally evolved separately from common ancestors. They suggest that the reason the two carnivorous giants such as the *Tyrannosaurus rex* and *Giganotosaurus,* resembled each other was due to similar environmental conditions. And when the landmasses began to break up, the animals continued to evolve separately.

Besides finding such large animals from long ago, scientists are also excited about another possibility: there is no doubt that environmental conditions differed greatly on all the continents. If this truly caused distinct differences in the dinosaurs, there are probably many different types of dinosaurs still to be discovered all around the world. But time will tell if scientists can determine the true reasons why the South American dinosaurs were giants of the Cretaceous world.

BUILDING DINOSAUR SKELETONS

What did **all dinosaur skeletons** have **in common**?

All dinosaurs had bony internal skeletons and four limbs—the common body "blueprint" for tetrapod vertebrates. Since dinosaurs evolved from the same general group of tetrapod vertebrate ancestors, they all share this common body blueprint.

What do **homologous** and **analogous** mean?

In terms of studying any animal skeleton—including dinosaurs—homologous is a word used to describe anatomical structures in organisms derived from the same such structure in a common ancestor. Analogous describes anatomical structures in different organisms that serve the same function, but are not derived from the same ancestral structure—such as the wings of pterosaurs, bats, and birds.

In general, how do scientists decide the **bone positions** of dinosaur skeletons?

Determining where bones go in a dinosaur skeleton is not an easy task. Scientists have to compare every bone with other dinosaur skeletons, and with modern species of rep-

A museum worker cleans up a dinosaur skeleton at the Denver Museum of Natural History. (Photo courtesy of Dave G. Houser/Corbis.)

tiles—and hope to find a skeleton in a "death pose" that was close to its living structure. Many times in the past, certain parts of a skeleton were put in the wrong place. For example, heads of certain dinosaurs have been put on the wrong skeleton. And the thumb spike of the *Iguanodon* was first interpreted as a nose spike.

How are **bone positions** in a dinosaur skeleton **further determined**?

The positions of bones in dinosaur skeletons are determined using what scientists call an "anatomical direction system," and only includes what is internal (in other words, it is not based on external conditions). This system uses pairs of names to determine certain directions based on the average (or standard) posture of tetrapods—with the back up, belly down, head pointing forward, and all four legs on the ground.

Each pair of names denotes opposite directions, similar to when we refer to north and south. Here are four examples of such paired names:

Anterior and posterior: The direction of anterior is toward the tip of the snout, while the posterior direction is toward the tip of the tail. This is analogous to front and back, respectively.

Dorsal and ventral: Dorsal means toward and beyond the spine, while ventral means toward and beyond the belly. These are analogous to up and down, respectively.

How many bones made up the average dinosaur skeleton?

Although the largest dinosaurs may have had a few more bones in their necks and tails, the number of bones in the average dinosaur was approximately 200.

Medial and lateral: These are directions referenced to an imaginary plane located in the center of the body, running from tail to snout. Medial means closer to this central reference; lateral means farther out.

Proximal and distal: These are normally used to indicate directions in the limbs and sometimes the tail. Proximal means closer to the trunk or base of a limb, while distal means farther out from the trunk or from the base of the limb.

How are **paired names** used in the **anatomical direction system?**

Most commonly, these names are used to describe the positional relationships of the skeletal bones to each other. For example, the hip bones of a dinosaur are posterior to the shoulder bones; that is, they are more toward the tail. Or when the lower jaw is ventral to the upper jaw, it is "down" from it.

This system can also describe how the skeletal structure is composed. For example, the muzzle of a dinosaur projects anteriorly from the eyes, meaning the muzzle points forward from the eyes.

Still another way that these names can be used is to describe what surface of a particular bone is being viewed. This is especially useful when looking at drawings or photographs of dinosaur bones. If the caption says that you were looking at the ventral view of the skull, you would be looking at the bottom; the dorsal view would be at the top of the skull.

What are the **major parts** of a dinosaur skeleton?

A dinosaur skeleton is divided into two major parts—the skull, and all the rest of the bones, which are normally referred to as the postcranium (posterior to the cranium). This postcranium can be further divided into the bones of the spine, trunk, and tail (axial skeleton), and the bones of the limbs and limb girdles (appendicular skeleton).

What comprises the **skull**?

The skull of a dinosaur is made up of the teeth and all the bones in the head. These bones can occur in pairs, on opposite sides of the head, or singly—usually around the middle plane of the skull. There are two major sections of the skull. The upper part, or

This dinosaur skeleton is exhibited in the Tyrrell Museum of Paleontology in Drumheller, Alberta, Canada. (Photo courtesy of Robert Holmes/Corbis.)

cranium, contains the braincase, nostrils, upper jaw, and eye sockets. The other section is the lower jaw, which is made up of the right and left lower jaws (mandibles).

What are some examples of the **bones** in a dinosaur **skull**?

Examples and locations of dinosaur skull bones include the cheekbone (jugal), located below the eye opening (orbit); the postorbital, a small bone located behind the eye opening; and the lacrimal, a bone that separates the eye opening and the opening forward of the eye.

What are some interesting **details** of a dinosaur **skull**?

First, there were more than 30 bones in the skull of a dinosaur. Most dinosaurs had unusually rigid joints between their skull bones, called sutures (similar to sutures in a human skull). And there were also kinetic skulls, such as the *Allosaurus fragilis,* in which several of the skull bones were joined but could still move—probably so they could stretch parts of the skull in order to gobble down extremely large chunks of meat.

What kind of **openings** are found in dinosaur **skulls**?

There were many openings in various dinosaur skulls. Most dinosaur skulls included a pair of external nostrils, a pair of eye openings (called orbits), and large openings

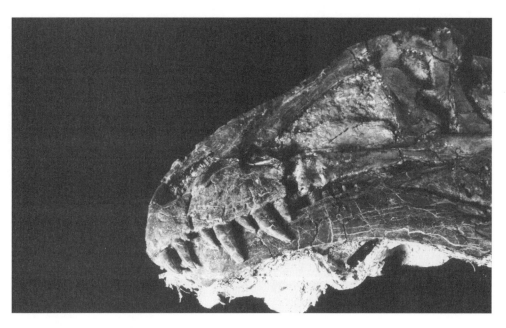

The skull of an *Acrocanthosaurus,* a dinosaur from the early Cretaceous period. (Photo courtesy of Francois Gohier/Photo Researchers Inc.)

that provided space for huge jaw muscles. More specialized openings included a hole in front of the eye, one behind the nostril, one in the lower jaw, one behind the eye, and one in the rear of the skull for the spinal cord. In fact, the presence and location of these special holes determine the difference between certain types of dinosaurs.

What **bones** held the dinosaur's **teeth**?

Dinosaurs had two bones in the upper jaw that held teeth. The larger bone holding the majority of the upper teeth was located toward the back of the snout (called the maxilla). The smaller bone holding fewer teeth (called the premaxilla) was located at the front of the skull. Teeth were held by the dentary section of the lower jaw; these teeth, of course, are called dentary teeth.

What is the **axial skeleton**?

The axial skeleton is one of the two sections of the entire dinosaur skeleton. It is made up of the trunk, spine, and tail—essentially forming the "foundation" to which the animal's limbs and skull were attached.

What are some of the **bones** of the **axial skeleton**?

The axial skeleton includes the so-called "backbone" of the dinosaur and the ribs.   **195**

Together with some other minor bones, the backbone and ribs formed the foundation to which the skull and limbs were attached.

The backbone (or vertebral column) was divided into four segments: the neck (cervical), the back (dorsal), hip (sacral), and the tail (caudal). It included numerous individual bones known as vertebrae.

The ribs were long, narrow bones attached to the vertebrae of the cervical and dorsal segments. These were paired bones—one on each side of the backbone—and extended downward to protect the internal organs. They included the neck ribs and the belly ribs (gastralia, or the bones that protected the digestive tract and other internal organs).

What were the **vertebrae** of a dinosaur?

Vertebrae were the numerous individual bones that made up the backbone (vertebral column) of the dinosaur. Each individual vertebra was a roughly cylindrical-shaped piece of bone (centrum); on top of the vertebrae were neural arches, triangular arches of bone covering the spinal cord. The spinal cord in a dinosaur would run between the centrum and neural arch. A bony neural spine projected up from the neural arch, and was where the back muscles were attached. Some dinosaurs, in addition to these basic features, had very complex vertebrae with all sorts of ridges and projections.

Each segment along the backbone had vertebrae that were specifically shaped to help that segment function. For example, the hip vertebrae (sacral) were fused together in dinosaurs in a structure called a sacrum; this provided support and strength for the hips. The neck (cervical) vertebrae were specifically shaped to provide flexibility, allowing the dinosaur to move its head around freely.

How many **vertebrae** did a dinosaur have?

It's impossible to pinpoint how many vertebrae each dinosaur had, as they varied greatly among all groups. In general, the neck bones held 9 to 19 vertebrae, the back

The lower vertebrae of a *Tyrannosaurus rex*. (Photo courtesy of Corbis.)

had 15 to 17 of these bones, the hips held 3 to 10 vertebrae—and the tail had from 35 to 82 vertebrae, depending on the dinosaur!

What were **zygapophyses**?

Zygapophyses were fingerlike projections extending forward and backward from the neural arches (the structures covering the spinal cord) of each vertebra. Zygapophyses projecting forward were called prezygapophyses; those projecting backward were postzygapophyses. These protrusions interacted with the projections on the neighboring vertebra, and controlled the amount of movement between each vertebra.

How was the **vertebral column** in **ornithischian dinosaurs** strengthened?

The vertebral column in ornithischian dinosaurs was strengthened by means of structures called "ossified tendons." These were actually tissues that connected the vertebrae together. They became filled with calcium, literally turning to bone (called ossifying). The result of this was a stiffening and strengthening of the connection between vertebrae—resulting in a strengthened backbone.

On ornithischian dinosaurs, ossified tendons appear as bony strands that look like spaghetti. Different names are given to them depending on where they are located on the dinosaur. For example, those between the tail vertebrae are called hypaxial tendons. In ornithischian dinosaurs, one purpose of the ossified tendons was to stiffen the base of the tail, making it more rigid with respect to the hips, while the tip of the tail was left mobile and flexible.

How were connections between **theropod dinosaurs' vertebrae** strengthened?

Some advanced species of theropod dinosaurs had strengthened vertebrae connections, but this was not accomplished by means of ossified tendons, as with the ornithischian dinosaurs. The theropod's prezygapophyses elongated and grew over several vertebrae—sometimes as many as 12 vertebrae—to strengthen and stiffen the area.

What were **chevrons** and **neural spines**?

On dinosaur tails, chevrons were downward-projecting bony structures found on the vertebrae. The neural spine projected up from the neural arch along the length of the backbone—and was where the back muscles were attached (this also forms the bumps down your own spine).

What is the **appendicular skeleton**?

The appendicular skeleton is the second section comprised of the postcranium. This section of the dinosaur skeleton included the bones of the forelimbs and hindlimbs, and the girdles that attached these limbs to the trunk.

How were the **arm (forelimb) bones attached** to the dinosaur's backbone?

The arm bones of a dinosaur were attached to the backbone by means of a pectoral girdle. This girdle was roughly C-shaped and attached to the front of the body. It consisted of bones such as the shoulder blade (scapula), collarbones (clavicles), and breastbone (sternum).

What bones made up the **arms and hands** of a dinosaur?

There were numerous bones of the dinosaur's arms, varying in size from large to small. Each of the two arms had a large upper arm bone (humerus); these bones extended from the shoulder to the elbow. They were joined by the two forearm bones (ulna and radius) that extended from the elbow to the hand.

The hands (manus) of a dinosaur were composed of a wrist, palm, and fingers attached to the end of the forearm bones. The wrist was made up of numerous small bones (carpals); the palm of the hand had longer bones (metacarpals). The fingers, also known as digits, were also made up of small bones (phalanges).

How were the **leg (hindlimb) bones attached** to the dinosaur's backbone?

The two dinosaur legs were attached to the backbone by means of pelvic girdles (pelves). There were two pelvic girdles—one on each side of the skeleton for each of the two legs.

Each girdle was composed of three bones: the ilium, pubis, and ischium. The ilium, the largest bone, was connected to the sacrum (an area of fused hip vertebrae). The pubis and ischium bones were attached to the bottom of the ilium, with the pubis attached toward the front and the ischium attached towards the rear.

Together, the ilium, pubis, and ischium formed a round hole in the pelvic girdle. This hole (acetabulum) was the hip

This dinosaur skeleton is featured in a museum in Ulan Bator, Mongolia. (Photo courtesy of Dean Conger/Corbis.)

socket where the hindlimbs were attached. In dinosaurs, this hip socket was open all the way through the pelvic girdle and is an identifying trait for dinosaurs. In many other animals, the hip socket has a bony wall at the back of the hole.

What bones made up the **legs and feet** of a dinosaur?

The bones that made up dinosaur legs were similar to the arm bones. The thighbone (femur) was a single upper leg bone attached to the pelvic girdle. The lower end of this bone joined the two bones of the lower leg at the knee; these leg bones were the inner shinbone (tibia) and outer bone (fibula).

What was unique about bipedal dinosaur feet?

The feet of dinosaurs were very different from those of humans. And because of their unique foot structure, most dinosaurs walked on their toes!

The long bones of the feet (metatarsals) were bunched together for strength. They were oriented upward toward the ankle joints at an angle, essentially lifting the metatarsals off the ground. This meant that only the toes made contact with the ground as the dinosaur walked or ran. In humans, the foot bones are parallel to the ground—so that the whole foot, not just the toes, makes contact.

The toes of most dinosaurs' feet were normally long and slender, which allowed the animals to grip the ground and have better balance. Most of the dinosaurs had only three toes for walking or running. We see the result in former muddy or sandy areas—as dinosaur trackways complete with birdlike footprints.

The dinosaur foot (pes) was made up of the ankle, foot bones, and toes. Attached to the lower leg bones were the small bones of the ankles (tarsals). The dinosaur feet were made up of longer foot bones (metatarsals) and the short bones of the toes (phalanges).

Did all dinosaurs have **long and slender toes**?

No, not every dinosaur had three long and slender toes. There were some exceptions: For example, large quadrupeds, such as the sauropods, had feet more like those of today's elephant—with short and broad toes.

What do the terms **digitigrade** and **plantograde** mean?

The term digitigrade literally means "toe-walking." Dinosaurs held their foot bones off the ground in the digitigrade position, so that these animals walked only on their toes. In contrast, human foot bones are oriented so the entire sole makes contact with the ground. This is called plantograde, or "sole-walking."

What was the advantage to the dinosaurs of **walking on their toes**?

Walking on toes increased a dinosaur's leg length, which in turn increased the animal's stride lengths. This translated into more speed, especially for bipedal (two-legged) dinosaurs such as the theropods, or some herbivores like the ornithopods; the advantage was better hunting or ability to escape, respectively. This type of motion also saved energy because the body didn't have to be raised and lowered every time the foot was lifted.

What was **unique** about the feet of most **quadruped** dinosaurs?

Unlike the bipedal types, the feet of most quadruped (four-footed) dinosaurs had shorter foot bones and a set of broad, stubby toes. This arrangement of foot bones was very similar to the feet of modern elephants.

Footprints of these types of dinosaurs were short and round, indicating that the bones of the feet were raised off the ground by a thick, fibrous, wedge-shaped heel pad. This heel pad enabled these huge animals to conserve a large amount of energy as they moved around. The ankle did not have to be raised and lowered during walking, a motion that would have lifted the entire body weight up and down. For dinosaurs like the large sauropods, this motion would have meant expending a great deal of energy!

What were **osteoderms**?

Osteoderms were bony growths located on the outside of some dinosaurs' skins, and were anchored in the skin by connective tissue. The most familiar examples of osteoderms were the spikes and plates that made up the armor of stegosaurs and ankylosaurs.

How did the **stiffened tail** of certain theropod dinosaurs **move**?

The stiffened tail of certain theropod dinosaurs moved completely opposite to those of ornithischian dinosaurs: the base of an ornithischian dinosaur's tail was stiffened, with a mobile tip. In contrast, certain theropod dinosaurs had a mobile base area, with a stiffened and rigid tail end—a consequence of elongated prezygapophyses and chevrons.

Can you tell the **difference** between **male and female dinosaurs** from their bones?

It is really not possible (at present) to determine the gender of a dinosaur by looking at its fossil bones. There are few clues to determine a dinosaur's gender, although some scientists believe certain species may have had features that distinguished gender. For example, some hadrosaurs ("duck-billed" dinosaurs) sported certain types of bony head crests. But just which gender *had* the crest is unknown. Currently, scientists are trying to base dinosaur gender ideas on examples from today's animal world—and even then, it's still almost impossible to determine a male from a female dinosaur.

Did **dinosaurs differ** in **bone structure**?

Overall, each dinosaur had a skeleton made up of the same basic structures: the skull, spine, ribs, shoulders, hips, legs, and tail. But individual dinosaur fossil bones do have structural differences. This is apparently dependent on several factors, including where the bones were located in the dinosaur; the bone's purpose or purposes; and the species of dinosaur. In general, dinosaurs that depended on speed needed long, light bones, while larger, slower-moving dinosaurs needed strong, solid bones.

What are some **specific differences** between dinosaur **bone structures**?

Some of the best examples of the differences between dinosaur bone structures are seen in the bipedal and quadrapedal herbivores. The large, heavy sauropods walked on all fours; they needed strong legs to support their enormous weight, so their bones were huge and solid. The smaller, fast-running bipedal herbivores like *Dryosaurus* needed to be fast; thus, they had long, thin-walled bones. These bones were essentially hollow tubes, and the insides were filled with a light bone marrow. This gave them a strong, flexible, but lightweight, structure, enabling them to move swiftly when circumstances demanded it—such as running from a predator.

What were some **features** of **theropod** dinosaur bones?

The carnivorous theropod dinosaurs all had hollow limb bones. Many also had air-filled (pneumatic) bones in the front part of their bodies—with some theropods having this type of bone present as far back as the middle of their tail.

How did the **pneumatic theropod bones** get their air supply?

There were numerous routes by which the pneumatic bones of the theropod dinosaurs obtained their air supply. For example, the vertebrae and ribs at the front of the body and neck were supplied with air from sacs and tubes connected to the lungs. In some advanced theropods, air was routed through tubes from the throat to the bones of the braincase. And bones around the eye and roof of the mouth obtained air from tubes extending from air sacs associated with the nose.

What do dinosaur bones tell us about a **dinosaur's stance**?

All dinosaur skeletons show that these creatures had a "fully improved stance." In other words, dinosaur legs were held straight under their bodies at all times. This enabled dinosaurs to grow bigger, cover longer distances, and move faster, compared to their reptile cousins that had their legs spread out on either side of their body. The dinosaur stance also enabled some of the animals to become bipedal; it also helped all

What bone discovery points to birds evolving from small theropod dinosaurs?

Recently, scientists discovered a wishbone as part of a dinosaur skeleton: the V-shaped wishbone was found in the shoulder region of a *Velociraptor* and measures about 4 inches (10 centimeters) long. A wishbone is an essential part of a bird's ability to fly, as it acts as a spring to lift the wings in flight. The discovery of a wishbone in a dinosaur skeleton makes it more likely that birds evolved from small theropod dinosaurs, not from some other reptiles.

dinosaurs with something called "locomotor stamina"—the ability to run and breathe at the same time.

What can paleontologists tell about the **lifestyle** of a **large herbivore** from its fossil bones?

The bones of giant dinosaurs like the *Diplodocus* tell scientists the large herbivore's legs were thick and widely spaced, acting as pillars to hold up the cross beams of its shoulder bones and hip girdle. The vertebrae across the hip were fused for strength, allowing it to support an almost 11-ton body weight. The legs ended in short, broad feet (similar to an elephant's) with claws on the back foot used as an antislip device. The bone structure limited the dinosaur to a normal walking pace of approximately 4 miles (6.4 kilometers) per hour, although they could have moved modestly faster for short periods of time. Thus, they were thought to be large, slow-moving, four-legged walkers. In addition, the large adult herbivores (sauropods) were probably relatively immune from predators because of their large size.

What were **unique skeletal features** of **large sauropods**?

There were a number of unique skeletal features of large sauropods—designed mostly to support their massive size and weight. These dinosaurs were similar in construction to a suspension bridge: The front and rear legs acted as underlying supports for the backbone; in turn, the backbone was supported from above by ligaments and muscles of the back. The vertebrae of the backbone were joined together so the neck, back, and tail bend slightly upward at the ends, spreading the massive weight toward the ends.

The top leg bone was shaped to swing underneath the body. The knee was constructed so the leg could move back and forth, similar to the knee of humans. The ankle had very limited movement, with no possible sideways motion. These and other skeletal features helped the large sauropods to support and move their tremendous bulk.

What can paleontologists tell about the **lifestyle** of a **small herbivore** from its fossil bones?

One good example is the *Hypsilophodon,* a small herbivore (ornithischian) with a much different skeleton from its larger sauropod cousins. The small dinosaur's entire structure seemed "shrunk down"—giving it strength with minimum weight. Its bones were hollow and thin-walled for lightness, and the thighbone was very short for rapid stride movements. The small dinosaur's feet were long and thin, with long upper foot bones (metatarsals), and it had short, sharp claws for gripping the ground. The long tailbone was stiffened by bony rods, and probably swung from side to side, helping it to quickly change directions. All of these structures paint a picture of a small, two-legged herbivore using its bony features to swiftly run and maneuver as a defense against predators.

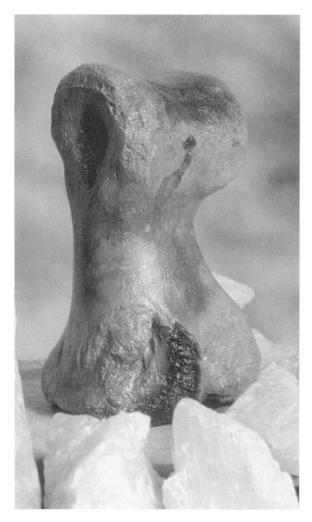

A toe bone from a *Tyrannosaurus.* Paleontologists can learn much about a dinosaur's lifestyle from the animal's bones. (Photo courtesy of Corbis.)

What can paleontologists tell about the **lifestyle** of a **midsize herbivore** from its fossil bones?

A good example of a midsize herbivore is the *Iguanodon* (ornithischian), a 33-foot- (10-meter-) long animal that weighed approximately four tons. The skeleton of the *Iguanodon* was very similar in structure to the smaller *Hypsilophodon,* but the bone proportions were different. The thighbone was much heavier and longer, and the upper part of the foot bone was shorter. This prevented the *Iguanodon* from running very fast, but did provide support for its heavier weight. The vertebrae along the dinosaur's spine were wide and tall, strengthened along the whole length by numerous bony tendons. Thus, the dinosaur walked on two legs, with a nearly horizontal posture; its back legs supported most of its weight. The huge shoulder bones, long arm bones, and fused wrist bones (carpals) gave the *Iguanodon* the ability to drop down on all fours for locomotion when the situation demanded it.

What can paleontologists tell about the **lifestyle** of a **large carnivore** from its fossil bones?

The *Tyrannosaurus* is currently the most recognizable of the large carnivorous dinosaurs (theropods). Its skeleton had heavy, large bones, with massive vertebrae, hip girdle, and thigh bones. The upper foot bones (metatarsals) were locked together for strength, while the toes were powerful and short. The knees show evidence of thick cartilage, similar to modern birds.

There are two scenarios concerning the speed and mobility of the *Tyrannosaurus* based on the animal's skeletal structure—and both sides point to the same evidence to bolster their claims. One group feels that the skeletal structure of a *Tyrannosaurus* caused the animal to move at a slow pace, which limited its main hunting abilities to scavenging or camouflage and ambush. The other group feels that the dinosaur's bone structure, along with the animal's massive musculature, enabled the *Tyrannosaurus* to run and sprint, making it an active, dangerous hunter.

Until more direct evidence is gathered, the most agreed-upon theory is based on a major deduction: the *Tyrannosaurus* would need more meat than was available from scavenging—thus it would have to hunt. And to hunt, it would have to at least match the speed of its prey. In other words, it would have to keep up with such dinosaur prey as the herbivores *Triceratops* and *Edmontosaurus* (ornithischians)—both of which are thought to have reached speeds of 9 to 12 miles (14 to 19 kilometers) per hour for short bursts.

ABNORMAL DINOSAUR BONES

What do **dinosaur bones** indicate about the **health** of these animals?

Dinosaurs, in general, seem to have been relatively healthy animals, if the evidence from—and the interpretation of—the fossil records are to be believed. A few fossilized bones have shown evidence of abnormalities, such as asymmetrical bone growth, healed traumatic and repetitive stress fractures, arthritis, ossification (the development of bonylike material) of spinal ligaments, and the fusion of the animal's spinal bones (or vertebrae).

What caused **asymmetrical bone growth** in dinosaurs?

Asymmetrical bone growth could have occurred, for example, when a tendon was ripped off the bone. This probably happened during some form of exertion, such as running after prey for carnivores, or trying to escape a predator for herbivores. If bone growth continued in this area after the tendon was torn, it would often grow back in an abnormal shape.

What caused **traumatic** and **repetitive stress fractures** in dinosaur bones?

Another feature that has been seen in some dinosaur bones, such as *Tyrannosaurus* and *Iguanodon,* are healed traumatic fractures. Such fractures may have occurred during struggles with other dinosaurs or even during mating activity.

Another type of fracture, called a stress fracture, apparently occurred in dinosaurs as a result of repetitive stresses to the bone. Stress fractures found in ceratopsians, such as the *Triceratops,* have often been blamed on foot stamping, sudden accelerations in response to predators, or even fractures brought about during long migrations.

Do **dinosaur bones** show evidence of **arthritis,** a common affliction in humans?

Yes, certain dinosaur bones show signs of certain types of arthritis—in particular, osteoarthritis and inflammatory arthritis. In humans, osteoarthritis, or degenerative arthritis, is common in the elderly. In general in humans, degenerative arthritis is caused by the increased deterioration of cartilage around the bone due to age, or from a propensity toward this type of arthritis. Inflammatory arthritis, or gout, in humans usually occurs when crystals of uric acid are deposited in a joint. The excess amounts of uric acid are usually unexplainable, but it has often been tied to dietary excesses.

In the vast majority of cases, dinosaur bones show almost no sign of osteoarthritis, leading some paleontologists to theorize these creatures had highly constrained joints, or bone joints with little rotational movement. Two specimens of *Iguanodon,* however, were found to have evidence of osteoarthritis in the ankle bones—weight-bearing parts of the body. Because scientists don't know the lifespans of dinosaurs, they also don't know whether or not the arthritis was caused by old age. In addition, two tyrannosaurid dinosaur remains show evidence of inflammatory arthritis in the hand and toe bones—possibly the result of a rich, red meat diet.

The first three neck vertebrae of the *Triceratops* may have been a developmental adaptation: stiffening in this area may have evolved to better support the animal's massive skull. (Photo courtesy of Hulton-Deutsch Collection/Corbis.)

What **bone phenomena** do both **humans** and **dinosaurs** share?

Humans and dinosaurs share a process called "diffuse idiopathic skeletal hyperostosis" (DISH)—or when the ossification (when something becomes bonylike) of the spinal ligaments stiffens the spinal area. Although it sounds bad, it is a normal process and not recognized as a disease in either humans or dinosaurs.

Bone fossils of creatures such as ceratopsians, hadrosaurs, iguanodonts, pachycephalosaurs, and some sauropods all show DISH—a stiffening of the dinosaurs' tail area that made it easier to hold the tail off the ground. Dinosaurs that used their tails as weapons, such as the stegosaurs, needed them to be flexible like whips—so they do not show evidence of this spinal ligament fusion. The discovery of DISH in dinosaurs dovetails nicely with a newer theory: many dinosaurs did not drag their tails, but rather held them off the ground as a form of counter-balance.

Another bone-related phenomenon humans and certain dinosaurs share is vertebral fusion, where the bones of the spine (the vertebrae) actually become joined and ossified together (as opposed to the spinal ligaments in the DISH process). In adult ceratopsians, such as the *Triceratops,* this fusion was limited to the first three neck (cervical) vertebrae, leading to speculation that this was not a disease, but a developmental adaptation: stiffening in this area may have evolved to better support the animal's massive skull. More recent fossil findings reveal that smaller, perhaps younger ceratopsians had incomplete fusion in this area; whereas the fusion was complete in larger, presumably older animals.

How were **dinosaurs' bony skeletons** held together?

Similar to those of humans, dinosaur skeletons were held together by a combination of ligaments, muscles, and tendons. The ligaments and tendons probably served the same function as those in modern humans: to connect the many tissues of the body to the skeleton. Muscles in dinosaurs also served the same function as in human bodies—to give the animals both strength and dexterity. In addition, some specialized muscles and tendons, such as those of the jaw, acted together in certain ways. For example, the model of a *Tyrannosaurus'* jaw is complex, with the muscles and tendons interacting in just the right way to allow the jaw to expand to its enormous size—and quickly snap shut to hold on to its prey.

How do paleontologists tell how **dinosaur muscles** were connected?

Some fossil bones have "muscle scars," or roughened patches, where the muscles were apparently attached. These scars often make it possible to estimate the position and size of some of the main muscles. From a mostly complete skeleton of a dinosaur, scientists can estimate where many of the muscles were located; how they worked with and against each other to move the dinosaur; and the general size and shape of the animal. Over the years, scientists' overall view of how a particular dinosaur behaved had a great influence on how they determined muscle size and brawn. Early ideas of a slow-moving *Tyrannosaurus* led to suggestions of a relatively weak and puny set of muscles; the newer idea of the *Tyrannosaurus* as an active hunter has led scientists to suggest that the animals had large, strong muscles.

SPECIFIC DINOSAURS
AND THEIR BONES

What **bone adaptations** did early birds like **Archaeopteryx** have?

The early birds—of which *Archaeopteryx* is the most well known—had hollow, pneumatic (containing air in the bone cavities) bones that provided lightness and strength.

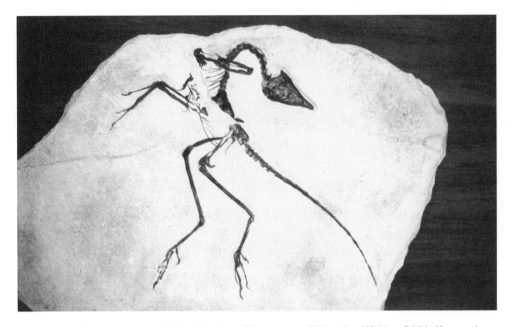

This fossil of an *Archaeopteryx* doesn't show its feathers. (Photo courtesy of University of Michigan Exhibit, Museum of Natural History.)

Some bones, particularly in the arm and wrist area, eventually became fused. There was not much difference in bones between the earliest birds and the smaller, carnivorous theropods. Only the presence of feathers truly distinguished the early birds from the land-limited small carnivores.

What were the purposes of **bony head projections** on some **dinosaurs**?

Although the true purposes are not known at present, scientists do have some theories as to the function of certain dinosaurs' bone head projections: the researchers believe these odd-shaped head projections would catch the eye, and thus, were used to attract mates or warn an enemy. Some projections could have been used for attack or defense, and others for some sort of sound generation.

Which group of **dinosaurs** had the most **prominent head projections**?

The hadrosaurs ("duck-billed" dinosaurs) had the most prominent head projections. All of their bodies were very similar, and resembled the earlier iguanodontids. One set of the hadrosaurs looked like many other reptiles, but with small crests. The other set of hadrosaurs had the most striking features on their heads—specifically, large, spectacular, and distinctive bony crests adorning their heads.

209

The duck-billed dinosaurs, or hadrosaurs, featured prominent head projections like the crest on this *Corythosaurus*. (Photo courtesy of University of Michigan Exhibit, Museum of Natural History.)

One fine example of dinosaurs with head projections is the *Corythosaurus,* a hadrosaur with a crest resembling a dinner plate on end. Another, the *Parasaurolophus,* had a long, hollow, horn-shaped crest rearing backward on top of its skull. The *Saurolophus* had a prominent bony ridge on top of its skull, sweeping back to form a spike; and the *Tsintaosaurus* had a forward-pointing hollow tube on top of its skull.

What **purpose** did the **long, hollow crest** serve on the skull of dinosaurs such as the *Parasaurolophus*?

No one really knows the true purpose of this dinosaur's (or any other dinosaur's) hollow crest. Several theories have been proposed in the past, such as the hollow crest being used as a snorkel while looking for food near or in water. This is now known to be impossible, as the crest had no opening at the end. Another idea was that the crest served as a foliage deflector as the animal searched for food or ran from predators. This idea has not been disproved, but it is highly unlikely.

Currently, scientists believe this dinosaur's 3-foot- (1-meter-) long, hollow chamber, with its complex arrangement of tubes and chambers, acted as a resonator. Air from the dinosaur's lungs was blown through the tubes, giving off a distinctive low sound. These sounds could have been used for communication, aggressive displays during mating season, or to sound the alarm when a predator was near.

Visitors walk among the saurischian (meaning "lizard-hipped") skeletons at the Metropolitan Museum of Art in New York. (Photo courtesy of Michael S. Yamashita/Corbis.)

A little boy gets a first-hand look at the skull of a *Triceratops* at a museum in Florida. (Photo courtesy of Gregory Smith/Associated Press.)

The 36-foot-long *Suchomimus tenerensis* had razor teeth, a long pointy snout, and foot-long claws, all of which was ideal for catching fish. This fossil was found in the Sahara. (Photo courtesy of Dennis Cook/ Associated Press.)

A child examines a fossilized *Triceratops* skull at the Royal Tyrrell Museum in Alberta, Canada. (Photo courtesy of Michael S. Yamashita/Corbis.)

Paleontologist Paul Sereno walks behind a model of the five-foot-long *Carcharodontosaurus* skull his team discovered in the Moroccan Sahara. This is the most complete skull ever found from the close of the dinosaur era in Africa. (Photo courtesy of Denis Paquin/Associated Press.)

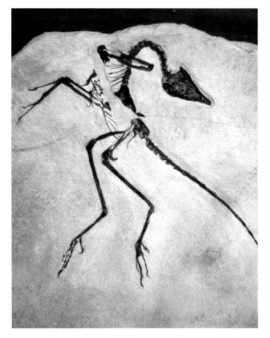

The *Archaeopteryx* may be the first ancestor of the birds. This fossil doesn't show the creature's feathers. (Photo courtesy of University of Michigan Exhibit, Museum of Natural History.)

Fossil of the *Sinosauropteryx,* a small, chicken-like creature with downy fluff. (Photo courtesy of David Bubier/Academy of Natural Sciences/Associated Press.)

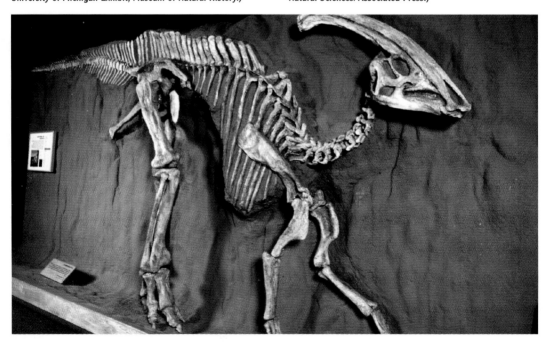

The skull of the *Parasaurolophus* features a hollow crest that may have been used for communication. (Photo courtesy of Francois Gohier/Photo Researchers Inc.)

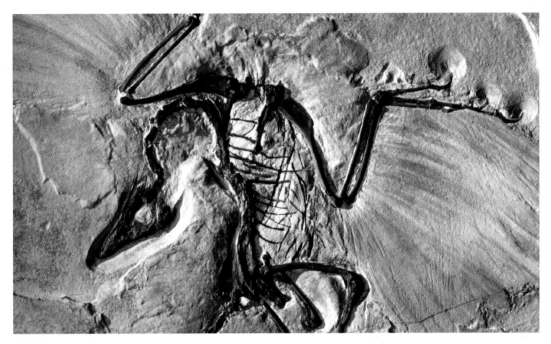

Seven fossils and one wing of the *Archaeopteryx* have been found to date. This *Archaeopteryx* fossil features wing impressions. (Photo courtesy of James L. Amos/Corbis.)

This fossilized baby dinosaur, dubbed *Scipionyx samniticus*, found in Italy during the 1980s, was so well preserved that scientists can see muscle fibers and the intestine. (Photo courtesy of Soprintendenza Archaeologica/Associated Press.)

The first dinosaur track ever to be described was a three-toed track, mentioned in an 1836 lithograph, similar to this fossilized footprint. (Photo courtesy of JLM Visuals.)

LEFT: This is possibly the biggest fecal fossil from a meat-eater found to date, from a juvenile *Tyrannosaurus rex.* The fossil—17 inches long, 5 inches high, and 6 inches wide—was found on a hillside in 1995 in Saskatchewan, Canada. (Photo courtesy of U.S. Geological Survey/Associated Press.)

BELOW: These are among 100 dinosaur eggs, measuring 5 inches in length and 3 inches in diameter, discovered in Portugal in 1997. Some of the eggs contained embryo elements of a carnivorous theropod. (Photo courtesy of Luisa Ferreira/Associated Press.)

Jellyfish were among the first soft-bodied creatures to appear in the oceans. (Photo courtesy of
Jeffrey L. Rotman/Corbis.)

This recreation of the Cambrian period shows
some of the vast marine life that existed. (Photo
courtesy of University of Michigan Exhibit,
Museum of Natural History.)

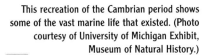

A scene in Colorado, 150 million years ago

These U.S. postage stamps were among the new dinosaur designs in 1997, and testify to our fascination with dinosaurs. (Photo courtesy of U.S. Postal Service/Associated Press.)

RIGHT: Dinosaurs—including the big purple guy named Barney—are beloved by children. (Photo courtesy of Associated Press.) **BELOW:** A still from the motion picture *The Lost World: Jurassic Park 2.* While not absolutely precise, the two *Jurassic Park* films present the most accurate dinosaur portrayals to date. (Photo courtesy of Universal Pictures/Associated Press.)

The *Ornithomimus,* whose fossilized head is shown here, was a type of dinosaur that resembled modern-day birds such as ostriches. (Photo courtesy of Michael S. Yamashita/Corbis.)

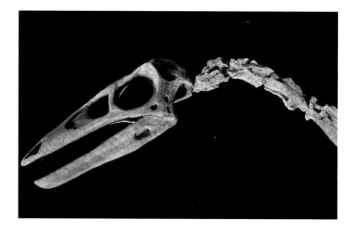

Many scientists believe that birds, such as these ostriches, descended from dinosaurs—or perhaps *are* modern-day dinosaurs! (Photo courtesy of Field Mark Publications.)

Crocodylomorphs, a group that includes alligators like this one, existed during the Triassic period. (Photo courtesy of Field Mark Publications.)

A *Plateosaurus* roams the land during the Triassic period. (Image courtesy of University of Michigan Exhibit, Museum of Natural History.)

Paleontologists clean and prepare dinosaur fossils for display. (Photo courtesy of Philippe Plailly/Photo Researchers Inc.)

Paleontologist Peter Larson cleans the jawbone of the *T. rex* nicknamed "Sue," whose skeleton was found in South Dakota in 1990. (Photo courtesy of Corbis.)

A Brazilian scientist studies a 220-million-year-old bone—one of the oldest dinosaur fossils ever found. (Photo courtesy of Ricardo Chaves/Associated Press.)

Environmentalist Dr. Vikas Amte examines some fossils of dinosaur eggs in Pisdura, India, in early 1997. (Photo courtesy of Sherwin Crasto/Associated Press.)

A park service worker chips rock away from dinosaur bones at Dinosaur National Monument, located in Utah and Colorado. (Photo courtesy of James L. Amos/Corbis.)

A team excavates dinosaur bones near Kauchanaburi, Thailand. (Photo courtesy of Bill Wassman/Stock Market.)

Model of a Pterosaur, one of the winged creatures of the Cretaceous period. While they were not dinosaurs, Pterosaurs were reptiles and were thus related to dinosaurs. (Photo courtesy of University of Michigan Exhibit, Museum of Natural History.)

This model of a *Torosaurus* was part of the Dinofest exhibition in Philadelphia in 1998. (Photo courtesy of Dan Loh/ Associated Press.)

Mammoths, like this one, evolved after mastodons, more than 10,000 years ago, toward the end of the Great Ice Age. (Photo courtesy of Jonathan Blair/Corbis.)

Museum goers in Paris, France, gaze up at a model of an *Allosaurus,* a carnivore from the Jurassic period. (Photo courtesy of Jonathan Blair/Corbis.)

In Alberta, Canada's Dinosaur Provincial Park, a *Styracosaurus* model stands on a riverbank. Scientists theorize that the *Styracosaurus* dinosaurs traveled in herds. (Photo courtesy of Jonathan Blair/Corbis.)

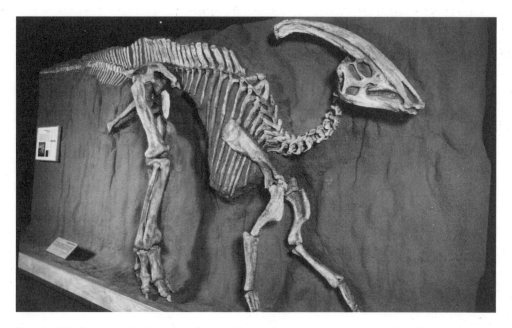

The skull of the *Parasaurolophus* featured a hollow crest that may have been used for communication. (Photo courtesy of Francois Gohier/Photo Researchers Inc.)

Has anyone speculated on the **type of sounds** certain dinosaurs made?

Scientists have recently reproduced and released a recording of sounds a *Parasaurolophus* might have made using its skull crest. A full-scale model of this dinosaur's skull crest—reproducing exactly the shape and size of the internal chambers and tubes—was used to duplicate the possible sound. Blowing through the crest produces a low, oboe-like sound—a strange noise still like no other living creature has made in our time.

Which dinosaurs had a **large skull** with an integral **bony neck frill**?

The group of dinosaurs with large, triangular-shaped skulls (when viewed from above), horns, curved beaks, and large, bony neck frills were the ceratopsians, or "horned faces." They were ornithischians, were herbivorous, and evolved during the late Cretaceous period. These dinosaurs were stocky and walked on four legs, similar to modern rhinoceroses.

The large bony neck frill, which is the dominant feature of these animals, is used by paleontologists to loosely group these animals into long-frilled and short-frilled types. The reason for the neck frill is unknown, although there are several theories. One suggests that the frills were used to make the animal look much larger in order to scare away potential predators. Another theory states that groups of the animals may have gathered together en masse, using not only their bulk and head armor to scare away predators, but the frills to look more menacing in a massive threat display.

211

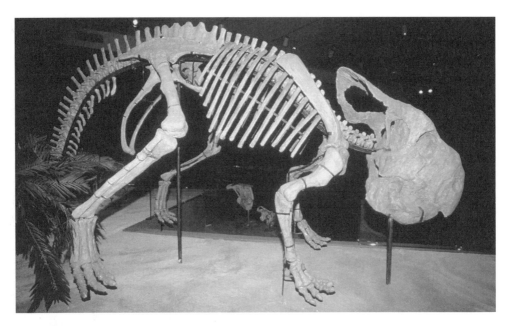

Skeletal mount of a *Protoceratops*, which had a well-developed neck shield. (Photo courtesy of Kevin Schafer/Corbis.)

How big were the **early ceratopsians**?

The *Psittacosaurus* was an early ceratopsian that seemed to bridge the gap between ornithopods and later ceratopsians. It had a curved beak, but no neck frill. The dinosaur was approximately 6.5 feet (2 meters) long; when it was on its two hind legs, it would reach up to about the shoulder height of an average human. A more recognizable early ceratopsian dinosaur was the *Protoceratops,* with a well-developed neck shield, but no horn. This animal was approximately 6 feet (1.8 meters) long, and walked on all fours, rising up to mid-thigh height of an average human.

Which **dinosaur** was the most well known of the **ceratopsians**?

The ceratopsian most people recognize is the *Triceratops*—a three-horned, large, herbivorous quadruped with a short neck frill. This animal was one of the largest of the ceratopsians, weighing up to 5.4 tons; it had an average length of 29.5 feet (9 meters). It also had a long horn above each eye, and a shorter one on the front snout. The head alone of the *Triceratops* could be up to 6.5 feet (2 meters) long!

What does the **skull** of the ***Triceratops*** tell us about the way it lived?

The *Triceratops,* like most of the ceratopsians, had a distinctive skull, with a large, bony frill, horns, and a narrow but deep, beaklike snout, similar to the beak of a par-

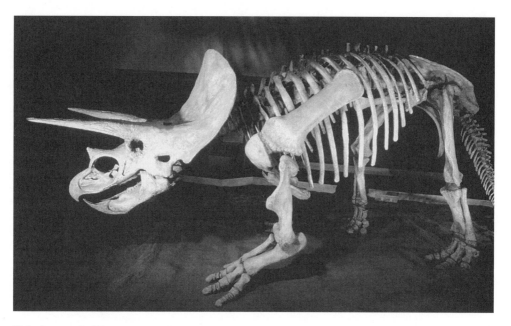

Skeletal mount of a *Triceratops,* a member of the ceratopsian family. (Photo courtesy of University of Michigan Exhibit, Museum of Natural History.)

rot. The teeth grew so that the cutting edges were almost vertical, allowing the *Triceratops* to slice plants like scissors; the continual growth of the teeth provided a self-sharpening edge. This allowed them to eat the low-lying, tough vegetation they found on the ground.

The long horns were probably used for display purposes, as shoving matches to establish dominance and territory, and as protection against predators. The bony neck frill acted as a protection for the brain, served as an attachment point for the powerful jaw muscles, and was perhaps used for territorial or mating displays.

What purpose did the **bony plates** on the back of the *Stegosaurus* serve?

Originally, the bony plates of the *Stegosaurus,* a herbivore, were thought to form a single row down the animal's spine; now paleontologists feel there were two staggered rows of plates, with a row on either side of the spine. Scientists also once thought the bony plates functioned as a defense from predators, or to attract mates. More recent studies in wind tunnels have shown that the staggered arrangement of plates is the most efficient pattern for shedding heat in a light breeze. Thus, the function of these plates is now thought to be one of heat regulation.

DINOSAUR ANATOMY

DINOSAUR SKIN

Are there any **fossils** of **dinosaur skin**?

The rarest types of dinosaur fossils are those showing skin texture—but not the actual skin itself. The fossilization process that produced such rare fossils required very specific conditions: the body of the dinosaur needed to be in a dry environment, which would allow some parts to mummify (dry up and shrivel). These mummified parts would then leave impressions on surrounding rock.

What was a **dinosaur's skin** like?

The few fossils of dinosaur skin uncovered to date show that most dinosaur skin was tough and scaly, like that of modern reptiles. For example, there was the tough, wrinkled skin with bony plates of the Cretaceous period hadrosaur *Edmontosaurus.* Similar to the hadrosaurs, ornithopods had thick, wrinkled skin with embedded bony knobs of various sizes. Some small theropods, like the recently discovered *Sinosauropteryx,* may have had featherlike features on its skin for heat regulation.

Did all **dinosaurs** have the **same type of skin**?

The amount of fossilized skin uncovered to date is extremely small, and most of our ideas of dinosaur skin come from extrapolation from modern reptiles. The chances of all dinosaurs having the same skin is probably small, since, over millions of years, these animals adapted to their environment and specialized needs. Chances are, their skin would have adapted too.

These dinosaur skin casts illustrate various dinosaur skin types. (Photo courtesy of University of Michigan Exhibit, Museum of Natural History.)

In fact, today's reptiles do not have the same types of skin. For example, consider the various reptilian skins—from heads to tails—of the large and small lizards, turtles, crocodiles, skinks, various snakes, and even worm lizards. They vary from a lizard's protective covering of scales or plates to the hard bony shell of turtles—all different adaptations to their specific needs and environments.

Did dinosaurs get **sunburned**?

It was very hot and humid during the Mesozoic era—so there may have been a great deal of sunshine. But it's doubtful that a dinosaur would get sunburned. It is thought that dinosaur skins were thick, similar to modern reptiles like turtles and crocodiles—not at all like a human's skin.

Have any dinosaur **embryo skin impressions** been found?

Yes, for the first time ever, the skin impressions of dinosaur embryos have been discovered at a large nesting site in the Patagonian badlands of Argentina. The eggs at the site—named "Auca Mahuevo" by paleontologists because of the large number of dinosaur eggs found there—are approximately 70 to 90 million years old, placing them in the late Cretaceous period.

Some of the eggs contained embryos, with patches of fossilized baby dinosaur skin. The skin had a scaly surface, similar to that of modern lizards. One skin impression had a distinct stripe of larger scales near its center—a section that probably ran down the dinosaur's back.

Has any **other information** been uncovered from dinosaur **embryo skin impressions**?

Yes, scientists have found that some dinosaur embryo skin impressions also indicate a possible growth pattern of armored plates. The dinosaur eggs found at Auca Mahuevo, Argentina, were thought to have been laid by large sauropods—probably titanosaurids whose remains are found nearby. Unlike any other known sauropods, the titanosaurids had bony, armored plates embedded in their skin. The fossilized embryo skins showed no signs of armored plates, indicating that these plates probably

This fossilized baby dinosaur, dubbed *Scipionyx samniticus*, found in Italy during the 1980s, was so well preserved that scientists can see muscle fibers and the intestine. The creature, from a previously unknown species, was a two-legged meat-eater that lived some 113 million years ago. (Photo courtesy of Soprintendenza Archaeologica/Associated Press.)

grew after the dinosaurs hatched. This type of growth pattern is similar to modern-day crocodiles and armored lizards—the adults have armored plates that the juveniles lack.

Have any other **soft parts** of **dinosaurs** been found?

Some impressions of soft parts of dinosaurs have been found in the past, but they are rare. Some fossils display the outlines of internal organs, and some animals have fossilized remains of what they had just eaten.

Did dinosaurs have lips?

Although dinosaurs have been portrayed in pictures and movies as having lips, this is really only an educated guess on the part of scientists. No known fossils have dinosaur lip impressions. Recently, a paleontologist compared hundreds of dinosaur fossils with some modern relatives, such as birds, turtles, and crocodiles. None of the bones examined had any of the structural features needed to make lips work. So, although having dinosaurs with lips may make them look interesting, at this time there is no scientific basis for these features.

But an even more exciting finding was recently uncovered: the fossil of a small, baby carnivorous dinosaur, hardly more than a hatchling, was discovered in Italy. The dinosaur was actually found by an amateur collector in the southern part of the country in 1981, but he thought it was just the fossil of a bird. In 1993, the fossil collector saw the movie *Jurassic Park* and realized his fossil looked very similar to the movie's *Velociraptor* (in reality, true *Velociraptors* were smaller). In 1998, after the fossil was examined by paleontologists, it was determined to be the bones of a young dinosaur—and was also the first dinosaur ever discovered in Italy.

This dinosaur, called *Scipionyx samniticus,* is about 113 million years old; and although it is a distant cousin of both the *Tyrannosaurus rex* and *Velociraptor,* it is considered to be an entirely new family. The fossil also shows something that usually does not survive millions of years of fossilization: soft parts, including a fossilized digestive tract running down through the skeleton, from the throat to the base of the tail. Even the wrinkles in the dinosaur's intestines were preserved.

Did dinosaurs have **cheeks**?

Although there is no fossil evidence of dinosaur cheeks, it is extremely probable that specific herbivorous dinosaurs had these features. For example, all of the ornithischian dinosaurs had rows of teeth set in from the jaw margin. This left a gap, or pocket, in the skull that was probably covered by skin—forming cheeks.

What was the **advantage** of having **cheeks** for a **herbivorous** dinosaur?

Herbivorous dinosaurs with cheeks would have been very efficient feeders. Present-day reptiles do not have cheeks. So when they gather and chew on a piece of plant material, the part outside the mouth often falls to the ground. Animals with cheeks are able to keep and chew all of the plant material they gather. The plant material not being chewed is stored in the cheek until it's brought into the mouth. No doubt some dinosaurs did have such cheeks, making the feeding process much more efficient.

What **color or colors** were the dinosaurs?

No one, as yet, has been able to tell anything about the color of a dinosaur's skin. The skin "fades" as it is mummified, and the rocks eventually give their own color to the fossil. But paleontologists theorize that dinosaurs, like some modern animals, used color and patterns to camouflage and identify themselves. Therefore, dinosaurs' skin colors probably ranged from light and dark browns to greens in various patterns—all earth colors, allowing them to hide or blend in with their environment.

But there may have also been brightly colored, smaller dinosaurs. After all, today's birds—thought to be directly related to the dinosaurs by many paleontologists—are often brightly colored in order to attract a mate, and warn other birds (and even predators) from their territory.

There is also some evidence that crocodiles and birds, the closest living relatives of dinosaurs, may have color vision. This suggests that dinosaurs may have responded to colors in their environment—especially bright colors for territorial or mating displays. It's also interesting to note that crocodiles with color vision are themselves not brightly colored at all.

TEETH AND CLAWS

What is a good description of **animal teeth**?

Teeth are found in the mouths of many animal species, from mammals to reptiles. In most cases, teeth are a direct means of survival: without teeth, an animal cannot digest, capture, or tear apart its prey or vegetation. Depending on the animal— whether it is a herbivore, a carnivore, or an omnivore—teeth are used mostly for chewing, cutting or slicing plants, or tearing apart flesh.

Most teeth are made of hardened calcium with a covering of enamel. Some animals have only one or two sets of teeth; others shed teeth many times over their lifetime. Still others grow one set, continually growing the same teeth back as they wear down.

What was the **composition** of dinosaur **teeth**?

Dinosaur teeth were formed from two materials, called dentine and enamel, both more durable and tougher than bone. Dentine was the softer of the two, and formed the core of each tooth; the outer surface was covered with the harder enamel.

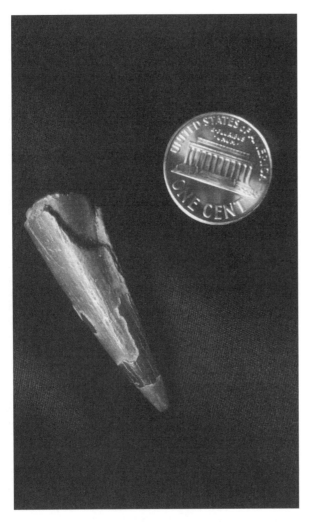

The tooth of a *Spinosaurus*. (Photo courtesy of University of Michigan Exhibit, Museum of Natural History.)

Where were **teeth located** in a dinosaur?

Dinosaur teeth grew out of sockets located in the jawbones. The lower tooth-containing jawbone is known as the dentary; the upper teeth were located in the premaxilla and maxilla bones of the upper jaw.

What do scientists know in general about **dinosaur teeth**?

Scientists know that most dinosaurs had more teeth than humans. In addition, the dinosaurs would shed their teeth throughout their life, much like animals such as sharks do today; for example, the hadrosaurs had hundreds of teeth waiting to replace their worn-out teeth. Other dinosaurs, such as the ornithomimids (ornithomimosaurs), had no teeth at all, but a beak similar to a bird. Some dinosaurs also had a combination of a beak and teeth.

There were many differences in the way their teeth were aligned. In humans, most of the teeth are aligned so we can chew plants; the canines represent our carnivorous past. Dinosaurs had all different kinds of teeth alignment: some were similar to that of today's carnivorous crocodile reptiles; others had teeth perfect for gnashing tough plants. Similar to modern animals, teeth alignment depended on what the dinosaur ate.

Why did **herbivorous** (plant-eating) dinosaurs' **teeth differ** from those of the **carnivores** (meat-eaters)?

The plant-eating dinosaurs had very different teeth from those of the carnivores—

Is it true that some dinosaurs had self-sharpening teeth?

Yes, some dinosaurs did have self-sharpening teeth, such as the ornithopods and ceratopsians. Both were members of the Cerapoda group, all of which had cheek teeth with thickened enamel on one side only. The other side of the teeth—the actual surface used to chew the plants—had only the softer dentine. As the animal chewed, the upper and lower teeth ground against each other, with the softer dentine wearing away faster than the harder enamel. This made these dinosaur teeth self-sharpening.

mainly because of the plants the herbivores had to eat. Meat can be readily cut up by sharp teeth, swallowed in large chunks, and digested easily in the gut. But living on a diet of plants is a much harder proposition. The cellulose found in plant tissue is much tougher than meat. Thus, plants must be cut into small pieces and thoroughly ground down by the teeth, a process that prepares the plant tissue for digestion in the gut. Once in the gut, microbes further break down the tough plant tissue—a long and rough process for the plant-eaters.

What special way did **ornithischian dinosaurs feed** on plants?

The ornithischian dinosaurs had a sharp, horny beak at the front of their mouth, with an array of rear teeth. The beak was probably used for cropping plant material, such as grass, fruits, leaves, bark, or twigs. The tooth batteries were then used to grind or cut the plants, preparing them for digestion. Each group of herbivorous dinosaurs had uniquely functioning and aligned teeth—no doubt reflecting the specific types and toughness of the plants they fed on.

How did the **teeth function** in the dinosaur *Iguanodon*?

In the *Iguanodon,* numerous sharp teeth were set in rows in the upper and lower jaws—and at steep angles to each other. When the teeth were pressed together, the upper jaw was forced outward. This created a grinding motion between the teeth that crushed the plant tissue.

How did the **teeth function** in the dinosaur *Triceratops*?

In the *Triceratops,* numerous teeth were interlocked in rows in the upper and lower jaws. These teeth were very sharp and formed a scissorlike blade running along the jaws. When pressed together, they passed each other vertically—similar to the action of scissor blades—and then sliced plants into short chunks.

What can scientists tell from the **shape** of **herbivorous dinosaurs' teeth**?

From the shape of the teeth, scientists can often interpret how different dinosaurs processed their food. In general, the teeth of herbivorous dinosaurs were very closely spaced, with either no gaps or a few, small gaps between them. A herbivore's teeth were mostly the same size for a simple reason: the herbivores chewed mostly on softer plants—thus, they didn't break their teeth as much as did the carnivores that chewed on hard bones.

Teeth varied between the herbivorous dinosaurs. For example, the teeth of some large sauropods, like *Diplodocus,* were located in a short row at the front of the mouth. These teeth were about the size and shape of the average pencil. These

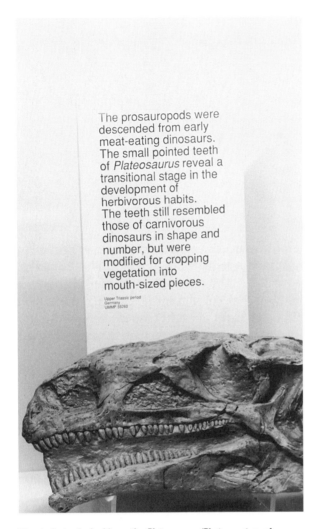

The prosauropods were descended from early meat-eating dinosaurs. The small pointed teeth of *Plateosaurus* reveal a transitional stage in the development of herbivorous habits. The teeth still resembled those of carnivorous dinosaurs in shape and number, but were modified for cropping vegetation into mouth-sized pieces.

Upper Triassic period
Germany
UMMP 55260

Mount of a toothy herbivore, the *Plateosaurus.* (Photo courtesy of University of Michigan Exhibit, Museum of Natural History.)

teeth were inadequate for extensive chewing, and paleontologists theorize the teeth were simply used to rake off the tender leaves from the treetops. This organic material was swallowed whole—leaving the breakdown of the plant material to the digestive tract of these animals.

The *Edmontosaurus,* a hadrosaur, did not have the same type of teeth as *Diplodocus.* After cutting or pulling the vegetation, its tongue would push the material back toward multiple rows of teeth located in its cheeks, called tooth batteries. Here, the upper teeth meshed with the lower teeth, with each tooth having dips and ridges. Combined with the powerful jaw muscles and cheeks, this grinding machine of a dinosaur allowed even the toughest plant material to be ground up before being digested. (And an average mouth contained close to 1,000 teeth!) Because of this grinding mechanism, paleontologists feel that the *Edmontosaurus* lived on mostly tough organic material, such as conifer needles, pine cones, and bark—in other words, food that most other herbivorous dinosaurs could not eat.

Yet another dinosaur—and one of the most common animals of its time during the late Cretaceous—was the *Protoceratops,* a herbivore with a sharp, narrow beak that easily sliced off vegetation. The scissorlike teeth at the back of its mouth would finely cut and chop the organic material, but not grind it, before it was swallowed. This allowed the *Protoceratops* to subsist on the tough, low-growing plants, such as palms and cycads.

Dagger-like teeth

The skull of the allosaur was built to eat meat—large amounts of it. The powerfully muscled jaws were lined with dagger-like teeth, used for tearing and slicing. Allosaurs did not chew their food, but simply gulped down the chunks of meat torn from their hapless prey.

Throughout an allosaur's life, its teeth were continuously shed and replaced by new ones growing from within the jaw bones. This section of jaw shows teeth in several stages of growth, with some recently emerged from the jawbone.

The *Allosaurus*'s huge, sharp teeth were well adapted for eating meat. (Photo courtesy of University of Michigan Exhibit, Museum of Natural History.)

What can scientists tell from the **shape** of **carnivorous dinosaurs' teeth**?

The teeth of carnivorous dinosaurs were much different from those of herbivores. In general, a carnivore's teeth had large gaps between them; the teeth acted as daggers, powered by the force of the jaw muscles and the dinosaur's weight. The teeth in a carnivorous dinosaur were different sizes, since new teeth were continually growing to replace those lost or broken—mostly from biting into bone or even fighting with other carnivores.

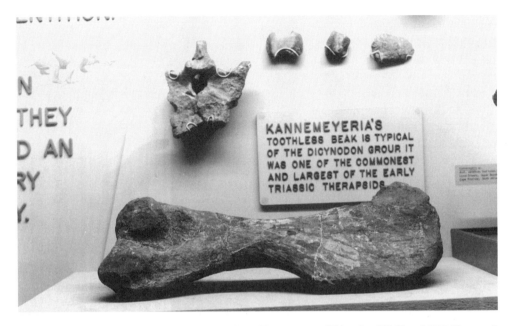

The *Kannemeyeria,* whose beak is shown here, was toothless. (Photo courtesy of University of Michigan Exhibit, Museum of Natural History.)

A typical large carnivore, like an *Allosaurus,* had backward curving, knifelike teeth; each tooth had serrations on the front and back edges. Paleontologists theorize a large carnivore like the *Allosaurus* would practice what is called macropredation. It would run into its victim, with its mouth open as wide as possible to drive the teeth in as far as possible. Closing its jaws, it would begin to jerk its powerful neck, ripping off a huge chunk of meat. The animal would then swallow this chunk whole, letting its digestive system take care of the rest. It would continue tearing off pieces of its prey until it was full.

What was **unusual** about the teeth of a *Tyrannosaurus rex*?

The teeth of a *Tyrannosaurus rex* were unusual in their shape. Most carnivorous dinosaurs had somewhat flat teeth, similar to razor-edged knife blades. However, a *Tyrannosaurus rex* had teeth shaped like giant spikes—almost like large, sharp bananas with serrations.

Are there any known **toothless theropod** dinosaurs?

There are several toothless theropod dinosaurs currently known—all from the group called the coelurosaurs. They include the ornithomimosaurs and oviraptorosaurs (oviraptorids).

What **adaptations** did **toothless dinosaurs** have?

Toothless dinosaurs, such as the *Kannemeyeria,* had beaks that they used in place of teeth. In addition, some had strong jaw muscles that—when combined with short, deep skulls—could crush their prey.

What did the **ornithomimosaurs eat**?

No one has found any fossil records of what ornithomimosaurs ate, but there are some theories. Such ornithomimosaurs as the *Ornithomimus, Struthiomimus,* and *Gallumimus* were similar in form to modern ostriches, so they probably ate the same kinds of food. Although they had weak jaw muscles, their beaks allowed them to eat anything small enough to be swallowed—such as small mammals, amphibians, lizards, fruits, and berries.

Clawed hands

With eight-foot strides of its long, powerful rear legs, allosaurus could overtake almost any prey, and then grab and hold its victim with the sharp curved claws on its front limbs. In life, the claw seen here was covered by a horny sheath, making it even longer and sharper.

This *Allosaurus* claw would have been a menace to its prey. (Photo courtesy of University of Michigan Exhibit, Museum of Natural History.)

What did the **oviraptorosaurs eat**?

Oviraptorosaurs such as *Oviraptor* and *Caenagnathus* were members of the Maniraptora group. They had strong toothless jaws for crushing their prey—although there is considerable debate as to the nature of that prey!

Although the oviraptorosaurs had powerful jaw muscles, their beaks were hollow and filled with air. Some paleontologists believe this indicates that these dinosaurs could not crush anything hard. Speculation on what oviraptorosaurs ate ranges from other dinosaurs' eggs, plants, and mollusks to eating food similar to that of the ornithomimosaurs.

Bone structure of the hand of an *Allosaurus,* a carnivorous dinosaur. (Photo courtesy of Michael S. Yamashita/Corbis.)

Were the **arms** of **carnivorous dinosaurs** used for anything?

The arms of some carnivorous dinosaurs were equipped with ferocious claws, which allowed the animal to grasp prey while the animal ripped off large chunks of meat with its mouth, or to hold down prey while the animal bit and slashed, trying to bring down its victim. Others, such as a *Deinonychus,* would hold down its victim with its long arms, positioning itself to slash the prey with its large, hind claws.

What were the **dromaeosaurids** and what type of **claws** did they have?

The dromaeosaurids take their name from the first dinosaur fossil of their type found: the *Dromaeosaurus,* or "running reptile." This group includes species such as the *Dromaeosaurus, Velociraptor, Deinonychus,* and the more recently discovered *Utahraptor.* These dinosaurs were fast-running meat-eaters, with long legs and light bone structures. They exhibited a blend of features from both the carnosaurs and the coelurosaurs—with some unique characteristics of their own.

Probably the most well-known feature of the dromaeosaurids was their large, sickle-shaped claws on the second toe of their foot. These huge, curved claws were probably used to tear and rip apart their prey. Dinosaurs from this group are known colloquially as "raptors." The best-known raptors are the "velociraptors" from the movies *Jurassic Park* and *The Lost World.* In reality, true *Velociraptors* were smaller than those portrayed in the movies; the movie raptors were closer in size to the

**What was the most savage
predatory dinosaur known to have walked the planet?**

This is a subjective call, and the answer probably depends on who was chasing whom at the time! Whether you feel the larger, but slower carnosaurs, like *Tyrannosaurus* or *Giganotosaurus,* were more savage, or the smaller, but quicker dromaeosaurids, like *Utahraptor* or *Deinonychus* took the prize, in the end, the victim usually ended up eaten. It would be like asking which animal is more savage—a lion or a polar bear. In their own way, and in their own habitat, each is a major predator in our modern world.

Deinonychus, a dromaeosaurid that was about twice the size of a *Velociraptor.* Overall, they were all thought to be vicious pack hunters you wouldn't want to meet in a dark alley—or in the tall grass!

What features did **raptors (dromaeosaurids)** share with **birds**?

Dromaeosaurid dinosaurs shared many features with birds: they both had hollow bones (some with holes) that made them lighter and stronger. The raptors also evolved in such a way that they eventually lost or fused some bones in the same areas as did birds.

How did the **dromaeosaurid carnivorous** dinosaurs **capture their prey**?

These large dinosaurs probably ran down their victims, grasping them with powerful front-arm claws resembling grappling hooks. They would then bite the prey with their backward-sloping needle-sharp teeth. Then they would slash and disembowel the prey with large, curving toe claws, which could be flexed in a wide arc to better penetrate their victims. When running, this toe claw could be raised up and back—preventing the claw from hitting the ground and becoming rounded.

What is the **largest raptor claw** found to date in **North America**?

The largest raptor claw found to date in North America belongs to a *Utahraptor.* This dinosaur had a length of about 20 feet (6 meters) and a height of about 7 feet (2 meters); the estimated weight of this animal is between 1,000 to 1,700 pounds. It had large, crescent-shaped claws on its forefeet and hind feet, with the two large foot claws measuring 12 inches (30.5 centimeters) in length. While the dinosaur was alive, the claws were covered with a sheath of keratin and were somewhat larger (they probably shrunk during fossilization). *Utahraptors* lived during the Cretaceous period.

What is the **largest raptor** found to date in the **world**?

The largest raptor that has been found to date in the world is the *Megaraptor namunhuaiquii*. *Megaraptor* means "giant thief," while *namunhuaiquii* is an Indian word meaning "foot lance." The raptorial claw of this dinosaur, measuring about 15 inches (38 centimeters) long, was discovered in the Patagonia region of Argentina. Paleontologists estimate that the *Megaraptor* was about 25 feet (7.6 meters) long, and lived roughly 100 million years ago during the Cretaceous period. This dinosaur does not seem to be closely related to the dromaeosaurids of North America and Asia—but may be a case of parallel evolution, in which two types of organisms form at the same time in a different regions of the world. Future digs should locate more bones and produce further data.

DINOSAUR METABOLISM

What is **animal metabolism**?

All animals have a certain metabolism. Simply put, the animal takes in foodstuff; in turn, the body uses a complex chain of specific physical and chemical processes to turn the food into energy for the animal.

Why is the **debate** over dinosaur **metabolism** so important?

An understanding of dinosaur metabolism is important because it determines the way we visualize the behavior of these animals. If dinosaurs were cold-blooded (similar to today's reptiles) they were probably mostly sluggish, with only occasional burst of quickness. In addition, they probably would not have been very smart creatures. They probably spent most of their time basking in the sun, moving only to obtain more food, similar to modern crocodiles.

On the other hand, if dinosaurs were warm-blooded (similar to today's mammals) they were probably active, social animals. They would have been quick, alert, and intelligent. They would have spent much of their time actively grazing—similar to modern antelope, or hunting in packs, similar to lions.

Do scientists know what **type of metabolism** dinosaurs had?

Currently, scientists do not know too much about dinosaur metabolism. There is a wealth of conflicting evidence, most of it indirect. Some of the problem may be that various types of dinosaurs had different metabolisms. For example, the large plant-eating dinosaurs might have needed a much different metabolism than the small, quick theropods.

Paleontologists are currently divided on their opinions of dinosaur metabolism, generally falling into three camps. Some interpret the available evidence as meaning dinosaurs were indeed cold-blooded. Others firmly believe that dinosaurs were warm-blooded. And the last group thinks dinosaurs had a unique physiology—a combination of both cold- and warm-blooded traits.

What do the terms **ectothermic** and **endothermic** mean?

Ectothermic and endothermic are terms used to describe the heat source animals use to maintain an activity temperature—or a safe body temperature for that organism. Ectothermic means the animal must depend on an external source of heat, such as sunlight. Endothermic means the animal uses an internal source of heat for this purpose. For example, reptiles, such as snakes, are primarily ectothermic, and known as "cold-blooded"; mammals are primarily endothermic, and known as "warm-blooded."

What do the terms **poikilothermic** and **homeothermic** mean?

Poikilothermic and homeothermic are terms used to describe an animal who either can or cannot maintain a steady internal temperature in its normal environment, regardless of changes in daily ambient temperatures. Poikilothermic means the animal cannot maintain a steady internal temperature, while homeothermic means the animal can maintain a steady internal temperature. For example, reptiles are poikilothermic; mammals are homeothermic.

What do the terms **tachymetabolic** and **bradymetabolic** mean?

Tachymetabolic and bradymetabolic are terms used to describe the rate at which an animal's metabolism, or body chemistry, runs. Tachymetabolic animals, such as modern birds, have a high rate of metabolism; bradymetabolic animals, such as reptiles, have a slow rate of metabolism.

How were **dinosaurs described in the past**?

Up until about 1970, most scientists felt that the dinosaurs were cold-blooded, that is, ectothermic and poikilothermic, similar to many modern reptiles. Thus, dinosaurs were viewed as sluggish, stupid creatures. Mammals, on the other hand, were warm-blooded, or endothermic and homeothermic, and were quick, agile—and thus, intelligent. This notion of cold-bloodedness colored all aspects of the way dinosaurs were viewed, including their behaviors (dull and stupid) and social structures (none).

Who first **proposed** that dinosaurs were **warm-blooded**?

In the late 1960s and early 1970s, paleontologists John H. Ostrom (b. 1928) and Robert T. Bakker (b. 1945) first suggested that dinosaurs were not sluggish, stupid, cold-blooded animals. Their work paved the way for the theory that many of these animals were actually agile, dynamic, and smart.

In 1969, John Ostrom published a description of the *Deinonychus,* a Cretaceous period carnivorous dinosaur. Based on his study of the creature, he theorized that dinosaurs may have been warm-blooded. In 1975, Robert Bakker summarized his ideas about dinosaur endothermy in an article published in *Scientific American.* This set off a new era in dinosaur paleontology that has continued through today—especially in advancing ideas on how dinosaurs truly regulated their bodies' metabolism and heat.

Why did **Robert Bakker** believe **dinosaurs** were **endothermic homeotherms**?

Some of the reasons paleontologist Robert Bakker gave for dinosaurs being endothermic homeotherms, or warm-blooded, are: dinosaurs had complex bone structures (with evidence of constant remodeling), a feature of modern mammals, not reptiles; dinosaurs had an upright structure, similar to birds and modern mammals; dinosaurs (at least the small theropods) had, from the evidence to date, active lifestyles; predator-to-prey ratios were closer to that of modern mammals than reptiles; and dinosaurs were found in polar regions.

What is the **predator-to-prey ratio**?

The predator-to-prey ratio is a mathematical concept used by scientists to estimate the maximum number of predators that can be supported by a given population of prey animals in a specific location. Predatory animals, being carnivorous, depend on other animals for their sustenance; an overabundance of predators in a given area leads to the rapid depletion of the prey animal population and perhaps the starvation death of some predators. An area that has too few predators sees a rapid increase in the population of the prey animals, leading to overgrazing and starvation of the prey animals. Over time, an optimum balance between the predators and their prey is reached and can be described by the predator-to-prey ratio.

On the African veldt, where lions prey on animals such as gazelles and wildebeests, the carnivores usually constitute 1 to 6 percent of the total animal population, which is typical of a mammal-type community. The ratio is low because these predators are endothermic, or warm-blooded, and need large amounts of food to sustain their metabolism; a given population of prey can only support a very small number of these predators.

> ## What can dinosaur bones tell us about the animals' internal heat regulation?
>
> **D**inosaur bones, like modern reptile bones, often show signs of not growing—as if these animals went through periods of little or no growth. One of the reasons for a lack of growth could be hibernation during periods of seasonal cold, indicating that the animals used an ectothermic (external) method of heat regulation. Mammals and birds, on the other hand, are endothermic (warm-blooded), and show no lines of arrested growth. Thus, the presence or absence of these lines give paleontologists clues about the way dinosaurs regulated their internal temperature.

Scientists estimate that an animal community with ectothermic, or cold-blooded, predators would have a ratio approximately 10 times larger, since ectotherms do not need as much food to sustain their metabolism. A given population of prey could support a much larger number of this type of predator.

What does the **predator-to-prey ratio** tell paleontologists about **dinosaurs**?

The predator-to-prey ratio tells paleontologists that the predatory dinosaurs (carnivorous theropods) were probably endothermic, or warm-blooded. For example, the different kinds of dinosaurs collected from the Oldman rock formation in Alberta, Canada, show that for every *Tyrannosaurus rex*, there were approximately 20 herbivorous dinosaurs—giving a predator-to-prey ratio of 5 percent. This is comparable to ratios found in modern mammalian communities.

Can scientists really use the **predator-to-prey ratio** in reference to **dinosaurs**?

There are essentially two reasons to question that the predator-to-prey ratio applies to certain dinosaurs—especially when interpreting whether the dinosaurs were truly warm-blooded. First, the assumption that the number of carnivorous dinosaurs was limited only by the available food supply may be true. But this also may not be true, as the number of carnivorous dinosaurs may have been limited by other, unknown factors.

Second, the predator-dinosaur-to-prey-dinosaur ratio makes the assumption that the current, known numbers of fossils accurately reflect dinosaur populations. Considering the long, hazardous process of fossilization, and the difficulty in collecting and identifying remains, the known fossil record may not really reflect the true dinosaur population. These cautions make the fixing of a ratio—and the extrapolation to warm-bloodedness—a somewhat nebulous process. Further data and research are needed in order for scientists to understand if and how the ratio applied to dinosaurs.

Can **bone tissue** tell us anything about dinosaur metabolism?

So far, the study of bone tissue cannot tell us anything definite about dinosaur metabolism. The highly vascular bone structure normally seen in warm-blooded animals has also been seen in saurischian dinosaur bones, such as the *Apatosaurus* and *Diplodocus,* and in ornithischian dinosaurs such as the *Iguanodon, Triceratops,* and *Stegosaurus.*

Although this would indicate some form of warm-bloodedness, this type of bone structure has also been seen in some modern cold-blooded animals. Apparently, a highly vascular bone structure is found in all animals with fast growth rates. It can also be found in large animals that need strong bones to support their weight. Thus, having this type of bone tissue is not an indication of cold- or warm-bloodedness—and cannot be used to determine dinosaur metabolism.

What kind of **heart** did dinosaurs have?

Fossil evidence of the soft internal parts of dinosaurs—including the heart—is sadly lacking. But based on indirect evidence, paleontologists have extrapolated that dinosaurs had a divided heart capable of keeping the blood at two different pressures.

Dinosaur bone tissue shows evidence of blood vessels. Therefore, a heart was necessary to drive the circulatory system, sending blood around the body. Dinosaurs with extremely long necks (such as the large sauropods) and those with heads held upright needed a high blood pressure. This would allow the blood to pump all the way to the brain when the animal was reaching for food. But such a blood system would have too high a pressure to safely circulate to the lungs for oxygenation. Thus, scientists believe dinosaurs probably had a divided heart—capable of supplying blood at two different pressures into two separate circulatory systems.

Does a **divided heart** in dinosaurs mean they were **warm-blooded**?

A divided heart is essential for warm-blooded animals. But even if dinosaurs did have this type of heart, it doesn't necessarily mean they were warm-blooded. In particular, all modern animals with divided hearts aren't necessarily warm-blooded. For example, the modern alligator has a divided heart, but it is still cold-blooded. The presence of a divided heart only shows that dinosaurs had the *potential* to be warm-blooded.

What does **theropod dinosaur brain size** tell us about their metabolism?

Unlike most of the other dinosaurs, some of the smaller theropods (carnivores) had large brains relative to their body size. The brains were equivalent to those found in similar-sized mammals. To function properly, large brains need a steady temperature, and constant supply of food and oxygen—all of which could indicate a *potential* for a higher metabolism associated with warm-bloodedness.

Could a dinosaur's **bipedal stance** indicate **warm-bloodedness**?

No, the bipedal stance of some dinosaurs does not indicate that they were warm-blooded. For example, the modern chameleon has an upright posture and is cold-blooded. Even crocodiles can walk in a semi-erect way—so posture is not an indication of warm-bloodedness.

Could a **dinosaur's speed** indicate **warm-bloodedness**?

No, a dinosaur's walking or running speed does not indicate that they were warm-blooded—even though studies of dinosaur tracks and bones show that some were capable of running at high speeds. To compare, some modern cold-blooded reptiles can move very quickly—they just lack the stamina to continue this pace for very long.

What do **dinosaurs' noses** tell us about their metabolism?

Some scientists believe that dinosaurs' noses are evidence for their cold-bloodedness. Respiratory turbinates are small scrolls of bone or cartilage in the nose covered with membranes—and the absence of these bones in dinosaurs' noses is probably a good indication that the animals were not warm-blooded. These turbinates are found in all warm-blooded animals, having evolved independently in mammals and birds; no known cold-blooded animals have them.

Warm-blooded animals breath quite rapidly. The warm, exhaled air passes over the turbinates and cools, causing the moisture in the air to condense out onto the membranes. In turn, this prevents dehydration.

If dinosaurs were truly warm-blooded, they would need to have respiratory turbinates to prevent dehydration. Scientists recently used computer-aided tomography (CAT) scans to study dinosaur fossil skulls for any signs of respiratory turbinates. So far, the remains of *Velociraptor* and *Nanotyrannus* do not show any signs of these structures. Further analysis is planned to study fossil skulls from all the major groups of dinosaurs.

Were any **dinosaurs warm-blooded**?

No one really knows for sure. Besides the issue of how the dinosaurs died off, the question of whether or not any dinosaurs were warm-blooded is one of the most highly debated issues in paleontology. The debate will continue until more fossil evidence is found to support dinosaur warm-bloodedness.

Is there any evidence that *Tyrannosaurus rex* was **warm-blooded**?

There may be some emerging evidence for this scenario: the measurement of oxygen isotope ratios from a *Tyrannosaurus rex* fossil skeleton indicates that this dinosaur may have been warm-blooded. The data suggests a fairly uniform body temperature, with the dinosaur's heat distributed uniformly over its body—similar to modern mammals and birds.

Scientists measured the relative ratios of oxygen-16 and oxygen-18 isotopes in the phosphate of numerous samples taken from a recently discovered, well-preserved, and nearly complete *Tyrannosaurus rex* skeleton. Using these ratios, the researchers determined which parts of the animal were the warmest. Although this technique did not determine the actual body temperatures of the *Tyrannosaurus rex,* it did show how the heat was distributed across the body.

The results indicate that this dinosaur was fairly evenly heated, with a less than four-degree variation in body temperature from location to location. The end of the tail was a little colder than the base, and the feet were a little colder than the core of the body. This type of heat distribution is typical of warm-blooded animals; cold-blooded animals that rely on the external environment for their heat have variations in the temperatures across their bodies—with the greatest variations occurring in their extremities.

How did the **largest dinosaurs** possibly regulate their **internal temperature**?

Although there is still a lot of debate on this subject, with new findings almost every day, the general agreement is that the largest dinosaurs were ectothermic homeotherms. In other words, the animals received the majority of their heat externally—most likely from the sun (similar to modern reptiles). But, because of their very large mass, they were also able to maintain a constant internal temperature. A large mass takes a long time to heat up or cool down, thus maintaining an even core temperature; this property is known as mass homeothermy.

How did the **smaller dinosaurs** possibly regulate their **internal temperature**?

A recent study of small, herbivorous dinosaurs from Australia belonging to the hypsilophodontids seems to indicate that these dinosaurs were indeed endothermic (warm-blooded). They lived in cold southern Australia, south of the Antarctic Circle, approximately 100 million years ago. But their bones show no signs of arrested growth—rather the animals had consistent, rapid growth. This would indicate that these dinosaurs did not hibernate, but were able to maintain an elevated internal temperature even in the cold. It would appear this species of dinosaurs, at least, may have been endothermic.

The fossilized remains of another small dinosaur were recently found northeast of Beijing, China, and may also be a link to endothermic dinosaurs. This animal had a long tail, and was about the size of a large turkey. Estimates place the age of this dinosaur, called *Sinosauropteryx*, between 120 and 140 million years old or even older. What was exciting about this discovery was the appearance of featherlike features along the animal's neck, back, and tail. Scientists think that these featherlike features were not useful for flight—rather *Sinosauropteryx* was warm-blooded and used these feathers to retain heat.

Other dinosaur bones found to date have also been intriguing. For example, those bones showing alternating lines of bone growth, then no bone growth, could indicate that the species' physiologies lie somewhere between modern reptiles and mammals.

Fossil of the *Sinosauropteryx*, a small, chicken-like creature with downy fluff. (Photo courtesy of David Bubier/Academy of Natural Sciences/Associated Press.)

Why are the fossil remains of *Scipionyx samniticus* so interesting?

The recent discovery of a baby theropod dinosaur called *Scipionyx samniticus* shows many fossilized soft parts—one of the first times such interior detail has ever been discovered. The fossilized remains also show these dinosaurs probably had a unique metabolism that help them dominate the land during the Mesozoic era.

What was **unique** about the **metabolism** of *Scipionyx samniticus?*

Scipionyx samniticus was probably cold-blooded like a reptile—but apparently also

235

had the metabolic capacity of a modern mammal or bird. Paleontologists illuminated the animal's fossil remains under ultraviolet light to make the soft parts more visible, revealing the liver, large intestine, windpipe, and some muscles. The body cavity of *Scipionyx samniticus* was also found to be divided into two parts by a diaphragm. The top part contained the lungs and heart, while the liver and entrails were located in the bottom part. The very presence of a diaphragm—also found in humans and other mammals—reveals that *Scipionyx samniticus* (and perhaps other theropod dinosaurs) had a much greater breathing capacity than most modern-day reptiles. Oxygen could be quickly pumped into the lungs and bloodstream, giving them more energy than other dinosaurs.

Because they were cold-blooded, they had low metabolic rates while resting, enabling them to conserve energy. But they could also, with their enhanced breathing capacity, move extremely fast and aggressively for relatively long periods of time.

In essence, they were turbocharged reptiles, combining the quickness and ruthlessness of a komodo dragon or crocodile with the long-term stamina of a tiger or lion. This ability to conserve energy most of the time—combined with ability to run long enough and fast enough to chase down any prey they wanted—enabled these animals to dominate over the other life-forms during the Mesozoic era.

Did the *Scipionyx samniticus'* unique metabolism contribute to its **extinction**?

Yes, it is possible that the unique metabolism of the *Scipionyx samniticus* (and possibly other theropod dinosaurs) contributed to its extinction. Theropod dinosaurs were essentially cold-blooded; they depended on the external environment to maintain their body temperature. This was fine for the animals during most of the Mesozoic era, as the climate was warm.

Dinosaurs may have been in decline for 6 to 8 million years before the end of the Cretaceous period. But before the end, the climate became cooler—either by natural global cooling or possibly by the impact of an asteroid or comet (or many) on the earth. The animals' unique metabolism made them sensitive to the climatic cooling—and thus, this specialization may have also contributed to their extinction.

Do scientists **agree** about the *Scipionyx samniticus'* **unique metabolism**?

No. Some scientists believe there is little proof—mainly because there is only one such beautifully preserved sample of the remains. Others also believe that the interpretation of the fossil may be incorrect. For example, the supposed liver in the fossil remains could easily be a smudge from the animal's stomach contents.

SIZE OF DINOSAURS

What was the purpose of the **different sizes** and **shapes** of dinosaurs?

Similar to today's animals, the different sizes and shapes were the result of adaptations to the many dinosaurs' surrounding environments. In particular, the dinosaurs were probably typical of most animals: they needed to adapt to the prevailing conditions and changing food supplies in order to survive. And many times these adaptations took the form of certain sizes and shapes—and probably even colors.

Was there an **upper limit** to the **size of a dinosaur**?

The answer to this question probably depends on the availability and locality of the dinosaur's food supply. In general, to support a larger weight, the dinosaur's bone size must have also increased, or else the bones would literally break under the animal's own weight. Additionally, as the bones became thicker to support the increasing weight, the animal would have become more and more cumbersome, limiting its ability to obtain food. Thus, for each dinosaur species, there was probably a definite limit to its size.

What was the **average size** among the **dinosaurs**?

The popular conception of dinosaurs is one of hugeness. But dinosaurs came in all sizes and shapes and types and they were extremely diverse, much like today's birds. They ranged in size from the gigantic sauropods, like *Brachiosaurus,* to small, chicken-sized ones like *Compsognathus,* and every size in between. Because we have only found relatively few fossils, it's hard to say what the average size of dinosaurs was.

How do scientists determine the **weight** of a dinosaur?

It's not easy to determine the weight of a dinosaur. Scientists can only estimate the animals' weight by looking at the bones of the animals—remains that have been sitting in rock for more than 65 million years!

One method of determining a dinosaur's weight is by studying the cross-sectional area of a limb bone; that way, scientists estimate the weight borne by the limb. But it's not only the weight times four legs—it's also the position of the legs, the posture of the animal, and the limb shape. Some scientists have also tried to extrapolate the weight of a dinosaur by comparing the animals to modern living species—but apparently, there is really no linear relationship.

Skeletal mount of a *Brachiosaurus,* a gigantic sauropod. (Photo courtesy of Gail Mooney/Corbis.)

What are the **problems** with **estimating** dinosaur **weight**?

There are the questions concerning proportions—in which dinosaur artists interpret the animals' postures differently. Another problem is truly determining just how much flesh an animal possessed, which would also add to the weight. In addition, some dinosaurs had hollow bones—probably less dense than those of crocodiles. But how much less dense were these bones?

What is the **largest dinosaur fossil** found to date?

Because so many different large dinosaur fossils have recently been found, it is difficult to definitively point to the largest dinosaur fossil.

On one end of the scale were the large sauropods, of which the *Brachiosaurus* ("arm lizard") is the most familiar. Many scientists believe the *Brachiosaurus* is one of the largest dinosaurs, mainly because paleontologists have found so many complete fossil skeletons of these huge species, and thus know more about them. This large plant-eater measured about 70 feet (22 meters) long, about the length of two large school buses, and 40 feet (12.2 meters) high—or about as tall as an average three-story building. One of the largest whole skeleton specimens of the *Brachiosaurus* is in the Humboldt Museum in Berlin, and it measures 72.75 feet (22.2 meters) long and 46 feet (14 meters) high. The weight of this specimen is estimated to have been about

Fossilized remains of a *Compsognathus,* the smallest dinosaur. (Photo courtesy of University of Michigan Exhibit, Museum of Natural History.)

34.7 tons. The average weight of a typical *Brachiosaurus* is disputed, ranging from 32 to 78 tons—but either way, they were enormous animals.

Bone fragments have also been found of dinosaur species even larger than the *Brachiosaurus.* For example, the *Supersaurus, Ultrasaurus, Argentinosaurus,* and *Amphicoelias* are all very large-boned animals, most of them carnivores. Since complete skeletons of these dinosaurs have not been found to date, their exact size cannot be determined. But some scientists believe some of these species may have been one-and-a-half to two times larger than the *Brachiosaurus.*

Which **carnivorous** dinosaur was **biggest**?

The favorite contender is the theropod *Tyrannosaurus,* the Cretaceous period carnivore found in North America and Asia; it measured over 40 feet (12 meters) in length. The two new challengers are the *Giganotosaurus* of South America, and the *Charcharodontosaurus* of North Africa, two huge meat-eaters.

So far, the *Tyrannosaurus* seems to be in the lead, thanks to a huge fossil of a *Tyrannosaurus'* pubis bone found in 1997 in Fort Peck, Montana. This creature was so massive, scientists have given the fossil its own name: *Tyrannosaurus imperator.* This tyrannosaur's pubis bone measures 52.4 inches (133 centimeters) long; the pubis bone of *Giganotosaurus* measures only 46.5 inches (118 centimeters) in length—which

239

would make the Montana *Tyrannosaurus* about 15 to 20 percent larger than any other known meat-eating dinosaur.

No doubt, this is only the beginning. The hunt for the largest carnivore—and dinosaur—will continue. Paleontologists will find new dinosaur bones, and one of them may one day prove to be the largest dinosaur ever known.

What are the **smallest dinosaur fossils** found to date?

The smallest adult dinosaur fossil found to date is that of the *Compsognathus* ("pretty jaw"). The animal was slightly larger than a turkey, with a total length of approximately 3 feet (1 meter), and weighed approximately 6.5 pounds. This small carnivore, nicknamed "Compy," lived during the Jurassic period, and was a fast-running and agile predator, probably subsisting on insects, frogs, and small lizards.

The smallest dinosaur fossil so far uncovered, regardless of age, is that of the *Mussaurus*, or "mouse lizard." Fossils of this animal were found in 1979 in South America. Once thought to be the smallest dinosaur, it is now known the *Mussaurus* fossils were actually hatchlings of *Coloradisaurus*, which, when fully grown, would be larger than a *Compsognathus*. Their eggs measure only 1 inch (2.54 centimeters) long; the fossil hatchlings measure only 7.8 to 16 inches (20 to 40 centimeters) long.

Which **dinosaur** had the **longest neck** of any animal known?

Although the true longest-neck prize is highly debated, it is thought that the *Barosaurus*, or "heavy lizard," had the longest neck of any known dinosaur. The reason for the debate is that fossils of the *Barosaurus* are some of the rarest known. Because there are not many other specimens to back up the longest-neck claim, many scientists do not believe this animal is the winner.

Even though there is still debate, the *Barosaurus*, related to the *Diplodocus*, did have an enormously long neck—thought to be longer than the *Brachiosaurus*. Fossil remains of the *Barosaurus* have been found in the western United States and in Africa. The only mounted skeleton in the world of *Barosaurus* is found in New York City, at the American Museum of Natural History—depicted rearing up on its hind legs, confronting a predator.

Most of the longest necks belonged to the sauropod (herbivore) dinosaurs, creatures who probably needed the longer necks to reach food in the higher tree branches. Other major contenders include the usual favorite, the *Brachiosaurus*, a sauropod that reached a height of 40 feet (12.2 meters)—with much of that height a combination of its long neck and front legs. Still another long-necked dinosaur was the *Mamenchisaurus*, a sauropod dinosaur with a 33-foot- (10- meter-) long neck.

Where have dwarf dinosaur fossils been found?

Dwarf dinosaur fossils have been found in Hateg, Romania. During the late Cretaceous period, much of the land area of Eastern Europe was inundated by the waters of the Tethys Ocean. Thus, the land existed in the form of islands.

Dinosaurs, along with other animals and plants, were isolated on these islands, cutting off the flora and fauna from other larger landmasses. Over time, the dinosaurs on these islands became smaller in response to the limited ecological environment. For example, the *Telmatosaurus,* a primitive hadrosaur found in Hateg, was about 15 feet (5 meters) long, and weighed approximately 1,103 pounds, or just over a half ton. This is about one-third the length and one-tenth the weight of other *Telmatosaurus* fossils found in other parts of the world. The larger dinosaurs were able to take advantage of greater territories and habitats, growing much more than their smaller, island-bound cousins.

What **fossil find** may lead scientists to the **longest dinosaur** ever found?

The longest dinosaur ever found may not be known for a while. The fossils of a possible 150-foot (46-meter) Jurassic period dinosaur called a *Seismosaurus* is still being dug out from a chunk of sandstone found in New Mexico. It will take years to carefully dig out the specimen for display. Because of the hard sandstone surrounding the skeleton, scientists can only uncover a few square inches of bone per day.

What was the **longest predatory dinosaur**?

Scientists believe that the carnivore *Spinosaurus aegypticus* may have been up to 56 feet (17 meters) long—one of the largest predators, if not the longest. The animal's long spine evolved during the early Cretaceous period. (In fact, the entire vertebra of a *Spinosaurus* is taller than the average-size human.) The tall spines formed a skin-encased sail-like structure; some scientists suggest that the long spine was needed to hold the sails. No one knows the function of the structure, but there are some theories: One states that because the animals lived in the tropics close to sea level, the sails may have been used to cool off the animals. Another idea is that the sails were used for attracting potential mates or for scaring off potential rivals—or even other dinosaur predators.

DINOSAUR BEHAVIOR

DINOSAUR DELICACIES

What did **dinosaurs eat**?

Based on the popular representations of dinosaurs in the media, these large, vicious creatures could eat anything they wanted—and some probably did! In reality, there is very little direct evidence of what the dinosaurs ate. But, from rare evidence and other factors, paleontologists have made some assumptions about dinosaur diets.

Since dinosaurs lived on our planet for about 150 million years, they must have slowly adapted to the changing flora and fauna. Overall, there were apparently two major types, and one minor type of dinosaurs: herbivores, carnivores, and omnivores, respectively. Most of the dinosaurs were herbivores, or animals that ate available plants; the carnivorous dinosaurs, of course, ate other animals, including dinosaurs; and very few dinosaurs were omnivores, or animals that ate meat and plants.

What **food was available** to the dinosaurs?

The food available to the dinosaurs gradually evolved over the millions of years of the Mesozoic era—just like the dinosaurs themselves. Most of the dinosaurs ate plants. Fossil evidence of pollen and spores indicates that there were hundreds to thousands of different types of plants growing during the Mesozoic era, most with edible leaves. Some examples of possible dinosaur delicacies included ferns, mosses, horsetail rushes, cycads, ginkos, and evergreen conifers like pine trees and redwoods (grass had not yet evolved). Toward the end of the Mesozoic era, with the advent of flowering plants, fruits also became available.

For dinosaurs of the carnivorous persuasion, there was also a large selection of food choices in the Mesozoic "cafeteria." These include the early mammals, eggs, tur-

What evidence do paleontologists use to determine the diets of dinosaurs?

Because the actual, physical evidence of dinosaur diets is so rare (the soft parts of a dinosaur are rarely fossilized), paleontologists have turned to indirect evidence to form some idea of the feeding habits of dinosaurs. These include coprolites (fossils of excrement), trackways, fossil assemblages, and tooth marks on bones.

tles, and lizards that shared the landscape with the dinosaurs. Of course, there were also other dinosaurs to be hunted or scavenged.

Did **dinosaurs** need **water**?

It is probably safe to assume that dinosaurs, like all living creatures, needed water to live. They probably obtained water much like modern reptiles, either directly from a water source; or from their food, such as the plants they ate (in the case of herbivores), the animals they consumed (carnivores), or both (omnivores).

What are **coprolites**?

Coprolites, or scat, are the fossilized droppings, or feces, of dinosaurs. Because of the soft nature of this fecal material, soft dinosaur droppings would often disintegrate before they had a chance to fossilize. And if they dropped in the "wrong" place (such as the shore of the ocean where the waves would wash the material away), the chances of the dung becoming fossilized were almost nonexistent.

Also, the shapes and sizes of most coprolites are not readily distinguishable between animals. Thus, there are, at present, few coprolites unequivocally traced back to dinosaurs—but the ones that have been traced offer tantalizing clues to dinosaur diets. In particular, such coprolites give us an insight into what the animal was eating, how it ate, and what happened afterward in terms of digestion.

What factors influenced the **fossilization** of **coprolites**?

The preservation and subsequent fossilization of coprolites depended on a number of factors, including the organic content and amount of water present in the deposited feces. It also included, of course, where the animal dropped the feces and the method of burial—all keys to the formation of coprolites.

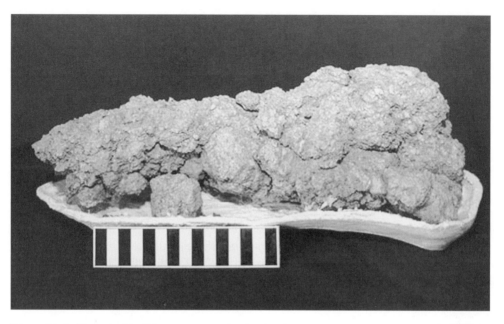

This possibly the biggest fecal fossil from a meat-eater found to date, from a juvenile *Tyrannosaurus rex*. The fossil, some 17 inches long, 5 inches high, and 6 inches wide, was found sticking out of a hillside in 1995 in Saskatchewan, Canada. (Photo courtesy of U.S. Geological Survey/Associated Press.)

There is one good example of content importance: the feces of carnivorous dinosaurs were more likely to become fossilized that those of the herbivores because of their higher mineral content. These minerals were from bits of bone within the feces—in other words, from the consumption of other animals!

Are all **coprolites large**—especially those from the larger dinosaurs?

Not all coprolites are large. Individual coprolites can be small—less than 3 inches (10 centimeters) long—even though they came from a large dinosaur. A modern example of this phenomena is the mule deer and elk of North America. These animals deposit many pellets that are less than a third of an inch (1 centimeter) in size, even though these are relatively large animals.

In terms of dinosaurs, evidence for this phenomena comes from a probable sauropod coprolite found in the Morrison formation of eastern Utah. Although this coprolite is about 16 inches (40 centimeters) in diameter, it is probably from a mass of smaller individual pellets that merged together—no doubt due to a high water content.

What have paleontologists **learned** from **dinosaur coprolites**?

Paleontologists have found—in coprolites thought to be from herbivorous dinosaurs—quantities of cycad leaf cuticles, conifer stems, or conifer wood tissues, giving some clues as to what these dinosaurs ate. Also, in some cases, the nature of the fragments shows these dinosaurs were well equipped to chew up and digest the tough, woody food available at the time.

Several coprolites from carnivorous dinosaurs have also been found. One recent find was astounding. In 1998, near the town of Eastend, Saskatchewan, Canada, scientists found a huge coprolite, almost as large as a loaf of bread. The 65-million-year-old coprolite measures 17 inches (43 centimeters) and is thought to be from a *Tyrannosaurus rex*; it is one of the largest coprolites ever found. The analysis of the coprolite also produced an intriguing suggestion: the remains look as if the *Tyrannosaurus* did not swallow the bones of its prey somewhat whole—but actually chewed and pulverized the animal's bones. This is contrary to what paleontologists have believed for a long time—that these carnivores "gulped and swallowed" their prey. But the verdict is still out on the subject until scientists find more such coprolites.

What **other information** can be obtained from **coprolites**?

The discovery of coprolites at a location can indicate the presence of dinosaurs—especially in areas that lack skeletal remains or other trace fossils. In addition, the possible surrounding habitats when the feces were deposited can also be inferred. For example, one possible habitat could be a floodplain near a river. The dinosaur's feces deposited on an arid floodplain could have dried slightly before a flood rapidly buried the remains. Other habitats that could have been prime places for coprolite formations include muddy areas surrounding lakes or estuaries, around swamps, and around streams and watering holes.

Did **dinosaurs urinate**?

No one knows if dinosaurs urinated, as the soft anatomical parts to indicate such an activity do not readily fossilize. But it is probably safe to assume they did, if modern reptiles and birds are similar to their ancient cousins, the dinosaurs. In fact, they may have excreted a solid form of urea, or guano, similar to modern birds and reptiles.

What do **trackways** tell paleontologists about **dinosaur diets**?

Trackways, the multiple fossilized footprints of dinosaurs, have given paleontologists some idea of the feeding habits of many dinosaurs. For example, an early Cretaceous period site in Texas, as well as a late Cretaceous period site in Bolivia, show footprints of what appears to be a pack of theropods actively stalking a herd of sauropods. In a

The ferocious teeth of a *Tyrannosaurus rex,* a carnivore. (Photo courtesy of Michael S. Yamashita/Corbis.)

Cretaceous period site in Australia, fossilized tracks suggest a herd of over 100 small coelurosaurs and ornithopods stampeded as a large, single therapod stalked the group. In a Utah coal mine, Cretaceous period footprints of herbivorous dinosaurs clustered around fossil tree trunks give some indication of their foraging behavior.

What are **fossil assemblages,** and what do they tell us about **dinosaur diets**?

Fossil assemblages are groups of fossils from different dinosaurs. For example, one assemblage found in the sandstones of the Gobi Desert in Mongolia is of a carnivorous *Velociraptor* intertwined with a herbivorous *Protoceratops*. The *Velociraptor's* clawed feet were attached to its prey's throat and belly, while the *Protoceratops'* jaws had trapped the arm of the predator. This assemblage suggests the struggling dinosaurs, predator and prey, died together as a massive sandstorm overcame them.

In 15 sites in Montana, major fossil assemblages have been found. The teeth of the carnivorous dinosaur *Deinonychus* was found in association with the fossil remains of the herbivorous dinosaur *Tenontosaurus*. Dinosaur teeth were continually shed, as new ones grew in, and vigorous biting could have increased tooth loss. Since there is lack of *Deinonychus* teeth found with the remains of other dinosaurs, paleontologists have concluded that the *Tenontosaurus* was the favorite prey of this predator.

What do **tooth marks** tell us about **dinosaur diets**?

Another piece of evidence used by paleontologists to determine dinosaur diets are tooth marks. Most of the grooves or punctures found associated with fossilized dinosaur bones were the result of attacks by carnivorous dinosaurs. Most of the time, however, this evidence does not reveal whether the victim was actively hunted or scavenged—and except in certain cases, the identity of the predator cannot be determined.

In one instance, the spacing of the scoring found on the bones of an *Apatosaurus,* a herbivore, matched the spacing of teeth from the jaw of an *Allosaurus,* a carnivore. In another case, dental putty was used to make molds of puncture marks found in a *Triceratops'* (a herbivore) pelvis, and an *Edmontosaurus'* (another herbivore) phalanx. The resulting molds nicely matched the fossilized teeth of the suspected predator, a carnivorous *Tyrannosaurus.* In one rare instance, a *Tyrannosaurus* tooth was found stuck in the fibula of a herbivorous hadrosaur, *Hypacrosaurus.* And of course, in the most obvious cases (and the most rare), predators could be identified if the fossil bones—and teeth—of the two animals were locked in mortal combat.

To what **group** did all the **meat-eating dinosaurs** belong?

All of the carnivorous, or meat-eating dinosaurs, belonged to the theropods, or bipedal (two-footed) carnivores. These dinosaurs, along with the large, herbivorous sauropods, made up the saurischian dinosaurs. This group represents a wide range of dinosaur species—from the large *Tyrannosaurus* to the small *Compsognathus*.

What were some of the **major types** of **theropod** dinosaurs?

The major types of dinosaurs making up the theropods were divided into two lineages: the coelurosaurs and the carnosaurs. This simple classification does not reflect the true relationships of the theropods, and is usually not used by paleontologists to classify the animals. But there is no universally accepted alternative classification of the animals—mainly because there are so many fossils (many of which changed dramatically over the Mesozoic era) and interpretations.

Thus, in general, the theropods were represented by the coelurosaurs and carnosaurs. The smaller, more nimble, meat-eating dinosaurs with longer grasping arms and long, narrow jaws were known as coelurosaurs, or "hollow-tailed lizards." They developed during the middle Jurassic period and roamed the land until the end of the Cretaceous. They could run very fast and catch insects and small mammals; some were also thought to be cannibals. One of the most well-known coelurosaurs is the *Compsognathus.*

The large, big-headed dinosaurs, with powerful legs and small arms, were known as carnosaurs, or "flesh lizards." These dinosaurs pursued and ate other dinosaurs, using numerous backward-curving teeth and clawed feet—and in many cases, weight—to catch prey. One well-known carnosaur is the *Allosaurus*. The popular carnivore *Tyrannosaurus* was once classified under the carnosaurs, but it is now thought that it is more closely related to the smaller coelurosaurs of the Cretaceous period.

What adaptations enabled **carnivorous dinosaurs** to **eat meat**?

All of the carnivorous dinosaurs shared many adaptations specific to catching, killing, eating, and digesting meat. These animals had larger, sharper, and more pointed teeth than their herbivorous cousins—and were used to kill the victim and tear the flesh off the body. To power these teeth—and to break down the nutritious bone marrow from their prey—carnivores needed strong jaws and muscles.

This *Tyrannosaurus* skull illustrates the carnivore's massive jaw and teeth, used for shearing its meat. (Photo courtesy of University of Michigan Exhibit, Museum of Natural History.)

The carnivores also had clawed feet for slashing their victims, with the dromaeosaurids possessing the epitome of this adaptation—large, sickle-shaped foot claws. The theropods, being bipedal, had their arms and hands free to grasp their prey; their fingers often had claws used to slash and hold the victim. And being bipedal, they had the relative speed and agility to catch their prey. It is thought by some scientists that for successful hunting, the theropods had good eyesight, a keen sense of smell, and a large brain (in proportion to the body) to calculate hunting strategies.

What did the **carnivorous dinosaurs** prefer to **eat**?

Little is known about the various carnivorous dinosaurs' food preference, but it was

> ## What plants did the herbivorous dinosaurs probably eat that are still present today?
>
> Descendants of the conifers, flowering plants, horsetails, ferns, and cycads continue to grow today, and probably their ancestors served as meals for ancient herbivorous dinosaurs.

probably limited to animals that were sick and ailing (thus easy to kill), or animals that were not as large as the predator—similar to how predators today search for a meal. The carnivores' digestive tracts were probably perfect for breaking down the proteins they needed to survive. And the digestive system was probably not as complex as that of an herbivore, as meat is easier to digest than plants.

The only chance scientists have had so far to view the carnivorous digestive tract was recently found: one of the few fossils found contains the intestines of a small carnivorous dinosaur, called *Scipionyx samniticus,* and nicknamed "Skippy." This dinosaur is about 113 million years old, and is a distant cousin of both the *Tyrannosaurus rex* and *Velociraptor.* Its intestines shows that the digestive tract was short—at least for this younger carnivore.

To what **groups** did the **plant-eating dinosaurs** belong?

All of the ornithischians, or "bird-hipped," dinosaurs were herbivores; as were the sauropods of the saurischians, or "lizard-hipped," dinosaurs (the other half of the saurischians were the theropods, or meat-eating dinosaurs). The largest dinosaurs found to date have been herbivores—specifically, members of the sauropods, such as the *Brachiosaurus* and *Supersaurus.*

What **adaptations** did the **herbivorous dinosaurs** have that enabled them to eat plants?

Some herbivorous dinosaurs did not chew at all, but merely swallowed whole the vegetation they pulled off a tree or bush. They had larger (and probably more rugged) digestive tracts than carnivorous dinosaurs in order to digest the tough, fibrous plants they ate. Some herbivores, such as the *Ankylosaurus,* even had fermentation chambers along their digestive tract, in which tough fibers would be broken down by bacteria. In addition, some herbivores had gastroliths, or "gizzard stones," in their digestive tract, which would grind up the fibrous plants, helping to digest the material. (It is interesting to note that this method is similar to how birds

The club tail of the herbivore *Ankylosaurus*. (Photo courtesy of University of Michigan Exhibit, Museum of Natural History.)

swallow stones to grind up ingested matter in their digestive tracts—and that birds are thought to be directly related to dinosaurs.) These stones were deliberately swallowed, and are often found with fossils of herbivores. Both of these actions prepared the vegetation for digestion.

Other herbivorous dinosaurs, like the hadrosaurs, also known as the "duck-billed" dinosaurs, had special teeth that would grind up the food before swallowing. Ceratopsians, like the *Triceratops,* had sharp teeth and powerful jaws that enabled them to cut through tough plants. And still other herbivores had cheek pouches, apparently used to store food for later ingestion.

What was an **omnivorous dinosaur**?

An omnivorous dinosaur was one that ate both plants and meat. There are only a few known omnivores among the dinosaurs, including *Ornithomimus* and perhaps *Oviraptor,* although new fossil finds may change scientists' opinion about the latter. A diet of an omnivorous dinosaur could have included different types of plants, insects, eggs, and small animals. These dinosaurs were probably rare, and only ate that way out of necessity—such as the sudden lack of meat or plants in their surrounding habitat. Other believe these dinosaurs were omnivores by accident—eating insects and small animals as they ate the plants around them.

Have any **fossilized stomach contents** of dinosaurs been found?

Although rare, some dinosaur stomach remains have been found over the years. The best examples are from carnivorous dinosaurs. The fossilized remains of a lizard (*Bavaisaurus*) were found in the gut region of a carnivorous dinosaur called *Compsognathus*—no doubt the dinosaur's last meal. In addition, *Coelophysis* fossils have been found with the fossilized remains of other *Coelophysis* dinosaurs inside the gut region, indicating these dinosaurs probably engaged in cannibalism. Whether this was active predation or scavenging has not been determined.

The stomach contents of herbivorous dinosaurs have not been as definitive, however, due to the organic nature of the material. One case was reported in the early 1900s, where the fossilized remains of an *Edmontosaurus* had been found with conifer seeds, twigs, and needles in the body cavity. However, it could not be determined if these were actual stomach contents, or just debris that had subsequently washed into the carcass.

DINOSAURS IN MOTION

What are some major **questions** associated with the **movement** of dinosaurs?

When paleontologists study the movement of dinosaurs, the most prevalent questions concern the postures that dinosaurs typically adopted, their speed of movement, both normal and maximum, and any hunting or herding behavior.

What **evidence** do we have concerning the **movement** of dinosaurs?

There are three main sources of evidence that help us to understand the movement of dinosaurs: homologies, analogies, and footprints.

Homologies are comparisons in the anatomical structures in organisms derived from the same such structures in a common ancestor. Because the vast majority of evidence we have about dinosaurs are their bones, the reconstruction of the skeleton and muscles can be very useful in helping to understand their movement. And, to make these reconstructions as accurate as possible, scientists use modern homologues. Unfortunately, the closest relations to the dinosaurs, such as the birds and crocodiles, have all evolved highly modified structures—making a direct comparison to the dinosaurs very chancy.

In addition to homologies, scientists can observe the movement of modern animals with similar structures and probable behaviors (analogies). For example, the probable motion of ornithomimids is based on that of the ostrich because this modern bird has a similar structure; the movement of the large sauropods is modeled on that of modern elephants. But these analogies are only as good as the similar structure the scientists is examining. And, unfortunately, it may not be truly representative of the actual motion or behavior of the dinosaur. In other words, ostriches are not theropod dinosaurs, and elephants are not sauropods.

The third and most direct evidence for dinosaur movement are the trace fossils called footprints. These records give scientists a wealth of clues about the speed, gait, posture, and sometimes behavior of these long-dead animals. And from the inferred motion represented by these footprints, paleontologists can sometimes obtain evidence of

Fossilized dinosaur footprint found in Spain in 1994. (Photo courtesy of Francesca Muntada/Corbis.)

the animals' behavior. For example, the lack of tail drag marks shows a dinosaur with an erect posture; some trackways show that certain dinosaurs exhibited a herding behavior.

What is an **important factor** in determining the **probable motion** of dinosaurs?

One of the most important factors in determining the probable motion of dinosaurs is their posture. Without an accurate knowledge of the animals' postures, their motion—whether obtained through the use of homologies, analogies, trackways, or a combination of these—can be misleading or downright wrong.

From the evidence of footprints, dinosaurs had an erect (or upright) posture, with their limbs directly under their bodies. This structure resulted in a motion similar to modern mammals, with the limbs held out to the sides and the upper bones nearly

253

parallel to the ground. Surprisingly, this posture was more similar to modern mammals than lizards, which have a sprawling posture.

But there were also variations within this erect posture, leading to some very unique movements. Some dinosaurs were bipedal, walking only on their hind limbs; others were quadrupeds, walking on all four limbs. Other dinosaurs spent most of their time on all fours, but were capable of standing on their hind limbs. Still others reversed this action, spending most of their time on two hind limbs, but capable of moving on all fours. And in the end, each had a distinct motion and behavior—all based on their respective postures.

What are the **problems** with determining dinosaur **motion from footprints**?

Although footprints are the most direct evidence scientists have to determine the motion of dinosaurs, they are not perfect. Many times footprints of the same dinosaur types formed differently in various types of sediments. The tracks of dinosaurs can also represent different speeds or gaits, and are also dependent on the conditions of the muds and sands in which they were made. And there is currently a poor correlation between known dinosaur tracks and skeletons. All of these factors make the interpretation of the dinosaur motions from footprints a combination of science, detection, and intuition.

What branch of **science** is concerned with the study of **footprints**?

The branch of science concerned with the study of footprints is called ichnology. In fact, ichnofossils are fossil traces left by animals—fossils that are not part of the organisms' body.

What conditions might lead to the **best footprints**?

Recent experiments show that the best footprints aren't made in fresh, new mud. Instead, the presence of a coating on top of older mud leads to the best tracks.

Fresh mud tends to be sticky and flows readily. Footprints made in this type of mud are poorly preserved, with little detail. Fresh, sticky mud adheres to the feet, leaving at best a partial impression in the ground; as the foot is lifted, some of the surrounding mud flows into the footprint. Footprints made in this type of mud seem to be typical of most of the known dinosaur tracks.

On the other hand, older coated mud seems to be a much better medium for making and preserving finely detailed footprints. This type of mud is commonly found around ponds, and is sometimes covered with a greenish coating of algae and bacteria.

What are dinosaur trackways?

Dinosaur trackways are fossil footprints of dinosaurs, and they are found all over the world. These trackways developed as dinosaurs (and other animals) walked in the soft sediment or sand along the shorelines of beaches, rivers, ponds, and lakes. Almost immediately after the animals walked by, the tracks were quickly buried in sediment, eventually becoming fossil footprints (also called ichnotaxia). Because such places were good sources of water and food—including lush plants for the herbivores and plenty of animals for the carnivores—they became natural pathways for all types of dinosaurs.

So far, the problem with the dinosaur trackways is that it is impossible to tell which dinosaur made the footprints. Scientists can only generally determine what type of dinosaur left the tracks; for example if the tracks belonged to a biped or quadruped dinosaur, and whether it was a sauropod or a theropod.

Experiments have shown that the coating acts as a binding agent. It keeps the muddy surface together and prevents flow into the footprint after the foot is lifted. It also acts as a parting agent, preventing the mud from sticking to the feet—allowing deep prints with fine detail. A third benefit to the coating is that it slows down the drying of the mud, allowing the prints to be formed.

Tracks made in this coated mud can be deep, very clear, well-preserved, with plenty of anatomical detail. The most well-known dinosaur footprints were probably made under these conditions.

What **other factors** affect how a **track is formed**?

Footprints, or tracks, are created by the holistic interaction of two factors: the actual motion of the animal's foot (and body), and the nature of the ground it walked on. Both of these factors are not separate and distinct, but depend on the other—in a sort of feedback loop.

As the animal moves, its weight presses on the ground, causing it to yield. The amount and type of yielding depends on the state of the ground—whether it is mud or sand, wet or almost dry. In turn, the state of the ground influences how the animal moves over it. Deep, wet, sticky mud results in a much different movement than firm, almost dry sand. This interaction between the ground and movement determines whether or not all the fine details of the animal's anatomy are preserved—and what type of movement is represented by the resulting tracks.

What are some of the **largest dinosaur trackways**?

Some of the largest dinosaur trackways are called megatrack sites, where footprint-bearing rock can extend for hundreds or even thousands of miles. Several Jurassic and Cretaceous sites in North America have such trackways. For example, tracks in the Entrada sandstone beds in eastern Utah (from the middle Jurassic) cover about 116 square miles (300 square kilometers); the density of the prints is estimated to be between 1 and 10 per 10.8 square feet (1 square meter).

What do **dinosaur trackways** found in rock tell us about the **behavior** of some dinosaurs?

Dinosaur trackways can tell us a few things about dinosaur behavior. For sauropods, the tracks are usually of more than one creature, and heading in the same direction, indicating a social herding behavior or even a migration. Some trackways include footprints of large theropods—some prints indicating a pack behavior to stalk large sauropods.

What do **dinosaur tracks** tell us about **locomotion** of some dinosaurs?

Dinosaur trackways confirm that certain dinosaurs walked and ran on all four legs (quadrupeds) and others on two legs (bipeds). The tracks also show that some dinosaurs walked in an erect fashion, and walked by putting one foot almost directly in front on the other. In addition, some dinosaurs ran quickly or walked slowly—probably depending on whether the animals were browsing, wading, trotting, running after prey, or running from predators. One interesting observation: so far, no tail marks—indicating the dinosaurs dragged their tails along behind them—have been found along trackways. Because of this, scientists believe dinosaurs probably held their tails erect.

Where did a **dinosaur stampede** take place?

There is such a special place in Australia, discovered in 1960. There, in the Lark Quarry Environment Park, south of Wilton, on the eroded edge of the Tully Range, are hundreds of dinosaur footprints preserved in rock. The footprints were made as dinosaurs walked in mud around a prehistoric lake.

Typical for animal life, most of the tracks were made as large carnivores hunted for prey along the edge of the lake. In particular, large carnosaurs trapped groups of coelurosaurs and ornithopods; in one instance, a carnosaur attacked an unfortunate animal, pursuing its victim along the muddy shore—and causing the rest of the surrounding dinosaurs to stampede in panic.

The Dinosaur Freeway is a large trackway of dinosaur footprints extending along the Front Range of the Rocky Mountains—from around Boulder, Colorado, to eastern New Mexico. In the middle Cretaceous period, this area was a coastal plain with a wide shoreline, a good source of water and food.

Although there is no longer a large lake with carnivorous dinosaurs, the area still holds a bit of danger: it isn't easy to get to. The drive to Lark Quarry takes one and a half to two hours by car—and the roads are dangerous, sometimes impassable, in wet weather.

How do paleontologists determine **speeds of dinosaurs** using the **trackways**?

Although it is difficult to tell the type of dinosaur that made a track, scientists can tell the relative speed of the animals as they moved along the trackways. By measuring the distance between the footprints, and the size of the tracks, they can tell that some dinosaurs ran much faster than first assumed. In other words, these tracks prove that the old idea—that dinosaurs were slow and sluggish—wasn't always true!

How are dinosaur **speeds calculated**?

Using measurements of stride and footprint lengths, dinosaur speeds are calculated using something called dynamic similarity. This pretends that all animals are the same size and move their limbs at the same rate. The concept of dimensionless speed is also used—originally developed in the shipbuilding industry to estimate ship speeds from small models.

Paleontologists first measure the distance between footprints in a trackway (stride length) as well as the length of the footprints themselves. The estimated leg length is then determined by multiplying the footprint length by a known constant; for example, the constant for theropods is 4.5. The relative stride length is determined by dividing the measured stride length by this estimated leg length. The resulting number would be referenced to a standard graph to obtain a dimensionless speed for the particular dinosaur. To get a real world speed, this dimensionless speed is used, along with the estimated leg length and the acceleration of gravity. This results in a more familiar number: speed in miles per hour or kilometers per hour.

What is the **speed**—from stride and leg length—of **humans**?

Scientists have tried out this "stride and leg length" method to determine the speed of humans. The formula estimates the human speed at approximately 14 miles (23 kilometers) per hour, just about right for sprinters.

What are some calculated **speeds of dinosaurs**?

Using measured stride and footprint lengths, scientists have calculated the speeds of over 60 dinosaurs. One of the real-life factors scientists had to keep in mind while formulating these calculations is the gait of the dinosaurs when they made the tracks: the difference between walking and running and the transitions between these movements. Another factor in the formula is the actual leg bone lengths of the dinosaurs—which helped scientists determine the reasonable speed types for the various dinosaurs. For example, the similar lengths of the femur and tibia bones in the legs of a *Tyrannosaurus rex* suggest a slower attainable speed than of the ornithomimids, which had a shorter femur and longer tibia. With all these caveats in mind, some examples of the calculated speeds of dinosaurs include:

Speed (miles/kilometers per hour)	Dinosaur
Up to 25/40	Small theropods and ornithopods
Up to 16/25	Ceratopsians
Up to 4 to 5/6 to 8	Armored dinosaurs, such as ankylosaurs and stegosaurs
Up to 7.5 to 11/12 to 17	Sauropods
Up to 37/60	Ornithomimids
Up to 12/20	Large theropods and ornithopods

What was the **fastest dinosaur**?

It is difficult to name the fastest dinosaur based on the few trackways found, but some information has been gathered by analyzing the tracks. The speediest dinosaurs were probably the small, bipedal carnivores, especially those with long, slim hindlimbs and light bodies. These swift dinosaurs probably didn't run any faster than the fastest modern land animals. One carnivorous dinosaur called an *Ornithomimus* is thought to have run about 43 miles (70 kilometers) per hour—about the speed of a modern African ostrich.

Where are dinosaur **tracks** being **studied by different scientists**?

A very good example of the interdisciplinary study of dinosaur tracks is currently ongoing at the Red Gulch Dinosaur Tracksite, located in Wyoming. A large number of fossil footprints were recently discovered on public lands at the site—a place once known as the Sundance Sea. A coordinated project is currently underway to study them using several earth science disciplines—including spatial documentation and analysis, geology, and vertebrate paleontology.

The spatial documentation and analysis team will measure, map, describe, and analyze the precise location and relationships of the dinosaur tracks using photogra-

What unique equipment was used to map the Red Gulch Dinosaur Tracksite?

The unique piece of equipment used to map the Red Gulch Dinosaur Tracksite was a radio-controlled model airplane! The airplane contained a camera that could take aerial photographs of the tracksite at a height of approximately 144 feet (44 meters). These pictures will help scientists determine whether the dinosaurs were traveling as a herd or family, and also in what direction they were moving.

phy and computer techniques. New state-of-the-art applications, using the latest technologies, will be developed to help determine any hidden trends and relationships among the tracksite features. This data will be shared with the geology and vertebrate paleontology teams.

The geology team will study the middle Jurassic period sedimentary rocks in which the dinosaur footprints formed, determining the local environment at the time the dinosaurs created the footprints. From this data, they hope to gain a more complete understanding of the Sundance Sea's regional history, where the ancient shorelines were located, what the sea levels were during this time—and even what the climate was like.

The vertebrate paleontologists will concentrate their efforts on the actual tracks, studying them in place, as well as taking molds and casts for later inspection. The shapes of these footprints—compared to other known tracks and skeletons—will help reveal which dinosaurs made these tracks. And the study of the location and distribution of the tracks will reveal the behavior of individuals and groups, as well as the habitat and community structure.

What might the **Red Gulch Dinosaur Tracksite** reveal?

The current interdisciplinary study of the Red Gulch Dinosaur Tracksite has the potential to tell scientists a great deal about the dinosaurs that made the tracks. It will also tell us more about the environment during the middle Jurassic period in this part of the world and how the sedimentary layer was deposited. All are clues that will help reconstruct the world of these animals.

Scientists hope to identify the specific dinosaurs that made the tracks, as well as whether or not the animals were bipedal or quadrupedal. In addition, the footprints may show evidence of behavior patterns, including whether these dinosaurs were solitary or lived in family groups. The way these dinosaurs lived and what they ate might also be discovered.

In addition to information about the dinosaurs themselves, the study may tell us about the conditions and environment in which they were made. The conditions of the terrain which the dinosaurs crossed to make these tracks might be one finding; another would be to discover what the climate was like at the time—for example, hot and humid, like a rain forest, dry like a desert, or cool, like a mountain area. If the footprints were made near a coastline, perhaps scientists can tell whether they were made at low tide, or during a period when the ocean was receding—gaining some understanding of what the coastal area was like. And finally, the tracks may reveal their age, and whether they were all made at the same time or over a longer span.

What **preliminary findings** come from the **Red Gulch** Dinosaur Tracksite study?

There have been many preliminary findings from the Red Gulch Dinosaur Tracksite study. For example, at least two different kinds of dinosaurs made the tracks—and many were made by small theropods. The tracks don't follow the same path, but go in all different directions; individual footprints also go in all directions, crossing each other in places. Some of the footprints are very small, not exceeding 3.5 inches (9 centimeters) long, while others are larger, on the order of 8 inches (20 centimeters) long. The smaller footprints could have been made by juveniles or by very small adult dinosaurs. So far, there isn't enough evidence to determine whether the tracks were made by a herd of dinosaurs, or just a few animals that lingered in the area for a period of time.

As far as the surrounding conditions during this time, scientists now believe that the waters of the ocean didn't cover all of Wyoming during the middle Jurassic period as previously thought. They also think the dinosaurs walked on a tidal flat's slimy ooze when they made the footprints at the Red Gulch Dinosaur Tracksite.

Did **dinosaurs** travel in **herds**?

Yes, dinosaurs did apparently live and travel in herds—and it was probably because of the old expression, "safety in numbers." Scientists have deduced this behavior based on dinosaur trackways, and huge collections of dinosaur bones that indicate massive kills (places in which large amounts of dinosaurs bones are found in one place).

In particular, many herbivores apparently traveled in herds, based on the multiple tracks left along the dinosaur trackways. The tracks also show that many herbivores held the young in the center of the herd—similar to elephant herds—probably to protect them.

Some dinosaur fossils have been found in massive collections—indicating many dozens of animals were killed in one spot. Some scientists believe such collections of animal bones show the creatures exhibited a herding behavior. In many cases, while in the herd, these animals were swiftly killed off, perhaps from a major flood, volcanic action, or a huge sandstorm. For example, the bonebeds of about 100 *Styracosaurus*

In Alberta, Canada's Dinosaur Provincial Park, a *Styracosaurus* model stands on a riverbank. Scientists theorize that the *Styracosaurus* dinosaurs traveled in herds. (Photo courtesy of Jonathan Blair/Corbis.)

dinosaurs, a herbivore, have been discovered, as have dinosaur bones that represent dozens of *Protoceratops* and *Triceratops*.

One particular herbivore called a *Maiasaura* (a hadrosaur) is also thought to have lived in herds—and probably returned to the same nesting grounds every year. Fossil bones of these animals were found in a huge group of about 10,000 animals in Montana. The animals all died suddenly, apparently when a volcano erupted—smothering the animals with volcanic gases and covering the creatures with a thick layer of ash.

Did **dinosaurs migrate**?

Yes, certain dinosaurs apparently migrated, similar to certain animals today. They probably migrated for the same reasons, too: seeking new food sources as the seasons changed, and migrating for purposes of mating and nesting. Similar to determining the herding behavior of dinosaurs, scientists have deduced dinosaur migrating behavior based on trackways, and huge collections of bones that indicate massive kills.

Did **dinosaurs hunt in packs**?

Yes, paleontologists speculate that certain carnivorous dinosaurs exhibited a social behavior called pack hunting. The large theropods, like *Tyrannosaurus* and *Giganotosaurus,* show some evidence of hunting in packs, similar to modern-day lions.

In a recent discovery in Argentina, scientists found a huge collection of dinosaur bones of the *Giganotosaurus*—a carnivorous dinosaur that grew to 45 feet (13.7 meter) long and weighed about 8 tons. The bones of four or five *Giganotosaurus* indicate that they died together on the Patagonian plains, swept away by a fast-flowing river. The bones show that two of the animals were very big, but the others were smaller. Scientists believe this shows that there was some kind of social behavior—probably that the animals hunted in packs. In particular, each animal within the group would have different characteristics, giving the pack a great range of capabilities—such as going after smaller and larger animals.

Other evidence shows that at least some of the dromaeosaurids, or "raptors," engaged in pack hunting. When the first fossils of a dinosaur called *Deinonychus* were found—a 6-foot- (1.8-meter-) tall, 9-foot- (2.8-meter-) long Cretaceous period predator of western North America—the remains of many of these carnivores were clustered near the body of a large herbivore, *Tenontosaurus*. Paleontologists theorized that these predators perished during the struggle with the larger dinosaur—indicating that the hunt was being conducted by a group.

Did any dinosaurs live in the **cold polar regions**?

Yes, paleontologists believe that while most flourished in tropical or temperate climates, some dinosaurs actually lived in the cold weather regions of the ancient world. Fossils of these polar dinosaurs have been uncovered on the North Slope of Alaska. Others have been found at Dinosaur Cove, at the southeastern tip of Australia, and dated at 105 to 110 million years ago. Although this part of Australia is presently at approximately 39 degrees south latitude, at the time of the polar dinosaurs, it was much farther south, and lay within the Antarctic Circle. For three months during the winter, the night lasted 24 hours a day, and temperatures fell well below zero degrees Fahrenheit (-17.8 degrees Celsius). The dinosaur fossils uncovered in this area show that the animals were well adapted to these harsh conditions—and that they apparently had keen night vision and may have been warm-blooded. They were generally small animals, ranging in size from about that of chicken to that of a human, with the largest carnivore about 9 feet (3 meters) high.

Did any **dinosaurs** climb or live in **trees**?

No known dinosaurs climbed or lived in trees. At one time, the foot bones of the *Hypsilophodon,* a small herbivorous ornithopod, were thought to have the big toe facing opposite to the other toes, similar to a bird's foot. Scientists speculated, based on this erroneous assumption, that this dinosaur lived in trees, perching on branches, similar to today's Australian tree kangaroo. When the true foot bone structure was discovered, it was realized that *Hypsilophodon* was a swift land runner, using its speed and agility to escape predators—not to live in trees.

Did any dinosaurs fly?

No known nonavian (or nonbird) flying dinosaur has ever been discovered—but there were creatures that flew at the time of the dinosaurs. The first and most prolific were the pterosaurs. These contemporaries of the dinosaur lived throughout the Mesozoic era and appeared to be close relatives of the dinosaurs, evolving from the archosaurs. The dinosaurs dominated on land; the pterosaurs dominated the air.

The connection of dinosaurs to birds is still highly debated. But if dinosaurs and birds are truly so closely related, then it could be said that avian dinosaurs, or birds, would eventually evolve, take to the air—and endure until today.

What was the purpose of the giant *Apatosaurus'* tail tip?

Some scientists believe the *Apatosaurus* (formerly known as the *Brontosaurus*) may have moved its 45-foot (14-meter) tail like a bullwhip—with its 6-foot (1.8-meter) skinny tip creating a loud crack. Recent computer models have compared the movement of a model *Apatosaurus* tail with the motion of a bullwhip. These studies show it is not only feasible the tail moved in this way, but the relatively slow motion at the base of the tail would translate into supersonic speeds at the tip. This would have created a loud sonic boom of about 200 decibels—much louder than the 140 decibels of a jet taking off!

In the past, paleontologists thought the tail of sauropods like the *Apatosaurus* were mainly used for balance or to swat rivals. But the tip of the tail contained tiny, fragile bones that could have easily broken in a fight. Now, some scientists think the loud crack from the tail tip could have been used to scare away predators, establish dominance in a herd, resolve disputes, and even to attract a mate.

DINOSAUR YOUNG

What do **dinosaur eggs** look like?

Scientists have collected fossil dinosaur eggs, sometimes finding more than a dozen in a nestlike area. The fossilized eggs are usually the color of the rock in which they are found; and similar to fossil dinosaur bones, their structures have been fossilized and replaced by minerals over time.

Dinosaur egg casts. (Photo courtesy of University of Michigan Exhibit, Museum of Natural History.)

Although the eggs are fossilized, scientists have discovered that dinosaur eggs probably looked similar to those of modern birds, reptiles, and some primitive mammals. Most of the eggs were rounded or elongated, with hard shells. They contained an amnion, a membrane that kept the egg moist—a kind of "private pond" for the young animal growing in the egg. The eggs appeared to be similar in other ways, too: the surface of the shell allowed for the exchange of gases necessary for the dinosaur young to survive (many of the fossilized eggs exhibit a mottled surface that indicates the shell had pores); and the young would crack its way out of an egg when it was ready to enter the world.

No one really knows if the majority of eggs laid by the dinosaurs were soft-, flexible-, or hard-shelled eggs. The eggshell would have to be relatively strong to support the weight of the brooding parents, or the overburden of nesting material; and the shell would still have to allow for the exchange of necessary gases. In reality, hard-shelled eggs have the best chance of fossilizing, as they are harder. Thus, most shells that scientists find today may not truly represent all the eggs that dinosaurs laid—just the hardest ones that survived.

Did all **dinosaurs lay eggs**?

As far as paleontologists can determine, all dinosaurs reproduced by laying eggs. The first fossilized dinosaur eggs were found in France in 1869, but not everyone agreed the eggs were from dinosaurs. Although it may seem somewhat obvious to us now, it took time before scientists agreed that dinosaurs nested, laid, and hatched eggs. The proof was found in the Gobi Desert in the 1920s, where both nests and eggs of a group of *Protoceratops* were found. Since that time, over 200 sites with fossil eggs of various dinosaurs have been found all over the world, including those in the United States, France, Mongolia, China, Argentina, and India.

However, it should also be noted that there are some modern lizards—which are reptiles—that do not lay eggs; rather they give birth to live young (called viviparity). Some scientists suggest that this is a result of adapting to colder climates. And although the idea is highly debated (and no real physical evidence has been found), some scientists speculate that polar dinosaurs may have reproduced in this way.

Environmentalist Dr. Vikas Amte examines some fossils of dinosaur eggs in Pisdura, India, in early 1997. Villagers discovered more than 300 eggs, along with some fossils of bone fragments, shells, and fecal matter, while plowing their fields. (Photo courtesy of Sherwin Crasto/Associated Press.)

Where was the **first clutch** of **dinosaur eggs** discovered?

The first known clutch (nest) of dinosaur eggs was found by Roy Chapman Andrews in 1922, in the Gobi Desert, south of the Altai Mountains. The eggs were found in one of the most prolific fossil beds in the area, a sedimentary layer known as the Nemget formation, also known for the more than 100 fossil skeletons of the small horned dinosaur *Protoceratops*.

What is the largest dinosaur egg known?

The largest dinosaur egg fossil to date is about 12 inches (30 centimeters) long and 10 inches (25 centimeters) wide; it may have weighed about 15.5 pounds. It is thought to be from a giant, 100-million-year-old herbivore called a *Hypselosaurus*. To compare, the prize for the largest bird egg (and largest flightless bird) on earth belongs to the African ostrich, with eggs up to 6.8 inches (17 centimeters) long by 5.4 inches (14 centimeters) wide, and weighing up to 3.3 pounds.

What did a **dinosaur nest** look like?

Not all dinosaur nests looked alike. Many were simple pits dug into the soil or sand; others were more complicated, including deep, mud-rimmed nests with grasslike linings. Some dinosaurs even had a certain way of laying their eggs. For example, the *Maiasaura,* a herbivore, would arrange the eggs in a spiral, making sure to allow enough space between hatchlings to aid them in escape from predators. *Protoceratops* also apparently laid their eggs in a spiral fashion.

What else has been **discovered** about dinosaur **nesting sites**?

At some sites, many nests were spaced closely together—similar to the colonies or rookeries associated with certain modern sea birds. Evidence shows that certain nesting sites were used over and over again by various dinosaurs. In addition, not only were some dinosaurs' eggs arranged in a spiral pattern in the nest, but they had a particular vertical orientation, perhaps to minimize breakage. Other nests contained the fossilized bones of young dinosaurs in a wide range of sizes—indicating that the parents cared for the juveniles for an extended period before the young left the nest.

What dinosaur was **named** as a consequence of its **nesting behavior**?

The name of the 26-foot (8-meter) hadrosaur *Maiasaura,* or "good mother lizard," was based on fossil finds in Montana: the nesting colony spanned 2.5 acres and contained 40 nests, each containing up to 25 grapefruit-sized eggs. This herbivorous dinosaur showed an advanced social and breeding behavior, including returning to the same nesting sites every breeding season; refurbishing existing nests; placing nests one dinosaur length apart (about 25 to 30 feet [7.6 to 9.1 meters]) so there was room for movement back and forth; incubating eggs using a warm compost layer; and feeding the nest-bound young with vegetation until they were ready to leave.

How have the **latest findings** of *Oviraptor* changed our image of this dinosaur?

The dinosaur *Oviraptor,* or "egg thief," was previously thought to have been a dinosaur egg consumer, as its fossilized remains were often found near nests. Recently, scientists uncovered an 80-million-year-old fossil that shows this bipedal, carnivorous dinosaur—approximately the size of a modern ostrich—apparently brooding or guarding a nest of 15 large eggs.

The fossil, uncovered in Mongolia's Gobi Desert in the mid-1990s, is the first hard evidence to date showing the behavior of this dinosaur; other theories on the dinosaur's behavior have been inferred from indirect data. The *Oviraptor* was found lying

Like most reptiles and birds, sauropods laid eggs. This is a cast of an egg, attributed to a sauropod called *Hypselosaurus*, whose fossils are found in southern France and northern Spain.

Fossilized egg of the *Hypselosaurus,* about twice the size of an ostrich's egg. (Photo courtesy of University of Michigan Exhibit, Museum of Natural History.)

on its clutch of eggs, with its legs tucked tightly against its body, and the arms turned back to encircle the nest. This is similar to the nesting behavior of modern birds—and suggests such behavior may have started long before the advent of wings and feathers.

How did **dinosaur eggs hatch**?

Similar to modern birds and reptiles, a dinosaur young cracked its way out of an egg when it was ready to enter the world. Also similar to these modern species, certain dinosaur species were apparently too small and weak to leave the nest after hatching. In most cases, the baby dinosaurs probably remained nestbound for many weeks after

they hatched, and had to be fed and tended by the adults. Scientists have deduced this from several nest sites that show the fragments of trampled egg shells, and remains that look like regurgitated leaves and berries. And similar to the young of most species, dinosaur hatchlings were no doubt especially susceptible and vulnerable to attacks from predators that hunted around the nesting sites.

Zoologist Peter Larson attempts to free and restore a fossilized egg nest. (Photo courtesy of Corbis.)

How can **parental care traits** of dinosaurs be extrapolated from living animals?

Of course, the parental care traits of dinosaurs cannot be directly observed, because they've been extinct for 65 million years. Therefore, paleontologists have had to resort to observing the closest living relatives of the dinosaurs—the birds and crocodiles. They believe that these modern animals probably had many of the same traits, including construction of nests or mounds; nesting together in rookeries; guarding the nest by one or both of the parents; warning and recognition sounds made by the young; and family group cohesiveness during the hatchling stage. In fact, many of these traits have been confirmed by recent fossil findings.

Did all dinosaurs have the **same parental care methods**?

No, not all dinosaurs shared the same parental care methods. Just as they were different in size and shape, their methods of taking care of their young also differed.

Are there any **examples** of the dinosaur **parenting care methods**?

Yes, there are some examples of parenting care methods—painstakingly pieced together mostly from known fossil nesting sites around the world. The first example is the *Orodromeus,* an ornithopod that lived in Montana during the Cretaceous period. This dinosaur laid its eggs in spirals, with the large ends up and tilted toward the center; the average clutch included 12 eggs. The young were hatched with well-developed limb bones and joints, suggesting the young could walk almost immediately. This is supported by the low number of crushed eggs in the nest site, indicating the young left quickly. Fossil evidence shows the young stayed in groups—but it is not known for how long.

The *Maiasaura* were also ornithopods in Montana during the Cretaceous period. These dinosaurs made nests in shallow holes, spaced apart from the surrounding nests by about the length of an adult dinosaur. On average, there were 17 eggs per clutch. The fossil evidence to date suggests that the hatchlings had poorly formed limb joints, which meant the young had to stay in the nest for a long period of time. This conclusion is supported by the numerous fossils of hatchlings found in the nests, along with trampled and crushed eggs. This means that the young *Maiasaura* needed a large amount of parental care and attention, with some estimates having the young staying in the nest for approximately 8 to 9 months.

Oviraptor was a theropod living in Mongolia during the Cretaceous period. And one of the most exciting recent fossil finds was that of an *Oviraptor* in a nesting position—suggesting a brooding behavior, similar to modern birds. In contrast to this nurturing attitude, the *Coelophysis*—theropods of the Triassic period in Arizona—probably ate their young, as seen in many fossil remains.

OLDER DINOSAURS

How **long** did **dinosaurs live**?

Scientists do not know the exact lifespan of the dinosaurs, but they estimate that dinosaurs lived about 75 to 300 years. This educated guess is based on examining the microstructure of dinosaur bones, which indicate that the dinosaurs matured slowly. This is similar to ancestors of the dinosaur, including crocodiles, whose eggs take about 90 days to hatch, and whose lifespans can extend from 70 to 100 years.

Does the **microstructure** of dinosaur **bones** indicate the **age** of these animals?

Yes, paleontologists have discovered that the bones of dinosaurs have growth rings, similar to those found in the trunks of trees—with each year of dinosaur growth recorded in the rings. The ring features are very small; to see them, the bones have to be cut into thin sections and examined under a microscope using polarized light. These growth rings are known scientifically as lines of arrested growth (LAG); they are assumed to form at the rate of one ring per year.

Using this technique, scientists have estimated the age of certain dinosaurs—and they vary greatly. For example, the bones of a ceratopsian dinosaur *Psittacosaurus* indicate that this particular animal was about 10 to 11 years old when it died; a second analyzed dinosaur, a *Troodon,* was 3 to 5 years old; the bones of a sauropod called *Bothriospondylus* show it was 43 years old; a *Massospondylus,* a prosauropod, was 15 years old; and a ceratosaur called *Syntarsus* was 7 years old.

What are some of **problems** with using dinosaur **growth rings**?

Although the analysis of growth rings (LAG) in dinosaur bones has yielded some estimates of growth rates, the technique is not without its problems. It is not known if LAGs truly form in one year; for example, one hadrosaur fossil supposedly had a different number of growth rings in its legs and arms. Second, the growth rates may be size dependent—in other words, a larger dinosaur may grow slower—just like elephants grow much slower than mice. Third, some animals may have had indeterminate growth like crocodiles. And finally, different species may have had different metabolisms—and if they were a combination of warm- and cold-blooded creatures, it would even mean more misinterpretation!

What is **another way** to estimate a dinosaur's **lifespan**?

Another way to estimate a dinosaur's lifespan is to compare it to the known life spans of living animals—based on body size. In general, larger animals tend to live longer than smaller ones. Using this method, the lifespan of very large sauropods like *Apatosaurus* and *Diplodocus* was probably on the order of 100 years. Smaller dinosaurs would have had a shorter lifespan.

Do scientists definitely know the **growth pattern** of dinosaurs?

No, scientists really don't know for certain what kind of growth pattern the dinosaurs had—and there are several reasons why. First, not all dinosaurs shared the same growth rate. Different types of dinosaurs probably grew at varying rates, complicating the analysis.

The second reason for the uncertainty in growth rates has to do with climate: dinosaurs inhabiting warmer regions of the planet probably grew more rapidly than those living in colder climates. Another reason has to do with the metabolic rate of dinosaurs—which is an area of intense speculation. Warm-blooded vertebrates with

How did dinosaurs sleep?

No one really knows the sleeping habits of the dinosaurs. It is not easy to infer such activities based on just the fossil record, as sleeping leaves no definitive physical trace. After all, no one knew sharks slept until recently—and sharks are common in today's oceans.

Still, scientists have inferred the sleeping habits of some of the dinosaurs. For example, most of the smaller animals probably slept like modern reptiles, just flopping down on the ground like a crocodile. Others, such as the huge *Tyrannosaurus,* probably had a much harder time sleeping lying down. Once it had lain down, it would have been difficult for it to get up using its small arms. Other larger dinosaurs would probably find their enormous weight would get in the way—thus, the only way larger dinosaurs could sleep was standing up. It is interesting to note that modern birds (which many scientists believe are close relatives to the dinosaurs) sleep standing up.

higher metabolic rates can grow up to 10 times faster than cold-blooded vertebrates. Dinosaurs with potentially higher metabolic rates, such as the small theropods, might have grown faster than the slow-moving sauropods—though not larger.

What are the **estimated growth rates** for a **ceratopsian** and **sauropod** dinosaur?

Even though there are concerns with determining growth rates, some scientists have tried to estimate the numbers. In particular, the growth rates were calculated for species where there is fossil evidence from both eggs and adults—using the maximum growth rate of living reptiles as a guide.

For example, an adult *Protoceratops,* a ceratopsian of the Cretaceous period in Mongolia, weighed approximately 390 pounds (177 kilograms); the hatchling weighed approximately 1 pound (.43 kilograms). (It's assumed the hatchling weight was 90 percent of the egg weight.) From this data, the researchers calculated the time the young *Protoceratops* needed to reach adulthood was approximately 26 to 38 years.

On the other end of the size scale was an adult *Hypselosaurus,* a sauropod of the Cretaceous period in France. This large dinosaur weighed approximately 11,700 pounds (5,300 kilograms) at adulthood; the hatchling weighed approximately 5 pounds (2.4 kilograms). The scientists calculated the time needed to reach adulthood for this animal at 82 to 188 years!

271

What are the **problems** with estimating dinosaur **growth rates** based on **modern reptiles**?

If we look to the modern relatives of the dinosaurs to determine growth patterns, we are again baffled: all these animals also show different types of growth patterns. Reptiles continue to grow as long as they live, though the rate slows with age, called indeterminate growth. On the other hand, birds cease growing as they reach adulthood; this is called determinate growth.

Some, if not all, dinosaurs probably had a much different metabolism than modern cold-blooded reptiles, which would drastically alter the growth rate calculations. Also, the actual growth rate depends on the climate where the dinosaur lived—animals that live in warmer climates grow faster than those in colder ones.

Did dinosaurs **see in color** or **black and white**?

Because eyes are soft parts of an animal, they do not survive the fossilization process. Thus, scientists have no idea what a dinosaur eye looked like, much less if the animals could see in color or black and white. And it's hard to guess: just look at the diversity of modern animals—and the diversity of eyes, and how and what various animals see.

Did **dinosaurs** have **binocular vision** similar to humans?

The majority of dinosaurs had monocular vision, with eyes set into the sides of their heads, and little overlap between the right and left fields of view. Thus, they had good peripheral vision, but the binocular vision was modest—similar to modern reptiles like the alligator. (One of the animals with the best pairs of eyes is the modern house cat. It has binocular vision that takes in 130 degrees in front of them, and has peripheral vision that stretches back farther than any other animal.)

But some scientists believe there were exceptions, and that some dinosaurs may have had binocular vision similar to a human's depth perception. In particular, predators such as the *Tyrannosaurus* may have been able to see depth, suggesting that the animals were hunters, not scavengers as some paleontologists believe. In addition, over time, some carnivores may have evolved facial traits that actually enhanced the animals' ability to see depth. And some dinosaurs may have developed sight similar to a hawk: the raptor can see its prey from far away, but its binocular vision does not kick in until it swoops down from the sky to take down its prey. More work is being done to determine how dinosaurs saw the world. Scientists are using model dinosaur heads and laser beams to ascertain sight position.

How large was a **dinosaur's brain**?

No one really knows the true size of dinosaur brains because, as with all soft parts of the dinosaur, brains did not survive the fossilization process. Therefore, scientists can only infer the size of the animals' brains by examining the brain case, or the part of the skull housing the brain. When studying dinosaurs scientists found that different dinosaurs had different sized brains, based on the volume of the brain case. For example, sauropods' brains were small in comparison with their body weight; whereas, some dinosaurs, such as the *Velociraptor,* had very large brains in comparison with their body weight.

Were the **dinosaurs intelligent**?

Since there are no dinosaurs living today, there is no way scientists can determine a dinosaur's intelligence quotient—or IQ.

However, they can judge how relatively intelligent dinosaurs were by taking a ratio of brain weight (based on the skull volume) to body weight, then comparing these ratios for various dinosaurs. This ratio is called the encephalization quotient (EQ). Based on this idea, the smartest dinosaurs had the larger brain to body weight ratios than the less intelligent ones.

The following table lists some types of dinosaurs and their EQs. Note that the dromaeosaurids and troodontids are thought to be some of the smartest dinosaurs. The troodontids include the *Troodon,* a carnivore; the dromaeosaurid dinosaurs include the *Velociraptor,* a 6-foot (1.8-meter) carnivore with clawed feet, sharp, pointed teeth—and an animal that probably roamed in packs.

Some Dinosaur Encephalization Quotients

Dinosaur	EQ (approximate)
Dromaeosaurids	5.8
Troodontids	5.8
Carnosaurs	1.0 to 1.9
Ornithopods	0.9 to 1.5
Ceratopsians	0.7 to 0.9
Stegosaurs	0.6
Ankylosaurs	0.55
Sauropods	0.2
Sauropodomorphas	0.1

What are the **encephalization quotients** for some **typical mammals**?

The encephalization quotient (EQs) for some typical mammals are based on the same formula as for the dinosaurs: the ratio of the brain to body weight. The following table lists the EQs of some well-known mammals.

Some Mammal Encephalization Quotients

Mammal	Animal Type	EQ
Human	Primate	7.4
Bottlenose dolphin	Cetacean	5.6
Bluenose dolphin	Cetacean	5.31
Chimpanzee	Primate	2.5
Rhesus monkey	Primate	2.09
Cat	Carnivore	1.71
Langur	Primate	1.29
Squirrel	Rodent	1.10
Rat	Rodent	0.40

WHAT HAPPENED?

THE CRETACEOUS EXTINCTION

What is an **extinction**?

An extinction is the sudden or gradual dying out of a species. There are a multitude of reasons for extinction, ranging from disease, human intervention, climate changes, volcanic eruptions, or colliding space bodies. Each one can cause the extinction of one or many species of animals, depending on the severity.

When did the idea of **extinction** become accepted?

During the seventeenth and eighteenth centuries, scientists knew that fossils were the ancient remains of plants and animals. However, most still felt that these fossils represented known, living species—species that would shortly be discovered living in some remote, unexplored part of the globe.

This changed radically in the 1750s. Explorers in North America found the remains of what they thought were elephants—but in reality, the animals were mastodons and mammoths, animals now known to have lived more than 10,000 years ago toward the end of the Great Ice Age. As these and other fossils from the New World were examined, scientists realized the fossils were actually the remains of recently extinct species. In 1796, Baron Georges Cuvier (1769–1832) of the Museum of Natural History in Paris (the first comparative anatomist) published a series of papers proving these "fossil elephants" and giant mammal bones from other parts of the world did indeed represent extinct species.

What is the evidence for dinosaur and other life-form extinction?

There are several indicators of dinosaur and other life-form extinction in the fossil record. But one of the best ways to determine an extinction is by the lack of fossils in a rock layer. For example, above the top rock layers from the Cretaceous period, there are no known fossils of dinosaurs; and just above the top rock layers from the Permian period, the number of fossils—from animals to plants—greatly diminishes. The reason is logical: the animals that die leave behind fossils; when they become extinct, no more fossils are left behind. Such evidence in rock layers makes it seem as if one minute the organisms were there, and the next they disappeared. In reality, most of the extinctions took place over thousands of years.

What is the **"fern spike"**?

The "fern spike" is a layer of rock filled with fern spores, and occurs after a major cataclysmic or localized extinction. Scientists believe that after a major mass extinction, most plants would be wiped out. The first plants to recover are the ferns, which spread their spores into the air—thus the "fern spike." This evidence in rock layers is often used to determine the line between the time before and after a massive global or local extinction.

What were the major **extinctions** during the **earth's** long history?

About five major extinctions have occurred over our planet's long history. Some of the extinctions greatly affected the animals and plants on land, while other extinctions mainly occurred in the oceans. Most of the major extinctions are based on the fossil record, and usually indicate a time when a large percent of the plants and animals living on the earth went extinct, usually for unknown reasons. The following table lists some major extinctions and the time periods between which each extinction happened.

Major Extinctions

Time Period	Date (millions of years ago)	Percent of Species Extinct (approximate)
Cambrian–Ordovician	438	85
Devonian–Carboniferous	360	82
Permian–Triassic	250	97
Triassic–Jurassic	208	76
Cretaceous–Tertiary	65	76

Asteroid 243 Ida. A large asteroid impact could have caused highly acidic rainfall over the planet. (Photo courtesy of National Aeronautics and Space Administration/Corbis.)

How many species of **dinosaurs** were living at the end of the **Cretaceous period**?

No one knows the exact number of dinosaur species living at the end of the Cretaceous period, as scientists do not have a complete dinosaur fossil record. The nature of fossilization, that is that not all animals were in the right place at the right time in order to become a fossil, and the process of erosion has wiped away much of the evidence over time. Although scientists know there were probably many more dinosaurs, only a few species were still alive toward the end of the Cretaceous period—and most of them lived on the North American continent.

How many **other organisms** became **extinct** at the end of the **Cretaceous period**?

No one knows the exact number of other organisms—land animals, marine animals, and plants—that became extinct at the end of the Cretaceous period. But based on the fossil record, scientists believe that about 76 percent of all species on the globe went extinct at the end of the Cretaceous period.

Why did certain **plants and animals survive** through the end of the **Cretaceous period**?

Until a definite reason for the extinction is determined, it is difficult to answer such a question. Apparently, some species were not affected by the occurrence. In fact, noc-

277

turnal mammals—probably through luck or inborn tolerance to harsh environmental conditions—survived. They quickly exploited all the new nooks and crannies available to them, and soon dominated the planet.

Why aren't **huge amounts** of **dinosaur bones** found in late Cretaceous period rock layers?

This is another mystery surrounding the whole question of dinosaur extinction at the end of the Cretaceous period: if indeed the dinosaurs were suddenly killed off by a catastrophe, there should be a thick layer of bones—or a "bone spike"—in the fossil record. However, no such bone spike has been found to date at the boundary between the Cretaceous and Tertiary periods. Equally puzzling, few dinosaur bones have been found within a foot or so below this boundary.

One possible theory to explain these "missing" dinosaur bones (if they truly are missing) involves acid rain. Models have shown that one consequence of a large asteroid impact would be highly acidic rainfall over the planet. This acidic water could have dissolved most of the dinosaur bones lying on the surface, and would have also penetrated below the surface into the upper soil zones. Combined with bacteria, the water would become even more acidic—dissolving any bones found there. Only already fossilized bones would resist the acidic water. And since the fossilization process takes a very long time, none of the more recent dinosaur bones would have been spared.

This theory—and it is only a theory at present—neatly explains why there are so few dinosaur bones found in rock below the boundary, and none at the boundary itself. Supporting evidence comes from the boundary layer itself: in many places around the world, a relatively thin layer of clay exists that could have formed from the erosion of rocks due to acid rain.

What **"bone spike"** was found in late Cretaceous period rock layers?

A late Cretaceous "bone spike," the thick layer of bones found in the fossil record around the time of a catastrophic extinction, has not been found until recently. A large bed of fossil fish bones from this time has been discovered on Seymour Island, Antarctica, covering more than 31 square miles (50 square kilometers). Although there is a possibility that the fish were killed off by volcanic activity, climate change, or some other environmental cause, their bones lie immediately above the iridium-rich layer that marks the end of the Cretaceous period. In other words, it's highly likely that the fish were victims of the catastrophic extinction that also affected the dinosaurs.

SOME THEORIES OF DINOSAUR EXTINCTION

How long ago did the **dinosaurs** disappear?

Based on the dinosaur fossil record, larger and smaller dinosaurs died out about 65 million years ago. More recently, many scientists point out that not all dinosaurs disappeared—citing birds as direct descendants of the dinosaur.

What are the **two general theories** as to how fast the dinosaurs went **extinct**?

The two general theories are catastrophism and gradualism. Catastrophism is the rapid change in conditions found on the planet, such as changes in the atmosphere, that led to the death of most species of dinosaurs. Gradualism maintains that the dinosaurs died out slowly, over a period of many hundreds of thousands or millions of years. This may be due, for example, to changes of climate caused by continental drift. Some scientists feel both theories are correct, with slow and rapid changes coming together at the end of the Cretaceous period—and leading to the extinction of the dinosaurs.

What is the **"disease" theory** of **dinosaur extinction**?

The "disease" theory of dinosaur extinction (which falls under the umbrella theory of gradualism) states that dinosaurs eventually died out because of disease. Some say biological changes, brought about by changes in their evolution, made the animals less competitive with other organisms—including mammals that had just started appearing. Others say a major disease, from rickets to constipation, wiped out the dinosaurs, with some dinosaur bones definitely showing signs of these diseases over time. Another idea is that overpopulation led to the spread of major diseases among certain species of dinosaurs—and eventually to them all.

What **other disease** could have led to dinosaur extinction?

According to recent findings, dinosaurs and other animals may have gone extinct because of epidemics of cancer. And these epidemics may have been caused by a massive burst of neutrinos from dying stars in our galaxy.

What are **neutrinos**?

Neutrinos are weakly interacting elementary particles from a star. Neutrinos are very strange: they have no electric charge and apparently no effective mass. In fact, neutrinos from the Sun can pass through the entire Earth—and us—with little chance of being stopped. But if there is a massive burst of neutrinos, that is when the trouble starts. And one of the ways to get a burst of neutrinos is by the collapse of dying stars.

How would a massive influx of **neutrinos** from a dying star have **led to cancer** in dinosaurs?

A massive influx of neutrinos from a dying star in our galaxy could have passed through our planet—with some of these particles colliding with the nuclei of atoms in living tissue. These collisions would cause the nuclei to recoil, similar to what happens to a billiard ball when hit by the cue ball. Damage to an organism's DNA (deoxyribonucleic acid) would result, which could lead to cancer-causing mutations.

And not just the dinosaurs would have been affected: the neutrino influx associated with a collapsing star would result in approximately 19,000 nuclei recoils in each kilogram of tissue for an organism living on Earth. Estimates have placed the number of resulting malignant cells per kilogram of living tissue at about 12. And each of these malignant cells would have the potential to produce a tumor.

Obviously, larger animals, such as the dinosaurs, would have a higher potential for developing cancer because they had more tissue. Compounding the problem, skin does not protect an organism from neutrinos; the particles penetrate through the entire body of a living organism. This means malignant cells could have formed in the very sensitive interior tissue, such as the bone marrow.

Could a **star collapse** near our solar system?

Scientists calculate that a dying star could collapse about once every 100 million years—and within a radius of approximately 20 light years from Earth. It may sound like a long distance, but in astronomical terms, it is not!

Could the **atmosphere** have caused the extinction of the dinosaurs?

Some scientists have proposed an atmospheric cause for the extinction of the dinosaurs—in particular, they point to a reduction in the amount of oxygen present in the atmosphere during the Cretaceous period. Researchers recently measured microscopic air bubbles trapped in amber. The study showed that the amount of oxygen present 2 million years before the end of the Cretaceous period was approximately 35 percent—and just after the end of the Cretaceous, the amount was down to 28 percent.

Would a **lower oxygen level** affect dinosaurs?

Yes, with a lower oxygen level, the dinosaurs could have experienced extreme respiratory stress. This is similar to what humans encounter when living or working at extremely high altitudes without supplemental oxygen.

Today's atmospheric oxygen level is 21 percent, but modern animals have the proper physiology to live in this atmosphere. Dinosaurs first evolved when the atmosphere was oxygen rich, and had the right physiology for this environment. Studies of an *Apatosaurus* skeleton show a limited capacity to breath, with relatively small nostrils and probably no diaphragm. This was fine as long as the atmosphere was rich in oxygen—but it was inadequate when the oxygen levels fell.

Under this scenario, dinosaurs may have experienced three different events leading their gradual extinction. First was a cooling climate toward the end of the Cretaceous period. Second, the oxygen levels might have fallen, making it extremely difficult to breath. This probably led to a reduction in dinosaur diversity—shrinking the number of genera from 35 about 10 million years before the end of the Cretaceous period to only 12 at the end. At that point, a third and final catastrophic event may have occurred: an asteroid impact or impacts, and/or volcanic activity—which finally pushed the remaining dinosaurs to extinction.

What could have **caused lower oxygen levels** at the end of the Cretaceous period?

The reduction in oxygen levels in the planet's atmosphere toward the end of the Cretaceous period may have been caused by volcanic activity. Volcanic activity could have increased, modifying the relative amounts of atmospheric gases, such as carbon dioxide and oxygen. In turn, this would influence the evolution of life on the planet. This is known as the "Pele hypothesis," after the Polynesian goddess of volcanoes.

What is the **"mammal" theory** of **dinosaur extinction**?

The "mammal" theory of dinosaur extinction (which falls under the umbrella theory of gradualism) states that dinosaurs were slowly wiped out by mammals, animals that only appeared at the end of the Mesozoic era (the end of the Cretaceous period). The mammals could have eaten many of the dinosaurs eggs (thus, the dinosaurs had difficulty reproducing) or the mammals could have taken over territories from the dinosaurs. On a smaller scale, such events happen today, especially when an introduced species takes over another species by eating the native organism's young or by taking over the territory and eating the available food supply.

What is the **"poison plant" theory** of **dinosaur extinction**?

The "poison plant" theory of dinosaur extinction involves the development of angiosperms (flowering plants), a new type of plant that flourished during the Cretaceous period. Some of the plants were no doubt poisonous to dinosaurs, as the plants probably developed protective toxins (poison) in order not to be eaten by animals. The more prolific plant-eating dinosaurs may have died out as the plants became more toxic to them and, in turn, the carnivores had fewer plant-eating dinosaurs to eat.

But this theory is too simplistic. There were many plants in the world, including varieties that were nonpoisonous. In addition, the idea does not explain the mass extinction of marine organisms at the end of the Cretaceous period—animals that had nothing to do with flowering plants on land.

Did **dinosaurs** get blown away by **hurricanes**?

No one really knows, but several researchers think this may have been possible. These scientists studied huge hurricanes called hypercanes, monster storms that grew much larger than modern hurricanes, especially if the ocean water was greatly warmed. They believe a large impacting meteorite struck or a major volcano erupted into shallow ocean waters, causing the ocean water temperatures to rise—doubling the temperatures we currently find in the tropics. This increase in water temperature could have created hypercanes that grew to immense sizes. In turn, the storms could have carried water vapor, ice crystals, and dust high into the atmosphere—blocking sunlight and destroying the protective ozone layer that shields animals from the ultraviolet radiation from the sun. The effect could have devastated the dinosaurs. Scientists admit the idea is a little far-fetched—but it is not impossible.

How could a **hypercane** form from an **asteroid impact**?

An asteroid larger than 6 miles (10 kilometers) in diameter impacting into a shallow sea would create a hot spot about 31 miles (50 kilometers) wide, heating the water to approximately 122 degrees Fahrenheit (50 degrees Celsius). A hypercane would form in a day over the area, with an eye a few miles across, and a pressure below 300 millibars—less than one-third the normal atmospheric pressure. This storm would have winds up to 984 feet (300 meters) per second, or about 90 percent the speed of sound! The resulting low pressure would suck in dust and water vapor—and send it soaring high into the atmosphere.

What **effects** would a **hypercane** have on our planet?

By its very nature, a hypercane would send material such as water vapor and dust into the upper atmosphere. Once there, high altitude clouds would form. Some scientists believe the clouds would reflect the sun's rays, with less thermal radiation reaching the planet below—thus, cooling the global climate. Other scientists think that these same clouds would increase the greenhouse effect, causing a global warming. In either case, the global climate would be radically altered.

The hypercane would also eventually destroy a great deal of life on the planet—not only because the immediate destruction caused by the hypercane, but through an indirect effect, too. The water droplets sent high into the upper atmosphere by a hypercane could react with the sun's ultraviolet radiation to form hydroxyl radicals. These radicals could then combine with chlorine, another material sent into the upper atmosphere by the storm. This combination would destroy large amounts of the upper atmospheric ozone layer, allowing the ultraviolet radiation of the sun to reach the earth's surface. Such an intense bombardment of ultraviolet radiation would kill organisms on land and in the upper ocean. And over time, it could break down the entire global food chain.

Could the **asteroid impact at Chicxulub** have generated a hypercane?

The asteroid impact at Chicxulub in the Yucatan Peninsula of Mexico could have indeed generated a hypercane. Approximately 65 million years ago, this area was covered by a shallow sea. The impact of the asteroid would have pushed the seawater aside, creating a crater on the seabed. The crater's interior would have become very hot from the enormous amount of impact energy; the returning seawater would heat up—generating a hypercane.

What is the **"human" theory** of **dinosaur extinction**?

There is no such thing! The idea of humans living at the same time as dinosaurs (at least nonavian ones) seems to have been propagated by the B-movies of the 1950s and 1960s, in which dinosaurs attacked humans. In reality, mammals did evolve about the same time as the dinosaurs, but the mammals were not humanlike. The dinosaurs died out about 65 million years ago; the first hominids appeared about 3 to 4 million years ago; and finally *Homo sapiens sapiens* appeared about 90,000 years ago.

THE IMPACT THEORY

What is the **"impact" theory** of **dinosaur extinction**?

The impact theory is one of the newest ideas in the catastrophic camp of dinosaur extinction. This theory states that a large object (or objects), such as an asteroid or comet, collided with our planet, resulting in a large impact crater, giant waves in the oceans that smashed onto land at heights of 2 to 3 miles (3.2 to 4.8 kilometers), and radical, rapid changes in the planet's weather, temperature, amount of sunshine, and climate.

What is an **asteroid**?

An asteroid is a large rocky body found in outer space. They range from about the size of a boulder to about 6 miles (10 kilometers), and generally are classified as carbonaceous, stony, or metal. The majority of asteroids are found along the plane of the solar system, called the ecliptic. They are often also called minor planets because of their large size and propensity to orbit along the same plane as the major planets. Most of the asteroids revolve around the Sun in a tight band between the orbits of Mars and Jupiter, called the asteroid belt. Italian astronomer Giuseppe Piazzi (1746–1826) discovered the first asteroid, Ceres, in 1801.

Where did the **asteroids come from**?

The majority of these space objects are thought to have formed at the beginning of the solar system, about 4.6 billion years ago. There are several theories as to asteroid ori-

> ## How many near-Earth objects are there?
>
> Scientists currently believe there are about 2,000 near-Earth objects (mostly asteroids or burned-out comets) larger than a half mile (1 kilometer) in diameter that revolve around the Sun in short-period orbits. These objects can occasionally intersect the orbit of Earth. But most of the time, we pass right by each other or we are far from each other when the object crosses Earth's orbit. The only problem is that scientists estimate only about 7 to 10 percent of this estimated population has been discovered. There are scientists searching the sky, but they are few in number; therefore, we don't know the actual orbits of most of these near-Earth objects.

gin. Scientists once believed that the asteroids were leftovers from a shattered planet, but further analysis showed there are few, if any, sources—internal or external—that would have enough energy to crack a planet. A more accepted theory is that the asteroids formed at the same time as the other planets, but the gravitational pull of Jupiter did not allow huge chunks of rock called planetesimals to create a planet. Instead, the rocks settled between the orbits of Mars and Jupiter, colliding and creating the smaller asteroids we see today.

Where are **asteroids found** in our **solar system**?

The majority of the asteroids stay within the asteroid belt, a band of chunks of rock between the orbits of Mars and Jupiter. Over hundreds of thousands of years, because of the gravitational pull of the planets or other space objects, an asteroid may stray from the belt. Such asteroids that come close to Earth or cross Earth's orbit are called near-Earth asteroids (the ones that cross Earth's path are also called Earth-crossing asteroids). It is known that in the past, some near-Earth asteroids struck Earth, creating impact craters on the planet's surface. Meteor Crater in Arizona is a good example of an impact crater formed by an asteroid. There also seems to be an association between some of the larger Earth-impact craters and the extinction of a large number of species during the planet's long history.

What is a **comet**?

Comets are a collection of dust, gases, and ice that orbits the Sun. Once described as "dirty snowballs," many comets are now thought to be more like "mudballs," most carrying more dust than ice. In general, comets are composed of carbon dioxide, frozen water, methane, ammonia, and materials such as silicates and organic compounds.

A comet as seen from Earth in March 1976. (Photo courtesy of National Aeronautics and Space Administration.)

Where do comets **originate**?

Short-period comets, or those that complete their orbits every few to 200 years, are thought to have originated in the Kuiper Belt, a fat disk of comet-like objects that probably exists beyond the orbit of Neptune and Pluto. Long-term comets, or those that travel into the solar system every thousands of years (or may never return at all), are thought to originate in the Oort Cloud, a theoretical cloud of comets proposed by Dutch astronomer Jan Oort (1909–92). The cloud surrounds the solar system about 100,000 astronomical units from the Sun. (One astronomical unit is equal to about 93 million miles [149,637,000 kilometers], the average distance between Earth and the Sun.)

Have there been any **recent comets**?

Comets are relatively common in the solar system, so the chances of seeing one are good. Two comets recently readily visible to the naked eye added to our knowledge of comets: Comet Hyakutake in 1996 was merely a ball of ice, measuring only about 1 to 1.8 miles (2 to 3 kilometers) in diameter. Comet Hale-Bopp, about 10 times as big as Hyakutake, entered our sky in 1997. In addition, the discovery of Shoemaker-Levy 9, now thought to have been a fragmented comet, made scientists aware of the impact of space objects on other planets: the comet broke up into about 22 fragments, with each piece plunging into the atmosphere of Jupiter in July 1994. It

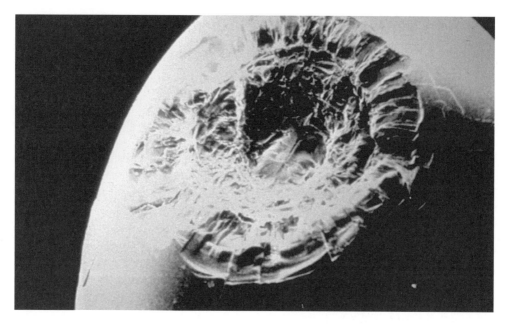

Simulation of a crater on a planet as caused by a meteorite. (Photo courtesy of JLM Visuals.)

was the first time humans had ever witnessed the impact of a space object on another planet.

Who **first formulated** the **impact scenario**?

In 1980, American physicist Luis Alvarez (1911–88) proposed that a large asteroid or comet hit the planet about 65 million years ago. His son, geologist Walter Alvarez (b. 1940), discovered a high concentration of iridium at the Cretaceous-Tertiary (K-T) boundary in Italy. Iridium is an element associated with extraterrestrial impacts. Because of this find, and the realization that the dinosaurs and many other species died out at the end of the Cretaceous, Louis and Walter Alvarez, along with colleagues Frank Asaro and Helen Michel, proposed that the extinctions at the K-T boundary were caused by the impact of a large space object. The iridium anomaly has since been found in over 50 K-T boundary sites around the world.

What is an **impact crater**?

An impact crater is a large impression on the surface of a planet, most often caused by a collision with a large space object, such as a comet or an asteroid. All planets and most satellites have impact craters—and even asteroids have impact craters. The

287

Moon is our most obvious example of impacts on a planetary body, as the surface is dotted with hundreds of craters.

How many **impact craters** are on our **planet**?

To date, scientists have identified about 150 impact craters on planet Earth. The majority have been found on the surface; less than a dozen or so are buried or are deep in the oceans. There were probably many more craters, but erosion—from wind, water, or the movement of the continental plates—has erased any evidence of their existence. In addition, there may be many more craters under the thick, vegetative growth of the jungles, in high mountains, or buried deep under sediment on land or in the oceans. The largest crater, the Vredefort crater in South Africa, is also one of the oldest, with an age of over 2 billion years; another large impact crater, the Sudbury in Canada, is also a major source of certain metals. Craters on the planet Mars dwarf Earth's craters. The largest impact crater (also called a basin) on Mars is Hellas Planitia, measuring 1,243 miles (2,000 kilometers) in diameter.

The following table lists craters discovered around the world and their diameter:

Name	Location	Diameter (miles/kilometers)
Vredefort	South Africa	186/300
Sudbury	Ontario, Canada	155/250
Chicxulub*	Yucatan, Mexico	105/170
Manicouagan	Quebec, Canada	62/100
Popigai	Russia	62/100
Acraman	South Australia, Australia	56/90
Chesapeake Bay	Virginia, USA	53/85
Puchezh-Katunki	Russia	50/80
Morokweng	South Africa	44/70
Kara	Russia	40/65
Beaverhead	Montana, USA	37/60

*Crater thought to be associated, or at least partially associated, with the extinction of the dinosaurs.

What is **shocked quartz**?

Shocked quartz is just what it sounds like: the mineral quartz, made of silicon, that has been shocked by the huge impact from an asteroid or comet. Scientists have discovered many sites of shocked quartz in rock layers associated with impact craters around the world.

What **evidence** supports the **impact theory**?

The most compelling evidence for this theory is the Chicxulub crater in Yucatan Peninsula, Mexico, an impact crater that was discovered by geologists in 1992. This 150-mile- (241-kilometer-) wide crater—although recent measurements of the underground crater reveal it may be as large as 186 miles (300 kilometers) in diameter—is thought to be the result of a collision with an asteroid 6 to 12 miles (10 to 20 kilometers) in diameter. The crater was created approximately 64.98 million years ago, in the right time frame for the extinction of the dinosaurs; it may be totally or partially associated with the extinction of the dinosaurs. The crater is buried, and was actually found in the 1960s during a subsurface survey taken by an oil company. It took years before a geologist looking at the data noticed the circularity of the feature—and brought the impact crater to the attention of the scientific community.

Have any **asteroid pieces** been found at the **Chicxulub** crater?

A piece of the asteroid that impacted at Chicxulub 65 million years ago has recently been found at the bottom of the Pacific Ocean—far away from the impact site. Samples have also been found in the crater itself.

What are the **samples** from the **Chicxulub crater** like?

The samples found at the Chicxulub crater are extremely tiny nuggets of almost pure iridium. There have been two of these tiny pieces found to date, with the smallest weighing about 100 trillionths of a gram and the other about twice that size.

Although space objects do contain tiny nuggets of metals, none are in as pure a state as the iridium found in the Chicxulub crater. Scientists speculate that the high energy of impact vaporized all the metals except iridium; this metal needs even higher temperatures to vaporize. Thus, extremely tiny nuggets of pure iridium were left behind in the crater after the impact. These nuggets have been extremely hard to find: it has taken years of searching the rocks from the crater, and the use of sophisticated analytical instruments such as the scanning electron microscope (SEM).

What **Chicxulub fragment** was found in the **Pacific Ocean**?

Scientists believe a coarse-grained tenth-of-an-inch- (2.5-millimeter-) long pebble is from the object that impacted at Chicxulub crater. The rock was found during a portion of the work done by the international Ocean Drilling Project. While examining a core of dark brown clay taken from the northwest Pacific seafloor, scientists noticed a light brown patch containing the pebble.

This pebble contains chromium, iridium, and iron in amounts similar to those found in other space objects such as meteorites. It was also found at the base of the

Cretaceous-Tertiary (K-T) boundary layer—and may be part of the object that created the K-T layer itself.

Scientists think the crater at Chicxulub was formed by an asteroid traveling at a low angle from the southeast. If so, the debris could have been splattered as far as 5,593 miles (9,000 kilometers) due west into the Pacific Ocean, which is where the fragment was found. Millions of years of ocean sediments subsequently covered this pebble—until it was brought up by a drilling core.

Alternatively, the fragment could have broken off before the impact of the asteroid. If the impacting object was a comet—as some scientists speculate—the fragment could have been part of the debris from its tail.

Why was the **impact angle** at Chicxulub so important?

The asteroid impact angle (20 degrees) at Chicxulub was very important because it determined how the energy was distributed. If the impact had occurred straight down (perpendicular to Earth) most of the energy would have been directed into the planet's interior. But the shallow impact angle of the Chicxulub object meant that debris—in the form of vaporized and molten rock—was scattered forward toward the northwest. This instantly destroyed all living organisms, including dinosaurs, over western North America. The material forced into the upper atmosphere by this angled impact would have cooled the climate over a period of months—effectively killing off the remaining dinosaurs.

What **evidence** do scientists have of the **angled impact** at Chicxulub?

There are many pieces of evidence for an angled impact at Chicxulub, including the shape of the crater, the discovery of a fragment of the asteroid in the North Pacific, and the proof in rock layers. Here is some of the evidence:

1) Most craters, whether on Earth or other planets of our solar system, are circular, reflecting a very high, if not perpendicular, angle of impact. Scientists think that

the Chicxulub crater is not circular, but elongated, or asymmetrical, which would indicate a shallow angle of impact. Although the crater has been buried over the millions of years since the impact and cannot be seen by the naked eye, measurements of Earth's gravitational field around the impact site can reveal the hidden details. These measurements show distortions in the gravitational field that were caused by the compression and ejection of material when the asteroid struck. This data is mapped in the form of contour lines; these lines form concentric arcs to the southeast of the crater, while fanning outward to the northwest, which is just what you would expect for an angled impact. The shape of the crater, outlined by these contour lines, is analogous to the patterns of debris seen around asymmetric craters on the Moon. And these results can be experimentally replicated using a high-speed gun that shoots projectiles at rock at a shallow angle.

2) A fragment of the asteroid that caused the impact crater at Chicxulub was recently found in the North Pacific, which is again consistent with the direction the debris would have been sent in from this shallow impact.

3) Pollen data from this time shows that ferns suddenly proliferated just after the impact. This "fern spike" came after spores colonized the newly exposed ground. The fern spike, along with extinctions of other plants, was strongest in western North America—the area where the low-lying debris cloud from the angled impact would have had the most immediate and severe consequences.

4) Lastly, the North American sediment records include two layers from the time of the Chicxulub impact—evidence also consistent with an angled impact. The first layer was quickly put down by the low-flowing debris cloud just after the impact; the second layer formed by the material thrown high into the atmosphere that eventually settled back to the surface.

How many **impact craters** are associated with **dinosaur extinction**?

Currently, there is only one Earth-impact crater associated with dinosaur extinction—the Chicxulub crater in Mexico. In addition, tiny glass fragments from the impact ejecta (the rock and soil that sprayed from the crater when it formed) were found in 1990 in the Caribbean Ocean, on the island of Haiti. The ejecta debris appears to fall in line with the Chicxulub crater. Another crater, the Manson structure in Iowa, was once thought to have been made at the end of the Cretaceous, but subsequent studies show it is not the correct age.

Is there any evidence of **multiple impacts** causing dinosaur extinction?

No, as of yet, there is no evidence of multiple impacts causing the dinosaur extinctions. And, so far, the only crater associated with the Cretaceous period extinctions is the Chicxulub crater on the coast of Yucatan, Mexico. Recently, two new impact crater sites were found in Belize and Mexico, about 290 miles (480 kilometers) and 140 miles (230 kilometers) from the Chicxulub crater, respectively. These sites are thought to be from the ejecta of Chicxulub—the material thrown up from the crater that landed nearby.

If dinosaurs did become extinct from impacts, **how did they die**?

After the impact, scientists theorize that several events occurred. Right after the impact, huge amounts of dust and debris from the impact would have been thrown high into the atmosphere. The dust would have been carried by the upper winds all around the world, filtering or blocking out the sunlight. Heat from the blast may have created firestorms—huge forest fires that added smoke, ash, and particles to the already dust-filled atmosphere. If the dust-filled winds did not kill the animals, the lack of sunlight would kill off plants, creating a serious crisis: the animals feeding off of the vegetation would die, and in a domino-like effect, the rest of the other organisms in the food chain would die off, including the dinosaurs.

How can **impact** from an asteroid affect **plants**?

An impact from an asteroid can affect plants in a number of ways. In particular, the debris thrown into the atmosphere can block the sunlight, killing off plants. And other plants can be directly affected by minerals or chemicals from the actual impact.

For example, the plants dinosaurs depended on for sustenance may have been poisoned by nickel after the impact of a space body. This theory holds that nickel, which is common in space objects such as meteorites and asteroids, was vaporized on impact. The metal particles were injected into the atmosphere, along with other material and debris, eventually falling to the surface of the planet. If, as some scientists think, the form of nickel present in the asteroid was water-soluble, then it would have easily found its way into plants and poisoned them.

How much **nickel** could **enter the Earth's ecosystem** through an impact?

The amount of nickel sent into the Earth's ecosystem by an impact would depend on the impact itself. Using the Chicxulub crater as an example, scientists have estimated that the amount of nickel introduced into the Earth's ecosystem was approximately 10 to 100 times the amount normally present. This is about 3 to 30 times the toxic amount!

The asteroid that impacted the Yucatan Peninsula was probably about 6 miles (10 kilometers) wide, with a density of approximately 3,000 kilograms per cubic meter. If it totally vaporized on impact—and the resulting material eventually settled evenly to the Earth's surface—it would produce a layer a few tenths of an inch (a few millimeters) thick. The nickel concentration in this layer would be between 130 and 1,300 parts per million (ppm); the normal amount of nickel in the soil is 15 ppm, with 40 ppm being toxic.

What would happen if an **asteroid** or **comet impacted** the **planet** today?

The effects of an asteroid or comet impact on our modern planet would depend on a number of variables, including the size, speed, and composition of the object, and the location of the impact.

Recent advanced computer simulations show that the impact of an asteroid 3 miles (5 kilometers) in diameter in the mid–Atlantic Ocean would produce huge tsunamis (similar to seismic sea waves caused by earthquakes, and which are usually called tidal waves) that would spread out in all directions. These waves would be large and powerful enough to completely inundate the upper East Coast of the United States, extending inward to the Appalachian Mountains; a similar scenario would play out in Western Europe. A smaller asteroid of approximately 1,300 feet (400 meters) in diameter, striking in the same place, would still generate tsunami waves up to 300 feet (90 meters) high on all the surrounding coastlines, leading to considerable destruction and loss of life.

If an asteroid measuring more than 1 mile (1.6 kilometers) in diameter struck the planet's land surface or a shallow water area, the impact would throw large amounts of dust into the atmosphere, blocking the rays of the sun. The result would be darkness, a mini ice age, disrupted weather and climate, and the cessation of plant growth for a year, if not longer. This would be a catastrophe without precedent in the history of the human race. Scientists feel the impact of a large asteroid or comet more than 3 miles (5 kilometers) in diameter would eliminate most flora and fauna from the planet, certainly destroying life as we know it.

What is the **frequency** with which **different-sized impactors** hit Earth?

Although there is still debate on what impactors enter Earth's atmosphere, here is one estimate. And remember, the majority strike our oceans:

Type of Impactor	Frequency of Strikes
pea-sized meteoroids	10 per hour
walnut-sized meteoroids	1 per hour
grapefruit-sized meteoroids	1 every 10 hours
basketball-sized meteoroids	1 per month
165-foot (50-meter) meteoroid	1 per 100 years (this would destroy an area the size of the state of New Jersey if it struck land)
6-mile- (1-kilometer-) wide asteroids	1 per 100,000 years

Has there been any evidence of a recent killer asteroid?

Yes, scientists believe they have found evidence of a killer asteroid during the present era. This huge rock smashed into southeastern Argentina about 3.3 million years ago—possibly killing off 36 species of animals because of the local climate change. Neither the asteroid itself nor a crater were found, but glassy fragments (called escoria) were dug up from the soil. These fragments indicate intense heating that only could have come from a space object striking Earth.

Unlike the asteroid(s) that supposedly struck at the end of the Cretaceous period, the Argentina hit did not affect the global climate. But the strike apparently did change the local climate, cooling down the temperatures. This killed off many animals in the region, including giant armadillos, ground sloths, and a large-beaked carnivorous bird.

Which asteroids have come close to Earth in recent times?

On June 30, 1908, a small asteroid of about 100 to 200 feet (30 to 60 meters) in diameter, with a mass between 10,000 and 100,000 tons, exploded about 3 miles (5 kilometers) above the ground near Tunguska, Siberia, destroying hundreds of square miles of remote forest lands. Fortunately, this object had a grazing trajectory instead of coming straight down, and was composed of mostly volatiles, rather than iron-nickel metal. Even so, it released the energy equivalent to a nuclear bomb, with the effects felt hundreds of miles away.

In 1972, a small, 1,000-ton asteroid skimmed our outer atmosphere, but few knew about it. Other asteroids have just passed by: On March 23, 1989, asteroid 1989 FC, with the kinetic energy of over 1,000 one-megaton hydrogen bombs, passed close by Earth; in the 1991 to 1994 time frame, four asteroids came closer to Earth than half the distance to the Moon. Geographos, a very massive, cigar-shaped asteroid 3.2 miles by 1.2 miles (5.1 by 1.9 kilometers) in length, passed near Earth in 1969 and 1994.

The larger objects are the most devastating, and get the most attention. But the smaller asteroids, approximately 328 feet (100 meters) in diameter, are more of a present danger, since they strike Earth approximately once every 100 years.

Are there any asteroids heading for Earth in the future?

Only in fairly recent times have scientists become aware of the dangers posed by the potential impact of asteroids and comets. Therefore, they are just beginning to search the skies for objects that might, sooner or later, impact the planet on which we live.

The estimates for the number of near-Earth objects (NEOs) are high. These objects revolve around the Sun with orbits that occasionally cross or closely approach Earth's orbit. Scientists believe there could be 1,600 to 2,000 objects that are larger than just over a half mile (1 kilometer) in diameter; 300,000 NEOs over 328 feet (100 meters); and probably about 100,000 smaller ones that scientists are unable to detect. To date, only 7 percent of the NEOs larger than just over a half mile (1 kilometer) have been discovered.

Recently, scientists found an asteroid, named 1997 XF11, and calculated its orbit. It appeared that a collision in the near future was imminent. After further study, however, it was concluded that this asteroid, though making several close passes by Earth, posed no danger for at least the next century.

The following table lists just a few of the asteroids that will come within .2 astronomical units (18,600,000 miles or 29,927,400 kilometers) of our planet during the next 33 years. One astronomical unit is equivalent to 93,000,000 miles (149,637,000 kilometers); for comparison, the mean distance to the Moon is 238,866 miles (384,400 kilometers).

Object Name	Date of Encounter	Distance from Earth, in astronomical units (AU)
1863 Antinous	April 1, 1999	.1894
6489 Golevka *	June 2, 1999	.0500
4486 Mithra*	August 14, 2000	.0465
2100 Ra-Shalom	September 6, 2000	.1896
4179 Toutatis	October 31, 2000	.0739
3362 Khufu	December 29, 2001	.1597
3362 Khufu	December 25, 2002	.1498
2100 Ra-Shalom	August 17, 2003	.1745
3362 Khufu	December 20, 2003	.1946
4179 Toutatis*	September 29, 2004	.0104
1862 Apollo	November 6, 2005	.0752
4450 Pan*	February 19, 2008	.0408
1620 Geographos	March 17, 2008	.1251

* listed by some scientists as potentially hazardous

What **other theory** involves a large **catastrophe** that may have led to the **extinction** of the dinosaurs?

Some scientists feel that an incredibly large volcanic eruption occurred in the right time frame. The lava flows of this eruption, called the Deccan Traps, formed the highlands of India. The volcanic event could have produced enough ash to block out much of the sunlight, leading to changes in temperature and climate. Some "catastrophists" feel there were two impacts in this time frame—one in the Yucatan, Mexico, and the other in India, which triggered the volcanic eruption.

STILL OTHER THEORIES

Did **changes in Earth's environment** lead to dinosaur extinction?

Although the predominate dinosaur extinction theory is that an asteroid impact dramatically changed Earth's climate, there are some paleontologists who think otherwise. These scientists believe changes in Earth's environment played a much more important role in the extinction of life-forms on the globe—and the impact 65 million years ago just killed off the remaining species.

Recent studies of the fossil record have examined changes in a wide range of plant and animal species' populations toward the end of the Cretaceous period. Only single-celled marine life showed a sudden decline at the end of this period. Other species declined gradually, with a few groups showing no change. And there was no evidence for a catastrophic mass extinction in the fossil record.

Instead, the majority of extinctions may have occurred gradually, due to environment changes such as falling sea levels and volcanic eruptions. The sea level apparently dropped by approximately 328 feet (100 meters) during this time; also, debris from volcanic eruptions in India may have been thrown into the atmosphere. Both could have contributed to a gradual extinction of many flora and fauna species.

What is the **problem** with the **environmental theory** of dinosaur extinction?

The main problem with the environmental theory of dinosaur and other life-form extinctions lies in the conflicting evidence in the fossil record. For example, evidence for the environmental theory includes ammonite fossil records (hard-shelled relatives of squid): one record shows they were in decline for approximately 11 million years before finally going extinct, but other fossil evidence indicates the impact at Chicxulub suddenly killed off from one-half to three-quarters of ammonite species along the coasts of France and Spain.

Unfortunately, the fossil record of Cretaceous period dinosaurs is very limited for the last 10 million years. In fact, the only good dinosaur records from this time are in western North America—and this evidence is limited to the last 2 million years of the

What are killer cosmic clouds?

Killer cosmic clouds are large areas in outer space, probably bigger than our entire solar system, that have much higher concentrations of hydrogen than normal. For the past five million years, our planet has been traveling in a relatively empty, typical region of space—with a density of less than one particle (mostly hydrogen) per cubic inch. Killer clouds are found where new stars are being formed and have much higher densities, on the order of hundreds of particles of hydrogen per cubic inch.

Cretaceous period. Thus, this poor, discontinuous dinosaur fossil record may simply indicate an apparent, not actual, reduction in their diversity.

What newly discovered phenomena may be **heading our way** in about **50,000 years**?

The newly discovered phenomena are killer cosmic clouds, found in localized areas of outer space. Theoretical physicist Gary P. Zank believes the clouds would be bad for life on Earth—and may have been the reason dinosaurs died out approximately 65 million years ago. Smaller and less dense clouds, called Local Fluff, could hit our area at any time. The next large, dense cloud we might encounter will be 50,000 years from now, when we meet up with the Aquila Rift, an area of new star formation.

What **effect** could these **killer clouds** have **on Earth** and its life forms?

Some scientists believe that a killer cloud could collapse the solar system's heliosphere—a bubble of space produced by the solar wind that partially protects our planet (and the other planets and satellites in our solar system) from cosmic rays. Cosmic rays are high-speed particles from outer space that constantly hit the heliosphere, but most are deflected by this shield. And that's good, because exposure to the powerful radiation from these rays could kill a human being. If the heliosphere around our planet collapsed from the introduction of a cosmic cloud, much higher levels of cosmic radiation would strike Earth, dramatically altering life—although scientists are not sure how much or in what ways.

Could a **killer cosmic cloud** have caused the **extinction** of the **dinosaurs**?

If supercomputer models are correct, then higher concentrations of hydrogen could have formed a wall and caused the heliosphere around Earth to collapse. This could have allowed more cosmic radiation to penetrate to Earth's surface, resulting in changes to the flora and fauna. If this did occur, such an increase in cosmic rays, with elevated levels of radiation, could have directly killed the dinosaurs. Another scenario is that the rays negatively affected the vegetation eaten by the herbivorous dinosaurs and other animals. These animals would have then died off, leaving no prey for the carnivorous dinosaurs, which also then died.

Is there any **proof** that Earth has encountered a **cosmic cloud** in the past?

Scientists do not know what happened 65 million years ago—or any other time in the past. But we don't have to wait 50,000 years until we reach Aquila Rift to obtain proof of cosmic clouds. Some scientists believe that, from time to time, our planet could have encountered smaller, less dense clouds of hydrogen, known as Local Fluff. These less devastating encounters, predict the models, would have only weakened the heliosphere, resulting in slight increases in cosmic rays hitting Earth.

One of the known side effects of cosmic rays striking Earth is the production of the rare metal beryllium. An increase of this metal could be proof that we had encountered one of these relatively benign clouds in the past. Ice cores taken from the South Pole do indeed show an increase in beryllium levels at approximately 35,000 and 60,000 years ago, leading scientists to speculate that contacts were made with Local Fluff. What were the effects of these minor encounters? Scientists speculate the effect of the Earth coming into contact with Local Fluff might have produced anything from an ice age to an increased greenhouse effect.

Is there such a thing as the **true story** of **dinosaur extinction**?

Many scientists believe that dinosaurs became extinct not due to one reason, but to a combination of reasons, most of which are have been covered in this text. In addition, some scientists believe that dinosaurs were already gradually declining when the catastrophe occurred. There is a chance that they would have become extinct anyway—with or without a catastrophic occurrence.

What do the **Cretaceous period extinctions** tell us about our **modern world**?

According to one theory, extinctions at the end of the Cretaceous period were due to a combination of environmental change and impacting space objects—both responsible for the elimination of the dinosaurs and other life-forms. In this scenario, the environment was already stressed by natural events, leading to the gradual decline and disappearance of many species of flora and fauna. The impact that finally wiped out many of the remaining species did not have to be large or catastrophic—it was just the final straw in a long series of changes, pushing the environment and life-forms over the edge.

Our modern world has created a large number of environmental changes and stresses, most of it manmade. More species are declining or have gone extinct than ever before. A small catastrophe—such as the impact of a relatively small space object or a large amount of volcanic activity—could tip our already fragile ecosystem over the edge. And, in turn, this could lead to a rapid climate change and the loss of innumerable species of plants and animals. The resulting changes in climate and loss of our food supply would directly effect our own species' ability to survive.

A healthier and more resilient ecosystem might be able to survive and adapt to a catastrophe like the one at the end of the Cretaceous period. Many people believe it is up to us to work toward the health and well-being of our planet—to firm up its immune system, so to speak. Otherwise, someday we may become just fossils of a species driven to extinction by a combination of self-induced environmental stress and a natural catastrophe.

AFTER THE DINOSAURS

WHAT SURVIVED?

What was intriguing about the extinction at the end of the Cretaceous period?

The extinction at the Cretaceous-Tertiary (K-T) boundary is particularly intriguing because of the fossil record; according to the evidence, the extinctions in the ocean and on land occurred at the same time.

What groups survived the extinction at the end of the Cretaceous period?

The survivors include most land plants and land animals—insects, snails, frogs, salamanders, crocodiles, lizards, snakes, turtles, and certain marsupials and mammals. Most marine invertebrates also survived, including starfishes, sea urchins, mollusks, arthropods, and most fishes.

What was a common characteristic of the surviving land animals?

The land animals that survived were all small in stature, such as mammals, frogs, and snakes; the larger animals, such as the dinosaurs, did not survive this extinction. In fact, some scientists estimate that no animal heavier than 55 pounds (25 kilograms) survived on land.

How did the end of the Cretaceous period rank among the planet's extinctions?

The mass extinction at the end of the Cretaceous period was the second largest in geologic history; around 76 percent of all species disappeared. The largest mass extinction

The groups that did not survive the massive extinction include the dinosaurs, pterosaurs, and some families of birds and marsupial mammals on land. In the oceans, mosasaurs, plesiosaurs, some families of teleost fishes, ammonites, belemnites, rudist, trigoniid, and inoceramid bivalves became extinct; as well as over half the ocean's various plankton groups. Some groups appear to have vanished rather suddenly and completely at the end of the Cretaceous period, like the switching out of a light, whereas others were already gradually diminishing in diversity in the last 10 million years of the Cretaceous period.

was at the end of the Permian period, about 250 million years ago, in which about 90 to 97 percent of all species disappeared.

What types of **plants did not disappear** at the end of the Cretaceous period?

Although many species of plants disappeared at the end of the Cretaceous period, many ferns and seed-producing plants continued to survive into modern time.

What percent of **marine animals** went **extinct** at the end of the Cretaceous period?

The marine biota was hit very hard by the Cretaceous extinctions. About 15 percent of all marine families died out—and perhaps 80 to 90 percent of all species. Here are some examples of the approximate percents of certain groups that went extinct:

Marine Group	Percentage Extinct
Ammonites	100%
Corals	65%
Marine reptiles	93%
Ostracodes	50%
Planktonic foraminifera	83%
Sea urchins	54%
Sponges	69%

Marsupials, distant relatives of this opossum, remained after the dinosaurs' extinction. (Photo courtesy of D. Robert Franz/Corbis.)

What percent of **land animals** went **extinct** at the end of the Cretaceous period?

At the end of the Cretaceous period, many land animals became extinct; for example, about 25 percent of all land animal families disappeared. About 56 percent of the reptiles in general died out—and 100 percent of all nonavian (nonbird) dinosaurs and pterosaurs became extinct.

Why did **certain animals survive** and other animals did not?

No one is really sure why certain animals died out and others did not. In some ways, the animal extinctions at the end of the Cretaceous period were very selective.

Are **mammals** surviving **relatives** of the dinosaurs?

No, mammals are not the surviving relatives of the dinosaurs. The earliest mammals were descendants from certain types of reptiles—but they are not in the same line as the dinosaurs.

What **mammals** lived at the **end of the Cretaceous** period?

Mammals had been around for millions of years before the end of the Cretaceous period; in fact, the first group of true mammals, the morganucodontids, evolved in the

An alligator lizard, one of the 6,000 reptile species alive today. (Photo courtesy of Field Mark Publications.)

late Triassic period. And they were a successful group of animals for about 150 million years before the dinosaurs became extinct.

By the end of the Cretaceous period, some mammals had developed many innovations vital to their survival: many stopped laying eggs and were able to deliver live young. Various mammal species eventually grew specialized teeth for a variety of tasks—such as cutting, gnawing, and grinding—for the better processing of food. They developed better ways to compete for food, such as having more energy in proportion to their size, or adapting to changing diets by becoming omnivores (plant- and meat-eating animals).

The therian mammals—marsupials and placentals—became the apparent heirs to the land the dinosaurs (and other organisms) left behind. Some mammal subgroups had already disappeared before the demise of the dinosaurs; others made it through the end of the Cretaceous period; and some even survive to this day.

Why did the **mammals** come to **dominate** in the **Cenozoic** era?

Mammals came to dominate the Cenozoic era (our present time) because there was "suddenly" little competition. The larger predatory reptiles had disappeared, and the mammals quickly filled the available ecological niches.

When did modern reptiles evolve?

The earliest turtles evolved during the Triassic period, but they probably could not withdraw into their shells like modern turtles. Lizards and snakes have poor fossil records. This is probably due to the animals' tendencies to live in dry uplands, far from the areas that are most likely to produce fossils (most animal bones survive if they are quickly buried with sediment, such as along riverbanks). It is thought that lizards appeared in the late Triassic; the earliest remains of snakes are found in the late Cretaceous (in North America and Patagonia, South America).

Are **mammals** the **most abundant animals** on the planet today?

No, mammals are not the most abundant animals—in terms of species or individuals—on our planet. There are many more kinds of fish, reptiles, and birds, and there are even more invertebrate species on earth, including insects and mollusks.

What are the **closest living relatives** to the dinosaurs?

The closest living relatives to the dinosaurs are thought to be certain modern reptiles and birds.

What is a **reptile**?

Modern reptiles include the alligators and crocodiles, turtles, lizards, and snakes. They all have several typical characteristics: they have a protective covering of scales or plates, five clawed toes on each foot (with exceptions, of course, such as snakes), and lungs instead of gills. Most lay eggs (although most poisonous snakes in the United States, except coral snakes, produce live young) and eat animals (the land tortoise is one exception).

How did **reptiles** fare at the end of the **Cretaceous period**?

After the Cretaceous period, most reptiles were wiped out. About 6,000 reptiles species exist today, fewer in number and much smaller in size than their ancestors—but greater in diversity.

What reptile **species survived** past the end of the **Cretaceous** period?

One interesting group of reptiles—also close relatives of the dinosaurs—are the crocodiles. They appear to have evolved from archosaurian ancestors during the late Trias-

A modern crocodile, relatively unchanged since the Triassic. (Photo courtesy of Danny Lehman/Corbis.)

sic; but unlike most of their contemporaries, they survived to the present day. They are also remarkable: these moderate- to large-sized semi-aquatic predators have remained relatively unchanged since the Triassic period.

What are the types of **modern crocodiles**?

There are two types of modern crocodiles found in tropical and subtropical environments: the gavialids are found in India; they eat fish and have slender snouts. The crocodylids are found almost worldwide, and consist of crocodiles and alligators. They have long bodies, and powerful tails used for swimming or defense. Their limbs allow the animals to maneuver and steer in the water; on land, they use their limbs to walk with a slow gait, with their bellies held high off the ground. These animals choose from a wide variety of food, including fish, large vertebrates, and carrion.

What is the difference between an **alligator** and a **crocodile**?

Although there are some overlapping habitats of alligators and crocodiles, it is rare to see these reptiles together. The best way to tell the difference between the two animals is by checking the size and head: crocodiles are slightly smaller and less bulky than alligators. In addition, the crocodile has a narrower snout, with a pair of

Alligators, like this one in Florida, are slightly larger and more bulky than crocodiles, and have a broader snout. (Photo courtesy of Field Mark Publications.)

enlarged teeth in the lower jaw that fit into a "notch" on each side of the snout. The alligator has a broader snout, and all the teeth in its upper jaw overlap with those in the lower jaw.

How would **dinosaurs** have **evolved** if they had **not gone extinct** 65 million years ago?

One theory comes from Dale Russell, curator of fossil vertebrates at the Canadian Museum of Nature, Ottawa, Canada, who believes that dinosaurs were evolving toward more humanlike features toward the end of the Cretaceous period. These features included a larger brain, forward focused eyes, and bipedalism. Extrapolating from these tendencies, Russell "evolved" a dinosaur. He called the bipedal creature he came up with a dinosauroid, which, though reptilian in many ways—including its extremities and somewhat scaly skin—also looked very humanoid.

Are there any descendants of the **dinosaurs** living **today**?

Some scientists believe that modern birds are not only close relatives of dinosaurs, but are actually the descendants of dinosaurs—or may actually *be* dinosaurs.

307

MODERN BIRDS

What are **birds**?

Birds are members of the animal kingdom; they have their own class, known as Aves. (A possible origin of the word bird is thought to be the Old English *brid,* which originally referred to the young of animals.) Birds are vertebrate animals, warm-blooded, and reproduce by laying eggs. They have four limbs, with the front two limbs modified into wings.

How are **birds classified**?

Birds have a class all their own, called Aves. Within this broad class is a subclass called the Neornithes; this grouping includes the approximately 9,000 species of living, or recent, birds. In turn, this grouping is further divided into four suborders, based on the palate anatomy of the birds. (There also are some different classification systems for birds, including one that divides the Neornithes only into the Palaeognathae and the Neognathae; for our purposes, we will use the four-suborder classification.) The four suborders are the Palaeognathae, which are divided into two subgroups, the ratites (such as ostrich, rhea, emu, and other large, flightless birds) and the tinamous (such as the South American tinamous); Impennes (penguins); the Odontognathae (fossil birds); and Neognathae (all other living birds, from hummingbirds to plovers).

What are some of the **species of birds** living in the **modern** world?

There are literally thousands of modern bird species; the following lists some of these groups, from the primitive to the more advanced species (this listing is only one classification—there are others in use):

Select Bird Groupings	Examples of Species
Ratites	Ostriches, rheas, emus
Tinamous	Tinamous
Grebes	Grebes
Loons	Loons
Penguins	Penguins
Tube-nosed	Tube-noses, such as albatrosses
Marine birds	Diving-petrels, shearwaters
Pelicans and relatives	Pelicans, boobies, gannets, cormorants, frigatebirds
Long-legged wading birds	Storks, herons, ibises, flamingos
Waterfowl	Ducks, geese, swans

Select Bird Groupings	Examples of Species
Birds of prey	Falcons, hawks, eagles, kites, osprey, new world vultures
Game birds	Curassows, grouse, quail, pheasants
Cranes, rails, and relatives	Bustards, cranes, kagu, cootes, sungrebes
Shorebirds, gulls, auks, and relatives	Avocets, plovers, sandpipers, gulls, terns
Pigeons and doves	Pigeons and doves
Parrots	Parrots, lories
Cuckoos and relatives	Cuckoos
Owls	Owls
Nightjars and relatives	Nightjars, frogmouths, potoos
Swifts and hummingbirds	Swifts, hummingbirds
Colies	Colies
Kingfishers and woodpeckers	Hornbills, kingfishers, motmots, todies, toucans, woodpeckers
Perching birds	Buntings, grosbeaks, tanagers, crows, jays, finches, thrushes

Why are **birds unique**?

The feature unique to birds, and what makes them so adaptable and fascinating, is a body covered with feathers. These lightweight structures provide insulation from the changing temperatures; are used as ornamentation and coloration for establishing dominance and attracting mates; and, most importantly, give the animals the ability to fly freely through the air. There are exceptions: although certain birds, such as penguins, possess feathers, they cannot fly.

What is the composition of **feathers**?

Feathers are light, strong, and flexible structures—composed mostly of keratinous, or protein, material.

Are bird **feathers** all **alike**?

No, there are specialized feathers found on specific parts of a bird's body. Each of these specialized feathers have definite purposes; for example, there are contour, semi-plume, down, filoplume, and powder feathers. Different species of birds have varying amounts of these types of feathers. Some species also have very specialized feathers, unique to those types of birds. For example, the crest feathers on blue jays and the bristles found on the toes of barn owls are both specialized feathers unique to these species of birds.

The peacock's feathers distinguish this creature from any other. Birds are thought by some to be descendants of the dinosaurs. (Photo courtesy of Field Mark Publications.)

What are **contour feathers**?

Contour feathers are found on a bird's outer body, wings, and tail. These feathers are usually stiff and large when present on the wings and tail, helping the bird to fly. Another type of contour feather grows around the ears.

What are **filoplume feathers**?

Filoplume feathers are the hairlike features associated with the contour feathers of a bird.

What are **semiplume feathers**?

Semiplume feathers provide a bird with insulation and flexibility—and for birds who frequent the water, buoyancy. These feathers are hidden beneath the contour feathers and are found on most of the bird's body.

What are **down feathers**?

Most people are familiar with down feathers since they fill many pillows and comforters. This is because these feathers are small, fluffy, and soft—and are great insulators. For the birds, they also act as insulators beneath certain contour feathers.

How do birds replace their feathers?

Birds replace their feathers by molting (the periodic natural shedding of old feathers and the growing of new ones)—from one to even three times per year. Many birds molt at different times of the year. For example, male goldfinches molt from a dull greenish yellow to bright yellow during the spring. This periodic shedding of old feathers—and the replacement by new feathers—is logical: feathers are incapable of further growth, and many get worn down, broken, and faded over the year just from normal wear-and-tear; molting replaces these damaged feathers. It is also a way for the males to look "enticing" to a potential mate—which is why many molts coincide around the mating season.

What are **powder feathers**?

Powder feathers do not really look like feathers—even though they are called a feather. Instead, they look like a powdery substance. Many scientists believe this powdery "feather" protects the bird from moisture, somewhat similar to how humans use talcum powder!

Are there **different** types of **bird molts**?

Yes. There is the complete molt, in which all the feathers are replaced. Most birds do not lose all their feathers at the same time, although there are exceptions: for example, some aquatic birds molt completely, remaining on the surface until their feathers grow back. There are also partial molts, in which feathers on certain parts of the bird's body—such as the head, body, or tail—are replaced. Some birds even molt the wing and tail feathers a few at a time and equally on either side of the body, allowing the bird to still fly and maneuver during the molt.

Do we know **how birds fly**?

Yes, we now know how birds fly. Since humans have watched birds in flight, they have dreamed of trying to fly—to move through the atmosphere using wings and feathers. But the actual mechanics of flight itself were hard to understand until the twentieth century. By then, detailed photographic pictures of birds in flight were possible; later on, computer models broke down the true way of flight—although artist Leonardo da Vinci's (1452–1519) flight drawings centuries before were surprisingly accurate for his time!

The combination of feathers, skeletal structure, and flexibility allows a bird to fly. Simply put, each wing has a duel use: the inner feathers are moved by the shoulder joint creating a lifting surface, generating the force necessary to stay in the air; the primary feathers move as the wrist moves forward and down, then upward and back during each flap, producing the power needed to move through the air.

Are birds the **only vertebrates** capable of **flying**?

No, bats are the other vertebrates capable of flight. Insects can fly, but they are considered to be invertebrates—and gliding, such as that done by a flying squirrel, doesn't count.

What type of **vocalizations** do birds make?

Birds exhibit many different forms of vocalizations—many of which make them unique. In particular, birds can make calls, or brief, simple sounds, for many purposes. They can be used to attract a mate, warn the young and others of danger, or assemble others of the flock together. Calls are also used in migration to keep the groups in contact with one another—such as the calls of Canadian geese as they fly south or north during the changing seasons.

Birds also have a song—and it is just as it says: a song, or elaborate vocalization, by a bird is used mostly for claiming territory or attracting a mate. Most of the songs are simple and repetitive; though they are greatly varied throughout the many songbird species. Songs include the hooting of an owl, and the many songs of a cardinal.

Many scientists believe the more complex birds songs are instinctive. For example, a song sparrow raised by a canary has been found to still sing a song sparrow melody.

Were **bird vocalizations** at the end of the **Mesozoic era** similar to those of **modern** birds?

It is difficult to know whether birds at the end of the Mesozoic era called and sang similar to modern birds. Scientists assume that older and modern birds made similar calls—after all, their head structures are relatively the same. And they probably made calls and songs for the same reasons—especially the males' songs for keeping territory and mating.

What is a **bird nest**?

Birds all seem to nest, or have a "home" where they lay and raise their young. Not all nesting sites are the familiar mud, grass, and twig structures made by many of today's songbirds; some are along rock ledges, on bare rocks, along building ledges, under bridges, in dead trees, or in depressions on the ground—all depending on the bird. There are usually a number of reasons why a bird chooses a certain site. Most birds chose a site somewhat out of the way from predators, but the majority chose a site nearest to a food supply.

It is unknown if birds have always nested, but it is interesting to note that some scientists have found evidence of dinosaurs nesting in colonies—similar to many modern birds. Because it is thought that dinosaurs and birds are related (and birds may even *be* dinosaurs, according to some scientists), this may indicate that early birds nested in ways similar to modern birds.

Do **birds** have an anatomy similar to **humans**?

No, birds differ in their anatomy—especially because they have beaks and feathers. But humans' and birds' internal systems, although mechanically different, do have similar functions: for example, birds have circulatory, respiratory, digestive, and skeletal systems, as do humans.

Circulatory system: A bird's circulatory system distributes oxygen and other materials to the organs and muscles of the bird's body; carbon dioxide and waste products are removed. This is similar to humans; but in the case of the bird, the driving mechanism, the heart, works much faster, generating a high pressure with rapid contractions.

Respiratory system: A bird's respiratory system, similar to humans, takes in oxygen for energy and removes carbon dioxide. But there is a definite difference: a bird's lungs do not inflate and deflate with each breath. Instead, a constant amount of air is always in the bird's lungs.

Digestive system: A bird's digestive system is similar to humans, as it digests the food the animal swallows. But the similarities end there: various species of birds have specialized digestive systems that allow them to eat certain foods. For example, there are seed-eating and flesh-eating birds—each digestive tract depends on the type of food and the particular species. Owls eat food, such as mice, by swallowing the entire animal; other birds only eat seeds. Birds also have a very rapid and highly efficient digestive tract that allows them to keep high internal temperatures—sometimes in the range of 101 to 112 degrees Fahrenheit (38 to 44 degrees Celsius). To compare, the human digestive structure allows us to eat both plants and animals (omnivores)—and our metabolisms are much slower.

Skeletal system: The only similarity between a bird and human skeleton is that they are both made of bones that provide a framework for the body. Although there are few similarities, the skeletal structures of birds and humans differ greatly. Birds have light, hollow, air-filled, strong bones; humans have thicker, marrow-filled bones. Both a bird's and human's bones and attached muscles allow each animal to walk and move in specific ways.

Ostriches lay the largest eggs of any bird. (Photo courtesy of Field Mark Publications.)

Which birds lay the **largest** and **smallest eggs**?

Ostriches lay the largest eggs, averaging approximately 6.8 by 5.4 inches (17.3 by 13.7 centimeters) in diameter. These eggs are small compared to those of the extinct elephant bird of Madagascar whose eggs averaged approximately 13 inches (33 centimeters) long, with a diameter of 9.5 inches (24 centimeters) at the widest part. These eggs weighed approximately 18 pounds each and had a capacity of two gallons—which means each egg could hold six ostrich eggs inside its shell.

The smallest eggs known are laid by the hummingbirds. The smallest of the hummingbirds, the vervain hummingbird *Mellisuga minima,* lays eggs less than a half-inch (1.3 centimeters) long.

What is **bird migration**?

The word migration comes from the Latin *migrare,* meaning "to go from one place to another." When discussing birds, migration is the regular, periodic movements of bird species from one area to another.

Year after year, many species of birds mate and nest in specific areas of the world. Most of these areas are only hospitable during the warmer months of the year; when the cold weather arrives, the birds migrate to warmer climates. These trips can be as long as thousands of miles. For example, the American golden plover breeds north of

What are bird beaks?

Bird beaks, which vary greatly in size, form, and color, are important to the animal's survival. The beak is the "instrument" a bird uses to gather and break up food—not to mention how they preen themselves, itch, collect material for nesting, and protect their territory. Without it, the animal would not survive long.

It is interesting to note that many plant-eating dinosaurs developed beaklike mouths, such as the *Triceratops*. But in this case, the dinosaurs' beaks were mainly used to cut the thick, tough plants these animals ate to survive.

Canada and Alaska during the Northern Hemisphere's spring and summer. In the Northern Hemisphere's fall, the plovers journey to southeastern South America to spend the "winter"—which is the summer season in the Southern Hemisphere— allowing the birds to find plenty of food. When spring arrives again in the Northern Hemisphere, the trip is reversed, and the plovers migrate back to the northern nesting grounds to breed.

In addition to the obvious reasons for migration, such as warmth and the availability of food and water, scientists believe breeding in areas with longer daylight hours presents more opportunity to gather food for nestlings. All of these factors help ensure the survival of the brood—and with it, the continuation of the species.

Do all **birds fly**?

The vast majority of birds fly. They are only incapable of flight during relatively short periods while they molt (the periodic natural shedding of old feathers and the growing of new ones).

True flightless birds are very unusual. There are some familiar examples of flightless birds throughout the world: the African ostrich; the South American rhea; and the emu, kiwi, and cassowary of Australia are all land, but flightless, birds. The penguins of the Southern Hemisphere also are incapable of air flight. They have feathers for insulation and breeding purposes, but use a different means of locomotion—their sleek bodies "flying" through the oceans using flipperlike wings.

All of these flightless birds have wings, but over millions of years of evolution, have lost the ability to fly—even though they probably descended from flying birds. These species may have lost their ability to fly through the gradual disuse of their wings. Perhaps they became isolated on oceanic islands and had no predators, thus, they had no need to fly and escape danger. Another possibility is that food became abundant, eliminating the necessity to fly long distances to search for food.

What do **birds eat**?

The answer is simple: taken as a group, birds eat just about everything. Over millions of years, birds have evolved certain features that allow them to obtain food from many animal and plant sources. Wherever there was an ecological niche with abundant food sources, birds adapted to exploit those resources.

Some birds eat mostly insects; others, like penguins, prefer to dine on seafood. Some birds, such as ducks or geese, float on the water, dipping or diving to extract plants from oceans, lakes, and rivers; while still others, such as raptors, swoop out of the sky, killing and devouring small land-dwelling mammals. Individual bird species not only exploit specific chosen food sources—but also have developed physical (and sometimes internal) characteristics to maximize their ability to harvest the food.

Overall, the list of what certain birds eat is enormous. A sampling of this menu includes: one-celled protozoans; jellyfishes; sea urchins; starfishes; marine and earthworms; crabs; shrimps; barnacles; all types of insects (including centipedes, millipedes, flies, butterflies, spiders, ticks, and scorpions); slugs; snails; squids; mussels; fishes; salamanders; frogs; toads; lizards; snakes; small mammals such as shrews, mice, rats, ground and tree squirrels, rabbits, and skunks; and larger mammals such as marmots, foxes, porcupines, young deer, and antelope. It seems that for every animal around, there is a bird species that will eat it!

Some birds also prey on each other, such as various large predatory birds (eagles, hawks, and owls) that kill and eat smaller birds. Many birds, like crows, jays, and magpies, eat the eggs and young of other birds.

Plants are not immune from being eaten, either. Specific birds have adapted to feasting on algae, sea lettuce, lichens, grasses, herbs, flower nectar, leaves and buds of trees, mosses, ferns, berries, fruits, tree sap, acorns, nuts, seeds of all kinds, and corn and rice. Again, it seems for almost every plant, there is a bird eating some part of it.

Where are **birds** found around the **world**?

Birds can be found in almost every part of the world: high mountain regions; ocean shores; arid grasslands; the middle of large oceans; warm climates; and even frigid, ice-locked areas. Over millions of years, birds evolved characteristics that allowed them to adapt to their chosen habitats.

Most living species (approximately 85 percent) of birds live in the tropical regions of the world, and two-thirds of those are found in the humid tropical climates. The remaining 15 percent of birds live in the temperate or cold climates.

Worms are a favorite delicacy of many birds. (Photo courtesy of Field Mark Publications.)

The factors influencing the distribution of birds over the world include the amount and distribution of landmasses and oceans over geologic time; physical barriers to movement, such as mountain ranges and deserts; a region's climate and environmental conditions; and the ability (or inability) of individual bird species to travel distances.

Were any **birds** around when **dinosaurs** roamed the earth?

Yes, scientists believe that the ancient ancestors of several modern birds were around during the latter part of the Cretaceous period. Originally, scientists thought that only aquatic birds, such as ancestors of the loons, seabirds, and albatrosses, populated the earth during prehistoric times. But recently, ancient bones resembling a modern parrot were found—although its identification has been debated. If the bones are confirmed, and more such bones are found, scientists will know that certain birds also flew when the dinosaurs roamed the earth about 65 to 70 million years ago.

THE LINK BETWEEN
BIRDS AND DINOSAURS

Did some **early scientists** believe **birds** were **related to dinosaurs**?

Yes, some early scientists believed there were similarities between birds and reptiles. It was noted as far back as 400 years ago. But the idea did not come to the forefront of science until the mid-nineteenth century—especially after the 1855 discovery of an unusual fossilized skeleton in a German rock quarry: the remains (subsequently called *Archaeopteryx lithographica*) exhibited a mixture of dinosaur- and birdlike features.

Who first published papers noting the **resemblance** of **birds to dinosaurs**?

In 1867, American paleontologists Edward Drinker Cope (1840–97) and Othniel Charles Marsh (1831–99) were the first to publish papers noting the resemblance of birds to dinosaurs.

What is *Archaeopteryx lithographica*?

Archaeopteryx lithographica is one of the world's most famous fossils. The first fossil of an *Archaeopteryx lithographica*—thought by many modern paleontologists to represent the oldest bird yet discovered—was found in 1855, in the Solnhofen quarries in southern Germany. The fossil would not be recognized as a bird until 1970. The fossil remains—a small bird about the size of a crow—were found in sedimentary rock from the upper Jurassic period, and six more fossil skeletons have been uncovered over the years.

Archaeopteryx lithographica, literally meaning "ancient wing from lithographic limestone," fossils are dated at 125 to 147 million years old (most scientists use 150 million years as the date). The fossils, though not recognized as birds, were used by some paleontologists (such as Thomas Henry Huxley, 1825–95) to confirm Darwin's theory of evolution; later, for other scientists, the *Archaeopteryx lithographica* represented the transition between dinosaurs and birds—and provided proof for the argument that birds descended from dinosaurs.

Have **other** skeletons of *Archaeopteryx lithographica* been found?

Yes, an almost complete skeleton was found in 1861. It was referred to as the "London specimen" and was the basis for a continuing debate between supporters and detractors of Charles Darwin's newly published theory of evolution. A third skeleton was discovered in 1877, and is referred to as the "Berlin specimen." Subsequent finds over the years bring the current total to seven—the latest found in 1992.

Thomas Henry Huxley first noted the shared characteristics of birds and dinosaurs. (Photo courtesy of Gale Group.)

What is the nature of the *Archaeopteryx lithographica* fossils **found** to date?

There have been seven actual specimens and one feather found of the *Archaeopteryx lithographica* to date. Here is a list of the discoveries made so far:

The Berlin specimen was found in 1877 near Blumenberg, Germany, and sports a complete head (although it was badly crushed). The Berlin Museum of Natural History bought the specimen from the son of amateur collector and local doctor, Carl Haberlein.

The London specimen was found in 1861 near Langenaltheim, Germany. It was eventually bought by the British Museum of Natural History (under the instruction of British naturalist Richard Owen, 1804–92) from Carl Haberlein. At that time, it cost a small fortune—700 UK pounds—but the amount also paid for over 1,000 other fossils from the Solnhofen quarries in southern Germany.

The Maxburg specimen was found in 1958 near the same place as the London specimen: Langenaltheim. The fossil represents the animal's torso only, and was the only specimen privately owned. It was found by Eduard Opitsch, who died in 1992; after his death, the specimen was found to be missing, and is thought to have been secretly sold. Thus, the whereabouts of this specimen remains a mystery today.

The Haarlem (or Teyler) specimen was found near Reideburg, Germany, in 1855—five years before the feather was discovered. Because it was not known to be a fossil of an early bird, it was classified as a *Pterodactylus crassipes,* or pterodactyl (not even a dinosaur); in 1970, paleontologist John H. Ostrom (b. 1928) examined the fossil and found evidence of feathers—and thus, its true identity.

What was the birdlike animal named *Confuciusornis sanctus*?

The *Confuciusornis sanctus,* discovered in the northeast province of Liaoning, China, was a pigeon-sized flying creature that may have been slightly younger than the *Archaeopteryx.* (Its actual age is still debated, but it may be about 140 million years old.) This animal had a horny, toothless beak; before it was discovered, scientists thought toothless beaks did not appear until the late Cretaceous period, about 70 million years ago. This creature also had feathers along its leg, making this the earliest known record of contour feathers on any animal.

The Eichstatt specimen was found in 1951 and is the smallest of all the *Archaeopteryx lithographica,* measuring about two-thirds the size of the other specimens; it also has the most well-preserved head found so far. It has a different tooth structure and its shoulder bones are less ossified than the other specimens—making many scientists believe this animal is an example of a different genus. Other scientists believe that the fossil represents a juvenile *Archaeopteryx lithographica,* or a species from an area with different food—thus the different structures.

The Solnhofen specimen was found in the 1960s near Eichstatt, Germany, and was at first thought to be a *Compsognathus.* But after preparing the specimen in the lab, scientists noticed that its arms were too long for its body size; they also found feathers—and the creature joined the list of *Archaeopteryx lithographica.*

The Solnhofen-Aktien-Verein specimen is the latest fossil of an *Archaeopteryx* to be discovered; it has a small ossified sternum and feather impressions. Interestingly enough, it was described in 1994—and was classified as a new species: *Archaeopteryx bavarica.*

Has anyone found an *Archaeopteryx lithographica* fossil feather?

Besides the seven actual specimens of the *Archaeopteryx lithographica,* one fossil feather has been found. It was discovered in 1860 near the Solnhofen quarries and described in 1861. It was also a surprise to scientists, not because it was old—but because of the feather's exquisite detail.

Did some scientists believe *Archaeopteryx lithographica* was a transition between dinosaurs and modern birds?

Yes, some scientists did believe *Archaeopteryx* was the transition between dinosaurs and modern birds—mainly because the fossilized skeletons exhibited a mixture of dinosaur- and birdlike features. The dinosaur (or reptilian) characteristics include such features as bony tails, teeth, and claws on the fingers; the birdlike characteristics include such features as feathers, wishbones, and beaks. Today, many scientists believe *Archaeopteryx lithographica* may have just been a link in dinosaur progression, eventually evolving into modern birds.

Not everyone, however, believes *Archaeopteryx lithographica* was a direct link to the dinosaurs. Some scientists believe birds and dinosaurs evolved separately from a common reptilian ancestor—but so far, no one has yet found acceptable fossil evidence to support or disprove this idea.

Has there been a recent revival of the idea that **birds** are the **descendants of dinosaurs**?

Yes, the idea that birds descended from dinosaurs was revived in 1969 by paleontologist John Ostrom (b. 1928). He suggested that dinosaurs may have been warm-blooded—thus, more active and similar to birds; and Robert T. Bakker's (b. 1945) article in *Scientific American* the next year pursued the same theory. At this time, scientists also began to delve deeply into dinosaur physiology (cells and tissues), noticing the physiological similarities and differences between dinosaurs and other species such as birds. And it is these studies, in combination with skeletal evidence, that scientists hope will lead to the correct answer about bird lineage.

DINOSAURS AROUND US?

What are the major camps in the **dinosaur-bird evolution debate**?

There are several camps of paleontologists in the dinosaur-bird evolution debate. One group believes birds descended from certain dinosaurs about 70 million years ago. Another camp believes birds evolved separately from dinosaurs about 200 million years ago. And there is another group that has emerged: scientists who believe that birds are actually dinosaurs. Right now, there are not enough fossils to come to a definite conclusion—and all sides have good arguments.

What **characteristics** are seemingly shared by **dinosaurs** and **birds**?

Not all dinosaur characteristics are similar to those of modern birds—but there are many similarities. For example, some dinosaurs had features such as bony tails, claws on the fingers, beaks, and, on some, feathers.

How did feathers evolve?

Scientists really don't know yet how feathers evolved. Some scientists believe feathers probably evolved as modified scales. These changed scales were not intended for flight, but for insulation to preserve the reptile's heat. Eventually, they evolved into feathers.

Other scientists believe feathers evolved from scutes—similar to the thick scales on the top of a bird's foot. Analysis shows that the bird scutes, scuttelae, claw sheaths, beak sheaths, and scales around a bird's eyes have the same chemical composition as feathers—and they are controlled by the same genes. Crocodiles, a sister group of the dinosaurs, also have scutes, with similar (but not identical) chemical composition as bird scutes. Scientists also know that dinosaurs had scutes, too—but they don't know the composition. Of course, some scientists speculate that scutes evolved from feathers!

Feathers are only one major characteristic that links dinosaurs to birds. Scientists have found feathered dinosaur fossils of the *Archaeopteryx lithographica,* and more recently, another specimen was found in northeast China, the *Sinosauropteryx prima*. These fossils exhibit featherlike impressions in the sedimentary rock in which they were found.

Other links between dinosaurs and birds involve certain skeletal similarities. For example, fossils of the dinosaur *Deinonychus* have many birdlike characteristics: the large head was balanced on a slender, almost birdlike neck; and the chest was short, with the arms folding inward in a resting position, similar to the wings of a bird at rest. The creature's foot was the most extraordinary of any dinosaur: it had a huge claw on the second toe. In many ways, the feet of the *Deinonychus* appear to be enlarged representations of a bird's feet.

Which **dinosaurs** are thought to have evolved into **birds**?

Paleontologists who believe birds evolved from dinosaurs think that the most likely bird ancestors were the small, carnivorous theropods. At least one fossil finding seems to indicate that dromaeosaurs, a subgroup of the theropods, eventually branched into many lines, including birds. This subgroup line also included such dinosaur species as *Velociraptor, Deinonychus,* and *Utahraptor.*

What is **cladistic analysis**?

Cladistic analysis is a relatively new method used to determine an organism's family tree. The older system of classification, developed by Swedish botanist Carl von Linne

(1707–78; also known as Carolus Linnaeus) in the eighteenth century, categorizes plants and animals by organisms' overall similar characteristics. A cladistic analysis uses specific characteristics, such as wrist bones, and relates them to previous and following generations, thus tracing the evolution of these structures. The more characteristics previous and following generations share, the more likely they are related. (A cladogram represents a diagram of all the clades, or groups of organisms.)

How is a **cladistic analysis accomplished**?

Cladistic analysis is not easy. Scientists have to study the minute details of early animal fossils, noting the slightest differences in bones and joints. Each different characteristic is assigned a code, then added to a computer database. The computer then sorts out the information, producing what looks like a "family tree," linking together past and modern animals by these detailed characteristics.

What does **cladistic analysis** tell us about **birds and dinosaurs**?

According to cladistic analysis, birds share some 132 characteristics with dinosaurs. Some scientists believe this hard evidence indicates that birds are, indeed, a kind of dinosaur. But many scientists still disagree.

What is the **latest theory** stating **birds** are truly **dinosaurs**?

One recent theory goes one step further than "birds are descendants of dinosaurs"—some paleontologists now feel modern birds are *truly* dinosaurs. This theory states that dinosaurs eventually evolved certain birdlike characteristics, such as light weight, agility, wings, feathers, and beaks. These specialized characteristics enabled the animals to somehow survive the extinction at the end of the Mesozoic era—and to continue evolving into modern birds.

Do all paleontologists believe that **birds and dinosaurs** are related?

No, not all paleontologists believe that birds are dinosaurs—or even that birds evolved directly from dinosaurs. Many feel birds and dinosaurs descended from a common, older ancestor, and developed many superficial similarities over millions of years due to what is called convergent evolution: because both dinosaurs and birds developed body designs for bipedal motion, they eventually started to resemble each other.

There are four major reasons why some scientists feel there is not a direct dinosaur-bird link: the timing problem, body size differences, skeletal variations, and the mismatch in finger evolution. First, in regard to timing, there is some fossil evidence that birdlike dinosaurs evolved 30 to 80 million years after the *Archaeopteryx lithographica,* which seems to put the cart before the horse—or the bird before the birdlike dinosaur, if you will. This is the opposite of what you would expect if birds descended from dinosaurs.

Second, some scientists feel it was nearly impossible for theropods to give rise to birds because of differences in body size. They point out that these carnivorous dinosaurs were relatively large, ground-dwelling animals, with heavy, balancing tails and short forelimbs—not the sort of body that could evolve into a lightweight, flying creature.

Third, although birds and dinosaurs have skeletons that appear, in some ways, to be similar, there are many variations as well: the teeth of theropods were curved and serrated, but early birds had straight, unserrated, peglike teeth; dinosaurs had a major lower jaw joint that early birds did not; the bone girdle of each animal was very different; and birds have a reversed rear toe for perching, while no dinosaur had a reversed toe.

Fourth, there is a discrepancy between the fingers of dinosaurs and birds: dinosaurs developed hands with three digits, or fingers, labeled one, two, and three—corresponding to the thumb, index, and middle fingers of humans. The fourth and fifth digits, corresponding to the ring and little finger of humans, remained as tiny bumps, which have been found on early dinosaur skeletons. However, as recent studies of embryos have shown, birds developed hands with fingers two, three, and four, corresponding to the index, middle, and ring fingers of humans. Fingers one and five, corresponding to our thumb and little finger, were lost. Some paleontologists wonder how a bird hand with fingers two, three, and four, could have evolved from a dinosaur hand with fingers one, two, and three. These scientists assert that such an evolution is impossible.

THE SEARCH FOR THE MISSING LINK

Is there any fossil evidence that **not all dinosaurs became extinct**?

Several recent fossil discoveries are used by some scientists as proof that not all dinosaurs become extinct—but rather are the animals we call birds. The latest fossil findings of *Caudipteryx zoui* and *Protarchaeopteryx robust* from China are seen by some paleontologists as proof that birds not only descended from dinosaurs, but are dinosaurs. The remains of these two 120-million-year-old species were found in Liaoning Province in northeast China; two fossils were that of *Protarchaeopteryx robust,* while a third fossil was that of a *Caudipteryx zoui.*

The *Protarchaeopteryx robust* fossils indicate this animal was a relative of *Archaeopteryx lithographica:* it was turkey-sized, and covered with down- and quill-like feathers. The *Caudipteryx zoui* fossil remains show features of a theropod dinosaur, but it was also covered with down- and quill-like feathers. The wing feathers were not swept back (as needed for flight), but were symmetrical in shape.

Both animals had the shape of swift, long-legged runners and, based on their skeletal characteristics, were more closely related to dinosaurs than birds; and even though they had feathers, neither appeared capable of flight. This seems to indicate that certain dinosaurs developed feathers for reasons other than flight. These feathered dinosaurs did not go extinct at the end of the Cretaceous period—and some scientists believe they continued to evolve into modern birds.

What recent fossil discovery indicates a **link** between **birds and dromaeosaurs**?

One fossil that may link birds and dinosaurs is named *Rahona ostromi,* or "Ostrom's menace from the clouds," in honor of American paleontologist John Ostrom (b. 1928, now professor emeritus of geology at Yale University). This fossil was found in 1995 off the eastern coast of Africa, on the island of Madagascar. Dating of the fossil indicates that the animal lived about 65 to 70 million years ago, or during the late Cretaceous period of the Mesozoic era. The fossil remains show a primitive bird about the size of a modern raven, with a 2-foot (.6-meter) wing span; it also has tiny bumps along the wing bones indicating where the flight feathers were attached.

Many paleontologists are convinced that *Rahona ostromi* had feathers and could fly. The first toe of each foot points backward, indicating the animal had a perching foot, similar to modern birds. But it also retained many dinosaur-like features—the most interesting of which is on the second toe of each foot: *Rahona ostromi* had a sickle-shaped killing claw on each of its second toes, a feature found in the subgroup of theropod dinosaurs known as dromaeosaurids. Apparently, *Rahona ostromi* was an animal with both bird- and dinosaur-like characteristics.

What is the birdlike animal named *Unenlagia comahuensis*?

Unenlagia comahuensis, or the "half-bird from northwest Patagonia," was a dinosaur living approximately 90 million years ago. Similar to many other recent reptile discoveries, scientists are taking a close look at the animal's birdlike characteristics. In fact, some scientists believe that *Unenlagia comahuensis* is the actual missing link between birds and dinosaurs.

What characteristics did *Unenlagia comahuensis* share with the birds?

Some scientists believe that the *Unenlagia comahuensis* had several characteristics in common with birds—including arms that could flap like wings and a birdlike pelvis. In particular, the 5-foot- (1.5-meter-) tall dinosaur had a shoulder blade (scapula) that

What is the birdlike animal named *Shuvuuia deserti?*

The 70-million-year-old fossil remains of *Shuvuuia deserti*—derived from the Mongolian word for "bird" and the Latin word for "desert"—were recently found in the Gobi Desert of Mongolia. This was the first skull found from an animal belonging to a group called the *Alvarezsauridae*, which some scientists believe represents an advanced stage in the transition from dinosaurs to birds. *Shuvuuia deserti* was flightless, turkey-sized, walked on two legs, had a long tail and neck, and short forearms ending in a single, blunt claw.

Although it was more advanced than the earlier *Archaeopteryx lithographica*, *Shuvuuia deserti* did not look like a stereotypical modern bird—leading paleontologists to conclude that birds in the late Cretaceous period were as diverse as they are today. Although many of these primitive species during the Cretaceous period were quite different, they did have some unique characteristics that are also found in modern birds. In the case of *Shuvuuia deserti*, the similarity was prokinesis—the up and down, independent movement of the snout that allowed the mouth to open wide.

shared some characteristics with birds; the forearm socket in this bone pointed out toward the side rather than down and back, as seen in other primitive birdlike animals such as the *Deinonychus*. In addition, the *Unenlagia*'s triangular pelvis looks like a cross between a *Deinonychus* and *Archaeopteryx*.

What is the birdlike animal named *Sinosauropteryx prima*?

Fossils of a *Sinosauropteryx prima*, found in China, are of a theropod dinosaur with what appears to be feathers. Some scientists believe the dinosaur had featherlike structures that were used for movement; other scientists believe the structures were probably protofeathers, an early step toward the evolution of bird feathers.

The *Sinosauropteryx* is one of the "Chinese feathered" dinosaurs, and is younger than the 140-million-year-old *Archaeopteryx*. Some scientists believe they are one of the most primitive coelurosaurs, as seen from their skeletal features.

What were the **protofeathers** like on *Sinosauropteryx?*

The protofeathers on the *Sinosauropteryx* appear to be covered with hollow filaments. These may have been the forerunners of bird feathers.

What do the *Sinosauropteryx* and other similar dinosaurs tell us about the **evolution of feathers**?

Dinosaurs like the *Sinosauropteryx,* other similar dinosaurs, and fossil feathers from the same period, give scientists a better idea about the evolution of feathers. In particular, it is thought that feathers evolved rapidly, in terms of geologic time. Feathers evolved highly adaptable properties over time—and in terms of survival, they gave the animals an aerodynamic body and provided insulation for warmth, two features needed to survive a rough, predatory-ridden world.

What was the **original purpose** of **feathers** on dinosaurs?

Based on the recent fossil discoveries of feathered, flightless dinosaurs, some paleontologists now think feathers were originally developed for insulation or ornamentation purposes.

Were **birds** the **only animals** that sported **feathers**?

Because geologic time takes in so many millions of years, some scientists believe there were other early animals that sported some type of feather or protofeather. Because many researchers believe that modern birds are direct descendants of two-legged, meat-eating dinosaurs, and since there was a wide range of these prehistoric theropods, there's a chance other dinosaurs had feathers—either as juveniles or all their lives. Some species kept their feathers (descendants of birds, for example), while others did not. The reason for the lack of evidence may be because feathers were not preserved, or maybe such fossils have yet to be discovered.

How did early feathered animals eventually **develop flight**?

There are several theories on how early feathered animals developed flight. One theory states that gliding creatures increased their surface area from the body outward—but flying animals increased it away from their center of gravity—giving them lift and more maneuverability to escape predators. Another theory states that wing motions evolved from the hunting techniques of the coelurosaurs. The skeletal structure of these dinosaurs allowed them to swing their arms down from above and behind their shoulders—easily grabbing prey. Both these theories imply that birds developed flight from the ground up, not from the trees down, also known as the cursorial theory.

Other paleontologists believe that flight developed as animals lived in trees (the arboreal, or tree, theory), flying by jumping and getting enough acceleration to generate lift. Still others believe that some animals ran and flapped their wings, increasing their angle of attack on the down stroke, generating enough lift to fly—especially if they were running downhill.

> ## What baby bird fossil seems to link dinosaurs and birds?
>
> **A** 135-million-year-old baby bird was found in the Pyrenees mountains of northern Spain. It had wings, feathers, and tiny holes in its immature bones just like modern birds, but also had a head and neck similar to carnivorous dinosaurs, with sharp teeth and powerful neck muscles for chewing.

Have any carnivorous **dinosaur** fossils shown traces of a **beak**?

In the Red Deer River Badlands of western Canada, the remains of a carnivorous ornithomimid dinosaur were found that included traces of keratin around the front of the animal's skull. Keratin, the material found in hair and fingernails, is also found in the beaks of birds. This was also the first carnivorous dinosaur with evidence of a beak—and it showed that dinosaurs could make the transition from teeth to a beaklike structure.

What does the internal structure of *Scipionyx samniticus* reveal about the **ancestry** of birds?

Recent studies of the *Scipionyx samniticus'* interior structure and unique metabolism has led some scientists to say that none of the known groups of dinosaurs could have been the ancestors of birds. This is because birds have an entirely different lung structure than the *Scipionyx samniticus,* a small theropod—and a much different metabolism. However, this is based on the findings from one fossil, one of very few to have internal parts preserved. These results will have to be carefully integrated with other findings, such as the presence of feathers and common skeletal features.

U.S. DINOSAUR DISCOVERIES

EARLY U.S. DINOSAUR HISTORY

Where and when were dinosaur **fossils first discovered** in the United States?

The first dinosaur fossils found in the United States were discovered in 1787 in New Jersey, by Caspar and Matelock Wistar of Philadelphia. They read a description of their findings before the American Philosophical Society, but the report of their discovery would not be published for 75 years.

Where were the bones of an **_Anchisaurus_** first found in the United States?

The Connecticut valley of the northeastern United States was the scene of the first *Anchisaurus* discovery. Solomon Ellsworth Jr. and Nathan Smith found the bones in 1818—but mistook the remains for human bones.

Where were the first **dinosaur footprints** found in the United States?

The first dinosaur footprints in the United States were found in 1800, by Pliny Moody (a student at Williams College) on his farm in Connecticut. Even though each footprint was about 1 foot (.3 meter) long, scientists from Yale and Harvard universities theorized that the dinosaur prints were the "footprints of Noah's raven," in reference to the great flood from the Bible.

What was the **first dinosaur track** to be **described**?

The first dinosaur track to be described anywhere was a three-toed track from the east bank of the Connecticut River near Holyoke, Massachusetts. This large footprint cast was originally named *Orinithichnites giganteus,* but was later renamed *Eubrontes giganteus.* A lithograph of this track was incorporated into William Buckland's (1784–1856) *Bridgewater Treatise* in 1836.

What early United States **expedition** mentioned a **giant leg bone** that was probably from a dinosaur?

The early United States expedition was that of army officers Meriwether Lewis (1774–1809) and William Clark (1770–1838)—two explorers sent out by President Thomas Jefferson to find a northwest passage to the Pacific coast. Along the way, in 1806, they recorded finding a giant leg bone near Billings, Montana—almost certainly that of a dinosaur.

When were the **first fossils** found in the Western Hemisphere accurately identified as belonging to a **dinosaur**?

In 1856, American paleontologist Joseph Leidy (1823–91), professor of anatomy at the University of Pennsylvania, accurately identified several fossil bones as being those of dinosaurs. These fossil remains were among the first to be collected in the American West, by an official geological survey team in 1855; the bones were found in the area now known as Montana. The remains were mostly fossil teeth—subsequently shown to be from *Trachodon* and *Deinodon* dinosaurs.

Who first suggested that some **dinosaurs** were **bipedal**?

Originally, dinosaurs were thought of as either giant, sprawling lizards, or bulky, quadrupedal (four-footed) reptiles with some mammal-like features. But, in 1858, American paleontologist Joseph Leidy (1823–91) described an almost complete skele-

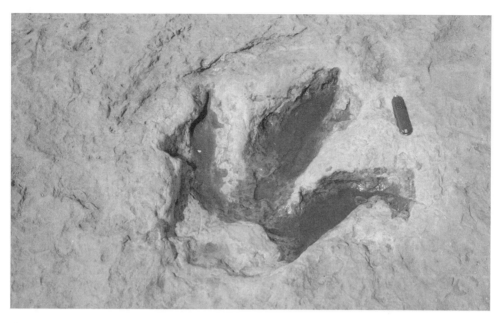

The first dinosaur track ever to be described was a three-toed track, mentioned in an 1836 lithograph, similar to this fossilized footprint. (Photo courtesy of JLM Visuals.)

ton discovered by William P. Foulke at Haddonfield, New Jersey. The fossil skeleton, named *Hadrosaurus,* was more complete than any yet discovered. It also indicated that the dinosaur was bipedal (two-footed)—a radical notion for the time.

What was the **first mounted dinosaur cast** in the United States to reflect a **bipedal stance**?

In the 1860s, at the Philadelphia Academy of Sciences, a mounted cast skeleton of a *Hadrosaurus* was the first to reflect a bipedal stance. Named and described by American paleontologist Joseph Leidy (1823–91) in 1858, this *Hadrosaurus* was the first cast skeleton in North America to be free-mounted. Working with Leidy on this project were American paleontologist Edward Drinker Cope (1840–97) and Benjamin Waterhouse Hawkins (1807–89), sculptor of the Crystal Palace England dinosaurs in England.

What was the **first mounted dinosaur skeleton** in the Western Hemisphere?

In the Western Hemisphere, the first skeleton composed of real dinosaur bones was mounted in 1901 at Yale's Peabody Museum of Natural History in Connecticut. A skeleton of an *Edmontosaurus* was mounted in an erect, bipedal, running stance.

Are there **dinosaur reconstructions** in New York City's **Central Park**?

No, but there used to be dinosaur reconstructions there. In 1868, sculptor Benjamin Waterhouse Hawkins (1807–89), who made the sculptures at Crystal Palace in England, was commissioned to make several dinosaur reconstructions in New York City's Central Park. According to reports, Hawkins tangled politically with "Boss Tweed" and his gang; Tweed smashed the models and threw them in the park's lake. All that is left are the drawings of the dinosaurs. There are other reports, too, concerning these dinosaur reconstructions—some say the dinosaurs are buried under the park, but the original story remains the most accepted.

Who was **O. C. Marsh**?

O. C. (Othniel Charles) Marsh (1831–99) was an American paleontologist who made numerous contributions to the field. In addition to his contributions to the evolutionary history of the horse, he discovered and named numerous dinosaurs during the "Bone Wars" of the late 1800s. In 1866, he helped establish, with the financial backing of his uncle, George Peabody, the Peabody Museum of Natural History at Yale University in Connecticut; he was also a professor at Yale.

In 1882, Marsh published the first dinosaur classification, which formed the foundation for the modern dinosaur classification. In the same year, Marsh was appointed as an official vertebrate paleontologist of the United States Geological Survey.

Who was **Edward Drinker Cope**?

Edward Drinker Cope (1840–97) was an American paleontologist who spent eight years with the U.S. Geological Survey and who was the most prolific namer of reptiles, both extinct and living. He named over 1,000 new species, including many fish and mammal species; and in his lifetime he was considered one of the top experts on amphibians. For a time, Cope worked as a freelance scholar associated with the Philadelphia Academy of Science. He was also a professor—at Haverford College (1860) and the University of Pennsylvania (from 1889 to 1897). Cope was owner and editor of *American Naturalist* from 1878 until his death.

Othniel Charles Marsh published the first dinosaur classification. (Photo courtesy of Archive Photos, Inc.)

What **scientific journal** is named after Edward Drinker **Cope**?

The scientific journal *Copeia,* devoted to fish and snakes, is named in honor of Edward D. Cope. This is because Cope—in spite of being so involved in the "Bone Wars" of the late 1800s—was still considered one of the top authorities on living and extinct animals of his day.

Who was **Charles H. Sternberg**?

Charles H. Sternberg (1850–1943) began as a collector of dinosaurs for American paleontologist Edward Drinker Cope. Later he became known as a professional fossil col-

335

lector for a number of institutions from 1876 to the early 1900s. His collecting took him through the dinosaur beds across the border from Montana and the Dakotas, on into Canada. He and his sons made important discoveries in the badlands of Alberta, Canada, forming the core of many dinosaur collections in Toronto and Ottawa, Ontario, New York, and at other worldwide dinosaur institutions.

What is the **Morrison formation**?

The world-famous Morrison formation is a specific layer of sedimentary rock made up of deposits of sand, mud, and volcanic ash. It formed over the period of roughly 8 million years, from approximately 156 to 141 million years ago, during the late Jurassic period. This rock is one of the richest dinosaur fossil spots in the United States, usually yielding excellent specimens. It was first discovered near Morrison, Colorado, in the late 1800s—hence its name.

What **Colorado sites** have been historically fruitful in terms of **dinosaurs finds**?

Colorado contains four major historically significant dinosaur sites, especially in terms of the nature and number of finds. These sites are Dinosaur Ridge, Garden Park, the Grand Junction area, and Dinosaur National Monument. The reason there have been numerous good finds in these areas is the presence of exposed rocks from the Morrison formation of the Jurassic period.

What is **Dinosaur Ridge**?

Dinosaur Ridge is composed of mostly rock of the Morrison formation, and is located north of the town of Morrison and just west of Denver, Colorado. This site was first discovered in 1877 by Arthur Lakes (1844–1917)—and was subsequently excavated during the great "Bone Wars"; the fossil site was worked by American paleontologist O. C. Marsh (1831–99) and his crew.

What is the significance of the **Hogback Ridge** on the Colorado and Utah border?

From 1909 to 1922, the Hogback Ridge at Split Mountain was worked by American paleontologist Earl Douglass (b. 1938) for the Carnegie Museum. On October 4, 1915, President Woodrow Wilson would designate the spot as Dinosaur National Monument—both because of its importance to paleontology, and to stop any future development of the area.

In 1909, Douglass found the dorsal bones of *Apatosaurus* at this site; it took six more years to remove the skeleton from the rock and mount it at the Carnegie Muse-

> ## Where and what is Como Bluff?
>
> Como Bluff is a long east–west oriented ridge located in southern Wyoming and the site of a famous Jurassic dinosaur fossil bed excavated during the great "Bone Wars" of the late 1800s. It was discovered by two employees of the Union Pacific Railway, W. E. Carlin and Bill Reed, as a new rail line was being built through the general area. They secretly contacted American paleontologist O. C. Marsh (1831–99), trying to sell him some gigantic bones. Marsh subsequently sent his assistant, S. W. Williston (1851–1918), to investigate the situation. Williston informed Marsh that the bones "extend for seven miles and are by the ton . . . the bones are very thick, well preserved, and easy to get out." Because of Williston's words, Marsh hired Carlin and Reed to work the beds exclusively for him, and to send the fossil bones back to Yale University. From samples of bones uncovered at Como Bluff, Marsh named the dinosaurs *Stegosaurus, Allosaurus, Nanosaurus, Camptosaurus,* and *Brontosaurus* (now known as *Apatosaurus*). Excavations at Como Bluff were discontinued after 1889.

um. After 1922, Douglass worked the quarry for two more years (for the University of Utah and the Smithsonian Institution) finding a *Diplodocus* that is currently mounted at the Smithsonian Institution. Today, tourists at the visitors center at Hogback Ridge can view the quarry face that acts as the north wall of the building—the bones left in place after the overlying rocks were removed.

When was the **first complete fossil** skeleton of a *Stegosaurus* found in the United States?

In 1886, near Canyon City, Colorado, the fossilized remains of *Stegosaurus* were found by paleontologist O. C. Marsh's crew. The animal's dorsal armor plates were arranged in two rows along the back, with the plates alternating position. This skeleton was subsequently displayed in the Smithsonian Institute in Washington as it was found in the field.

When was the first *Triceratops* fossil discovered in the United States?

A fossilized skull of a three-horned, Cretaceous period, herbivorous dinosaur was discovered by American paleontologists John Bell Hatcher (1861–1904) and O. C. Marsh (1831–99) in 1888, in the Judith River beds of Montana. This dinosaur would subsequently be named *Triceratops*.

Where and when was the first skeleton of a *Brachiosaurus* found in the United States?

In 1900, the first *Brachiosaurus*, or "arm reptile," was discovered in the area of Grand Junction, Colorado. The dinosaur earned this name since its front legs were longer than its hind legs; it was regarded as the largest known dinosaur at that time. The *Brachiosaurus* was discovered by Elmer Riggs, assistant curator of paleontology at the Field Columbian Museum (now the Field Museum of Natural History) in Chicago, and H. W. Menke.

The area where the bones were discovered and quarried is now known as Riggs Hill. Riggs broke with the conventional thought of his day, and suggested that the sauropod was not amphibious (living on land and in water)—but a land-dwelling animal with habits similar to those of the modern elephant.

When was the first *Tyrannosaurus rex* fossil discovered in the United States?

The first *Tyrannosaurus rex* skeleton discovered in the United States was in 1902 by Barnum Brown—perhaps the greatest collector of dinosaurs. Brown, working for the American Museum of Natural History, discovered the remains in the area of Hell Creek, Montana.

Where is the **largest known accumulation** of **theropod skeletons** found in the United States—or in the world?

The largest mass accumulation of theropod skeletons in the United States (and the world) was found at the Ghost Ranch quarry, in northwestern New Mexico. In 1947, George Whitaker and E. H. Colbert, members of an expedition from the American Museum of Natural History, found over 100 skeletons of the late Triassic period dinosaur *Coelophysis*. They found the dinosaur skeletons in Arroyo Seco ("dry canyon") on the lands of the Ghost Ranch.

The skulls in this bone bed show considerable variations in size, ranging from 3 to 10 inches (8 to 26 centimeters) in length, indicating the presence of juveniles and adults. In 1948, during further excavations, George Whitaker and Carl Sorenson discovered two skeletons of *Coelophysis* with juveniles inside the stomach areas—thought to indicate that this species was cannibalistic.

It is still a mystery why so many of these animals ended up in such a small area. Some paleontologists suggest that a herd of *Coelophysis* was overwhelmed by a flood, perhaps while crossing a river. If this is true, then this discovery became the first evidence for herding behavior among a dinosaur species.

Where was the **first** known fossilized **dinosaur skin** found in the United States?

In 1908, the fossil impression of a duck-billed dinosaur's skin was discovered in Wyoming, by paleontologist Charles H. Sternberg (1850–1943) and his sons, Charles M., George, and Levi Sternberg.

Where was an **almost complete skeleton** of an *Apatosaurus* found in the United States?

In 1909, American paleontologist Earl Douglass (b. 1938) discovered an *Apatosaurus* (formerly known as *Brontosaurus*) skeleton in the Carnegie Quarry (now Dinosaur National Monument) on the border between Utah and Colorado. Through 1923, further excavations in this area uncovered the largest known concentration of Jurassic period dinosaurs in the United States.

RECENT DINOSAUR FINDS

What is the **significance** of the *Maiasaura* dinosaur discovery in the United States?

In 1978, American paleontologists John R. Horner (b. 1946) and Bob Makela discovered the fossilized remains of what would subsequently be called *Maiasaura,* or "good mother lizard," in Montana. This is the first known nest of baby dinosaurs, and indicates the young had been cared for by adult dinosaurs. Starting in 1979, and working into the 1980s, Horner uncovered evidence of herding behavior in the dinosaurs—providing new insights into the social behavior of these dinosaurs. The herd is estimated to have been almost 10,000 dinosaurs strong.

Where is one of the **largest sets** of **dinosaur tracks** in the United States?

In 1989, paleontologists found approximately 1,000 well-preserved dinosaur footprints in a quarry in Culpeper, Virginia. These tracks were dated to about 210 million years ago.

Where did scientists recently find a **detailed set of dinosaur tracks** in the United States?

One of the most detailed and lengthy set of dinosaur tracks was recently found at a place now called the Red Gulch Dinosaur Tracksite, located in Wyoming. A large num-

Paleontologist Peter Larson examines the teeth of "Stan," a *Tyrannosaurus rex* discovered in 1992 in South Dakota. Stan is the second most complete *T. rex* skeleton in the world, next to "Sue." (Photo courtesy of Greg Latza/Associated Press.)

ber of fossil footprints—of both quadrupedal (four-footed) and bipedal (two-footed) dinosaurs—were discovered on public lands at the site, in an area once known to be part of the Sundance Sea.

Where was the **first** skeleton of *Supersaurus* found in the United States?

The "home" of the *Supersaurus*—believed to be one of the world's largest dinosaurs—is the Dry Mesa Quarry, on the Uncompahgre Plateau in western Colorado. This site was first explored in 1971, by Ed and Vivian Jones, amateur paleontologists from Delta, Colorado. It is also home of another large dinosaur, the *Ultrasaurus*.

Where was the **first** skeleton of a *Utahraptor* found in the United States?

In 1991, paleontologist Jim Kirkland found the first skeleton of *Utahraptor,* a large dromaeosaurid with long foot claws, in the Gaston Quarry, Utah. The quarry itself had been discovered in 1989 by Robert Gaston.

What famous dinosaur is nicknamed **"Sue"**?

"Sue" is the nickname given to the most complete *Tyrannosaurus rex* skeleton yet discovered. "Sue" represents almost 90 percent of the total skeleton, compared to other *T. rex* skeletons, which are usually only 40 to 50 percent complete. This alone makes it an important specimen.

But the legal controversy surrounding the ownership of the bones made "Sue" a household name. The remains were found in 1990 by Sue Hendrickson, for whom it is named. Hendrickson came upon the fossilized bones while walking on a Cheyenne River Reservation ranch in South Dakota owned by Maurice Williams. The complete remains, eventually totaling 130 crates and boxes, were excavated by Peter Larson and associates of the Black Hills Institute. In 1992, a subsequent legal dispute over ownership of the bones led to an FBI raid on Larson's museum to seize the remains, followed by a lengthy court battle. The case ended in Larson's incarceration and the ownership of the bones was given to Williams, who in turn decided to sell them at a public

Paleontologist Peter Larson cleans the jawbone of the *T. rex* nicknamed "Sue," whose skeleton was found in South Dakota in 1990. (Photo courtesy of Corbis.)

auction. In October 1997, the remains were auctioned by Sotheby's, with the winning bid of $8.36 million submitted by the Chicago Field Museum of Natural History.

The museum plans to restore the dinosaur bones and exhibit "Sue" in her own gallery, a task that should be finished around the turn of the century. Until then, visitors can watch the restoration process through a glass wall at the Fossil Preparation Laboratory. And for those who cannot make it to Chicago, two replicas are being made—one will tour the United States, while the other will go on display at Walt Disney World in Florida.

What discovery in the United States led to new theories about dinosaur **behavior and physiology**?

The discovery and description of *Deinonychus,* "terrible claw," by paleontologist John H. Ostrom (b. 1928) of the Yale Peabody Museum turned out to be the catalyst that changed people's perceptions about dinosaurs. In 1964, *Deinonychus* bones were excavated from the Cloverly formation rocks of the lower Cretaceous period in Montana; Ostrom presented his findings in 1969. The information from these fossils, and other fossil finds related to *Deinonychus,* increased our knowledge of dromaeosaurids—which may have been the most aggressive and maybe the most intelligent of the theropods.

341

Based on fossil evidence found during the excavation, Ostrom concluded that these animals may have hunted in packs, indicating a social structure. Also, the animals' skeletons were light and slender, with a stiffened tail for balance, long clawed arms for grasping, sharp backward-curving teeth for tearing flesh, and a huge sickle-shaped claw on the second toe of the foot for slashing. The animal was built for speed and agility, quite unlike the perception of dinosaurs up until that time. From these findings, Ostrom theorized that *Deinonychus* may have been warm-blooded. This radical notion opened up new thinking about dinosaur physiology—and led to the modern ideas of dinosaurs as active, social animals.

Where has the world's **largest *Tyrannosaurus rex*** been found?

The current size champion was found in the summer of 1997 in a late Cretaceous period bone bed near the Fort Peck reservoir in Montana. This area is in the badlands of eastern Montana; the remains were found in the Hell Creek rock layer, a geological formation well known for its dinosaur bones. The site appears to have been a river channel; the bones of dead dinosaurs were washed into the channel and collected in one place.

This skeleton, though only partially excavated, appears to be nearly complete, and is the largest specimen of a *Tyrannosaurus rex* yet found. Its pubis bone is at least 52 inches (133 centimeters) long; the previous largest known *Tyrannosaurus rex* skeleton had a pubis bone approximately 48 inches (122 centimeters) long. The skull of this animal measures approximately 6.6 feet (2 meters) long. In fact, this is the largest carnivorous animal found to date on the planet—eclipsing the claim of the *Gigantosaurus*.

Have **dinosaur fossils** been found in any United States **metropolitan areas**?

Dinosaur fossils have been found in the Denver, Colorado, metropolitan area, exposed during recent construction projects. This urban area lies on top of a treasure trove of fossils, both dinosaur and others. Evidence suggests that millions of years ago this area was part of a tropical rain forest; during excavation for Denver International Airport in 1989, bone and plant fossils were found. There are other examples, too. Recently, the remains of four *Triceratops* were discovered during the construction of

> ### What special tool was used to uncover the oldest dinosaur eggshell ever found in New Mexico?
>
> The special tool used to uncover a 1-square-inch (2.54-centimeter), 150-million-year-old dinosaur eggshell was a toy backhoe! This "sophisticated paleontological device" was wielded by three-year-old David Shiffler of New Mexico. His family had stopped along the Rio Puerco after a camping trip. Seizing the opportunity, David began to dig in a sandy spot with his toy backhoe, uncovering a small object he declared was a dinosaur eggshell. David's father later took the object to paleontologists, who confirmed that it was indeed a dinosaur eggshell from the late Jurassic. This makes the dinosaur eggshell the oldest one found in New Mexico—and one of the oldest found anywhere. It also means that David is one of the youngest people to make a major paleontological discovery.

fairways at The Heritage at Westmoor golf course; at a subdivision south of the golf course, bones from five dinosaurs, a crocodile, and a mammal were found.

What **heavily armored dinosaur fossils** were recently found in **Utah**?

Scientists recently discovered two new species of heavily armored dinosaurs (or anky-losaurids) in Utah, about 100 miles southwest of Salt Lake City. The species were both about 30 feet (9 meters) in length. One is an ankylosaur, or club-tailed armored dinosaur, and is the oldest ever found. The other fossil is that of a nodosaur, a clubless armored dinosaur, the largest on record. Most ankylosaurids were from Asia; these animals were thought to have crossed over a land bridge to North America about 100 million years ago.

Where was the world's **oldest** and most primitive **duck-billed dinosaur** recently found?

The world's oldest and most primitive duck-billed dinosaur, *Protohadros byrdi,* was recently discovered in a road cut near Flower Mound in northcentral Texas. When this dinosaur died almost 95.5 million years ago, the middle of North America had a shallow seaway, and northern Texas was a wooded marsh.

Where has a **fossil impression** of a **duckbill dinosaur's skin** been discovered?

A fossil impression of a duckbill dinosaur's skin has been discovered near Deming, New Mexico—and is the first dinosaur skin found in that state. Discovered in association with the fossilized bones making up the backbone of a duck-billed dinosaur, the skin impression exhibits a three-dimensional pattern. It is thought that these types of dinosaurs inhabited the area about 70 million years ago.

Dinosaur fossil skin impressions are extremely rare. There are only a dozen of them from duck-billed dinosaurs, and only a very few have been found in association with dinosaur bones. This recent find shows that these dinosaurs had lizardlike skin and lacked hair or feathers.

Where have the remains of a *Parasaurolophus* been found in the United States?

Recently, the skull of the crested duck-billed dinosaur *Parasaurolophus* was discovered eroding out of an arroyo in northwestern New Mexico. This skull included the lower left jaw and a nearly complete tubular nasal crest—measuring over 4 feet (1.2 meters) long. The remains of this late Cretaceous period dinosaur are extremely rare, with less than six known specimens, making it even rarer than *Tyrannosaurus rex* remains. This newly discovered skull is the most complete one of *Parasaurolophus* from New Mexico, and will help paleontologists sort out the relationships between the different-named species of this dinosaur.

Have **East Coast dinosaur tracks** recently been found by an **amateur paleontologist**?

Yes, a large number of dinosaur and flying reptile tracks from around 105 to 115 million years ago have recently been found in local stream beds by Ray Stanford, an amateur paleontologist living in the area around Washington, D.C. Collected over a period of four years, the hundreds of rocks containing dinosaur tracks are stored at Stanford's house. They are placed in piles for each type of dinosaur and "labeled" by a representative toy dinosaur. Stanford's finds have astonished professional paleontologists, who had thought that tracks like these didn't exist in this area.

Does this **collection** of East Coast dinosaur **tracks** contain any **surprises**?

Besides the unexpected discovery of these tracks on the East Coast, there are up to a dozen species of dinosaurs represented by the footprints—with several species previously unknown. There appear to be several different species of herbivorous dinosaurs, and perhaps a young ankylosaur.

Where were the **fossilized remains** of a **Jurassic period tree** recently found?

The fossilized remains of a Jurassic period tree were recently discovered in the Garden Park Fossil Park near Canon City, Colorado—by a teenager on a school outing. While

What discovery in Pennsylvania helps us understand the Triassic period extinction?

Three skulls from animals belonging to the genus *Hypsognathus* were recently uncovered in Pennsylvania. Two were found in a mudstone deposit at a construction site in Exeter Township, while a third was found in the town of Pennsburg. These sites are located in the area between Allentown and Pottstown, Pennsylvania, and were part of the Newark rift basin millions of years ago, formed as the supercontinent Pangea began to break apart. The remains of these animals have been dated to just 500,000 years before the extinction at the end of the Triassic period, approximately 200 million years ago—presenting paleontologists with a rare fossil record of animals that lived during this time.

The *Hypsognathus* reptiles were 1-foot- (.3-meter-) long, horned herbivores, somewhat analogous to modern-day groundhogs. They lived during the Triassic period among animals such as amphibians and reptiles, including the relatively new and small dinosaurs. Scientists believe something happened about 200 million years ago—a mass extinction that changed the course of evolution, allowing the dinosaurs to dominate, growing into larger and more diverse forms. Evidence for this mass extinction has been very rare, mainly due to a lack of skeletal remains from this time period. The discovery of the *Hypsognathus* skulls shows these animals lived right up to the boundary between the Triassic and Jurassic—lending support to the mass extinction theory.

scraping in the dirt, the teenager found what he thought was a bone; a tour guide realized the fossil's true identity.

The fossilized tree, believed to be a type of conifer, is currently being carefully dug out; it will eventually be lifted out of the ground with a crane. This is the first Jurassic period (about 150 million years old) tree from Garden Park—and perhaps the entire Front Range of Colorado.

Where have many **Cretaceous period fossils** been found in the **western United States**?

A large number of Cretaceous period fossils, both plants and animals, have recently been uncovered in Emery County, Utah. The more than 6,000 fossils include approximately 80 different types of animals. The specimens at this dig are thought to be about 100 million years old—and are the first fossils found in this area from a span of time ranging from about 145 to 65 million years ago (the end of the Cretaceous period).

These fossils will help shed some light on the great changes that occurred during this time period, but have remained a mystery due to lack of fossil evidence.

What are some **findings** from the **Utah Cretaceous** period fossils?

There have been some very interesting findings associated with the Cretaceous fossils found in Emery County, Utah. For example, the early dominant dinosaurs in North America during this period appear to have been the large, long-necked sauropods. But their huge numbers, combined with their huge appetites, caused them to essentially clear-cut the existing forests. The new flowering plants then moved in and took over—being fast growing and capable of rapid colonization.

These early flowering plants grew low to the ground as bushes and shrubs; the long-necked sauropods faded from the scene, apparently having eaten themselves out of a food supply. To take advantage of these low-lying plants, new forms of dinosaurs emerged and became dominant; these included such animals as the duckbills and the short, squat-horned dinosaurs.

Another finding concerns the ancestry of these North American dinosaurs: nearly all of the dinosaurs found at this site were first discovered in Asia. It is now thought that the North American Cretaceous period dinosaurs were the descendants of dinosaurs that first arose in Asia. This is the first evidence showing that these dinosaurs came from Asia—and most of these dinosaurs were present in North America by about 100 million years ago.

INTERNATIONAL DINOSAUR DISCOVERIES

EARLY DINOSAUR HISTORY OUTSIDE THE UNITED STATES

Who wrote the earliest **description** of **dinosaur bones**?

The author's name was Chang Qu; around 300 B.C., he wrote about "dragon bones" found in Wucheng, China (now Sichuan Province). These bones were often ground up by the Chinese and used as medicine or for magical potions. More than 1,500 years later, these "dragon bones" would be recognized as dinosaur fossils.

When was *Scrotum humanum* discovered?

Around 1676, the Reverend Plot of England reported a fossil bone find: A "human thigh bone of one of the giants mentioned in the Bible." In 1763, R. Brooke named the bone based on its shape. He referred to it as *Scrotum humanum*—the genitals of a giant man. Today, the bone is thought to be from a megalosaurid dinosaur, from the distal end of a femur. The name *Scrotum humanum*—though unofficially the first assigned name given to dinosaur bones—has never been used, since it was an erroneous designation.

Who first published a **scientific name** for fossil **dinosaur** bones?

In 1822, English surgeon and paleontologist James Parkinson (1755–1824) published the name *Megalosaurus,* based on fossil findings in England; unfortunately, he did not provide a description.

Who **first** published information on fossils **classified as a dinosaur**?

Although James Parkinson published the name *Megalosaurus* in 1822, the first officially recognized scientific naming and description of a dinosaur was by William Buckland (1784–1856), a professor at Oxford University in England. In 1824, Buckland published his studies of a Cretaceous period carnivore whose fossils had been found in Stonesfield, England, describing the animal based on fossilized jaws and teeth. He also used the name *Megalosaurus,* and presented his data at a meeting of the Geological Society of London. This was subsequently accepted as the first dinosaur to be described.

Who **first proposed extinctions** had occurred during the earth's history?

Baron Georges Cuvier (1769–1832), a French scientist at the National Museum of Natural History in Paris, was the first to propose the idea of extinctions. Around 1800, his work with mammoth and mastodon bones (although they were not labeled such until later) that had recently been found in North America led to his theory of extinction. He was able to show that these creatures recently went extinct—refuting claims that all creatures that ever existed were still alive and living on unexplored areas of the earth.

Cuvier is considered to be the father of modern paleontology and comparative anatomy. His confirmation of the extinction process opened the door for the study of more ancient animals—the dinosaurs.

Who **first recognized** certain fossils as **giant reptiles**?

Gideon Mantell (1790–1852), an English country doctor and fossil collector, was the first to recognize certain fossils as giant reptiles. The well-known story—but perhaps not completely true—is that Mantell's wife, Mary Ann, found some fossilized teeth in rocks along the roadside while accompanying her husband on a house call. (Some people believe that Mantell actually found the fossils.) The rocks had come from the Bestede Quarry, Cuckfield, Sussex, England. In 1822, Mantell's examination of these teeth—and of subsequent remains from the same area—led him to the first reconstruction of what is now known as a dinosaur. In 1825, a year after William Buckland's published description of *Megalosaurus,* Mantell published a description of this ancient reptile. He named it *Iguanodon,* or "iguana tooth," as the teeth, though much larger, matched those of the modern lizard.

This was the second published description of a creature that became known as a dinosaur. Mantell subsequently used a pictorial representation of the *Iguanodon* on the coat of arms for his residence, Maidstone, Kent, England.

What town features the dinosaur *Iguanodon* on their **civic coat of arms**?

The town of Maidstone, Kent, England, has the *Iguanodon* embedded on its coat of arms. In 1834, fossil collector Gideon Mantell made an identification of a partial skeleton as being an *Iguanodon;* the fossil remains had been dug up by W. H. Bensted in his own quarry. Though Mantell purchased the skeleton for his own collection, the town still felt a sense of ownership and, in 1949, petitioned the Royal College of Arms to add the dinosaur to part of their civic shield. Their request was approved.

What **other discovery** can be attributed to **Gideon Mantell**?

Gideon Mantell also scientifically described the first known dinosaur skin in 1852. This was from the forelimb of a *Pelorosaurus becklesii* dinosaur.

Who **coined** the word **palaeontology**?

In 1830, Sir Charles Lyell (1797–1875), a Scottish geologist, coined the word palaeontology, or "discourse on ancient things." Between 1829 and 1833, Lyell recognized that this was a separate field of science. In general, "paleontology" is the spelling used in the United States.

Where were the first **life-sized dinosaur models** publicly displayed?

The first life-sized dinosaur models were publicly displayed at Sydenham Park, site of the relocated Crystal Palace in southeast London, England. The year was 1854, and the sculpting of these figures by Benjamin Waterhouse Hawkins (1807–89) had been supervised by paleontologist Sir Richard Owen. The figures were placed in the park, later renamed the Crystal Palace Park; the dinosaurs were all portrayed as giant, elephantine lizards. These figures were enormously popular with the public. And although the Crystal Palace itself burned down years ago, the sculptured dinosaurs can still be viewed on the grounds.

Who was first to reconstruct the way **dinosaurs behaved**?

Louis Dollo (1857–1931), a French mining engineer, was the first to interpret the remains of dinosaurs. Dollo did this with an eye toward reconstructing their lifestyles. In 1878, the remains of approximately 40 *Iguanodon* were discovered in the Fosse Sainte-Barbe coal mine near the town Bernissart in southwestern Belgium. Their excavation took three years. Dollo spent the rest of his life assembling, studying, and interpreting the fossil remains.

In 1882, he started as an assistant naturalist at the Royal Natural History Museum in Brussels, Belgium; in 1904, he became director of the museum, based on the strength of his scientific discoveries associated with the *Iguanodon.* Not only did he assemble the bones for exhibit and write papers concerning his findings, but he attempted to portray the behavior of these animals.

Who **first classified dinosaurs** based on the structure of the pelvic area?

In 1887, English paleontologist Harry Govier Seeley (1839–1909) realized there were two distinct groups of dinosaurs. He classified them as Ornithischia ("bird-hipped") and Saurischia ("lizard-hipped"), based primarily on the bone structure of the pelvic area. This system of classification was widely adopted and is still in use today. Seeley also grouped the dinosaurs with crocodiles, birds, and extinct reptiles known as thecodonts; this common ancestral group is now known as the archosaurs.

Why are the **Solnhofen quarries** of Germany so **important** to paleontology?

The Solnhofen quarries of Bavaria, Germany, are important not just because they are home to the oldest known bird fossils, the *Archaeopteryx lithographica;* this area is also what paleontologists call a *Lagerstatten*—German for "fossil lode" or "storehouse." Because of their unique prehistoric conditions, these sites have preserved numerous animals, giving us a virtual snapshot of ancient fauna. There are only approximately 100 fossil sites around the world designated as *Lagerstatten*—each representing different time periods, and all rich in fossil varieties.

What were the **conditions** that **formed the rock** in the **Solnhofen quarries**?

The Solnhofen quarries were the site of a quiet, warm-water, anoxic (lacking oxygen) lagoon. It lay behind reefs on the northern shores of the Tethys Ocean approximately 150 million years ago. The tropical climate at this time was perfect for the animals and plants living along its shores. And the ocean itself teemed with life beyond the stagnant lagoon.

Storms would sweep in dead or dying animals from the ocean; dying land creatures either fell into the lagoon, or drifted into it from the shore. Their bodies fell to the bottom of the lagoon and were covered by soft lime mud; little oxygen was present to decompose the organisms. The ensuing fine limestone rock preserved, in exquisite detail, the remains of over 600 species, including the smallest dinosaur, *Compsognathus;* pterosaurs by the hundreds; numerous insects; and, of course, the remains of *Archaeopteryx lithographica.*

When was the most spectacular **dinosaur fossil expedition** mounted?

The most spectacular dinosaur fossil expedition ever mounted began in 1909 and lasted through 1912. The expedition took place in German East Africa—now known as Tanzania—around the village of Tendaguru.

In 1907, W. B. Sattler found gigantic fossil bones weathering out of the surface rock as he explored the area around Tendaguru for mineral resources. After reporting his findings, the area was subsequently visited by noted paleontologist Professor Eberhard Fraas, who took samples back to Germany. There, Dr. W. Branca, the director of the Berlin Museum, realized the importance and scope of the findings—and started raising funds for an expedition.

The expedition began in 1909—a search larger in scope than anything to date. In the first year, 170 native laborers were employed by the expedition; in the second year 400 were used. The third and fourth years saw 500 natives at work on the dig sites, which were located in an area extending almost 2 miles (3 kilometers) between Tendaguru Village and Tendaguru Hill. The laborers were accompanied by their families; thus, the expedition had to accommodate upward of 700 to 900 people. As if that weren't enough, after the fossils were mapped, measured, excavated, and encased in plaster, they had to be hand carried from Tendaguru, in the interior, to Lindi, on the coast—a trek that took four days. There, the enormous number of bones, eventually totaling 250 tons, were shipped to Germany for preparation, study, and reconstruction.

Fossilized *Albertosaurus* head at Royal Tyrrell Museum in Alberta, Canada. (Photo courtesy of Michael S. Yamashita/Corbis.)

Which dinosaur remains were excavated during the **Tendaguru expedition**?

The Tendaguru expedition was itself spectacular—and so were the dinosaur fossils discovered at the site. Among the findings were three types of theropods—the small, agile *Elaphrosaurus,* and the larger *Ceratosaurus* and *Allosaurus.* Six herbivorous dinosaurs were also found: the tiny ornithopod *Dryosaurus; Kentrosaurus,* a stegosaur; and four sauropods, *Dicraeosaurus, Barosaurus, Tornieria,* and the largest one of the time, *Brachiosaurus.* The reconstructed skeleton of a Tendaguru *Brachiosaurus* at the Berlin Museum is the largest complete dinosaur skeleton in the world.

In addition to these spectacular dinosaur finds, the expedition also uncovered remains of pterosaurs, fishes, and a tiny mammal jawbone. All of the animals were similar to those found earlier in the Morrison formation in the western United States, indicating that migration between North America and Africa was relatively easy during the time of these animals.

Where were the **first *Albertosaurus*** fossil remains found?

The first fossil remains of the late Cretaceous dinosaur *Albertosaurus* were found in the badlands of the Red Deer River Valley of Alberta, Canada. Geologist Joseph Burr Tyrrell found the fossil remains in the spring of 1884, as he led an expedition near present-day Drumheller for the Geological Survey of Canada.

In the early 1900s, the discovery of these and other remains brought numerous paleontologists to the area, including Barnum Brown of the American Museum of Natural History, and Charles H. Sternberg (1850–1943) and sons for the Canadian Geological Survey. The friendly rivalry between Brown and the Sternbergs was dubbed the "Great Canadian Dinosaur Rush."

Today, the badlands of the Red Deer River Valley in Alberta, Canada, are recognized as one of the world's leading fossil collecting areas, with some 25 species of dinosaurs so far uncovered. The significance of this area led to the establishment of the Royal Tyrrell Museum, established in June 1990, in Drumheller.

How did the "badlands" of the Red Deer River Valley form?

The badlands of the Red Deer River Valley, in Alberta, Canada, were carved by meltwater torrents when the ice sheets retreated approximately 10,000 to 15,000 years ago. There is some evidence that flash floods, rather than rivers, were the agents that created the present badlands topography. These landscapes include narrow, winding gullies and channels; heavy erosion; steep slopes; and little or no vegetation.

During the time of the dinosaurs, this area included numerous deltas and river flood plains that extended out into a shallow, inland sea. The late Cretaceous deposits of sand and mud often included the bodies of dinosaurs. Over millions of years, as material was laid down layer upon layer, the deposits turned into rock, fossilizing the dinosaur bones.

The advance and retreat of four glacial ice sheets over millions of years—along with other natural erosional processes by wind and water—caused significant wearing away of the area. The material on top was removed, and the exposed Cretaceous period sedimentary rocks were carved into the badlands of today. The Cretaceous layer is known as the Horseshoe Canyon formation—and is continually eroding, exposing fresh dinosaur fossils.

RECENT FINDS

ASIA

What great Jurassic and early Cretaceous period discovery was made in Asia?

The site of spectacular fossils, including many dinosaur remains, was found in Liaoning Province, northeast China, near the village of Beipiao. Included in the finds were the first fossilized internal organs of dinosaurs—and the first fossil of a dinosaur containing the remains of a mammal it might have eaten.

This site has so far yielded the remains of *Confuciusornis,* the oldest beaked bird; the possibly feathered dinosaur *Sinosauropteryx prima;* the oldest modern bird *Liaoningornis; Protarchaeopteryx,* perhaps a primitive bird older than *Archaeopteryx lithographica;* and many other species of dinosaurs, mammals, insects, and plants.

The fossils found at the site were preserved in great detail. This was because the prolific rock layer is from a lacustrine (lake) deposit and covered with a fine volcanic ash. Paleontologists speculate that a brief catastrophe, such as a volcanic eruption, killed and quickly buried everything in the area. Thus, even impressions of soft body parts, such as feathers and organs, were preserved.

What **Cretaceous dinosaur fossils** were recently found in **Mongolia**?

At Ukhaa Tolgod, in the Gobi Desert of Mongolia, lies what is billed as one of the greatest Cretaceous fossil finds in history. Starting in 1993, the discoveries include the remains of more than 13 troodontid skeletons; over 100 uncollected dinosaur specimens; numerous mammals; and a nest-brooding adult *Oviraptor.*

The reason for the huge number and extraordinary states of preservation is thought to be due to a series of catastrophic occurrences. These events swiftly buried the animals, precluding any damage by the elements or scavengers. Scientists believe normally stable sand dunes became drenched with rain water, triggering sudden debris flows that trapped—and preserved—the animals.

What recent events in **Russia** have highlighted **crime** in dinosaur **fossil collecting**?

In 1996, the remains of five dinosaurs disappeared from the fossil repository of the Paleontological Institute of the Russian Academy of Sciences in Moscow, and are believed to have been stolen. They included a lower jaw and maxilla with teeth from the large carnivore *Tarbosaurus efremovi;* a skull of *Breviceratops kozlowskii,* a late Cretaceous herbivore; and two skulls of *Protoceratops.*

AUSTRALIA

Who found the **first evidence** of **dinosaurs in Australia**?

The first evidence of dinosaurs in Australia was found in 1906 by a Mr. Ferguson, a
government geologist: a small carnivorous dinosaur claw was discovered on the

The Gobi Desert has been the site of many remarkable fossil finds. (Photo courtesy of Dean Conger/Corbis.)

Gippsland coast of eastern Victoria. Since then, many more dinosaurs have been discovered in states such as Queensland, South Australia, and New South Wales. These discoveries include sauropods and iguanadons, such as the *Muttaburrasaurus,* which is unique to Australia.

What fossil was **stolen** from a **site in Australia**?

In 1996, fossil collectors stole a dinosaur footprint from a site in northwest Australia, approximately 1,800 miles (3,000 kilometers) from Sydney. This was the world's only known fossil footprint made by a *Stegosaurus,* and represented a loss not only to science, but to the aborigines of Australia, who regarded the location of the footprints as one of their sacred sites. The thieves apparently used power tools to remove the rock containing the trace fossil. Under aboriginal law, this offense is punishable by death.

Has the **stolen** Australian *Stegosaurus* **footprint** been recovered?

Yes, approximately one year after thieves made off with the only known fossil footprint made by a *Stegosaurus,* police recovered it and arrested two Australian men. The recovered block of rock containing the footprint weighed approximately 66 pounds (30 kilograms); measured 23 inches (60 centimeters) by 15.5 inches (40 centimeters); and was 5 inches (13 centimeters) deep.

The men attempted to sell the fossil footprint in Asia, but were unsuccessful. Police believe this may have been due to the size of the rock—or perhaps the weight. Police would not elaborate on how the fossil was recovered.

POLAR REGIONS

In what northern locale were **dinosaur footprints** found in 1960?

The Arctic island of West Spitzbergen (in the Svalbard island group) in the Northern Hemisphere is where an international team of geologists discovered dinosaur footprints. These tracks were thought to have been made by *Iguanodon,* an early Cretaceous period dinosaur.

Where were the **first duck-billed dinosaur fossils** found outside the Americas?

The first duck-billed dinosaur (a plant-eating hadrosaur) fossils found outside the Americas were discovered on Vega Island, off the eastern side of the Antarctic Peninsula. A tooth found there was dated at approximately 66 to 67 million years old; this finding gives more credence to theories about a land bridge connecting South America and Antarctica during this time. It also indicates that this cold climate and ecosystem were once lush and robust enough to support large plant-eaters.

EUROPE

What **European island** recently became a hotspot for dinosaur **fossil discoveries**?

The small Isle of Wight, 3 miles (4.8 kilometers) off the southern coast of England, has recently become a major hotspot for paleontologists—and it's evolving into one of the

> ## Why is it interesting that dinosaurs lived in Australia?
>
> One reason is because of Australia's climate which, during the realm of the dinosaur, was very cold. This is because millions of years ago Australia was within the polar circle and still attached to Antarctica.

world's best dinosaur fossil discovery sites. This island was once home to Queen Victoria, and is best known as a holiday destination. But the quality of its dinosaur fossils—and the time period from which they originate—make this island the focus of paleontologists worldwide.

The uniqueness of the dinosaur fossils found on the Isle of Wight is in their age: they are from the early Cretaceous period, which lasted from approximately 141 to 93 million years ago. Fossils from this period are rare; most sites around the world yield fossils from the Triassic or Jurassic periods. Thus the Isle of Wight dinosaur fossils are essentially a window into a unique period of time, and constitutes a resource not found elsewhere in the world. On top of this, the fossils are well preserved and articulated, meaning the bones are still joined together, not strewn around.

Why are dinosaur fossils relatively **easy to find** on the **Isle of Wight**?

The dinosaur fossils on the Isle of Wight are relatively easy to find because they are concentrated in two small areas. There is a 6-mile- (10-kilometer-) long fossil-containing area along the southern coast of the island, and another half-mile- (0.8-kilometer-) long area on the eastern coast. In many other of the top fossil sites in the world, the bones of dinosaurs are distributed over thousands of square miles, making the search for them more diffuse and difficult.

The continual uncovering of dinosaur bones on the Isle of Wight is due to a unique combination of physical factors. The rock containing the dinosaur bones has been pushed to the surface by geological pressures; in other parts of the world, this type of rock may be buried underground—sometimes up to 1,000 feet (305 meters) below the surface.

The fossil-bearing rock itself is a soft rock, consisting mainly of sandstones and mudstones, which makes the rock susceptible to erosion. And the Isle of Wight certainly has erosion: more than 3 feet (1 meter) of rock is worn away every year in certain exposed areas. The engine for this high rate of erosion is the sea. Every fall and winter, the flow of the tides, combined with high seas and gales from the English Channel, batter the rocks that make up the sea cliffs on the island.

But this has been a boon to scientists: the erosion exposes dinosaur bones, which literally fall onto the beaches at the feet of eagerly awaiting paleontologists. Among the many finds on the Isle of Wight are several new discoveries. The skeleton of the first small, meat-eating dinosaur found in England, a new species, was found in a crumbling cliff by an amateur collector. In 1997, a smaller version of a *Tyrannosaurus rex,* another new species called *Neovenator salerii,* was also discovered. And a very well-preserved *Iguanodon* was recently uncovered.

What **small, unusual carnivorous dinosaur** was found on the Isle of Wight?

The fossil remains of a 12-foot (3.7-meter) carnivorous dinosaur was recently discovered on the Isle of Wight off the southern coast of England. This new species of dinosaur was catlike, with unusually long hind legs on which it ran at high speed; it was also equipped with claws and razor-sharp teeth. Though not yet named, this is the first small, meat-eating dinosaur found in Britain. It is unusual because it appears to be from the early Cretaceous period—and remains from this time are not often found in this area.

What was *Neovenator salerii* like?

Neovenator salerii ("Salero's new hunter") was a carnivorous dinosaur similar to *Tyrannosaurus rex* that was between 24 and 28 feet (7.5 and 8.5 meters) in length. About 120 million years ago, it would have been the main predator in the area now called the Isle of Wight.

Neovenator salerii was named for the Salero family, who are the first natives of the Isle of Wight to have a dinosaur named after them. They owned the land on which the dinosaur was found. The fossil remains were very well preserved, with almost no signs of crushing. This made it easier to compare the bones to other known species—and to determine that this was an entirely new type of carnivorous dinosaur.

What was *Valdosaurus?*

Valdosaurus ("wealden lizard") was a small- to medium-sized ornithopod dinosaur whose remains have been found on the Isle of Wight. Only a few partial, fragmented remains have been found over the years. What little evidence there is suggests that this dinosaur was about 14 feet (4.25 meters) long and about 4 feet (1.2 meters) high at the hips.

The excavated leg bones of *Valdosaurus* are comparable to those of *Dryosaurus,* a dryosaurid ("oak lizard") known from the upper Jurassic period of North America, which lived some 30 million years earlier. Using *Dryosaurus* as a guide, *Valdosaurus* may have been a fast-running biped (two-footed) with long hind legs, short front limbs, a small skull, and stocky build. From the shape and size of the hindlimb bones, scientists know that *Valdosaurus* was an agile and fast runner; there is currently no evidence of any armor plates, sharp teeth, horns, or claws. Thus *Valdosaurus* probably was a grazing dinosaur, eating ferns and cycad-like fronds. But it remained continually alert for predators, using its running ability as a defense against attacks.

Have any **sauropod** fossil remains been found on the **Isle of Wight**?

Yes, the fossil remains of a sauropod have been found on the Isle of Wight. In 1992, while exploring the cliffs on the southwest coast of the Isle of Wight, the local official paleontologist discovered a whitish bone sticking out. As excavation of this site progressed, more and more large bones were uncovered—including 3- to 6.5-foot- (1- to 2-meter-) long arm bones, 6.5-foot- (2-meter-) long ribs, and giant vertebrae.

This sauropod appears to have been a species of *Brachiosaurus,* but the final description and naming will have to wait until more of the bones have been cleaned and more research has been done.

Where are the **oldest fossilized dinosaur embryos** found?

The oldest fossil embryos were discovered among approximately 100 dinosaur eggs recently found in the area around Lourinha, a small town about 37 miles (60 kilometers) north of Lisbon, Portugal.

The embryos—identified as those of theropods—were dated at approximately 140 million years old. They are the oldest embryos to date, and the only ones currently known from the Jurassic period. Until this finding, all other fossilized dinosaur embryos came from the Cretaceous period, with the oldest of those being approximately 80 million years old.

Where is the **world's largest paleontological institute** located?

The world's largest institute is located in Moscow, Russia, and is known as the Paleontological Institute of the Russian Academy of Sciences. No other institute in the world has more paleontologists under one roof, with research interests ranging from the dinosaurs of Mongolia and mammals from Georgia (near Russia) to the origins of life itself. There are extensive collections of fossils from all over the former Soviet Union and the world, along with a Museum of Paleontology and great public exhibits. The exhibits include Mongolian dinosaurs, synapsids from the Perm region (of Russia), and Pre-Cambrian fossils from Siberia.

Unfortunately, with all of these wonderful resources and exhibits, the institute and museum are largely underfunded and remain relatively unknown to those outside the paleontological world, unlike more popular museums such as the American Museum of Natural History in New York City.

SOUTH AMERICA

Where were the remains of the **oldest known dinosaur** discovered?

The fossil remains of *Eoraptor* ("dawn hunter") were discovered in the Ischigualasto formation rock layer in Argentina—the same area where the second oldest dinosaur, the *Herrerasaurus,* was found. In 1991, Ricardo Martinez made the first find of a *Eoraptor;* this was followed by the discovery of another skeleton in the 1990s, by Fernando Novas and Paul Sereno. In 1993, the analysis of these remains led Sereno to name *Eoraptor* the "first," or most primitive known, form of dinosaur.

Eoraptor was smaller than *Herrerasaurus,* being about 3 feet (1 meter) long. It had all the dinosaur characteristics found in *Herrerasaurus,* but its skull was a basic design. It also had a few specializations that would allow it to be placed in any of the major dinosaur groups. The primitive dinosaurs probably represented 5 percent of the total animal population in the beginning of the late Triassic period. But they would soon spread throughout the world—and dominate the land in the Jurassic and Cretaceous periods.

Where was the **second oldest dinosaur** found?

In 1959, the remains of a *Herrerasaurus*—thought by some paleontologists to be the second oldest known dinosaur—were discovered in Argentina. The remains were found in a layer of rock known as the Ischigualasto formation; the area is located in the Ischigualasto valley, or the "valley of the moon."

The discoverers were Victorino Herrera, a goat-herder, and Osvaldo Reig, a paleontologist. In 1988, a complete skull and skeleton of *Herrerasaurus* was found in the

These are among 100 dinosaur eggs, measuring 5 inches in length and 3 inches in diameter, discovered in Portugal in 1997. Some of the eggs in one clutch contained embryo elements of a carnivorous theropod. (Photo courtesy of Luisa Ferreira/Associated Press.)

same area by Paul Sereno and Fernando Novas. This 10- to 20-foot- (3- to 6-meter-) long reptile had numerous characteristics enabling it to succeed at its carnivorous lifestyle: recurved teeth, powerful hind limbs, a bipedal stance, and strong arms. It was excavated from rock laid down during the beginning of the late Triassic period, approximately 230 million years ago.

Where was a *Giganotosaurus carolinii* found?

A *Giganotosaurus carolinii,* one of the contenders for the world's largest carnivorous dinosaur, was discovered in Argentina by Ruben Carolini, an auto mechanic and amateur fossil hunter. Although this dinosaur had a similar appearance to *Tyrannosaurus rex,* paleontologists don't think the two were related.

Where have a **group** of *Giganotosaurus* remains been discovered?

The skeletal remains of a group of *Giganotosaurus* have been discovered in Neuquen, a southern province of Argentina. There were bones of four or five of these Cretaceous period theropods—two were very large and the others smaller. Paleontologists believe this discovery is the most important evidence to date of a social, pack-hunting behavior on the part of large carnivorous dinosaurs.

Approximately 90 million years ago, when these animals died, this region was similar to the present-day pampas of northern Argentina. The climate was warm and rainy, and the land was essentially low scrub, dotted with araucaria trees. After the group of *Giganotosaurus* died, a west-flowing river swept their bodies away. A local goat herder found the deposit containing the dinosaur bones in an area that is now a sandy rise in a desert.

What great **fossil find** was made in **Argentina** that helped **link dinosaurs to birds**?

In the Patagonia region of Argentina, paleontologists have uncovered fossil remains of a dinosaur creature that embodies many physical characteristics that strengthen the argument that birds are descendants of dinosaurs. Named *Unenlagia comahuensis,* this meat-eating creature stood nearly 4 feet (1.2 meters) tall and was nearly 7 feet (2.1 meters) long. Even though it could not fly and did not have wings, its bone structure was similar to that of ancient birds, allowing the dinosaur to tuck its upper arm bones close to its body, similar to the way modern birds fold their wings.

What major **dinosaur egg** discovery was made in **South America**?

Thousands of fossilized dinosaur eggs—along with parts of teeth, skin, and bones from the unhatched embryos—have been discovered in the northwestern Patagonian province of Neuquen, Argentina, in a place called Auca Mahuida. Paleontologists have nicknamed the site "Auca Mahuevo" after *huevo,* the Spanish word for "egg."

Among the thousands of eggs are the first embryos ever found of a sauropod dinosaur, the large, four-footed plant-eaters; in addition, some eggs contained the first embryonic skin ever found of a dinosaur. Approximately 70 to 90 million years ago, this area of South America looked like the plains of the American Midwest; now, it resembles the Badlands of South Dakota, with erosion continually exposing rocks, bones, and eggs.

How do paleontologists know which **dinosaur** laid the **eggs** found at **Auca Mahuevo**?

Paleontologists have used two clues to identify the type of dinosaur that laid the eggs at the recently discovered site in northwest Patagonia, Argentina: the embryonic teeth and the skin found in association with the eggs.

The embryos had tiny, peglike teeth, a characteristic of the sauropods. Paleontologists noted spots on the teeth had been rubbed flat by friction, indicating that the embryonic dinosaurs ground their teeth even before they were hatched. Some scientists believe this shows that the young were exercising their jaw muscles.

Why was the discovery of *Giganotosaurus* important?

The discovery of *Giganotosaurus* cleared up a mystery: why *Tyrannosaurus rex* had never migrated into South America. Both of these dinosaurs occupied the same position on top of the food chain—and it now appears that the roughly equal-sized *Giganotosaurus* kept the *T. rex* out of South America. In turn, *T. rex* kept *Giganotosaurus* out of North America. Other dinosaurs, such as the smaller theropods and larger herbivores, freely wandered between the two landmasses where there was a land bridge between them.

The embryonic skin found in some eggs has clearly visible scales. And based on the patterns in the skin, paleontologists believe the eggs were laid by *Titanosaurs*. This species of sauropod dinosaur grew to approximately 45 feet (14 meters) long—and were the only sauropods to survive to the end of the Cretaceous period.

What is the **importance** of this discovery of **thousands of dinosaur eggs** at one site in Argentina?

There are three reasons why the discovery of thousands of dinosaur eggs in the northwestern Patagonian province of Neuquen, Argentina, is important—above and beyond the findings of embryonic bones, teeth, and skin. First, this shows that sauropods laid eggs, rather than giving live birth, as had been suggested by some scientists. Second, it indicates that these dinosaurs repeatedly converged to one place to lay their eggs; until now, there was no true evidence for such behavior. And third, it solves a 100-year-old mystery: large, round dinosaur eggs, similar to those found at Auca Mahuevo, had been previously found in Africa, India, China, Europe, and South America—but the dinosaur that laid them remained unknown. Now, paleontologists can conclude that a species of sauropod laid these types of eggs.

Are the **dinosaur eggs** in Argentina being **mapped**?

Yes, the site in the Neuquen Province of Argentina, where thousands of dinosaur eggs have been found, is being mapped by scientists. The first stage of this project is to map one sector of the site, an area approximately 11 miles (18 kilometers) long and 3 to 4 miles (4 to 6 kilometers) wide, containing about 200 dinosaur eggs. Work on this part is almost complete, and a map showing the positions of all the eggs will be published in the near future. This mapping will help scientists understand the reproductive patterns of these dinosaurs. And it may also shed some light on

363

whether this was just an area for these dinosaurs to deposit their eggs, or something more structured, like a nest.

How is the **age** of these South American dinosaur **eggs** being **determined**?

Initially, the age of these dinosaur eggs was estimated at 70 to 90 million years old. This was based on the types of animal fossils found in the same geological formation. But in order to make the date more accurate, paleontologists are using two different methods.

The first method is to determine if there is a pattern of magnetic field reversal locked in the rocks. Many times over the past millions of years, the magnetic field of the earth has flipped, or reversed, so that a compass would point south instead of north. Eventually, the field flipped back to its "normal" position. Magnetic particles in mud orient themselves to reflect the magnetic field direction present at the time; the mud eventually solidifies to become rock, locking in the pattern. Successive layers of rock will show a distinct pattern of normal and reversed magnetic field orientation. At the dinosaur egg site, rock samples from different layers representing various ages are being collected and analyzed for their magnetic field orientation. Any pattern found will be compared to a corresponding pattern in the known geologic record—allowing a closer estimate of the age of the eggs.

The second method used to date these dinosaur eggs deals with volcanic ash, which can be analyzed in a laboratory and dated to within about 200,000 years. This would give paleontologists a reference point in the sedimentary rock layers and pinpoint the eggs' ages to within about 1 million years. Fortunately, a layer of ash deposited from an ancient volcano was found at the site, and scientists are now determining if the ash is well preserved enough to obtain a date.

What discovery shows a **relationship** between dinosaurs in the **Northern and Southern Hemispheres**?

The discovery of the foot of *Araucanoraptor argentynus* in Neuquen, Argentina, is another piece of evidence that dinosaurs migrated into the Southern Hemisphere— and were therefore related to those found in the Northern Hemisphere. This particular dinosaur was a 90-million-year-old theropod originally thought to have never made it to the Southern Hemisphere.

For a long time, paleontologists believed that dinosaurs from the Northern Hemisphere were completely different from those found in the South. Fossil finds like those of *Araucanoraptor argentynus* show that they were indeed related. In fact, *Araucanoraptor argentynus* was related to the *Troodon,* whose fossil remains have been found in Canada.

The 36-foot-long *Suchomimus tenerensis* had razor teeth, a long pointy snout, and foot-long claws, all of which were ideal for catching fish. This fossil was found in the Sahara. (Photo courtesy of Dennis Cook/Associated Press.)

AFRICA

Where were fossil remains of a *Suchomimus tenerensis* recently **found**?

The remains of a *Suchomimus tenerensis*—a large fish-eating dinosaur with a long, crocodile-like snout—were recently found in the Tenere Desert of Niger, a central African country. Fossils of this Cretaceous dinosaur were located in rock strata called the Elrhaz formation. Approximately 100 million years ago, this area had a lush climate with plenty of water and supported many types of animals, including giant crocodiles, large fish, and many different species of dinosaurs—including the newly discovered *Suchomimus tenerensis*. Over time, the remains of this African dinosaur had been swept into a river, tumbled, then covered by sediment. The winds of the desert eroded the sands covering the remains, exposing it to the light of day.

What **mysteries** did the remains of the dinosaur *Majungatholus* solve?

The discovery of *Majungatholus,* on the island of Madagascar off the southeast coast of Africa, cleared up three mysteries that had been puzzling paleontologists for years: the name of the dinosaur that left behind numerous fossil teeth on Madagascar; why the remains of a Northern Hemisphere pachycephalosaur were present on the island; and how the dinosaurs got from South America to Madagascar.

365

How did the *Majungatholus* remains explain the **fossil teeth** found on Madagascar?

Paleontologists discovered hundreds of dagger-like fossil teeth throughout Madagascar over 100 years ago, but no one knew what type of dinosaur had shed the teeth (during a meal, some carnivorous dinosaurs shed a few of their teeth, similar to modern sharks and crocodiles). In 1996, an expedition went to Madagascar to find the dinosaur associated with these teeth. One day, while digging into a hill, a paleontologist found some tailbones. Further digging exposed an upper jawbone of a large carnivorous dinosaur—and the jaw contained the same teeth found scattered throughout Madagascar. The mystery had been solved at last!

The dinosaur responsible for the fossil teeth was named *Majungatholus,* a distant relative of *Tyrannosaurus rex.* It was approximately 20 to 30 feet (6 to 9 meters) long and lived in Madagascar about 70 million years ago. The skull of the dinosaur had a stubby remnant of a horn set between the eyes; some of the skull bones had an unusually rough texture, perhaps echoing patterns in the overlying skin. Paleontologists speculate that the combination of horn and texture on the head may have been used to threaten enemies or attract a mate.

How did the *Majungatholus* remains explain **dinosaur migration** from South America to Madagascar?

The *Majungatholus* was very similar to another dinosaur found in Argentina, although the latter animal had two horns; other bone fragments found in India were also very similar, indicating these dinosaurs were all from the same group. However, no evidence has been found to date of any of these dinosaurs in Africa.

Approximately 120 million years ago, South America, Africa, Antarctica, Madagascar, Australia, and India were all joined together in one supercontinent called Gondwana, or Gondwanaland. Scientists originally believed a piece of the landmass containing South America and Africa first split away from Gondwanaland, then pulled apart to form the South Atlantic Ocean. As the breakup of Gondwanaland continued, Madagascar ended up as an island to the east of Africa. The discovery of *Majungatholus*—and its similarity to dinosaurs in India and South America—made this scenario unlikely. How could this group of dinosaurs get from South America to Madagascar without first going through Africa?

To answer this question, scientists modified the sequence by which Gondwanaland broke up. Now they believe the landmass of Africa broke off from Gondwanaland first, becoming isolated from the rest of the supercontinent. South America and the Indian subcontinent, which included Madagascar, remained connected to Antarctica as recently as 80 million years ago by means of land bridges. The group of dinosaurs to which *Majungatholus* belonged, as well as many other dinosaurs, could have migrated freely

How did the *Majungatholus* remains explain the pachycephalosaur?

At the turn of the century, fragments of a dinosaur skull were found in Madagascar. One of these fragments had a protrusion, which led some paleontologists to believe these were the remains of a pachycephalosaur, or "dome-headed" dinosaur. This group of dinosaurs was herbivorous and may have used their thickened skulls as battering rams. Scientists named this dinosaur *Majungatholus,* but for many years it was only known from a few fossil fragments. The problem was, pachycephalosaurs had only been found in the Northern Hemisphere. And how this dinosaur got to Madagascar was unknown.

With the recent discovery of more complete remains of a *Majungatholus,* the mystery was finally solved. The older skull fragments matched those of the newly discovered dinosaur. Paleontologists realized that the protrusion on the original bones had been wrongly identified as a dome—in reality, it was a horn. There had not been a pachycephalosaur in Madagascar after all—the *Majungatholus* was a large, carnivorous dinosaur with a small horn between its eyes.

from South America to India and Madagascar by way of Antarctica. This would account for the remains found in those continents, and also for the lack of them in Africa.

Where have the remains of a *Carcharodontosaurus* been found?

The remains of a *Carcharodontosaurus,* a large theropod that rivaled the *Tyrannosaurus rex* in size, were recently found in Morocco. The skull alone measured almost 5.5 feet (1.7 meters). The first *Carcharodontosaurus* was discovered in 1931, identified from an incomplete North African skull and few bones; the remains were later destroyed during World War II. The most recent remains were found in 1996—and are even larger than the old specimen.

DIGGING FOR DINOSAURS

FINDING DINOSAUR FOSSILS

What is the first precaution amateur diggers should take before searching for dinosaur fossils?

The first and most important precaution amateur diggers should take before searching for dinosaur fossils—or any other fossils—is to make sure they have permission to search the area, from the person, organization, or government agency that owns the lands. In addition, would-be diggers must verify that they can collect and keep any specimens they find on the land. Without permission, they may be arrested and charged with trespassing, destruction of property, or even theft.

How do paleontologists or amateur collectors find dinosaur fossils?

The key to finding dinosaur fossils (or fossils of any kind) is to search in the right types of rocks. This generally means searching in sedimentary rock—or rocks composed of materials such as sand or mud that were deposited in a lake, river, or ocean. However, not all sedimentary rock contains fossils, much less dinosaur fossils. The right combination of factors must have existed for a dinosaur to have been transformed into a fossil in sedimentary rock.

To find dinosaur fossils, paleontologists must locate sedimentary rocks laid down during the right time—in this case, periods within the Mesozoic era. For example, if the paleontologist is interested in Jurassic period dinosaurs, then he or she should be looking for rocks deposited during that time. Once the fossil hunter knows which age of rocks he or she is looking for, the location of such rocks can be determined from a

369

A team excavates dinosaur bones near Kauchanaburi, Thailand. (Photo courtesy of Bill Wassman/Stock Market.)

geologic map of the area. These maps pinpoint the locations of the various rock types exposed at the surface, and show an area's topography (height of the land).

Once a location with the right type of rock is determined, the paleontologist explores the area on foot, checking for exposed rock, and features that may have led to exposed rock, such as folds and faults. The paleontologist also looks for areas where erosion—due to action by water, wind, or even humans—continually wears away the sedimentary rock. This ensures a continuing exposure of the rock and of any fossils within the rock.

The last step is to continually search the area, which often leads to spotting an exposed bone or other fossil part. This may all sound very simple, but it is not: patience and perseverance are the key ingredients at this stage of the search. Once the paleontologist makes a dinosaur or other fossil find, then the excavation, transportation, and restoration processes begin.

How can **geologic maps** be obtained?

Geologic maps can be obtained through many sources. In particular, there are topographic maps published by the United States Geological Survey. These maps can also be obtained, although at less quality, from the government agency's Internet site, which you can find in the next chapter of this book.

> ## What is a dig site?
>
> **A** dig site is a localized area where numerous fossil remains are found and excavated by paleontologists. For example, if a herd of dinosaurs drowned while crossing a flood-swollen river, their bodies could have been deposited in a bend of the river. There, their bodies would be quickly covered over with mud, and fossilization would take place. Millions of years later, if a fossil collector discovered a few exposed fossils—and subsequent exploratory digging uncovered a large amount of fossils—then the area would become an active dig site.
>
> A site where excavation is currently ongoing (or was worked in the past) is generally referred to as a quarry—after all, fossil hunters are digging into the rock! Many times these quarries are named after the collectors who found the first fossil remains there. Others are named after nearby towns.

Where are **dinosaur dig sites** usually **located**?

Dinosaur remains can be found worldwide—from the barren deserts of Mongolia to the cold slopes of the Antarctic. This is because, at the time dinosaurs roamed the land, all of today's landmasses were connected or close by—allowing dinosaurs to freely move about.

Still, all dinosaur dig sites have something in common: the action of natural or human agents have eroded the land, exposing the buried, fossil-bearing rock to the light of day. In many cases, the best place to discover the first bones that signal a major find is where this erosional action continues today. In the Gobi Desert, the passing of another sandstorm means a fresh batch of bones will be waiting on the surface. Bases of sea cliffs, where the water batters the rock during high tides or storms, will have new fossils exposed. Areas of heavy downpours, flash flooding, and excavation in a commercial quarry are all good places to find the bones that will trigger the start of the formal digging process.

What **methods** do paleontologists use to find **buried dinosaur bones**?

Predicting where dinosaur bones lie beneath the surface of the ground is a very difficult task, and for many years this process has depended on the experience and intuition of the field worker. If a paleontologist knew where dinosaur bones and skeletons were precisely located underground, this would eliminate many of the current hit-and-miss searches for new discoveries. And it would make excavations of known locations much more efficient.

Park service staff at Utah's Dinosaur National Monument chip rock away from dinosaur bones in a fossil bed. (Photo courtesy of James L. Amos/Corbis.)

There are currently no methods specifically developed to find dinosaur bones beneath the ground. But there are a few instruments paleontologists have adapted from diverse fields such as hydrology and archaeology to search rock layers for clues. Some of the most promising ones include ground-penetrating radar; acoustic diffraction tomography; proton free precession magnetometry; and radiation detection using scintillation counters.

Unfortunately, all of these techniques have limitations: none of them can give the paleontologist an "X-ray of the ground" to reveal the location of buried bones. And an experienced engineer is needed to operate the equipment, understand the theory behind the instrument's design, and interpret the generated data.

How do paleontologists use **ground-penetrating radar**?

Ground-penetrating radar is a technique in which radio waves are transmitted deep into the ground from a lawnmower-sized mobile unit. Some of these waves are reflected and travel back to the surface, where they are detected, recorded, and printed out. There are various reasons why the radio waves are reflected, including changes in the types of rock, cracks in the ground, changes in the amount of water in the rock, or a boundary between rock and a dinosaur bone. It takes considerable talent and intuition to figure out which reflections are due to the presence of dinosaur bones, and which reflections are not. And there are no positive images of bones produced by this technique—just indications of possible sites.

What is **acoustic diffraction tomography**?

Acoustic diffraction tomography is also known as seismic tomography. And it is a technique that cannot, by any stretch of the imagination, be called subtle—at least not in its execution. An instrument known as a "betsy" (essentially a high-powered 8-gauge Magnum shotgun mounted on wheels) is used to fire a lead slug into the ground at a predetermined point. This generates a seismic shock wave in all directions. The wave is detected by hydrophones suspended in vertical, pipe-lined, water-filled holes dug deep into the ground—preferably twice as deep as the suspected location of any bones.

A paleontologist exposes dinosaur tracks in a Mojave formation at the Dinosaur Trackway Site in the Painted Desert near Cameron, Arizona. (Photo courtesy of Tom Bean/Corbis.)

The exact arrival time of the shock wave is recorded by the hydrophones. Any discrepancy in arrival time, whether too slow or too fast, can indicate the presence of something buried between the hydrophones and the site where the "betsy" was fired. If slugs are fired into the ground at different places, the results, along with geometric calculations, can give the paleontologist an idea of where and how deep to dig, and the approximate size of the object. But again, short of digging, there is no real way of knowing whether or not the object is a dinosaur bone.

What is **proton free precession magnetometry**?

This technique measures the differences in the intensity of the earth's magnetic field along a predetermined grid. The instrument is very precise, and has the advantage of being portable; it is mounted on a pole and can be carried in the field. Because the magnetic properties of buried dinosaur bones can be different from the surrounding rock (due to their chemical composition), differences in the magnetic field intensity may mean there are bones beneath the surface. However, materials other than dinosaur bones may also produce these differences—leading paleontologists to fall back on the tried-and-true method of excavation to determine the cause of the anomalous readings.

What is **radiation detection** with **scintillation counters**?

Scintillation counters are instruments sensitive enough to detect the radiation coming from objects below the surface. Some dinosaur bones, because of the location in which they were buried, may contain radioactive isotopes of uranium. These isotopes decay over time, producing radiation levels above the normal background level for that area. These slight increases can be detected by the scintillation counters. However, this technique is only useful for bones that are buried at very shallow depths below the surface.

How has a newly invented instrument called a **scintillation counter** been used to find dinosaur bones?

Although past attempts to develop an effective scintillation counter instrument to locate dinosaur bones have failed, an amateur inventor and radiation analyst recently invented one that does work—and it works very well! The instrument containing the scintillation counter is placed on a handcart and pushed across the ground like a lawnmower; similar to a Geiger counter, it clicks as it detects radiation. The areas of increased radiation, or "hot spots," are noted and mapped on a grid. After the background radiation is filtered out, the remaining hot spots are areas where dinosaur bones are present—and can be dug out by paleontologists.

Has the **scintillation counter** instrument **found any** new dinosaur **species**?

Yes, using this recently invented device, two new dinosaur species have been discovered in Utah. They are a duck-billed hadrosaur and a nodosaur from the Cretaceous period. The discovery of these animals will give paleontologists information about a relatively unknown period in Utah's history, which ranged from about 150 million years ago, the time of the large sauropods, to approximately 70 million years ago, during the time of the *Triceratops* and *Tyrannosaurus rex*. The recently discovered dinosaurs will be named after the inventor, and his wife and assistant.

These fossilized dinosaur bones lie exposed in the rock that formed around them at the Dinosaur Quarry in Dinosaur National Monument, Utah. (Photo courtesy David Muench/Corbis.)

How is **modern technology** helping map and study **dinosaur fossil** finds?

At a dig site, the exact location of fossil discoveries can now be determined using the global positioning systems (GPS)— instruments that use satellite technology to pinpoint a location on Earth. This technique eliminates errors due to poor maps, shifting landmarks, and inaccurate compass readings. The orientation and distribution of the fossil bones in all three dimensions can also be obtained using electronic distance measurement (EDM) and other survey devices. (There are also some high-resolution GPS devices capable of providing this data.) These instruments minimize the errors inherent in using compasses and tape measures.

There is another advantage to using these techniques: the data can be fed directly into a computer. With the help of such programs as geographic information systems (GIS) and computer-aided design (CAD), a three-dimensional map of a quarry site, showing the location and orientation of all the bones, can be generated. The paleontologist can then study the site from different orientations, attempting to answer questions such as: What social structure did these dinosaurs have? Or, what caused dinosaur bones to be concentrated in this location?

How do paleontologists **dig for dinosaurs**?

Once an initial bone find has been made and evaluated, and the decision made to dig further, the process of excavating the rest of the bones commences. This is, contrary to the perception given in the media, a long, hard, labor-intensive practice, especially if the dinosaur was large, and a complete skeleton is present. The overlying rock must first be removed, using appropriate tools. These tools can range from dynamite, bulldozers, and jackhammers to picks and shovels. Once this overlying layer has been removed, finer tools, such as dental picks and toothbrushes, are used to expose the

A dinosaur dig site. (Photo courtesy of James L. Amos/Corbis.)

upper bone surfaces. To prevent these exposed bones from drying out, cracking, or oxidizing, they are stabilized by applying appropriate chemical hardeners.

The exposed bone surfaces are then completely mapped, and a plan for the excavation of the entire skeleton is made. The first step is to isolate each bone, or group of bones, by digging vertical trenches around each, leaving a substantial thickness of rock in place for protection. Any bones exposed on the sides by this trenching should be stabilized, and each bone must be numbered with permanent ink and recorded on the map records.

The exposed bones on the top and sides are covered with layers of damp newspapers, tissues, or paper towels; then, top and sides are covered with a jacket of plaster-soaked burlap strips. When dry, this jacket locks the bones into the rock, preventing any cracking or damage. Next, the rock on the underside of this block is carefully removed, a little bit at a time. Any exposed bones are again stabilized, and the newly exposed areas are jacketed. Pieces of wood or metal are used to prop up the jacketed block as the amount of rock on the underside is slowly reduced.

Once this rock is small enough, and all of the rest of the block has been jacketed, the block can be turned over. But before that, labels are placed on the jacket using permanent ink, indicating the mapping number for each bone inside, an orientation arrow, the date, the site name and number, and any other information needed by the museum for restoration. After the block has been turned over, any remaining exposed

Who first developed a method to protect excavated dinosaur bones?

Not only did a plethora of dinosaur bones come out of the rivalry between American paleontologists Edward Drinker Cope (1840–97) and O. C. Marsh (1831–91), but new methods to protect the precious excavated dinosaur bones were also developed. For example, Cope's crew preserved fossils using jackets of burlap bags dipped in a paste of overcooked rice. This pasty rice mix was slathered over the burlap covering the bone; as it dried, it hardened enough to allow the bones to be safely shipped back to the eagerly awaiting scientist.

area of rock is jacketed—and this bone or group of bones is ready for transportation to the museum.

What is **grid mapping**?

Grid mapping is a standardized method for recording the positions of bones found at a dinosaur dig. Long pegs are notched at equal intervals along their length, usually at every 4 inches (10 centimeters); they are pounded into the ground around the outside of the fossil discovery. These pegs are placed at 1-yard (1-meter) intervals, forming a square or rectangle around the fossil of interest. The pegs must be pounded into the ground to the same heights so they are level. String then connects all the pegs; the string is attached to the first, or highest, notches on each peg. This forms a large grid with many squares measuring 1 yard (1 meter) on each side.

A survey grid consists of a wood frame 1 yard (1 meter) square that holds a wire mesh with 4-inch (10-centimeter) squares. It is placed in one of the larger string grids on top of the fossil remains. Then the paleontologist uses graph paper to draw (to scale) what he or she sees beneath each of the smaller wire mesh squares. This process is repeated for each large square by moving the survey grid frame. When all of the grid squares have been mapped, the string is removed, and the excavation continues down to the next notch on each peg. The mapping process is repeated for this layer—and any subsequent layers—until the fossil is removed. This gives a "three-dimensional map" of the excavated fossils and the site.

Why is **grid mapping** important?

The grid mapping process may be long and tedious, but the recorded information is crucial to the paleontologist. The position in which the dinosaur was found may give information about its morphology, and how it lived. The relative positions of the bones often form the basis for reconstruction of the skeleton. Any other fossils around the

A park service worker chips rock away from dinosaur bones at Dinosaur National Monument, located in Utah and Colorado. (Photo courtesy of James L. Amos/Corbis.)

bones are also helpful: shells, plant material, or other bones may give clues as to what this dinosaur ate, and what other creatures existed at the same time. If there are enough clues, paleontologists can reconstruct how the animal died and became fossilized. Unless this important data is recorded during the excavation, such details will be lost.

What types of **tools** are used at **dinosaur digs**?

There are a large variety of tools used at dig sites. But the excavation of any one fossil is a unique process—and may only require a few of them. Also, different stages of the excavation process may require different tools. With that in mind, the following table provides a general list of the major tools that might come in handy at dig sites. (Note: Some dig sites may be miles from roads, with tools carried in—so light weight and multiple uses are important considerations.)

Tool	Comments
Shovel or spade	A lightweight model is used for digging out loose material.
Geologic hammer	These hammers have a square at one end and a chisel or pick at the other end. They are indispensable, general-purpose tools.
Club hammer	This tool is used for hitting heavy chisels. Geologic hammers are often substituted for this tool.
Rock saw and stonemason's chisels	These are chisels with an assortment of blade widths. They are used for removing rock from around fossil.
Trowel or old knife	Trowels or old knives are used to scrape away soft rock.

Tool	Comments
Brushes	All types of brushes, from tooth- to paintbrushes, are used on a dig. They are good for removing loose rock.
Strainer or sieve	Strainers or sieves are useful for separating small fossil pieces from loose rock or washing samples.

What kind of **clothing and equipment** is taken into the field?

The best clothing and equipment would be similar to hiking or rock-hunting clothes and equipment. Of course, the clothing and equipment must be suitable for the local environment. For example, clothing for a dinosaur dig in the Gobi Desert would be much different than for one in Antarctica. And equipment needed for a day dig at a local quarry would be different than the equipment needed for a months-long expedition in a remote part of the world.

The following table provides a general guide to clothing and equipment; it is by no means complete. If people are inexperienced in hiking or working in the outdoors, professionals recommend that they seek more specific advice from those who are experienced—such as geologists, backpackers, paleontologists, and mountain climbers. There are numerous books on preparing for the outdoors, and outdoor stores can be gold mines of advice. Also, many organizations sponsoring dinosaurs digs have lists of required clothing and equipment to use as guidelines.

The following is a list of the proper clothing need to engage in any type of digging situation.

Clothing and Equipment	Comments
Appropriate clothing for weather and local conditions	Long-sleeved shirts, T-shirts, shorts, long pants, sweaters, jackets, underwear. Temperature can be controlled through the shedding or adding of multiple layers of clothing. Diggers should take enough for the length of the expedition.
Backpack	Used to carry tools, food, water, and extra clothing.
Sturdy boots	For hiking to the dig site and for protection from falling rocks and hard surfaces.
Gloves	For hand protection during digs. Also to keep hands warm in colder climates.
Safety helmet	Protection from falling rocks if working in an area with cliffs, or collecting in a working quarry.
Rain gear	Protection from getting wet; can also be used to stay warm.
Flashlight	For illumination at night or under dark overhangs.
Hat	Protection from sun or rain. Use when there is no danger from falling rocks.
Sunglasses/sunblock	Protection from the sun's ultraviolet rays.

Clothing and Equipment	Comments
Goggles	Eye protection from flying rock chips.
Canteens	For carrying water in remote areas.
Camera/video camera	To record excavation of fossils.
Compass/map	For finding directions in remote locations.
First aid kit	In case of injury or other medical emergencies.
Tent/sleeping bag/cooking gear	For shelter, rest, and cooking food at remote site.

How are **dinosaur fossils distinguishable** from other fossils?

There are a number of ways amateur diggers can determine if a fossil is from a dinosaur. There are numerous fossil guides and books that describe fossil identities. It's helpful to have some knowledge of taxonomy (the classification of plants and animals) as well as a general knowledge of biology and geology.

Fossil clubs, colleges, universities, and natural history museums can also help with fossil identification. Often museum and university personnel will help their patrons identify fossils, although sometimes a fee may be charged for this service. If they cannot identify the fossils, they often provide referrals.

If the fossil does not correspond to anything known, it might be a new dinosaur species. In this case, the finding is very important to scientific knowledge, and the fossil founder may be asked to donate the specimen to the museum or university for their collection—not only for the collection but for additional scientific study. The founder's name might even be used as the basis for the scientific name of the new species—which many people find exciting! Also, amateurs might be asked to assist with further excavation at the dig site.

Can **amateurs find dinosaur fossils** of new or important species?

With the right tools and knowledge of where to look, amateurs are just as competent at finding dinosaur fossils as professional paleontologists. In fact, most dinosaur finds are made by amateur collectors. This is mainly because there are far more amateurs who have time to devote to searches. There are numerous examples from around the world of discoveries made by amateurs that have led to profound leaps in scientists' knowledge of dinosaurs.

Who recently discovered the remains of the **oldest known horned dinosaur**?

Christopher Wolfe, an eight-year-old third-grader from Phoenix, Arizona, discovered the remains of the oldest known horned dinosaur during a trip to western New Mexico. As he climbed up a hill, he was attracted to a blackish purple object on the ground, which turned out to be a fossilized piece of the small horn that protected the dinosaur's eye. The rest of the fossilized remains include jaw parts, teeth, brain case, and other pieces. The dinosaur was approximately 90 million years old—the oldest known horned dinosaur—and was named *Zuniceratops christopheri* after its discoverer.

Dinosaur bone fossils at Dinosaur National Monument in Colorado. (Photo courtesy of Tom Bean/Corbis.)

Why are **construction sites** important to the **discovery** of dinosaur fossils?

In some areas, construction sites are important because they expose layers of dinosaur fossil–containing rock that would otherwise remain buried beneath the surface. For example, the Denver, Colorado, area has few natural outcrops with eroded dinosaur bones. Construction sites in this area are an important manmade substitute for the natural actions of uplifting and erosion—allowing discoveries to be made that would not otherwise be possible.

What **problems** are associated with dinosaur discoveries at **construction sites**?

One problem that occurs when dinosaur fossils are found at a construction site is the reluctance of the crews to report the findings. This happens because they fear that the project might be canceled to protect the bones. For example, during the 1970s, a construction crew putting in a pipeline around Denver uncovered many dinosaur bones— but didn't tell anyone. Only long after the project was completed, and it was too late, did a worker report the findings.

Paleontologists are now working with contractors to allay their fears of being shut down if dinosaur fossils are found on a construction site. Scientists can step in to remove the precious bones—and the construction can then proceed.

Are **road** and **railway cuts** important places to find dinosaur fossils?

Yes, road and railway cuts are important places to finding dinosaur fossils. Similar to construction sites, these cuts can expose dinosaur bone–containing rock to view, and erosion continually brings new material to the surface. Many fossils, dinosaur and otherwise, have been discovered at these manmade sites.

What are some examples in which amateurs found dinosaur sites?

One good example is the site of what is now the Mygatt-Moore Quarry near Fruita, Colorado: it was discovered on a late March hike in 1981, by Grand Junction, Colorado, residents Pete and Marilyn Mygatt, and J. D. and Vanetta Moore. They were amateur rock and fossil hunters who had "cabin fever" that day—and decided to go for a hike near the Utah border. During a lunch break, Pete Mygatt noticed a rock and picked it up. It split apart, revealing a partial tail vertebra of what was later identified as an *Apatosaurus*. This site is now named the Mygatt-Moore Quarry, and has yielded eight species of dinosaurs, including *Mymoorapelta,* a small armored dinosaur, and the first ankylosaur from the Jurassic period found in North America.

Another example is Rob Gaston, a local Fruita, Colorado, artist who found some of the earliest dinosaur tracks in western Colorado. His discoveries led to the discovery of the Gaston Quarry, where the *Utahraptor* was subsequently found.

How can paleontologists determine the **location** where a **dinosaur actually died**?

One of the main problems paleontologists have is determining where a dinosaur actually died—in other words, where the animal was originally buried. Did the animal die and was buried at the site where the bones were found? Or were the bones later transported to the site, perhaps by the action of water?

For many years, the only way to determine the original burial location was to observe the amount of abrasion on the bones. Dinosaur bones without much abrasion were probably found close to the original site of burial; those bones with a large amount of abrasion had probably been moved over a relatively long distance. But there are problems associated with using the amount of abrasion on the bones as a clue. It turns out that the amount of abrasion can be influenced by the degree of weathering, the freshness of the bone, and other factors.

What **new method** is being used to determine a fossil bone's **original burial place**?

A new geochemical technique is now being used to determine a fossil bone's original burial site. This technique analyzes the rare earth elements present in bones and the surrounding sedimentary rock; rare earth elements are normally present in rocks and soil in small amounts.

Dinosaur bones contain calcium phosphate (apatite) and proteins. When the animal dies, the protein rots away. After burial, the calcium phosphate reforms into a slightly different crystalline structure, and rare earth elements in the surrounding soil may replace some of the calcium ions in the bone structure. The relative proportions of the different rare earth elements present in a bone are a signature that is established soon after burial—and remains fixed. If the rare earth element signature in a bone matches the surrounding sediment, it is likely that this was the original site of burial. However, if the signature of the bone is different from the surrounding sediment, then it is likely the bone was transported from its original burial site.

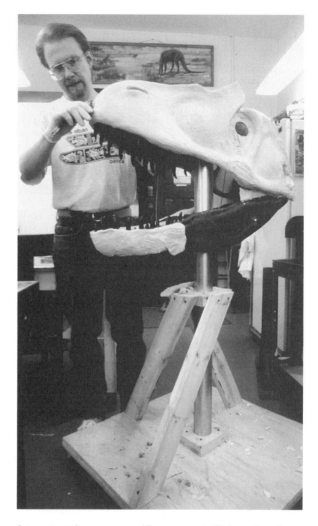

A museum worker prepares an *Allosaurus* mount. (Photo courtesy of University of Michigan Exhibit, Museum of Natural History.)

Where has the **rare earth element technique** been used to study **bones**?

The rare earth element technique has been used on bone samples from the Rhaetic Bone Bed located in Great Britain, a late Triassic period marine unit. Bone and sediment samples were analyzed from Aust, near Bristol, and from the Westbury Garden Cliff, located on the other side of the River Severn. The Aust samples appeared heavily abraded, while the Westbury samples were almost free of wear. The rare earth element signatures from the Westbury bones and sediment were the same, suggesting that this was the original burial site; the signatures from the bones and sediment from Aust were different, suggesting the bones had been transported from somewhere else.

Interestingly enough, this analysis also found the signatures of bones from both Aust and Westbury were the same. This suggests the Aust bones were buried first in an

383

environment similar to Westbury—if not Westbury itself—then later uncovered and transported to the Aust location!

PUTTING DINOSAURS TOGETHER

What happens to **excavated dinosaur bones** after they reach a museum?

It depends on whether or not the museum or institute plans to exhibit the find in the near future. If there are no immediate plans for the bones, they will be placed in safe storage until time and funds are available for their preparation. However, if the skeleton is to be put on display relatively quickly—as in the case of a new, spectacular species—then the bones will go through a fairly standard preparation process.

Simply put, the bones must be removed from the encasing rock during the preparation process. Next, any missing parts must be identified and substitutes found. Lastly, the bones are attached together and the entire skeleton is mounted for display. This process is tedious and time consuming. For example, it took seven years of work until the *Apatosaurus* at the American Museum of Natural History was exhibited to the public.

How are **dinosaur bones prepared** for study and display?

The process of preparing dinosaur bones excavated from the field is generally done in a laboratory, where a wide variety of tools and chemicals are available. The first step in preparation is to remove the rock from around the bones, using hand tools, dental picks, needles, microscopes, small pneumatic tools—or anything else that does the job. This technique is laborious and exacting, and can only be mastered through hours of hands-on experience.

Once the bones are exposed, they are repaired, if necessary, and stabilized to prevent further degradation. There are a wide variety of glues and adhesives that serve this purpose. Weak or cracked bones may require the addition of structural supports, such as fiberglass or steel bands.

How are **dinosaur bones mounted** for display?

Once the fossilized dinosaur bones have been prepared and stabilized—and any missing pieces obtained or substituted—the skeleton is ready to be free-mounted. The purpose of the mounted dinosaur is to display the skeleton as it might have looked in real life.

A paleontologist works at cleaning and preparing this dinosaur mount for display. (Photo courtesy of Corbis.)

As with any large-scale project, the first step involves planning. Sketches and scale models are made, showing what the display will look like. Any variations to the posture—perhaps to reflect new information or to make the display more lifelike—can be made at this stage, avoiding costly changes during actual assembly. The sketches and models will also show whether the skeleton will fit into its designated exhibition space. It would be very costly and time consuming—not to mention embarrassing—to find out during assembly that the skeleton does not "fit." A good, final sketch can also be used as a guide during the actual assembly, as well as showing where extra support is needed.

Next, a strong steel armature is constructed and the individual dinosaur bones attached to it—in their proper places, of course. The armature is custom made to provide enough support, but shaped to be unobtrusive. Because dinosaur bones are very brittle, no stress can be placed on them; the armature is designed to support the weight of all the bones. Attachment of the bones to the armature is made using pins, bolts, or steel straps. Sometimes, it becomes necessary to hang cables from above to provide more support for parts of the skeleton.

Once the entire skeleton is mounted, there are still a few more details: the base on which the skeleton rests must be made visually appealing; barriers must be placed around the mount to protect it from the curious; and labels and display information created and positioned. At last, the dinosaur skeleton, which has remained hidden for millions of years, is ready to be viewed by the public.

When a dinosaur skeleton considered for exhibition has missing bones (which is the case for the vast majority of fossil finds), these bones must be restored. This is accomplished in a variety of ways. Some missing bones can be replaced with fossil bones or casts from another individual of the same dinosaur species; two or more partial skeletons can be combined to produce one complete skeleton, which is often done; or, if these methods cannot be used, the missing bones can be sculpted from a variety of materials such as wood, epoxy, or ceramic.

Do **dinosaur bones** ever get **"rearranged"** after they are mounted?

Yes, dinosaur bones have been rearranged after they were mounted. This is because the field of dinosaur study is constantly changing as more bones are found, or more studies are made. For example, in early 1999, scientists designed a computer model of a sauropod dinosaur—the animals with a neck up to 40 feet (12 meters) in length. Most of these dinosaurs were posed by museums with long S-shaped necks that would allow them to reach high into the tall trees to gather leaves. But the computer model indicated that the animals could not lift their heavy necks—the vertebrae were too heavy. These dinosaurs probably kept their necks straight out and may have chewed on lower-lying shrubs. Thus many museums may be rearranging their sauropod mounts in the future to more accurately reflect the shape scientists believe was the "true shape" of a sauropod's neck.

How will **modern technology** help paleontologists **prepare, reproduce,** and **study** dinosaur fossil finds in the near future?

New technologies are rapidly changing the way paleontologists prepare, reproduce, and study dinosaur fossils. For example, computer-aided tomography (CAT) uses X-rays to generate a three-dimensional image of an internal structure of an object. In fact, it has already been used to determine if fossilized eggs contain baby dinosaur remains. Only those rocks containing fossils, or those eggs that contain baby dinosaurs, will be prepared, eliminating much of the destructive guess work. In the near future, lab workers will also have a three-dimensional image of a specimen to help them in the preparation process.

Once fossil remains have been prepared, precise measurements will be made using new instruments such as electronic calipers, or two- and three-dimensional digitizers. This data will be sent directly to a computer, which will guide machinery to automatically

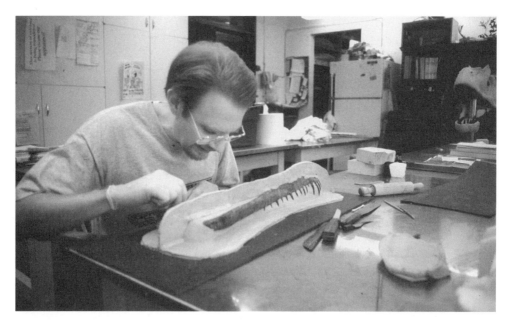

The initial stages of preparing a pterosaur mount. (Photo courtesy of University of Michigan Exhibit, Museum of Natural History.)

generate reproductions of the remains in materials such as metal or plastic. This will make highly accurate casts available to more scientists—and the public—at lower costs. Another exciting possibility: three-dimensional data might be obtained from such nondestructive techniques as CAT, allowing paleontologists to make highly accurate reproductions of dinosaur fossils—without ever removing the fragile bones from the encasing rock!

The research into dinosaur behavior and physiology will be greatly enhanced by the combined use of three-dimensional imaging, modeling, and virtual reality. Scientists will be able to study individual specimens, or even complete skeletons, from any angle or view—perhaps even from the inside looking out. And with data stored on computers, pale-ontologists will have much quicker access to rare specimens. Such systems as the World Wide Web (WWW) will allow scientists to study a rare specimen on the computer—without having to travel to the few museums and institutions that house the actual fossils.

GETTING EDUCATED

Where can those interested obtain more **education** in **dinosaur paleontology**?

There are numerous opportunities available at all levels for those interested in more education and experience in dinosaur paleontology. Colleges and universities often   387

A museum worker cleans the fossilized remains of an *Albertosaurus* in the laboratory at the Royal Tyrrell Museum in Alberta, Canada. (Photo courtesy of Michael S. Yamashita/Corbis.)

offer courses in this specific subject, or the field of paleontology in general. Most colleges will allow a person to audit a course or take courses for credit even if he or she is not working toward a degree. If the student is really ambitious, he or she can take courses that could lead to a degree in paleontology, with an emphasis on dinosaurs. Some organizations offer formal instruction in conjunction with dinosaur digs—and often for college credit.

Because of the interest in fossil collecting in general—and dinosaurs in particular—some museums and colleges are starting programs geared toward "professionalizing" the amateur fossil collector. These programs are intended to give the amateur the same level of practical field knowledge as the professional paleontologist. They can be certification programs—or can even lead to an associate's degree.

What **formal studies** are required to become a **professional paleontologist**?

The field of paleontology is an interdisciplinary field, requiring knowledge from many other fields of science; for example, biology, geology, physics, and chemistry. Because the field requires a broad range of knowledge, there are relatively few educational institutions that offer degrees in paleontology, or in the more specialized field of dinosaur paleontology. However, while the goal is challenging, it is not impossible.

Paleontologists clean and prepare dinosaur fossils for display. (Photo courtesy of Philippe Plailly/Photo Researchers Inc.)

For high school students, the best strategy would be to take as many science and math courses as possible, such as physics, chemistry, biology, geology, computers, calculus, and algebra. A foreign language would also be helpful. The student should also read as much as possible on fossils and dinosaurs; visit museums with dinosaur displays; talk to dinosaur paleontologists for information; and perhaps volunteer to participate in dinosaur digs.

In college, the more science courses you take, the better. Most paleontologists have degrees in zoology or geology, and some have degrees in both. Zoology is useful for understanding the biology and taxonomy (classification) of animals, in this case dinosaurs; geology is needed to understand the fossil environment, as well as interpreting the natural processes that occurred when the animal lived. A double major in zoology and geology would be ideal; but if that is not possible, a major in one and minor in the other would suffice. Any other course to broaden the student's knowledge would be useful, such as statistical analysis and ecology. Conversing with professional paleontologists would help give the student a working knowledge about the field of paleontology, how it works, and what is required to succeed in the field.

Most professional paleontologists have advanced degrees; a master's degree or Ph.D. in paleontology can be obtained at a few universities. The student should carefully research the particular emphasis at their chosen school and check out the academic interests of the faculty, making sure there is a match with the student's own interests.

What does a professional paleontologist do?

The work of a professional paleontologist varies, depending on where he or she works. Most paleontologists in the United States are college or university professors; some also work in museums, as independent consultants, or for government surveys.

In general, professional paleontologists can conduct research, and write and publish academic research papers. They also curate, catalogue, and inventory fossils in a museum or university. They can run a research program, teach, or engage in a combination of these activities. Most of this work requires an advanced degree, although there are notable exceptions.

For people with undergraduate degrees, paleontology work can include preparing fossils, excavating and collecting fossils, mounting specimens for display, and casting specimens.

Where can those interested get information about **participating in dinosaur digs**?

The best way for novices to obtain education, training, and experience is to participate in an organized dig. Depending on the program, there are opportunities ranging from one-day digs in pleasant surroundings, to longer expeditions in distant lands like Mongolia. Some programs include formal instruction for college credit—so amateurs are encouraged to check the details of the program in which they are interested.

The choices of dinosaur digs are limitless and can sometimes seem overwhelming. The programs listed below represent only a sampling of those offered by museums, education institutions, and private concerns. Information about other opportunities can be found on the Internet, or in the classified ad sections of magazines dealing with paleontology, science, or nature. (Note: Some institutions charge fees for participating in the dinosaur digs.)

Exposaur Excursions
Opportunities to dig in the Drumheller area
Box 7500
Drumheller, Alberta, Canada T0J 0Y0
(888) 440-4240; FAX: (403) 823-7131

Dinosaur Research Expeditions
Six-day expeditions to recover fossil eggs and embryos from the badlands of Montana with Vickie Clouse of Montana State University—Northern
(800) 662-6132 ext. 3716

Judith River Dinosaur Institute
Five days of dig site instruction at an established dinosaur site in the Judith River

formation of Montana
Box Y
Mata, Montana 59583
(406) 654-2323

Museum of the Rockies
A variety of programs at Egg Mountain
Montana State University
600 W. Kasy Blvd.
Bozeman, Montana 59717-2730
(406) 994-2251

Timescale Adventures
Hands-on programs at active research sites near the Rocky Mountains
P.O. Box 356
Choteau, Montana 59422

Dinamation International Society Expeditions
Paleontological expeditions to sites around the world
Director of Expeditions
550 Crossroads
Court Fruita, Colorado 81521
(800) DIG-DINO

Wyoming Dinosaur Center
Day-long informational dig with scientists from the Center
P.O. Box 868
Thermopolis, Wyoming 82443
(800) 455-DINO or (307) 864-2997

Western Paleo Safaris
Week-long educational outings in search of fossils in the American West
P.O. Box 1042
Laramie, Wyoming 82073
(888) 875-2233 (PIN 7737)

Grand River Museum
Two-week-long sessions at the Hell Creek formation in South Dakota
Grand River Museum
Lemmon, South Dakota 57638

Are there **certification programs** in the field of dinosaur paleontology?

In response to the growing number of fossil collectors interested in dinosaur paleontology and field work, a number of museums and institutions are offering programs designed to turn amateurs into "para-paleontologists." Students are trained to collect and prepare dinosaur fossils. With this training, some people may make the transition into a full-time paleontological career.

What are some **examples of certification programs**?

The Denver Museum of Natural History in Denver, Colorado, has a Paleontology Certification Program for adults (17 years of age and older). It is offered to people who want to learn more about paleontology and develop skills in the collection and preservation of fossils. Established in 1990, the core certification program includes a series of required courses. These courses provide an introduction to the history of life revealed through the fossil record, and knowledge of the theories and techniques of paleontology. After obtaining the basic Certificate of Competency—which requires completing the mandatory classes, passing a final exam, and receiving approval of a museum committee—the student can continue studies in fossil preparation or field work. After courses in hands-on laboratory methods and a final exam, the student obtains a Lab Specialization Certificate; or, after additional related classwork, six days of actual field work, and a final exam, the student can obtain a Field Specialization Certificate. Some students pursue both areas of interest. Classes are usually held in the evenings, with field trips on the weekends.

Another program is offered by Montana State University—Northern, located in Havre, Montana. The university is starting a program in paleontology technology, with options to earn an associate of science degree in this field, or to have paleontology technology as a minor. These programs will combine an emphasis on scientific research with practical training in this field. Those interested should contact the university at (800) 662-6132 for more information about this proposed program.

LEARNING MORE

RESOURCES

Where is the **best information** on dinosaurs located?

There are numerous resources available about dinosaurs. Most local libraries and bookstores have good selections of the latest dinosaur books. There are museums located around the world with permanent exhibits of dinosaur fossils, skeletons, and reconstructions—and most are extremely informative. Sometimes television specials or movies appear about dinosaurs; many of these can also be obtained in VCR format (often from a local library) for home viewing. In addition, there are traveling exhibits of animated dinosaurs; and there are parks and trails around the world where visitors can travel in the footsteps of early dinosaur explorers—and maybe observe digs still in process. In addition, dinosaur fans can connect to the Internet (either at home or in a local library) and find innumerable sites dealing with dinosaurs and related subjects.

How can dinosaur fans find **dinosaur books** at the library or bookstore?

Many local libraries have a wealth of information about dinosaurs. A card catalog or computer search system is a good place to start gathering information. Library patrons should look under the subject *dinosaurs*. Most of the adult nonfiction books on dinosaurs are located in the science section, with Dewey Decimal numbers ranging from 567.91 to 568.19. Reference librarians are available to assist patrons with this process.

Many juvenile sections of libraries seem to have a large selection of books on dinosaurs, albeit on a less technical level than their adult counterparts. The same Dewey Decimal numbers apply here: with a prefix J (for juvenile), dinosaur aficionados should look in the range 567.91 to 568.19.

A little boy gets a first-hand look at the skull of a *Triceratops* at a museum in Florida. (Photo courtesy of Gregory Smith/Associated Press.)

Additionally, books about dinosaurs are usually found in the science and/or nature section of the local bookstore. There may also be books of a less technical nature (and often more pictorial) found in a separate children's section.

What are some **books** that deal with **general dinosaur information**?

The following is a list of just a few of the books that contain general information about dinosaurs:

Creagh, Carson, Angela C. Milner, and Simone End. *Dinosaurs (The Nature Company Discoveries Library)*. Alexandria, VA: Time Life Books, 1995. Covers diet, possible causes of extinction, coloration, and dinosaurs' relation to birds. Illustrations and diagrams, glossary, index.

Currie, Philip J., and Kevin Padian, editors. *Encyclopedia of Dinosaurs*. San Diego, CA: Academic Press, 1997. Illustrations include color plates; also a chronology of dinosaur history; index.

Dodson, Peter. *The Horned Dinosaurs: A Natural History*. Princeton, New Jersey: Princeton University Press, 1996. Comprehensive study of horned dinosaurs, the rhinoceros-like creatures that were among the last dinosaurs to walk the earth.

Farlow, James O., and M. K. Brett-Surman. *The Complete Dinosaur*. Bloomington, IN: Indiana University Press, 1997. Comprehensive, easy-to-use reference. Illustrations; chronology; glossary. Also, a list of science fiction and fantasy books about dinosaurs.

Glut, Donald F. *Dinosaurs: The Encyclopedia*. Foreword by M. K. Brett-Surman. Jefferson, NC: McFarland & Co., 1997. Heavily illustrated general reference book; 1,000 pages in hardcover. Glossary; index.

The Great Dinosaur Fact File. Cherry Hill, NJ: Dinosaurs to Go!, semiannual. Directory covers all recognized dinosaurs from around the world, including more than 625 dinosaur genera and museums where they are displayed.

Horner, John R., and Don Lessem. *The Complete T rex: How Stunning New Discoveries Are Changing Our Understanding of the World's Most Famous Dinosaur*. New York: Simon & Schuster, 1993. Dinosaur experts cover recent findings and their impact on the science of paleontology.

Horner, John R., and Edwin Dobb. *Dinosaur Lives: Unearthing an Evolutionary Saga*. New York: HarperCollins, 1997. Celebrated paleontologist Horner recounts his discoveries of dinosaur eggs, babies, nests; also examines the impact dinosaurs have on our lives.

Lambert, David. *Dinosaur Data Book: The Definitive Illustrated Encyclopedia of Dinosaurs and Other Prehistoric Reptiles.* Revised and updated edition. New York: Grammercy, 1998. Illustrated factbook; updated to account for recent dinosaur discoveries. Also, information on dinosaurs in popular media.

Norman, David. *Dinosaur! The Definitive Account of the "Terrible Lizards"—from Their First Days on Earth to Their Disappearance 65 Million Years Ago.* Reprint. New York: MacMillan General Reference, 1995. World-renowned paleontologist takes readers on a tour of the Mesozoic era. Covers the latest theories of how dinosaurs lived and theories on their extinction. Full-color illustrations.

Russell, Dale A. *An Odyssey in Time: The Dinosaurs of North America.* Reprint. Toronto: University of Toronto Press, 1992. The curator of the National Museum of Natural Sciences (Ottawa, Ontario) gives a readable, intelligent account of prehistoric North America and its dinosaurs. Color illustrations; maps; bibliography.

Weishampel, David B., Peter Dodson, and Halszka Osmolska. *The Dinosauria (Centennial Book).* Berkeley, CA: University of California Press, 1992. Comprehensive reference book for paleontologists, geologists, students, and serious amateurs. Illustrations; extensive bibliography.

Weishampel, David B., and Luther Young. *Dinosaurs of the East Coast.* Baltimore, MD: Johns Hopkins University Press, 1996. Survey of East Coast dinosaur findings and their importance in recreating the fossil records of dinosaurs in the region. More than 130 illustrations.

What are some **books** explaining dinosaurs' **evolution** and **extinction**?

The question of dinosaur evolution and extinction has been addressed in numerous books. The following are just some examples avid readers might want to check out:

Archibald, J. David. *Dinosaur Extinction and the End of an Era: What the Fossils Say.* New York: Columbia University Press, 1996. Addresses problems with the theory that an asteroid impact caused the extinction of the dinosaurs.

Bakker, R. T. *Dinosaur Heresies: New Theories Unlocking the Mystery of the Dinosaurs and Their Extinction.* Reprint. Kensington Publishing, 1996. Dispels common misconceptions about dinosaurs, presenting new evidence that the creatures were warmblooded, agile, and intelligent.

Dingus, Lowell, and Timothy Rowe. *The Mistaken Extinction: Dinosaur Evolution and the Origin of Birds.* New York: W. H. Freeman, 1997. Examines the theory that dinosaurs didn't disappear; they merely took flight. Illustrations.

Fastovsky, David E., and David B. Weishampel. *The Evolution and Extinction of the Dinosaurs.* Illustrated by Brian Regal. New York: Cambridge University Press, 1996. Highly readable reference presents "dinosaurs as professionals understand them." Illustrations; subject index.

Officer, Charles B., and Jake Page. *The Great Dinosaur Extinction Controversy.* Perseus Press, 1996. Debunks popular theory that a catastrophic collision between earth and a giant meteor caused the extinction of dinosaurs; offers alternative explanations for the mass extinctions at the end of the Cretaceous period.

Powell, James Lawrence. *Night Comes to the Cretaceous: Dinosaur Extinction and the Transformation of Modern Geology.* New York: W. H. Freeman, 1998. Describes the debate over the impact theory.

Shipman, Pat. *Taking Wing: Archaeopteryx and the Evolution of Bird Flight.* New York: Simon & Schuster, 1998. Story of how the 1861 discovery of the fossil skeleton of a transitional bird-reptile changed theories of evolution. Illustrations.

Are there any **books** about **fossils**?

The following are some books about fossils that may be of interest to the general reader:

The Audubon Society Field Guide to North American Fossils. New York: Alfred A. Knopf, 1982. An all-color, illustrated guide to fossils. Includes more than 470 identification pictures and 15 maps.

Fenton, Carroll Lane, and Mildred Adams Fenton. *The Fossil Book.* Revised and expanded edition by Patricia Vickers Rich, Thomas Hewitt Rich, and Mildred Adams Fenton. NewYork: Doubleday, 1958, 1989. Called "the classic work for fossil collectors and enthusiasts." More than 1,500 illustrations.

Lauber, Patricia. *Dinosaurs Walked Here and Other Stories Fossils Tell.* New York: Simon & Schuster, 1987. Through dozens of photos, explains how to identify fossils and tells what they reveal about the prehistoric world.

Webby, B. D., editor. *Fossil Collections of the World: An International Guide.* Lawrence, KS: International Palaeontological Association of the Paleontological Institute. Directory covering institutions and organizations holding fossil collections; includes description of holdings. Index. Published irregularly.

Wolberg, Donald, and Patsy Reinard. *Collecting the Natural World: Legal Requirements and Personal Liability for Collecting Plants, Animals, Rocks, Minerals, and Fossils.* Geoscience, 1995. Discusses all applicable federal and state laws; a reference for the amateur collector.

Are there any dinosaur **field guides**?

The following are few of the dinosaur field guides available:

Costa, Vincenzo. *Dinosaur Safari Guide: Tracking North America's Prehistoric Past.* Stillwater, MN: Voyageur Press, 1994. Complete descriptions of and directions to more than 170 dinosaur and other prehistoric creature sites, museums, fossil exhibits, track sites, and parks in the United States and Canada.

Gaffney, Eugene S. *Dinosaurs.* Illustrated by John Dawson. New York: Golden Books Adult Publishing Company, 1990. A field guide to dinosaurs most likely to be found in museums.

Morell, Mark A., and Eugene Gaffney. *Discovering Dinosaurs in the American Museum of Natural History.* New York: Alfred A. Knopf, 1997. Written by curators at the American Natural History Museum. Guidebook also provides summaries of the museum's dig sites, recounts stories of the paleontologists who discovered the bones, and presents information on 40 specimens. More than 150 illustrations, charts, and maps (in color and black and white).

Wallace, Joseph E. *Dinosaurs: Audubon Society Pocket Guides.* New York: Alfred A. Knopf, 1993. Guide explains the lives and behavior of the world's prehistoric animals; also discusses their extinction. Full-color paintings and skeletal line drawings are from museum specimens around the world. Also includes maps.

Will, Richard, and Margery Read. *Dinosaur Digs: Places Where You Can Discover Prehistoric Creatures.* Castine, ME: Country Roads Press, 1992. A directory of museums and parks; photos.

Are there any **books** about dinosaur **expeditions** and **paleontologists**?

There are numerous books describing the exciting dinosaur expeditions and the fascinating scientists in the field of paleontology. The following is a representative sampling of the books on these subjects:

Colbert, Edwin H. *The Great Dinosaur Hunters and Their Discoveries.* Reprint. New York: Dover Publications, 1984. Includes chapters on first discoveries, skeletons in the earth, two evolutionary streams, the oldest dinosaurs, Jurassic giants of the Western world, Canadian dinosaurs, and Asiatic dinosaurs.

Doescher, Rex A., editor. *Directory of Paleontologists of the World, 5th edition.* Lawrence, KS: International Palaeontological Association, 1989. Lists more than 7,000 paleontologists (name, office address, area of specialization or interest, and affiliation).

Horner, John R., and James Gorman. *Digging Dinosaurs: The Search That Unraveled the Mystery of Baby Dinosaurs.* Reprint. Illustrated by Donna Braginetz and Kris Ellingsen. New York: HarperPerennial, 1996. One of the world's leading paleontologists chronicles the search that unraveled the mystery of baby dinosaurs. The book is credited with revolutionizing the way people think about dinosaurs; considered a classic.

Jacobs, Louis L. *Quest for the African Dinosaurs: Ancient Roots of the Modern World.* New York: Villard Books, 1993. After discovering a major fossil site in Malawi (Africa), Jacobs and his team went on to identify 13 kinds of vertebrate animals that "give a window into the world of this part of Africa 100 million years ago."

Lessem, Don. *Kings of Creation: How a New Breed of Scientists Is Revolutionizing Our Understanding of Dinosaurs.* Illustrated by John Sibbick. New York: Simon & Schuster, 1992. Dinosaur expert Lessem takes readers on a journey through dinosaur time.

Novacek, Michael. *Dinosaurs of the Flaming Cliffs.* Illustrated by Ed Heck. New York: Anchor Books/Doubleday, 1996. Chronicles the groundbreaking discoveries made by one of the largest dinosaur expeditions of the late twentieth century.

Psihoyos, Louie, and John Knoebber. *Hunting Dinosaurs.* New York: Random House, 1994. Recounts the experiences of paleontologists who have scoured remote lands in search of evidence of dinosaurs. Full-color photos; charts and maps.

Are there any dinosaur **books** that are suitable for **children** and **families**?

There are a large number of books that are suitable for the whole family and children of all ages. The following is a listing of some of these books:

Arnold, Caroline. *Dinosaurs All Around: An Artist's View of the Prehistoric World.* Photos by Richard Hewett. New York: Clarion Books, 1993. Through illustrations, the reader is taken on a visit to a workshop where a life-size dinosaur model is being constructed. Information about dinosaurs and how conclusions are made from the study of fossils.

Benton, Michael J. *Dinosaur and Other Prehistoric Animals Fact Finder.* New York: Kingfisher Books, 1992. Alphabetical guide to 200 dinosaurs and other prehistoric creatures.

Benton, Michael J. *The Penguin Historical Atlas of the Dinosaurs.* London: Penguin Books, 1996. Plots the development of dinosaurs from their emergence from the ocean, their dispersal across the shifting continents, and their gradual evolution, to their sudden and mysterious extinction 64 million years ago. More than 60 full-color maps; more than 70 illustrations (color and black and white); index.

Cooper, John A. *Dinosaurs* (CD-ROM). Illustrated by Chris Leishman. New York: Smithmark Publishers, 1997. Interactive multimedia product.

Dixon, Dougal. *Dinosaur: An Interactive Guide to the Dinosaur World.* New York: DK Publishing, 1994. Action pack includes book, press-out scale model, 3-D diorama, wall chart, and game for ages 9 to 12; hands-on learning.

Eldredge, Niles, Douglas Eldredge, and Gregory Eldredge. *The Fossil Factory: A Kid's Guide to Digging Up Dinosaurs, Exploring Evolution and Finding Fossils.* Reading, MA: Addison-Wesley Longman, 1989. Covers facts about the earth's life-forms; includes activities and a guide to more than 50 sites where children can look for fossils.

Kitamura, Satoshi. *Paper Dinosaurs: A Cut-Out Book.* New York: Farrar, Straus & Giroux, 1995. Kids ages 8 to 11 can create their own world of dinosaurs.

Kricher, John C. *Peterson First Guides: Dinosaurs.* Illustrated by Gordon Morrison. New York: Houghton Mifflin, 1990. Gives the names and characteristics of dinosaurs and covers theories about how they lived. Field guide format useful for museum visits.

Lambert, David, and John H. Ostrom. *The Ultimate Dinosaur Book.* New York: DK Publishing, 1993. A-to-Z dinosaur dictionary covers all known species of dinosaurs; full color photos, diagrams, and illustrations.

Lindsay, William. *On the Trail of Incredible Dinosaurs.* New York: DK Publishing, 1998. Published in association with the American Museum of Natural History. Covers four dinosaurs. Photographs of realistic scale models bring creatures to life. Full color.

Lindsay, William. *Tyrannosaurus.* New York: DK Publishing, 1993. Published in association with the American Museum of Natural History, Lindsay describes the discovery and excavation of fossil evidence for the *Tyrannosaurus.*

Norman, David. *The Humongous Book of Dinosaurs.* New York: Stewart, Tabori and Chang, 1997. Describes all known dinosaurs, their world, and the scientists who study them. Includes special glasses for viewing the 3-D illustrations.

Norman, David. *The Illustrated Encyclopedia of Dinosaurs.* New York: Random House Value Publishing, 1995. Heavily illustrated book covers 68 dinosaurs. Glossary.

Parker, Steve. *Dinosaurs and How They Lived.* Illustrated by Guiliano Fornari Sergio. New York: DK Publishing, 1991. Parker traces discoveries of recent years, describing breakthroughs and changes in our understanding of these creatures. Full color. For young readers.

Parker, Steve. *Inside Dinosaurs and Other Prehistoric Creatures.* Illustrated by Ted Dewan. New York: Delacorte Press, 1994. Cutaway color illustrations take kids on a guided tour of the anatomy of dinosaurs.

Pearce, Q. L. *How to Talk Dinosaur with Your Child.* Los Angeles: Lowell House, 1991. Explains how parents can share dinosaur facts with their children and foster a love of science.

Stevenson, Jay, and McGhee, George R. *The Complete Idiot's Guide to Dinosaurs.* Alpha Books, 1998. As the book says, a complete guide to dinosaurs, including descriptions of more than 300 known dinosaur species.

Walker, Cyril, and David Ward. *Fossils.* New York: DK Publishing, 1992. Eyewitness Handbook covers 500 vertebrate, invertebrate, and plant fossils, including descriptions, informal names, range, distribution, and occurrence.

Whitfield, Philip. *Macmillan Children's Guide to Dinosaurs and Other Prehistoric Animals.* New York: Simon & Schuster Children's, 1992. For ages 7 to 10. Describes the pre-historic animals that lived in different parts of the world during each geological period, from the Triassic through the Cretaceous.

What **magazines** carry articles relating to **dinosaurs**?

Sometimes, it seems as though articles about dinosaurs are everywhere, especially when there is a major discovery or change in an existing theory. Usually, magazines that cover the natural sciences, such as *National Geographic, Nature, Natural History, New Scientist, The Sciences,* and *Scientific American* (just to name a few), are good bets for dinosaur articles on a continuing basis. There are even some specialized magazines dealing only with the subject, such as *Prehistoric Times.*

What are some of the **publications** that often deal with the topics of **dinosaurs** and **paleontology**?

The following list contains some of the numerous publications that deal with dinosaurs and paleontology, including phone numbers and addresses:

American Paleontologist
Paleontological Research Institution
1259 Trumansburg Rd.
Ithaca, NY 14850

(607) 273-6623
(607) 273-6620 fax
Newsletter publishes articles about paleontology and earth science. Quarterly.

Dinosaur Report
Dinosaur Society
200 Carleton Ave.
East Islip, NY 11730
(516) 277-7855
(516) 277-1479 fax
Email: dsociety@aol.com
http://www.dinosociety.org
Reports on paleontological issues and news. Quarterly.

Discover: The World of Science
114 5th Ave.
New York, NY 10011
(212) 633-4817 fax
http://www.discover.com
Covers science, from astronomy to zoology. Monthly.

Journal of Paleontology
Museum of Natural History and Department of Geology
Rm. 245 NHB
1301 W. Green St.
Urbana, IL 61801
(217) 333-3833
(217) 244-4996 fax
Email: fossils@hercules.geology.uiuc.edu
Scientific journal. Bimonthly.

National Geographic
National Geographic Society
1145 17th St. NW
Washington, DC 20036-4688
(202) 857-7000
(800) NGS-LINE
(202) 429-5712 fax
http://www.nationalgeographic.com
Covers history, culture, the environment, and science. Monthly.

Natural History Magazine
American Museum of Natural History
Exhibition Department
Central Park West at 79th St.
New York, NY 10024
(212) 769-5500
(212) 769-5511 fax
http://www.amnh.org/welcome/smp_publications.html

Covers natural science, anthropology, archeology, and zoology. 10/year.

Nature: International Weekly Journal of Science
Nature Publishing Co.
345 Park Ave. S, 10th Fl.
New York, NY 10010-1707
(212) 726-9200
(212) 696-9006 fax
http://www.nature.com (searchable archive; free registration required)

Paleoclimates
The University of Arizona
Gould-Simpson Bldg.
Tucson, AZ 85721
(520) 621-4595
(520) 621-2672 fax
Journal on the interdisciplinary subject of paleoclimatology, the study of past climate change. Includes articles on all aspects of the climate and environment of the Quaternary period and earlier times. Quarterly.

Popular Science
Times Mirror Magazines, Inc.
2 Park Ave.
New York, NY 10016
http://www.popsci.com (searchable archive)
General interest science magazine. Monthly.

Rocks & Minerals
Heldref Publications
Helen Dwight Reid Educational Foundation
1319 18th St. NW
Washington, DC 20036-1802
(202) 296-6267
(800) 365-9753
(202) 296-5149 fax
http://www.heldref.org/ (subscription information)
Magazine for students of mineralogy, geology, and paleontology. Bimonthly.

Rotunda: The Magazine of the Royal Ontario Museum
Attn: Publications Dept.
100 Queen's Park
Toronto, ON, Canada M5S 2C6
(416) 586-5590
(416) 586-5827 fax
http://rom.on.ca
Coves art, archaeology, natural sciences, astronomy. 3 times/year.

Are there any **children's publications** that often deal with dinosaurs and paleontology?

Yes, the following lists two of the children's publications that deal with dinosaurs and paleontology:

Dino Times
 Dinosaur Society
 200 Carleton Ave.
 East Islip, NY 11730
 (516) 277-7855
 (516) 277-1479 fax
 Email: dsociety@aol.com
 http://www.dinosociety.org
 Magazine for children; includes news on current dinosaur studies. Monthly.

National Geographic World
 National Geographic Society
 1145 17th St. NW
 Washington, DC 20036-4688
 (202) 857-7000
 (800) NGS-LINE
 (202) 429-5712 fax
 http://www.nationalgeographic.com
 Magazine featuring factual stories on natural history, outdoor adventure, sports, science, and history for children ages 8 to 13. Monthly.

Why **visit a museum** that has dinosaur exhibits?

There are many reasons for dinosaur fans to visit a museum that features dinosaurs. Maybe they have always wanted to participate in a dinosaur dig. Maybe they have seen specials on television, or read about digs in a book—and find they are interested in learning more about the animals. Perhaps they want to encourage a budding paleontologist in their family. Or perhaps they want to experience the thrill of seeing a fossil that was buried for 65 million years—or hold a bone in their hands that is *very* old. Teachers may want to show their students all about how to collect, or help them understand dinosaurs a little bit better. Or they may want to learn how paleontologists really explore, dig, collect, and excavate dinosaur bones. There are many reasons to seek out information about dinosaurs in museums—and plenty of museums to visit.

What are some of the top **U.S. museums** with **dinosaur collections** and **exhibits**?

There are numerous museums with dinosaur collections and exhibits in the United States. Some are small museums, often associated with a university or college that offers courses or majors in paleontology; others are small museums started by ama-

Many museums have dinosaur exhibits open to the public. (Photo courtesy of Gail Mooney/Corbis.)

teurs or professionals with a special interest in dinosaur collection and education. It would be impossible to list all the museums with dinosaur collections in the United States. The following table lists some of the more well-known museums with dinosaur collections (skeletons, casts, or fossil remains) in the 48 contiguous states.

Location (alphabetical by state)	Museum Name	Comments
Flagstaff, AZ	Museum of Northern Arizona	Displays of *Coelophysis* and *Scutellosaurus*.
Los Angeles, CA	Los Angeles County Museum	Displays of *Camptosaurus, Dilophosaurus, Edmontosaurus,* and *Tyrannosaurus*.
Boulder, CO	University of Colorado Museum	
Denver, CO	Denver Museum of Natural History	
Grand Junction, CO	Dinosaur Valley, Museum of Western Colorado	
New Haven, CT	Peabody Museum, Yale University	
Chicago, IL	Field Museum of Natural History	

Location (alphabetical by state)	Museum Name	Comments
Ann Arbor, MI	University of Michigan Exhibit Museum of Natural History	
Bozeman, MT	Museum of the Rockies	Exhibit of the *Maiasaura*
New York City, NY	American Museum of Natural History	
Cleveland, OH	Cleveland Museum of Natural History	
Philadelphia, PA	Academy of Natural Sciences	
Houston, TX	Houston Museum of Natural Science	
Provo, UT	Earth Science Museum	Displays of a *Supersaurus* and *Ultrasaurus*.
Salt Lake City, UT	Utah Museum of Natural History	Displays of *Allosaurus*, *Barosaurus, Camptosaurus,* and *Stegosaurus*.
Washington, D.C.	National Museum of Natural History (at the Smithsonian Institution)	
Laramie, WY	University of Wyoming Geological Museum	Displays of *Anatosaurus, Apatosaurus, Anchiceratops,* and *Tyrannosaurus*.

Which **museums** in the **United States** have **paleontological displays** as part of their permanent exhibits?

The following museums offer paleontological displays as part of their permanent exhibits; they are listed in alphabetical order by state and include addresses and phone numbers. (Many museums also maintain their own websites, which often include information about exhibits, schedules, and even virtual tours.)

Alaska
University of Alaska Museum
    907 Yukon Dr.
    Fairbanks, AK 99775
    (907) 474-7505
    Fossils from dinosaurs and prehistoric mammals.

Arizona
Museum of Northern Arizona
    Fort Valley Rd.
Flagstaff, AZ 86001

A child on an educational journey at a museum. (Photo courtesy of Michael S. Yamashita/Corbis.)

(602) 774-5211
Exhibits include a 3-D skeleton reproduction.

Mesa Southwest Museum
   53 North Macdonald St.
   Mesa, AZ 85201
   (602) 644-2230
   (602) 644-2169
   Features displays on dinosaurs in Arizona.

Arizona Museum of Science and Technology
   80 North St.
   Phoenix, AZ 85004
   (602) 256-9388
   Displays include dinosaur fossils and casts of skulls of *Tyrannosaurus rex* and *Triceratops*.

Arkansas

Arkansas Museum of Science and History
   MacArthur Park
   Little Rock, AR 72202
   (501) 324-9231
   Displays include dinosaur track castings and information on how fossils are formed.

California

Museum of Natural History
University of California
Berkeley, CA 94720
(510) 642-1821

The Page Museum at the La Brea Tar Pits
5801 Wilshire Blvd.
Los Angeles, CA 90036
(323) 936-2230
Thousands of Ice Age mammals and birds died in the infamous asphalt pits, often referred to as the Death Trap of the Ages. According to museum scientists, the sticky tar trapped and preserved in pristine condition some 4 million fossils, many of which have been recovered and are on display. From time to time, the museum holds public viewings of pit excavations.

Colorado

Denver Museum of Natural History
2001 Colorado Blvd.
Denver, CO 80205
(303) 370-6357
Features fossil displays and dioramas plus the Prehistoric Journey exhibit, which includes several dinosaur skeletons.

Devil's Canyon Science and Learning Center
550 Jurassic Court
Fruita, CO 81521
(303) 858-7282
Robotic dinosaurs are on display, courtesy of a cooperative effort between the museum and Dinamation International Society. Working fossil lab.

Museum of Western Colorado and Dinosaur Valley
P.O. Box 20000-5020
Grand Junction, CO 81502-2020
(303) 242-9210
Exhibits include five animated scale models of dinosaurs and a working fossil lab.

Connecticut

Peabody Museum of Natural History
Yale University
170 Whitney Ave.
New Haven, CT 06511
(203) 432-3775
Features the renowned Great Hall of Dinosaurs. Displays include the Deinonychus, the small but deadly meat-eater, which was discovered in 1964 by the Peabody's (now-retired) curator, Dr. John H. Ostrom.

Illinois

Chicago Academy of Science
2001 North Clark St.
Chicago, IL 60614
(312) 871-2668
Features include an Ice Age cave and the Dinosaur Alcove.

Field Museum of Natural History
Roosevelt Rd. and Lake Shore Dr.
Chicago, IL 60605
(312) 922-9410
In 1994 the world-renowned Field moved its extensive dinosaur displays into the museum's new hall (called the Elizabeth Morse Genius Dinosaur Hall) and reassembled the skeletons according to the most up-to-date research.

Indiana

Wayne Geology Museum
2101 Coliseum Blvd. East
Fort Wayne, IN 468050
(219) 481-6100
Indiana University and Purdue University paleontological exhibits are housed here.

Kansas

Dyche Museum of Natural History
University of Kansas
Jayhawk Blvd.
Lawrence, KS 66045
(913) 864-4540
Displays include the fossils of a prehistoric bird with a 25-foot (7.6-meter) wingspan, marine animals, and prehistoric sea turtles.

Louisiana

Audubon Institute
6500 Magazine St.
New Orleans, LA 70118
(504) 861-2537
Pathways to the Past at the institute's natural history museum explores the dinosaur-bird connection. Includes hands-on learning for all ages.

Massachusetts

Pratt Museum of Natural History
Amherst College
Amherst, MA 033103
(800) 723-1548
Begun as the private collection of a fossil-hunter enthusiast (who was then president of Amherst College), the museum displays fossils of prehistoric bird tracks and dinosaur bones from the area.

Michigan

University of Michigan Museum of Natural History
1109 Geddes Ave.
Ann Arbor, MI 48109
(734) 763-6085
Prehistoric life is on display in the museum's Hall of Evolution.

Minnesota

The Science Museum of Minnesota
30 E. 10th St.
St. Paul, MN 55101
(612) 221-9444
The museum has a Paleontology Hall, featuring impressive displays—including a dinosaur egg.

Missouri

St. Louis Science Center
5050 Oakland Ave.
St. Louis, MO 63110
(314) 289-4444
The science center includes a fossil center, dinosaur models, educational videos, and Dinosaur Park.

Montana

Museum of the Rockies
Montana State University
600 West Kagy Blvd.
Bozeman, MT 59717
(406) 994-DINO
Renowned paleontological display includes locally discovered fossils, including those of the *Maiasaura*. Exhibits focus on how the species lived. The museum also runs the Paleo Field School, which leads students on explorations of Montana dig site. Call the school at (406) 994-2251 for more information.

Nevada

Las Vegas Natural History Museum
900 Las Vegas Blvd. North
Las Vegas, NV 89101
Prehistoric room includes an extensive dinosaur collection.

New Jersey

New Jersey State Museum
205 West State St.
Trenton, NJ 08625
(609) 292-6308
The excellent collection of fossils and other paleontological exhibits here bears testimony to New Jersey's rich prehistory. Children's exhibits.

New Mexico

Ruth Hall Museum of Paleontology
  Ghost Ranch Conference Center
  Abiquiu, NM 87501
  (505) 685-4333
  More than 100 complete skeletons of the small, carnivorous dinosaur *Coelophysis* are on display.

New Mexico Museum of Natural History
  1801 Mountain Rd., NW
  Albuquerque, NM 87104
  (505) 841-8837
  Excellent paleontological exhibit takes many forms—most notably an elevator (called the Evo-lator) that takes visitors on a ride through evolutionary history. Also, fossils, reconstructions, and sculptures.

New York

American Museum of Natural History
  79th St. and Central Park West
  New York, NY 10024
  (212) 769-5100
  A national treasure, this world-renowned museum features three dinosaur halls. Extensive displays are must-sees for any aspiring paleontologist.

North Carolina

Natural Science Center
  4301 Lawndal Dr.
  Greensboro, NC 27401
  (919) 288-3769
  Features a Dinosaur Gallery, *Tyrannosaurus rex* restoration model, and a skeletal mount of a *Triceratops*.

North Carolina Museum of Natural Science
  102 North Salisbury St.
  Raleigh, NC 27604
  (910) 733-7450
  Skull replicas, a prehistoric bird hall, and a hall of mammals.

North Dakota

Dakota Dinosaur Museum
  1226 Simms Rd.
  Dickinson, ND 58601
  (701) 227-0431
  Full-scale dinosaur skeletons, models, and fossils. Fossil lab.

Ohio

McKinley Museum of History
  800 McKinley Monument Dr. NW

Canton, OH 44708
(216) 455-7043
A robotic model of an *Allosaurus* greets visitors to the museum's Discovery World, featuring dinosaur reproductions, skulls, and a dig-site reproduction.

The Cleveland Museum of Natural History
University Circle
1 Wade Oval Dr.
Cleveland, OH 44106
(216) 231-4600
Excellent prehistoric displays include an Ice Age mammal exhibit.

Oklahoma

Oklahoma Museum of Natural History
1335 Asp Ave.
Norman, OK 73019
(405) 325-4712
The paleontological offerings include a dinosaur collection as well as a prehistoric mammals exhibit.

Pennsylvania

Academy of Natural Science Museum
1900 Benjamin Franklin Parkway
Philadelphia, PA 19103
(215) 299-1000
International museum of natural history founded in 1812, the Academy of Natural Science boasts a newly renovated dinosaur hall, which includes numerous life-size skeletons, nests, and even a huge footprint. Visitors can explore the dinosaur discovery process from beginning to end.

Wagner Free Institute of Science
17th St. and Montgomery Ave.
Philadelphia, PA 19121
(215) 763-6529
Many of the museum's displays of dinosaur bones and other fossils were first mounted in 1865 and are typical of that era, providing visitors a historical perspective on paleontological exhibits.

The Carnegie Museum of Natural History
4400 Forbes Ave.
Pittsburgh, PA 15213
(412) 622-3131
Extensive collection of dinosaur skeletons, prehistoric mammals, and marine reptiles.

South Dakota

Black Hills Institute of Geological Research
217 Main St.
Hill City, SD 57745
(605) 574-4289

The institute offers an impressive fossil lab and museum. One of the institute's volunteers happened to find "Sue"—the most complete *Tyrannosaurus rex* ever discovered.

Texas

Shuler Museum of Paleontology
Southern Methodist University
Dallas, TX 75275
(214) 768-2000
The work and discoveries of renowned paleontologist Dr. Louis Jacobs are on display.

Fort Worth Museum of Science and History
1501 Montgomery St.
Fort Worth, TX 76107
(817) 732-1631
Extensive displays include Texas findings as well as the interactive Dino Dig exhibit, a reproduction of a famous dig site.

Utah

Dinosaur National Monument
Jensen, UT 84035
(801) 789-2115
This national monument is one of the richest dinosaur beds ever discovered. Excavation work is still underway but the public is welcome to explore the findings at the year-round visitor center.

Utah Museum of Natural History
University of Utah
President's Circle
Salt Lake City, UT 84112
(801) 581-4303
Highlights include skeletal mounts, extensive fossil displays, and reconstructions.

Virginia

Virginia Museum of Natural History
1001 Douglas Ave.
Martinville, VA 24122
(703) 666-8600
Paleontological display includes a computerized *Triceratops* model.

Washington

Pacific Science Center
200 Second Ave. North
Seattle, WA 98372
(206) 443-2001
Fossils, footprints, cutaway model of a *T. rex* leg, and hands-on exhibits for children.

Burke Museum
University of Washington
Seattle, WA 98195

A child examines a fossilized *Triceratops* skull at the Royal Tyrrell Museum in Alberta, Canada. (Photo courtesy of Michael S. Yamashita/Corbis.)

(206) 543-5590
Featuring the Life and Times of Washington State—a hands-on exhibit that begins 545 million years ago. Replicas include carnivorous dinosaurs. Fossil exhibit.

Washington, D.C.

The National Museum of Natural History
The Smithsonian Institution
10th St. and Constitution Ave.
Washington, D.C. 20560
(202) 357-1300
Among the best—and certainly most extensive—paleontological displays anywhere. In addition to numerous displays of dinosaurs, ancient mammals, and ancient marine life-forms, the museum features a working laboratory.

Wisconsin

Milwaukee Public Museum
800 West Wells
Milwaukee, WI 53233
(414) 278-2702
The museum's dinosaurs exhibit includes recreations of a *Triceratops* and a *T. rex* in their habitats.

Wyoming

Wyoming Dinosaur Center
  Thermopolis, WY 80443
  (307) 864-5522
  The dinosaurs once roamed here, and the museum is situated to take advantage of that.
  The center not only offers extensive exhibits, but also gives tours of the bone beds
  where paleontologists are at work on excavations.

What are some of the top **Canadian museums** with **dinosaur collections** and **exhibits**?

Canada has numerous museums with dinosaur collections and exhibits, including
skeletons, casts, and fossil remains. The following list represents some of the more
well-known Canadian museums.

Location	Museum Name	Comments
Alberta	Dinosaur Provincial Park	The park is an excavation in progress.
Ottawa, Ontario	National Museum of Natural Sciences	
Alberta	Provincial Museum of Alberta	
Quebec	Redpath Museum	Displays of *Majungatholus, Saurornithoides,* and *Zephyrosaurus.*
Toronto, Ontario	Royal Ontario Museum	
Drumheller, Alberta	Tyrrell Museum of Paleontology	

What are some **museums** in **Canada** that have **paleontological displays** as part of their permanent exhibits?

The following are phone numbers and addresses of two of the leading Canadian museums that have paleontological displays as part of their permanent exhibit:

Royal Tyrrell Museum of Paleontology
  Drumheller, Alberta T0J 0Y0
  (403) 823-7707
  Features numerous skeletal mounts in what is probably Canada's most extensive paleontological collection.

Royal Ontario Museum
  100 Queen's Park
  Toronto, Ontario, Canada M5S 2C6

413

(416) 586-5590

The museum's paleontological exhibit showcases more than 10 different dinosaurs. Features live-action puppetry and animation and includes interviews with leading paleontologists.

What are some of the top **museums outside North America** with **dinosaur collections** and **exhibits**?

Dinosaur museums are not only restricted to the United States and Canada. Many famous collections of dinosaur bones are found in such places as Europe, Africa, and Asia.

Location	Museum Name and Comments
Cape Town, South Africa	South African Museum: Displays of *Anchisaurus, Heterodontosaurus, Massospondylus,* and *Melanorosaurus.*
Buenos Aires, Argentina	Museo Argentino de Ciencias Naturales: Displays of *Antarctosaurus, Mussaurus, Noasaurus, Saltasaurus,* and *Titanosaurus.*
Birmingham, England	Birmingham Museum
London, England	British Museum of Natural History
London, England	Crystal Palace Park: Displays of Benjamin Waterhouse Hawkins's nineteenth-century dinosaur models.
Dorchester, England	The Dinosaur Museum
Cambridge, England	Sedgwick Museum
Oxford, England	University Museum
Paris, France	National Museum of Natural History: Displays of *Compsognathus, Diplodocus, Iguanodon, Protoceratops, Tarbosaurus,* and *Triceratops.*
Berlin, Germany	Natural History Museum, Humboldt University: Displays of *Archaeopteryx, Brachiosaurus, Dicraeosaurus, Dryosaurus, Elapbrosaurus,* and *Kentrosaurus.*
Chorzow, Poland	Dinosaur Park: Displays of *Saichania, Saurolophus,* and *Tarbosaurus.*
Warsaw, Poland	Institute of Palaeobiology: Displays of *Deinocheirus, Gallimimus, Homalocephale, Nemegtosaurus, Pinacosaurus, Proceratops, Opishthoceolicaudia, Saichania, Tarbosaurus,* and *Velociraptor.*
Edinburgh, Scotland	Royal Scottish Museum

Have any **museums reposed** their **dinosaur skeletons**?

A number of museums around the world have changed their dinosaur exhibits to reflect revised thinking about the animals. One of them is the American Museum of Natural History in New York City. Here, the "new" *Tyrannosaurus rex* is portrayed as a ferocious, stalking carnivore whose tail waves in the air. The original version of the *Tyrannosaurus rex* stood straight up—but scientists now think this posture would have dislocated many of his vertebrae! The dinosaur's tail is now horizontal for balance, and his head is held lower, as though he is hunting.

Also at the American Museum of Natural History—in an exhibit sure to generate a lot of controversy—a *Barosaurus* is posed rearing up on its hind legs to protect its young from an attacking *Allosaurus*. This is certainly not the traditional view of this extremely large, plant-eating sauropod.

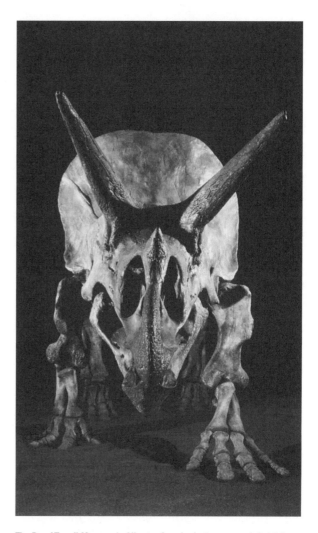

The Royal Tyrrell Museum in Alberta, Canada, features several skeletal mounts, including this rather imposing one of a *Triceratops*. (Photo courtesy of Francois Gohier/Photo Researchers Inc.)

Another example of a skeleton that has been reconstructed based on more up-to-date research is at the Carnegie Museum of Natural History in Pittsburgh. The museum has a *Tyrannosaurus rex* posed in a more lifelike posture—as if it is confronting prey or another *Tyrannosaurus rex*.

And if certain scientists are correct, museums may be reposing their long-necked sauropods. Most of these dinosaurs are posed with long S-shaped necks, reaching high into the tall trees to gather leaves. But a recent computer model of dinosaurs with

415

necks up to 40 feet (12 meters) long indicates that these animals could not lift their heavy necks—the vertebrae were too heavy—that they probably kept their necks held straight out. The sauropods may have chewed on lower-lying shrubs, not tall trees.

How can a dinosaur **fashion statement** be made?

Dinosaur fans who find themselves reading about dinosaurs, digging for dinosaur fossils, collecting dinosaur stamps, and even dreaming about dinosaurs are certainly ready for the next step! After exploring the great dinosaur exhibits at the American Museum of Natural History (Central Park West at 79th St., New York, NY 10012), visitors will want to stop by their gift shop. There, they can purchase a *Tyrannosaurus rex* T-shirt featuring the finest specimen of a *T. rex* skull ever described. Or they can buy a cladistics T-shirt, featuring the evolution of different dinosaur species. Don't forget the baby—Dino Babywear includes colorful renditions of *Triceratops* and *Stegosaurus*. For more formal wear, there is the *Tyrannosaurus rex* 100 percent silk tie that features everyone's favorite theropod in a stalking posture.

The gift shop has something for the office, too. There is the *Tyrannosaurus rex* mousepad, in various colors. Also available are mousepads depicting early Jurassic or Cretaceous period scenes, reproduced from the mural in the Hall of Vertebrate Origins. Of course, there are matching mugs for those who want to reflect on prehistory during coffee breaks or long meetings.

Where can **animated, life-like dinosaurs** be seen?

A tremendous exhibit of animated, robotic *life-sized* dinosaurs can be found at the Devil's Canyon Science and Learning Center, the permanent home of the Dinamation International Society. The center is located just south of Interstate 70, in Fruita, Colorado, a short distance west of Grand Junction. The highlights of the animated dinosaurs include a *Utahraptor* eating its prey, and a *Dilophosaurus* spitting a stream of water at unwary visitors (to simulate the animal's poison it would spray to keep away predators or to catch prey). There are also numerous static and hands-on exhibits, a gift shop, and a preparation laboratory. The center is located in the middle of dinosaur country, with numerous interpretive trails and working quarries within a short driving distance. This is not to be missed!

MEDIA SOURCES

Where can **television** or **video specials** on **dinosaurs** be found?

Most of the television specials on dinosaurs are found on stations with a predilection toward science and nature. For example, the Public Broadcasting System (PBS) and the Discovery Channel offer nature shows. Viewers should check local guides for times and dates of upcoming dinosaur programs. Also, Internet surfers should consult these shows' websites for archival information on past programming.

Both PBS and the Discovery Channel often offer videos of their shows on dinosaurs. These tapes can be ordered directly, or sometimes can be found in a local libraries' video section. They may also make their way to several local video rental stores, shelved in the documentary or nature sections.

What are some examples of **educational videos** that deal with dinosaurs?

The following is a list of some of the many educational videos available that feature dinosaurs:

Bill Nye the Science Guy: Dinosaurs—Those Big Boneheads (1994). Bill Nye takes a look at dinosaurs and what has been discovered about their lifestyles. In another episode, Bill Nye explains how the earth's surface and its inner mantle differ.

Common Fossils of the United States (1990). A look at the varieties of fossils common to the United States, including their age and the environments that produced them.

Digging Dinosaurs (1988). This video provides an informative introduction to paleontology for young children, and an excellent presentation to be shown before or after field trips to natural history museums.

Digging Up Dinosaurs (1992). Introduction to paleontology in two parts. Part one includes treks led by Martin Lockley to a site in the Dinosaur National Monument in Utah, and by Scott Madsen to a site where microfossils were uncovered. Part two includes a trek to a site where an *Allosaurus* was uncovered and reveals the process of excavating, casting, and repairing the bones.

Dinosaur (1997). Follows paleontologists as they uncover fossil bones in Dinosaur National Monument.

Dinosaur Footprints of the Peace River Valley. In northeastern British Columbia, the Peace River Canyon contains one of the largest concentrations of dinosaur footprints in the world. The film observes a team of paleontologists mapping the area and making molds of the prints.

Dinosaur Hunt (1998). Three-part series features aspects of the dinosaur and the hunt for fossils, including the chaos that erupts when a fossil is found, whether dinosaurs and birds are biologically related, and the false mystique of the *Tyrannosaurus rex.* Three hours on three videocassettes.

Dinosaur! With Walter Cronkite (1991). Hosted by Walter Cronkite. A four-part boxed set that traces the discovery of dinosaurs from the first paleontological find to the latest breakthroughs. Includes animatronics, dramatic re-enactments, and visits to archeological sites. A companion book written by paleontologist David Norman is also available.

The Dinosaurs! (1993). Paleontologists reconstruct the existence of these prehistoric reptiles from ancient artifacts in this four-tape series.

417

Dinosaurs Are Very Big (1994). Part of the "Digging Dinosaurs" collection that takes a look at some of the dinosaurs that roamed the earth in the past. Uses computer animation with visits to digs and museums to help explain the differences between the various dinosaurs.

Dinosaurs! Dinosaurs! (1995). Reveals how paleontologists have relied on fossilized remains to determine the appearance of dinosaurs living 70 million years ago. Animated dinosaur models enhance realistic footage.

Dinosaurs: Then and Now (1995). Centers on an animated journey from the birth of the solar system to the recent discovery of the fossil of *Utahraptor,* the "super slasher."

The Fascinating World of Prehistoric Animals (1993). Two programs introduce the world of prehistoric animals and dinosaurs. Each program is available individually or together on one tape.

Giant Dinosaurs (1993). Features the *Torosaurus, Braceosarus, Diplodocus,* and other dinosaurs in full-color graphics and computer animation. Accurate information and realistic representation make this an interesting and educational presentation.

Invasion of the Dinosaurs (1993). A brief overview of the era of the dinosaur as well as descriptions of some of the better-known creatures, with life-size Dinomation replicas used as educational models.

Invasion of the Robot Dinosaurs (1991). Realistically animated dinosaurs live again at the Museum of Natural History. Examine the lives of *Tyrannosaurus rex, Triceratops,* and others—how they lived and how they may have died. Informative fun for the whole family.

Lost Worlds, Vanished Lives (1991). Naturalist David Attenborough looks at the world of paleontology. He examines the earth's fossil records, as well as computer-enhanced studies of dinosaurs, to offer new insights into humankind's earliest ancestors. On four cassettes.

Nova: The Case of the Flying Dinosaur (1992). Discusses whether or not birds are the direct descendants of dinosaurs.

Paleo World (1994). Three-volume series looks at the Jurassic era of prehistory, examining predators, early mammals, and ideas on evolution. Available as a boxed set or individually.

Reading Rainbow: Digging Up Dinosaurs (1983). Voice(s) by Jerry Stiller, hosted by LeVar Burton. Burton takes viewers back in time to do some dinosaur watching.

The Return of Dinosaurs. Hosted by Gary Owens and Eric Boardman. Hosts Owens and Boardman join a group of kids at the Natural History Museum in Los Angeles for a dinosaur bone hunt and lots of dino-info. At the Canadian Museum of Paleontology the viewer sees how fossils are dug up and reconstructed for museum display.

What are some examples of **children's videos** that deal with dinosaurs?

The following is a list of a few of the children's videos available that explore the world of dinosaurs:

Adventures in Dinosaur City (1992). Cast: Omri Katz, Shawn Hoffman, Tiffanie Poston, Mimi Maynard, Pete Koch, Megan Hughes, Brett Thompson. Directed by Tony Doyle. Modern-day preteen siblings are transported back in time to the stone age. There they meet their favorite TV characters (they're dinosaurs) and help them solve prehistoric crimes. Family film may amuse kids, but adults should stick to *Jurassic Park*.

Adventures in Dinosaurland (1983). Animated story of a little dinosaur who takes kids back to the stone age.

Age of Dinosaurs (1988). A series that's perfect for little kids who are curious about dinosaurs.

All About Dinosaurs (1990). Children in grade school can learn all about the prehistoric creatures that fascinate them so.

Dinosaurs (1988). Music and dinosaurs combine to provide kids with an educational experience.

Donny Deinonychus: The Educational Dinosaur: Vol. 1 (1993). Narrated by Ruth Buzzi and Richard Moll. Two debut episodes of a nonviolent educational series for children that shares the story of prehistory while teaching basic morals, values, judgments, and courtesies. In "Donny Deinonychus" Donny the Parrot is the victim of a misdirected scientific experiment and metamorphoses into his prehistoric ancestor, Donny Deinonychus (Dine-non-i-kus), whose parrot memory is erased and replaced by that of a dinosaur. Donny wants only to get back "home" to prehistory and flees the house with Professor Stevens hot on his trail. In "Stormy, the Long Lost Friend" Donny introduces Stormy the *Triceratops* and explains that even though someone may be scary looking, they may not necessarily be bad.

The Land Before Time (1988). Voices: Pat Hingle, Helen Shaver, Gabriel Damon, Candice Houston, Burke Barnes, Judith Barsi, Will Ryan. Directed by Don Bluth. Lushly animated children's film about five orphaned baby dinosaurs who band together and try to find the Great Valley, a paradise where they might live safely. Charming, coy, and shamelessly tearjerking; producers included Steven Spielberg and George Lucas.

The Land Before Time 2: The Great Valley Adventure (1994). Sequel to 1988's animated adventure finds dinosaur pals Littlefoot, Cera, Ducky, Petrie, and Spike happily settled in the Great Valley. But their adventures don't stop as they chase two egg-stealing *Struthiomimus* and retrieve an egg of unknown origin from the Mysterious Beyond.

The Land Before Time 3: The Time of the Great Giving (1995). Directed by Roy Allen Smith. Littlefoot and his pals try to find a new source of water when the Great Valley experiences a severe water shortage.

The Land Before Time 4: Journey through the Mists (1996). The little dinosaurs travel through the land of the mists in search of a rejuvenation flower that can save the life of Littlefoot's sick grandpa.

King Kong's vision of dinosaurs was enacted through the cinematic technique of claymation. (Photo courtesy of Kobal Collection.)

The Land Before Time 5: The Mysterious Island (1997). Directed by Charles Grosvenor. When a swarm of insects devour all the plants in the Great Valley, the herds are forced to move. But with the adults fighting, Littlefoot and his pals go off on their own. They cross the Big Water to a mysterious island, which just happens to be the home of their old friend, the baby *T. rex,* Chomper. And it's up to Chomper to protect his plant-eating friends from the island's meat-eaters, who look on the little band as dinner.

What are some **films**—good and bad—with **dinosaurs** as a major theme?

The following are just some of the films, old and new, good and bad, that feature dinosaurs:

At the Earth's Core (1976). Cast: Doug McClure, Peter Cushing, Caroline Munro, Kevin Connor, Godfrey James, Keith Barron. Directed by Cy Grant. A Victorian scientist invents a giant burrowing machine, which he and his crew use to dig deeply into the earth. To their surprise, they discover a lost world of subhuman creatures and prehistoric monsters. Based on Edgar Rice Burroughs's novels.

Dinosaur Island (1993). Cast: Ross Hagen, Richard Gabai, Tom Shell, Steve Barkett, Toni Naples, Antonia Dorian, Peter Spellos, Griffin Drew. Directed by Jim Wynorski and Fred Olen Ray. Five military men survive a plane crash and discover an island where scantily clad (leather bikinis being the fashion choice) lascivious ladies live. Will the awesome power of testosterone overcome the fierce dinosaurs that stand between the men and their objects of desire?

A still from the motion picture *The Lost World: Jurassic Park 2*. (Photo courtesy of Universal Pictures/Associated Press.)

Hollywood Dinosaur Chronicles (1987). Hosted by Doug McClure. As soon as filmmaking was invented, dinosaurs became stars! Here are a few of those very early appearances. From the silents, *Gertie the Dinosaur* and *Lost World,* to recent productions like *Godzilla* and *Baby,* all the best of the extinct critters is represented here.

Jurassic Park (1993). Cast: Sam Neill, Laura Dern, Jeff Goldblum, Richard Attenborough, Samuel L. Jackson. Directed by Steven Spielberg. Michael Crichton's spine-tingling thriller translates well (but not faithfully) due to its main attraction: realistic, rampaging dinosaurs. Genetically cloned from prehistoric DNA (deoxyribonucleic acid), all is well until they escape from their pens—smarter and less predictable than expected. Contrived plot and thin characters (except Goldblum), but who cares? The true stars are the dinos, an incredible combination of models and computer animation. Violent, suspenseful, and realistic with gory attack scenes. Not for small kids, though much of the marketing is aimed at them. Spielberg knocked his own *E.T.* out of first place as "JP" became the highest-grossing movie of all time. Also available in a letterbox version.

The Land That Time Forgot (1975). Cast: Doug McClure, John McEnery, Susan Penhaligon, Kevin Connor. Directed by James Cawthorn. A World War I veteran, a beautiful woman, and their German enemies are stranded in a land outside time filled with prehistoric creatures. Based on the 1918 novel by Edgar Rice Burroughs. Followed in 1977 by *The People That Time Forgot.*

The Lost Continent (1951). Cast: Cesar Romero, Hillary Brooke, Chick Chandler, John Hoyt, Acquanetta, Sid Melton, Whit Bissell, Hugh Beaumont. Directed by Sam New-

421

field. An expedition searching for a lost rocket on a jungle island discovers dinosaurs and other extinct creatures.

The Lost World: Jurassic Park 2 (1997). Cast: Jeff Goldblum, Julianne Moore, Vince Vaughn, Arliss Howard, Pete Postlethwaite, Peter Stormare, Vanessa Lee Chester, Directed by Steven Spielberg. Sequel to *Jurassic Park,* proves only that Spielberg has tapped this well one too many times. It's four years after the first adventure and the surviving dinos have peacefully set up house on a deserted island near Costa Rica. Mathematician Ian Malcolm (Goldblum, reprising his role) reluctantly becomes part of an expedition to monitor the beasts, only because his paleontologist girlfriend (Moore) is so gung-ho. Other characters exist, but are reduced to the role of entrees. More dinos (two *T. rexes,* a clan of *Raptors,* and bite-sized newcomers *Compsognathus*), thrilling special effects, and more gore make up for thin subplots involving a rich businessman who wants to use the dinosaurs for a new zoo and another who hunts them for sport. Ironically, Spielberg's predictability owes much to better films such as *King Kong, Aliens,* and *Godzilla.* Still, *T. rex* and buddies, the true stars, rise to the occasion to entertain in an otherwise lackluster sequel. Based on Michael Crichton's book.

Massacre in Dinosaur Valley (1985). Cast: Michael Sopkiw, Suzanne Carvall. A dashing young paleontologist and his fellow explorers go on a perilous journey down the Amazon in search of the Valley of the Dinosaur.

One Million B.C. (1940). Cast: Victor Mature, Carole Landis, Lon Chaney Jr. Directed by Hal Roach and Hal Roach Jr. The strange saga of the struggle of primitive cavemen and their battle against dinosaurs and other monsters. Curiously told in flashbacks, this film provided stock footage for countless dinosaur movies that followed. Portions of film rumored to be directed by cinematic pioneer D. W. Griffith.

One Million Years B.C. (1966). Cast: Raquel Welch, John Richardson, Percy Herbert, Robert Brown, Martine Beswick. Directed by Don Chaffey. It's Welch in a fur bikini and special effects expert Ray Harryhausen doing dinosaurs so who cares about a plot (which involves Welch and her boyfriend, who's from a rival clan). Remake of the 1940 film *One Million B.C.*

The People That Time Forgot (1977). Cast: Doug McClure, Patrick Wayne, Sarah Douglas, Dana Gillespie, Thorley Walters, Shane Rimmer. Directed by Kevin Connor. Sequel to *The Land That Time Forgot,* based on the Edgar Rice Burroughs novel. A rescue team returns to a world of prehistoric monsters to rescue a man left there after the first film.

Pterodactyl Woman from Beverly Hills (1997). Cast: Beverly D'Angelo, Moon Zappa, Brion James, Brad Wilson, Aron Eisenberg. Written and directed by Philippe Mora. California housewife Pixie Chandler (D'Angelo) is the victim of an eccentric witch doctor (James) when her paleontologist husband Dick (Wilson) disturbs an ancient burial site and the doc curses Pixie by turning her into a dinosaur. This is the first so-called family release from those madcap Troma people who brought you the *Toxic Avenger.*

Return to the Lost World (1998). Cast: John Rhys-Davies, David Warner, Darren Peter Mercer, Geza Kovacs. Directed by Timothy Bond. Rival scientists Challenger and Summerlee set out for the Lost World and find it threatened by oil prospectors. With a volcano about to explode the scientists set out to save their prehistoric paradise and its dinosaur inhabitants. Based on a story by Sir Arthur Conan Doyle. Sequel to *The Lost World.*

Sir Arthur Conan Doyle's The Lost World (1993). Cast: Patrick Bergin. Zoologist George Challenger (Bergin) recruits a team of scientists to help him find a mythic land where dinosaurs and other prehistoric creatures exist. Lots of cliches although the special effects aren't bad.

Teenage Caveman (1958). Cast: Robert Vaughn, Darrah Marshall, Leslie Bradley, Frank De Kova. Directed by Roger Corman. A teenage boy living in a post-apocalypse yet prehistoric world journeys across the river, even though he was warned against it, and finds an old man who owns a book about past civilizations in the twentieth century. Schlocky, and one of the better bad films around. The dinosaur shots were picked up from the film *One Million B.C.*

A scene from the B-movie *Carnosaur*, which came close to realistically portraying dinosaurs. (Photo courtesy of Kobal Collection.)

Theodore Rex (1995). Cast: Whoopi Goldberg, Armin Mueller-Stahl, Richard Roundtree, Juliet Landau. Written and directed by Jonathan Betuel. Futuristic comedy finds cynical, seasoned cop Katie Coltrane (Goldberg) furious at being teamed with Teddy, who just happens to be an eight-foot-tall, three-ton, returned-from-extinction *Tyrannosaurus rex* (who has a taste for cookies). And Teddy's not exactly the brightest dinosaur on the block, which makes Katie's job all the harder when they stumble across a major crime caper.

Two Lost Worlds (1950). Cast: James Arness, Laura Elliott, Bill Kennedy. Directed by Norman Dawn. A young hero battles monstrous dinosaurs, pirates, and more in this film when he and his shipmates are shipwrecked on an uncharted island. Don't miss the footage from *Captain Fury, One Billion B.C.,* and *Captain Caution.*

423

The Valley of Gwangi (1969). Cast: James Franciscus, Gila Golan, Richard Carlson, Laurence Naismith, Freda Jackson. Directed by James O'Connolly. One of the best prehistoric-monster westerns ever made. Cowboys discover a lost valley of dinosaurs and try to capture a vicious, carnivorous allosaurus. Bad move, kemosabe! The creatures move via the stop-motion model animation by special effects maestro Ray Harryhausen, here at his finest.

Which **movies depict dinosaurs** in realistic ways?

Most movies have an unrealistic and unprofessional portrayal of dinosaurs as real animals—and even show the dinosaurs as contemporaries of humans! In addition, the special effects tend to be poor, ranging from an obvious stuntman in a rubber suit, to the stiff, jerky, stop-motion action of small models.

The most realistic portrayal of dinosaurs can be seen in *Jurassic Park* and *The Lost World: Jurassic Park 2*. The combination of state-of-the-art special effects, such as computer graphics imaging (CGI), and input on behavior and motion of dinosaurs from paleontologists such as Robert Bakker, brings these creatures to awe-inspiring—and sometimes terrifying—life.

How accurate was the movie *Jurassic Park*?

In the movie *Jurassic Park* scientists took blood (DNA) from an ancient mosquito—an insect that had fed on a dinosaur just before being trapped in tree resin that eventually became hardened amber. The first mistake the movie made was to use amber from the Dominican Republic: Such amber is only 20 to 40 million years old, and dinosaurs died out about 65 million years ago. Amber from Switzerland, Kuji, Japan, or even Israel would have been more appropriate, as the amber that formed in these areas is from the Cretaceous period.

Another problem is the ecosystem used in the film: Not only is the island too small for all those creatures to flourish, but there is nowhere known on earth where herbivores and carnivores live separately—except maybe in a zoo. Still another problem is the actual use of the "dinosaur DNA" to clone the dinosaurs. Just the total process, based on what scientists know now, would take years: scientists would have to get the correct DNA sequence, and using a frog to fill in the DNA sequences would not result in a perfect dinosaur. There is a long list of why dinosaur DNA cloning would not work (at this present time).

The book *The Science of Jurassic Park: The Lost World; or, How to Build a Dinosaur* by Rob Desalle and David Lindley explores the "reality" of the movie in detail. In the meantime, viewers should take this movie (and those like it) for what it truly is—entertainment.

A scene from the film *Jurassic Park*. (Photo courtesy of Kobal Collection.)

Have there been any **successes** in using **DNA** to **recreate ancient life-forms**?

So far, no ancient life-forms have been recreated using preserved deoxyribonucleic acid (DNA). However, scientists have recently brought back to life ancient bacteria that were present in the guts of bees trapped for 20 to 45 million years in amber—the first time this has been accomplished. These bacteria, new to our modern world, may be useful in some industrial processes, or might be a source of new pharmaceuticals.

Was the *Tyrannosaurus rex* in the movie *Jurassic Park* running at the correct speed?

Scientists have calculated the speed of the *T. rex* in the movie *Jurassic Park,* and discovered the animal was moving only about 12 miles (19 kilometers) per hour. In reality, trackways thought to be from *T. rex* show the animals could move at 20 miles (32 kilometers) per hour. And if the jeep was going 40 miles (64 kilometers) per hour, it could easily have escaped the huge predator!

What were the first **dinosaur bones** in **outer space**?

The first, and so far, only dinosaur to make the journey into outer space was a *Coelophysis.* But it was not a living dinosaur—and the journey did not happen millions of years ago. On January 22, 1998, the Space Shuttle *Endeavor* lifted off from the Kennedy

THE WORLD OF DINOSAURS

These U.S. postage stamps were among the new dinosaur designs in 1997. (Photo courtesy of U.S. Postal Service/Associated Press.)

Space Center at Cape Canaveral, Florida, bound for a rendezvous with Russia's *MIR* space station. Aboard the shuttle was the fossilized skull of a *Coelophysis,* a small, carnivorous dinosaur that lived in North America about 220 million years ago. The skull had been found—along with numerous other fossilized bones and skulls—at the famous Ghost Ranch, New Mexico, quarry. The *Coelophysis* skull was one of a group of lightweight items that a shuttle normally carries on each trip. These items are not on board for research purposes, but to give them the uniqueness of having been in space.

Are there any **stamps** depicting **dinosaurs**?

There are many stamps issued by different countries depicting all types of dinosaurs. Although the images of dinosaurs have been seen on stamps as early as 1935, dinosaurs on postage stamps appeared in 1958 in China. Since then, many countries have followed suit.

Stamps (postage or otherwise) depicting dinosaurs have generated enough interest to have their own advertisements in numerous stamp magazines. In addition, there are several international stamp-collecting houses that, for a fee, will automatically send interested parties new dinosaur stamps when they are issued by most countries.

For information about dinosaur stamps, the books *Dinosaur Stamps of the World* by Baldwin and Halstead (1991) and *Dinosaurs Resurrected* by Hasegawa and Shiraki (1994) are recommended, as is the periodical *Biophilately.*

What did the most **recent dinosaur stamps** depict?

The U.S. stamps are part of two separate scenes on a large stamp sheet—the entire page called "The World of Dinosaurs." The scenes represent Colorado 150 million years ago, toward the end of the Jurassic period, and Montana 75 million years ago, during the Cretaceous period. In the Colorado scene, dinosaurs represented are *Ceratosaurus, Camptosaurus, Camarasaurus, Goniopholis, Brachiosaurus, Stegosaurus, Allosaurus,* and *Opisthias,* with cycads, pterosaurs, and sundry other organisms of that time. The Montana scene includes *Edmontonia, Einiosaurus, Daspletosaurus, Palaeosaniwa, Corythosaurus, Ornithomimus,* and *Parasaurolophus,* with dinosaur hatchlings, birds, frogs, mammals, and other organisms of that time.

Are any **models** of **dinosaurs** available?

Models of dinosaurs seem to be everywhere, from discount department stores to museum gift shops. Unfortunately, many of the inexpensive models are not accurate, reflecting the attitude that the models are "only for kids."

The first dinosaur models were marketed to the public during the mid-1800s, through the Ward's catalog of scientific supplies; they were plaster-cast miniature replicas of the life-size models sculpted by Benjamin Waterhouse Hawkins (1807–89) for the exhibit at the Crystal Palace grounds in London, England. During the 1940s, the SRG company produced the metal cast figures, which were usually sold in museum shops; they were among the few small replicas available to the general public at that time.

Today, numerous companies are making dinosaur models available for sale in toy stores, museum shops, and department stores. Many of the replicas trade off accuracy for price, being viewed as toys or media tie-ins. Some, however, are quite accurate, and are backed by large museums—such as the hard-rubber figures found at the Carnegie Museum of Natural History (in Pittsburgh, Pennsylvania). These models can also be found in stores specializing in nature or museum gifts.

There are also smaller, private firms dealing in accurate dinosaur models. These companies can usually be found in magazines that specialize in nature and science; a good place model builders can look for these sources is *Prehistoric Times,* a magazine devoted to the dinosaur collector and enthusiast. A few of these companies are the Dinosaur Studio, Battat Dinosaur Resin Replicas, and Link & Pin Hobbies.

Are there **sculptures** of dinosaurs?

Yes, there are many sculptures of dinosaurs around the world—too many to mention in this text. Some sculptures are merely representations of dinosaurs to attract attention, such as those found at a roadside diner near dinosaur country in the western United States.

427

But other sculptures are more accurate, detailed—and works of art. For example, the Royal Tyrrell Museum of Paleontology in Alberta, Canada, holds the largest collection of Brian Cooley's dinosaur sculptures, including his first, an *Albertosaurus*. Other sculptures include an *Edmontonia* and a small pachycephalosaur, *Stegoceras*. And the Travel and Interpretive Center at Milk River, Alberta, Canada, also has a dinosaur: those people who cross into Canada from the United States around Sweetgrass, Montana, are greeted by a 36-foot- (11-meter-) high sculpture of a *Tyrannosaurus rex*.

Are there any **traveling exhibits** of **dinosaurs**?

There are indeed exhibits of dinosaurs, both static and animated, that make their appearance at fairs, convention centers, malls, and schools. The schedule and location of each varies, those interested should call for the latest information. The following table lists some traveling dinosaur exhibits and their contact information.

Dinamation International
    189A Technology Dr.
    Irvine, CA 92718
    (714) 753-9630

The Dinosaurs of Jurassic Park
    Dinosaur Society
    200 Carleton Ave.
    East Islip, NY 11730
    (516) 277-7855

Mr. Buddy Davis
    1040 Henpeck Rd.
    Utica, OH 43080
    (614) 668-3321

Kokoro Dinosaurs
    6005 Yolanda Ave.
    Tarzana, CA 91356
    (818) 996-8303

Jurassic Journey/Dino Discovery
    1024 County Rd. #365
    Taylor, MO 63471
    800-723-9571

Are there any **dinosaur meetings** worth attending?

Many meetings dealing with dinosaurs may be too technical for the average person. But the Dinofest®, which bills itself as the "World's Fair of Dinosaurs," certainly has something for everyone—for every age and interest level. There are exhibits, animated dinosaurs, technical symposia, and everything related to dinosaur paleontology. A

Dinofest® will be held in St. Louis, Missouri, in the year 2000. The scheduled happenings can be accessed by calling (800) 736-1420, or by contacting the Internet site: http://www.dinofest.org.

Are there any **outdoor sites** devoted to **dinosaur education** and **discovery?**

There are numerous sites for the dinosaur enthusiast that have an outdoor, "hands-on" component. The following are just a few examples:

Cleveland-Lloyd Dinosaur Quarry, Price, Utah: This quarry was discovered in 1928, and has so far yielded over 10,000 dinosaur bones. It is still being worked today; most of the bones collected are from the dinosaur *Allosaurus.* There are tours to the quarry site from a visitors center.

Dinosaur National Monument, Vernal, Utah: The Dinosaur National Monument is located on the border of northeast Utah and northwest Colorado. It covers about 211,272 acres (85,500 hectares) and has the largest concentration of fossilized dinosaur bones in the United States. The visitors center is built around one of the quarry faces, and visitors can observe paleontologists removing dinosaur bones from the rock.

Dinosaur Provincial Park, Patricia, Alberta, Canada: This is one of the richest dig sites in the world, and it is the source of many of the fossils in the Royal Tyrrell Museum. Some areas are open to the public to explore and hike through.

Dinosaur Ridge, Morrison, Colorado: This tour takes a drive up the Alameda Parkway as it climbs the ridge through the rocks of the Morrison formation; this is also where famed American paleontologist O. C. Marsh (1831–91) and his crew uncovered numerous types of dinosaur fossils. There are dinosaur tracks and fossilized remains of *Apatosaurus* still present.

Rabbit Valley Research Nature Area/Trail Through Time, Grand Junction, Colorado: An approximately 2-mile (3.2-kilometer) hike along a historic trail, complete with interpretive trailside markers. Highlights include *Camarasaurus* bones still in the rock, and the active Mygatt-Moore Quarry, where the remains of more than a dozen dinosaur species have been found.

Riggs Hill Trail/Dinosaur Hill Trail, Grand Junction, Colorado: These short (approximately 1-mile) trails take the hiker through areas of historical paleontological dig sites. Complete with interpretive trailside markers, Riggs Hill is the site of the world's first *Brachiosaurus* discovery in 1900. It also contains the Holt Quarry, where partial skeletons of *Stegosaurus, Allosaurus,* and *Brachiosaurus* were excavated in 1937. Dinosaur Hill contains the quarry where an *Apatosaurus* (*Brontosaurus*) was excavated in 1901.

Wyoming Dinosaur Center, Thermopolis, Wyoming: The center has a working fossil lab, and exhibits of numerous dinosaur skeletons. But the real centerpiece is the trip to the actual bone beds of the Morrison and Cloverly formation. There, excavations of camarasaurs, stegosaurs, an allosaur, and Wyoming's first *Brachiosaurus* are being carried out; visitors can ask questions of the paleontologists as they work.

429

Where can amateurs visit a working **quarry** that specializes in dinosaur **tracks**?

In South Hadley, Massachusetts, is a place called the Nash Dino Land, on Amherst Road, off Route 116—where the world's largest dinosaur footprint quarry is located. The area is located in what is known as the Connecticut River valley, and is filled with Triassic and Jurassic period rock layers. In 1802, a local farmer, Pliny Moody, was farming his fields when his plowshare caught on a heavy rock. The rock showed huge footprints, originally thought to be from a giant bird; they were later identified as dinosaur footprints. More than a century later, a young man named Carlton Nash found out about the dinosaur footprints, and was eventually able to purchase a 2-acre (.80-hectare) area that now contains the quarry.

Nash and his family began running the operation in 1939, and except for a stretch of time during World War II, the Nash Dino Land (also called the Nash Dinosaur Track Quarry) has been in continuous business. Over the years, the quarry has produced more than 5,000 dinosaur footprints, with more discovered as the new rock layers are revealed. Found there have been the first ganoid fish ever found in dinosaur track layers; the largest footprint known from Triassic period layers; and a breast and tail imprint—possibly the only ones known in existence.

Are there dinosaur **tracks for sale** at the **Nash Dino Land** quarry?

Yes, there are plenty of dinosaur tracks for sale at the Nash Dino Land quarry. Famous visitors have visited the quarry—some even buying a slab of dinosaur footprints—including Barnum Brown, General George Patton, and Dale Carnegie, to mention only a few.

Are there any **travel guides** to **museums** and **public dinosaur sites**?

One of the best travel guides that encompasses museums and public sites in the United States and Canada is *Dino-Trekking: The Ultimate Dinosaur Lover's Travel Guide,* by Kelly Milner Halls (1996). Though ostensibly written for children, this book is suitable for anyone with an interest in seeing dinosaurs—whether indoors or outside. It contains descriptions of museums and public dinosaur sites, and lists places carrying dinosaur products.

DINOSAURS ON THE INTERNET

How can information about **dinosaurs** on the **Internet be accessed**?

Anyone who has access to the Internet—whether through a local library, education institution, or home computer—can reach a dinosaur site. There are so many resources dealing with dinosaurs on the Internet that it would take a complete book to list them all. The easiest way for dinosaur hunters to begin their cyberspace journey is to access one of the many search engines on the World Wide Web. Browsers should type "dinosaur" in the appropriate box, click on "go" (or "search"), and stand back. A list of thousands of sites mentioning the word dinosaur will appear. Some reliable search engines are listed in the following table.

Search Engine	Internet Address
AltaVista	http://www.altavista.digital.com/
Excite	http://www.excite.com/
HotBot	http://www.hotbot.com/
Lycos	http://www.lycos.com/
Northern Light Search	http://www.northernlight.com/

What are some examples of **Internet sites** that contain information on dinosaurs?

The following lists some Internet sites that contain lots of useful information on dinosaurs and the prehistoric world in which they lived:

Carnegie Museum of Natural History: Mix and match dinosaurs at the Carnegie Museum of Natural History site. DinoScience challenges visitors to match the right dinosaur skull with its skeleton. A fun way to learn, for dinosaur lovers of all ages. (http://www.clpgh.org/cmnh/discovery/dinoscience).

Dinamation: The site of the Dinamation International Society, which promotes science education and research, and of the Dinamation International Corporation, which produces a line of scientifically accurate products for all ages. Those interested visit to learn about their work in robotic dinosaurs and find out about where they can see these creatures in person. Also, there's plenty of online information—including a weekly term, a "Dinosaur of the Month" feature, and details about the Devil's Canyon Science and Learning Center. (http://www.dinamation.org).

"Dino" Don: Dinosaur expert and writer "Dino" Don Lessem put together and maintains this excellent site offering "Dinosaurs, dinosaurs, and more dinosaurs!" It's dino-everything: art, dictionary, contest, news, digs, scientists, books, links, and "all manner of cool stuff" for children of all ages. (http://www.dinodon.com).

Dinofest: In the spring of 1998, Philadelphia's Academy of Natural Sciences presented Dinofest, called "The World's Fair of Dinosaurs." Those interested should visit this award-winning site to see the archives from the exhibit. Also, dinosaur news and a kids' art show are featured (http://www.acnatsci.org/dinofestarchive/ index.html). The promotional site for the show can still be visited at (http://www3.phillynews.com/packages/dinofest/), where more information on Dinofest is available along with lessons, games, links and resources, as well as video tours.

This model of a *Torosaurus* was part of the Dinofest exhibition in Philadelphia in 1998. (Photo courtesy of Dan Loh/Associated Press.)

"Dino" Russ's Lair: Sponsored by the Illinois State Geological Survey (as part of its educational extension program) and known as "Dino Russ's Lair" (after its keeper, Russell Jacobson), visitors find information on art, digs, eggs, exhibits, real-world places to visit, tracks, organizations, links, and software. National Geographic Society Online named it one of best dinosaur sites on the Web. (http://denr1.igis.uiuc.edu/isgsroot/dinos/vertpaleo.html).

Dinosaur Eggs: *National Geographic* takes visitors behind the scenes of the Great Dinosaur Egg Hunt. Follow fossil researchers as they "hatch" fossilized dinosaur eggs; tour a museum of hatchlings. (http://www.nationalgeographic.com/dinoeggs/index.html).

The Dinosaur Interplanetary Gazette: Featuring "245 million years of dinosaur news at Dinosaur Central," this mega-site of paleo-info includes news, discoveries, articles about dinosaurs in the media, book reviews, and much more. The National Education Association gave this jam-packed site the nod for its informative content. (http://www.dinosaur.org/frontpage.html).

Dinosaur News: Visit the online magazine *New Scientist* to find links to several brief but informative articles on the latest dinosaur theories and findings. (http://rexfiles.new scientist.com).

The Dinosaur Pages: This award-winning site moved recently and is under reconstruction, but is still worth visiting for its rich content. T. Mike Keesey began this project while he was a college student and he's collected loads of information about dinosaurs. Provides a list of links to other paleo-related sites on the Internet. (http://www.gl.umbc.edu/~tkeese1/dinosaur/index.htm).

The Dinosaur Society: Founded in 1991, the Dinosaur Society is dedicated to dinosaur research and educating people about dinosaurs. Their honored site is true to that goal: It features a dig visit, society news, dinosaur art, gift shop, links, publications lists, and much more. For enthusiasts of all ages, but especially fun for kids—who will probably find it interesting enough to want to sign up to be a member of the society. (http://www.dinosociety.org/homepage.html).

Dinosauria Online: Read articles by paleontologists and others, and get in on discussions about dinosaurs at this award-winning site. Plenty of content, plus picture gallery, a store, and a searchable vertebrate catalog. For the amateur and serious dinosaur enthusiast alike. (http://www.dinosauria.com).

Dinosaurs in New Mexico: Exhibits, research, collections info, and links, all courtesy of the New Mexico Museum of Natural History and Science. (http://www.aps.edu/htmlpages/dinosinnm.html).

Dinosaurs in the Gobi Desert: During the summer of 1998 the Discovery Channel sent a correspondent along on a 20-day paleontological expedition through the Gobi Desert. Those who want to learn more should visit this website to read daily dispatches from the paleontologists, learn about their finds, and check out online areas such as the Bone Zone, Paleo-Talk, and an email exchange between visitors to the web-site and a paleontologist from the American Museum of Natural History. (http://www.discovery.com/area/specials/gobi/gobi.html).

Expedia's Mungo Park: Fossil hunters should join world-renowned paleontologists Jack Horner and Phil Currie on an expedition to some of North America's richest fossil sites. Visitors can read their dispatches, find out what detours they took, and get a dossier and resource information for planning their own (real-world) expedition. (http://www.mungopark.com).

Field Museum of Natural History: Information on the Field Museum's new Elizabeth Morse Genius Dinosaur Hall and the McDonald's Fossil Preparation Laboratory, where visitors can watch museum staff and volunteers ready fossilized *Tyrannosaurus rex* bones for study. Also, listing of current exhibitions; museum news. (http://www.fmnh.org/exhibits/perm_exhibits_nature. Htm).

Paleontological Research Institution: The site of the Ithaca, New York–based Paleontological Research Institution. Educational resource provides information on PRI's collection of fossils (many of which can be viewed online). Also worth reviewing is "What Is It?"— a new feature challenging visitors to look at a fossil and try to identify it (not as easy as it sounds since these are fossils that have stumped the PRI experts). (http://www.englib.cornell.edu/pri).

Is there information on the **Internet** about **museums** exhibiting **dinosaurs fossils**?

Many museums have their own websites, with details and pictures. Typing in the name of a particular museum in a search engine connects viewers to that particular institution's web page.

A quick reference guide to museums in the United States can be found at the Cyberspace Museum of Natural History and Exploration Technology—the Paleontology Museum Database Page (http://www.cyberspacemuseum.com/paleodbase.htm). This site lists the museums found in each of the states. Clicking on the name of any museum takes viewers to a page that gives its location, telephone number, hours, fees, and a list of the dinosaurs currently on exhibit.

Another site that lists selected museums around the world is Dinosaur Dreaming—Other Dinosaur and Palaeo Websites (http://www.earth.monash.edu.au/dinodream/resource/dinosite.htm). Viewers click on the museum of interest to access a particular institution.

Is it possible to **tour museums** over the **Internet**?

Yes, many museums have websites on the Internet that allow viewers to take a virtual tour; the following are some examples:

American Museum of Natural History: Get an online preview of the famed museum's dinosaur hall, which includes the world's tallest free-standing dinosaur skeleton. Includes floor plans to help guide tourists. (http://www.amnh.org/exhibitions/index. html).

Dinosaur Hall: The Dinosaur Hall at Philadelphia's Academy of Natural Sciences features five different guided online tours of exhibits: From the Fossils; The Big Dig; Fossil Prep Lab; Bones, Guts, and Behavior; and Science through Art. Also, a kids section and links for teachers, as well as academy news, museum info, and newsletter of online events round out this website. (http://www.acnatsci.org/dinosaurs/dinonew.html).

Field Museum of Natural History: Visitors can begin an online tour of the Field's Life Over Time exhibit, tracing 3.8 billion years of the evolution of life on earth—single cells to dinosaurs to humans. (http://www.fmnh.org/exhibits/web_exhibits.htm).

National Museum of Natural History: Those interested can visit the virtual exhibits at the Smithsonian online. Dinosaurs are on the first floor of the Museum of Natural History; a floor plan helps viewers navigate through the halls. (http://www.nmnh.si.edu/Virtual-Tour/Tour/First/ Dinosaurs/index.html).

Peabody Museum: Yale University's Peabody Museum online features the famous mural, *The Age of Reptiles,* painted by Rudolph Zallinger between 1942 and 1947 (http://www.peabody.yale.edu/mural). The Peabody's home page (at http://www.peabody. yale.edu/) offers museum news, events and exhibits info, and historical information (including a "who was who" among paleontologists).

University of California Museum of Paleontology: Visitors browse the extensive online exhibit, Paleontology without Walls. Features illustrations, but is text-heavy; older students will find it highly informative. Online visitors can choose their paradigm for touring the museum: Phylogeny—the Family Tree of Life or Geological Time or Evolutionary Thought. (http://www.ucmp.berkeley.edu/exhibit/ exhibits.html).

Virtual Dinosaurs: Virtual tours, 3-D Zone, Kid-space, Hands-On Zone, and Cool Science are among the possibilities for exploration at the interactive site of Questacon, the Natural Science and Technology Centre in Canberra, Australia. Features online dinosaur activities for children as well as quick-time videos of their robotic dinosaurs, including the *Muttaburrasaurus,* which was discovered in Australia. (http://sunsite.anu.edu.au/Questacon/).

Virtual Reality Fossils: Britain's Natural History Museum (London) lets explorers investigate and manipulate virtual fossils online (provided they have a VRML-capable browser). The site also explains how the museum made the 3-D exhibits and provides links to the VRML software so viewers can download it if they don't already have it. (http://www.nhm.ac.uk/museum/tempexhib/VRML/index.html).

What **dinosaur research societies** or **organizations** exist?

There are numerous dinosaur-oriented societies and organizations in existence worldwide. Some are local in scope, and sponsored by local universities; while others are larger, nonprofit or profit groups sponsoring digs, buying land for preservation purposes, and educating the public. Internet addresses for some of these associations are listed in the following chart.

Organization Name	Internet Address
The Dinosaur Society	http://www.dinosociety.org/
Dinamation International Society	http://www.dinamation.org/
Denver Dinosaur Trackers Research Group	http://carbon.cudenver.edu/public/trackers/
Dinosaur Dreaming	http://www.earth.monash.edu.au/dinodream/
The Paleobiological Fund	http://members.aol.com/cpaleo/
The Society of Vertebrate	http://eteweb.lscf.ucsb.edu/svp/Paleontology

What other **organizations** are there in **natural history** on the Internet?

Other scientific organizations that represent the field of natural history, including exploration, geology, and biology, are as follows:

Academy of Natural Sciences
   1900 Benjamin Franklin Pkwy.
   Philadelphia, PA 19103
   (215) 299-1000
   (215) 299-1028 fax
   http://www.acnatsci.org
   Founded: 1812. Natural science research institution and museum with extensive historical and scientific collections of shells, insects, fish, birds, fossils, plants, minerals, and microscopic organisms. Conducts research programs and expeditions.

American Federation of Mineralogical Societies
   P.O. Box 26523
   Oklahoma City, OK 73126-0523
   (405) 682-2151
   http://www.galstar.com/~mela/afms.html
   Founded: 1947. Promotes popular interest and education in the earth sciences, particularly geology, mineralogy, paleontology, lapidary, and related subjects.

American Museum of Natural History
   Central Park West at W. 79th St.

New York, NY 10024-5192
(212) 769-5100
http://www.amnh.org
Founded: 1869. Promotes the study of evolutionary biology. Serves as a research, education, and exhibition center for the study of the zoological, anthropological, and mineralogical sciences. Maintains the Naturemax Theater and permanent exhibits on meteorites, minerals and gems, birds, mammals, reptiles and amphibians, dinosaurs (early and late), the biology of invertebrates, ocean life, and more. Also prepares temporary exhibitions of international significance several times a year.

International Society of Cryptozoology
P.O. Box 43070
Tucson, AZ 85733
(520) 884-8369
(520) 884-8369 fax
http://www.izoo.org/isc/
Founded: 1982. Members include biological scientists and other individuals interested in animals of unexpected size, form, or occurrence in time or location. Association investigates and discusses reports of animals such as giant octopuses (spanning 150 feet [46 meters] or more); lake monsters in Loch Ness, Scotland, and other lakes; large, long-necked animals in Central African swamps that resemble Mesozoic sauropod dinosaurs; and large, unknown hominoids. Disseminates cryptozoological information among biological scientists, including information on cryptozoological claims, and analyses of evidence such as photographs, sonar tracks, footprint casts, and tissue and hair samples. Serves as a forum for public discussion and education; provides information to authorities and the news media.

National Geographic Society
17th & M St. NW
Washington, D.C. 20036
(202) 857-7000
(202) 775-6141 fax
http://www.nationalgeographic.com
Founded: 1888. Sponsors expeditions and research in geography, natural history, archaeology, astronomy, ethnology, and oceanography; sends writers and photographers throughout the world; disseminates information through its magazines, maps, books, television documentaries, films, educational media, and information services for media.

Paleontological Research Institution
1259 Trumansburg Rd.
Ithaca, NY 14850
(607) 273-6623
(607) 273-6620 fax
Email: WDA1@cornell.edu
http://www.englib.cornell.edu/PRI
Founded: 1932. Professional and amateur paleontologists, geologists, conchologists, and allied scientists or persons interested in the promotion of natural history. Receives,

collects, preserves, and makes accessible to students and scientists paleontological and geological type specimens and exhibits; conducts scientific explorations, research, investigations, and experiments; collects and preserves scientific data, reports, graphs, maps, documents, and publications.

Paleontological Society
  Box 28200-16
  Lakewood, CO 80228-3108
  (303) 236-9228
  (303) 236-5690 fax
  http://tigger.cc.uic.edu/orgs/paleo/homepage.html
  Email: twhenry@usgs.gov
  Founded: 1908. Members include professionals and amateurs interested in the study of paleontology.

Society for Sedimentary Geology
  1731 E. 71st St.
  Tulsa, OK 74136-5108
  (918) 493-3361; 800-865-9765
  (918) 493-2093 fax
  http://www.ngdc.noaa.gov/mgg/sepm/sepm.html
  Founded: 1926. Professional society of geologists interested in sedimentary paleontology and related disciplines. Sponsors continuing education courses; K-12 earth science education; conducts technical sessions, geological workshops, research conference, and field trips.

Society for the Preservation of Natural History Collections
  National Museum of Natural History
  Smithsonian Institution
  MRC-176, Div. Fishes
  Washington, DC 20560
  (202) 786-2426
  (202) 357-2986 fax
  http://www.uni.edu/museum/spnhc
  Founded: 1985. Individuals interested in the development and preservation of natural history collections. Encourages research on the requirements for preserving, storing, and displaying natural history collections; provides and maintains an international association of persons who study and care for natural history collections. Conducts educational programs.

Society for the Study of Evolution
  Business Office
  P.O. Box 1897
  Lawrence, KS 66044
  (800) 627-0629
  (913) 843-1274 fax
  http://lsvl.la.asu.edu/evolution/
  Founded: 1946. Professional society of biologists concerned with organic evolution.

Where are actual **dinosaur fossils** or **reproductions for sale**?

There are numerous companies that specialize in the production and sale of dinosaur fossils and reproductions. Advertisements for these companies can be found in many nature and science magazines; the following list is of selected companies that have websites on the Internet.

Company Name	Website Address
Black Hills Institute of Geological Research	http://www.global-expos.com/BHIGR/
Extinctions	http://www.extinctions.com/
The Fossil Company	http://www.fossil-company.com/
Skullduggery, Inc.	http://skullduggery.com
Western Paleontological Laboratories, Inc.	http://www.itsnet.com/~western/wplhome.html

Are there **dinosaur posters and prints** for sale on the Internet?

One Internet source that carries dinosaur posters and prints is http://www.monstrosities.com/Products/, which also features videos, models, books, and toys.

Can Internet browsers view some examples of **dinosaur artwork** on any websites?

The following are some Internet sites that contain examples of dinosaur artwork:

Dinosaur Cartoons by Charley Parker: Charley Parker was the talent behind the Dinofest website's cartoons, which originally appeared in *Isaac Asimov's Science Fiction* magazine. Interested parties who visit his site click through an entertaining gallery of dinosaur cartoons (http://www.zark.com/extra/dinotoons/dinos.html).

Pictures-a-Go-Go: Dinosaur expert David Goldman and Syracuse University offer this vault of dinosaur pictures, with an A-to-Z index of links to sites where viewers can see dinosaur and other paleontological art. Viewers should try linking to the site, which is regularly updated (http://web.syr.edu/~dbgoldma/pictures.html).

Walters & Kissinger: The curators of the Dinofest Art Show, Robert F. Walters and Tess Kissinger, give online visitors an inside peek on what they're working on in their complete dinosaur art studio, including paintings and sculptures. Viewers might enjoy linking to the site (http://www.dinoart.com).

Dinosaur Resources

Books

GENERAL/REFERENCE

Alexander, R. McNeill. *The Dynamics of Dinosaurs and Other Extinct Giants.* Reprint. New York: Columbia University Press, 1989. Applies simple physics and engineering principles to understand the mechanics of animals—living and extinct.

Colbert, Edwin H. *Men and Dinosaurs.* New York: Dutton, 1968. Outlines the history of dinosaur collecting. Considered a seminal work by paleontologists and students of paleontology.

Creagh, Carson, Angela C. Milner, and Simone End. *Dinosaurs (The Nature Company Discoveries Library).* Alexandria, Virginia: Time Life Books, 1995. Covers diet, possible causes of extinction, coloration, and dinosaurs' relation to birds. Illustrations and diagrams, glossary, index.

Currie, Philip J., and Kevin Padian, editors. *Encyclopedia of Dinosaurs.* San Diego: Academic Press, 1997. Illustrations include color plates; also a chronology of dinosaur history; index.

Dodson, Peter. *The Horned Dinosaurs: A Natural History.* Princeton, New Jersey: Princeton University Press, 1996. Comprehensive study of horned dinosaurs, the rhinoceros-like creatures that were among the last dinosaurs to walk the earth.

Farlow, James O., and M. K. Brett-Surman. *The Complete Dinosaur.* Bloomington: Indiana University Press, 1997. Comprehensive, easy-to-use reference. Illustrations; chronology; glossary. Also, a list of science fiction and fantasy books about dinosaurs.

Glut, Donald F. *The Dinosaur Dictionary.* Introductions by Alfred Sherwood Romer and David Techter. New York: Bonanza Books, 1972. General-use dictionary of dinosaur and paleontology terms. Available at some public libraries.

439

Glut, Donald F. *The Dinosaur Scrapbook.* Introduction by Ray Harryhausen and Robert A. Long. Secaucus, New Jersey: Citadel Press, 1980. Dinosaurs in the mass media.

Glut, Donald F. *Dinosaurs: The Encyclopedia.* Foreword by M. K. Brett-Surman. Jefferson, North Carolina: McFarland & Co., 1997. Heavily illustrated general reference book. 1,000 pages in hardcover. Glossary; index.

The Great Dinosaur Fact File. Cherry Hill, New Jersey: Dinosaurs To Go!, semiannual. Directory covers all recognized dinosaurs from around the world, including more than 625 dinosaur genera and museums where they are displayed.

Harper, David. *Basic Paleontology.* London: Addison-Wesley Longman, 1997. Thirteen subject chapters cover the basics. Geological time scale; glossary; index.

Horner, John R., and Don Lessem. *The Complete T. rex: How Stunning New Discoveries Are Changing Our Understanding of the World's Most Famous Dinosaur.* New York: Simon & Schuster, 1993. Dinosaur experts cover recent findings and their impact on the science of paleontology.

Horner, John R., and Edwin Dobb. *Dinosaur Lives: Unearthing an Evolutionary Saga.* New York: HarperCollins, 1997. Celebrated paleontologist Horner recounts his discoveries of dinosaur eggs, babies, nests; also examines the impact dinosaurs have on our lives—from blockbuster films like *Jurassic Park* and *Lost World* to cutting-edge research on how dinosaurs evolved.

Lambert, David. *Dinosaur Data Book: The Definitive Illustrated Encyclopedia of Dinosaurs and Other Prehistoric Reptiles.* Revised and updated edition. New York: Grammercy, 1998. Illustrated factbook; updated to account for recent dinosaur discoveries. Also, information on dinosaurs in popular media.

Lockley, Martin. *Tracking Dinosaurs: A New Look at an Ancient World.* New York: Cambridge University Press, 1991. Nontechnical study of the prehistoric reptiles' footprints. Reviews and dispels popular myths and misconceptions.

Norman, David. *Dinosaur! The Definitive Account of the "Terrible Lizards"—from Their First Days on Earth to Their Disappearance 65 Million Years Ago.* Reprint. New York: MacMillan General Reference, 1995. World-renowned paleontologist takes readers on a tour of the Mesozoic era. Covers the latest theories of how dinosaurs lived and theories on their extinction. Full-color illustrations.

Russell, Dale A. *An Odyssey in Time: The Dinosaurs of North America.* Reprint. Toronto: University of Toronto Press, 1992. The curator of the National Museum of Natural Sciences (Ottawa, Ontario) gives a readable, intelligent account of prehistoric North America and its dinosaurs. Color illustrations; maps; bibliography.

Spinar, Zdenek V. *Life Before Man.* Revised edition. With Michael J. Benton, consulting editor. New York: Thames and Hudson, 1995. Sequence of more than 200 illustrations (most of them color) reconstructs in detail the conditions on earth from its beginnings more than four billion years ago to the arrival of *Homo sapiens*.

Weishampel, David B., Peter Dodson, and Halszka Osmolska. *The Dinosauria (Centennial Book).* Berkeley: University of California Press, 1992. Comprehensive reference book for paleontologists, geologists, students, and serious amateurs. Illustrations; extensive bibliography.

Weishampel, David B., and Luther Young. *Dinosaurs of the East Coast.* Baltimore, Maryland: Johns Hopkins University Press, 1996. Survey of East Coast dinosaur findings and their importance in recreating the fossil records of dinosaurs in the region. More than 130 illustrations.

EVOLUTION AND EXTINCTION

Archibald, J. David. *Dinosaur Extinction and the End of an Era: What the Fossils Say.* New York: Columbia University Press, 1996. Addresses problems with the theory that an asteroid impact caused the extinction of the dinosaurs.

Asimov, Isaac. *Did Comets Kill the Dinosaurs?* Milwaukee, Wisconsin: Gareth Stevens Media, 1988. The renowned scientist Asimov addresses the theory.

Bakker, R. T. *Dinosaur Heresies: New Theories Unlocking the Mystery of the Dinosaurs and Their Extinction.* Reprint. Kensington Publishing, 1996. Dispels common misconceptions about dinosaurs, presenting new evidence the creatures were warm-blooded, agile, and intelligent.

Chatterjee, Sankar. *The Rise of the Birds: 225 Million Years of Evolution.* Baltimore, Maryland: Johns Hopkins University Press, 1997. In 1983 in fossil beds in west Texas, Chatterjee discovered the Protoavis, a primordial bird. The book examines the origins of birds and the dinosaur link.

Dingus, Lowell, and Timothy Rowe. *The Mistaken Extinction: Dinosaur Evolution and the Origin of Birds.* New York: W. H. Freeman, 1997. Examines the theory that dinosaurs didn't disappear; they merely took flight. Illustrations.

Fastovsky, David E., and David B. Weishampel. *The Evolution and Extinction of the Dinosaurs.* Illustrated by Brian Regal. New York: Cambridge University Press, 1996. Highly readable reference presents "dinosaurs as professionals understand them." Illustrations; subject index.

Officer, Charles B., and Jake Page. *The Great Dinosaur Extinction Controversy.* Perseus Press, 1996. Debunks popular theory that a catastrophic collision between Earth and a giant meteor caused the extinction of dinosaurs; discusses how the hypothesis became widespread and offers alternative explanation for the mass extinctions at the end of the Cretaceous period.

Powell, James Lawrence. *Night Comes to the Cretaceous: Dinosaur Extinction and the Transformation of Modern Geology.* New York: W. H. Freeman, 1998. Describes the debate over the impact theory.

Shipman, Pat. *Taking Wing: Archaeopteryx and the Evolution of Bird Flight.* New York: Simon & Schuster, 1998. Story of how the 1861 discovery of the fossil skeleton of a transitional bird-reptile changed theories of evolution. Illustrations.

Sutcliffe, Antony J. *On the Track of Ice Age Mammals.* Cambridge, Massachusetts: Harvard University Press, 1985. Unravels the puzzle of worldwide animal extinction; examines causes and consequences of drastic fluctuations in the earth's climate.

Ward, Peter D. *The Call of Distant Mammoths: Why the Ice Age Mammals Disappeared.* New York: Springer-Verlag, 1997. Addresses the question of why the great mammals that once walked the earth are now largely extinct outside of Africa; builds a case for human hunting of these mammals (versus climate change) as the culprit for their extinction.

Wicander, Reed, and James Monroe. *Historical Geology: Evolution of Earth and Life through Time.* West Publishing, 1993. Includes several chapters devoted to prehistoric life.

FOSSILS

The Audubon Society Field Guide to North American Fossils. New York: Alfred A. Knopf, 1982. An all-color, illustrated guide to fossils. Includes more than 470 identification pictures and 15 maps.

Fenton, Carroll Lane, and Mildred Adams Fenton. *The Fossil Book.* Revised and expanded edition by Patricia Vickers Rich, Thomas Hewitt Rich, and Mildred Adams Fenton. New York: Doubleday, 1958, 1989. Called "the classic work for fossil collectors and enthusiasts." Guide to the earth's life forms—including flying and gliding reptiles and hairy reptiles. More than 1,500 illustrations.

Lauber, Patricia. *Dinosaurs Walked Here and Other Stories Fossils Tell.* New York: Simon & Schuster, 1987. Through dozens of photos, explains how to identify fossils and tells what they reveal about the prehistoric world.

Webby, B. D., editor. *Fossil Collections of the World: An International Guide.* Lawrence, Kansas: International Palaeontological Association of the Paleontological Institute, n.d. Directory covering institutions and organizations holding fossil collections; includes description of holdings. Index. Published irregularly.

Wolberg, Donald, and Patsy Reinard. *Collecting the Natural World: Legal Requirements and Personal Liability for Collecting Plants, Animals, Rocks, Minerals, and Fossils.* Geoscience, 1995. Discusses all applicable federal and state laws; a reference for the amateur collector.

GUIDEBOOKS

Costa, Vincenzo. *Dinosaur Safari Guide: Tracking North America's Prehistoric Past.* Stillwater, Minnesota: Voyageur Press, 1994. Complete descriptions of and directions to more than 170 dinosaur and other prehistoric creature sites, museums, fossil exhibits, track sites, and parks in the United States and Canada.

Gaffney, Eugene S. *Dinosaurs.* Illustrated by John Dawson. New York: Golden Books Adult Publishing Company, 1990. A field guide to dinosaurs most likely to be found in museums. For all ages.

Halls, Kelly Milner. *Dino-Trekking: The Ultimate Dinosaur Lover's Travel Guide.* Illustrated by R. C. Spears. New York: John Wiley & Sons, 1996. Guidebook to more than 300 paleontological exhibits in the United States and Canada. Covers museums, science centers, parks and monuments, track sites, roadside attractions, and amusement parks.

Morell, Mark A., and Eugene Gaffney. *Discovering Dinosaurs in the American Museum of Natural History.* New York: Alfred A. Knopf, 1997. Written by curators at the American Natural History Museum exhibits. Guidebook also provides summaries of the museum's dig sites, recounts stories of the paleontologists who discovered the bones, and presents information on 40 specimens. More than 150 illustrations, charts, and maps (in color and black & white).

Wallace, Joseph E. *Dinosaurs: Audubon Society Pocket Guides.* New York: Alfred A. Knopf, 1993. Guide explains the lives and behavior of the world's prehistoric animals; also discusses their extinction. Full-color paintings and skeletal line drawings are from museum specimens around the world. Maps.

Will, Richard, and Margery Read. *Dinosaur Digs: Places Where You Can Discover Prehistoric Creatures.* Castine, Maine: Country Roads Press, 1992. A directory of museums and parks; photos.

PALEONTOLOGISTS AND EXPEDITIONS

Colbert, Edwin H. *The Great Dinosaur Hunters and Their Discoveries.* Reprint. New York: Dover Publications, 1984. Includes chapters on first discoveries, skeletons in the earth, two evolutionary streams, the oldest dinosaurs, Jurassic giants of the western world, Canadian dinosaurs, and Asiatic dinosaurs.

Doescher, Rex A., editor. *Directory of Paleontologists of the World, 5th edition.* Lawrence, Kansas: International Palaeontological Association, 1989. Lists more than 7,000 paleontologists (name, office address, area of specialization or interest, and affiliation).

Horner, John R., and James Gorman. *Digging Dinosaurs: The Search That Unraveled the Mystery of Baby Dinosaurs.* Reprint. Illustrated by Donna Braginetz and Kris Ellingsen. New York: HarperPerennial, 1996. One of the world's leading paleontologists chronicles the search that unraveled the mystery of baby dinosaurs. The book is credited with revolutionizing the way people think about dinosaurs; considered a classic.

Jacobs, Louis L. *Quest for the African Dinosaurs: Ancient Roots of the Modern World.* New York: Villard Books, 1993. After discovering a major fossil site in Malawi (Africa), Jacobs and his team went on to identify thirteen kinds of vertebrate animals that "give a window into the world of this part of Africa one hundred million years ago."

Lessem, Don. *Kings of Creation: How a New Breed of Scientists Is Revolutionizing Our Understanding of Dinosaurs.* Illustrated by John Sibbick. New York: Simon & Schuster, 1992. Dinosaur expert Lessem takes readers on a journey through dinosaur time.

Novacek, Michael. *Dinosaurs of the Flaming Cliffs.* Illustrated by Ed Heck. New York: Anchor Books/Doubleday, 1996. Chronicles the groundbreaking discoveries made by of one of the largest dinosaur expeditions of the late twentieth century.

Psihoyos, Louie, and John Knoebber. *Hunting Dinosaurs.* New York: Random House, 1994. Recounts the experiences of paleontologists who have scoured remote lands in search of evidence of dinosaurs. Full-color photos; charts and maps.

Simpson, George Gaylord. *Concession to the Improbable: An Unconventional Autobiography.* New Haven, Connecticut: Yale University Press, 1978. The life of one of the world's great paleontologists.

Simpson, George Gaylord. *Discoverers of the Lost World.* New Haven, Connecticut: Yale University Press, 1984. An account of some of those who unearthed long-buried mammals of South America, which was cut off from other land masses during most of the Age of Mammals. Covers the careers of more than 20 researchers.

Wilford, John Noble. *The Riddle of the Dinosaur.* Illustrated by Doug Henderson. New York: Alfred A. Knopf, 1985. The life and behavior of the giant beasts in the days of their dominion. Chronicles the adventures and achievements of paleontologists.

BOOKS FOR CHILDREN AND FAMILIES

Aliki. *Digging Up Dinosaurs.* New York: Thomas Y. Crowell, 1988. Introduces various types of dinosaurs, explaining how scientists find, preserve, and reassemble dinosaur skeletons.

Aliki. *Dinosaurs Are Different.* DemcoMedia, 1986. Explains how scientists categorize dinosaurs (including orders and suborders).

Arnold, Caroline. *Dinosaurs All Around: An Artist's View of the Prehistoric World.* Photos by Richard Hewett. New York: Clarion Books, 1993. Through illustrations, the reader is taken on a visit to a workshop where a life-size dinosaur model is being constructed. Information about dinosaurs and how conclusions are made from the study of fossils.

Benton, Michael J. *Dinosaur and Other Prehistoric Animals Factfinder.* New York: Kingfisher Books, 1992. Alphabetical guide to 200 dinosaurs and other prehistoric creatures.

Benton, Michael J. *The Penguin Historical Atlas of the Dinosaurs.* London: Penguin Books, 1996. Plots the development of dinosaurs from their emergence from the ocean, their dispersal across the shifting continents, and their gradual evolution, to their sudden and mysterious extinction 64 million years ago. More than 60 full-color maps; more than 70 illustrations (color and black & white); index.

Clark, Neil, and William Lindsay. *Dinosaurs.* New York: DK Publishing, 1995. A guide for the dinosaur enthusiast as well as teachers; compendium of all dinosaur groups and detailed information on their lifestyles and environment. Author Clark is a curator at the Hunterian Museum in Glasgow, Scotland.

Cooper, John A. *Dinosaurs* (CD-ROM). Illustrated by Chris Leishman. New York: Smithmark Publishers, 1997. Interactive multimedia product.

Dixon, Dougal. *Dinosaur: An Interactive Guide to the Dinosaur World.* New York: DK Publishing, 1994. Action Pack includes book, press-out scale model, 3-D diorama, wall chart, and game for ages 9–12; hands-on learning.

Eldredge, Niles, Douglas Eldredge, and Gregory Eldredge. *The Fossil Factory: A Kid's Guide to Digging Up Dinosaurs, Exploring Evolution and Finding Fossils.* Reading, Massachusetts: Addison-Wesley Longman, 1989. Covers facts about the earth's life forms; includes activities and a guide to more than fifty sites where children can look for fossils.

Gabriel, Diane L., and Judith Love Cohen. *You Can Be a Woman Paleontologist.* Illustrated by David A. Katz. Cascade, 1994. Good information for aspiring paleontologists—regardless of gender. Discusses career options, encourages reading and study. Also available in a Spanish-language edition, *Tu puedes ser una paleontologa.*

Kitamura, Satoshi. *Paper Dinosaurs: A Cut-Out Book.* New York: Farrar, Straus & Giroux, 1995. Kids ages 8–11 can create their own world of dinosaurs.

Kricher, John C. *Peterson First Guides: Dinosaurs.* Illustrated by Gordon Morrison. New York: Houghton Mifflin, 1990. Gives the names and characteristics of dinosaurs and covers theories about how they lived. Field guide format useful for museum visits.

Lambert, David, and Ralph E. Molnar. *The Visual Dictionary of Dinosaurs.* New York: DK Publishing, 1993. Part of the Eyewitness series, dictionary provides readers of all ages. More than 200 color illustrations; charts; index.

Lambert, David, and John H. Ostrom. *The Ultimate Dinosaur Book.* New York: DK Publishing, 1993. A-to-Z dinosaur dictionary covers all known species of dinosaurs; full-color photos, diagrams, and illustrations.

Lauber, Patricia. *Living with Dinosaurs.* Illustrated by Douglas Henderson. New York: Bradbury Press; Toronto: Collier Macmillan Canada, 1991. Recreates life among the dinosaurs of North America 75 million years ago.

Lindsay, William. *On the Trail of Incredible Dinosaurs.* New York: DK Publishing, 1998. Published in association with the American Museum of Natural History. Covers four dinosaurs. Photographs of realistic scale-models bring creatures to life. Full color.

Lindsay, William. *Prehistoric Life.* New York: DK Publishing, 1994. Part of the Eyewitness series. Illustrations tell the story of evolution on earth.

Lindsay, William. *Tyrannosaurus.* New York: DK Publishing, 1993. Published in association with the American Museum of Natural History, Lindsay describes the discovery and excavation of fossil evidence for the Tyrannosaurus.

Norman, David, and Angela Milner. *Dinosaur.* New York: DK Publishing, 1989. Part of the Eyewitness series. Introduction to dinosaurs covers fossils, skeleton reconstruction. Heavily illustrated.

Norman, David. *The Humongous Book of Dinosaurs.* New York: Stewart, Tabori and Chang, 1997. Describes all known dinosaurs, their world, and the scientists who study them. Includes special glasses for viewing the 3-D illustrations.

Norman, David. *The Illustrated Encyclopedia of Dinosaurs.* New York: Random House Value Publishing, 1995. Heavily illustrated book covers 68 dinosaurs. Glossary.

445

Parker, Steve. *Dinosaurs and How They Lived.* Illustrated by Guiliano Fornari Sergio. New York: DK Publishing, 1991. Parker traces discoveries of recent years, describing breakthroughs and changes in our understanding of these creatures. Full color. For young readers.

Parker, Steve. *Inside Dinosaurs and Other Prehistoric Creatures.* Illustrated by Ted Dewan. New York: Delacorte Press, 1994. Cutaway color illustrations take kids on a guided tour of the anatomy of dinosaurs.

Pearce, Q. L. *How to Talk Dinosaur with Your Child.* Los Angeles: Lowell House, 1991. Explains how parents can share dinosaur facts with their children and foster a love of science.

Preston, Douglas. *Dinosaurs in the Attic: An Excursion into the American Museum of Natural History.* New York: St. Martin's Press, 1993. Readers can "travel" to the ends of the earth in this chronicle of the expeditions, discoveries, and scientists behind the greatest natural history collection ever assembled. 16 pages of photos.

Stevenson, Jay, and George R. McGhee. *The Complete Idiot's Guide to Dinosaurs.* Alpha Books, 1998. As the book says, a complete guide to dinosaurs, including descriptions of more than 300 known dinosaur species.

Walker, Cyril, and David Ward. *Fossils.* New York: DK Publishing, 1992. Eyewitness Handbook covers 500 vertebrate, invertebrate, and plant fossils, including descriptions, informal names, range, distribution, and occurrence.

Whitfield, Philip. *Macmillan Children's Guide to Dinosaurs and Other Prehistoric Animals.* New York: Simon & Schuster Children's, 1992. For ages 7–10. Describes the prehistoric animals that lived in different parts of the world during each geological period, from the Triassic through the Cretaceous.

Museums

The following museums (listed by state/province) offer paleontological displays as part of their permanent exhibits. Many museums also maintain their own Websites, which often include information about exhibits, schedules, and even virtual tours. For a selected listing, check the Websites information (in this Resources section).

ALASKA

University of Alaska Museum
907 Yukon Dr.
Fairbanks, AK 99775
(907) 474-7505
Fossils from dinosaurs and prehistoric mammals.

ARIZONA

Arizona Museum of Science and Technology
80 North St.
Phoenix, AZ 85004
(602) 256-9388
Displays include dinosaur fossils and casts of skulls of *Tyrannosaurus rex* and *Triceratops*.

Mesa Southwest Museum
53 North Macdonald St.
Mesa, AZ 85201
(602) 644-2230
(602) 644-2169
Features displays on dinosaurs in Arizona.

Museum of Northern Arizona
Fort Valley Rd.
Flagstaff, AZ 86001
(602) 774-5211
Exhibits include a 3-D skeleton reproduction.

ARKANSAS

Arkansas Museum of Science and History
MacArthur Park
Little Rock, AR 72202
(501) 324-9231
Displays include dinosaur track castings and information on how fossils are formed.

CALIFORNIA

Museum of Natural History
University of California
Berkeley, CA 94720
(510) 642-1821

The Page Museum at the La Brea Tar Pits
5801 Wilshire Blvd.
Los Angeles, CA 90036
(323) 936-2230
Thousands of Ice Age mammals and birds died in the infamous asphalt pits, often referred to as the Death Trap of the Ages. According to museum scientists, the sticky tar trapped and preserved in pristine condition some four million fossils, many of which have been recovered and are on display. From time to time, the museum holds public viewings of pit excavations.

COLORADO

Denver Museum of Natural History
    2001 Colorado Blvd.
    Denver, CO 80205
    (303) 370-6357
    Features fossil displays and dioramas plus the Prehistoric Journey exhibit, which includes several dinosaur skeletons.

Devil's Canyon Science and Learning Center
    550 Jurassic Court
    Fruita, CO 81521
    (303) 858-7282
    Robotic dinosaurs are on display, courtesy of a cooperative effort between the museum and Dinamation International Society (see entry under Organizations). Working fossil lab.

Museum of Western Colorado and Dinosaur Valley
    PO Box 20000-5020
    Grand Junction, CO 81502-2020
    (303) 242-9210
    Exhibits include five animated scale models of dinosaurs and a working fossil lab.

CONNECTICUT

Peabody Museum of Natural History
    Yale University
    170 Whitney Ave.
    New Haven, CT 06511
    (203) 432-3775
    Features the renowned Great Hall of Dinosaurs. Displays include the Deinonychus, the small but deadly meat-eater, which was discovered in 1964 by the Peabody's (now-retired) curator, Dr. John H. Ostrom.

ILLINOIS

Chicago Academy of Science
    2001 North Clark St.
    Chicago, IL 60614
    (312) 871-2668
    Features include an Ice Age Cave and the Dinosaur Alcove.

Field Museum of Natural History
    Roosevelt Rd. and Lake Shore Dr.
    Chicago, IL 60605
    (312) 922-9410
    In 1994 the world-renowned Field moved its extensive dinosaur displays into the muse-

um's new hall (called the Elizabeth Morse Genius Dinosaur Hall) and reassembled the skeletons according to the most up-to-date research.

INDIANA

Wayne Geology Museum
    2101 Coliseum Blvd. East
    Fort Wayne, IN 468050
    (219) 481-6100
    Indiana University and Purdue University paleontological exhibits are housed here.

KANSAS

Dyche Museum of Natural History
    University of Kansas
    Jayhawk Blvd.
    Lawrence, KS 66045
    (913) 864-4540
    Displays include the fossils of a prehistoric bird with a twenty-five-foot wingspan, marine animals, and prehistoric sea turtles.

LOUISIANA

Audubon Institute
    6500 Magazine St.
    New Orleans, LA 70118
    (504) 861-2537
    Pathways to the Past at the institute's natural history museum explores the dinosaur-bird connection. Includes hands-on learning for all ages.

MASSACHUSETTS

Pratt Museum of Natural History
    Amherst College
    Amherst, MA 03103
    (800) 723-1548
    Begun as the private collection of a fossil-hunter enthusiast (who was then president of Amherst College), the museum displays fossils of prehistoric bird tracks and dinosaur bones from the area.

MICHIGAN

University of Michigan Museum of Natural History
  1109 Geddes Ave.
  Ann Arbor, MI 48109
  (734) 763-6085
  Prehistoric life is on display in the museum's Hall of Evolution.

MINNESOTA

The Science Museum of Minnesota
  30 E. 10th St.
  St. Paul, MN 55101
  (612) 221-9444
  The museum has a Paleontology Hall, featuring impressive displays—including a dinosaur egg.

MISSOURI

St. Louis Science Center
  5050 Oakland Ave.
  St. Louis, MO 63110
  (314) 289-4444
  The science center includes a fossil center, dinosaur models, educational videos, and Dinosaur Park.

MONTANA

Museum of the Rockies
  Montana State University
  600 West Kagy Blvd.
  Bozeman, MT 59717
  (406)-994-DINO
  Renowned paleontological display includes locally discovered fossils, including those of the female lizard Maiasaura. Exhibits focus on how the species lived. The museum also runs the Paleo Field School (tel. (406)-994-2251), which leads students on explorations of Montana dig sites.

NEVADA

Las Vegas Natural History Museum
  900 Las Vegas Blvd. North

Las Vegas, NV 89101
Prehistoric room includes an extensive dinosaur collection.

New Jersey

New Jersey State Museum
205 West State St.
Trenton, NJ 08625
(609) 292-6308
The excellent collection of fossils and other paleontological exhibits here bears testimony to New Jersey's rich prehistory. Children's exhibits.

New Mexico

New Mexico Museum of Natural History
1801 Mountain Rd., NW
Albuquerque, NM 87104
(505) 841-8837
Excellent paleontological exhibit takes many forms—most notably an elevator (called the Evo-lator) that takes visitors on a ride through evolutionary history. Also, fossils, reconstructions, and sculptures.

Ruth Hall Museum of Paleontology
Ghost Ranch Conference Center
Abiquiu, NM 87501
(505) 685-4333
More than 100 complete skeletons of the small, carnivorous dinosaur Coelophysis are on display.

New York

American Museum of Natural History
79th St. and Central Park West
New York, NY 10024
(212) 769-5100
A national treasure, this world-renowned museum features three dinosaur halls. Extensive displays are must-sees for any aspiring paleontologist.

North Carolina

Natural Science Center
4301 Lawndal Dr.
Greensboro, NC 27401

451

(919) 288-3769
Features a Dinosaur Gallery, *Tyrannosaurus rex* restoration model, and a skeletal mount (of a *Triceratops*).

North Carolina Museum of Natural Science
102 North Salisbury St.
Raleigh, NC 27604
(910) 733-7450
Skull replicas, a prehistoric bird hall, and a hall of mammals.

North Dakota

Dakota Dinosaur Museum
1226 Simms Rd.
Dickinson, ND 58601
(701) 227-0431
Full-scale dinosaur skeletons, models, and fossils. Fossil lab.

Ohio

The Cleveland Museum of Natural History
University Circle
1 Wade Oval Dr.
Cleveland, OH 44106
(216) 231-4600
Excellent prehistoric displays include an Ice Age mammal exhibit.

McKinley Museum of History
800 McKinley Monument Dr. NW
Canton, OH 44708
(216) 455-7043
A robotic model (of an *Allosaurus*) greets visitors to the museum's Discovery World, featuring dinosaur reproductions, skulls, and a dig-site reproduction.

Oklahoma

Oklahoma Museum of Natural History
1335 Asp Ave.
Norman, OK 73019
(405) 325-4712
The paleontological offerings include a dinosaur collection as well as a prehistoric mammals exhibit.

PENNSYLVANIA

Academy of Natural Science Museum
    1900 Benjamin Franklin Parkway
    Philadelphia, PA 19103
    (215) 299-1000
    International museum of natural history founded in 1812, the Academy of Natural Science boasts a newly renovated dinosaur hall, which includes numerous life-size skeletons, nests, and even a huge footprint. Visitors can explore the dinosaur discovery process from beginning to end.

The Carnegie Museum of Natural History
    4400 Forbes Ave.
    Pittsburgh, PA 15213
    (412) 622-3131
    Extensive collection of dinosaur skeletons, prehistoric mammals, and marine reptiles.

Wagner Free Institute of Science
    17th St. and Montgomery Ave.
    Philadelphia, PA 19121
    (215) 763-6529
    Many of the museum's displays of dinosaur bones and other fossils were first mounted in 1865 and are typical of that era, providing visitors a historical perspective on paleontological exhibits.

SOUTH DAKOTA

Black Hills Institute of Geological Research
    217 Main St.
    Hill City, SD 57745
    (605) 574-4289
    The institute offers an impressive fossil lab and museum. One of the institute's volunteers happened to find Sue—the most complete Tyrannosaurus rex ever discovered.

TEXAS

Fort Worth Museum of Science and History
    1501 Montgomery St.
    Fort Worth, TX 76107
    (817) 732-1631
    Extensive displays include Texas findings as well as the interactive DinoDig exhibit, a reproduction of a famous dig site.

Shuler Museum of Paleontology
    Southern Methodist University
    Dallas, TX 75275

(214) 768-2000
The work and discoveries of renowned paleontologist Dr. Louis Jacobs are on display.

UTAH

Dinosaur National Monument
  Jensen, UT 84035
  (801) 789-2115
  This national monument is one of the richest dinosaur beds ever discovered. Excavation work is still underway but the public is welcome to explore the findings at the year-round visitor center.

Utah Museum of Natural History
  University of Utah
  President's Circle
  Salt Lake City, UT 84112
  (801) 581-4303
  Highlights include skeletal mounts, extensive fossil displays, and reconstructions.

VIRGINIA

Virginia Museum of Natural History
  1001 Douglas Ave.
  Martinville, VA 24122
  (703) 666-8600
  Paleontological display includes a computerized *Triceratops* model.

WASHINGTON

Burke Museum
  University of Washington
  Seattle, WA 98195
  (206) 543-5590
  Featuring the Life and Times of Washington State—a hands-on exhibit that begins 545 million years ago. Replicas include carnivorous dinosaurs. Fossil exhibit.

Pacific Science Center
  200 Second Ave. North
  Seattle, WA 98372
  (206) 443-2001

  Fossils, footprints, cutaway model of a *T. rex* leg, and hands-on exhibits for children.

Washington, D.C.

The National Museum of Natural History
   The Smithsonian Institution
   10th St. and Constitution Ave.
   Washington, DC 20560
   (202) 357-1300
   Among the best—and certainly most extensive—paleontological displays anywhere. In addition to numerous displays of dinosaurs, ancient mammals, and ancient marine life-forms, the museum features a working laboratory.

Wisconsin

Milwaukee Public Museum
   800 West Wells
   Milwaukee, WI 53233
   (414) 278-2702
   The museum's dinosaurs exhibit includes recreations of a *Triceratops* and a *T. rex* in their habitats.

Wyoming

Wyoming Dinosaur Center
   Thermopolis, WY 80443
   (307) 864-5522
   The dinosaurs once roamed here, and the museum is situated to take advantage of that. The center not only offers extensive exhibits, but also gives tours of the bone beds where paleontologists are at work on excavations.

Canada

Royal Ontario Museum
   100 Queen's Park
   Toronto, Ontario, Canada M5S 2C6
   (416) 586-5590
   The museum's paleontological exhibit showcases more than ten different dinosaurs. Features live-action puppetry and animation and includes interviews with leading paleontologists.

Royal Tyrrell Museum of Paleontology
   Drumheller, Alberta, Canada T0J 0Y0
   (403) 823-7707
   Features numerous skeletal mounts in what is probably Canada's most extensive paleontological collection.

Organizations

Academy of Natural Sciences
  1900 Benjamin Franklin Pkwy.
  Philadelphia, PA 19103
  (215) 299-1000
  (215) 299-1028 fax
  http://www.acnatsci.org
  Founded: 1812. Natural science research institution and museum with extensive historical and scientific collections of shells, insects, fish, birds, fossils, plants, minerals, and microscopic organisms. Conducts research programs and expeditions.

American Federation of Mineralogical Societies
  PO Box 26523
  Oklahoma City, OK 73126-0523
  (405) 682-2151
  Founded: 1947. Promotes popular interest and education in the earth sciences, particularly geology, mineralogy, paleontology, lapidary, and related subjects.

American Museum of Natural History
  Central Park West at W. 79th St.
  New York, NY 10024-5192
  (212) 769-5100
  http://www.amnh.org
  Founded: 1869. Promotes the study of evolutionary biology. Serves as a research, education, and exhibition center for the study of the zoological, anthropological, and mineralogical sciences. Maintains the Naturemax Theater and permanent exhibits on meteorites, minerals and gems, birds, mammals, reptiles and amphibians, dinosaurs (early and late), the biology of invertebrates, ocean life, and more. Also prepares temporary exhibitions of international significance several times a year.

Dinamation International Society
  550 Jurassic Court
  Fruita, CO 81521
  800-DIG-DINO
  (303) 858-3532
  Email: dis@gj.net
  http://www.dinamation.org
  Promotes education, research, and preservation in the biological, earth, and physical sciences, with an emphasis on dinosaurs and paleontology.

Dinosaur Society
  200 Carleton Ave.
  East Islip, NY 11730
  (516) 277-7855
  (516) 277-1479 fax
  Email: dsociety@aol.com
  http://www.dinosociety.org
  Founded: 1991. Promotes research and education in the study of dinosaurs. Assists

merchandisers in accurately presenting products portraying dinosaurs to reflect current scientific knowledge. Operates speakers' bureau. Offers children's services and travel programs.

International Society of Cryptozoology
PO Box 43070
Tucson, AZ 85733
(520) 884-8369
(520) 884-8369 fax
Founded: 1982. Members include biological scientists and other individuals interested in animals of unexpected size, form, or occurrence in time or location. Association investigates and discusses reports of animals such as giant octopuses (spanning 150 feet or more); lake monsters in Loch Ness, Scotland, and other lakes; large, long-necked animals in Central African swamps that resemble Mesozoic sauropod dinosaurs, and large, unknown hominoids. Disseminates cryptozoological information among biological scientists, including information on cryptozoological claims, and analyses of evidence such as photographs, sonar tracks, footprint casts, and tissue and hair samples. Serves as a forum for public discussion and education; provides information to authorities and the news media.

National Geographic Society
17th & M St. NW
Washington, DC 20036
(202) 857-7000
(202) 775-6141 fax
http://www.nationalgeographic.com
Founded: 1888. Sponsors expeditions and research in geography, natural history, archaeology, astronomy, ethnology, and oceanography; sends writers and photographers throughout the world; disseminates information through its magazines, maps, books, television documentaries, films, educational media, and information services for media.

Paleontological Research Institution
1259 Trumansburg Rd.
Ithaca, NY 14850
(607) 273-6623
(607) 273-6620 fax
Email: WDA1@cornell.edu
http://www.Englib.cornell.edu/PRI/
Founded: 1932. Professional and amateur paleontologists, geologists, conchologists, and allied scientists or persons interested in the promotion of natural history. Receives, collects, preserves, and makes accessible to students and scientists paleontological and geological type specimens and exhibits; conducts scientific explorations, research, investigations, and experiments; collects and preserves scientific data, reports, graphs, maps, documents, and publications.

Paleontological Society
Box 28200-16
Lakewood, CO 80228-3108

(303) 236-9228
(303) 236-5690 fax
Email: twhenry@usgs.gov
Founded: 1908. Members include professionals and amateurs interested in the study of paleontology.

Society for Sedimentary Geology
1731 E. 71st St.
Tulsa, OK 74136-5108
(918) 493-3361; 800-865-9765
(918) 493-2093 fax
http://www.ngdc.noaa.gov/mgg/sepm/sepm.html
Founded: 1926. Professional society of geologists interested in sedimentary paleontology and related disciplines. Sponsors continuing education courses; K–12 earth science education; conducts technical sessions, geological workshops, research conference, and field trips.

Society for the Preservation of Natural History Collections
National Museum of Natural History
Smithsonian Institution
MRC-176, Div. Fishes
Washington, DC 20560
(202) 786-2426
(202) 357-2986 fax
http://www.uni.edu/museum/spnhc
Founded: 1985. Individuals interested in the development and preservation of natural history collections. Encourages research on the requirements for preserving, storing, and displaying natural history collections; provides and maintains an international association of persons who study and care for natural history collections. Conducts educational programs.

Society for the Study of Evolution
Business Office
PO Box 1897
Lawrence, KS 66044
800-627-0629
(913) 843-1274 fax
Founded: 1946. Professional society of biologists concerned with organic evolution.

Society of Vertebrate Paleontology
W. 436 Nebraska Hall
Lincoln, NE 68588-0542
(402) 472-4604
(402) 472-8949 fax
Founded: 1940. Serves the common interests of people concerned with the history, evolution, comparative anatomy, and taxonomy of vertebrate animals, as well as the field occurrence, collection, and study of fossil vertebrates and the stratigraphy of the beds where they are found.

Regional Organizations

Santa Rosa Mineral and Gem Society
    PO Box 7036
    Santa Rosa, California 95407-7036
    (707) 528-7610

Garden Park Paleontology Society
    PO Box 313
    Canon City, Colorado 81215-0313
    (719) 269-7150
    (800) 987-6379
    (719) 269-7227 fax
    Email: depot@ris.net

Florida Paleontological Society
    Florida Museum of Natural History
    Gainesville, Florida 32611
    (904) 392-1721
    (904) 392-8783 fax

Kentucky Paleontological Society
    365 Cromwell Way
    Lexington, Kentucky 40503
    (606) 223-8884

Los Alamos Geological Society
    PO Box 762
    Los Alamos, New Mexico 87544
    (505) 661-6171
    (505) 672-3107
    Email: hoffmans@ix.netcom.com

North Dakota Paleontological Society
    PO Box 1921
    Bismarck, North Dakota 58502-1921
    (701) 255-3658

Central Texas Paleontological Society
    16420 Edgemere
    Pflugerville,Texas 78660
    (512) 251-2848
    (512) 280-0368

Publications

The following publications, many of them general-interest science magazines, cover new findings relevant to paleontology.

American Paleontologist
Paleontological Research Institution
1259 Trumansburg Rd.
Ithaca, NY 14850.
(607) 273-6623
(607) 273-6620 fax
Newsletter publishes articles about paleontology and earth science. Quarterly.

Dinosaur Report
Dinosaur Society
200 Carleton Ave.
East Islip, NY 11730
(516) 277-7855
(516) 277-1479 fax
Email: dsociety@aol.com
http://www.dinosociety.org
Reports on paleontological issues and news. Quarterly.

Discover: The World of Science
114 5th Ave.
New York, NY 10011
(212) 633-4817 fax
http://www.discover.com
Covering science, from astronomy to zoology. Monthly.

Explorer
The Cleveland Museum of Natural History
University Circle
1 Wade Oval Dr.
Cleveland, OH 44106-1767
(216) 231-4600
(216) 231-5919 fax
Email: pubs@cmnh.org
http://www.cmnh.org
Magazine featuring articles on natural history and science. Quarterly.

Journal of Paleontology
Museum of Natural History & Dept. of Geology
Rm. 245 NHB
1301 W. Green St.
Urbana, IL 61801
(217) 333-3833
(217) 244-4996 fax
Email: fossils@hercules.geology.uiuc.edu
Scientific journal. Bimonthly.

National Geographic
National Geographic Society
1145 17th St. NW

Washington, DC 20036-4688
(202) 857-7000
(800) NGS-LINE
(202) 429-5712 fax
http://www.nationalgeographic.com
Magazine covering history, culture, the environment, and science. Monthly.

Natural History Magazine
American Museum of Natural History
Exhibition Department
Central Park West at 79th St.
New York, NY 10024
(212) 769-5500
(212) 769-5511 fax
http://www.amnh.org/welcome/smp_publications.html
Covering natural science, anthropology, archeology, and zoology. 10/year.

Nature: International Weekly Journal of Science
Nature Publishing Co.
345 Park Ave. S, 10th Fl.
New York, NY 10010-1707
(212) 726-9200
(212) 696-9006 fax
http://www.nature.com (searchable archive; free registration required)

Paleoclimates
The University of Arizona
Gould-Simpson Bldg.
Tucson, AZ 85721
(520) 621-4595
(520) 621-2672 fax
Journal on the interdisciplinary subject of paleoclimatology, the study of past climate change. Includes articles on all aspects of the climate and environment of the Quaternary and earlier times. Quarterly.

Paleontological Journal
John Wiley & Sons, Inc.
605 3rd Ave.
New York, NY 10158
(212) 850-6000
(800) 225-5945
English-language translation of a periodical on the paleontology of Eurasia. Quarterly.

Popular Science
Times Mirror Magazines, Inc.
929 Pearl St., Ste. 200
Boulder, CO 80302
http://www.popsci.com (searchable archive)
General interest science magazine. Monthly.

Quaternary Research: An Interdisciplinary Journal
  Academic Press
  525 B St., Ste. 1900
  San Diego, CA 92101-4411
  (619) 699-6825
  (800) 894-3434
  (619) 699-6380 fax
  Publishing articles from disciplines contributing to the knowledge of the Quaternary
  Period; includes studies from geology, paleontology, and oceanography. Bimonthly.

Rocks & Minerals
  Heldref Publications
  Helen Dwight Reid Educational Foundation
  1319 18th St. NW
  Washington, DC 20036-1802
  (202) 296-6267
  (800) 365-9753
  (202) 296-5149 fax
  http://www.heldref.org/ (subscription information)
  Magazine for students of mineralogy, geology, and paleontology. Bimonthly.

Rotunda: The Magazine of the Royal Ontario Museum
  Attn: Publications Dept.
  100 Queen's Park
  Toronto, ON, Canada M5S 2C6
  (416) 586-5590
  (416) 586-5827 fax
  http://rom.on.ca
  Covering art, archaeology, natural sciences, astronomy. 3 times/year.

Children's Publications

Dino Times
  Dinosaur Society
  200 Carleton Ave.
  East Islip, NY 11730
  (516) 277-7855
  (516) 277-1479 fax
  Email: dsociety@aol.com
  http://www.dinosociety.org
  Magazine for children; includes news on current dinosaur studies. Monthly.

National Geographic World
  National Geographic Society
  1145 17th St. NW
  Washington, DC 20036-4688
  (202) 857-7000

(800) NGS-LINE
(202) 429-5712 fax
http://www.nationalgeographic.com
Magazine featuring factual stories on natural history, outdoor adventure, sports, science, and history for children ages 8 through 13. Monthly.

Dinosaurs on Video

The following listing includes fictional films featuring dinosaurs, educational videos, and documentaries focusing on the creation and extinction of dinosaurs.

Adventure at the Center of the Earth (1963). Mexican horror film featuring dinosaurs, cyclops, bat-creatures, and a rat-faced monster. In Spanish without subtitles.

Adventures in Dinosaur City (1992). Cast: Omri Katz, Shawn Hoffman, Tiffanie Poston, Mimi Maynard, Pete Koch, Megan Hughes, Brett Thompson. Directed by Tony Doyle. Modern-day pre-teen siblings are transported back in time to the stone age. There they meet their favorite TV characters (they're dinosaurs) and help them solve prehistoric crimes. Family film may amuse kids, but adults should stick to *Jurassic Park*.

Adventures in Dinosaurland (1983). Animated story of a little dinosaur who takes kids back to the stone age.

Age of Dinosaurs (1988). A series that's perfect for little kids who are curious about dinosaurs.

All About Dinosaurs (1990). Children in grade school can learn all about the prehistoric creatures that fascinate them so.

The Asteroid and the Dinosaur (1981). Scientists explain a theory that a giant asteroid collided with the earth millions of years ago, tossing a killing cloud of dust and debris into the atmosphere.

At the Earth's Core (1976). Cast: Doug McClure, Peter Cushing, Caroline Munro, Kevin Connor, Godfrey James, Keith Barron. Directed by Cy Grant. A Victorian scientist invents a giant burrowing machine, which he and his crew use to dig deeply into the Earth. To their surprise, they discover a lost world of subhuman creatures and prehistoric monsters. Based on Edgar Rice Burrough's novels.

Attack of the Super Monsters (1984). Group of prehistoric monsters are developing dastardly plots below the Earth to ruin the human race.

Baby. . . Secret of the Lost Legend (1985). Cast: William Katt, Sean Young, Patrick McGoohan, Julian Fellowes. Directed by Bill W. L. Norton. A sportswriter and his paleontologist wife risk their lives to reunite a hatching brontosaurus with its mother in the African jungle. Although this Disney film is not lewd in any sense, beware of several scenes displaying frontal nudity and some violence.

Bill Nye the Science Guy: Dinosaurs—Those Big Boneheads (1994). Bill Nye takes a look at dinosaurs and what has been discovered about their lifestyles. In another episode, Bill Nye explains how the Earth's surface and its inner mantle differ.

Box Investigates. . . Children visit Box's Science Lab, where they discover and investigate the worlds of dinosaurs, animals, and insects. Includes guide.

Cadillacs and Dinosaurs: "Wild Child" and "Pursuit" (1995). In "Wild Child," Jack and Hannah struggle to rescue a kidnapped child from the evil dino-poachers. In "Pursuit," Jack fights to clear his name when he is wrongly accused of stealing a dinosaur-killing weapon. Animated.

Carnosaur (1993). Cast: Diane Ladd, Raphael Sbarge, Jennifer Runyon, Harrison Page, Clint Howard, Ned Bellamy, Adam Simon. Directed by Nigel Holton. Straight from the Corman film factory, this exploitive quickie about dinosaurs harkens back to '50s-style monster epics. Predictable plot with extremely cheap effects. Genetic scientist Dr. Jane Tiptree (Ladd) is hatching diabolic experiments with chickens when things go awry. The experiments result in a bunch of lethal prehistoric creatures wreaking havoc among the community.

Carnosaur 2 (1994). Cast: John Savage, Cliff DeYoung, Arabella Holzbog, Ryan Thomas Johnson. Directed by Louis Morneau. Technicians investigating a power shortage at a secret military mining facility encounter deadly dinos. Entertaining schlock.

Carnosaur 3: Primal Species (1996). Cast: Scott Valentine, Janet Gunn, Rick Dean, Rodger Halstead, Tony Peck, Jonathan Winfrey. Directed by Kevin Kiner. Terrorists get big surprise when the cargo they hijack turns out to be three very hungry dinos who make snacks of them all. Then it's up to commando Valentine, scientist Gunn, and some soldiers to get rid of the beasts.

Caveman (1981). Cast: Ringo Starr, Barbara Bach, John Matuszak, Dennis Quaid, Jack Gilford, Shelley Long, Cork Hubbert. Written and Directed by Carl Gottlieb. Starr stars in this prehistoric spoof about a group of cavemen banished from different tribes who band together to form a tribe called "The Misfits."

Clifford (1992). Cast: Martin Short, Charles Grodin, Mary Steenburgen, Dabney Coleman, Sonia Jackson. Directed by Paul Flaherty. Short plays a 10-year-old in an effort delayed by movie studio Orion's past financial crisis. Creepy little Clifford's uncle Martin (Grodin) rues the day he volunteered to babysit his nephew to prove to his girlfriend (Steenburgen) how much he likes kids. Clifford terrorizes Grodin in surprisingly nasty ways when their plans for visiting Dinosaurworld fall through, although Grodin sees to well-deserved revenge. Not just bad in the conventional sense, but bad in a bizarre sort of alien fashion that raises questions about who was controlling the bodies of the producers. To create the effect of Short really being short, other actors stood on boxes and sets were built slightly larger than life.

Common Fossils of the United States (1990). A look at the varieties of fossils common to the U.S., including their age and the environments that produced them.

The Crater Lake Monster (1977). Cast: Richard Cardella, Glenn Roberts, Mark Siegel, Bob Hyman. Directed by William R. Stromberg. The dormant egg of a prehistoric creature hatches after a meteor rudely awakens the dozing dino. He's understandably miffed and begins a revenge campaign. Prehistoric yawner.

Digging Dinosaurs (1988). This video provides an informative introduction to paleontology for young children, and an excellent presentation to be shown before or after field trips to natural history museums.

Digging Dinosaurs: A Search for the Creatures of the Mesozoic Era (1987). Follows the excitement of a paleontological dig in Western Montana.

Digging Dinosaurs—2 Pack (1994). Two-part set aimed at teaching younger audiences about dinosaurs. Covers the different types of dinosaurs, as well as how and where dinosaur bones have been found. Includes computer animation, actual footage of dinosaur digs, and visits to museums and paleontology labs.

Digging Up Dinosaurs (1992). Introduction to paleontology in two parts. Part one includes treks lead by Martin Lockley to a site in the Dinosaur National Monument in Utah, and Scott Madsen to a site where microfossils were uncovered. Part two includes a trek to a site where an *Allosaurus* was uncovered, the process of excavating, and casting and repairing the bones.

Dino Riders: The Adventure Begins (1988). The Dino Riders must save themselves from the evil Vipers.

Dinosaur (1989). Visit to the Dinosaur Quarry in Dinosaur National Monument, an archaeologist's oasis where an abundance of dinosaur fossils, bones, and skeletons have been excavated.

Dinosaur (1997). Follows paleontologists as they uncover fossil bones in Dinosaur National Monument.

Dinosaur (1980). Hosted by Christopher Reeve. Directed by Robert Guenette. An introduction to dinosaurs and the prehistoric world they inhabited millions of years ago. An Emmy Award–winning animated film depicting the environment and lives of the dinosaurs.

The Dinosaur Age (1958). This video presents a look at how we have come to learn about dinosaurs through fossils.

Dinosaur Families (1994). Part of the "Digging Dinosaurs" collection. This section covers the family structure of the dinosaurs and how paleontologists and children can dig for dinosaur bones.

Dinosaur Footprints of the Peace River Valley. In northeastern British Columbia, the Peace River Canyon contains one of the largest concentrations of dinosaur footprints in the world. The film observes a team of paleontologists mapping the area and making molds of the prints.

Dinosaur Hunt (1998). Three-part series features aspects of the dinosaur and the hunt for fossils, including the chaos that erupts when a fossil is found, whether dinosaurs and birds are biologically related, and the false mystique of the *Tyrannosaurus rex*. Three hours on three videocassettes.

The Dinosaur Hunters (1972). An unusual film asking: How did dinosaurs function? What did they eat? How did they reproduce? How did they defend themselves?

Dinosaur Island (1993). Cast: Ross Hagen, Richard Gabai, Tom Shell, Steve Barkett, Toni Naples, Antonia Dorian, Peter Spellos, Griffin Drew. Directed by Jim Wynorski and Fred

Olen Ray. Five military men survive a plane crash and discover an island where scantily clad (leather bikinis being the fashion choice) lascivious ladies live. Will the awesome power of testosterone overcome the fierce dinosaurs that stand between the men and their objects of desire?

The Dinosaur Who Wondered Who He Was (1976). A long time ago, a little creature hatched, grew into a big dinosaur, and had a lot to learn about the world and himself.

Dinosaur! With Walter Cronkite (1991). Hosted by Walter Cronkite. A four-part boxed set that traces the discovery of dinosaurs from the first archeological find to the latest breakthroughs. Includes animatronics, dramatic re-enactments, and visits to archeological sites. A companion book written by paleontologist David Norman is also available.

The Dinosaurs! (1993). Paleontologists reconstruct the existence of these prehistoric reptiles from ancient artifacts in this four-tape series.

Dinosaurs! Features an animated, live action, and claymated look at dinosaurs, featuring Fred Savage.

Dinosaurs (1988). Music and dinosaurs combine to provide kids with an educational experience.

Dinosaurs (1979). An introduction to the study of dinosaurs and the means used by modern science to attempt to answer the many questions afforded by their history.

Dinosaurs: A Closer Look (199?). Five lessons explore perspective, classification, adaptation, and a global view of dinosaurs. Narrative CAV videodisc sequences contribute content information bolstered by student readings, group activities, and class discussions.

Dinosaurs: A First Film (1979). This animated program shows the changes in dinosaurs, the variety of dinosaurs, and the change in climate that led to their downfall.

Dinosaurs: Age of Reptiles (1979). Paleontologists are seen working with other scientists to reconstruct dinosaurs via fossils.

Dinosaurs: Age of the Terrible Lizard (1970). An animated but completely factual account of the Dinosaur Age: major types of dinosaurs, behavior characteristics, evidence of evolutionary development.

Dinosaurs and Other Creature Features (1996). Introduces a host of creatures including dinosaurs, vampire bats, black widow spiders, and more; lessons include music videos.

Dinosaurs Are Very Big (1994). Part of the "Digging Dinosaurs" collection that takes a look at some of the dinosaurs that roamed the earth in the past. Uses computer animation with visits to digs and museums to help explain the differences between the various dinosaurs.

Dinosaurs! Dinosaurs! (1995). Reveals how paleontologists have relied on fossilized remains to determine the appearance of dinosaurs living 70 million years ago. Animated dinosaur models enhance realistic footage.

Dinosaurs! Dinosaurs! (1994). Hosted by Leslie Nielsen. From dig site to museum laboratory, details how scientists study the characteristics and living habits of dinosaurs.

Dinosaurs, Dinosaurs, Dinosaurs (1987). Cast: Gary Owens and Eric Boardman. Owens is slowly turning into a dinosaur and partner Boardman must learn all he can in order to stop the changes. A semi-educational program that re-creates the world of dinosaurs.

Dinosaurs: Fantastic Creatures That Ruled the Earth. Attempts to dispell myths that have surrounded dinosaurs and offers answers to commonly asked questions.

Dinosaurs: Messages in Stone (1994). Graphically explores the making of a mold from extant dinosaur fossils and discusses theories of dinosaur behavior. Animated dinosaur models enhance realistc footage.

Dinosaurs: Piecing It All Together. Combines animation with comments from paleontologists and paleoartists to answer many questions associated with the history, life, and extinction of dinosaurs.

Dinosaurs: Puzzles from the Past (1981). Explains to youngsters that dinosaurs were different from today's reptiles. They were built differently, moved differently, and roamed the earth for millions of years before they gradually and mysteriously disappeared.

Dinosaurs: Terrible Lizards (1976). Discusses a variety of dinosaurs, explores methods used by paleontologists, and shows how a dinosaur skeleton is assembled and reconstructed for museum display.

Dinosaurs: Terrible Lizards (1970). Brings the age of the dinosaur to realistic life. An overview of what they looked like and how they lived and died.

Dinosaurs: The Ageless Quarry. Recounts the events of June 9, 1884, when geologist Joseph B. Tyrell discoved a fossilized dinosaur bone in Drumheller, Alberta, ushering in the Alberta dinosaur rush. Today the site is the toast of paleontologists worldwide for its rich fossil content and fascinating Tyrell Museum of Paleontology.

Dinosaurs: Then and Now (1995). Centers on an animated journey from the birth of the solar system to the recent discovery of the fossil of Utahraptor, the "Super Slasher."

Dinosaurus! (1960). Cast: Ward Ramsey, Kristina Hanson, Irvin S. Yeaworth Jr. Directed by Paul Lukather. Large, sadistic dinosaurs appear in the modern world. They eat, burn, and pillage their way through this film. Also includes a romance between a Neanderthal and a modern-age woman.

Donny Deinonychus: The Educational Dinosaur, Vol. 1 (1993). Narrated by Ruth Buzzi and Richard Moll. Two debut episodes of a non-violent educational series for children that shares the story of prehistory while teaching basic morals, values, judgments, and courtesies. In "Donny Deinonychus" Donny the Parrot is the victim of a misdirected scientific experiment and metamorphosizes into his prehistoric ancestor, Donny Deinonychus (Dine-non-i-kus), whose parrot memory is erased and replaced by that of a dinosaur. Donny wants only to get back 'home' to prehistory and flees the house with Professor Stevens hot on his trail. In "Stormy, the Long Lost Friend" Donny introduces Stormy the Triceratops and explains that even though someone may be scary looking, they may not necessarily be bad.

EPIC: Days of the Dinosaurs (1987). Narrated by John Huston. Directed by Yoram Gross. An animated fable about two babies born into a pack of dingoes in a prehistoric world. They must fight for superiority over the mystical powers of nature.

Exploring Dinosaurs (1992). Rather than a lemonade stand, Jeff sets up a dinosaur information booth from which he shares with customers the wonders of the dinosaur kingdom, including their form, diet, habitat, and extinction. Models, archaeological findings, and artwork help illustrate Jeff's findings. Comes with teacher's guide and blackline master.

Eyewitness Dinosaur. Investigates paleontology, explaining the process of discovery from digging to reconstruction.

The Eyewitness Video Series (1996). Features the world of living things. Focuses on evolutionary process, habitats, and more.

The Fascinating World of Prehistoric Animals (1993). Two programs introduce the world of prehistoric animals and dinosaurs. Each program available individually or together on one tape.

Fossils: Clues to the Past (1983). Explains what fossils are, how they are formed, what they can tell us, and how their age can be determined.

Giant Dinosaurs (1993). Features the *Torosaurus, Braceosarus, Diplodocus,* and other dinosaurs in full-color graphics and computer animation. Accurate information and realistic representation make this an interesting and educational presentation.

The Great Dinosaur Discovery (1976). The discovery of the "world's largest dinosaur" is documented—a gigantic new sauropod estimated to have been over 60 feet tall, 100 feet long, and weighing near 100 tons. Filmed on the site as the actual discoveries were made.

Hollywood Dinosaur Chronicles (1987). Hosted by Doug McClure. As soon as filmmaking was invented, dinosaurs became stars! Here are a few of those very early appearances. From the silents *Gertie the Dinosaur* and *Lost World,* to recent productions like *Godzilla* and *Baby,* all the best of the extinct critters is represented here.

Hot-Blooded Dinosaurs (1977). Sheds new light on the intriguing puzzle of how dinosaurs lived. From *Nova.*

The Infinite Voyage: The Great Dinosaur Hunt (1989). An episode of "The Infinite Voyage," wherein via new research and computer graphics revolutionary discoveries about dinosaurs are being plumbed.

Invasion of the Dinosaurs (1993). A brief overview of the era of the dinosaur as well as descriptions of some of the better-known creatures, with life-size Dinomation replicas used as educational models.

Invasion of the Robot Dinosaurs (1991). Realistically animated dinosaurs live again at the Museum of Natural History. Examine the lives of *Tyrannosaurus rex, Triceratops,* and others, how they lived and how they may have died. Informative fun for the whole family.

Jurassic Park (1993). Cast: Sam Neill, Laura Dern, Jeff Goldblum, Richard Attenborough, Samuel L. Jackson. Directed by Steven Spielberg. Michael Crichton's spine-tingling thriller translates well (but not faithfully) due to its main attraction: realistic, rampaging dinosaurs. Genetically cloned from prehistoric DNA, all is well until they escape from their pens—smarter and less predictable than expected. Contrived plot and thin characters (except Goldblum), but who cares? The true stars are the dinos, an incredible combination of models and computer animation. Violent, suspenseful, and realistic with gory attack scenes. Not for small kids, though much of the marketing is aimed at them. Spielberg knocked his own *E.T.* out of first place as "JP" became the highest-grossing movie of all time. Also available in a letterbox version.

King Dinosaur (1955). Cast: Bill Bryant, Wanda Curtis, Patti Gallagher, Douglas Henderson. A new planet arrives in the solar system, and a scientific team checks out its giant iguana–ridden terrain.

The Land Before Time (1988). Voices: Pat Hingle, Helen Shaver, Gabriel Damon, Candice Houston, Burke Barnes, Judith Barsi, Will Ryan. Directed by Don Bluth. Lushly animated children's film about five orphaned baby dinosaurs who band together and try to find the Great Valley, a paradise where they might live safely. Works same parental separation theme as Bluth's *American Tail*. Charming, coy, and shamelessly tearjerking; producers included Steven Spielberg and George Lucas.

The Land Before Time 2: The Great Valley Adventure (1994). Sequel to 1988's animated adventure finds dinsosaur pals Littlefoot, Cera, Ducky, Petrie, and Spike happily settled in the Great Valley. But their adventures don't stop as they chase two egg-stealing Struthiomimuses and retrieve an egg of unknown origin from the Mysterious Beyond.

The Land Before Time 3: The Time of the Great Giving (1995). Directed by Roy Allen Smith. Littlefoot and his pals try to find a new source of water when the Great Valley experiences a severe water shortage.

The Land Before Time 4: Journey Through the Mists (1996). The little dinosaurs travel through the land of the mists in search of a rejuvenation flower that can save the life of Littlefoot's sick grandpa.

The Land Before Time 5: The Mysterious Island (1997). Directed by Charles Grosvenor. When a swarm of insects devour all the plants in the Great Valley, the herds are forced to move. But with the adults fighting, Littlefoot and his pals go off on their own. They cross the Big Water to a mysterious island, which just happens to be the home of their old friend, the baby T-rex, Chomper. And it's up to Chomper to protect his plant-eating friends from the island's meat-eaters, who look on the little band as dinner.

Land of the Lost (1992). Cast: Timothy Bottoms. Tom Porter and his children Kevin and Annie are transported back to prehistoric times where they are joined by a mysterious jungle girl and a monkey-boy named Stink. They must fight for survival in a jungle filled with gigantic dinosaurs, evil lizard-men, and other dangers.

The Land That Time Forgot (1975). Cast: Doug McClure, John McEnery, Susan Penhaligon, Kevin Connor. Directed by James Cawthorn. A WWI veteran, a beautiful woman, and their German enemies are stranded in a land outside time filled with prehistoric creatures. Based on the 1918 novel by Edgar Rice Burroughs. Followed in 1977 by *The People that Time Forgot*.

The Land Unknown (1957). Cast: Jock Mahoney, Shawn Smith, William Reynolds, Henry (Kleinbach) Brandon, Douglas Kennedy. Directed by Virgil W. Vogel. A Naval helicopter is forced down in a tropical land of prehistoric terror, complete with ferocious creatures from the Mesozoic Era. While trying to make repairs, the crew discovers the sole survivor of a previous expedition who was driven to madness by life in the primordial jungle. Good performances from cast, although the monsters aren't that believable. Based on a story by Charles Palmer.

Legend of the Dinosaurs (1983). Slavering, teeth-gnashing dinosaurs are discovered on Mt. Fuji.

Life During the Mesozoic Era (19??). Takes at look at the different forms of life that existed during the Mesozoic Era (70 million to 220 million years ago). Comes with teacher's manual.

The Lost Continent (1951). Cast: Cesar Romero, Hillary Brooke, Chick Chandler, John Hoyt, Acquanetta, Sid Melton, Whit Bissell, Hugh Beaumont. Directed by Sam Newfield. An expedition searching for a lost rocket on a jungle island discovers dinosaurs and other extinct creatures.

Lost in Dinosaur World (1993). A ten-year-old boy and his seven-year-old sister have the experience of a lifetime when they get lost in a dinosaur park. Tension mounts as their parents are warned that it's almost feeding time for the dinosaurs. Fun and informative, offering a fair amount of scientific facts about dinosaurs and the world in which they lived.

The Lost World: Jurassic Park 2 (1997). Cast: Jeff Goldblum, Julianne Moore, Vince Vaughn, Arliss Howard, Pete Postlethwaite, Peter Stormare, Vanessa Lee Chester. Directed by Steven Spielberg. A sequel to *Jurassic Park,* this movie proves only that Spielberg has tapped this well one too many times. It's four years after the first adventure and the surviving dinos have peacefully set up house on a deserted island near Costa Rica. Mathematician Ian Malcolm (Goldblum, reprising his role) reluctantly becomes part of an expedition to monitor the beasts, only because his paleontologist girlfriend (Moore) is so gung-ho. Other characters exist, but are reduced to the role of entrees. More dinos (two T-rexes, a clan of Raptors, and bite-sized newcomers Compsognathus), thrilling special effects, and more gore make up for thin subplots involving a rich businessman who wants to use the dinosaurs for a new zoo and another who hunts them for sport. Ironically, Spielberg's predictablity owes much to better films such as *King Kong, Aliens,* and *Godzilla.* Still, T-rex and buddies, the true stars, rise to the occasion to entertain in an otherwise lackluster sequel. Based on Michael Crichton's book.

Lost Worlds, Vanished Lives (1991). Naturalist David Attenborough looks at the world of paleontology. He examines the Earth's fossil records, as well as computer-enhanced studies of dinosaurs, to offer new insights into humankind's earliest ancestors. On four cassettes.

A Magical Field Trip to the Dinosaur Museum (1991). Cast: Rosie O'Flanigan. Chris takes a trip to a dinosaur museum with his friend Nicole and Rosie O'Flanigan, which provides him with knowledge about dinosaurs and a great story to tell at school. Available at a special series price.

Maia: A Dinosaur Grows Up (1990). Learn what life was like 80 million years ago through the eyes and experiences of Maia, a duck-billed dinosaur.

Massacre in Dinosaur Valley (1985). Michael Sopkiw, Suzanne Carvall. A dashing young paleontologist and his fellow explorers go on a perilous journey down the Amazon in search of the Valley of the Dinosaur.

Message from a Dinosaur (1965). Shows how life of the past is reconstructed from fossil remains and how new forms of life evolved from adaptations to environmental changes.

More about Dinosaurs (1993). Part of the 14-part First Time Science Series that uses animation to outline factors leading to the extinction of the dinosaurs.

More Dinosaurs (1985). Cast: Hosted by Gary Owens and Eric Boardman. Owens and Boardman go on an African safari to investigate the legend of the living dinosaur and tour Dinosaur National Monument and the Smithsonian to learn more.

My Science Project (1985). John Stockwell, Danielle von Zerneck, Fisher Stevens, Raphael Sbarge, Richard Masur, Barry Corbin, Ann Wedgeworth, Dennis Hopper. Directed by Jonathan Betuel. Teenager Stockwell stumbles across a crystal sphere with a funky light. Unaware that it is an alien time-travel device, he takes it to school to use as a science project in a last-ditch effort to avoid failing his class. Chaos follows and Stockwell and his chums find themselves battling gladiators, mutants, and dinosaurs. Plenty of special effects and a likeable enough teenage movie.

Nature Connection: Badlands. Dr. Suzuki brings a group of children to Dinosaur Provincial Park where they learn about the creatures from the prehistoric era.

Nova: The Case of the Flying Dinosaur (1992). Discusses whether or not birds are the direct descendents of dinosaurs.

One Million B.C. (1940). Cast: Victor Mature, Carole Landis, Lon Chaney Jr. Directed by Hal Roach and Hal Roach Jr. The strange saga of the struggle of primitive cavemen and their battle against dinosaurs and other monsters. Curiously told in flashbacks, this film provided stock footage for countless dinosaur movies that followed. Portions of film rumored to be directed by cinematic pioneer D. W. Griffith.

One Million Years B.C. (1966). Cast: Raquel Welch, John Richardson, Percy Herbert, Robert Brown, Martine Beswick. Directed by Don Chaffey. It's Welch in a fur bikini and special effects expert Ray Harryhausen doing dinosaurs, so who cares about a plot (which involves Welch and her boyfriend, who's from a rival clan). Remake of the 1940 film *One Million B.C.*

One of Our Dinosaurs Is Missing (1975). Peter Ustinov, Helen Hayes, Derek Nimmo, Clive Revill, Joan Sims. Directed by Robert Stevenson. An English nanny and her cohorts help British Intelligence retrieve a microfilm-concealing dinosaur fossil from the bad guys that have stolen it. Disney film was shot on location in England.

The Outer Planets/Shooting Stars (1993). Part 6 of the 12-part Galactic Encyclopedia series. Focuses on the planets furthest from the sun—Uranus, Neptune, and Pluto—and speculates on whether a collision with a comet or asteroid is the possible cause of the extinction of dinosaurs.

Paleo World (1994). Three-volume series looks at the Jurassic era of pre-history, examining predators, early mammals, and ideas on evolution. Available as a boxed set or individually.

The People That Time Forgot (1977). Cast: Doug McClure, Patrick Wayne, Sarah Douglas, Dana Gillespie, Thorley Walters, Shane Rimmer. Directed by Kevin Connor. Sequel to *The Land That Time Forgot,* based on the Edgar Rice Burroughs novel. A rescue team returns to a world of prehistoric monsters to rescue a man left there after the first film.

Planet of Dinosaurs (1980). James Whitworth. Directed by James K. Shea. Survivors from a ruined spaceship combat huge savage dinosaurs on a swampy uncharted planet.

Prehistoric World (1988). Hosted by Gary Owens and Eric Boardman. A companion to *More Dinosaurs* and *Dinosaurs, Dinosaurs, Dinosaurs,* examines prehistoric mammals. Kids can see recreations of the saber tooth tiger, woolly mammoth and other animals, as well as a trip to the La Brea Tar Pits.

Prehysteria (1993). Cast: Brett Cullen, Austin O'Brien. Directed by Albert Band. Fantasy/adventure about a widower, his 11-year-old son and teenage daughter, and what happens when some mysterious eggs from South America accidentally wind up at their farm. Imagine their surprise when the eggs hatch and out pop a brood of pygmy dinosaurs. The dinosaurs are cute (as is the family).

Prehysteria 2 (1994). Cast: Dean Scofield, Kevin R. Connors, Jennifer Harte, Bettye Ackerman, Larry Hankin, Greg Lewis, Alan Palo, Michael Hagiwara, Owen Bush. Directed by Albert Band. While their adoptive family is on vacation the pygmy dinosaurs get loose and aid a lonely rich boy whose governess is plotting to send him to military boarding school.

Prehysteria 3 (1995). Cast: Fred Willard, Bruce Weitz, Whitney Anderson. Directed by Julian Breen. The mini-dinos take up miniature golf. Seems Thomas MacGregor's (Willard) putt-putt business is about to sink when his daughter Ella (Anderson) finds the pygmy dinosaurs and a promotional bonanza is born. But Thomas's evil brother Hal (Weitz) hatches a plot to take over the now-successful enterprise.

Pterodactyl Woman from Beverly Hills (1997). Cast: Beverly D'Angelo, Moon Zappa, Brion James, Brad Wilson, Aron Eisenberg. Written and directed by Philippe Mora. California housewife Pixie Chandler (D'Angelo) is the victim of an eccentric witch doctor (James) when her paleontologist husband Dick (Wilson) disturbs an ancient burial site and the doc curses Pixie by turning her into a dinosaur. This is the first so-called family release from those madcap Troma people who brought you the *Toxic Avenger.*

Reading Rainbow: Digging Up Dinosaurs (1983). Voice(s) by Jerry Stiller, hosted by LeVar Burton. Burton takes viewers back in time to do some dinosaur watching.

Return of the Dinosaurs (1983). A comet is about to collide with the Earth. Never fear! The dinosaur patrol will interfere (and ultimately save the planet).

The Return of Dinosaurs. Hosted by Gary Owens and Eric Boardman. Hosts Owens and Boardman join a group of kids at the Natural History Museum in Los Angeles for a dinosaur bone hunt and lots of dino-info. At the Canadian Museum of Paleontology the viewer will see how fossils are dug up and reconstructed for museum display.

Return to the Lost World (1993). Cast: John Rhys-Davies, David Warner, Darren Peter Mercer, Geza Kovacs. Directed by Timothy Bond. Rival scientists Challenger and Summerlee set out for the Lost World and find it threatened by oil prospectors. With a volcano about to explode the scientists set out to save their prehistoric paradise and its dinosaur inhabitants. Based on a story by Sir Arthur Conan Doyle. Sequel to *The Lost World*.

Sir Arthur Conan Doyle's The Lost World (1998). Cast: Patrick Bergin. Zoologist George Challenger (Bergin) recruits a team of scientists to help him find a mythic land where dinosaurs and other prehistoric creatures exist. Lots of cliches although the special effects aren't bad.

64,000,000 Years Ago (1987). Chronicles the days when magnificent, majestic dinosaurs ruled the earth.

Son of Dinosaurs (1990). Cast: Gary Owens, Eric Boardman, Kenneth Mars, Alex Rodine, James Stewart. Owens and Boardman are back as those intrepid dinosaur hunters, this time as sworn "Protectors" of the discovery of a lifetime—a dinosaur egg containing a live embryo. But watch out. . .there's a man who'll stop at nothing to steal the precious egg.

Sound of Horror (1964). Cast: James Philbrook, Arturo Fernandez, Soledad Miranda, Ingrid Pitt. Directed by Jose Antonio Nieves-Conde. Efforts to keep budgets down back-fire on this Spanish production. A dinosaur egg hatches, and out lashes an invisible predator. Yes, you'll have to use your imagination as archaeologists are slashed to bits by the no-show terror.

Sound of Thunder. A man goes on safari 60 years into the past to hunt *Tyrannosaurus rex.*

Story of Dinosaurs (1993). Part of the 14-part First Time Science Series that uses animation to summarize the life and habits of dinosaurs.

Super Mario Bros. (1993). Cast: Bob Hoskins, John Leguizamo, Dennis Hopper, Annabel Jankel, Samantha Mathis, Lance Henriksen, Fisher Stevens, Fiona Shaw, Richard Edson. Directed by Rocky Morton. This $42 million adventure fantasy is based on the popular Nintendo video game. The brothers are in hot pursuit of the Princess Daisy, who's been kidnapped by evil slimebucket Hopper and taken to Dinohattan, a fungi-infested, garbage-strewn, rat-hole version of Manhattan. Hopper will amuse the adults, doing a gleeful reptilian version of Frank Booth from *Blue Velvet*. Hoskins and Leguizamo act gamely in broad Nintendo style, enthusiastically partaking in high-tech wizardry and the many gags. Hits bullseye of target audience—elementary and junior high kids—with frenetic pace, gaudy special effects, oversized sets, and animatronic monsters.

T. Rex Exposed (1991). Presents facts and myths surrounding the *Tyrannosaurus rex,* and includes footage of the 1990 Montana excavation of one of the largest and most complete *T. rex* skeletons to date.

Tammy and the T-Rex (1994). Cast: Terry Kiser, John Franklin, Paul Walker, Denise Richards. Directed by Stewart Raffill. All Michael (Walker) wanted was a date with the lovely Denise (Richards)—he didn't expect to almost die for her. Nor did he expect a mad scientist to transplant his brain into a mechanical three-ton dinosaur. Part teen angst—part camp horror—all good-natured hooey.

Teenage Caveman (1958). Cast: Robert Vaughn, Darrah Marshall, Leslie Bradley, Frank De Kova. Directed by Roger Corman. A teenage boy living in a post-apocalypse yet prehistoric world journeys across the river, even though he was warned against it, and finds an old man who owns a book about past civilizations in the 20th century. Schlocky, and one of the better bad films around. The dinosaur shots were picked up from the film *One Million B.C.*

Teenage Mutant Ninja Turtles: Turtles at the Earth's Core (1991). The Turtles have a fantastic adventure in a land populated by dinosaurs.

Theodore Rex (1995). Cast: Whoopi Goldberg, Armin Mueller-Stahl, Richard Roundtree, Juliet Landau. Written and directed by Jonathan Betuel. Futuristic comedy finds cynical, seasoned cop Katie Coltrane (Goldberg) furious at being teamed with Teddy, who just happens to be an eight-foot-tall, three-ton, returned-from-extinction *Tyrannosaurus rex* (who has a taste for cookies). And Teddy's not exactly the brightest dinosaur on the block, which makes Katie's job all the harder when they stumble across a major crime caper.

Two Lost Worlds (1950). Cast: James Arness, Laura Elliott, Bill Kennedy. Directed by Norman Dawn. A young hero battles monstrous dinosaurs, pirates, and more in this cheapy when he and his shipmates are shipwrecked on an uncharted island. Don't miss the footage from *Captain Fury, One Billion B.C.,* and *Captain Caution,* and Arness long before his Sheriff Dillon fame and his "big" role in *The Thing.*

Unknown Island (1948). Cast: Virginia Grey, Philip Reed, Richard Denning, Barton MacLane. Directed by Jack Bernhard. Scientists travel to a legendary island where dinosaurs supposedly still exist. Bogus dinosaurs and cliched script.

The Valley of Gwangi (1969). Cast: James Franciscus, Gila Golan, Richard Carlson, Laurence Naismith, Freda Jackson. Directed by James O'Connolly. One of the best prehistoric-monster westerns out there. Cowboys discover a lost valley of dinosaurs and try to capture a vicious, carnivorous allosaurus. Bad move, kemosabe! The creatures move via the stop-motion model animation by special effects maestro Ray Harryhausen, here at his finest.

VITSIE Video Sitter: Dinosaurs (1990). The Vitsie series designed for young children has received an Award of Excellence from the Film Advisory Board. *Dinosaurs* lets the little ones play and sing while learning about the ancient reptiles.

We're Back! A Dinosaur's Story (1993). Voices: John Goodman, Felicity Kendal, Walter Cronkite, Joey Shea, Jay Leno, Julia Child, Kenneth Mars, Martin Short, Rhea Perlman. Directed by Dick Zondag. Animated adventures of a pack of revived dinosaurs who return to their old stomping grounds—which are now modern-day New York City. Smart-mouth human boy Louie and his girlfriend Cecilia take the dinos under their wing (so to speak), wise them up to modern life, and try to prevent their capture by the evil Professor Screweyes. Slow-moving with some violence. Adapted from the book by Hudson Talbott.

What Ever Happened to the Dinosaurs? (1992). Informative video explores the current theories about dinosaurs with the help of four curious kids.

When Dinosaurs Ruled the Earth (1970). Cast: Victoria Vetri, Robin Hawdon, Patrick Allen, Drewe Henley, Sean Caffrey, Magda Konopka, Imogen Hassall. Directed by Val Guest. When *One Million Years B.C.* ruled the box office the Brits cranked out a few more lively prehistoric fantasies. A sexy cavegirl, exiled because of her blond hair, acquires a cave-beau and a dinosaur guardian. Stop-motion animation from Jim Danforth, story by J. G. Ballard. Under the name Angela Dorian, Vetri was Playmate of the Year in 1968 (A.D.).

Where Did They Go? A Dinosaur Update (1988). The fun and excitement of dinosaurs have been captured for children to enjoy.

A Whopping Small Dinosaur (1988). This documentary follows a team of dedicated paleontologists into the Painted Desert, where the bones of a "whopping small dinosaur" are removed from the ground, shipped to a museum, and then assembled.

Dinosaur Websites

Dinofest®: http://www.acnatsci.org/dinofestarchive/index.html. In the spring of 1998, Philadelphia's Academy of Natural Sciences presented Dinofest®, called "The World's Fair of Dinosaurs." Visit this award–winning site to see the archives from the exhibit. Also, dinosaur news, and kids' art show. The promotional site for the show can still be visited (at http://www3.phillynews.com/packages/dinofest/), where more info on Dinofest is available along with lessons, games, links and resources, as well as video tours.

Dinosaur Eggs: http://www.nationalgeographic.com/dinoeggs/index.html. National Geographic Magazine takes visitors behind the scenes of the Great Dinosaur Egg Hunt. Follow fossil researchers as they "hatch" fossilized dinosaur eggs; tour a museum of hatchlings.

Dinosaurs in the Gobi Desert: http://www.discovery.com/area/specials/gobi/ gobi1.html. During the summer of 1998 the Discovery Channel sent a correspondent along on a 20-day paleontological expedition through the Gobi Desert. Visit this website to read daily dispatches from the paleontologists, learn about their finds, and check out online areas such as the Bone Zone, Paleo-Talk, and an email exchange between visitors to the website and a paleontologist from the American Museum of Natural History.

Dinosaurs in Print: http://www.lhl.lib.mo.us/pubserv/hos/dino/welcome.htm. View the publications that told the world about dinosaurs. The Linda Hall Library (Kansas City, Missouri) hosts this web exhibition, which consists of a hypertext catalog of pictures and text from some eighty works about dinosaur discovery and theory published between 1824 and 1969.

Expedia's Mungo Park: http://www.mungopark.com. Join world–renowned paleontologists Jack Horner and Phil Currie on an expedition to some of North America's richest fossil sites: Read their dispatches, find out what detours they took, and get a dossier and resource information for planning your own (real-world) expedition.

Giganotosaurus: http://www.giganotosaurus.com. "Dino" Don Lessem takes you on a tour of discovery of this remarkable animal—the largest carnivorous dinosaur ever found, even bigger than *T. rex*. For all ages.

Haddonfield Hadrosaurus: http://www.levins.com/dinosaur.html. Haddonfield, New Jersey, was home to the first dinosaur skeleton ever excavated (in 1858). The Hadrosaurus found there and the site where it was found are celebrated as the beginning of modern

475

paleontology. Visit this website to see photos, graphics, and maps, and to find information for planning a visit to this historic site. (The feature is by Hoag Levins.)

Bill Nye the Science Guy: http://nyelabs.kcts.org/nyeverse/episode/e03.html. Kids' favorite scientist and host of the popular TV show, Nye turns his attention to dishing up the dirt on dinosaurs. Forget about *Jurassic Park* ("Jurassic Shmurassic") and get the facts about dinosaurs. Also follow simple instructions for making you own "fossils."

Sue: The Tyrannosaurus Rex: http://www.sothebys.com/search/index.html. Visit the site of Sotheby's Auction House: A search here (keyword = Sue) pulls up excellent archival articles on how the *T. rex* was discovered (in August 1990 in South Dakota), the significance of the find, the restoration of the skeleton, and the auction (in October 1997). Also, you can view quick-time videos of Sue's skull, tooth, vertebrae, and forelimb.

WaybackMachine: http://www.discovery.com:80/area/wayback/wayback970324/wayback1.html. Travel in Discovery Channel's Wayback Machine to 1902, and be there as renowned paleontologist Barnum Brown finds an almost-complete skeleton of a *Tyrannosaurus rex*—in a desolate spot in Montana. Dinosaur enthusiasts of all ages will enjoy the trip.

Virtual Tours

American Museum of Natural History: http://www.amnh.org/exhibitions/index.html. Get an online preview of the famed museum's dinosaur hall, which includes the world's tallest free-standing dinosaur skeleton. Includes floor plans to help guide you.

Children's Museum of Indianapolis: http://www.childrensmuseum.org/dino.htm. Online exhibit of dinosaurs is specifically geared toward kids. Also, dinosaur fact sheets and FAQ.

Dinosaur Hall: http://www.acnatsci.org/dinosaurs/dinonew.html. The Dinosaur Hall at Philadelphia's Academy of Natural Sciences features five different guided online tours of exhibits: From the Fossils; The Big Dig; Fossil Prep Lab; Bones, Guts, and Behavior; and Science through Art. Also, a kids section and links for teachers, as well as academy news, museum info, and newsletter of online events.

Field Museum of Natural History: http://www.fmnh.org/exhibits/web_exhibits.htm. Visit this page to begin an online tour of the Field's Life Over Time exhibit, tracing 3.8 billion years of the evolution of life on earth—from single cells to dinosaurs and humans.

Finland's Museum of Natural History: http://www.fmnh.helsinki.fi/. English-language site of the Finnish Museum of Natural History (part of Helsinki University) offers information about and pictures from its exhibitions and collections. At press time, the museum was showing After the Ice Age, an exhibition about how the Ice Age affected the biology and geology of Finland, and about what happened as the icecap withdrew. Previous exhibitions include Dinosaurs—Rulers of Their Time; Backyard Monsters; and Treasures of the Museum.

Florida Museum of Natural History: http://www.flmnh.ufl.edu/. The Florida Museum of Natural History (Gainesville) offers virtual exhibits and a photo gallery to online visitors as part of their museum outreach program.

Hall of Archosaurs: http://www.ucmp.berkeley.edu/diapsids/archosy.html. Learn about the dinosaur family tree at the University of California Museum of Paleontology. Click on a map to explore the major dinosaur phyla, a grouping that includes all descendants, living or extinct, known and unknown, of an inferred common ancestor. Not geared for young children, but terrific for older students.

Honolulu Community College Dinosaur Exhibit: http://www.hcc.hawaii.edu/dinos. Take a narrated tour (conducted by history instructor Rick Ziegler) of the Honolulu Community College's exhibit of replicas of fossils from the American Museum of Natural History.

La Brea Tar Pits: http://www.lam.mus.ca.us/nhm/dino/kiosk and http://www.lam.mus.ca.us/page. Educational website of the Natural History Museum of Los Angeles County features ten different dinosaurs. Also, the Page Museum at the La Brea Tar Pits, where scientists discovered an unusually diverse assemblage of extinct Ice Age plants and animals, offers a look at fossils, kids' stuff, and a calendar of events at its searchable site.

National Museum of Natural History: http://www.nmnh.si.edu/VirtualTour/Tour/First/Dinosaurs/index.html. Visit the virtual exhibits at the Smithsonian. Dinosaurs are on the first floor of the Museum of Natural History; a floor plan helps you navigate through the halls.

Peabody Museum: http://www.peabody.yale.edu/mural. Visit Yale University's Peabody Museum online to view the famous mural, *The Age of Reptiles,* painted by Rudolph Zallinger between 1942 and 1947. The Peabody's homepage (at http://www.peabody.yale.edu/) offers museum news, events and exhibits info, and historical information (including a "who was who" among paleontologists).

Russian Paleontological Institute: http://www.ucmp.berkeley.edu/pin/pinentrance.html. Visit the Russian Paleontological Institute, hosted by the University of California. Includes sections on Pleistocene mammals, Mongolian dinosaurs, and Tertiary mammals. Graphics and (English-language) text.

Time Traveling: http://www.washington.edu/burkemuseum/ltws.html. The University of Washington offers virtual tours of its Burke Museum of Natural History and Culture, featuring the Life and Times of Washington State exhibit—a hands-on adventure that begins 545 million years ago. Also, info on exhibits, collections, news, and events at the museum.

T. rex at the University of California Museum of Paleontology: http://www.ucmp.berkeley.edu/trex/trexpo.html. Visit the T. rex skeleton at the University of California Museum of Paleontology, and learn more about these huge creatures, the world they lived in, and how scientists excavated the skeleton. Also, read the scientists' write-up on "Building the Perfect Beast," which tells the story of how they reconstructed the forty-foot skeleton.

University of California Museum of Paleontology: http://www.ucmp.berkeley.edu/exhibit/exhibits.html. Browse the extensive online exhibit, Paleontology without Walls. Features illustrations but it's text-heavy, so it's not kid-friendly, but older students will find it highly informative. Online visitors can

477

choose their paradigm for touring the museum: Phylogeny—the Family Tree of Life or Geological Time or Evolutionary Thought.

Virtual Dinosaurs: http://sunsite.anu.edu.au/Questacon/. Virtual tours, 3-D Zone, Kidspace, Hands-On Zone, and Cool Science are among the possibilities for exploration at the interactive site of Questacon, the Natural Science and Technology Centre in Canberra, Australia. Features online dinosaur activities for children as well as quick-time videos of their robotic dinosaurs, including the Muttaburrasaurus, which was discovered in Australia.

Virtual Reality Fossils: http://www.nhm.ac.uk/museum/tempexhib/VRML/index.html. Britain's Natural History Museum (London) lets you explore and manipulate virtual fossils online (provided you have a VRML–capable browser). The site also explains how they made the 3-D exhibits and provides links to the VRML software so you can download it if you don't already have it.

ART

Dinosaur Cartoons by Charley Parker: http://www.zark.com/extra/dinotoons/dinos.html. Charley Parker was the talent behind the Dinofest® website's cartoons, which originally appeared in Isaac Asimov's *Science Fiction*. Visit his site to click through an entertaining gallery of dinosaur cartoons.

Pictures-a-Go-Go: http://web.syr.edu/~dbgoldma/pictures.html. Dinosaur expert David Goldman and Syracuse University offer this vault of dinosaur pictures. A-to-Z index of links to sites where you can view dinosaur and other paleontological art. Updated regularly.

Walters & Kissinger: http://www.dinoart.com. The Curators of the Dinofest® Art Show, Robert F. Walters and Tess Kissinger give online visitors an inside peak on what they're working on in their complete dinosaur art studio (includes paintings and sculptures).

INFORMATION AND NEWS

Carnegie Museum of Natural History: http://www.clpgh.org/cmnh/discovery/dinoscience. Mix and match dinosaurs at the Carnegie Museum of Natural History site. DinoScience challenges visitors to match the right dinosaur skull with its skeleton. A fun way to learn, no matter what your age.

Dinamation: http://www.dinamation.org. The site of the Dinamation International Society, which promotes science education and research, and of the Dinamation International Corporation, which produces a line of scientifically accurate products for all ages. Visit to learn about their work in robotic dinosaurs and find out about where you can see their creatures in person. Also, plenty of online information—including a weekly term, a "Dinosaur of the Month" feature, and details about the Devil's Canyon Science and Learning Center.

"Dino" Don: http://www.dinodon.com. Dinosaur expert and writer "Dino" Don Lessem put together and maintains this excellent site offering "Dinosaurs, dinosaurs, and more dinosaurs!" It's dino-everything: art, dictionary, contest, news, digs, scientists, books, links, and "all manner of cool stuff" for children of all ages.

"Dino" Russ's Lair: http://denr1.igis.uiuc.edu/isgsroot/dinos/vertpaleo.html. Don't be put off by the URL; this site is worth the visit. Sponsored by the Illinois State Geological Survey (as part of its educational extension program) and known as "Dino Russ's Lair" (after its keeper, Russell Jacobson), visitors will find information on art, digs, eggs, exhibits, real-world places to visit, tracks, organizations, links, and software. National Geographic Society Online named it one of best dinosaur sites on the Web.

The Dinosaur Interplanetary Gazette: http://www.dinosaur.org/frontpage.html. Featuring "245 million years of dinosaur news at Dinosaur Central," this mega-site of paleo-info includes news, discoveries, articles about dinosaurs in the media, book reviews, and much more. The National Education Association gave this jam-packed site the nod for its informative content.

Dinosaur News: http://rexfiles.newscientist.com. Visit the online magazine New Scientist to find links to several brief but informative articles on the latest dinosaur theories and findings.

The Dinosaur Pages: http://www.gl.umbc.edu/~tkeese1/dinosaur/index.htm. This award-winning site moved recently and is under reconstruction, but is still worth visiting for its rich content. T. Mike Keesey began this project while he was a college student and he's collected loads of information about dinosaurs. Also, a list of links to other paleo-related sites on the Internet.

The Dinosaur Society: http://www.dinosociety.org/homepage.html. Founded in 1991, the Dinosaur Society is dedicated to dinosaur research and educating people about dinosaurs. Their honored site is true to that goal: It features a dig visit, society news, dinosaur art, gift shop, links, publications lists, and much more. For enthusiasts of all ages, but especially fun for kids—who will probably find it interesting enough to want to sign up to be a member of the society.

Dinosauria Online: http://www.dinosauria.com. Read articles by paleontologists and others, and get in on discussions about dinosaurs at this award-winning site. Plenty of content, plus picture gallery, a store, and a searchable vertebrate catalog. For the amateur and serious dinosaur enthusiast alike.

Dinosaurs in New Mexico: http://www.aps.edu/htmlpages/dinosinnm.html. Exhibits, research, collections info, and links, all courtesy of the New Mexico Museum of Natural History and Science.

Dinosaurs in the Gobi Desert: http://www.discovery.com/area/specials/gobi/gobi.html. During the summer of 1998 the Discovery Channel sent a correspondent along on a 20-day paleontological expedition through the Gobi Desert. Those who want to learn more should visit this website to read daily dispatches from the paleontologists, learn about their finds, and check out online areas such as the Bone Zone, Paleo-Talk, and an email exchange between visitors to the web-site and a paleontologist from the American Museum of Natural History.

Expedia's Mungo Park: http://www.mungopark.com. Fossil hunters should join world-renowned paleontologists Jack Horner and Phil Currie on an expedition to some of North America's richest fossil sites. Visitors can read their dispatches, find out what detours they took, and get a dossier and resource information for planning their own (real-world) expedition.

Field Museum of Natural History: http://www.fmnh.org/exhibits/perm_exhibits_nature. Information on the Field Museum's new Elizabeth Morse Genius Dinosaur Hall and the McDonald's Fossil Preparation Laboratory, where visitors can watch museum staff and volunteers ready fossilized *Tyrannosaurus rex* bones for study. Also, listing of current exhibitions; museum news.

National Geographic: http://www.nationalgeographic.com/index.html. The renowned magazine has run more than a few articles on dinosaur discoveries of recent years; readers can search the archives electronically to find stories.

Nova's **"Life with T. Rex":** http://www.pbs.org/wgbh/nova/trex. Information about life during the time of the *Tyrannosaurus rex* from Public Television's *Nova*. Includes information on the animals, plants, and insects that inhabited the earth during the time of the dinosaurs.

Paleontological Research Institution: http://www.englib.cornell.edu/pri. The site of the Ithaca, NY–based Paleontological Research Institution. Educational resource provides information on PRI's collection of fossils (many of which can be viewed online). Also "What Is It?"—a new feature challenging visitors to look at a fossil and try to identify it (not as easy as it sounds since these are fossils that have stumped the PRI experts).

Strange Science: http://www.turnpike.net/~mscott/. This site "follows the sometimes crazy assumptions of early fossil collectors," tracing the rocky road to modern paleontology and biology. Science isn't always as exact as we think it should be, and before great scientists and scholars arrived at the knowledge we take for granted today, they put forth some interesting (but erroneous) theories. Visit this site to learn about how scientific theory is formulated.

Tomorrow Morning's News: http://www.morning.com/archives/tm241/science.html. The Internet edition of Tomorrow Morning's News Stories for Kids features an archived article on the discovery of fossils in New Mexico; the finds are believed to be the remains of the oldest horned dinosaur ever found. Interesting reading for all ages, but definitely geared toward kids.

Wyoming Dinosaur Center: http://www.trib.com/DINO/facts.html. Fast facts and quick quizzes can be found at this site, sponsored by the Wyoming Dinosaur Center and Big Horn Basin Foundation.

Museum Sites (informational)

American Museum of Natural History: http://www.amnh.org/. A site for all ages; it offers information on the museum's dinosaur hall and newly renovated fossil halls (displaying the largest array of vertebrate fossils in the world). Visitors to the Manhattan museum can follow the story of vertebrate evolution, a story extending back some 500 million years, along a giant "family tree" of vertebrates. Online visitors can read museum news and learn about personalities in paleontology.

Carnegie Museum of Natural History: http://www.clpgh.org/cmnh/exhibits/index.html. Preview exhibits at Pittsburgh's Carnegie Museum of Natural History, featuring (at press time) China's feathered dinosaurs (at http://www.clpgh.org/cmnh/exhibits/feathered/index.html).

Children's Museum of Indianapolis: http://www.a1.com/children/dinoapat.htm. A brontosaurus by any other name. . . . Visit the Children's Museum of Indianapolis to view images and read up on the *Apatosaurus,* which used to be known as the *Brontosaurus.*

Dinosaur Hall: http://www.acnatsci.org/dinosaurs/dinonew.html. The Dinosaur Hall at Philadelphia's Academy of Natural Sciences features five different guided online tours of exhibits: From the Fossils; The Big Dig; Fossil Prep Lab; Bones, Guts, and Behavior; and Science through Art. Also, a kids section and links for teachers, as well as academy news, museum info, and newsletter of online events round out this website.

Field Museum of Natural History: http://www.fmnh.org/exhibits/perm_exhibits_nature.htm. Information on the Field Museum's new Elizabeth Morse Genius Dinosaur Hall and the McDonald's Fossil Preparation Laboratory, where visitors can watch museum staff and volunteers ready fossilized *Tyrannosaurus rex* bones for study. Also, listing of current exhibitions; museum news.

National Museum of Natural History: http://www.nmnh.si.edu/paleo/faq.html. The Natural History Museum at the Smithsonian Institution clears up the top ten misconceptions about dinosaurs. For information about the museum's exhibits (permanent and temporary), visit their homepage (at http://mnh.si.edu/museum/online.html).

Natural History of Texas: http://www.utexas.edu/depts/tnhc/. Information (mostly text, but some images) about the Texas Memorial Museum's holdings, including the research and collections of its Vertebrate Paleontology Laboratory.

NatureNet: http://www.vmnh.org/. Information, news, drawings, and photos of exhibits at the Virginia Museum of Natural History.

Peabody Museum: http://www.peabody. yale.edu/. Yale University's Peabody Museum home page offers museum news, events and exhibits info, and historical information (including a "who was who" among paleontologists). Peabody's website features the famous mural, *The Age of Reptiles,* painted by Rudolph Zallinger between 1942 and 1947 (http://www.peabody.yale.edu/mural).

Recreating Dinosaurs?: http://www.nhm.ac.uk/sc. London's Natural History Museum examines the possibility of recreating dinosaurs: In *Jurassic Park* and its sequel, *The Lost World,* dinosaurs are recreated from fragments of their DNA. Scientists in the film extracted the DNA from ancient bloodsucking insects trapped in amber. How possible is this? The museum's scientists find out. The site also offers information on the museum's exhibits.

Sue at the Field Museum: http://www.fmnh.org/new/trex.htm. The Field Museum of Natural History recently acquired the T. rex known as "Sue." Approximately 90% complete by bone count (and more than 90% complete by volume since most of the missing bones are relatively small), this example dwarfs all other known T. rex skeletons and became known as Sue after Susan Hendrickson, the field paleontologist who found it weathering out of the Dakota badlands. Visit the site to learn about the results of the CT scan on Sue's skull, read about the museum's plans for the T. rex, and read a list of Q&As about the famous skeleton.

T. rex and the "Death Star": http://www.mov.vic.gov.au/planetarium/trds.html. The planetarium at Australia's Museum of Victoria (Melbourne, Australia) provides information on the theory that an asteroid colliding into earth wiped out the dinosaur population sixty-five million years ago.

Links Pages

Paleobook: http://www.paleobook.com. Lists paleontological and archaeological books—fiction and nonfiction, for all age groups.

T. rex Surfs the Net: http://pioneer.mov.vic.gov.au/dinoExhibit/mainTrex.html. The Museum of Victoria, Australia, provides pages of links to other dinosaur sites on the Internet. Beware of some out-of-date connections; this site was last updated more than two years ago. Still worth the visit.

University of California Museum of Paleontology's Dinosaur Links: http://www.ucmp.berkeley.edu/diapsids/dinolinks.html. A treasure trove of dino-related information on the Internet.

University of California Museum of Paleontology's "Subway": http://www.ucmp.berkeley.edu/subway/subway.html. This site will lead you to many online destinations related to paleontology. Links include the National Science Foundation and natural history resources. Site map categorizes the possible destinations. (Beware of some links, since the site was last updated summer 1997.)

Bibliography

Bakker, Robert T. *The Dinosaur Heresies.* New York: William Morrow & Company, 1986.

Benton, Michael J. *Historical Atlas of Dinosaurs.* London, England: Penguin Books, 1996.

Bird, Roland T. *Bones for Barnum Brown.* Fort Worth: Texas Christian University Press, 1985.

Dixon, D., B. Cox, R. J .G. Savage, and B. Gardiner. *Dinosaurs and Prehistoric Animals.* New York: Macmillan Publishing, 1988.

Farlow, James O., and M. K. Brett-Surman, eds. *The Complete Dinosaur.* Bloomington: Indiana University Press, 1997.

Fraser, Nicholas C., and Hans-Dieter Sues, eds.*In the Shadow of the Dinosaurs.* New York: Cambridge University Press, 1997.

Gardom, Tim, and Angela Milner. *The Book of Dinosaurs.* Rocklin, California: Prima Publishing, 1993.

Halls, Kelly Milner. *Dino-Trekking: The Ultimate Dinosaur Lover's Travel Guide.* New York: John Wiley & Sons, Inc., 1996.

Horner, John R., and Edwin Dobb. *Dinosaur Lives.* New York: HarperCollins, 1997.

Jenkins, John T., and Jannice L. Jenkins. *Colorado's Dinosaurs.* Denver: Colorado Geological Survey, 1993.

Norman, David. *The Illustrated Encyclopedia of Dinosaurs.* New York: Crescent Books, 1985.

Officer, Charles, and Jake Page. *The Great Dinosaur Extinction Controversy.* New York: Addison-Wesley (Helix Books), 1996.

Parker, Steve. *The Practical Paleontologist.* New York: Simon & Schuster, 1990.

Psihoyos, Louis. *Hunting Dinosaurs.* New York: Random House, 1994.

Silbernagel, Bob. *Dinosaur Stalkers.* Fruita, Colorado: Dinamation International Society, 1996.

Wallace, Joseph. *The Complete Book of the Dinosaur.* New York: Gallery Books, 1989.

Wallace, Joseph. *Book of Dinosaurs and Other Ancient Creatures.* New York: Simon & Schuster, 1994.

Index

Handy Answers.
Courtesy of Mother Nature.
Uncover the mysteries of the world with these four *Handy Answer* reference books.

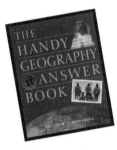

The Handy Geography Answer Book

Take a tour of the world the whole family will enjoy. Discover the differences between England, Great Britain and the United Kingdom. Find out who owns the oceans. Name the seven seas. *Handy Geography* has 1,000 common and not-so-common questions and answers about the natural features of the world and the ever-changing mark humans make on our planet. The non-technical explanations will appeal to adults and students alike. Entry topics cover a lot of ground, from trivia (such as "the highest" or "the deepest") to how the terrain affects the location of countries and cities and the people that inhabit them.

1998 • Matthew Todd Rosenburg • Paperback • 400 pp. with 16-page color insert
ISBN 1-57859-062-0 • **$19.95**

The Handy Science Answer Book

Can a bird fly upside down? Is white gold really gold? Why do golf balls have dimples? Who invented the Braille alphabet? Why is the sky blue? *Handy Science* holds the answers to those questions and nearly 1,400 others. The answers were compiled from the ready-reference files of the Science and Technology Department of the Carnegie Library of Pittsburgh. Everyone will enjoy hours of discovery on topics such as cars, outer space, math, the inner workings of the human body, computers and much more.

1996 • Paperback • 598 pp. • ISBN 0-7876-1013-5 • **$16.95**

The Handy Weather Answer Book

Find out if mobile homes really attract tornadoes, the difference between sleet and freezing rain and nearly 1,000 other questions. The clear-cut answers reside in this cornucopia of weather facts. *Handy Weather* covers such confounding and pertinent topics as hurricanes, thunder and lightning, droughts and flash floods, earthquakes and volcanoes. You'll also find coverage of weather-related phenomena like El Niño, the greenhouse effect, Aurora Borealis and St. Elmo's fire.

1996 • Walter A. Lyons, Ph.D. • Paperback • 398 pp. • ISBN 0-7876-1034-8 • **$16.95**

The Handy Bug Answer Book

For anyone who has asked the question, "Why in the world is the world full of bugs?" and for the child in the rest of us, there's *The Handy Bug Answer Book*. Dr. Gilbert Waldbauer shares his enthusiasm about the intricate and barely visible world of insects in this entertaining and highly accessible question and answer book. Organized by topics, *Handy Bug* answers nearly 800 questions on insect lives and habits. Uncover facts about their numbers, reproductive cycles, physical makeup and where they can be found. Discover which ones are true pests and which ones are beneficial to us and the differences between insect, spiders, millipedes and other invertebrates.

1998 • Dr. Gilbert Waldbauer • Paperback • 425 pp. with 16-page color insert
ISBN 1-57859-049-3 • **$19.95**

VISIBLE
INK
PRESS

Available at fine bookstores everywhere,
or at your favorite online bookseller.